Autism Spectrum Disorders

Autism
Spectrum Disorders

Issues in Assessment and Intervention

Patricia A. Prelock

pro·ed
An International Publisher

8700 Shoal Creek Boulevard
Austin, Texas 78757-6897
800/897-3202   Fax 800/397-7633
www.proedinc.com

© 2006 by PRO-ED, Inc.
8700 Shoal Creek Boulevard
Austin, Texas 78757-6897
800/897-3202   Fax 800/397-7633
www.proedinc.com

Library of Congress Cataloging-in-Publication Data

Prelock, Patricia A.
  Autism spectrum disorders : issues in assessment and intervention / by Patricia A. Prelock.
    p. cm.
  Includes bibliographical references and indexes.
  ISBN 1-4164-0129-6 (alk. paper)
  1. Autism in children—Handbooks, manuals, etc.   I. Title.

RJ506.A9P72   2006
618.92'85882—dc22

                                                                        2005010830

Art Director: Jason Crosier
Designer: Nancy McKinney
This book is designed in Myriad and Fairfield LH.

Printed in the United States of America

1 2 3 4 5 6 7 8 9 10   10 09 08 07 06

Contents

Contributors | xi

List of Illustrations | xiii

Foreword | xv

Preface | xvii

Acknowledgments | xxi

PART I

Assessment   1

CHAPTER 1

Autism and Related Disorders: Trends in Diagnosis and
Neurobiologic Considerations   3
With guest contributor Stephen H. Contompasis, MD

Introduction   4
Trends in the Diagnosis of Autism   5
Early Indicators of Autism Spectrum Disorders   14
Best Practice Guidelines for Diagnosis   22
Role of Practitioners in Diagnosis   26
Differential Diagnosis   28
Neurobiologic Considerations   32
Summary   36

Appendix 1.A
Summary of DSM–IV Diagnostic Criteria for Pervasive
Developmental Disorders   39

Appendix 1.B
Summary of Screening and Diagnostic Tools for ASD   43

Practice Opportunities   50
Suggested Readings   50
Resources   50
Glossary   54
References   55

CHAPTER 2

Learning To Work with Families To Support Children with ASD   65
With guest contributor Jean E. Beatson, EdD, RN

Introduction   66
Tenets of Family-Centered Care   67
Role of Cultural Competence   70
Barriers to Family–Professional Collaboration: What Are They and How Should We Respond?   72
Building Professional Relationships with Families Affected by ASD   81
Implications for Professionals and Families Affected by ASD   82
Summary   83
Practice Opportunities   84
Suggested Readings   84
Resources   85
Glossary   90
References   90

CHAPTER 3

An Interdisciplinary, Family-Centered, and Community-Based Assessment Model for Children with ASD   93

Introduction   94
A Disablement Framework To Guide Assessment   94
Ecological and Dynamic Assessment Approaches   95
Role of Families and Practitioners in Assessment   98
An Interdisciplinary Assessment Model for Children with ASD   101
Potential Limitations of the Community-Based Assessment Model   119
Summary   119

Appendix 3.A
Sample Information Form for Children   122

Appendix 3.B
Sample Preassessment Planning Meeting Format   131

Appendix 3.C
Sample of Follow-Up Planning   138

Appendix 3.D
Sample Report A   143

Appendix 3.E
Sample Report B   153

Practice Opportunities   161
Suggested Readings   161
Resources   162
Glossary   162
References   163

CHAPTER 4

Understanding and Assessing the Communication of Children with ASD   167

Introduction   168
Theoretical Views of Language Impairment in Children with ASD   168
Early Communication Challenges   169
Pragmatic Challenges for Verbal Children with ASD   174
Other Language Challenges   180
Creating Profiles of Communication Strengths and Challenges   185
Communication Assessment Across Impairment, Activity, and Participation   195
Summary   205

Appendix 4.A
Communication Assessment Interview   208

Practice Opportunities   211
Suggested Readings   211
Resources   212
Glossary   213
References   214

CHAPTER 5

Understanding and Assessing the Play of Children with ASD   221

Introduction   222
Principles of Play Development   223
Relationships Among Play, Language, and Cognition   226
Challenges in Play for Children with ASD   229
Creating Profiles of Play Strengths and Challenges   233
Play Assessment Across Impairment, Activity, and Participation   234
Summary   243
Practice Opportunities   245
Suggested Readings   246
Resources   246
Glossary   247
References   247

CHAPTER 6

Understanding and Assessing the Social–Emotional Development of Children with ASD   251

With guest contributor Amy Ducker, PhD

Introduction   252
Social–Emotional Development   253
Key Areas of Impairment   256
Impact of Deficits in Arousal and Attention   264
Creating Profiles of Social–Emotional Development   265

Social–Emotional Assessment Across Impairment, Activity, and Participation   282
Summary   288
Practice Opportunities   291
Suggested Readings   291
Resources   292
Glossary   294
References   295

CHAPTER 7

Sensory and Motor Considerations in the Assessment of Children with ASD   303

With guest contributors Ruth Dennis, EdD, OTR, and Susan Edelman, EdD, PT

Introduction   304
Descriptions of Sensory and Motor Characteristics in ASD   304
Relationships Between Sensory and Motor Characteristics   310
Assumptions About Sensory–Motor Functioning and Implications
    for Assessment and Intervention   323
Dimensions of Disability and Aspects of Sensory–Motor Function
    To Be Assessed in Children with ASD   324
Considerations for Assessment   326
Summary   332
Practice Opportunities   334
Suggested Readings   335
Resources   336
Glossary   338
References   339

PART 2

Intervention   345

CHAPTER 8

Making Intervention Decisions To Better Serve Children with ASD and Their Families   347

Introduction   348
Perspectives on Current Interventions   348
Visioning and Planning for Effective Intervention   356
Strategies for Difficult Decision Making   359
Considerations for Nonstandard Interventions   371
Curriculum Analysis and Intervention Planning   374
Summary   382

Appendix 8.A

Curriculum Analysis for Young Children with ASD and Individuals with ASD
Who Exhibit Limited Verbal and Cognitive Skills   384

Appendix 8.B
Language-Based Curriculum Analysis for Schoolchildren and
Adolescents with ASD   386

Practice Opportunities   389
Suggested Readings   389
Resources   390
Glossary   391
References   391

CHAPTER 9

Interventions To Support the Communication of Children with ASD   397

Introduction   398
Interventions for Supporting Limited Verbal Skills   399
Interventions for Supporting Verbal Skills   412
TEACCH Language and Communication Curriculum   431
Managing Unconventional Verbal Behavior   433
Expanding Conversational Abilities of Children with ASD   434
Supporting Communication and Language Intervention in the Home   437
Summary   440
Practice Opportunities   443
Suggested Readings   444
Resources   445
Glossary   451
References   452

CHAPTER 10

Interventions To Support the Play of Children with ASD   459

Introduction   460
Teaching Play   460
Summary   474
Practice Opportunities   474
Suggested Readings   475
Resources   475
Glossary   476
References   476

CHAPTER 11

Interventions To Support the Social–Emotional Needs of Children with ASD   479

Introduction   480
Models of Intervention   480

Strategies To Support Social Interaction and Social Communication 496
Other Intervention Suggestions To Support the Social Behavior of Children
  with ASD 521
Summary 525
Practice Opportunities 527
Suggested Readings 527
Resources 528
Glossary 533
References 533

CHAPTER 12

Health-Care Considerations for Children with ASD   541

With guest contributor Stephen H. Contompasis, MD

Introduction 542
Role of a "Medical Home" for Children with ASD 542
A Plan for Coordinated and Comprehensive Health Care for Children with ASD 544
Strategies To Support the Health Care of Children with ASD 545
Summary 562
Practice Opportunities 563
Suggested Readings 564
Resources 565
Glossary 567
References 568

CHAPTER 13

Inclusionary Practice for Children with ASD   573

Introduction 574
Inclusive Education for Children with ASD 575
Strategies for Effective IEP Teams 579
Supporting Integration and Transitions Within General Education Settings 581
Summary 594
Practice Opportunities 595
Suggested Readings 596
Resources 596
Glossary 597
References 598

Epilogue | 603

Author Index | 605

Subject Index | 613

About the Author and Contributors | 631

Contributors

Jean E. Beatson
Research Assistant Professor
University of Vermont
VT-ILEHP Program
210 Colchester Avenue, Farrell Hall
Burlington, VT 05405

Stephen H. Contompasis
Clinical Associate Professor
University of Vermont
VT-ILEHP Program
210 Colchester Avenue, Farrell Hall
Burlington, VT 05405

Ruth Dennis
Assistant Research Professor
University of Vermont
Center for Disability and Community
   Inclusion
3rd Floor, Mann Hall
Burlington, VT 05405

Amy Ducker
Clinical Director
Baird Center for Children and
   Families
1110 Pine Street
Burlington, VT 05401

Susan Edelman
Research Assistant Professor
University of Vermont
Center for Disability and Community
   Inclusion
3rd Floor, Mann Hall
Burlington, VT 05405

Patricia A. Prelock
Professor and Chair
Department of Communication
   Sciences
University of Vermont
407 Pomeroy Hall, 489 Main Street
Burlington, VT 05405

Illustrations

FIGURES

Figure 1.1	Diagnostic Criteria Checklist for Autistic Disorder	11
Figure 1.2	Checklist for Autism in Toddlers (CHAT)	13
Figure 1.3	Australian Scale for Asperger's Syndrome	15
Figure 1.4	Modified Checklist for Autism in Toddlers (M–CHAT)	18
Figure 1.5	Early indicators or red flags of autism spectrum disorder checklist	23
Figure 3.1	Agenda format for team meetings	99
Figure 3.2	Genogram	104
Figure 3.3	Ecomap	104
Figure 3.4	IFSP or IEP at-a-glance	107
Figure 3.5	Format for record review	113
Figure 3.6	Sample report format	117
Figure 4.1	Assessment of unconventional verbal behavior	189
Figure 4.2	Observational framework for examining semantic language in children with ASD	192
Figure 4.3	Observational framework for examining pragmatic language in children with ASD	198
Figure 5.1	Play assessment interview	237
Figure 5.2	Questions to guide play assessment	242
Figure 6.1	Assessment of pivotal response behaviors	270
Figure 6.2	Assessment of friendship behaviors	272
Figure 7.1	Components of sensory–motor functioning and concerns related to ASD	313
Figure 7.2	Hierarchical levels of CNS sensory and motor functioning	315
Figure 8.1	Mediation model: Position 1	365
Figure 8.2	Mediation model: Position 2	366
Figure 8.3	Mediation model: New position	367
Figure 8.4	Checklist for considering nonstandard or controversial practices	375
Figure 11.1	Sample assessment rubric for peer tutoring	499
Figure 11.2	Sample social stories for a third-grade student with ASD	516
Figure 12.1	Health care checklist for children with ASD	549
Figure 12.2	Format for observing suspected seizure activity	553
Figure 12.3	Assessment of pain or illness for children with ASD	560

TABLES

Table 1.1   Recommended Practice for Diagnosing Children with Suspected ASD   26

Table 1.2   Suggestions for Making Physician Referrals Regarding a Diagnosis of ASD   27

Table 2.1   Key Elements of Family-Centered Care   68

Table 2.2   Barriers to and Solutions for Establishing Family–Professional Partnerships   80

Table 3.1   Team Meeting Roles   100

Table 4.1   Selected Assessment Tools for Semantic Language   190

Table 4.2   Selected Assessment Tools for Pragmatic Language   196

Table 4.3   Dimensions of Disability and Aspects of Communication To Be Assessed in Children with ASD   200

Table 5.1   Dimensions of Disability and Aspects of Play To Be Assessed in Children with ASD   235

Table 6.1   Dimensions of Disability and Aspects of Social–Emotional Function To Be Assessed in Children with ASD   283

Table 7.1   Comparison of Features of the Neuromaturational and Dynamic Systems Models   322

Table 7.2   Dimensions of Disability and Aspects of Sensory–Motor Function To Be Assessed in Children with ASD   325

Table 9.1   Sample Communication Goals and Possible Strategies To Support Those Goals for Children with ASD   442

Table 9.2   Tips for Improving Listening and Speaking Skills in Children and Adolescents with ASD   444

Table 9.3   Tips for Supporting Language Use in Children and Adolescents with ASD   445

Table 10.1   Sample Play Goals and Possible Strategies To Support Those Goals for Children with ASD   462

Table 11.1   Sample Social Interaction Goals and Possible Strategies To Support Those Goals for Children with ASD   502

Table 12.1   Tenets for Establishing a Medical Home   543

Table 12.2   Problem List for Jason, a Child with ASD   547

Foreword

Since Leo Kanner introduced the word *autism* nearly 60 years ago, ideas of what it is and what it is not, as well as attitudes surrounding the disability, have undergone numerous changes. In the mid-1960s, many experts still subscribed to the idea that autism had psychological causes at its root. These professionals often pointed to familial dynamics that they believed had worked toward converting an otherwise socially and emotionally healthy child into one with autism. I should know: I was diagnosed during that time. Although none of the professionals whose help my parents sought directly blamed my mother for my condition, their implications, indirect comments, assumptions, and attempts to place limitations on our future as a family spoke volumes.

In the 35 years since my diagnosis, many positive changes have occurred with respect to autism spectrum disorder (ASD), two of the biggest being in the amount of information available and in experts' attitudes and understanding. What was once thought of as a psychological disorder caused by ice-sculpture parents is now widely regarded as having at its base a complex set of atypical neurological and genetic patterns. Even if it may not have taken much of the sting out of a diagnosis of autism, this shift has at least "liberated" parents by letting them off the hook and erasing much of the previous stigma.

Many of the attitude changes are well reflected and represented in this book by Dr. Patricia Prelock. The format and chapter order give readers a comprehensive set of well-prepared questions to consider while they chart the course toward dealing and coping with some of the mystery surrounding ASD. This well-researched text also offers a holistic, organic, and multifaceted approach and applies it to what has all too often gotten stuck between the lines: It goes well beyond the facts, statistics, and figures by dissecting the individual areas of play, language, and socialization affected. Moreover, Dr. Prelock's text takes family members and places them in the center ring of the treatment process, viewing them as a vital part of the professional team.

This textbook allows us to see autism through the lens of various perspectives, all of which lend credence to the notion that autism is not some hopeless esoteric disorder with inherent and debilitating limitations, as previously thought. Instead, what quickly emerges is the continuum on which it rests. By framing autism in terms of the diverse challenges it presents to a child's sense of play, language (spoken and nonspoken), motor development, and social skills, we're presented with a more holistic picture of the experience. At the same time, clinging to stereotypical and defeatist ways of dealing with ASD becomes as difficult as it is outdated.

I've spent nearly 10 years sharing with numerous audiences my experiences from the inside, specifically many of my struggles to merely make sense of a chaotic world, let alone fit into it. For me, autism affected all of the ingredients essential to effective communication and socialization as outlined in Dr. Prelock's book. In addition, experts knew even before they examined me what they were going to say to my parents who sought their help and expertise. Sadly, few of the basics, such as empathy and active listening, factored into the dialogue.

However, times and attitudes have changed from those dark days. This text takes many of those changes, methods of diagnosis, interventions, and approaches and, with eloquence and passion, displays them for the betterment of the reader. It's too bad my mother couldn't have read this book back in 1965.

—*Sean Barron*

Preface

This book is intended to serve two purposes. First, it is designed to provide a comprehensive text that can be used for coursework in the area of autism. Although the roles of communication, play, and social interaction in understanding and managing the needs of children with autism spectrum disorders (ASD) are emphasized, the text should have broad appeal to interdisciplinary professionals who are preparing students to work with individuals with ASD and their families. My hope, then, is that not only faculty in speech–language pathology, but also those in psychology, education, early childhood education, special education, social work, pediatrics, occupational therapy, physical therapy, nursing, and audiology, among others, will find this to be a useful resource. Second, the book is designed to serve as a practical resource for working professionals across a range of disciplines as well as families who are affected by ASD.

The reader will see that each chapter is designed in a similar way. The chapters begin with several key questions that should guide the readers' thinking. Those questions are revisited at the end of the chapter. Recognizing the value of key resources for supporting children with ASD and their families, each chapter includes a list of resources related to its particular content area. These lists are intended to expand the student's, practitioner's, and family member's repertoire of practical sources of support. All the chapters also include a number of practice opportunities for the reader and learner to apply the information presented, three to four suggested readings with a brief description of each, a list of resources for more information, and a glossary of key terms.

The specific content of the book was also strategically designed. The book is divided into two major sections: assessment and intervention. The discussion of assessment begins with diagnosis in Chapter 1, where issues of early identification, differential diagnosis, and neurobiological findings are considered. In Chapter 2, the role of families in the assessment and intervention of their children with ASD is emphasized. In Chapter 3, a field-tested interdisciplinary model for assessment and intervention planning is described to facilitate learning and practice. The World Health Organization framework guides the approach to assessment through the next four chapters. This framework was selected because it incorporates elements of both the traditional deficits perspective and the strengths perspective and considers factors both intrinsic and extrinsic to the individual. The most recent version of the framework, the *International Classification of Functioning,*

Disability and Health (ICF), describes dimensions of disability (impairment, activity, and participation) that are affected by contextual factors such as societal attitudes, cultural norms, education, and lifestyle (World Health Organization, 2001). Each of these dimensions is considered as the reader learns about creating assessment profiles for children with ASD across communication, play, social, and sensory areas in Chapters 4, 5, 6, and 7.

Evidence-based practice guides the intervention chapters. My goal was to present models of intervention and specific strategies that have a solid theoretical foundation, have application to children with ASD across a range of ages and ability levels, and have some evidence of positive effects for children with ASD. As will be noted, the range of evidence for the particular interventions discussed is significant. In Chapter 8, I have included some guidelines for considering the evidence and evaluating how practitioners might select interventions for individual children with ASD. The intervention chapters on communication, play, and social–emotional development, Chapters 9, 10, and 11, provide a comprehensive description of each intervention model or strategy, the intervention goals that might be considered, the perceived value for children with ASD, and the reported efficacy.

Chapter 12, "Health Care Considerations for Children with ASD," has been added because health care is a frequently ignored or poorly understood area of function for this population. I hope that students and practitioners reading this book will recognize how the health of the child with ASD affects that child's ability to communicate, play, and interact socially. The last chapter offers a discussion of inclusive practices for children with ASD. It assumes the competence of children with ASD and their families, recognizes the skill of general educators as teachers, and incorporates what we know from the literature that can support learning success.

Although I have individually discussed assessment and intervention issues affecting communication, play, and social–emotional development, I recognize the interrelationships among these areas of behavior. It will also become clear that as performance is evaluated in one area, valuable information related to other areas can be obtained. Similarly, many of the intervention strategies described to support one area may be useful in supporting performance in other areas. I chose to separate these dimensions of learning and behavior so that each could be carefully examined, but I expect that the reader will make clear connections and identify the interrelationships. Also, I chose not to include a chapter on interventions related to sensory motor development since my goal is that the practitioner will recognize that communication, play, and social–emotional development have clear sensory connections and that any intervention should consider the implications of sensory motor aspects of functioning. Further, a specific chapter to address problem behaviors was not included, as I am assuming that many problem behaviors are often attempts to communicate. With a solid understanding of ways to assess and support communication, which is addressed in this text, practitioners will have several strategies they can use to support positive behaviors in children with ASD. Several excellent resources are already available to expand one's knowledge and understanding of challenging behaviors and ways to manage these behaviors.

My hope is that by reading this book, the reader will be challenged to think in different ways. My primary goal is to facilitate the acquisition of knowledge and skills students and practitioners need to make a difference in the lives of children with ASD and their families. I also see this text as a potential resource for families seeking to understand the core deficit areas for their children with ASD and what can be done to address these deficit areas.

Autism is a pervasive developmental disorder, in that it affects all aspects of day-to-day functioning—ability to communicate, to play in meaningful ways, to interact with others, and to manage the activities of daily living. Over the last several years, our understanding of this disorder has evolved to recognize the variability in severity of symptoms and the likelihood that there is a neurobiological and genetic basis to the disorder. Although autism can be a devastating disorder for children and their families, current research indicates that with early detection and intervention, progress can be made. As you prepare to read this text, it is important that you understand the nuances of early and differential diagnosis, the need to assess the core areas of deficit, and the value of evidence-based intervention practices.

Reference

World Health Organization. (2001). *International classification of functioning, disability and health*. Geneva, Switzerland: Author.

Acknowledgments

For more than 20 years, I have been privileged to be part of the lives of many families and children affected by autism spectrum disorders (ASD). Families have taught me the value of hearing what they have to say and listening to what they want and need for their children and themselves. Children with ASD have expanded my understanding of what it means to have a perspective different from my own and to struggle in a world that seldom takes advantage of their unique interests and strengths. I am indebted to these families and children, who have graciously allowed me to participate in their journey of life and learning.

I wish to thank my colleagues, who have greatly contributed to the literature in the area of autism and have expanded and enriched my thinking on this topic. I also want to thank my guest contributors, Jean Beatson, Stephen Contompasis, Amy Ducker, Ruth Dennis, and Susan Edelman, for their input on selected chapters, which provided an interdisciplinary perspective on the issues facing children with ASD. Thanks are extended to Sean Barron, a trusted friend and colleague who shared personal insights that I respect.

I am particularly grateful to my husband, Bill Congleton, for his encouragement in completing this project. He tolerated many late nights and limited personal time but remained willing to read each chapter with an eye for understanding. His love and support have made a significant contribution to what I am able to do in the field of autism.

Assessment

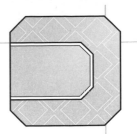

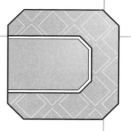

CHAPTER 1

Autism and Related Disorders
Trends in Diagnosis and Neurobiologic Considerations

Patricia A. Prelock and Stephen H. Contompasis

QUESTIONS TO CONSIDER

In this chapter, several questions will be addressed related to the diagnosis of autism spectrum disorders (ASD) and to the recognition of early indicators of these disorders. You will begin to understand the complex role of neurobiology in understanding the disorder. The following six questions provide a context for exploring the diagnosis, the function of the brain and individual genetic profiles in understanding the characteristics of the disorder, and the role of families and practitioners in making the diagnosis:

1. What are the trends in the diagnosis of ASD?
2. What are the early indicators for a diagnosis of ASD?
3. What are some guidelines for best practice in diagnosing ASD?
4. Who should make the diagnosis?
5. How should ASD be differentially diagnosed from related neuro-developmental disorders?
6. What are some neurobiological considerations in the understanding of ASD?

Introduction

Autism is currently seen as a common childhood disorder with core deficits in socialization, communication, play, and behavior, and as late as 2000 was believed to affect nearly 1 in 500 people (American Psychiatric Association, 2000; Filipek et al., 2000). The most recent reports of prevalence, however, indicate that the rate of occurrence for autism has increased to 3.4 per 1,000 or almost 1 in 250 (Yeargin-Allsopp et al., 2003). When the autism spectrum, including Asperger syndrome and pervasive developmental disorder not otherwise specified (PDD-NOS), is considered, some estimates have been as high as 60 in 10,000, or nearly 1 in 166 (Fombonne, 2003a). The reported increases raise several questions, including how autism has been described in the past, the criteria currently used to define the disorder, variability in diagnostic practices, and genetic and environmental factors that may be affecting the occurrence of the condition.

Leo Kanner, an American psychiatrist, first described autism in 1943. He identified several common characteristics in the children he studied, including poor social relatedness, impaired language for communication purposes, a desire for sameness, object fascination, cognitive potential (i.e., average or above average intelligence), and onset prior to 30 months. Over time, considerable variation has been reported in the manifestations of autism, both across and within individuals (Lord, 1997; Volkmar, Klin, & Cohen, 1997). Variability in symptom expression has increased the complexity in diagnosis, and the term *autism spectrum* has evolved to describe a range of impairment in social interaction, communication, and behavior. Equating autism with ASD, however, is somewhat misleading. There is clearly a relationship between those individuals representing a range of symptoms across the core deficit areas of social interaction, communication, and behavior, but determining the exact relationship will require better information on the underlying causes of autism and related conditions.

Although autism remains a behavioral disorder defined by its clinical manifestations, current research indicates that it is a brain disorder with a genetic basis. The increased incidence of the disorder in siblings supports a genetic basis. Further, advances in genetic testing are identifying specific gene locations linked to autism, and neuroscientists are increasing their awareness of how genes influence cell-to-cell signaling in the developing brain that refines neural connections and lend themselves to specific impairments in neurological function. Certainly, ongoing research in this area will contribute to the understanding of the disorder, its causes, and its long-term impact. Such research also gives hope to families and individuals affected by autism and the practitioners who serve them for a future of earlier diagnosis and better outcomes.

Trends in the Diagnosis of Autism

Prior to Kanner's 1943 description of autism, children with ASD were most likely considered mentally impaired or psychotic (Trevarthen, Aitken, Papoudi, & Robarts, 1998). Psychosis was often assumed because there was poor understanding of childhood disorders. Kanner was the first to recognize this population as a distinctive group. A year later, Hans Asperger described a similar condition, identifying children with higher cognitive skills and overall functioning but with the specific challenges in social understanding first reported by Kanner (Asperger, 1944; Frith, 1991). In contrast to Kanner's description of autism, Asperger characterized his population as exhibiting significant social problems despite their essentially appropriate verbal abilities.

Since Kanner (1943) first described autism, several diagnostic schemes have been used to define and redefine the disorder. It was not until the 1970s, however, that autism gained acceptance as a valid diagnostic category. In 1978, Rutter proposed a simplified set of criteria, including impaired social development, impaired language development, insistence on sameness, and onset prior to 30 months. In 1980, autism was officially included as a diagnostic category under "Pervasive Developmental Disorders" in *The Diagnostic and Statistical Manual of Mental Disorders–Third Edition* (DSM–III), representing Rutter's four major criteria (American Psychiatric Association [APA], 1980; Schopler, 1994). The DSM–III's diagnostic criteria failed to address developmental issues in the disorder, as it focused on younger children with more severe impairments. A revision (DSM–III–R; American Psychiatric Association, 1987) reduced the major criteria to three, not requiring onset prior to 30 months because of data that suggested onset may not occur until 36 months or even later (Schopler, 1994). No emphasis was given to historical information, and the specific criteria under each of the three major areas were increased in number and developmental orientation. Further, the DSM–III–R criteria were overinclusive and failed to correlate with the World Health Organization's *International Classification of Diseases* (ICD–10; World Health Organization, 1987). In 1994, the DSM–IV (American Psychiatric Association, 1994) was published, with another revision of the criteria for autism and an expansion of the definition to include progressive conditions such as Rett's Disorder and Childhood Disintegrative Disorder with shared "autistic" features. The revision occurred as a result of extensive field trials supporting the inclusion of an age of onset and a definition more aligned with the ICD–10 criteria (Volkmar et al., 1994). Problems remain with the DSM–IV criteria, however, in that they are less stringent and more inclusive than those of the ICD–10, and Asperger's Disorder and Pervasive Development Disorder Not Otherwise Specified (PDD-NOS) are not clearly defined (Tidmarsh & Volkmar, 2003).

The changing diagnostic criteria and the use of two different classification systems, one nationally (the DSM) and the other internationally (the

ICD), have certainly contributed to the inconsistency and reported confusions in the diagnosis of autism over the past several years (Volkmar, 1996). However, the core deficit areas that Kanner first described have remained the same, and the pervasive impairment in motivation for social interaction has continued as a hallmark of the disorder.

The most recent revision of the DSM (DSM–IV–TR; APA, 2000) includes additions to the text describing autism, specifically highlighting possible differences in the manifestations of certain behaviors for younger versus older children and including more descriptive examples of behaviors reported in the core deficit areas. No changes have been made, however, in the specific diagnostic criteria used to diagnose autism, either nationally or internationally, since 1994.

The diagnostic criteria in the DSM–IV (APA, 1994) and the DSM–IV–TR (APA, 2000, p. 75) in each of the core deficit areas are

1. qualitative impairment in social interaction, as manifested by at least two of the following:
   - marked impairment in the use of multiple nonverbal behaviors such as eye-to-eye gaze, facial expression, body postures, and gestures to regulate social interaction
   - failure to develop peer relationships appropriate to developmental level
   - a lack of spontaneous seeking to share enjoyment, interests, or achievements with other people (e.g., by a lack of showing, bringing, or pointing out objects of interest)
   - lack of social or emotional reciprocity
2. qualitative impairments in communication as manifested by at least one of the following:
   - delay in, or total lack of, the development of spoken language (not accompanied by an attempt to compensate through alternative modes of communication such as gesture or mime)
   - in individuals with adequate speech, marked impairment in the ability to initiate or sustain a conversation with others
   - stereotyped and repetitive use of language or idiosyncratic language
   - lack of varied, spontaneous make-believe play or social imitative play appropriate to developmental level
3. restricted repetitive and stereotyped patterns of behavior, interests, and activities, as manifested by at least one of the following:
   - encompassing preoccupation with one or more stereotyped and restricted patterns of interest that is abnormal either in intensity or focus
   - apparently inflexible adherence to specific, nonfunctional routines or rituals
   - stereotyped and repetitive motor mannerisms (e.g., hand or finger flapping or twisting, or complex whole-body movements)
   - persistent preoccupation with parts of objects

Pervasive Developmental Disorders

The DSM–IV proposes a concept of spectrum disorder, including classic Autistic Disorder, Rett's Disorder, Childhood Disintegrative Disorder, and Asperger's Disorder under the category of Pervasive Developmental Disorders (see Appendix 1.A for a description of each disorder, including diagnostic features, associated conditions, age, gender, prevalence, course, familial pattern, and differential diagnosis). It is important to read the comprehensive description of the diagnostic criteria within the DSM–IV–TR, which provides examples and identifies areas of controversy or difficulty in diagnosis. In the paragraphs that follow, each of the Pervasive Developmental Disorders is briefly described.

Autistic Disorder. The DSM–IV defines Autistic Disorder, or classic autism, by the presence of at least six of the diagnostic criteria previously listed. For a child to receive a diagnosis of Autistic Disorder, the following must be determined (APA, 2000, p. 75):

- at least two of the social impairment criteria are met;
- at least one of the communication impairment criteria is met;
- at least one of the restricted repetitive and stereotyped patterns of behavior, interests, and activities criteria is met;
- a delay or abnormal functioning is observed in social interaction, language used as social communication, or symbolic/imaginative play prior to age 3; and
- behavior cannot be accounted for as Rett's or Childhood Disintegrative Disorder.

The use of descriptors such as "marked impairments," "encompassing preoccupation," "delay in," and "apparently inflexible" makes consistent and accurate diagnosis a challenge. These terms may be perceived or interpreted differently by different practitioners, particularly by those with more or less experience diagnosing children along the autism spectrum.

Rett's Disorder. A diagnosis of Rett's Disorder requires attention to a very different set of criteria than the other disorders along the spectrum. For a child to receive a diagnosis of Rett's Disorder, the following criteria have to be met (APA, 2000, p. 77):

- apparently normal prenatal, perinatal, and postnatal development up to the first 5 months of life;
- normal head size up to 5 months, with a decrease in head growth between 5 and 48 months;
- loss of hand skills between 5 and 30 months and the presence of unusual behaviors such as hand wringing;
- normal psychomotor development up to 5 months, with significant deficits after onset;

- severe communication deficits; and
- decreased interest in social interaction at onset, which develops later in the course of the disorder.

Although not required for a diagnosis of Rett's Disorder, related symptoms often reported include breathing dysfunctions, EEG abnormalities, seizures, muscle rigidity or spasticity, scoliosis, bruxism, small feet in relation to stature, growth retardation, peripheral vasomotor disturbances, abnormal sleep patterns and agitation, dysphagia and nutritional deficits, decreased mobility with age, and constipation (Hagberg, Aicardi, Dias, & Ramos, 1983; Trevathan & Naidu, 1988). Four stages have also been described to characterize distinct periods of development in individuals with Rett's Disorder (Hagberg & Witt Engerstrom, 1986; Trevathan & Naidu, 1988; Van Acker, 1991; Witt Engerstrom, 1992). In Stage 1 there is an initial onset of unclear symptoms and developmental stagnation; Stage 2 signals a period of rapid deterioration and loss of previously acquired skills; stabilization occurs in Stage 3; and Stage 4 leads to some improvement in social skills, although motor deterioration usually occurs.

Recently, researchers have learned that a mutation in the MECP2 (methyl-CpG-binding protein) gene on the X chromosome accounts for most occurrences of typical forms of Rett's Disorder (Dragich, Houwink-Manville, & Schanen, 2000; Shahbazian & Zoghbi, 2001). Rett's Disorder occurs in about 1 in 10,000 girls (Hagberg, 1985; Witt-Engerstrom & Gillberg, 1987). Typically, a new and spontaneous mutation in the MECP2 gene on the X chromosome is thought to be represented as a dominant condition (X-linked dominant) that is usually lethal to the male fetus, although in rare instances severely affected males have been reported (Meloni et al., 2001; Villard et al., 2000). Research has also suggested that individuals with Rett's Disorder may not actually have a period of "normal" development and that the disorder may be more consistent with a curtailment of cerebral maturation versus cerebral degeneration (Bauman, Kemper, & Arin, 1995; Leonard & Bower, 1998).

Childhood Disintegrative Disorder. Previously referred to as Heller's Syndrome, dementia infantalis, or disintegrative psychosis, Childhood Disintegrative Disorder (CDD) has a later onset (after age 2) than Rett's Disorder and Autistic Disorder, although it shares with them many features in terms of loss of social, motor, and communication skills. For a child to receive a diagnosis of CDD, the following criteria have to be met (APA, 2000, p. 79):

- at least 2 years of normal development;
- marked regression in at least two areas of development, including receptive or expressive language skills, social or adaptive skills, bowel or bladder control, play skills, or motor skills;
- no specific medical cause or neurodegenerative syndrome to explain the marked regression noted; and

- deficits in social, communication, and restricted repetitive and stereotyped patterns of behavior typical of Autistic Disorder.

Volkmar's (1992) review of the literature, including case reports of CDD, suggests that this disorder differs from classic autism in four specific areas: reported age of onset (mostly 3 to 4 years of age); clinical features (e.g., loss of previously acquired skills following a course of normal development); course (deterioration in development, sometimes progressive); and prognosis (usually lifelong challenges and high level of care required). Although the actual nature of CDD is controversial, the similar clinical picture to Autistic Disorder suggests a possible neurological basis (Malhotra & Gupta, 1999). Childhood Disintegrative Disorder remains a rare diagnosis, with a period of regression being the defining feature and a generally poor prognosis reported.

Asperger's Disorder. Hans Asperger, a German psychiatrist, first described this disorder in 1944, but its English translation did not appear until much later (Frith, 1991). For a child to receive a diagnosis of Asperger's Disorder, the following criteria have to be met (APA, 2000, p. 84):

- no significant delays in language development;
- no significant delays in cognitive development prior to age 3;
- severe and sustained deficits in social interaction;
- development of restricted repetitive and stereotyped patterns of behavior, interests, or activities; and
- significant deficits in social, occupational, or other areas of functioning.

In his original characterization of autism, Asperger described the children he saw as using pedantic and stereotyped speech, displaying clumsiness, showing obsessive-type interests, and exhibiting deficient social behavior. Some clinical researchers view Asperger's Disorder not as a separate disorder but simply as a different level of severity or degree than classic autism; they suggest that use of the term ensures that the observed problems in social understanding are recognized (Howlin, 1987; Schopler, 1985; Tantam, 1988; Wing, 1981). Gillberg (1991) has also defined criteria for making a diagnosis of Asperger's Disorder, specifying six areas of impairment: reciprocal social interaction, interest development, self-imposed routines, speech and language development, nonverbal communication, and motor performance.

Asperger's Disorder is newly included in the DSM–IV (APA, 1994), and field studies have yet to distinguish whether individuals diagnosed with it are distinctly different from those diagnosed with PDD-NOS or Autistic Disorder (Freeman & Cronin, 2002). Interpretation of what is "normal" or typical language development is at the forefront of the argument. There is also some question about whether early language delay is a good predictor of autistic behavior in older children and whether it is a valid discriminator between Autistic Disorder and Asperger's Disorder (Eisenmajer et al., 1998). Whether children with typical vocabulary development and other autistic criteria may be underrecognized for having atypical pragmatic and semantic language difficulties that would satisfy the criteria for Autistic Disorder requires further research. Socially awkward children in their teens with advanced academic skills may slip under the "radar screen" of an autism diagnosis. As well, Asperger's Disorder may be diagnosed without an accurate appraisal of a child's early symptoms, which may have included delays in language and play and would have prompted a diagnosis of autism.

Pervasive Developmental Disorder Not Otherwise Specified (PDD-NOS). PDD-NOS is a "subthreshold" diagnostic category used in the DSM–IV to account for those children who appear to represent "atypical autism." For a child to receive a diagnosis of PDD-NOS, the following criteria have to be met (APA, 2000, p. 84):

- pervasive impairment in social interaction;
- pervasive impairment in communication skills OR presence of stereotyped patterns of behavior, interests, or activities, which does not meet the criteria for a specific Pervasive Developmental Disorder; and
- presence of impairments that do not meet the criteria for Autistic Disorder because of late age at onset, atypical symptoms, or subthreshold symptoms.

It is not unusual for practitioners to identify four or five symptoms of Autistic Disorder, make a diagnosis of PDD-NOS, and later identify additional symptoms that provide a more convincing diagnosis of classic autism. Buitelaar, Van der Gaag, Klin, and Volkmar (1999) have explored the boundaries of PDD-NOS. They suggest that the most effective scoring rule, based on the DSM–IV and the ICD–10 criteria, might be a total of three items from the core deficit areas (social interaction, communication, and behavior), with at least one of the items coming from social interaction. Also, the child would not meet the criteria for Autistic Disorder or another PDD.

Diagnostic Assessment Tools

Better understanding of the core features of autism has led to the development of both screening and diagnostic instruments, in addition to the use of the DSM–IV diagnostic criteria (see Figure 1.1 for a checklist format), to assist practitioners in the recognition of ASD and in earlier diagnosis. The use of more formal diagnostic instruments can also help to differentiate severity of presentation. Current tools often involve interviews with the family, which are completed by practitioners through observation and interviews or interactions with the child. Appendix 1.B provides a brief description of some of the tools currently being used in assessments of children suspected

Diagnostic Criteria Checklist for Autistic Disorder

Child's name: _____ Date: _____

Date of birth: ____/____/____ Person(s) completing checklist: _____

A. A total of six (or more) items from (1), (2), and (3), with at least two from (1) and one from each of (2) and (3):	Yes	No	Uncertain
(1) qualitative impairment in social interaction, as manifested by at least two of the following:			
(a) marked impairment in the use of multiple nonverbal behaviors such as eye-to-eye gaze, facial expression, body postures, and gestures to regulate social interaction			
(b) failure to develop peer relationships appropriate to developmental level			
(c) lack of spontaneous seeking to share enjoyment, interests, or achievements with other people (e.g., by a lack of showing, bringing, or pointing out objects of interest)			
(d) lack of social or emotional reciprocity			
(2) qualitative impairment in communication, as manifested by at least one of the following:			
(a) delay in, or total lack of, the development of spoken language (not accompanied by an attempt to compensate through alternative modes of communication such as gesture or mime)			
(b) in individuals with adequate speech, marked impairment in the ability to initiate or sustain a conversation with others			
(c) stereotyped and repetitive use of language or idiosyncratic language			

(continues)

FIGURE 1.1. Diagnostic Criteria Checklist for Autistic Disorder. *Note.* Adapted from the *Diagnostic and Statistical Manual of Mental Disorders–Fourth Edition–Text Revision* (p. 75), by American Psychiatric Association, 2000, Washington, DC: Author. Copyright 2000 by American Psychiatric Association. Adapted with permission.

	Yes	No	Uncertain
(d) lack of varied, spontaneous make-believe play or social imitative play appropriate to developmental level			
(3) restricted repetitive and stereotyped patterns of behavior, interests, and activities, as manifested by at least one of the following:			
(a) encompassing preoccupation with one or more stereotyped and restricted patterns of interest that is abnormal in either intensity or focus			
(b) apparently inflexible adherence to specific, nonfunctional routines or rituals			
(c) stereotyped and repetitive motor mannerisms (e.g., hand or finger flapping or twisting, or complex whole-body movements)			
(d) persistent preoccupation with parts of objects			
B. Delays or abnormal functioning in at least one of the following areas, with onset prior to age 3 years:			
(a) social interaction			
(b) language as used in social communication			
C. The disturbance is not better accounted for by Rett's Disorder or Childhood Disintegrative Disorder			

FIGURE 1.1. *Continued.*

of having ASD. Most of these tools demonstrate at least moderate sensitivity and good specificity. Formats for using three of the screening tools described, the *Checklist for Autism in Toddlers* (CHAT; Baron-Cohen, Allen, & Gillberg, 1992), the *Australian Scale for Asperger's Syndrome* (Garnett & Attwood, 1998), and the *Modified CHAT* (M–CHAT; Robins, Fein, Barton, & Green, 2001a), are provided as Figures 1.2, 1.3, and 1.4, respectively. Despite newer diagnostic criteria and improved tools, the diagnosis of autism remains challenging. Accurate diagnosis still relies heavily on clinical experience (Klin, Lang, Cicchetti, & Volkmar, 2000; Lord, 1995), and because

Checklist for Autism in Toddlers

Child's name: _____   Date: _____

Date of birth: ____/____/____   Person(s) completing checklist: _____

Section A—Ask the parent[a]	Yes	No
1. Does your child enjoy being swung or bounced on your knee?		
2. Does your child take an interest in other children?		
3. Does your child like climbing on things, such as up stairs?		
4. Does your child enjoy playing peek-a-boo or hide-and-seek?		
5. Does your child ever pretend, for example, to make a cup of tea using a toy cup and teapot, or pretend other things?		
6. Does your child ever use his or her index finger to point to ask for something?		
7. Does your child ever use his or her index finger to point to indicate interest in something?		
8. Can your child play properly with small toys (e.g., cars or bricks) without just mouthing, fiddling with, or dropping them?		
9. Does your child ever bring objects over to you, to show you something?		
Section B—Practitioner's observation[b]		
1. During the appointment, has the child made eye contact with you?		
2. Get the child's attention, then point across the room at an interesting object and say, "Oh look! There's a [name the toy]!" Watch the child's face. (To record yes on this item, ensure that the child has not simply looked at your hand, but has actually looked at the object you are pointing at.)		
3. Get the child's attention, then give the child a miniature toy cup and teapot and say, "Can you make a cup of tea?" Does the child pretend to pour out tea and drink it? (If you can elicit an example of pretending in some other game, score a yes on this item.)		

(continues)

FIGURE 1.2. Checklist for Autism in Toddlers (CHAT). [a]Look for difficulty responding to numbers 5 (pretend play) and 7 (proto-declarative pointing). [b]Look for difficulty responding to numbers 2 (gaze monitoring), 3 (pretend play), and 4 (proto-declarative pointing). *Note.* Adapted from "Can Autism Be Detected at 18 Months? The Needle, the Haystack, and the CHAT," by S. Baron-Cohen, J. Allen, and C. Gillberg, 1992, *British Journal of Psychiatry, 161,* pp. 839–843. Copyright 1992 by the British Journal of Psychiatry. Adapted with permission.

Section B—Practitioner's observation[b]	Yes	No
4. Say to the child, "Where's the light" or "Show me the light." Does the child point with his or her index finger at the light? (Repeat this with "Where's the teddy?" or some other unreachable object if child does not understand the word "light." To record yes on this item, the child must have looked up at your face around the time of pointing.)		
5. Can the child build a tower of bricks? (If so, how many? Number of bricks _____)		

FIGURE 1.2. *Continued.*

autism is a clinical diagnosis, it is crucial that individuals coordinating comprehensive diagnostic assessments for children suspected of autism be well trained and experienced (Freeman & Cronin, 2002).

Early Indicators of Autism Spectrum Disorders

In the last 10 years, clinical researchers have identified several early indicators, or red flags, to consider in the diagnosis of ASD. Two approaches have been used to identify these early indicators: retrospective video analysis and follow-up of early screenings in at-risk populations. Some researchers have completed retrospective video analysis of social, communication, and play behaviors in the first 2 years of life for children who later received a diagnosis of autism (Adrien et al., 1992; Baranek, 1999; Mars, Mauk, & Dowrick, 1998; Osterling & Dawson, 1994; Werner, Dawson, Osterling, & Dinno, 2000). For example, in an analysis of 11 family home movies using an infant behavioral evaluation scale, Adrien and colleagues (1992) found differences between children with and without a diagnosis of autism or pervasive developmental disorder in eye contact, emotional expression, attention to and initiation of communication, and motor performance during the first 2 years of life. In a review of videotapes of first birthday parties, Osterling and Dawson (1994) found that children 12 months of age who later received a diagnosis of autism were less likely to point, orient to their name, show objects, or look at others. This analysis was also done with same-age peers who did not have a diagnosis of autism. In a follow-up study, Werner et al. (2000) confirmed the failure to orient to name and indicated that this finding emerged as early as 8 to 10 months of age. Baranek (1999) explored the existence of sensory–motor behaviors in addition to social behaviors as early indicators of autism. In her retrospective analysis, she reviewed videotapes of 11 children with

Australian Scale for Asperger's Syndrome

Child's name: _____ Date: _____

Date of birth: ____/____/____ Person(s) completing checklist: _____

Questions	0	1	2	3	4	5
Social–Emotional						
1. Does the child lack understanding of how to play with other children (e.g., is unaware of rules for social play)?						
2. When free to play with other children such as during school lunchtime, does the child avoid social contact with them (e.g., finds secluded place or goes to the library)?						
3. Does the child appear unaware of social conventions or codes of conduct and make inappropriate actions and comments (e.g., making a personal comment to someone, unaware of how the comment could offend)?						
4. Does the child lack empathy (i.e., the intuitive understanding of another person's feelings; e.g., not realizing an apology would help the other person feel better)?						
5. Does the child seem to expect other people to know his or her thoughts, experiences, and opinions (e.g., doesn't realize you could not know about something that happened to the child because you were not with the child at the time)?						
6. Does the child need an excessive amount of reassurance, especially if things are changed or go wrong?						
7. Does the child lack subtlety in his or her expression of emotion (e.g., shows distress or affection out of proportion to the situation)?						
8. Does the child lack precision in his or her expression of emotion (e.g., not understanding the levels of emotional expression appropriate for different people)?						
9. Is the child uninterested in participating in competitive sports, games, and activities?						

(continues)

FIGURE 1.3. Australian Scale for Asperger's Syndrome. *Note.* 0 = rarely (ordinary level expected), 5 = frequently (most conspicuous). A "yes" answer to the majority of questions in the scale and a rating between 2 and 5 do not imply that the child has Asperger's syndrome but do suggest a need for further assessment. Adapted from "The Australian Scale for Asperger's Syndrome," by M. S. Garnett and A. J. Attwood, 1998, in *Asperger's Syndrome: A Guide for Parents and Professionals* (pp. 17–19), by T. Attwood (Ed.), Philadelphia: Jessica Kingsley. Copyright 1998 by Jessica Kingsley Publishers. Adapted with permission.

Questions	0	1	2	3	4	5
10. Is the child indifferent to peer pressure?						
Communication Skills						
11. Does the child take a literal interpretation of comments (e.g., is confused by phrases such as "pull your socks up," "looks can kill," or "hop on the scales")?						
12. Does the child have an unusual tone of voice (e.g., seems to have a "foreign" accent or a monotone that lacks emphasis on key words)?						
13. When you talk to the child, does he or she appear uninterested in your side of the conversation (e.g., doesn't ask about or comment on your thoughts or opinions on the topic)?						
14. When in a conversation, does the child tend to use less eye contact than you would expect?						
15. Is the child's speech overprecise or pedantic (e.g., talks in a formal way or like a walking dictionary)?						
16. Does the child have problems repairing a conversation (e.g., when confused, he or she does not ask for clarification but simply switches to a familiar topic or takes ages to think of a reply)?						
Cognitive Skills						
17. Does the child read books primarily for information, seeming uninterested in fictional works (e.g., is an avid reader of encyclopedias and science books but not keen on adventure stories)?						
18. Does the child have an exceptional long-term memory for events and facts (e.g., remembers the neighbor's car registration of several years ago, or clearly recalls scenes that happened many years ago)?						
19. Does the child lack social imaginative play (e.g., doesn't include other children in imaginary games or is confused by the pretend games of other children)?						
Specific Interests						
20. Is the child fascinated by a particular topic and avidly collects information or statistics on that interest (e.g., becomes a walking encyclopedia on vehicles, maps, or league tables)?						

(continues)

FIGURE 1.3. *Continued.*

Questions	0	1	2	3	4	5
21. Does the child become unduly upset by changes in routine or expectation (e.g., is distressed by going to school by a different route)?						
22. Does the child develop elaborate routines or rituals that must be completed (e.g., lining up toys before going to bed)?						
Movement Skills						
23. Does the child have poor motor coordination (e.g., is not skilled at catching a ball)?						
24. Does the child have an odd gait when running?						

Other Characteristics:

Check whether the child has shown any of the following:

A. unusual fear or distress due to

    1.   ordinary sounds (e.g., electrical appliances)   ——

    2.   light touch on skin or scalp   ——

    3.   wearing particular items of clothing   ——

    4.   unexpected noises   ——

    5.   seeing certain objects   ——

    6.   noisy, crowded places (e.g., supermarkets)   ——

B. a tendency to flap or rock when excited or distressed   ——

C. a lack of sensitivity to low levels of pain   ——

D. lateness in acquiring speech   ——

E. unusual facial grimaces or tics   ——

FIGURE 1.3. *Continued.*

autism, 10 with developmental disabilities, and 11 without disabilities at 9 to 12 months of age. She confirmed a failure to orient to name and added other early predictors, including aversion to social touch, poor visual attention, and excessive mouthing. Mars and her collaborators (1998) reviewed prediagnostic home videos of 25 children with ASD and 25 children with typical development between 12 and 30 months of age. They found that an absence of or failure to develop joint attention was the strongest early marker of an eventual diagnosis of ASD.

Modified Checklist for Autism in Toddlers

Child's name: _____ Date: _____

Date of birth: ____/____/____ Person(s) completing checklist: _____

Questions (to be answered by parents):	Yes	No
1. Does your child enjoy being swung or bounced on your knee?		
2. Does your child take an interest in other children?[a]		
3. Does your child like climbing on things, such as up stairs?		
4. Does your child enjoy playing peek-a-boo or hide-and-seek?		
5. Does your child ever pretend, for example, to talk on the phone or take care of dolls, or other things?		
6. Does your child ever use his or her index finger to point to ask for something?		
7. Does your child ever use his or her index finger to point to indicate interest in something?[a]		
8. Can your child play properly with small toys (e.g., cars or bricks) without just mouthing, fiddling with, or dropping them?		
9. Does your child ever bring objects over to you, to show you something?[a]		
10. Does your child look you in the eye for more than a second or two?		
11. Does your child ever seem oversensitive to noise (e.g., plugs ears)?		
12. Does your child smile in response to your face or your smile?		
13. Does your child imitate you (e.g., if you make a face, will your child imitate it)?[a]		
14. Does your child respond to his or her name when you call?[a]		
15. If you point at a toy across the room, does your child look at it?[a]		
16. Does your child walk?		
17. Does your child look at things you are looking at?		

(continues)

FIGURE 1.4. Modified Checklist for Autism in Toddlers (M–CHAT). [a]Items found to be the most discriminating (in descending order): #7, 14, 2, 9, 15, 13. *Note.* Adapted from "The Modified Checklist for Autism in Toddlers: An Initial Study Investigating the Early Detection of Autism and Pervasive Developmental Disorders," by D. L. Robins, D. Fein, M. L. Barton, and J. A. Green, 2001, *Journal of Autism and Developmental Disorders, 31*(2), pp. 131–144. Copyright 2001 by Springer Science+Business Media. Adapted with permission.

Questions (to be answered by parents):	Yes	No
18. Does your child make unusual finger movements near his or her face?		
19. Does your child try to attract your attention to his or her activity?		
20. Have you ever wondered if your child is deaf?		
21. Does your child understand what people say?		
22. Does your child sometimes stare at nothing and wander with no purpose?		
23. Does your child look at your face to check your reaction when faced with something unfamiliar?		

FIGURE 1.4. *Continued.*

Some researchers have begun examining videotapes as early as 4 to 6 months of age to identify possible movement differences in children who later received a diagnosis of autism. Teitelbaum, Teitelbaum, Nye, Fryman, and Maurer (1998) used a movement analysis system to examine the lying, righting, sitting, crawling, and walking behavior of 17 children with autism whose parents supplied videotapes of their children's first year of life. Some of the movement differences observed included asymmetry in stomach lying at 4 months, a delay in sitting stability at 6 months, asymmetry in arm support and leg movement during crawling, and asymmetry in arm and leg movement while walking. Teitelbaum and his colleagues confirmed the belief that movement disturbances exist in autism, are present at birth, and can serve as early markers in diagnosis. It should be noted, however, that there has been little follow-up on the movement analysis reported by Teitelbaum et al., and results should be interpreted with caution at present.

Other researchers have used prospective longitudinal studies in which children at risk are screened and followed over time to determine whether early indicators of an autism spectrum diagnosis are maintained and what might be predictive at 18, 24, and 36 months of age (Baird et al., 2000; Baron-Cohen et al., 1992; Baron-Cohen et al., 1996; Lord, 1995). For example, Baron-Cohen and colleagues (1992) followed 91 children from their 18-month pediatric checkup through their third year of life. Forty of the children were at risk for ASD based on family history, and 51 had no prior history of ASD. All of the children were given the *Checklist for Autism in Toddlers* (Baron-Cohen et al., 1992) at their 18-month checkup. This screening tool includes nine questions asked of parents to determine their child's engagement and symbolism in play, joint attention, and use of pointing. It also includes five key observations by the practitioner to assess the child's symbolic play, ability to use a meaningful point, and ability to establish joint attention. Follow-up at age 3 for all children revealed four children with a diagnosis of autism. All four children came from the at-risk group. Answers to specific questions and observations on the CHAT were reported as predictive of the diagnosis at age 3. These included the following:

- failure to point to express interest (protodeclarative pointing);
- failure to show interest in or joint attention for pleasure or connection with another (gaze monitoring); and
- failure to demonstrate symbolic play (pretend play).

A follow-up study with over 16,000 children by Baron-Cohen and colleagues (1996) confirmed the early markers (i.e., lack of protodeclarative pointing, gaze monitoring, and pretend play) and differentiated those markers likely to occur in children with developmental disorders other than autism. Most children identified on the CHAT will receive a diagnosis of autism or pervasive developmental disorder, making it a valuable screening tool for identifying very young children at risk for ASD (Baron-Cohen et al., 2000). Practitioners must be aware, however, that the CHAT is likely to miss some children who eventually receive a diagnosis of autism, suggesting the need for careful monitoring of children over time.

Using the M–CHAT, consisting of 23 questions asked of the primary caregivers, Robins et al. (2001a) found six items that predicted a later diagnosis of autism. They screened 1,293 children and identified lack of pointing, failure to respond to name, lack of interest in other children, failure to "show" objects, inability to follow a point, and failure to imitate another as the social–communication skills most often demonstrated by children who later received a diagnosis of autism. Although both the CHAT and the M–CHAT show promise in early diagnosis, additional research is critical (Charman et al., 2001; Freeman & Cronin, 2002).

In her longitudinal research with 30 children, Lord (1995) also identified early predictors of autism and specified the clearest discriminators at ages 2 and 3. She found that behaviors identified at age 2 that remained significant at age 3 for a diagnosis of autism were directing attention (showing, pointing, vocalizing, etc.) and attention to voice (particularly neutral voice). Clearest discriminators at age 3 included seeking to share enjoyment (best predictor), pointing to express interest (more refined form of directing attention), using another's body as a tool (hand leading), unusual hand and finger mannerisms, and attention to voice.

Most recently, Wetherby and her colleagues have been engaged in longitudinal research to identify precise early indicators of autism during the 2nd and 3rd years of life through their examination of videotaped communication samples (Shumway, Wetherby, & Woods, 2003; Wetherby & Woods, 2003; Wetherby et al., 2004). They used the *Communication and Symbolic Behavior Scales Developmental Profile* (CSBS DP; Wetherby & Prizant, 2002) Infant–Toddler Checklist as a screening tool for children with ASD and identified red flags for ASD from videotapes collected during the

2nd year of life and then again in the 3rd year of life. The *Systematic Observation of Red Flags for Autism Spectrum Disorders in Young Children* (SORF; Wetherby & Woods, 2002) was used to record the observed behaviors from the videotaped communication samples. Fifty-four children were drawn from a pool of 3,021 children who are part of an ongoing longitudinal study of the FIRST WORDS Project (http://firstwords.fsu.edu). Three groups of 18 children were formed: children with ASD, children with developmental delays, and children who were typically developing. Following analysis of the SORF assessment, Wetherby and colleagues found significant differences between children with ASD and children with developmental delays, and between children with ASD and those who were typically developing on 9 of the 29 items on the SORF (Wetherby & Woods, 2003; Wetherby et al., 2004). These included a lack of appropriate eye gaze; warm, joyful expressions with gaze; sharing enjoyment or interest; response to name; coordination of gaze, facial expression, gesture, and sound; showing a demonstration of unusual prosody; repetitive movements or posturing of body, arms, hands, or fingers; and repetitive movements with objects. Children with ASD also differed significantly from children who were typically developing by demonstrating a lack of the following 4 skills: responding to contextual cues, pointing, vocalizing with consonants, and playing with a variety of toys. A follow-up study examined whether these 13 differentiating behaviors were evident in a sample of 15 children later diagnosed with ASD in the 2nd and 3rd years of their life (Shumway et al., 2003). The researchers were also interested in identifying any changes in the pattern of red flags seen in 2nd versus 3rd year of life. Shumway and colleagues found that the same 13 distinguishing behaviors were observed for their sample of children, and that those behaviors persisted in the 3rd year of life, although there were some differences in persistence of certain behaviors from year 2 to year 3 and some instances of new red flags emerging in the 3rd year. The researchers concluded that young children with ASD fail to exhibit certain typical behaviors and do present with some atypical behaviors. Early identification of ASD was most often characterized by impairments in early social communication and by repetitive behaviors.

Current research provides much promise for infant diagnosis. Klin and his colleagues (2004) reported on a case study of a 15-month-old little girl with autism who was evaluated using a battery of motor, cognitive, communication, symbolic, and adaptive behavior measures to examine the child's autistic symptoms at 15, 23, and 34 months. They found value in the use of tools such as the *Mullen Scales of Early Learning* (Mullen, 1995), the CSBS DP (Wetherby & Prizant, 2002), the *MacArthur Communicative Development Inventories* (Fenson et al., 1993), the *Vineland Adaptive Behavior Scales* (Sparrow, Balla, & Cicchetti, 1984), the *Autism Diagnostic Observation Schedule–Generic* (ADOS–G; Lord, Rutter, DiLavore, & Risi, 1999), and the *Autism Diagnostic Interview–Revised* (Lord, Rutter, & LeCouteur, 1991) to document the child's profile of relative strengths and significant deficits that are characteristic of autism. Klin et al. also noted accelerated head growth between 6 and 9 months. Research investigating the eye movement of toddlers further reveals that 2-year-olds with autism are sensitive to changes in gaze direction and may process gaze information using different strategies than 2-year-olds without autism (Chawarska, Klin, & Volkmar, 2003). Certainly, infant research, particularly related to early diagnosis and understanding the developmental trajectory of communication, gaze monitoring, relating, attention shifting, and other adaptive behaviors, is critical to the current knowledge base on autism.

Early diagnosis, however, has its challenges. The existing screening instruments continue to have limitations such as methodological flaws and small numbers of children in the sampled populations, and they often miss children who later receive a diagnosis of autism (Bryson, Rogers, & Fombonne, 2003). Making a diagnosis at 2 and 3 years of age is also very different from making a diagnosis at 5 and 6 years of age (Lord & Risi, 2000). For example, even children who follow a typical course of development vary in their ability to establish joint attention, say their first word, and initiate social interaction. Clinicians appear to be more reliable in their diagnosis of children under 3 years of age when they consider the broader autism spectrum as compared to autism and PDD-NOS (Stone et al., 1999). The challenges in early diagnosis require practitioners to be cognizant of the subtle developmental differences in young children with and without autism, particularly in the areas of social impairment and spoken language delays, and to actively engage family members in the diagnostic process. It is imperative that practitioners across disciplines make a commitment to careful observation of the social interaction, communication, play, and behavior of young children. Having a developmental perspective on these areas of potential deficit and unusual behavior in very young children with ASD is critical to the assessment and intervention of children at risk (Watson, Baranek, & DiLavore, 2003). Further, language regression prior to age 3 is a serious concern, as is cognitive impairment; both require follow-up (Wilson, Djukic, Shinnar, Dharmanu, & Rapin, 2003). A checklist identifying the early indicators of autism is included in Figure 1.5 as a tool for practitioners to use in their office or school screenings, as well as for families to identify concerns when attending those screenings.

Best Practice Guidelines for Diagnosis

Recent literature has reported efforts to establish guidelines or best practice parameters for the diagnosis of autism (American Academy of Child and Adolescent Psychiatry, 1999; American Academy of Pediatrics, 2001; Filipek et al., 2000). These guidelines are helping practitioners to recognize or suspect autism in children, based on abnormal social and communication development at earlier ages.

The American Academy of Neurology and the Child Neurology Society Quality Standards Subcommittee (with representatives from nine different professional organizations and four parent organizations) published practice

Early Indicators or Red Flags of ASD Checklist

Child's name: _____ Date: _____

Date of birth: ____/____/____ Person(s) completing checklist: _____

Indicator	Yes	No	Uncertain/ Comments
1. Demonstrates poor social visual orientation and attention (Adrien et al., 1992; Baranek, 1999).			
2. Fails to point to express interest (pointing typically develops by 8–10 mos.; may be delayed or never develop in ASD) (Baron-Cohen et al., 1992; Lord, 1995; Osterling & Dawson, 1994; Wetherby & Woods, 2003). [a, b]			
3. Uses hand leading or another's body as a tool (sees hand as a tool, often replacing pointing) (Lord, 1995).[a]			
4. Mouths objects excessively (Baranek, 1999).			
5. Stops talking after using three or more meaningful words (Lord, 2000).			
6. Uses fewer than five meaningful words on a daily basis at age 2; lack of vocalizations with consonants (Lord, 2000; Wetherby & Woods, 2003). [b]			
7. Fails to look at others; abnormal eye contact or inappropriate eye gaze (Adrien et al., 1992; Osterling & Dawson, 1994; Wetherby & Woods, 2003).[c]			
8. Fails to show interest in other children, ignores people, prefers to be alone (Adrien et al., 1992).			
9. Fails to orient to name, shows delayed response to name, or lacks attention to voice (especially neutral voice) (Baranek, 1999; Lord, 1995; Osterling & Dawson, 1994; Wetherby & Woods, 2003).[c, d]			
10. Lacks symbolic play (e.g., pretending to make a meal, talk on the telephone); lacks conventional play with a variety of toys (Baron-Cohen et al., 1992; Wetherby & Woods, 2003).[c]			

(continues)

FIGURE 1.5. Early indicators or red flags of autism spectrum disorder checklist. *Note.* The presence of (a "yes" response to) at least two of these red flags may indicate the need for further assessment. [a]Clearest discriminators at age 3 (Lord, 1995). [b]Distinguishes children with ASD from children who are typically developing but not from children with developmental delays (Wetherby & Woods, 2003). [c]Distinguishes children with ASD from children with developmental delays and those who are typically developing (Wetherby & Woods, 2003). [d]Clearest discriminators at age 2 (Lord, 1995).

Indicator	Yes	No	Uncertain/ Comments
11. Exhibits unusual hand and finger mannerisms, repetitive movements or posturing of body, arms, hands, or fingers (Lord, 1995; Wetherby & Woods, 2003).[a, c]			
12. Displays aversion to social touch (Baranek, 1999).			
13. Lacks coordination of gaze, facial expression, gesture, and sound (Wetherby & Woods, 2003).[c]			
14. Lacks expressive postures and gestures or exhibits unusual postures (Adrien et al., 1992).			
15. Fails to share enjoyment or interest (Lord, 1995; Wetherby & Woods, 2003).[a, c]			
16. Fails to show objects; fails to show an interest in or joint attention to games for pleasure or connection with another; fails to spontaneously direct another's attention (Baron-Cohen et al., 1992; Lord, 1995; Osterling & Dawson, 1994; Wetherby & Woods, 2003).[c]			
17. Fails to show warm, joyful expressions with gaze; lacks emotional facial expression and social smile (Adrien et al., 1992; Wetherby & Woods, 2003).[c]			
18. Makes repetitive movements with objects (Wetherby & Woods, 2003).[c]			
19. Displays unusual prosody (Wetherby & Woods, 2003).[c]			
20. Fails to respond to contextual cues (Wetherby & Woods, 2003).[b]			

FIGURE 1.5. *Continued.*

parameters for screening and diagnosing autism in young children (Filipek et al., 2000). The committee recommended two levels of assessment:

Level 1—Routine developmental surveillance and screening of autism for all children to identify those at risk for autism or any type of atypical development, and

Level 2—Diagnosis and evaluation of autism to differentiate autism from other developmental disorders.

The multidisciplinary consensus panel proposed the following parameters for effective screening:

- formal hearing testing
- lead testing (if pica or the eating of nonfood substances is reported)

- further evaluation if
  —no babbling by 12 months
  —no gesturing by 12 months
  —no single words by 16 months
  —no two-word phrases by 24 months (spontaneous and not echolalic)
  —loss of language or social skills (at any age)
- monitoring of siblings' social, communication, and play skills
- use of some formal screening tool for autism (e.g., CHAT; Baron-Cohen et al., 1992)

These parameters are suggested as a practice guide for all those who come into contact with young children. Children who fail a screening at Level 1 would be referred for further assessment following the guidelines established for Level 2.

The proposed guidelines for diagnostic and evaluation procedures at Level 2 include the following:

- diagnosis by an experienced clinician
- examination of
  —familial prevalence
  —large head circumference without associated neuropathology
  —association with tuberous sclerosis complex (TSC)
  —patterns of decreased cognitive skills, especially verbal and adaptive functions
- observation of
  —verbal and nonverbal communication
  —specific deficits in speech and language
  —sensorimotor challenges
  —motor deficits
- consideration for
  —genetic testing
  —selective metabolic testing
  —sleep EEG

This collaborative effort represents the importance that practitioners across several disciplines are giving to assessing this challenging disorder and their willingness to partner with families and individuals with autism in the evaluation process.

The American Academy of Child and Adolescent Psychiatry outlines several guidelines for the assessment and treatment of individuals with autism. As part of the evaluation process, information is to be gathered regarding early health and medical history as well as psychosocial considerations and the child's intervention history (American Academy of Child and Adolescent Psychiatry, 1999). A medical assessment is also recommended, including audiological, visual, neurological, psychological, and communication evaluations.

The American Academy of Pediatrics has issued a technical report of the pediatrician's role in the diagnosis and management of ASD in children (American Academy of Pediatrics, 2001). Because pediatricians share the challenge of making an accurate and early diagnosis, collaboration between pediatricians and the families they serve is essential. The American Academy of Pediatrics provided 12 key recommendations that have implications for all practitioners involved in the diagnosis and assessment of children with ASD. These recommendations are summarized in Table 1.1.

Role of Practitioners in Diagnosis

Families, educators, and health care professionals can all make important contributions to identifying the signs of autism, but an experienced clinician in the area of autism is needed to make an appropriate diagnosis (Filipek et al., 2000). Experienced clinicians not only rely on their clinical judgment but support their clinical decision making through their understanding and

TABLE 1.1
Recommended Practice for Diagnosing Children with Suspected ASD

- Listen carefully to families when they share information about their child's development, value their insight, and address their concerns.
- Monitor all development at well-child visits, specifically language and social skill development.
- Consider using screening tools for autism or refer a child you suspect of having autism to a specialist or team with expertise in ASD.
- Refer children with language delays for audiologic and speech and language evaluations.
- Promote immunizations and reassure families of the lack of evidence of a causal relationship to ASD.
- Screen for lead with risk factors such as pica.
- Refer to genetics with the presence of dysmorphic features, history of Fragile X, or mental retardation with an undetermined etiology.
- Refer to neurology with suspected seizures or noted regression.
- Share current literature and provide contacts for support once a diagnosis has been made.
- Encourage families to seek genetic counseling as appropriate.
- Monitor younger siblings of children with a diagnosis of ASD.
- Seek opportunities for enrollment in early intervention or school programs for children with suspected delay or symptoms of ASD.
- Become familiar with the current approaches to intervention and be able to share the information with families both objectively and with compassion.
- Provide care coordination among interprofessional services.
- Encourage families to consent to tissue donation in the event of the death of a child with ASD.

Note. Adapted from "American Academy of Pediatrics Policy Statement on the Pediatrician's Role in the Diagnosis and Management of ASD in Children," by American Academy of Pediatrics, 2001, *Pediatrics, 107*(5), pp. 1221–1226. Copyright 2001 by American Academy of Pediatrics. Adapted with permission.

use of the criteria specified in the DSM–IV or the ICD–10, as well as assessment tools, rating scales, and checklists. Interdisciplinary teams with experience in diagnosing autism can often provide the most comprehensive overview of the child with ASD, but these teams must have experienced team members familiar with the range of symptoms and general course of the disorder.

External pressures, outside the practice of developmental diagnosis, can force the diagnostic process. Often, to qualify for particular services (e.g., developmental services or special education), a formal diagnosis must be offered by a licensed physician (pediatrician, developmental pediatrician, psychiatrist, or neurologist) or other licensed health practitioner (e.g., psychologist). This should not undermine the ability of other educational and health professionals to suspect and identify children appropriately. All disciplines need to work in concert with those able to provide a diagnosis, so that children can be found eligible for the services they need.

As practitioners and families make referrals to medical professionals for evaluation of a child suspected of ASD, there are some things that can be done ahead of time to make sure the physician has what is needed to make an informed decision. Prior to making a referral, team members can gather information, so that the medical visit is enriched by the knowledge and experience of those who interact with the child on a daily basis. Most physicians cannot visit a school or a child's home and have limited time to examine all the aspects of a child's daily life that provide critical information for making a diagnosis. Table 1.2 lists a number of activities that could

---

TABLE 1.2
Suggestions for Making Physician Referrals Regarding a Diagnosis of ASD

---

1. Send a videotape (30 minutes maximum) of the following:

    - the child engaged in both structured and unstructured tasks,
    - the child interacting with adults and with peers,
    - the child playing with objects,
    - the child working in a small group and independently (if appropriate), and
    - the child at school and at home or other setting.

2. Complete the *Checklist for Autism in Toddlers,* the *Modified Checklist for Autism in Toddlers,* or the Early Indicators or Red Flags of ASD Checklist with the family as a retrospective look at the child's early history (see Figures 1.2, 1.4, 1.5).

3. If you suspect Asperger syndrome in an older child, complete the *Australian Scale for Asperger's Syndrome* (see Figure 1.3).

4. Review the diagnostic criteria for autism (see Figure 1.1) and provide the physician with specific observations or examples in each of the areas listed (e.g., social interaction, communication, and behavior).

5. Provide the physician with a *brief* explanation of interventions that have been used to support the social interaction, communication, and behavior of the child, along with the successes and challenges of each.

be done in preparation for a referral. Not all of these activities would need to be done for each child, but team members may wish to consider many of them, especially when they believe the diagnostic process might be complex for a particular child. The team might also ask the physician to review the diagnostic criteria with the family during the visit, explaining the specific behaviors that were observed or not observed that would suggest or not suggest a diagnosis of autism spectrum disorder.

Diagnosing children on the fringes of autism can be frustrating even to experienced clinicians. Diagnostic uncertainty can be devastating to parents and others involved. Parents may understandably cling to the opinion of one professional in hopes that their child does not have autism and dismiss a professional who might view the child otherwise. In other circumstances, parents may express disappointment in the professional who "missed" or failed early on to "make the diagnosis" that was later confirmed. Most important, professionals must be honest with families and share what they know, what they do not know, what they suspect and why, and how they might proceed. The task of sharing difficult news should not determine if and when a practitioner decides to talk with families about a potential diagnosis. Bax (1999) has put it this way:

> Disclosing a neurodevelopmental disorder to parents is always difficult, in spite of current training to the task. Regardless of how well trained we are, we will always find the task difficult and often worry if we have got it "wrong." However, I have found myself almost thanked when telling parents that their child has a problem.... Another couple said ... "That's exactly what we think he's got wrong with him." These comments identify the failure of the appropriate professionals to see children with neurodevelopmental disorders as soon as their parents become concerned and to make a correct diagnosis. (p. 795)

It is also important to note that families and providers may become frustrated when children fail to meet the diagnostic criteria or fit a diagnosis of autism even though they exhibit some obvious social challenges and require services or additional supports. Honesty with families is just as critical in these situations. It is not appropriate to offer a diagnosis just so a patient can receive services. Teams must work cooperatively to define the issues facing a child with social, communication, or behavioral challenges who does not fit the diagnosis of autism, and collaboratively determine those services that will address the child's individual needs.

Differential Diagnosis

The differential diagnosis of children who present with differences in social and language development and rigid or repetitive behaviors includes the spectrum of autistic disorders and pervasive developmental disorders addressed earlier as well as disorders typically considered outside the spectrum. Disorders outside of the spectrum (albeit with some overlapping symptomatology) include specific language impairment, learning disabilities, mental retardation, obsessive-compulsive disorder, attention-deficit/hyperactivity disorder (ADHD), personality disorders, schizophrenia, and other mental disorders.

Specific Language Impairment and Autistic Disorder

Differential diagnosis in young children may be difficult as practitioners try to distinguish between the presence of a language disorder alone and the language symptoms of autism. Children with specific language impairment and autism may have similarities in early language delay and acquisition, but the language of children with autism is often more "disordered" in its pattern of expression (Noterdaeme, Sitter, Mildenberger, & Amorosa, 2000). For example, children with autism often use pronoun reversal, echolalia, metaphorical language, and stereotyped utterances (Klinger & Dawson, 1996). Although children with specific language impairment may experience secondary difficulties with socialization, they can often be differentiated from children with autism by their abilities to use gesture and eye contact to communicate. Further, they do not demonstrate the repetitive restrictive stereotyped behaviors typical of children with ASD.

Learning Disabilities and Autistic Disorder

Children with a variety of learning disabilities may have subsequent language and social challenges. Syndromes of nonverbal learning disability (NLD) and right hemispheric dysfunction are being recognized as having a profound impact on visual–spatial abilities and the "reading" of facial and gestural cues of others during social interaction, which may result in odd and antisocial behavior (Manoach, Sandson, & Weintraub, 1995; Rourke, 1989; Semrud-Clikeman & Hynd, 1990). Research is ongoing to determine the overlap or separation of NLD syndromes with diagnoses along the autism spectrum (Rourke, 2000; Volkmar & Klin, 1998). Cognitive testing that reveals a pattern of relatively lower verbal IQ can help to distinguish autism from NLD, which typically presents with relatively lower performance IQ.

Mental Retardation and Autistic Disorder

Autistic disorder and the range of pervasive developmental disorders are defined by the deviance in behavior displayed in comparison to mental age. Therefore, although many children with this diagnosis also exhibit mental retardation, at least 25% of children with autism have normal intellectual ability, which indicates it is a separate disorder from mental retardation (MR)

(Klinger & Dawson, 1996). Further, when comparing children with autism to children with MR of comparable developmental levels, children with autism demonstrate specific impairments in joint attention, symbolic play, imitation and theory-of-mind (Klinger & Dawson, 1996). Differential diagnosis between autism and MR is often difficult for individuals with lower cognitive abilities who also exhibit self-stimulatory behavior (Volkmar & Wiesner, 2004).

Obsessive-Compulsive Disorder and Autistic Disorder

Obsessive-compulsive disorder (OCD) is defined by the presence of obsessions (persistent ideas, thoughts, impulses, and images) and compulsions (repetitive behaviors). The clinical presentation and manifestation of the disorder should differentiate it from autism. OCD typically presents at younger ages (between 6 and 15 years) for males and older ages (between 20 and 29 years) for females (APA, 2000). Children who later present with OCD exhibit typical language and social development. Children and adults with autism may have "compulsive" repetitive behaviors and appear to be "obsessed" with specific thought patterns but by definition meet the criteria for autism; in general, OCD as a separate disorder is not considered in such cases.

Attention-Deficit/Hyperactivity Disorder and Autistic Disorder

ADHD and autism differ in onset, course, associated features, familial patterns, and prognosis, although challenges in attention affect children in both disorder groups (Lord, 2000). Children with autism may have variable attention (Allen & Courchesne, 2001), from being aloof and inattentive to details in their environment to being hyperalert or hyperfocused on areas of narrowed interest to the exclusion of other stimuli. Perhaps their attention is best described by the inability to appropriately focus on the more meaningful social information in their environment. Children with autism may also have reactions to sensory stimuli that distract them from their tasks or cause them to overact with increased physical activity. Most important, though, children with autism have deficits in joint attention, which requires them to direct their gaze and attention to the same object or event as another person and share the other's interest in that object or event (Lord, 2000). Many of these features of attention may be mistaken for ADHD; however, the pervasive nature of the social deficit in autism should distinguish it. Some studies have found that children with autism and decreased attention may benefit from the stimulant medication typically used for treating children with ADHD, although a greater incidence of medication side effects is reported for children with autism (Handen, Johnson, & Lubetsky, 2000). The DSM–IV schema suggest that ADHD should not be diagnosed when the symptoms of inattention occur exclusively during the course of a pervasive developmental disorder (APA, 1994). Recent research, however, calls for some reconsideration in making a comorbid diagnosis for children with autism who display significant ADHD-like symptoms (Goldstein & Schwebach, 2004).

Personality Disorders and Autistic Disorder

Personality disorders are characterized by maladaptive patterns for coping, experiencing, and relating (APA, 1994; Bleiberg, 2001). Although individuals with autism may exhibit unusual behaviors that could be confused with features of specific personality disorders, age of presentation (typically adolescence or beyond for personality disorders) and the persistent typical features of pervasive developmental disorder should distinguish them. Baltaxe, Russell, D'Angiola, and Simmons (1995) have suggested some continuity in the social language deficits observed in ASD and personality disorders, particularly in the use of referencing to support discourse cohesion. Further, individuals with ASD and other developmental disorders run a higher risk than the population at large for manifesting additional psychiatric disorders (Ghaziuddin, Weidmer-Mikhail, & Ghaziuddin, 1998; Gillberg & Billstedt, 2000; Volkmar, Cook, Pomeroy, Realmuto, & Tanguay, 1999; Wolff, 1973, 1989). Deterioration or changes in function or mental status should be thoroughly investigated, and treatment and therapeutic intervention should be offered. Interventions need to consider children's development and life experiences and those of their parents with a focus on the desired future for each child (Wolff, 1989).

Schizophrenia and Autistic Disorder

Predating current conceptual understanding of autism, infantile or childhood autism was once considered to be a form of schizophrenia. Schizophrenia is manifested by normal or near-normal development, less impaired intellectual abilities, and a gradual or sudden onset of psychotic symptoms, including delusions, hallucinations, disorganized speech, and unusual behavior appearing later in development (American Academy of Child and Adolescent Psychiatry, 1999). Typical onset of schizophrenia is in the teens to mid-30s and rarely occurs prior to age 7 (Klinger & Dawson, 1996). Childhood-onset schizophrenia is defined by the development of the first psychotic symptoms by age 12 and is rarer than adult presentation. Further, the marked social impairment and unusual behaviors typical of children with ASD are not seen in individuals with schizophrenia (Volkmar & Wiesner, 2004).

Neurobiologic Considerations

Research in the last 10 years has increased understanding of why autism might be seen in some children, the differences in the brain that could explain certain autistic behaviors, and the possible genetic links that exist in children and families affected by this disorder. In this section, the focus will be the anatomical abnormalities that have been reported in the brains of individuals with ASD, the connections between brain function and behavior related to ASD, and some speculation as to specific theorized etiologies used to explain why autism occurs.

Anatomical Abnormalities

In general, large brain size has been described in individuals with autism. Multiple studies suggest, however, that several areas of brain maldevelopment exist in autism, indicating a more complex neurobiological picture (Fidler, Bailey, & Smalley, 2000; Lainhart, Piven, Wzorek, & Landa, 1997). It seems that both the white and gray matter of the brain are affected and that this widespread brain involvement explains the pervasive nature of the disorder.

Courchesne and Pierce (2000) describe the involvement of several brain structures, including the cerebellum, the limbic system, the cerebrum, the basal ganglia, the superior olive, and the facial motor nucleus. There are also reports of a smaller cerebellar vermis and cortex, and most autopsy studies show some cerebellar abnormalities (Courschesne, Saitoh, et al., 1994). Bailey, Luthert, Dean, Harding, and Janota (1998) reported that 90% of the individuals they studied had fewer Purkinje neurons (important communication catalysts with other parts of the brain) than expected of individuals without autism. In fact, Bailey and colleagues indicated that individuals with autism had a 20% to 60% loss of these neurons. Considering the functions of the cerebellum, including learning, memory, sensory, motor, attention, language, face processing, and problem solving, it is not difficult to understand how differences in this area of the brain could explain some of the behavioral symptoms observed in children with ASD.

By means of autopsy and magnetic resonance imaging (MRI) studies, abnormalities in the limbic system have also been reported in most (Bauman & Kemper, 1988, 1994) but not all (Bailey et al., 1998) individuals with a diagnosis of autism. An increase in neurons as well as a reduction in their density has been described in the limbic system. Specifically, the amygdala, which makes an important contribution to emotional and social learning, has been identified as abnormal in size for this population (Abell et al., 1999; Aylward et al., 1999).

In contrast to the reduction of size in areas of the cerebellum, an increased volume of the cerebrum has been identified in 2- to 4-year-olds with autism. The corpus callosum, however, which supports communication across the two hemispheres of the brain, has been reported as smaller, with the posterior section most affected (Egaas, Courchesne, & Saitoh, 1995). A reduction in size in the corpus callosum might suggest less effective and efficient exchange and processing of information across the two hemispheres.

Other sites in the brain have also been reported as abnormal in individuals with autism, but to a lesser extent. Studies have shown abnormalities in the parietal lobe, the basal ganglia, and the brain stem. Rodier (2000) has described a smaller than normal facial nucleus (which controls muscles of facial expression), an absent superior olive (a relay station for auditory information), and a shortened brain stem.

Most recently, Boddaert and Zilbovicius (2002) described the benefits of improved functional brain imaging in identifying consistent dysfunction in the temporal lobes of children with autism. They reviewed research over the last 15 years and presented the key results of rest and activation studies, reporting that individuals with autism demonstrate different patterns of cortical activity in the left temporal lobe compared to normal controls.

Although multiple areas of the brain are known to be affected, as of yet no specific profiles have been developed. Researchers also know that abnormal neurodevelopment occurs early on (Nicolson & Szatmari, 2003). Research continues to investigate differences in the brains of individuals with autism while trying to understand and explain the behavior so often observed in this population.

Brain–Behavior Findings

Newer neuroimaging techniques such as functional MRI (FMRI), single-photon emission computed tomography (SPECT), and positron-emission tomography (PET) use differences in cellular metabolism to obtain "real time" pictures of regional brain function. Studies of the brain have been used to explain at least three general areas of abnormality most often observed in individuals with autism: social, attention, and restricted interests. Social abnormalities have been reported in the face perception, emotion processing, social cue orientation, and attention regulation of individuals with autism. Brain structures that have a role in social processing, specifically in self-awareness, includes abnormalities in the amygdala (Abell et al., 1999; Aylward et al., 1999; Baron-Cohen et al., 1999) and reduced activation of the fusiform gyrus while viewing pictures of faces (Courchesne & Pierce, 2000; Pierce & Courchesne, 2000; Schultz et al., 2000). It is postulated that such structural abnormalities might make the brain unable to support the level of activity required for facial processing, or it might be that the brain is structurally intact but decreased experience with faces causes underdevelopment. Either interaction is possible.

Attention abnormalities in autism occur in three general areas: disengagement, orienting, and attention shifting. Attention requires complex networking involving the cerebellum and the parietal lobes of the brain. The ability to *disengage,* or respond to unexpected information outside the immediate attentional focus, involves the parietal cortex. Townsend and

Courchesne (1994) found that individuals with reduced parietal volume are slow to disengage. This leads to a narrow distribution of visual spatial attention. *Orienting* is the ability to focus on places where information occurs. It serves to increase an individual's processing speed and accuracy. For individuals with autism, orienting is often slow and inaccurate for both social and nonsocial information (Harris, Courchesne, Townsend, Carper, & Lord, 1999; Townsend et al., 1999). *Attention shifting* requires an ability to change attention quickly from one source to another. This involves both the cerebellum and the parietal cortex (Allen, Buxton, Wong, & Courchesne, 1997). Individuals with autism often demonstrate slow and inaccurate attention shifting, particularly between sights and sounds, and often miss important information. It has been suggested that with Purkinje neuron loss, a disorganized path begins prenatally or in the early postnatal period that impinges on those processes underlying attention shifting and orienting (Courchesne, Townsend, et al., 1994). Thus, a young child with autism is already at a disadvantage in being unable to learn from joint interactions because of the inability to regulate a shift in attention or orient to important input.

The restricted interest, or failure to explore stimuli, characteristic of individuals with autism has been related to abnormalities in the cerebellar vermis. Studies have found that the greater the repetitive and stereotyped behavior observed, the greater the cerebellar vermis abnormality (Courchesne, Saitoh, et al., 1994; Courchesne, Yeung-Courchesne, Press, Hesselink, & Jernigan, 1988).

Severity of early behavioral impairments (e.g., orienting to social stimuli, motor imitation, shared attention, symbolic play) in autism has been linked to the medial temporal lobe and a related limbic structure, the orbital prefrontal cortex (Dawson, Meltzoff, Osterling, & Rinaldi, 1998). A recent review by Boddaert and Zilbovicius (2002) has also implicated the left temporal cortex as demonstrating abnormal patterns of activation in individuals with autism. This finding may be used to explain another area of abnormality reported for this population, which is language impairment. The left temporal lobe is important to the organization of language and behavioral responses to sound (Boddaert & Zilbovicius, 2002). Asymmetry in the volume of the frontal cortex, a region of the brain frequently associated with language functioning, also has been reported for boys with autism (Herbert et al., 2002). Most recently, frontal lobe involvement has been reported for individuals with autism (ages 6 to 47 years) with both lower and higher cognitive abilities, affecting their flexibility and ability to plan efficiently (Ozonoff et al., 2004).

Speculated Etiology

Families often search for a cause of their child's autism, as do researchers, to better understand the nature and course of the disorder, as well as to define methods for prevention and intervention. Although research is in the early stages, recent genetic findings have provided insight into the nature of the disorder. Twin studies have provided important confirmation that a genetic basis exists. Bailey and colleagues (1995) found that when one twin of an identical pair is diagnosed with autism, the second twin has a 60% chance of having the same diagnosis and an 86% chance of having some autistic symptoms. A recurrence rate of 3% to 8% has been noted in siblings, which is greater than the general population risk of 0.16%, although less than the 50% recurrence risk for a dominant trait or 25% recurrence risk for a recessive trait (Rodier, 2000).

Current research on the genetics of autism suggests that up to 5% to 10% of autism is secondary to a chromosome abnormality or a single gene disorder (Muhle, Trentacoste, & Rapin, 2004). The remaining 90% to 95% of cases are of unknown cause, but further advances in genetics may determine other single gene disorders not yet detectable. In addition, approximately 30% of children with autism have dysmorphic features such as microcephaly or brain abnormalities, whereas 70% have no physical abnormalities. Recurrence risks for autism appear to be different in subsequently born siblings based on the gender of the sibling, and not the gender of the child previously diagnosed with autism (Newschaffer, Fallin, & Lee, 2002). Recurrence risks also differ based on presence or absence of physical features in the previously diagnosed child. The reader is cautioned, however, that these and other cited recurrence risks are reported from small studies and have limitations for genetic counseling. For male siblings of an affected child, the risks are about 7% if the affected child has no physical manifestations and about 1% if the affected child has physical differences (Ritvo et al., 1989). For female siblings of an affected child, the risk is about 1% in either scenario. The likelihood of autism increases dramatically, toward 35%, if there are two previously affected siblings (Ritvo et al., 1989).

There is also evidence that several genes may be involved in the causation and pathogenesis of autism. Genetic studies of persons with autism and their close relatives have detected polymorphism (changes in the genetic code) on several chromosomes, suggesting some association between that defect and a gene for autism at that site. The most common polymorphisms have been found in chromosome 15 at 15q11 to 13. In linkage studies in families without structural chromosomal changes, the distal end of chromosome 7 (distal 7q) emerges as the region of greatest interest (Wassink & Piven, 2000). Other genes known for producing specific products, such as the neurotransmitters serotonin and gamma-aminobutyric acid (GABA), are being investigated for their possible link to symptomatology of autism (Lamb, Parr, Bailey, & Monaco, 2002).

More controversial but equally interesting to researchers and families are teratogens, such as toxins or viruses, which have been suggested as possible causal agents in autism. There is no substantial evidence for a causal relationship, although these agents can cause brain damage in the regions affected in autism. For example, prenatal and neonatal alcohol exposure and prenatal exposure to the valporic acid in seizure medication can cause Purkinje cell loss. Cytomegalovirus (CMV) interferes with cerebellar development and has impacted the play and social behavior of animals. It has also been suggested that the mumps, measles, and rubella (MMR) vaccine may serve as a risk factor when added to the genetic predisposition for autism, but no significant correlation has been found (Kaye, Maria Del Mar, & Jick, 2001; Madsen et al., 2002). Further, it has been found that prenatal exposure to thalidomide has led to autism in children, characterized by abnormalities in eye movement, facial expression, or both, suggesting initiation of the disorder in early gestation (Rodier, 2000). Clearly, the strongest causal evidence for autism implicates genes over toxins. The role of immunizations, however, continues to be worrisome for families. Families should be encouraged to talk openly with their primary health care providers about their concerns and worries regarding immunization. Primary health care providers have a responsibility to listen, hear the concerns families raise, inform families of what is known about the genetic connections to autism, and explain the role of immunizations in the health of their children.

Multiple theories regarding the cause of autism have been proposed, pursued, and rejected due to lack of scientific evidence. These include theories about food allergies or intolerances (to gluten, casein, lactose), toxins (mercury, pesticides), infections (candida or yeast), immunizations, gastrointestinal abnormality (secretin), vitamin or micronutrient deficiency (B_{12} and magnesium) and other metabolic abnormalities (thyroid, mitochondrial enzymes). Often a "pseudoscientific" approach toward causality is used. This approach lacks appropriate epidemiological validity. For example, proponents of the theory that immunizations cause autism might argue that the prevalence of autism has increased and the number of childhood immunizations has increased; therefore, immunizations cause autism. Epidemiologists point out several flaws in this thinking. The consensus of the American Academy of Neurology is that there is inadequate supporting evidence for hair analysis, celiac antibodies, allergy testing (particularly food allergies for gluten, casein, candida, and other molds), immunologic or neurochemical abnormalities, micronutrients such as vitamin levels, intestinal permeability studies, stool analysis, urinary peptides, mitochondrial disorders (including lactate and pyruvate), thyroid function tests, or erythrocyte glutathione peroxidase studies to explain the causes of autism (Filipek et al., 2000). The search for causes continues, although it is unlikely that research findings will lead to practical solutions very soon (Fombonne, 2003b). It is critical, therefore, that in the meantime, clinical researchers look into developing and evaluating interventions that will improve long-term outcomes for children with ASD.

Summary

This chapter provided information about both the history and the recent trends in diagnosis of ASD, as well as about the early markers, or red flags, practitioners might observe in very young children. The chapter also described the practice guidelines for the screening and assessment of children with ASD. Further, it explained who is involved in making a diagnosis and the challenges in distinguishing among related disorders, along with the neurobiological nature of ASD. The summary that follows refers to the questions at the beginning of the chapter and highlights the key points.

What are the trends in the diagnosis of ASD?

The prevalence of ASD is about 1 in 500, although some have reported even higher incidences. Over the last 30 years, the diagnosis of autism has been refined several times and characterized to include a spectrum of disorders with primary deficits in social reciprocity, communication, and repetitive behavior and interests. Both national (DSM) and international (ICD) classification systems have been used by practitioners to guide them in the diagnostic process. The continuing refinement of the definition and the use of two different classification systems has certainly contributed to some confusion in diagnosis, but the core deficits have remained consistent with those first described by Kanner in 1943.

What are the early indicators for a diagnosis of ASD?

Both retrospective video analysis and early screenings of at risk populations have been used to identify potential red flags of autism. Although the diagnosis of children under 3 years of age remains difficult because of variability in typical development and the manifestations of language and behavioral challenges in related disabilities, some consistent discriminators for distinguishing children with ASD have emerged. A frequently reported early indicator is the failure of a young child to establish joint attention, to show delight or pleasure in an experience or event shared with another. A delay in or absence of pointing and the presence of hand leading, as well as unusual hand or finger mannerisms, have been described. Other early markers include an absence of symbolic play, the inability to understand words out of context, the failure to use words meaningfully, and the cessation of talking after saying at least three meaningful words. Some research has even identified early motor behaviors (e.g., sitting, standing, crawling, walking) that reveal differences between children with an eventual diagnosis of ASD and age-matched peers. Research is likely to continue to reveal early indicators that lead to a suspicion of autism. Most important, though, earlier identification can lead to earlier intervention and, hopefully, to improved outcomes for children with ASD.

What are some guidelines for best practice in diagnosing ASD?

The American Academy of Pediatrics, the American Academy of Neurology, and the Child Neurology Society have defined a set of guidelines to support practitioners in both the screening and diagnosis of autism. These guidelines are important best practice recommendations for ensuring that children suspected of ASD are identified early and provided with the services needed. Understanding early language development and recognizing delays and differences in communication and social interaction are critical to the proposed guidelines. Speech, language, and hearing testing has an important role in both screening and diagnosis, as do lead testing for children with pica and monitoring the development of siblings.

Who should make the diagnosis?

An experienced clinician is most likely to provide consistent and reliable diagnoses of children along the autism spectrum. This is not to suggest, however, that families and other practitioners who have day-to-day experiences with a particular child have no information to contribute. In fact, the diagnostic process should involve an interdisciplinary team effort with information gathered from a variety of contexts across a number of settings.

How should ASD be differentially diagnosed from related neurodevelopmental disorders?

It is important that practitioners involved in the diagnosis of children with neurodevelopmental disabilities become familiar with the diagnostic criteria not only of the pervasive developmental disorders identified in the DSM–IV, but also of related disorders that may share one or more aspects of ASD. These include specific language impairment, nonverbal learning disabilities, mental retardation, obsessive-compulsive disorder, attention-deficit/hyperactivity disorder, and schizophrenia. Practitioners must understand the nature, age of onset, and course of a particular disorder, as well as its defining and associated features, to make an accurate, differential diagnosis.

What are some neurobiological considerations in the understanding of ASD?

There appear to be multiple anatomical abnormalities in the brains of individuals with ASD that confirm a biological basis to the disorder. The widespread abnormality reported in brain structures such as the cerebellum, cerebrum, limbic system, and brain stem, to name just a few, seems to explain the pervasive nature of the disorder. Both speculation and research regarding brain–behavior connections have suggested that the social deficits, attentional challenges, and restricted range of interests reported in children with ASD have a neurological basis. Further, genetic findings using twin and sibling studies, as well as genome-wide searches, indicate that several genes at different chromosome locations may be involved. Autism is a complex disorder, but ongoing neuroimaging and genetic studies will continue to provide greater understanding and a guide toward meaningful interventions.

APPENDIX 1.A
Summary of DSM–IV Diagnostic Criteria for Pervasive Developmental Disorders (PDDs)

Features

	Autistic Disorder 299.00	Rett's Disorder 299.80	Childhood Disintegrative Disorder 299.10	Asperger's Disorder 299.80
Diagnostic	Failure to develop peer relationships.	Development of multiple specific impairments after a period of normal development.	Marked regression in multiple areas following at least 2 years of normal development.	Severe and sustained impairment in social interaction.
	Lack of spontaneous seeking to share enjoyment, interests, etc.	Head circumference decreases at 5 to 48 months.	Significant loss of previously acquired skills in at least two of the following areas:	Development of restricted, repetitive patterns of behavior, interests, and activities.
	Lack of social and emotional reciprocity.	Loss of hand skills at 5 to 30 months and development of hand wringing or hand washing movements.	• receptive or expressive language • social skills or adaptive skills • bowel or bladder control • play • motor skills	Clinically significant impairment in social, occupational, or other important areas of functioning.
	Communication impairment.			
	Lack of varied, spontaneous make-believe play.	After onset, interest in social interaction decreases but develops again later in the course of the condition.	Social and communicative deficits and restricted, repetitive, and stereotyped behaviors typical of Autistic Disorder.	No clinically significant delays or deviance in language.
	Restricted, repetitive, and stereotyped patterns of behavior.	Problems in gait and trunk movement.		No clinically significant delays in cognitive development in the first 3 years; normal curiosity about the environment.
		Severe communication and psychomotor deficits.		Gross and sustained impairment in reciprocal interaction; may use multiple nonverbal behaviors to regulate social interaction and communication.
				Failure to develop peer relationships.
				Lack of spontaneous seeking to share enjoyment, interests, etc.
				Lack of social and emotional reciprocity.

(continues)

APPENDIX 1.A Continued.
Summary of DSM–IV Diagnostic Criteria for Pervasive Developmental Disorders (PDDs)

Features

Autistic Disorder 299.00	Rett's Disorder 299.80	Childhood Disintegrative Disorder 299.10	Asperger's Disorder 299.80
Associated Conditions			
MR (mild–profound).	MR (severe–profound).	MR (severe).	MR *not* observed, unless mild in school years with no delays in early years.
Uneven cognitive skills.	EEG abnormalities and seizure disorder.	EEG abnormalities and seizure disorder.	Strengths in vocabulary and rote memory.
V weaker than NV skills.	Nonspecific brain abnormalities.	Occasionally seen with medical condition (e.g., metachromatic leukodystrophy, Schilder's disease).	Challenges in visual–motor and visual–spatial skills.
Single-word vocabulary does not predict language.	Genetic mutation causal for some cases.		Mild motor clumsiness and awkwardness.
Hyperactivity, short attention span, impulsivity, aggression, self-injurious behaviors, temper tantrums.			Overactive and inattentive.
Over- or underreactive to sensory input.			Associated with other mental disorders, including Depressive Disorders.
Limitations in eating and sleeping.			
Abnormalities in affect or mood.			
EEG abnormalities.			
Group differences in serotonin activity.			
25% develop seizures, especially in adolescence.			
Micro- and macrocephaly.			

Age			
Prior to age 3. Generally no period of normal development. 20% report relatively normal development for 1 to 2 years.	Prior to age 4; between 5 and 48 months; usually at 12 or 24 months.	Prior to age 10, with at least 2 years of normal development. Most often diagnosed between age 3 and 4.	Looks different at different ages. Social disability becomes dramatic over time, including feelings of social isolation and victimization, often leading to depression and anxiety in adolescence and young adulthood.
Gender			
4–5:1 males to females; females more likely to exhibit severe MR.	Only reported in females.	More common among males.	5:1 males to females.
Prevalence			
2 to 20 cases in 10,000.	Rare.	Rare; may be underdiagnosed.	No reliable information available.
Course			
Onset prior to age 3. Manifestations in infancy more subtle. Developmental gains common. Language and intelligence strong predictors of prognosis. Nature of social interaction impairment may change over time and may depend on child's developmental level	Distinct developmental regression. Lifelong. Skill loss persists and in some cases is progressive. Recovery limited, although some modest developmental gains possible. Interest in social interaction may occur in later childhood or adolescence. Communication and behavioral deficits persist.	Onset prior to age 10 and requires at least 2 years of normal development. Potential early signs include increased activity level, irritability, and anxiety, followed by loss of speech and other skills; child may lose interest in environment. Skill loss reaches a plateau, and mild improvement may occur. If associated with progressive neurological condition, skill loss is progressive. Continuous and lifelong.	Continuous and lifelong. Verbal abilities sometimes mark the severity of the disorder, particularly in area of social adjustment. Behavior often misinterpreted as stubborn and willful. Prognosis better than in Autistic Disorder; many individuals employed and achieving personal self-sufficiency.

(continues)

APPENDIX 1.A *Continued.*

Summary of DSM–IV Diagnostic Criteria for Pervasive Developmental Disorders (PDDs)

		Features	
Autistic Disorder 299.00	**Rett's Disorder 299.80**	**Childhood Disintegrative Disorder 299.10**	**Asperger's Disorder 299.80**
Familial Pattern			
Increased risk among siblings (5%).	No information.	No information.	Increase among family members.
Risk of other developmental disabilities for siblings.			Increase of Autistic Disorder and other social difficulties.
Differential Diagnosis			
Periods of regression more severe than those reported in normal development.	Periods of regression more severe and prolonged than those reported in normal development.	Periods of regression more severe and prolonged than those reported in normal development.	Early cognitive and language skills not delayed and no regression.
Autistic Disorder used as additional diagnosis for individuals with MR if there are qualitative impairments in social and communication skills, and specific behaviors characteristic of Autism are present.		Clinically significant loss of previously acquired skills; MR likely.	Restricted behaviors primarily encompass pursuing a circumscribed interest for an inordinate amount of time.
			Interest in others but in an eccentric, one-sided, verbose, and insensitive manner.

Note. PDD–Not Otherwise Specified (NOS): Pervasive social impairment with either impairment in communication or the presence of stereotyped behaviors, interests, activities and not meeting all the criteria for PDD/Autism; also includes atypical autism (i.e., late onset, atypical symptoms, subthreshold symptoms). MR = mental retardation; V = verbal; NV = nonverbal; EEG = electroencephalogram. Adapted from the *Diagnostic and Statistical Manual of Mental Disorders–Fourth Edition–Text Revision* (pp. 70–84), by American Psychiatric Association, 2000, Washington, DC: Author. Copyright 2000 by American Psychological Association. Adapted with permission.

APPENDIX 1.B
Summary of Screening and Diagnostic Tools for ASD

Assessment Tool	Age	Type of Tool	Mode of Assessment	Areas of Assessment	Reliability and Validity
Asperger Syndrome Diagnostic Scale (Myles, Bock, & Simpson, 2001)	5 to 18 years	Diagnostic	Observational tool used by having sustained contact with the individual being assessed for at least 2 weeks	Probe areas: language, social, maladaptive, cognitive, and sensorimotor.	Internal consistency: strong with an alpha of .83 for the Asperger Syndrome Quotient (ASQ). Interrater reliability: strong, correlation coefficient of .93 for the ASQ. Content description validity: acceptable coefficients (.47–.67). Criterion prediction validity: accurate in distinguishing individuals with and without AS. Construct identification validity: all items significantly related to the ASQ, making strong contributions to the measured construct.
Australian Scale for Asperger's Syndrome (Garnett & Attwood, 1998)	School-age children with high cognitive skills	Screening	Rating scale for teachers or parents	Probe areas: social–emotional skills, communication skills, cognitive skills, specific interests, movement skills, behavior.	Not reported.

(continues)

APPENDIX 1.B *Continued.*
Summary of Screening and Diagnostic Tools for ASD

Assessment Tool	Age	Type of Tool	Mode of Assessment	Areas of Assessment	Reliability and Validity
Autism Behavior Checklist (ABC), subtest of *Autism Screening Instrument for Educational Planning–Second Edition* (Krug, Arick, & Almond, 1980, 1993)	All ages	Screening	Structured checklist completed by teacher and parent	Checklist of 57 non-adaptive behaviors comparing an individual to peers in five areas: sensory, relating, body and object use, language, and social interaction and self-help.	Standardized norms available for the teacher checklist only. Interrater reliability 95%; intrarater reliability (based on split-half reliability test) yielded .87 correlation. Content validity: 55 of 57 descriptors significant predictors of ASD. Criterion-related validity: 86% of individuals with autism had ABC scores within 1 standard deviation of the mean ABC profile. Poor convergent validity with other tools.
Autism Diagnostic Interview–Revised (ADI–R; LeCouteur et al., 1989; Lord et al., 1997; Lord, Rutter, & LeCouteur, 1994; Lord, Storoschuk, Rutter, & Pickles, 1993)	18 months through adult	Diagnostic	Structured parent interview	Probe areas: • reciprocal social interaction • communication and language • restricted, repetitive behaviors and interests	Internal consistency: alpha of .95 for social area; .84 for communication area; .69 for behavior area. Test–retest reliability exceeded 83%. Validity: individual items were strong discriminators between children with ASD and children with MR or speech–language impairment.

Autism Diagnostic Observation Schedule–Generic (ADOS–G; Lord, Rutter, DiLavore, & Risi, 1999; Lord et al., 2000)	2 years through adult	Diagnostic	Semistructured and standardized observational tool using four modules determined by expressive language level; combination of the ADOS (5–12 years) and the PL–ADOS (2–5 years) with two new modules added	Probe areas: communication, social interaction, and play.	Interrater reliability of individual items: kappas exceeded .60 for Module 1 with mean agreement of 91.5%; ranged from .40 to over .60 for Module 2 with mean agreement of 89%; ranged from .47 to .65 for Module 3 with mean agreement of 88.2%; ranged from .41 to .66 with mean agreement of 88.25%. Interrater agreement in diagnostic classification (Autism vs. nonspectrum): 100% for Modules 1 and 3, 91% for Module 2; 90% for Module 4. Test–retest reliability: excellent stability for social, communication, and total; good stability for behavior. Internal consistency: alphas of .86 to .91 (social); .74 to .84 (communication); .47 to .65 (behavior; across the four modules.
Autism Screening Questionnaire (ASQ; Berument et al., 1999)	Version 1: under 6 years Version 2: over 6 years	Screening	Rating scale indicating presence (scored as 1) or absence (scored as 0) of abnormal behavior, completed by primary caregiver	Probe areas: social interaction, language/communication, and repetition/stereotyped behavior.	Good discriminative validity between individuals with and without ASD. Sensitivity 0.85, specificity 0.75, predictive value 0.93.

(continues)

APPENDIX 1.B *Continued.*
Summary of Screening and Diagnostic Tools for ASD

Assessment Tool	Age	Type of Tool	Mode of Assessment	Areas of Assessment	Reliability and Validity
Autism Spectrum Screening Questionnaire (ASSQ; Ehlers, Gillberg, & Wing, 1999)	6 to 17 years	Screening	A 27-item checklist completed by parents or teachers	Assesses symptoms of ASD in children and adolescents with strong or mildly impaired cognitive skills. Uses a 3-point scoring scale: 0 = *normality*, 1 = *some abnormality*, 2 = *definite abnormality*.	Test–retest reliability: strong correlation coefficient of .94 for teacher sample, .96 for parent sample. Interrater reliability for parent and teacher at time 1, acceptable correlation coefficient of .66. Divergent validity: high correlation coefficient of .75 and .77 with Rutter Scale, .58 and .70 for parents and teachers, respectively, with Conners's Scale. Concurrent validity: ASSQ differentiated children with ASD from children with attention-deficit and behavioral disorders; the Rutter and Conner's Scales did not differentiate ASD.
Checklist for Autism in Toddlers (CHAT; Baron-Cohen, Allen, & Gillberg, 1992; Baron-Cohen et al., 1996)	18 months	Screening	Interview questions asked of parents; observation by practitioner	Probe areas: pretend play, taking an interest in other children, pointing, and gaze monitoring.	Readministration of CHAT found that children who failed the criterion items received a diagnosis of autism between 20 and 42 months. Less sensitive to milder symptoms of ASD: sensitivity 0.20 to 0.38, specificity 0.98.

Instrument	Age	Type	Format	Probe areas	Psychometric properties
Childhood Autism Rating Scale (CARS; Schopler, Reichler, DeVellis, & Daly, 1980; Schopler, Reichler, & Rochen-Renner, 1988)	24 months and older	Diagnostic	Structured interview and observation	Probe areas: • relating to people • imitation • emotional response • body use • object use • adaptation to change • visual response • listening response • taste, smell, and touch response and use • fear of nervousness • verbal communication • nonverbal communication • activity level • level and consistency of intellectual functioning • general impressions	Discriminates children with autism from children without autism but with other mental handicaps. Convergence with ADI good for children with autism. Internal consistency: alpha = .94; interrater reliability: 71%; test–retest reliability: correlation of .88 and kappa of .64; criterion-related validity: correlation of .84.
Gilliam Asperger's Disorder Scale (GADS; Gilliam, 2001)	3 to 22 years	Diagnostic	Behavioral rating scale used by parents, teachers, and practitioners with sustained contact with individual for at least 2 weeks	Probe areas: • social interaction • restricted patterns of behavior • cognitive patterns • pragmatic skills • early development (optional subscale)	Internal consistency: moderate to strong alphas for Asperger's Disorder Quotient (ADQ) (.87–.95); test–retest reliability: correlation coefficient .93; interrater reliability: correlation coefficient .89; content description validity: acceptable item discrimination coefficients; criterion prediction validity: strong degree of accuracy in discriminating between Asperger's Disorder (AD) and non-AD groups.

(continues)

APPENDIX 1.B *Continued.*

Summary of Screening and Diagnostic Tools for ASD

Assessment Tool	Age	Type of Tool	Mode of Assessment	Areas of Assessment	Reliability and Validity
Gilliam Asperger's Disorder Scale (Continued)					Construct identification validity: significant correlations for the subscales, indicating items across subscales measure same construct, i.e., behavioral characteristics of AD.
Gilliam Autism Rating Scale (GARS; Gilliam, 1995)	3 to 22 years	Diagnostic	Checklist used by parents, teachers, and practitioners to identify symptoms of autism and indicate severity	Probe areas: stereotyped behaviors, communication, social interaction, and developmental disturbances.	Internal consistency: alpha of .96 for total test; test–retest reliability: correlations ranged from .81 to .86; interrater reliability: correlations ranged from .72 to .95; content validity: item coefficients of .61 to .69; criterion-related validity: correlated with the ABC.
Krug Asperger's Disorder Index (KADI; Krug & Arick, 2004)	6 to 22 years	Diagnostic	Index completed by a parent, caregiver, or teacher at home or school	Probe areas: 32 items that help differentiate Asperger Disorder from other forms of high-functioning autism.	Standardized on 486 individuals with and without autism across 30 states and 10 countries.
Modified Checklist for Autism in Toddlers (M–CHAT; Charman et al., 2001; Robins, Fein, Barton, & Green, 2001a, 2001b)	18 months	Screening	Checklist completed by parents at pediatric visit	Probe areas: pretend play, social relatedness, communication, sensory, and motor.	Internal consistency: alpha of .85, sensitivity 0.87; specificity 0.99; positive predictive power 0.80; negative predictive power 0.99.

Instrument	Age	Type	Method	Probe areas	Psychometrics
Parent Interview for Autism (PIA; Stone & Hogan, 1993)	Preschool age and younger	Diagnostic	Structured interview with parents: questions about observable behaviors; ratings of frequency of occurrence	Probe areas: • social relating • affective responses • motor imitation • peer interactions • object play • imaginative play • language understanding • nonverbal communication • motoric behaviors • sensory responses • need for sameness	Internal consistency and test–retest reliability for total PIA .90. Construct validity: successfully differentiated children with ASD from children with MR. Concurrent validity with DSM–IV and CARS.
Screening Tool for Autism in Two-Year-Olds (STAT Stone, Coonrod, & Ousley, 2000)	24 to 35 month	Screening	20-minute play interaction with child	Probe areas: play (pretend and reciprocal social play), motor imitation, and nonverbal communicative development (requesting and directing attention).	Strong sensitivity (0.92) and specificity (0.85), differentiating children with ASD (100%) from children with other developmental disorders (97%). Concurrent validity (with ADOS): kappa of 0.95.
Systematic Observation of Red Flags for Autism Spectrum Disorders in Young Children (SORF; Weatherby & Woods, 2002)	12 to 36 months	Screening	Review of videotaped communication or behavior samples between child and caregiver	Probe areas: • reciprocal social interaction • unconventional gestures • unconventional sounds and words • repetitive behaviors and restricted interests • emotional regulation	Interrater reliability: mean 97.1%, range 89.7 to 100% across children, range 83 to 100% across items.

Practice Opportunities

1. Select a child with a diagnosis of autism and review with the family and team members the diagnostic criteria using the checklist in Figure 1.1. Use the checklist annually to determine which characteristics remain consistent and which have dissipated or diminished in degree of impairment.

2. In preparation for referring a child to an experienced diagnostician or diagnostic team for a potential diagnosis of ASD, complete the activities listed in Figure 1.7.

3. Identify a pediatrician or family practice physician in your area who serves the children in your program and meet with him or her to discuss the American Academy of Pediatrics guidelines for screening a child for ASD. Brainstorm a method for providing speech, language, and hearing screenings in collaboration with this physician.

Suggested Readings

Baron-Cohen, S., Allen, J., & Gillberg, C. (1992). Can autism be detected at 18 months? The needle, the haystack, and the CHAT. *British Journal of Psychiatry, 161,* 839–843.

This article describes the development and use of the *Checklist for Autism in Toddlers* for screening children who may be at risk for ASD at their 18-month pediatric checkup. Key indicators for autism are identified in the areas of joint attention, pointing, and gaze.

Lord, C. (1997). Diagnostic instruments in autism spectrum disorder. In D. J. Cohen & F. R. Volkmar (Eds.), *Handbook of autism and pervasive developmental disorders* (pp. 460–483). New York: Wiley.

In this chapter, Lord describes the methods and tools that have been used to support a diagnosis of ASD, describes the reliability and validity of the available tools, and offers important insight into the challenges of diagnosis in the first few years of life.

Zimmerman, S. (1996). *Grief dancers: A journey into the depths of the soul.* Golden, CO: Nemo Press.

In this family story, a mother shares her experiences in trying to understand the behaviors of her daughter. She searches for understanding and explanation from a variety of practitioners, none of whom can quite explain what is happening to her daughter. The mother eventually learns that her daughter has Rett's Disorder.

Resources

Books

Attwood, T. (1997). *Asperger's syndrome: A guide for parents and professionals.* Philadelphia: Jessica Kingsley.

Baron-Cohen, S., & Bolton, P. (1993). *Autism: The facts.* New York: Oxford University Press.

Boyd, B. (2003). *Parenting a child with Asperger syndrome: 200 tips and strategies.* New York: Jessica Kingsley.

Bruey, C. T. (2003). *Demystifying autism spectrum disorders: A guide to diagnosis for parents and professionals.* Bethesda, MD: Woodbine House.

Hagberg, B. (Ed.). (1993). *Rett syndrome: Clinical and biological aspects.* London: MacKeith Press.

Hermelin, B. (2001). *Bright splinters of the mind: A personal story of research with autistic savants.* New York: Jessica Kingsley.

Janzen, J. E. (1997). *Understanding the nature of autism: A practical guide.* Austin, TX: PRO-ED.

Janzen, J. E. (1999). *Autism: Facts and strategies for parents.* Austin, TX: Therapy Skill Builders.

Klin, A., Volkmar, F. R., & Sparrow, S. S. (2000). *Asperger syndrome.* New York: Guilford Press.

Ledgin, N. (1998). *Diagnosing Jefferson: Evidence of a condition that guided his beliefs, behavior, and personal associations.* Arlington, TX: Future Horizons.

Leventhal-Belfer, L., & Coe, C. (2003). *Asperger syndrome in young children: A developmental approach for parents and professionals.* New York: Jessica Kingsley.

Myles, B. S., & Simpson, R. L. (1998). *Asperger syndrome: A guide for educators and parents.* Austin, TX: PRO-ED.

Newport, J. (2001). *Your life is not a label: A guide to living fully with autism and Asperger's syndrome for parents, professionals and you!* Arlington, TX: Future Horizons.

Nowicki, S. (1997). *Helping the child who doesn't fit in.* Troy, MI: Quirk Roberts.

Ozonoff, S., Dawson, G., & McPartland, J. (2002). *A parent's guide to Asperger syndrome & high functioning autism: How to meet the challenges and help your child thrive.* New York: Guilford Press.

Powers, M. D., & Poland, J. (2002). *Asperger syndrome and your child: A parent's guide—Unlocking your child's potential.* New York: HarperCollins.

Richer, J., & Coates, S. (2001). *Autism: The search for coherence.* Philadelphia: Jessica Kingsley.

Satkiewicz-Gayhardt, V., Peerenboom, B., & Campbell, R. (1998). *Crossing bridges: A parent's perspective on coping after a child is diagnosed with autism/PDD.* Stratham, NH: Potential Unlimited.

Shore, S. M. (2001). *Beyond the wall: Personal experiences with autism and Asperger syndrome.* Shawnee Mission, KS: Autism Asperger Publishing.

Simpson, R. L., & Zionts, P. (2000). *Autism: Information and resources for parents, families, and professionals* (2nd ed.). Austin, TX: PRO-ED.

Szatmari, P. (2004). *A mind apart: Understanding children with autism and Asperger syndrome.* New York: Guilford Press.

Vermeulen, P. (2001). *Autistic thinking—This is the title.* Philadelphia: Jessica Kingsley.

Waltz, M. (1999). *Pervasive developmental disorders: Finding a diagnosis and getting help.* Sebastopol, CA: O'Reilly & Associates.

Weber, J. D. (Ed.). (1999). *Children with Fragile X.* Bethesda, MD: Woodbine House.

Whitman, T. L. (2004). *The development of autism: A self-regulatory perspective.* New York: Jessica Kingsley.

Willey, L. H. (1999). *Pretending to be normal: Living with Asperger's syndrome*. Philadelphia: Jessica Kingsley.

Wing, L. (2001). *The autistic spectrum: A parent's guide to understanding and helping your child*. Berkeley, CA: Ulysses Press.

Yapko, D. (2003).*Understanding autism spectrum disorders: Frequently asked questions*. New York: Jessica Kingsley.

Organizations and Web Sites

Asperger's Association of New England
http://aane.autistics.org
182 Main St.
Watertown, MA 02472
617/393-3824

Association for Persons with Severe Handicaps
http://www.tash.org
29 W. Susquehanna Ave., Ste. 210
Baltimore, MD 21204
410/828-8274
410/828-6706 (fax)

Autism Independent UK
http://www.autismuk.com
199/201 Blanford Avenue
Kettering, Northants
NN16 9AT
United Kingdom
01536-523274

Autism National Committee
http://www.autcom.org
PO Box 6175
North Plymouth, MA 02362-6175
610/649-0974 (fax)

Autism Network International
http://www.ani.autistics.us/
PO Box 35448
Syracuse, NY 13235-5448

Autism Research Institute
http://www.autism.com/ari/
4182 Adams Ave.
San Diego, CA 92116
619/281-7165
619/563-6840 (fax)

Autism Services Center
http://www.autismservicescenter.org

Autism Society of America
http://www.autism-society.org
7910 Woodmont Ave., Ste. 300
Bethesda, MD 20814-3015
800/328-8476
301/657-0881
301/657-0869 (fax)

Center for the Study of Autism
http://www.autism.org
PO Box 4538
Salem, OR 97302

Cure Autism Now
http://www.canfoundation.org
5455 Wilshire Boulevard, Ste. 715
Los Angeles, CA 90036
323/549-0500
323/549-0547 (fax)
888/8-AUTISM

Federation for Children with Special Needs
http://www.fcsn.org
fcsninfo@fcsn.org
1135 Tremont St., Ste. 420
Boston, MA 02120
617/236-7210
617/572-2094 (fax)

Indiana Resource Center for Autism
www.isdd.indiana.edu/~irca
2853 E. Tenth St.
Bloomington, IN 47408-2696
812/855-6508
812/855-9630 (fax)
812/855-9396 (TT)

**MAAP Services for More Advanced Persons with Autism
and Asperger's Syndrome**
http://www.maapservices.org
Chart@netnitco.net
PO Box 524
Crown Point, IN 46307
219/662-1311
219/662-0638 (fax)

National Alliance for Autism Research
http://www.naar.org
Naar@naar.org
414 Wall St.
Research Park
Princeton, NJ 08540
888/777-NAAR
609/430-9160
609/430-9163 (fax)

National Dissemination Center for Children with Disabilities
http://www.nichcy.org
PO Box 1492
Washington, DC 20013-1492
800/695-0285
202/884-8441 (fax)

Online Asperger Syndrome Information & Support
http://www.udel.edu/bkirby/asperger
bkirby@udel.edu

Yale Child Study Center
http://info.med.yale.edu/childstdy/autism

230 South Frontage Rd.
PO Box 207900
New Haven, CT 06520
203/785-2513
203/737-4197 (fax)

Glossary

Amygdala. An almond-shaped mass of gray matter in the anterior medial portion of the temporal lobe; it is part of the limbic system and is implicated in emotion.

Basal ganglia. Located in the floor of the lateral ventricles near the base of the cerebrum; includes areas important for movement (i.e., the putamen, caudate nucleus, globus pallidus, subthalamic nucleus, and substantia nigra).

Cerebellar vermis. Midline portion of the cerebellum that has a wormlike look.

Cerebellum. The smaller area of the brain above the pons and medulla that is important for balance and posture.

Cerebrum. The principal hemispheres of the brain.

CMV. Cytomegalovirus; a common, acquired virus that typically causes a benign mononucleosis-like illness with fever and sore throat; can infect fetus of a mother with no prior exposure or antibody response and cause microcephaly, deafness, and developmental delays.

Construct validity. Evidence supporting the theoretical framework or construct being measured by a test.

Content validity. Evidence substantiating that the test items sampled are representative of the area or domain being assessed and interpreted.

Cortex. Outermost layer (the gray matter) of the cerebral hemisphere.

Criterion validity. Correlation between scores on tests assessing similar or dissimilar constructs.

Disengaging. Ability to respond to unexpected information outside the immediate attentional focus.

Dominant mutation. A faulty gene inherited from one parent.

Embryogenesis. Pertaining to the development of the embryo and all embryonic structures from fertilization to the end of the 8th week of gestation, by which time rudiments of all major organ systems (including the nervous system) have developed.

Facial nucleus. Found in the brain stem; controls the muscles of facial expression.

Functional brain imaging. Research techniques (i.e., functional MRI, single-photon emission CT, and positron-emission tomography) that use differences in cellular metabolism to document "real-time" pictures of regional brain function during specific developmental activities; can show areas of dysfunction within the brain.

Fusiform gyrus. Temporal lobe structure involved in face perception.

Internal consistency reliability. Evidence that test items are homogeneous over the domain being assessed.

Limbic System. Borders the thalamus and the hypothalamus; formed of all the medial deep structures and includes the cingulate gyrus, the hippocampal formation, the amygdala, and the infraorbital cortex.

MMR. Mumps–measles–rubella vaccine, which is often given at a toddler's 12-month pediatric checkup.

Orienting. Ability to focus on places where information occurs.

Parietal lobe. Lies between the frontal and occipital lobes.

Polymorphism. Changes in the genetic code.

Purkinje neurons. Neurons that send projections out of the cerebellar cortex to deep cerebellar nuclei, from which areas messages go to other areas of the brain that influence movement.

Recessive mutation. An altered gene that requires two copies (from both parents) to represent itself.

Shifting attention. Ability to quickly change attention from one source to another.

Superior olive. Found in the brain stem; serves as a relay station for auditory information.

Teratogens. Anything that can cause disruption to the developing embryo or fetus, including infections, chemical agents, medications, temperature (high fever), or radiation.

Test–retest reliability. Stability of scores on a test from one time period to another.

Tuberous sclerosis complex (TSC). A neurocutaneous disorder that produces lesions or tubers affecting several organs, including the skin, heart, kidneys, brain, and lungs; often, children affected by this disorder have autism or display autistic characteristics.

Validity. The extent to which an instrument measures what it purports to measure.

Valporic acid. Brand name Depakote; an antiseizure medication that can have "teratogenic" effects on the developing embryo and fetus.

References

Abell, F., Krams, M., Ashburner, J., Passingham, R., Friston, K., Frackowiak, R., et al. (1999). The neuroanatomy of autism: A voxel-based whole brain analysis of structural scans. *NeuroReport, 10,* 1647–1651.

Adrien, J. L., Perrot, A., Sauvage, D., Leddet, I., Larmande, C., Hameury, L., et al. (1992). Early symptoms in autism from family home movies: Evaluation and comparison between 1st and 2nd year of life using I.B.S.E. Scale. *Acta Paedopsychiatrica, 55,* 71–75.

Allen, G., Buxton, R. B., Wong, E. C., & Courchesne, E. (1997). Attentional activation of the cerebellum independent of motor involvement. *Science, 275,* 1940–1943.

Allen, G., & Courchesne, E. (2001). Attention function and dysfunction in autism. *Frontiers in Bioscience, 6,* 105–119.

American Academy of Child and Adolescent Psychiatry. (1999). Practice parameters for the assessment and treatment of children with autism and other pervasive developmental disorders. *Journal of the American Academy of Child and Adolescent Psychiatry,* 38(Suppl. 12), 32S–54S.

American Academy of Pediatrics, Committee on Children with Disabilities. (2001). Technical report: The pediatrician's role in the diagnosis and management of autistic spectrum disorder in children. *Pediatrics, 107,* 1221–1226.

American Psychiatric Association. (1980). *Diagnostic and statistical manual of mental disorders* (3rd ed.). Washington, DC: Author.

American Psychiatric Association. (1987). *Diagnostic and statistical manual of mental disorders* (3rd ed. rev.). Washington, DC: Author.

American Psychiatric Association. (1994). *Diagnostic and statistical manual of mental disorders* (4th ed.). Washington, DC: Author.

American Psychiatric Association. (2000). *Diagnostic and statistical manual of mental disorders* (4th ed. text rev.). Washington, DC: Author.

Asperger, H. (1944). Die autistischen psychopathern in kindersalter. *Archives für Psyciatrie und Nervenkrankheiten, 117,* 76–136. (English translation in Frith, 1991)

Aylward, E. H., Minshew, N. J., Goldstein, G., Honeycutt, N. A., Augustine, A. M., Yates, K. O., et al. (1999). MRI volumes of amygdala and hippocampus in non–mentally retarded autistic adolescents and adults. *Neurology, 53,* 2145–2150.

Bailey, A., LeCouteur, A., Gottesman, I., Bolton, P., Simonoff, E., Yuzda, E., et al. (1995). Autism as a strongly genetic disorder: Evidence from a British twin study. *Psychological Medicine, 25,* 63–78.

Bailey, A., Luthert, P., Dean, A., Harding, B., & Janota, I. (1998). A clinicopathological study of autism. *Brain, 121,* 889–905.

Baird, G., Charman, T., Baron-Cohen, S., Cox, A., Swettenham, J., Wheelwright, S., et al. (2000). A screening instrument for autism at 18 months of age: A six-year follow-up study. *Journal of the American Academy of Child and Adolescent Psychiatry, 39,* 694–702.

Baltaxe, C. A. M., Russell, A., D'Angiola, N., & Simmons, J. Q. (1995). Discourse cohesion in the verbal interactions of individuals diagnosed with autistic disorder or schizotypal personality disorder. *Australia and New Zealand Journal of Developmental Disabilities, 20*(2), 79–96.

Baranek, G. T. (1999). Autism during infancy: A retrospective video analysis of sensory–motor and social behaviors at 9–12 months of age. *Journal of Autism and Developmental Disorders, 29,* 213–224.

Baron-Cohen, S., Allen, J., & Gillberg, C. (1992). Can autism be detected at 18 months? The needle, the haystack, and the CHAT. *British Journal of Psychiatry, 161,* 839–843.

Baron-Cohen, S., Cox, A., Baird, G., Swettenham, J., Nightingale, N., Morgan, K., et al. (1996). Psychological markers in the detection of autism in infancy in a large population. *British Journal of Psychiatry, 168,* 138–163.

Baron-Cohen, S., Ring, H. A., Wheelwright, S., Bullmore, E. T., Brammer, M. J., Simmons, A., et al. (1999). Social intelligence in the normal and autistic brain: An fMRI study. *European Journal of Neuroscience, 11,* 1891–1898.

Baron-Cohen, S., Wheelwright, S., Cox, A., Baird, G., Charman, T., Swettenham, J., et al. (2000). The early identification of autism: The Checklist for Autism in Toddlers (CHAT). *Journal of Developmental and Learning Disorders, 4*(1), 3–30.

Bauman, M. L., & Kemper, T. (1988). Limbic and cerebellar abnormalities: Consistent findings in infantile autism. *Journal of Neuropathology & Experimental Neurology, 47,* 369.

Bauman, M. L., & Kemper, T. (1994). *The neurobiology of autism.* Baltimore: Johns Hopkins University Press.

Bauman, M. L., Kemper, T. L., & Arin, D. M. (1995). Microscopic observations of the brain in Rett syndrome. *Neuropediatrics, 26,* 105–108.

Bax, M. (1999). Diagnosis made too late. *Developmental Medicine and Child Neurology, 41*(12), 795.

Berument, S. K., Rutter, M., Lord, C., Pickles, A., & Bailey, A. (1999). Autism Screening Questionnaire: Diagnostic validity. *British Journal of Psychiatry, 175,* 444–451.

Bleiberg, E. (2001). *Treating personality disorders in children and adolescents: A relational approach.* New York: Guilford Press.

Boddaert, N., & Zilbovicius, M. (2002). Functional neuroimaging and childhood autism. *Pediatric Radiology, 32,* 1–7.

Bryson, S. E., Rogers, S. J., & Fombonne, E. (2003). Autism spectrum disorders: Early detection, intervention, education and psychopharmacological management. *Canadian Journal of Psychiatry, 48,* 506–516.

Buitelaar, J. K., Van der Gaag, R., Klin, A., & Volkmar, F. (1999). Exploring the boundaries of Pervasive Developmental Disorder Not Otherwise Specified: Analyses of data from the DSM–IV Autistic Disorder field trial. *Journal of Autism and Developmental Disorders, 29,* 33–44.

Charman, T., Baron-Cohen, S., Baird, G., Cox, A., Wheelwright, S., Swettenham, J., et al. (2001). Commentary: The Modified Checklist for Autism in Toddlers. *Journal of Autism and Developmental Disorders, 31,* 145–151.

Chawarska, K., Klin, A., & Volkmar, F. (2003). Automatic attention cueing through eye movement in 2-year-old children with autism. *Child Development, 74*(4), 1108–1122.

Courchesne, E., & Pierce, K. (2000). An inside look at the neurobiology, etiology, and future research of autism. *Advocate, 33*(4), 18–22, 35.

Courchesne, E., Saitoh, O., Yeung-Courchesne, R., Press, G. A., Lincoln, A. J., Haas, R. H., et al. (1994). Abnormality of cerebellar vermian lobules VI & VII in patients with infantile autism: Identification of hypoplastic and hyperplastic subgroups with MR imaging. *American Journal of Roentgenology, 162,* 123–130.

Courchesne, E., Townsend, J. P., Akshoomoff, N. A., Yeung-Courchesne, R., Press, G. A., Murakami, J. W., et al. (1994). A new finding: Impairment in shifting attention in autistic and cerebellar patients. In S. H. Broman & J. Grafman (Eds.), *Atypical cognitive deficits in developmental disorders: Implications for brain function* (pp. 101–137). Hillsdale, NJ: Erlbaum.

Courchesne, E., Yeung-Courchesne, R., Press, G. A., Hesselink, J. R., & Jernigan, T. L. (1988). Hypoplasia of cerebellar vermal lobules VI and VII in autism. *New England Journal of Medicine, 318,* 1349–1354.

Dawson, G., Meltzoff, A. N., Osterling, J., & Rinaldi, J. (1998). Neuropsychological correlates of early correlates of early symptoms of autism. *Child Development, 69*(5), 1276–1285.

Dragich, J., Houwink-Manville, I., & Schanen, C. (2000). Rett syndrome: A surprising result of mutation in MECP2. *Human Molecular Genetics, 9*(16), 2365–2375.

Egaas, B., Courchesne, E., & Saitoh, O. (1995). Reduced size of corpus callosum in autism. *Archives of Neurology, 52,* 794–801.

Ehlers, S., Gillberg, C., & Wing, L. (1999). A screening questionnaire for Asperger syndrome and other high-functioning autism spectrum disorders in school age children. *Journal of Autism and Developmental Disorders, 29*(2), 129–141.

Eisenmajer, R., Prior, M., Leekam, S., Wing, L., Ong, B., Gould, J., et al. (1998). Delayed language onset as a predictor of clinical symptoms in pervasive developmental disorders. *Journal of Autism and Developmental Disorders, 28*(6), 527–533.

Fenson, L., Dale, P. S., Reznick, S., Thal, D., Bates, E., Hartung, J. P., et al. (1993). *The MacArthur Communicative Development Inventories.* San Diego: Singular.

Fidler, D. J., Bailey, J. N., & Smalley, S. L. (2000). Macrocephaly in autism and other pervasive developmental disorders. *Developmental Medicine and Child Neurology, 42*(11), 737–740.

Filipek, P. A., Accardo, P. J., Ashwal, S., Baranek, G. T., Cook, E. H., Dawson, G., et al. (2000). Practice parameter: Screening and diagnosis of autism: Report of the Quality Standards Committee of the American Academy of Neurology and the Child Neurology Society. *Neurology, 55,* 468–479.

Fombonne, E. (2003a). Epidemiological surveys of autism and other pervasive developmental disorders: An update. *Journal of Autism and Developmental Disorders, 33*(4), 365–382.

Fombonne, E. (2003b). Modern views of autism. *Canadian Journal of Psychiatry, 48,* 502–505.

Freeman, B. J., & Cronin, P. (2002). Diagnosing autism spectrum disorder in young children: An update. *Infants and Young Children, 14*(3), 1–10.

Frith, U. (1991). *Autism and Asperger syndrome.* New York: Cambridge University Press.

Garnett, M. S., & Attwood, A. J. (1998). The Australian Scale for Asperger's Syndrome. In T. Attwood (Ed.), *Asperger's syndrome: A guide for parents and professionals* (pp. 17–19). Philadelphia: Jessica Kingsley.

Ghaziuddin, M., Weidmer-Mikhail, E., & Ghaziuddin, N. (1998). Co-morbidity of Asperger syndrome: A preliminary report. *Journal of Intellectual Disability Research, 42*(4), 279–283.

Gillberg, C. (1991). Clinical and neurobiological aspects of Asperger syndrome in six family studies. In U. Frith (Ed.), *Autism and Asperger syndrome* (pp. 122–146). New York: Cambridge University Press.

Gillberg, C., & Billstedt, E. (2000). Autism and Asperger syndrome: Coexistence with other clinical disorders. *Acta Psychiatrica Scandinavia, 102*(5), 321–330.

Gilliam, J. E. (1995). *Gilliam Autism Rating Scale.* Austin, TX: PRO-ED.

Gilliam, J. E. (2001). *Gilliam Asperger's Disorder Scale.* Austin, TX: PRO-ED.

Goldstein, S., & Schwebach, A. J. (2004). The comorbidity of pervasive developmental disorders and attention deficit hyperactivity disorder: Results of a retrospective chart review. *Journal of Autism and Developmental Disorders, 34*(3), 329–339.

Hagberg, B. (1985). Rett's syndrome: Prevalence and impact on progressive severe mental retardation in girls. *Acta Scandinavia, 74,* 405–408.

Hagberg, B., Aicardi, J., Dias, K., & Ramos, O. (1983). A progressive syndrome of autism, dementia, ataxia, and loss of purposeful hand use in girls: Rett's syndrome—Report of 35 cases. *Annals of Neurology, 14,* 471–479.

Hagberg, B., & Witt Engerstrom, I. (1986). Rett's syndrome: A suggested staging system for describing impairment profile with increasing age towards adolescence. *Journal of Medical Genetics, 24*(Suppl.), 47–59.

Handen, B. L., Johnson, C. R., & Lubetsky, M. (2000). Efficacy of methylphenidate among children with autism and symptoms of attention-deficit hyperactivity disorder. *Journal of Autism and Developmental Disorders, 30*(3), 245–255.

Harris, N. S., Courchesne, E., Townsend, J., Carper, R. A., & Lord, C. (1999). Neuroanatomic contributions to slowed orienting of attention in children with autism. *Cognitive Brain Research, 8,* 61–71.

Herbert, M. R., Harris, G. J., Adrien, K. T., Ziegler, D. A., Makris, N., Kennedy, D. N., et al. (2002). Abnormal asymmetry in language association cortex in autism. *Annals of Neurology, 52*(5), 588–596.

Howlin, P. (1987). Asperger syndrome: Does it exist and what can be done about it? In *Proceedings of the First International Symposium on Specific Speech & Language Disorders in Children.* London: AFASIC.

Kanner, L. (1943). Autistic disturbances of affective contact. *Nervous Child, 2,* 217–250.

Kaye, J. A., Maria Del Mar, M. M., & Jick, H. (2001). Mumps, measles, and rubella vaccine and the incidence of autism recorded by general practitioners: A time-trend analysis. *Western Journal of Medicine, 174*(6), 387–390.

Klin, A., Chawarska, K., Paul, R., Rubin, E., Morgan, T., Wiesner, L., et al. (2004). Autism in a 15-month-old child. *American Journal of Psychiatry, 161*(11), 1981–1988.

Klin, A., Lang, J., Cicchetti, D. V., & Volkmar, F. R. (2000). Brief report: Interrater reliability of clinical diagnosis and DSM–IV criteria for autistic disorder: Results of the DSM–IV field trial. *Journal of Autism and Developmental Disorders, 30*(2), 163–167.

Klinger, L. G., & Dawson, G. (1996). Autistic disorder. In E. Mash & R. Barkely (Eds.), *Child psychopathology* (pp. 311–339). New York: Guilford Press.

Krug, D. A., & Arick, J. R. (2004). *Krug Asperger's Disorder Index*. Los Angeles: Western Psychological Services.

Krug, D. A., Arick, J., & Almond, P. (1980). Behavior checklist for identifying severely handicapped individuals with high levels of autistic behavior. *Journal of Child Psychology and Psychiatry, 21,* 221–229.

Krug, D. A., Arick, J. R., & Almond, P. J. (1993). *Autism Screening Instrument for Educational Planning–Second edition*. Austin, TX: PRO-ED.

Lainhart, J. E., Piven, J., Wzorek, M., & Landa, R. (1997). Macrocephaly in children and adults with autism. *Journal of the American Academy of Child and Adolescent Psychiatry, 36*(2), 282–290.

Lamb, J. A., Parr, J. R., Bailey, A. J., & Monaco, A. P. (2002). Autism: In search of susceptibility genes. *Neuromolecular Medicine, 2*(1), 11–28.

LeCouteur, A., Rutter, M., Lord, C., Rios, P., Robertson, S., Holdgrafer, M., et al. (1989). Autism Diagnostic Interview: A standardized investigator-based instrument. *Journal of Autism and Developmental Disorders, 19*(3), 363–387.

Leonard, H., & Bower, C. (1998). Is the girl with Rett syndrome normal at birth? *Developmental Medicine & Child Neurology, 40,* 115–121.

Lord, C. (1995). Follow-up of two-year-olds referred for possible autism. *Journal of Child Psychology and Psychiatry, 36*(8), 1365–1382.

Lord, C. (1997). Diagnostic instruments in autism spectrum disorder. In D. J. Cohen & F. R. Volkmar (Eds.), *Handbook of autism and pervasive developmental disorders* (pp. 460–483). New York: Wiley.

Lord, C. (2000). Autism spectrum disorders and ADHD. In P. J. Accardo & T. A. Blondis (Eds.), *Attention deficits and hyperactivity in children and adults* (pp. 401–417). New York: Marcel Decker.

Lord, C., Pickles, A., McLennan, J., Rutter, M., Bregman, J., Folstein, S., et al. (1997). Diagnosing autism: Analyses of data from the Autism Diagnostic Interview. *Journal of Autism and Developmental Disorders, 27*(5), 501–517.

Lord, C., & Risi, S. (2000). Early diagnosis in children with autism spectrum disorders. *Advocate, 33,* 23–26.

Lord, C., Risi, S., Lambrecht, L., Cook, E. H., Leventhal, B. L., DiLavore, P. C., et al. (2000). The Autism Diagnostic Observation Schedule–Generic: A standard measure of social and communication deficits associated with the spectrum of Autism. *Journal of Autism and Developmental Disorders, 30*(3), 205–223.

Lord, C., Rutter, M., DiLavore, P. C., & Risi, S. (1999). *Autism Diagnostic Observation Schedule–Generic*. Los Angeles: Western Psychological Services.

Lord, C., Rutter, M., & LeCouteur, A. (1991). *Autism Diagnostic Interview–Revised*. Chicago: University of Chicago Press.

Lord, C., Rutter, M., & LeCouteur, A. (1994). Autism Diagnostic Interview–Revised: A revised version of a diagnostic interview for caregivers of individuals with possible pervasive developmental disorders. *Journal of Autism and Developmental Disorders, 24*(5), 659–685.

Lord, C., Storoschuk, S., Rutter, M., & Pickles, A. (1993). Using the ADI–R to diagnose autism in preschool children. *Infant Mental Health Journal, 14*(3), 234–252.

Madsen, K. M., Hviid, A., Vesteraard, M., Schendel, D., Wohlfahrt, J., Thorsen, P., et al. (2002). A population-based study of measles, mumps, and rubella vaccination and autism. *New England Journal of Medicine, 347*(19), 1477–1482.

Malhotra, S., & Gupta, N. (1999). Childhood Disintegrative Disorder. *Journal of Autism and Developmental Disabilities, 29*(6), 491–498.

Manoach, D., Sandson, T., & Weintraub, S. (1995). The developmental social–emotional processing disorder is associated with right hemisphere abnormalities. *Neuropsychiatry, Neurophysiology, Behavioral Neurology, 8,* 99–105.

Mars, A. E., Mauk, J. E., & Dowrick, P. W. (1998). Symptoms of pervasive developmental disorders as observed in prediagnostic home videos of infants and toddlers. *Journal of Pediatrics, 132,* 500–504.

Meloni, I., Bruttini, M., Longo, I., Mari, F., Rizzolio, F., D'Adamo, P., et al. (2001). A mutation in the Rett's syndrome gene, MECP2, causes X-linked mental retardation and progressive spasticity in males. *American Journal of Human Genetics, 67*(4), 982–985.

Muhle, R., Trentacoste, S. V., & Rapin, I. (2004). The genetics of autism. *Pediatrics, 113*(5), 472–486.

Mullen, E. M. (1995). *Mullen Scales of Early Learning.* Circle Pines, MN: American Guidance Service.

Myles, B. S., Bock, S. J., & Simpson, R. L. (2001). *Asperger Syndrome Diagnostic Scale.* Austin, TX: PRO-ED.

Newschaffer, C. J., Fallin, D., & Lee, N. L. (2002). Heritable and nonheritable risk factors for autism spectrum disorders. *Epidemiologic Reviews, 24*(2), 137–153.

Nicolson, R., & Szatmari, P. (2003). Genetic and neurodevelopmental influence in autistic disorder. *Canadian Journal of Psychiatry, 48,* 526–537.

Noterdaeme, M., Sitter, S., Mildenberger, K., & Amorosa, H. (2000). Diagnostic assessment of communicative and interactive behaviours in children with autism and receptive language disorder. *European Child and Adolescent Psychiatry, 9*(4), 295–300.

Osterling, J., & Dawson, G. (1994). Early recognition of children with autism: A study of first birthday home videotapes. *Journal of Autism and Developmental Disorders, 24,* 247–258.

Ozonoff, S., Cook, I., Coon, H., Dawson, G., Joseph, R., Klin, A., et al. (2004). Performance on Cambridge Neuropsychological Test Automated Battery subtests sensitive to frontal lobe function in people with autistic disorder: Evidence from the Collaborative Programs of Excellence in Autism network. *Journal of Autism and Developmental Disorders, 34,* 139–149.

Pierce, K., & Courchesne, E. (2000). Exploring the neurofunctional organization of face processing in autism. *Archives of General Psychiatry, 57,* 344–345.

Ritvo, E. R., Jorde, L. B., Mason-Brothers, A., Freeman, B. J., Pingree, C., Jones, M. B., et al. (1989). The UCLA–University of Utah epidemiologic survey of autism: Recurrence risk estimates and genetic counseling. *American Journal of Psychiatry, 146,* 1032–1036.

Robins, D. L., Fein, D., Barton, M. L., & Green, J. A. (2001a). The Modified Checklist for Autism in Toddlers: An initial study investigating the early detection of autism and pervasive developmental disorders. *Journal of Autism and Developmental Disorders, 31*(2), 131–144.

Robins, D. L., Fein, D., Barton, M. L., & Green, J. A. (2001b). Reply to Charman et al.'s Commentary on the Modified Checklist for Autism in Toddlers. *Journal of Autism and Developmental Disorders, 31*(2), 149–151.

Rodier, P. M. (2000, February). The early origins of autism. *Scientific American,* 56–63.

Rourke, B. P. (1989). *Nonverbal learning disabilities: The syndrome and the model.* New York: Guilford Press.

Rourke, B. P. (2000). Nonverbal learning disabilities and Asperger syndrome. In A. Klin, F. R. Volkmar, & S. S. Sparrow (Eds.), *Asperger syndrome* (pp. 231–253). New York: Guilford Press.

Rutter, M. (1978). Diagnosis and definition of childhood autism. *Journal of Autism and Childhood Schizophrenia, 8,* 139–161.

Schopler, E. (1985). Editorial: Convergence of learning disability, higher-level autism and Asperger's syndrome. *Journal of Autism and Developmental Disorders, 15,* 359.

Schopler, E. (1994). Neurobiologic correlates in the classification and study of autism. In S. H. Broman & J. Grafman (Eds.), *Atypical cognitive deficits in developmental disorders: Implications for brain function* (pp. 87–100). Hillsdale, NJ: Erlbaum.

Schopler, E., Reichler, R., DeVellis, R., & Daly, K. (1980). Toward objective classification of childhood autism: Childhood Autism Rating Scale (CARS). *Journal of Autism and Developmental Disorders, 10,* 91–103.

Schopler, E., Reichler, R. J., & Rochen-Renner, B. (1988). *Childhood Autism Rating Scale.* Los Angeles: Western Psychological Services.

Schultz, R. T., Gauthier, I., Klin, A., Fulbright, R. K., Anderson, A. W., Volkmar, F., et al. (2000). Abnormal ventral temporal cortical activity during face discrimination among individuals with autism and Asperger syndrome. *Archives in General Psychiatry, 57,* 331–340.

Semrud-Clikeman, M., & Hynd, G. (1990). Right hemispheric dysfunction in nonverbal learning disabilities: Social, academic, and adaptive functioning in adults and children. *Psychological Bulletin, 107,* 196–209.

Shahbazian, M. D., & Zoghbi, H. Y. (2001). Molecular genetics of Rett's syndrome and clinical spectrum of MECP2 mutations. *Current Opinion in Neurology, 14*(2), 171–176.

Shumway, S., Wetherby, A. M., & Woods, J. (2003, November). *Red flags of autism spectrum disorders in the second and third years of life.* Paper presented at the Annual Convention of the American Speech-Language-Hearing Association, Chicago.

Sparrow, S. S., Balla, D., & Cicchetti, D. (1984). *Vineland Adaptive Behavior Scales.* Circle Pines, MN: American Guidance Service.

Stone, W. L., Coonrod, E. E., & Ousley, O. Y. (2000). Brief report: Screening Tool for Autism in Two-Year-Olds (STAT): Development and preliminary data. *Journal of Autism and Developmental Disorders, 30*(6), 607–612.

Stone, W. L., & Hogan, K. L. (1993). A structured parent interview for identifying young children with autism. *Journal of Autism and Developmental Disorders, 23*(4), 639–652.

Stone, W. L., Lee, E. B., Ashford, L., Brissie, J., Hepburn, S. L., Coonrod, E. E., et al. (1999). Can autism be diagnosed accurately in children under 3 years? *Journal of Child Psychology and Psychiatry, 40*(2), 219–226.

Tantam, N. (1988). Asperger's syndrome. *Journal of Child Psychology and Psychiatry, 29,* 245–255.

Teitelbaum, P., Teitelbaum, O., Nye, J., Fryman, J., & Maurer, R. G. (1998). Movement analysis in infancy may be useful for early diagnosis of autism. *Journal of Neuroscience, 95*(23), 13982–13987.

Tidmarsh, L., & Volkmar, F. R. (2003). Diagnosis and epidemiology of autism spectrum disorders. *Canadian Journal of Psychiatry, 48,* 517–525.

Townsend, J., & Courchesne, E. (1994). Parietal damage and narrow "spotlight" spatial attention. *Journal of Cognitive Neuroscience, 6,* 220–232.

Townsend, J., Courchesne, E., Singer-Harris, N., Covington, J., Westerfield, M., Lyden, P., et al. (1999). Spatial attention deficits in patients with acquired or developmental cerebellar abnormality. *Journal of Neuroscience, 19,* 5632–5642.

Trevarthen, C., Aitken, K., Papoudi, D., & Robarts, J. (1998). *Children with autism: Diagnosis and interventions to meet their needs* (2nd ed.). Philadelphia: Jessica Kingsley.

Trevathan, E., & Naidu, S. (1988). The clinical recognition and differential diagnosis of Rett syndrome. *Annals of Neurology, 23,* 425–428.

Van Acker, R. (1991). Rett syndrome: A review of current knowledge. *Journal of Autism and Developmental Disorders, 21,* 381–406.

Villard, L., Kpebe, A., Cardoso, C., Chelly, J., Tardieu, M., & Fontes, M. (2000). Two affected boys in a Rett's syndrome family: Clinical and molecular findings. *Neurology, 55*(8), 1188–1193.

Volkmar, F. R. (1992). Childhood Disintegrative Disorder: Issues for DSM–IV. *Journal of Autism and Developmental Disorders, 22,* 625–642.

Volkmar, F. R. (1996). Brief report: Diagnostic issues in autism. *Journal of Autism and Developmental Disorders, 26,* 155–158.

Volkmar, F., Cook, E. H., Jr., Pomeroy, J., Realmuto, G., & Tanguay, P. (1999). Practice parameters for the assessment and treatment of children, adolescents, and adults with autism and other pervasive developmental disorders. *Journal of the American Academy of Child Adolescent Psychiatry, 38*(12), 32–54.

Volkmar, F. R., & Klin, A. (1998). Asperger syndrome and nonverbal learning disabilities. In E. Schopler, G. B. Mesibov, & L. J. Kunce (Eds.), *Asperger syndrome or high-functioning autism?* (pp. 107–121). New York: Plenum Press.

Volkmar, F. R., Klin, A., & Cohen, D. J. (1997). Diagnosis and classification of autism and related conditions: Consensus and issues. In D. J. Cohen & F. R. Volkmar (Eds.), *Handbook of autism and pervasive developmental disorders* (2nd ed., pp. 5–40). New York: Wiley.

Volkmar, F. R., Klin, A., Siegel, B., Szatmari, P., Lord, C., Campbell, M., et al. (1994). Field trial for autistic disorders in DSM–IV. *American Journal of Psychiatry, 151*(9), 1361–1367.

Volkmar, F. R., & Wiesner, L. A. (2004). *Healthcare for children on the autism spectrum: A guide to medical, nutritional, and behavioral issues.* Bethesda, MD: Woodbine House.

Wassink, T. H., & Piven, J. (2000). The molecular genetics of autism. *Current Psychiatry Reports, 2,* 170–175.

Watson, L. R., Baranek, G. R., & DiLavore, P. C. (2003). Toddlers with autism: Developmental perspectives. *Infants & Young Children, 16*(3), 201–214.

Werner, E., Dawson, G., Osterling, J., & Dinno, N. (2000). Brief report: Recognition of autism spectrum disorder before one year of age: A retrospective study based on home videotapes. *Journal of Autism and Developmental Disorders, 30,* 157–162.

Wetherby, A. M., & Prizant, B. M. (2002). *Communication and Symbolic Behavior Scales Developmental Profile.* Baltimore: Brookes.

Wetherby, A. M., & Woods, J. (2002). *Systematic Observation of Red Flags for Autism Spectrum Disorders in Young Children.* Unpublished manual. Tallahassee: Florida State University.

Wetherby, A. M., & Woods, J. (2003, November). *Red flags of autism spectrum disorders in the second year of life.* Paper presented at the Annual Convention of the American Speech–Language–Hearing Association, Chicago, IL.

Wetherby, A. M., Woods, J., Allen, L., Cleary, J., Dickinson, H., & Lord, C. (2004). Early indicators of autism spectrum disorders in the second year of life. *Journal of Autism and Developmental Disorders, 34*(5), 473–493.

Wilson, S., Djukic, A., Shinnar, S., Dharmanu, C., & Rapin, I. (2003). Clinical characteristics of language regression in children. *Developmental Medicine & Child Neurology, 45,* 508–514.

Wing, L. (1981). Asperger's syndrome: A clinical account. *Psychological Medicine, 11,* 115 129.

Witt Engerstrom, I. (1992). Rett syndrome: The late infantile regression period—A retrospective analysis of 91 cases. *Acta Paediatrica, 81,* 167–172.

Witt-Engerstrom, I., & Gillberg, C. (1987). Rett's syndrome in Sweden. *Journal of Autism and Developmental Disorders, 17*(1), 149–150.

Wolff, S. (1973). *Children under stress.* Baltimore: Penguin Books.

Wolff, S. (1989). *Childhood and human nature: The development of personality.* New York: Routledge.

World Health Organization. (1987). *International classification of diseases* (10th rev.). Geneva, Switzerland: Author.

Yeargin-Allsopp, M., Rice, C., Karapukar, T., Doernberg, N., Boyle, C., & Murphy, C. (2003). Prevalence of autism in a U.S. metropolitan area. *Journal of the American Medical Association, 289*(1), 49–55.

CHAPTER 2

Learning To Work with Families To Support Children with ASD

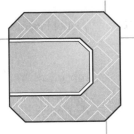

Jean E. Beatson and Patricia A. Prelock*

QUESTIONS TO CONSIDER

In this chapter, you will learn about the essential components for meeting the needs of children with autism spectrum disorders (ASD) as part of a family–professional team. Consider the following questions about the role of family-centered care and cultural competence when establishing relationships as collaborative teams:

1. What is family-centered care?
2. What role does cultural competence play in collaborating with families?
3. What are the barriers to family–professional collaboration?
4. How can professionals build relationships with families affected by ASD?

---

*The authors contributed equally to this chapter.

Introduction

Service delivery to any population of children with special needs requires a commitment to listening and communicating effectively. It demands recognition of the filter one uses to understand the perspective of others in the context of one's own. For example, read the following perspective offered by a parent who shares her experience of being around professionals working with her 7-year-old son with autism:

> I get really tired of them telling me that I'm so special doing this, and I'd like them to come [to our home] and see that Tommy [pseudonym] is no different than any other child…. He is a kid and a person. He comes to the table just like all the other kids, you know—there is no magic here.

As this mother spoke, it was apparent that the professionals working with her son perceived her "specialness" as something they could never achieve. Their perceptions allowed them to question whether Tommy could learn or even belonged in their school. This parent could do what they could never do; she was special, and they were not. This mother knew she was not special, and neither was her son. When she spoke these words, she was frustrated and full of anguish. It caused her to distrust the recommendations made by the service providers and teachers.

After her son's team experienced a shift in perspective about Tommy, a partnership between the parent and the professionals was built. The mother reported,

> I think their [the teachers' and providers'] attitude toward him has kind of shifted. [Before,] there was always this question in their minds about how much Tommy is really going to learn, is he retarded, and after the [negative] behaviors started, [they questioned] does he really belong here.

This mother explained that after the team was allowed to pose questions about Tommy's learning and behavior and explore the answers with a group of knowledgeable and family-centered consultants, the family and team built a shared understanding and perspective on who Tommy was within the context of his family. Because of that shift in perspective, a trusting family–professional collaboration took root. The mother and the team began to communicate and support each other, working together to solve issues as they arose.

It is useful to consider the essential relationship components within these two scenarios that supported the formation of a collaborative parent–professional partnership. Examining what is missing is as informative as examining what is present. In the first scenario, the professionals demonstrated little effective listening. This led to the parent's fear and frustration, particularly regarding educational plans for her son. The parent could not seriously entertain questions about whether her son should remain in the school because she strongly felt that the professionals had an incorrect view of her and her son.

In the second scenario, the mother and team had achieved a new understanding of Tommy, his capabilities, and his family. The team dynamic shifted when a group of knowledgeable, family-centered consultants made a home visit with members of the school team and created a time for the hard questions to be asked and answered. Out of this came a shared understanding of Tommy and team goals. Team members no longer placated the mother with compliments while ignoring her true concerns and angst for her son. Everyone became engaged in the day-to-day joys and struggles of working with Tommy. Effective listening, mutual respect, and a shared understanding led to the development of a trusting, collaborative relationship.

The role of families should be a primary concern in service delivery for children with ASD. Families are a constant in a child's life, and they provide a natural context for children with ASD to learn and generalize the skills that are critical to their success as communicators and social beings. In the sections that follow, we describe the tenets of family-centered care that are likely to affect the practice parameters for family-centered and culturally competent care. Barriers to effective practice and strategies to address these barriers will also be discussed.

Tenets of Family-Centered Care

Although the term *family-centered care* has been in use for more than 30 years, it was not formally defined until the late 1980s, when a group of families and professionals came together and described its key elements (Shelton & Stepanek, 1994). Table 2.1 highlights these elements.

One key element in family-centered care is the notion that families are a constant in the care provided for their children with special needs. Team members serving a particular child and family change yearly (Giangreco, Edelman, Nelson, Young, & Kiefer-O'Donnell, 1999). Professionals need to remember that families and children with ASD and other special needs are constantly forming and ending relationships with providers. When meeting a family and child with ASD, it would be prudent for the professional to ask, "What number am I in the long line of providers with whom you have collaborated?"

Inherent in the key elements of family-centered care is recognition of the diversity of families (Shelton & Stepanek, 1994, 1995). Each family has its own culture (Fadiman, 1997; Kavanagh, 1994; Patterson, 1995; Turnbull, Friesen, & Ramirez, 1998). Professionals are cautioned against using their own ethnocentric definitions of family and are urged instead to understand and respect how the family with which they are working identifies itself.

TABLE 2.1

Key Elements of Family-Centered Care

1. Incorporating into policy and practice the recognition that the family is the constant in a child's life, while service systems and the support personnel within those systems fluctuate.

2. Facilitating family–professional collaboration at all levels of hospital, home, and community care: care of an individual child; program development, implementation, evaluation, and evolution; and policy formation.

3. Exchanging complete and unbiased information between families and professionals in a supportive manner at all times.

4. Incorporating into policy and practice the recognition and honoring of cultural diversity, strengths, and individuality within and across all families, including ethnic, racial, spiritual, social, economic, educational, and geographic diversity.

5. Recognizing and respecting different methods of coping with and implementing comprehensive policies and programs that provide developmental, educational, emotional, environmental, and financial supports to meet the needs of families.

6. Encouraging and facilitating family-to-family support and networking.

7. Ensuring that hospital, home, and community service and support systems for children who need specialized health and developmental care and their families are flexible, accessible, and comprehensive in responding to diverse family-identified needs.

8. Appreciating families as families and children as children, recognizing that they possess a wide range of strengths, concerns, emotions, and aspirations beyond their need for specialized health and developmental services and support.

Note. Adapted from *Family-Centered Care for Children Needing Specialized Health and Developmental Services,* by T. L. Shelton and J. S. Stepanek, 1994, Association for the Care of Children's Health, 7910 Woodmont Avenue, Suite 300, Bethesda, MD 20814. Copyright 1994 by Association for the Care of Children's Health. Adapted with permission.

Within the mainstream culture in the United States, family is typically defined as mother, father, and children living together, with aunts, uncles, and grandparents, defined as "extended family," living elsewhere. Other cultural groups, however, define family differently; some have many generations living together with distinct roles for decision making and relationship building (Fadiman, 1997; Kavanagh, 1994). For example, the Native American concept of family includes extended family members, who often care for the children so that parents can work (Joe & Malach, 1992). Native Americans living on reservations are likely to live in extended family groups, whereas those living in the city are more likely to live in nuclear family groups. In both situations, elders are valued and sought for advice, and group consensus is usually sought before important decisions are made.

What is clear is that all families function in their own unique way, and it is the professional's responsibility not only to try to understand the values and uniqueness of each family, but also to be able to describe the values that drive his or her own professional behavior. A critical component of family-centered care is the recognition that all families have strengths (Ahmann, 1998; Dunst & Trivette, 1996; Dunst, Trivette, & Hamby, 1996; Kavanagh,

1994; Patterson, 1995; Weick & Saleebey, 1995). Looking for and articulating family strengths is essential to the collaborative process. The strengths of a family and child with ASD become the building blocks for effective services.

Beatson and Prelock (2002) investigated how parents of children with ASD experienced a family-centered assessment process through the Vermont Rural Autism Project (VT-RAP), a 3-year federal- and state-funded training project that was designed to prepare early childhood special educators, speech–language pathologists (SLPs), and other related service providers to enhance the quality of their assessment and intervention of children with ASD and their families. The overriding goal of the project was to create systems change across the state of Vermont by developing the expertise of community-based teams in assessment, program planning, and intervention for children with ASD. The assessment and intervention approach modeled throughout VT-RAP reflected a strengths-based (Dunst & Trivette, 1996) and family-centered (Shelton & Stepanek, 1994) framework. Families who participated in the project were an integral part of the assessment and intervention planning team and were recognized as having inherent strengths, on which program development and implementation were founded (Beatson & Prelock, 2002; Prelock, Beatson, Bitner, Broder, & Ducker, 2003). Children's needs, as perceived by their parents and community teams, guided the assessment process. Recognition of the expert knowledge parents bring to the assessment process also supported the family-centered and strengths-based approach.

Families have described the VT-RAP assessment and planning model as an effective approach not only to assessing their children's needs but also to facilitating the planning and implementation of the children's educational and community programs (Beatson & Prelock, 2002). One mother reported feeling rescued when the team serving her son and family finally shifted their attitude from one of pathology to seeing him as a young man with strengths and challenges, and as a person with autism. She said,

> It is a whole attitude shift, and once you make that, things fall into place. I think that's what RAP does. It pushes that button that gives people an attitude shift. I know it did for the school team. It made us feel like somebody was coming to our rescue, [like we had] dialed 911.

Family-centered care necessitates truly caring for families, realizing that all families have strengths and expertise, honoring the constancy of the family in the life of the child, being flexible in response to family-identified needs, and creating a context of growth and empowerment. Providers need to understand and respect the fact that families cope in different ways and may or may not seek the support of professionals at different times during their family life cycle. Incorporating family-centered care into practice leads to improved outcomes for families of children with special needs and disabilities, which include decreased hospitalizations, increased satisfaction, decreased costs, increased family involvement, and enhanced family coping

(Horst, Werner, & Werner, 2000). For families with children affected by ASD, family-centered care is critical, as the pervasiveness of the child's needs affects all aspects of family life.

Role of Cultural Competence

Family-centered care also requires that professionals be culturally competent. Culture is defined as the learned and shared rules and traditions that express the values and beliefs of a group and the individuals within that group (Kalyanpur & Harry, 1999). Moreover, culture promotes identity in individuals and groups (Kagawa-Singer, 1994). Everyone exists within a cultural framework. Culture is dynamic, ever changing and fluid.

Additionally, each service system—for example, health care (Fadiman, 1997; Kleinman, Eisenberg, & Good, 1978) and special education (Kalyanpur & Harry, 1999)—has its own culture. Consequently, when a provider and a family come together, it is a meeting of at least three cultures. Even an area of study as specific as child development is ruled by cultural beliefs (McCollum, Ree, & Chen, 2000). And of course, culture guides the style of parent–child interactions (Kalyanpur & Harry, 1999). As Brookins (1993) points out, developmental studies have focused mostly on White, middle-class children. More recently, scholars are recognizing that context is as important as biology (Brookins, 1993; Kalyanpur & Harry, 1999). However, the importance of context is still not being considered as it should be within school systems (Kalyanpur & Harry, 1999) and health care (Fadiman, 1997).

The cultural framework of a family or individual cannot be assumed, nor can one assume that the individual or family understands the culture of the provider or the system within which they are functioning (Fadiman, 1997). *Cultural competence* can be defined as the ability to collaborate across cultures in a respectful manner, leading to mutually desired outcomes (McCubbin, Thompson, Thompson, & Kaston, 1993). In order to accomplish this, providers must be prepared to explain their own cultural framework and know how to sensitively explore that of the individual or family with whom they are working (Dennis & Giangreco, 1996; Fadiman, 1997; Kalyanpur & Harry, 1999; Kleinman et al., 1978). Only then can mutual ground be found and meaningful goals and outcomes be realized (Bates, Rankin-Hill, & Sanchez-Ayendez, 1997).

Service systems offer rules and rituals that reflect their embedded cultural values (Bates et al., 1997; Brookins, 1993; Kalyanpur & Harry, 1999). Kalyanpur and Harry offer a detailed analysis of the cultural underpinnings of special education and the Individuals with Disabilities Education Act (IDEA) of 1990. In their comprehensive review of the literature, they found that special education reflects the five core American mainstream values of freedom of choice, individual rights, equality, achievement, and social mobility. As a result of the trend toward increasing diversity, tensions often surface in relation to conflicting goals. For example, how do educational programs support achievement and equal education in all populations? This tension has contributed to the categorization of children using a deficit-based model. Most Americans within the mainstream culture are comfortable with the system of evaluating individuals as normal versus not normal. Increasing numbers of individuals and families do not subscribe to that way of thinking, however (Kalyanpur & Harry, 1999).

As parents and providers work together to identify and support children with ASD, the Individuals with Disabilities Education Act of 1990 provides one vehicle that can be used to require service systems to respond to individual needs. IDEA contains six principles of law: zero reject, nondiscriminatory assessment, individualized and appropriate education, least restrictive environment, due process, and parent participation. These principles of law reflect core American values (Kalyanpur & Harry, 1999). The value of individual rights accounts for person-centered planning such as the Individualized Education Program (IEP) and the movement toward independence and self-determination.

The revered American value of freedom of choice is embedded in the goal of individual achievement, access to quality education, and involvement of parents (Kalyanpur & Harry, 1999). The reality, however, is that there is limited choice in the services offered to children with ASD and other special needs. Zero reject, nondiscriminatory assessment, and parent participation are supported in the core value of equality. Although most may say these principles and values are well intentioned, there are families who will be conflicted by the notion of individual rights over the common good, view disabilities differently, and favor status quo over equality (Dennis & Giangreco, 1996; Fadiman, 1997; Kalyanpur & Harry, 1999). For example, an Asian family may not value individual independence or personal choice, many Hawaiian children are not afforded much personal choice by their elders, and Latino parents may retain decision-making rights for their children until the children marry or move away (Dennis & Giangreco, 1996).

Some families' religious beliefs form the primary way they view and interact with the world. The story of one such family whose 4-year-old son was assessed through VT-RAP follows. The child's diagnosis was complicated by a seizure disorder, Crouzon's syndrome, and speech and language delay. Questions regarding mental retardation versus autism persisted. The family opted not to sort out the diagnosis as part of the assessment and, instead, wanted the VT-RAP team to focus on recommendations for intervention. On the assessment day, the mother, Alice (a pseudonym), welcomed the VT-RAP team into their home with homemade lasagna set up as a buffet lunch. A couple of months later, the school and VT-RAP assessment team sat around the family's living room reviewing the report and making action plans for implementing the recommendations. Alice said,

> We all sat on our living room floor and talked. It was very teary, heart-warming, and sincere. They became part of our family as well as helping us with Ricky [a pseudonym]. We got very attached to everyone. I can't put words to what it meant.

When asked about what happened for her son's team as a result of participating in VT-RAP, Alice said,

> The team got attached to Ricky. They learned a lot about Crouzon's and us as parents. There's so much. They learned there are parents out there that'll do anything. We put our trust in the Lord's hands. They saw our faith.

When asked from her perspective how the team's experience with VT-RAP affected the team's practice, she said, "In seeing our closeness, seeing our faith, we developed a friendship. The team was willing to listen and cared about how Jim [dad, pseudonym] and I felt. They respected the parents' feelings."

Seeing and understanding this family in the context of their faith enabled a trusting family–professional relationship to develop. Reaching this level of connection required the team to get down on the living room floor to share a meal, along with stories and knowledge. It was important to the parents that professionals would drive for over an hour to get to their home. That showed the parents that the professionals honored their family values and the role of the family.

It is not enough to describe one's own cultural values and to sensitively explore the cultural values of families. Professionals must also understand the cultural underpinnings of the systems with which they work. Once this triad of cultural understanding is reached, actions and reactions of colleagues and families begin to make more sense, and barriers to professional–family collaboration can be anticipated and avoided.

Barriers to Family–Professional Collaboration: What Are They and How Should We Respond?

The implementation of family-centered care frequently presents challenges. These might include role stress when family or other team members are stretched beyond their comfort zone, negotiation problems when there is a breakdown in communication between families and providers, or power struggles when there are more gatekeepers than collaborators (Newton, 2000). In addition, problems arise when there are differences in interaction styles among families and providers (Feldman, Ploof, & Cohen, 1999). Divergent beliefs regarding the nature of disability might also fuel problems in information dissemination and service provision (Fadiman, 1997; Groce & Zola, 1993; Joe & Malach, 1992; Kalyanpur & Harry, 1999; Laird, 1995). The real barrier to family–professional collaboration, however, arises when assumptions are made about what families believe and value or when diverse beliefs or values are disrespected (Fadiman, 1997; Kalyanpur & Harry, 1999;

Kleinman et al., 1978). Assessment results are influenced by the team's culture as much or even more than the "culture, strengths, and needs of the children who are evaluated and their families" (Westby & Ford, 1993a, p. 51). Without training and consciousness raising, there tends to be an embedded belief in the universality of knowledge on the part of the professional. Too often the resulting assumptions and misperceptions become another burden for the family to bear. These assumptions can, and often do, lead to completely erroneous plans being made for children by well-intentioned service providers, leaving the family at a minimum confused and at a maximum angry and headed toward mediation or legal action.

Honor the Family's Culture and Strengths

As one of many who work with families affected by ASD, it is the responsibility of each practitioner to honor the culture and strengths of the family (Fadiman, 1997; Weick & Saleebey, 1995). Understanding their own short tenure in the life of a child and family should motivate professionals to respect the culture of the family and decrease their expectations that the family will adapt to the culture of the professionals. When this basic tenet of family constancy in family-centered care is not embraced, a mutually trusting, caring relationship with the family is unlikely to develop.

A few years ago, one of the authors was working as a care coordinator for a Vietnamese refugee family with a 3-year-old girl who had a repaired cleft lip. Part of the care coordination involved organizing speech and language assessments, accompanying the mother and daughter to clinical appointments, making home visits, and helping with the problems associated with adapting to life in America. Four people lived in the home: the 3-year-old child; her grandmother, who spoke Vietnamese; her mother, who spoke some English; and her teenage sister, who was learning English quickly. One of the service providers expressed concern that the 3-year-old was not learning English and was not exposed to many other children. Thinking she was doing a good thing for the family, the provider enrolled the 3-year-old in a local preschool. The confused mother and grandmother dutifully dressed the little girl in her best clothes and sent her off to school at the allotted times. The little girl cried nonstop every day. The grandmother grew despondent now that her job of taking care of her granddaughter had been taken away from her. The mother was distressed by the unhappiness of both her mother and her daughter, and the family's real needs (i.e., English classes, transportation, employment, health care) were not being addressed. One day the schoolteacher spoke to the author (as care coordinator for the little girl) in frustration, saying that the little one cries all the time and comes dressed inappropriately for preschool. The author explained to the teacher that dressing up was a sign of respect, that the little girl missed her grandmother, and that the grandmother missed her. Suddenly, the situation became clear to everyone involved. The little girl left preschool, the grandmother resumed her responsibilities, and the providers began to recognize the family's point of view.

Understand Skills for Listening and Speaking

Lack of professional training in working together as equal partners is also a barrier to family–professional collaboration (Kalyanpur & Harry, 1999). Both families and professionals require some knowledge and understanding of the ways effective listening and speaking can occur. The goal of effective listening is to make sure that what is being said is heard and understood. Effective speaking is saying what you mean. The elements of effective listening and speaking are described in the paragraphs that follow, with examples from communication exchanges between family members and service professionals.

Effective Listening Components
- Paying attention to relevant verbal and nonverbal information
- Interpreting information
- Addressing questions posed
- Giving feedback on information shared
- Eliciting information

To be an effective listener as part of a parent–professional team, it is important to *attend to the relevant verbal and nonverbal information* that occurs within a conversation or team meeting. This requires communicative partners to be sure that what is said is what is meant. It also requires communicative partners to look for times when verbal information is not matched to nonverbal information. In the following example, a parent offers his perspective on the classroom intervention that his second grader with autism is receiving, and the speech–language pathologist (SLP) responds, recognizing a mismatch in what is said and what is potentially meant.

PARENT: I guess the classroom intervention is helping Carlos.
SLP: When you say that, I notice some hesitation.

Second, it is important that *information be interpreted with some immediacy* to ensure that the inferences made by a communicative partner are accurate. In the example that follows, Carlos's second-grade teacher offers some information, followed by Carlos's mother attempting to clearly interpret what was said.

TEACHER: Carlos continues to require repeated instructions. He never gets his work done.
PARENT: Do you mean he doesn't get any of his work done, or just those tasks that he has more difficulty understanding or that are not part of his interests?

Third, an effective listener *addresses any questions that are posed,* attending to both verbal and nonverbal information expressed by the speaker. Effective listening also requires an awareness of one's own agenda while engaged in a conversational exchange. For example, if a parent asks, "Does Carlos have the ability to understand what I say?" the SLP should be able to answer that question and not shift the discussion to a different topic that he or she is concerned with. The SLP might say the following:

> Both testing and my observations suggest that Carlos is able to understand what is being said to him, as long as the instructions are presented one at a time. He has difficulty sequencing and responding to a series of directions, especially those that include unfamiliar vocabulary and for which he has no visual cue.

Fourth, it is important to *provide feedback* about information that is shared conversationally. Effective listeners let the speaker know they are listening by indicating that the information has been heard, often reflecting on what has been said. In the next example, after a teacher has expressed her angst about meeting Carlos's learning needs, the SLP might respond,

> It must be challenging to have Carlos in class, particularly when you are required to follow a curriculum and introduce topics that are often difficult for him to understand and are less interesting to him.

Fifth, sufficient *information must be elicited* if team members are to understand what is important to them and what they need to know to provide the support a child with ASD requires. Some strategies that both parents and professionals can use include acknowledgment (e.g., I see the challenge you're facing.), support (e.g., How could we capitalize on Carlos's interests and still meet the curriculum objectives?), and clarification (e.g., Can Carlos understand the new topics introduced in the classroom if preteaching or visual supports are used?).

Effective Speaking Components
- Clear statement of point of view
- Simple presentation of meaningful information
- Use of feedback to ensure information presented is understood
- Use of advanced organizers
- Summarization

To be effective speakers in conversation, team members must *clearly state their point of view.* For example, stating, "Carlos never talks in the classroom" is not as clear or accurate as, "Carlos responds to questions in the classroom only when he is asked about trains or TV game shows, two of his favorite interests."

Information should be presented in a simple, meaningful way. As an example, notice the complexity of the first message that follows compared to the second message provided by a teacher while conversing with a parent:

> *Complex and less meaningful:* Carlos is reading at Level II but is unable to respond independently to comprehension questions.
>
> *Simple and more meaningful:* In the second-grade reader, Carlos should be able to read a short story of three to five pages and write answers to questions about the story using complete sentences. I brought an example of a story he read last week, the questions he was asked, and his responses.

It is important to *obtain feedback* to ensure that the information shared is understood during conversational exchanges. Using simple questions such as "Does this make sense to you?" or "Have you seen this behavior in Carlos?" can help both parents and service providers gain perspective, share mutual understanding, and clarify confusion or differences in experience.

Using advanced organizers (e.g., stating what is going to be discussed) is an effective way to prepare the listener for what is about to be said. Often at team meetings, a child's case manager has several items to be discussed. Highlighting the primary issues supports the listeners' ability to attend, organize their thinking, and prepare for what is to come. A teacher can prepare the team for the information she is about to share by saying something like, "I thought I'd begin by telling you what we are doing in class and then tell you where Carlos is having difficulty."

Finally, it is important for the speaker to *summarize what he or she has said*. This ensures that team members understand the issues presented, learn what works and does not work, and know the next steps, if any, that have been discussed and agreed upon. An example of summarization follows:

> It sounds like we have the same concerns about Carlos's expressive language at home and in school. He has difficulty starting and sticking with a conversation if the topic is anything other than trains or TV shows. We have discovered, however, that if he is presented with visual cues, such as written sentences or question starters, he can answer and ask questions in conversation around other topics.

Recognize Team Culture

Professional collaborators must understand their own cultural biases if they are to develop the flexibility and open-mindedness required to establish successful family–professional partnerships. They must also provide accurate information about a child's strengths and challenges if they are to function as knowledgeable team partners exchanging information across disciplines. Team culture consists of the values and beliefs that are characteristic of a team and reflect its history and learning over time (Briggs, 1997).

Recognizing team culture is important for several reasons. It provides insight into the attitudes and beliefs of a team, acknowledges current practice patterns, helps to frame roles and responsibilities, and creates a context for team members to interpret what is occurring and what will occur (Briggs, 1997; Westby & Ford, 1993b). Groups appear to share or hold in common things that influence their interactions among their own members and with members of other groups. Schein (1992) has defined the following commonalities among groups:

- behavioral regularities in interaction (e.g., formality of the language used);
- norms (e.g., often unspoken standards regarding relationships with families or other agencies);
- explicitly stated values (e.g., identifying a group as being family centered or interdisciplinary);
- guiding philosophy (e.g., mission statement);
- "game rules" for surviving as a team member (e.g., who you go to for answers);
- climate (e.g., homelike or cliniclike setting);
- expected competencies (e.g., shared skills or mental models);
- shared meanings and experiences (e.g., understanding what emerges from the group as a result of interactions over time); and
- integration of symbols that characterize the group (e.g., materials used by the group).

Team culture allows a group to differentiate between members and nonmembers and helps to determine the specific philosophical orientation held by the group (Briggs, 1997). It also serves to inform team members of what they value and how they are supposed to act. As perspective team members, both families and professionals must examine the level of congruence between the values espoused by a team and the underlying assumptions that appear to be guiding the team's actions (Westby & Ford, 1993a). Level of congruence is an important indicator of team health and can facilitate or hinder the development of family–professional partnerships.

Share an Understanding of Rights and Responsibilities

Existent within IDEA are tensions and paradoxes that can contribute to the erosion of family–professional relationships. Although the mandate for parent participation requires school personnel to involve parents in the decision-making process and establish collaborative partnerships, the principle of due process pits parents and professionals against each other and creates adversarial conditions (Kalyanpur & Harry, 1999). All parents interviewed in the VT-RAP study (Beatson & Prelock, 2002) were aware of the tension between maintaining working relationships with school professionals and advocating for what they considered to be appropriate plans for their children. Because of the broad and intensive needs experienced by the children with ASD and their families, programs were expensive and year-round. Parents and professionals alike consistently struggled with the conflicting realities of the children's needs, limited resources, and lack of training.

There are also cultural differences in understanding and actualizing the principle of due process. Families from lower socioeconomic classes (Humphry, 1994) and those who value harmony over individualism are less inclined to fight for their children (Kalyanpur & Harry, 1999), and their children often have inadequate programs. Many of the families participating within the Vermont Rural Autism Project fell into the category commonly referred to as the working poor. They did not understand their rights, nor did they have the language or knowledge needed to demand them.

As partners in the effort to support the needs of children with ASD, parents and professionals need to define the issues that affect practice and service, and then brainstorm ways to solve problems creatively. For example, Vermont developed a statewide task force to better meet the needs of young children with autism and to more carefully examine the variability in needs and the inequity of services across the state (Autism Task Force of Vermont, 1998). The resulting position statement led to the development of a statewide Autism Information Center to share up-to-date information and resources with parents and professionals, a rejuvenation of the Autism Society of Vermont with a focus on advocacy and support, and a specific allocation of funds from the Agency of Human Services to respond to the pervasive needs of children with ASD.

Learn the Language and Let the Power Go

The use of professional language and a hierarchy of power and knowledge constitute significant barriers to family–professional collaboration (Kalyanpur & Harry, 1999). Professional language and jargon often serve as a means of "alienation and disempowerment" (p. 49). One mother who was interviewed felt desperate to be seen as having important knowledge at her son's IEP meeting and spoke about the experience of appearing unknowledgeable because she did not use professional language:

> I need someone to help me, to guide me as to which way to go. I was lost at that IEP meeting. You know, I wanted to present myself professionally. I wanted someone to help me to present myself as a professional, to show that I do know what I am talking about.

Additionally, because teachers and special educators are formally trained and most parents are not, teachers' knowledge is often more valued than families' knowledge (Kalyanpur & Harry, 1999). Instead of perceiving knowledge as culturally situated (Laird, 1995), in most education settings, knowledge is accepted as an objective reality rather than a fluid, subjective discourse (Kalyanpur & Harry, 1999). When one sort of knowledge is valued over a different sort of knowledge, a power differential occurs; in this situation, the professionals are more powerful, and the parents less.

The tension between the principle of equality and the reality of the power imbalance "is also felt in the status parents are accorded in the decision-making process and the patterns of communication between parents and professionals in formal conferences" (Kalyanpur & Harry, 1999, p. 66). Ultimately, the IEP meeting can progress without the parents' input but not without the special educators' input. The power lies with the professional.

If parents are participating in the IEP meeting, other aspects of their lesser status may become apparent. For example, the order of speakers reflects those with greater status to those with lesser (Kalyanpur & Harry, 1999). Typically, psychologists or physicians are afforded the greatest status and speak first, then in descending order of power and status come the special educator, related service providers, the general education teacher, and finally the parents. Stylistic differences in communication are also hierarchical, with more formal communication having higher status and the narrative style, or storytelling, the least amount of status (Kalyanpur & Harry, 1999; Laird, 1995; Weick & Saleebey, 1995).

The power hierarchy at IEP meetings was apparent to VT-RAP parents. One of the parents, a teacher for many years, spoke movingly about his experience of being "on the other side of the IEP table." He suddenly felt anxious that his son's needs would not be met, that his program would be insufficient, and ultimately he felt at the mercy of the professionals sitting around the table. He experienced powerlessness. His wife, Emily (a pseudonym), had similar experiences. She told of being at an IEP meeting where, as people sat in a circle chatting before the meeting officially began, her son's special educator spoke to the person sitting on the other side of her making constant references to "the mother" wanting this or that. Finally, in an attempt to become a part of the conversation by using humor, Emily said, "Well, speaking as the mother …," whereupon the special educator turned, looked at her, said nothing, and then returned her attention to the other professional and continued in the same vein. Emily was effectively silenced. In their research, Kalyanpur and Harry (1999) found that that power differential creates an enormous barrier to family–professional collaboration.

One way to reduce the language barrier at team meetings is to assign someone a specific role as a "watchdog" for language use that might not be understood by all members of the team. The assignment of a "jargon buster" at a team meeting serves two important roles. First, it creates a vehicle in which clarification of terms is ensured. Second, it lessens the power differential between parents and professionals by recognizing that all members of the team need to be able to understand all the terminology used.

Another strategy to reduce the "power of the professional" at team meetings is to encourage parents to bring other family members, a friend, or other support person to a meeting. The presence of additional family supports addresses several barriers often experienced by families at team meetings with an overabundance of professionals. It evens out the "numbers" a bit between home and school. The family is provided with another filter through which to understand what is being said. And the family has someone with whom they can process and debrief the events of the meeting.

Changing the location of the meeting from the school to the home will also shift the power balance. Also, asking the parents or the regular education teacher to speak first can change the power differential. Spending a few moments at the beginning of the meeting to identify values and norms that the team promises to uphold, including, for example, the many different forms that knowledge takes (e.g., story, formal report), mutual respect, and everyone having equal importance, is essential to creating a collaborative and inclusive team dynamic. Table 2.2 highlights the primary barriers to establishing effective parent–professional interactions and presents possible actions to be taken by professionals to reduce those barriers.

TABLE 2.2

Barriers to and Solutions for Establishing Family–Professional Partnerships

Barriers	Solutions
Making inaccurate assumptions about the cultural framework of a family, including their values and beliefs.	• Understand and be able to explain your own cultural framework. • Sensitively explore the cultural framework of the family with whom you are working. • Honor the family's culture and strengths.
Lack of training in ways to work together as equal partners.	• Learn strategies for effective listening and speaking during team meetings and other conversational exchanges. • Establish team norms. • Attend workshops and conferences as a parent–professional team.
Possibility of litigation.	• Understand and respect the rights of individuals and their families. • Recognize the pressures of the service systems. • Brainstorm solutions that engage policymakers.
Language confusion.	• Assign a "jargon buster" at family–professional meetings.
Hierarchy of power.	• Encourage families to include additional family members or other support people at team meetings. • Attend workshops and conferences as a parent–professional team. • Change the location of team meetings to a neutral place or the home of a family member. • Change the order of speakers at team meetings, so families can share their thoughts and ideas before service providers.

Building Professional Relationships with Families Affected by ASD

Autism affects families of all cultural backgrounds, and professionals involved in the assessment of and intervention for children with ASD must be cognizant of the impact of culture on family functioning (Brown & Rogers, 2003; Department of Health and Human Services, 2002; Wing, 1993). Paramount to building professional relationships with families affected by ASD is the ability to assume a "posture of cultural reciprocity" (Kalyanpur & Harry, 1999, p. 115). Cultural reciprocity is a way to move from overt cultural awareness, noticing obvious differences in dress and language, to covert cultural awareness, noticing differences that are not easily seen, and finally to subtle cultural awareness. Subtle cultural awareness is attained when professionals recognize the values that underlie their actions and understand that those values are culture specific and therefore not universal. Optimally, the professional will understand how their personal values interface with those of the family they are serving and the service system within which both parties are interacting. Understanding this triad of cultures forms the bones of professional and family collaboration.

Kalyanpur and Harry (1999) articulated four steps to guide professionals in assuming a stance of cultural reciprocity. In the first step, professionals increase their knowledge about the cultural beliefs and values embedded in their own perspectives—for example, about a student with ASD. This is accomplished simply by asking themselves *why*. For example, "Why is it important to me that Johnny make eye contact with me when I speak to him?" Perhaps it is because of a belief that eye contact shows that Johnny is listening and respectful. Eye contact is not a universal sign of listening and respect, of course, but an American cultural value.

In the second and third steps of cultural reciprocity, the professionals find out whether the family shares their values and, if not, what the family's perspective is (Kalyanpur & Harry, 1999). Professionals can accomplish this simply and directly by explaining their values and assumptions, as well as those of the system within which they are working, and asking the family about their perspectives. Using Stephan as the example, the professional may say to the family, "In my culture, Stephan shows that he is listening and being respectful to me when I am speaking to him by making eye contact. Is this true in your family?" The family may say, "Looking directly at his elders is a sign of disrespect, and we do not allow it."

In the fourth step, the professional takes all this information and collaborates with the family to create a plan that adapts professional and systemic values with those of the family (Kalyanpur & Harry, 1999). This can be very exciting for all concerned because it is a creative and innovative aspect of professional and family collaboration. Returning to the example of Stephan, the professional and the family may agree that being respectful to teachers is important. The manner in which it is demonstrated may be adjusted. Paying attention and learning may be defined as important for both the family and the teacher, but the teacher may learn from the family other signs that Stephan exhibits when he is attentive. In this way, not only is culture bridged, the power differential is shifted because alternate ways of knowing are valued.

Implications for Professionals and Families Affected by ASD

Professionals who embark on the journey of providing culturally competent, family-centered care are inviting into their lives the unique opportunity to truly engage with themselves, with their practice, and with children with ASD and their families in a deeply caring and richly satisfying manner. The degree of self-awareness required will benefit professionals in all areas of their life. This level of self-awareness is dependent on developing an ongoing reflective practice and a willingness to openly engage in dialogue centered on values, beliefs, and the contextual nature of knowledge (Kalyanpur & Harry, 1999; Like, Steiner, & Rubel, 1996). Implementing the four steps in cultural reciprocity is one way to get at these basic assumptions.

An excellent place to begin making practice changes is in the IEP meeting. The professional can collaborate on determining the setting of the meeting, the order of speakers, the norms that govern the IEP team, and the composition of the team; defining the agenda; and sharing knowledge about the cultural underpinnings of the IEP ritual, the team's worldview, and that of the family. Attending to the team's culture can aid in producing a truly collaborative team with the family and child affected by ASD.

When true collaboration is happening, the implications for families are extraordinary. Every VT-RAP family interviewed described an experience of empowerment as the rituals around assessment of their children with ASD were changed in a way that adhered to the principles of family-centered, culturally competent care (Beatson & Prelock, 2002). Community meetings were held in homes. One team meeting had more family members in attendance than professionals. Families participated in the planning and assessment. Their top-priority questions and concerns were addressed, and they helped edit the report.

Another benefit for families engaged in the process of family-centered, culturally competent collaboration is that, although their family values and beliefs may differ from those of the American mainstream, they increase their knowledge about how things may be perceived in the world outside their family. This knowledge may assist them in negotiating the larger world around them.

Not only do children with ASD reap the benefits of the collaboration between the adults in their lives, they are also wonderful collaborators themselves. Children with ASD who participated in the Vermont Rural Autism Project were interviewed as part of the assessment. One teenager with ASD attended the planning meeting and made her desires, needs, and goals known. She, her parents, and the school team were able to understand the differences in their values, adapt expectations accordingly, and create a plan that would benefit all concerned.

When families and professionals bridge cultures, children are privy to a world that makes more sense to them. Instead of having to negotiate two opposing worlds, children can move comfortably between two different worlds that are in harmony. What remains congruent are the primary values and beliefs of all members of the team. Returning to Stephan one last time, what must his experience be if in one world someone puts her hands on his face to move his head to engage him visually and when he goes home he is reprimanded for staring into his grandfather's face when addressed?

Summary

This chapter described family-centered care and the role such care plays in the delivery of service to families affected by ASD. It also provided information on the barriers to family–professional collaboration and ways to improve those important relationships. The summary that follows refers to the questions at the beginning of the chapter and highlights key points.

What is family-centered care?

Families can and should identify its members and their respective roles. Recognizing that families are a constant in the child's life whereas professionals come and go, family-centered practitioners seek to know and understand how families conceptualize their strengths and challenges, and what guides the diversity of their values and beliefs.

What role does cultural competence play in collaborating with families?

Integral to the notion of family-centered care is cultural competence. Simply defined, *culture* is the worldview of an individual, family, team, or system. Cultural competence is the ability to meaningfully bridge the different cultures of professional, system, and family. The four steps of cultural reciprocity provide a framework for attaining cultural competence. One cannot assume mutual understanding of cultures between a family and a provider. There is limited research on the effects of cultural factors in autism, but providers must assume that the behaviors of children with ASD are affected by a social context that has a cultural basis (Brown & Rogers, 2003). Cultural competence requires providers to understand their own cultural background and how that background influences interactions with families.

What are the barriers to family–professional collaboration?

It has become apparent in service delivery that not understanding the cultural framework of family will limit the ability of service providers to respond to the values and beliefs the family holds paramount. Lacking a common language and understanding of the problems and issues facing a child with ASD, along with a hierarchical power base in team meetings, further complicates relationship building. Too often, fear of due process limits the open, respectful sharing that is required to move forward as a team. Finally, few families or service providers have had training or practice in working as equal partners to define problems and create reasonable solutions.

How can professionals build relationships with families affected by ASD?

Speech–language pathologists, special educators, nurses, and other professionals working with families affected by ASD have a mandate to know themselves well. They need to be able to describe their own values and beliefs as well as that of the system within which they work. They need to learn how to elicit the same information from families with authentic caring, compassion, and interest. Once such a relationship is created, true family–professional collaboration becomes a reality and the journey of meaningful service delivery begins.

Practice Opportunities

1. As you begin the development of a parent–professional partnership, identify at least three strengths of a family you are working with that has a child with ASD. For a family member answering this question, identify three strengths of the team that is working with you and your child with ASD.

2. What two questions might you ask yourself as you consider the cultural components that are likely to influence the development of a parent–professional partnership?

3. Identify two things that you will do differently both as a listener and as a speaker during team meetings with parents and professionals.

4. How will you reduce the language barrier and power differential that may exist during your parent–professional meetings?

Suggested Readings

Dunst, C. J., & Trivette, C. M. (1996). Empowerment, effective helpgiving practices and family-centered care. *Pediatric Nursing, 22,* 334–337.

> This article shares the tenets of family-centered practice and offers ideas for supporting the needs of families in a way that supports their empowerment.

Fadiman, A. (1997). *The spirit catches you and you fall down: A Hmong child, her American doctors, and the collision of two cultures.* New York: Farrar, Straus and Giroux.

> This book provides a provocative description of two cultures at odds, physicians practicing Western medicine and a Hmong family attempting to love their sick child, as both try to care for a young child with a severe seizure disorder. The power of the story is in the struggle of trying to understand why

each party feels and acts the way it does, and the challenges the participants experience in developing a family–professional partnership as a result of cultural misunderstandings.

Kephart, B. (1998). *A slant of sun.* New York: Norton.

This is the story of a mother's search for an understanding of the behaviors her son exhibits while celebrating his unique contribution to his family. Understanding how medical terms like Pervasive Developmental Disorder/Not Otherwise Specified are used to describe her son challenges her relationships with professionals. Ultimately, her love and her son's courage help him make language connections, evolve from his obsessive play, and decrease his frustrations.

RESOURCES

Resources Online

Attainment Company
  http://www.attainmentcompany.com
  800/327-4269

Future Horizons
  http://www.futurehorizons-autism.com
  800/489-0727

Jessica Kingsley Publishers
  http://www.jkp.com
  44(020)7833-2307

KidAccess
  http://www.kidaccess.com
  412/521-8552

Paul Brookes Publishing
  http://www.brookespublishing.com
  800/638-3775

Service Centers, Support Groups, and Newsletters

BBB Autism
  http://www.bbbautism.com

Center for Outreach & Services for the Autism Community
  1450 Parkside Ave., Ste. 22
  Ewing, NJ 08368
  609/883-8100

Exceptional Parent Magazine
  PO Box 3000, Dept. EP
  Danville, NJ 07834-9919
  800/247-8080

Family & Disability Newsletter
  Beach Center
  3111 Haworth Hall
  University of Kansas

Lawrence, KS 66045-7516
913/864-7600

Family Resource Associates
35 Haddon Ave.
Shrewsbury, NJ 07701
908/747-5310
800/501-0139

Family Village
http://www.familyvillage.wisc.edu

National Parent Network on Disabilities (NPND)
http://www.npnd.org
NPND@cs.net
1130 17th St. NW, Ste. 400
Washington, DC 20036
202/463-9403 (fax)

Parents Helping Parents
http://www.php.com
408/727-5775

Sibling Information Network
AJ Pappanikou Center
1776 Ellington Rd. South
Windsor, CT 06074
203/648-1205

Sibling Support Project
http://www.chmc.org/departmt/sibsupp
Dmeyer@chmc.org
Children's Hospital & Medical Center
4800 Sand Point Way NE
Seattle, WA 98105-0371
206/368-4911
206/368-4816 (fax)

Geneva Centre for Autism
http://www.autism.net
416/322-7877

Guidebooks

Aarons, M., & Gittens, T. (1992). *The handbook of autism: A guide for parents and profession-als.* New York: Routledge.

Baron-Cohen, S., & Bolton, P. (1993). *Autism: The facts.* New York: Oxford University Press.

Brill, M. T. (2001). *Keys to parenting the child with autism* (2nd ed.). New York: Barron's.

Gerdtz, J., & Bregman, J. (1990). *Autism: A practical guide for those who help others.* New York: Continuum.

Gerland, G. (2000). *Finding out about Asperger's syndrome, high functioning autism and PDD.* Philadelphia: Jessica Kingsley.

Harris, S. L. (1994). *Siblings of children with autism: A guide for families.* Bethesda, MD: Woodbine House.

Harris, S. L., & Weiss, M. J. (1998). *Right from the start: Behavioral intervention for young children with autism.* Bethesda, MD: Woodbine House.

Hart, C. (1993). *A parent's guide to autism: Answers to the most common questions.* New York: Pocket Books.

Hyatt-Foley, D., & Foley, M. G. (2002). *Getting services for your child on the autism spectrum.* Philadelphia: Jessica Kingsley.

Ives, M., & Munro, N. (2001). *Caring for a child with autism.* Philadelphia: Jessica Kingsley.

Janzen, J. E. (1999). *Autism: Facts and strategies for parents.* Austin, TX: Therapy Skill Builders.

Matthews, J., & Williams, J. (2000). *The self-help guide for special kids and their parents.* Philadelphia: Jessica Kingsley.

O'Neill, J. L. (1998). *Through the eyes of aliens: A book about autistic people.* Philadelphia: Jessica Kingsley.

Ozonoff, S., Dawson, G., & McPartland, J. (2002). *A parent's guide to Asperger syndrome & high-functioning autism: How to meet the challenges and help your child thrive.* New York: Guilford Press.

Paluszny, M. P. (1979). *Autism: A practical guide for parents and professionals.* Syracuse, NY: Syracuse University Press.

Powell, T., & Gallagher, P. A. (1993). *Brothers and sisters: A special part of exceptional families* (2nd ed.). Baltimore: Brookes.

Powers, M. D. (2000). *Children with autism: A parent's guide.* Bethesda, MD: Woodbine House.

Quinn, B., & Malone, A. (2000). *Pervasive developmental disorder: An altered perspective.* Philadelphia: Jessica Kingsley.

Schopler, E. (1995). *Parent survival manual: A guide to crisis resolution in autism and related developmental disorders.* New York: Plenum Press.

Siegel, B., & Silverstein, S. (1994). *What about me? Growing up with a developmentally disabled sibling.* New York: Plenum Press.

Simpson, R. L., & Zionts, P. (1992). *Autism: Information and resources for parents, families, and professionals.* Austin, TX: PRO-ED.

Stanton, M. (2000). *Learning to live with high functioning autism.* Philadelphia: Jessica Kingsley.

Stillman, W. (2002). *Demystifying the autistic experience: A humanistic introduction for parents, caregivers and educators.* Philadelphia: Jessica Kingsley.

Szatmari, P. (2004). *A mind apart: Understanding children with autism and Asperger syndrome.* New York: Guilford Press.

Welton, J. (2004). *Can I tell you about Asperger syndrome? A guide for friends and family.* New York: Jessica Kingsley.

Welton, J., & Telford, J. (2004). *What did you say? What do you mean? An illustrated guide to understanding metaphors.* New York: Jessica Kingsley.

Books by Families and Individuals with ASD

Andron, L. (2001). *Our journey through high functioning autism and Asperger syndrome.* Philadelphia: Jessica Kingsley.

Barron, J., & Barron, S. (2002). *There's a boy in here: Emerging from the bonds of autism.* Arlington, TX: Future Horizons.

Birch, J. (2002). *Congratulations! It's Asperger syndrome.* New York: Jessica Kingsley.

Davis, B., & Schunick, W. G. (2001). *Breaking Autism's barriers: A father's story.* Philadelphia: Jessica Kingsley.

Downey, M. K., & Downey, K. (2002). *The people in a girl's life: How to find them, better understand them and keep them.* Philadelphia: Jessica Kingsley.

Fleisher, M. (2003). *Making sense of the unfeasible: My life journey with Asperger syndrome.* New York: Jessica Kingsley.

Fling, E. R. (2000). *Eating an artichoke: A mother's perspective on Asperger syndrome.* Philadelphia: Jessica Kingsley.

Gilpin, W. (2002). *Much more … laughing and loving with autism.* Arlington, TX: Future Horizons.

Grandin, T. (1986). *Emergence: Labeled autistic.* Norvato, CA: Arena Press.

Grandin, T. (1995). *Thinking in pictures and other reports from my life with autism.* New York: Bantam Doubleday Dell.

Hall, K. (2000). *Asperger syndrome, the universe and everything.* Philadelphia: Jessica Kingsley.

Hart, C. (1989). *Without reason: A family copes with two generations of autism.* New York: Harper & Row.

Hoopmann, K. (2000). *Blue bottle mystery: An Asperger adventure.* Philadelphia: Jessica Kingsley.

Hoopmann, K. (2002). *Lisa and the lacemaker: An Asperger adventure.* Philadelphia: Jessica Kingsley.

Hoopmann, K. (2001). *Of mice and aliens: An Asperger adventure.* Philadelphia: Jessica Kingsley.

Johnson, C., & Crowder, J. (1994). *Autism: From tragedy to triumph.* Boston: Branden Books.

Kaufman, B. N. (1994). *Son rise: The miracle continues.* Tiburon, CA: H. J. Kramer.

Kephart, B. (1998). *A slant of sun.* New York: Norton.

Lawson, W. (2001). *Understanding and working with the spectrum of autism: An insider's view.* Philadelphia: Jessica Kingsley.

Ledgin, N. (2002). *Asperger's and self-esteem: Insight and hope through famous role models.* Arlington, TX: Future Horizons.

Leonard-Toomey, P. (Ed.). (1997). *In our words: Stories by brothers and sisters of children with autism and PDD.* Fall River, MA: Adsum.

Martin, E. P. (1999). *Dear Charlie: A guide for living your life with autism—A grandfather's love letter.* Arlington, TX: Future Horizons.

Maurice, C. (1993). *Let me hear your voice: A family's triumph over autism.* Austin, TX: PRO-ED.

McCabe, P., McCabe, E., & McCabe, J. (2002). *Living and loving with Asperger syndrome: Family viewpoints.* New York: Jessica Kingsley.

Mesner, A. W. (1996). *Captain Tommy.* Stratham, NH: Potential Unlimited.

Meyers, D. J. (Ed.). (1995). *Uncommon fathers: Reflections on raising a child with a disability.* Bethesda, MD: Woodbine House.

Meyers, D. J. (Ed.). (1997). *Views from our shoes: Growing up with a brother or sister with special needs.* Bethesda, MD: Woodbine House.

Mont, D. (2002). *A different kind of boy: A father's memoir about raising a gifted child with autism.* Philadelphia: Jessica Kingsley.

Morse, D., Gayhardt, V., & Wallace, R. S. (1998). *At home with autism: Three families' stories.* Stratham, NH: Potential Unlimited.

Mukhopadhyay, T. R. (2003). *The mind tree: A miraculous child breaks the silence of autism.* New York: Arcade.

Ogaz, N. (2002). *Buster and the amazing daisy: Adventures with Asperger syndrome.* Philadelphia: Jessica Kingsley.

Overton, J. (2003). *Snapshots of autism: A family album.* New York: Jessica Kingsley.

Park, C. C. (1982). *The siege: The first 8 years of an autistic child.* New York: Little, Brown.

Park, C. C. (2001). *Exiting Nirvana: A daughter's life with autism.* New York: Little, Brown.

Peers, J. (2003). *Asparagus dreams.* New York: Jessica Kingsley.

Powers, M. D. (Ed.). (1989). *Children with autism: A parent's guide.* Bethesda, MD: Woodbine House.

Prince-Hughes, D. (Ed.). (2002). *Aquamarine blue: Personal stories of college students with autism.* Athens, OH: Swallow Press and Ohio University Press.

Prince-Hughes, D. (2004). *Songs of the gorilla nation: My journey through autism.* New York: Harmony Books.

Pyles, L. (2001). *Hitchhiking through Asperger syndrome.* Philadelphia: Jessica Kingsley.

Rankin, K. (2000). *Growing up severely autistic: They call me Gabriel.* Philadelphia: Jessica Kingsley.

Reed, D. (1996). *Paid for the privilege: Hearing the voices of autism.* Madison, WI: DRI Press.

Romkema, C. (2002). *Embracing the sky.* Philadelphia: Jessica Kingsley.

Satkiewicz-Gayhardt, V., Peerenboom, B., & Campbell, R. (1998). *Crossing bridges: A parent's perspective on coping after a child is diagnosed with Autism/PDD.* Stratham, NH: Potential Unlimited.

Schneider, E. (1999). *Discovering my autism: Apologia pro vita sua.* New York: Jessica Kingsley.

Schneider, E. (2003). *Living the good life with autism.* New York: Jessica Kingsley.

Schulze, C. B. (1993). *When snow turns to rain: One family's struggle to solve the riddle of autism.* Rockville, MD: Woodbine House.

Seroussi, K. (2000). *Unraveling the mystery of autism and pervasive developmental disorder: A mother's story of research and recovery.* New York: Simon & Schuster.

Shaw, J. (2002). *I'm not naughty—I'm autistic: Jodi's journey.* Philadelphia: Jessica Kingsley.

Shore, S. (2001). *Beyond the wall: Personal experiences with autism and Asperger's syndrome.* Shawnee Mission, KS: Autism Asperger Publishing.

Stehli, A. (1991). *The sound of a miracle: A child's triumph over autism.* New York: Avon Books.

Stehli, A. (1995). *Dancing in the rain.* Westport, CT: Georgiana Organization.

Stone, F. (2004). *Autism—The eighth colour of the rainbow: Learn to speak autistic.* New York: Jessica Kingsley.

Willey, L. H. (1999). *Pretending to be normal: Living with Asperger's syndrome.* Philadelphia: Jessica Kingsley.

Williams, D. (1992). *Nobody nowhere: The extraordinary autobiography of an autistic.* New York: Avon Books.

Williams, D. (1994). *Somebody's somewhere: Breaking free from the world of autism.* New York: Times Books.

Williams, D. (1996). *Autism: An inside-out approach.* Philadelphia: Jessica Kingsley.

Williams, D. (1998). *Autism and sensing: The unlost instinct.* Philadelphia: Jessica Kingsley.

Williams, D. (1998). *Like colour to the blind.* Philadelphia: Jessica Kingsley.

Williams, D. (2002). *Exposure anxiety—The invisible cage: An exploration of self-protection responses in the autism spectrum.* Philadelphia: Jessica Kingsley.

Williams, D. (2004). *Everyday heaven.* New York: Jessica Kingsley.

Williams, D. (2004). *Not just anything: A collection of thoughts on paper.* New York: Jessica Kingsley.

Wilson, R. (2000). *The legendary blobshocker.* Arlington, TX: Future Horizons.

Zimmerman, S. (1996). *Grief dancers: A journey into the depths of the soul.* Golden, CO: Nemo Press.

Glossary

Collaborative teaming. An interactive process that enables individuals with different backgrounds and expertise to organize and work together to define and creatively solve problems as a team, recognizing that no single person could have produced such solutions.

Cultural competence. The ability to collaborate across cultures in a respectful manner leading to mutually desired outcomes.

Cultural reciprocity. A way to move from overt cultural awareness, noticing obvious differences in dress and language, to covert cultural awareness, noticing differences that are not easily seen, and then to subtle cultural awareness.

Culture. The learned and shared rules and traditions that express the values and beliefs of a group and the individuals within that group.

Family-centered care. Recognition of the family as a constant in the child's life, with a set of values and diverse beliefs, which are understood and respected in the care provided to the child.

IDEA. Individuals with Disabilities Education Act, a federal law designed to require educational service systems to be responsive to the individual needs of children and youth with disabilities.

VT-RAP. Vermont Rural Autism Project, a federally funded program (1997–2001) designed to train speech–language pathologists, early childhood special educators, and other related service providers to better meet the needs of children with ASD and their families in their home communities.

References

Ahmann, E. (1998). Examining assumptions underlying nursing practice with children and families. *Pediatric Nursing, 23,* 467–469.

Autism Task Force of Vermont. (1998). *Creating a comprehensive service delivery system for children in the State of Vermont with Autism Spectrum Disorder.* Position paper of the Vermont Autism Task Force, Montpelier.

Bates, M. S., Rankin-Hill, L., & Sanchez-Ayendez, M. (1997). The effects of the cultural context of health care on treatment of and response to chronic pain and illness. *Social Science Medicine, 45,* 1433–1447.

Beatson, J. E., & Prelock, P. A. (2002). The Vermont Rural Autism Project: Sharing experiences, shifting attitudes. *Focus on Autism & Other Developmental Disabilities, 17*(1), 48–54.

Briggs, M. H. (1997). Team culture. In M. H. Briggs, *Building early intervention teams: Working together for children and families* (pp. 23–34). Gaithersburg, MD: Aspen.

Brookins, G. K. (1993). Culture, ethnicity, and biocultural competence: Implications for children with chronic illness and disability. *Pediatrics, 91,* 1056–1062.

Brown, J. R., & Rogers, S. J. (2003). Cultural issues in autism. In S. Ozonoff, S. J. Rogers, & R. L. Hendren (Eds.), *Autism spectrum disorders: A research review for practitioners* (pp. 209–226). Washington, DC: American Psychiatric Publishing.

Dennis, R. E., & Giangreco, M. F. (1996). Creating conversation: Reflections on cultural sensitivity in family interviewing. *Exceptional Children, 63,* 103–115.

Department of Health and Human Services. (2002). *Report to Congress on autism.* Prepared by the National Institute of Mental Health, the National Institutes of Health, and the Department of Health and Human Services. Washington, DC: Department of Health and Human Services.

Dunst, C. J., & Trivette, C. M. (1996). Empowerment, effective helpgiving practices and family-centered care. *Pediatric Nursing, 22,* 334–337.

Dunst, C. J., Trivette, C. M., & Hamby, D. W. (1996). Measuring the helpgiving practices of human services program practitioners. *Human Relations, 49,* 815–835.

Fadiman, A. (1997). *The spirit catches you and you fall down: A Hmong child, her American doctors, and the collision of two cultures.* New York: Farrar, Straus and Giroux.

Feldman, H. M., Ploof, D., & Cohen, W. I. (1999). Physician–family partnerships: The adaptive practice model. *Developmental and Behavioral Pediatrics, 20,* 111–116.

Giangreco, M. F., Edelman, S. W., Nelson, C., Young, M. R., & Kiefer-O'Donnell, R. (1999, March). Changes in educational team membership for students who are deaf–blind in general education classes. *Journal of Visual Impairment and Blindness,* pp. 166–173.

Groce, N. E., & Zola, I. K. (1993). Multiculturalism, chronic illness, and disability. *Pediatrics, 91,* 1048–1055.

Horst, L., Werner, R. R., & Werner, C. L. (2000). Case management for children and families. *Journal of Child and Family Nursing, 3,* 5–14.

Humphry, R. (1994). Families who live in chronic poverty: Meeting the challenge of family-centered services. *The American Journal of Occupational Therapy, 49,* 687–692.

Individuals with Disabilities Education Act of 1990, 20 U.S.C. § 1400 *et seq.*

Joe, J. R., & Malach, R. S. (1992). Families with Native American roots. In E. W. Lynch & M. J. Hanson (Eds.), *Developing cross-cultural competence: A guide for working with young children and their families* (pp. 89–119). Baltimore: Brookes.

Kagawa-Singer, M. (1994). Cross-cultural views of disability. *Rehabilitation Nursing, 19,* 362–365.

Kalyanpur, M., & Harry, B. (1999). *Culture in special education: Building reciprocal family–provider relationships.* Baltimore: Brookes.

Kavanagh, K. H. (1994). Family: Is there anything more diverse? *Pediatric Nursing, 20,* 423–426.

Kleinman, A., Eisenberg, L., & Good, B. (1978). Clinical lessons from anthropological and cross-cultural research. *Annals of Internal Medicine, 88,* 251–258.

Laird, J. (1995, March). Family-centered practice in the postmodern era. *Families in Society: The Journal of Contemporary Human Services,* pp. 150–162.

Like, R. C., Steiner, P., & Rubel, A. J. (1996). Recommended core curriculum guidelines on culturally sensitive and competent health care. *Family Medicine, 28,* 291–295.

McCollum, J. A., Ree, Y., & Chen, Y. (2000). Interpreting parent–infant interactions: Cross-cultural lessons. *Infants and Young Children, 12,* 22–33.

McCubbin, H. I., Thompson, E. A., Thompson, M. A., & Kaston, A. J. (1993). Culture, ethnicity, and the family: Critical factors in childhood chronic illnesses and disabilities. *Pediatrics, 91,* 1063–1070.

Newton, M. S. (2000). Family-centered care: Current realities in parent participation. *Pediatric Nursing, 26,* 164–168.

Patterson, J. M. (1995). Promoting resilience in families experiencing stress. *Pediatric Clinics of North America, 42,* 47–63.

Prelock, P. A., Beatson, J., Bitner, B., Broder, C., & Ducker, A. (2003). Interdisciplinary assessment of young children with autism spectrum disorders. *Language, Speech & Hearing Services in Schools, 34*(3), 194–202.

Schein, E. H. (1992). *Organizational culture and leadership* (2nd ed.). San Francisco: Jossey-Bass.

Shelton, T. L., & Stepanek, J. S. (1994). *Family-centered care for children needing specialized health and developmental services.* Bethesda, MD: Association for the Care of Children's Health.

Shelton, T. L., & Stepanek, J. S. (1995). Excerpts from family-centered care for children needing specialized health and developmental services. *Pediatric Nursing, 21,* 362–364.

Turnbull, A. P., Friesen, B. J., & Ramirez, C. (1998). Participatory action research as a model for conducting family research. *Journal of the Association of Individuals with Severe Handicaps, 23,* 178–188.

Weick, A., & Saleebey, D. (1995, March). Supporting family strengths: Orienting policy and practice toward the 21st century. *Families In Society: The Journal of Contemporary Human Services,* 141–148.

Westby, C. E., & Ford, V. (1993a). Professional communicative paradigms in family-centered service delivery. *ASHA Monograph, 30,* 50–59.

Westby, C. E., & Ford, V. (1993b). The role of team culture in assessment and intervention. *Journal of Educational and Psychological Consultation, 4,* 319–341.

Wing, L. (1993). Definition and prevalence of autism. *European Child and Adolescent Psychiatry, 2,* 61–74.

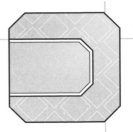

An Interdisciplinary, Family-Centered, and Community-Based Assessment Model for Children with ASD

Patricia A. Prelock

QUESTIONS TO CONSIDER

In this chapter, you will learn about an innovative model for addressing the assessment needs of children with autism spectrum disorders (ASD) as part of a family–professional team. The complexity of diagnosis and the importance of establishing collaborative partnerships have been discussed in Chapters 1 and 2, respectively. This chapter will take you to the next step, actually learning how to implement a dynamic assessment approach that is responsive to the needs of children with ASD, their families, and the practitioners who support them. Consider the following questions:

1. What components of a disablement framework should guide the assessment process for children with ASD?

2. How should ecological and dynamic assessment be incorporated into a functional evaluation process for children with ASD?

3. What role do families and practitioners play in the assessment of children with ASD?

4. What are the components of an interdisciplinary, family-centered, and community-based assessment model for children with ASD?

Introduction

Assessment is a process of gathering information to answer questions and make decisions (Schwartz, Boulware, McBride, & Sandall, 2001). The role of assessment, however, extends well beyond making a diagnosis or identifying deficits in skill development. Comprehensive, functional assessments can serve as road maps for intervention planning (Schwartz et al., 2001). To ensure that a child receives the full benefit of an intervention program, there must be a link between assessment and the goals and curriculum that are established for a child with ASD. In the sections that follow, I discuss some frameworks and approaches described in the literature that can guide the assessment of children with ASD and teach the consequences of this devastating health condition.

A Disablement Framework To Guide Assessment

In Chapter 1, we identified two classification systems, the *Diagnostic and Statistical Manual of Mental Disorders* (DSM) and the *International Classification of Diseases* (ICD), that have been used to make a diagnosis of autism. The ICD has a partner classification system, the *International Classification of Impairments, Disabilities and Handicaps* (ICIDH), which focuses not on diagnosis but on the consequences of a disease or health condition (World Health Organization [WHO], 1999). It is a disablement framework that has important implications for assessment. The most recent version of this classification model has been renamed the *International Classification of Functioning, Disability and Health* (ICF; WHO, 2001). The ICF can be used to enrich the diagnostic information provided by the ICD or the DSM (the classification system most often used in the United States), in that it examines an individual's functioning at the body, person, and society levels (WHO, 2001). Understanding the diagnosis and learning about the disablement, or functional, status of an individual are a powerful combination for creating a more meaningful picture of a child with ASD.

Historically, two models, the medical and social views, have been used to explain disablement. The medical view sees it as an individual problem created by disease, trauma, or health condition, with management directed at making personal adjustments and behavior changes (WHO, 1999). In contrast, the social view sees the problem as society's challenge to integrate individuals with disabilities. Management, therefore, would be directed toward social action and environmental change. The ICF has synthesized these polarized views to create an understanding of health on both the biological and the social levels (WHO, 1999, 2001).

The ICF can be used as a communication tool among a variety of disciplines and individuals with or affected by disability. It serves a valuable purpose in collecting data that can be used to assess the consequences of an individual's health condition and to identify needs for treatment. The structure of the ICF defines dimensions of classification: impairments, activities, and participation. These dimensions can be used alone or in relation to each other to describe the experiences/attributes and situations/circumstances of individuals with disabilities (WHO, 1999, 2001). For example, when a child is diagnosed with ASD, there are external signs of the disorder at the impairment, or body, level. The child may fail to point or look when called, scream when another person approaches, or engage in unusual finger and hand mannerisms (impairments). At the disability, or person, level, the child may limit engagement with others, avoid sitting in morning circle at school, and prefer to play only with trains (activities). The response at a handicap, or societal, level may lead to the child's restriction in participation. He is no longer invited to attend assemblies at school because of screaming, his parents seldom take him out to eat because of his inappropriate behavior, and he has no friends who come over to play with him (participation).

The dimensions of the ICF also include contextual factors through which the disablement process occurs. These factors are either environmental or personal. *Environmental factors* are outside or "extrinsic to" the child and might include societal attitudes, cultural norms, laws, educational systems, and architectural considerations. For example, a child with ASD might be placed in a class for children with similar disorders or integrated into a general education classroom, depending on the culture of the educational community. *Personal factors* are specific to the child and might include age, gender, other health conditions, past and current experiences, education, fitness, lifestyle, habits, and coping styles. For example, a child with ASD who is not toilet trained and limits his consumption of food by color would be particularly challenged in a classroom where all other students are toilet trained and choose from a menu of available cafeteria food.

An appreciation of the contextual factors that influence how individuals perceive both the medical and social aspects of their lives can improve and add depth to assessment results. Contextual factors broaden the scope of traditional assessment beyond a deficit focus toward a more holistic and dynamic view of the child's experience. Further, parents provide a valuable source of information across all dimensions. Studies have consistently shown that parents are reliable reporters of behaviors of their children with ASD (Lord & Risi, 2000).

Ecological and Dynamic Assessment Approaches

Ecological assessment considers the broader aspects of a child's environment. It involves observing children in their daily activities and learning about the skills they have an opportunity to use and develop (Haney & Cavallaro, 1996). It also requires asking the questions that probe for the relevant information (Westby, 1990). It can be used to understand who the child is in the context of his or her family through the use of genograms (McGoldrick & Gerson, 1985; McGoldrick, Gerson, & Shellenberger, 1999) and how the child and family are integrated as part of their community through the use of ecomaps (see "Genograms and Ecomaps" later in chapter) (Hartman & Laird, 1983). Ecological assessment helps an assessment team identify the supports and compromises faced by children with ASD and their families in those areas most important to them (e.g., interaction; physical, emotional, spiritual, and intellectual functions; safety; adaptive behavior; and quality of life). It also provides information about the significant resources available in a family's world, the resources or supports that are nonexistent or in short supply, and the nature of the relationships between the child, the family, and the environment. Several components of the assessment model described in this chapter integrate the notion and importance of ecological assessment. An ecological approach to assessment is also well suited to address the dimensions of the disablement framework discussed earlier, particularly at the societal or participation level.

The community-based assessment model described in this chapter also integrates a dynamic assessment approach (Notari-Syverson & Losardo, 1996; Pena, 1996). Dynamic assessment involves gathering structured and systematic observations within functional context-bound activities in multiple settings. Unlike a traditional assessment model of one-time information gathering, information is collected on an ongoing basis. Dynamic assessment involves a highly individualized continuum of interaction (moving from low to high structure), which is guided by intervention principles. The general framework focuses on a preassessment, diagnostic intervention, and outcome measurement period, allowing for potential change to be assessed (Pena, 1996).

Dynamic assessment has several requirements involving an assessment structure, roles in the examination scenario, test orientation, and interpretation of results. Assessment instruments are constructed to provide the examiner and the child with "teachable moments" that have implications for later instruction. These teachable moments during the assessment process provide the examiner with information about the child's learning ability as well as the child's capacity to manage change.

The examiner's role in dynamic assessment is one of teacher-observer versus examiner (Feuerstein, Rand, Jensen, Kaniel, & Tzuriel, 1987). Similarly, the child's role is one of learner-performer versus test taker. This paradigm shift in the assessment process is particularly well suited to meeting the needs of children with ASD. It enables the examiner and the child to establish two-way communication. For example, during an assessment of a preschool child with ASD, an examiner observed the child's interest in a fireman's hat in the dramatic play area. As a teacher, the examiner interacted with the child, building on the child's interest and creating a context for determining whether the child could play out a fire-fighter role. The examiner gave the child a string of beads and suggested he use the beads to extinguish a fire. The examiner observed the child become a learner-performer. The child acted out the suggested scenario using the beads as a fire hose to extinguish the imaginary fire. As an observer, the examiner then measured, or assessed, the child's ability to respond to a request, recognize a context [learner], and carry out a play event [performer]. Without this facilitation, the examiner may have perceived greater limits in the child's ability to perform (Pena, 1996).

Test orientation in dynamic assessment refers to the selection of assessment materials and tools that focus on the process versus the product of the assessment. Testing materials are selected because of the framework they provide for play-based and observation-based assessment within the areas found to be most challenging. For example, for children with ASD, tools and observation frameworks would be selected that support an assessment of the child's communication, social interaction, play, and behavior. The instruments and observation formats selected would also need to provide opportunities for interactions between the examiner and the child in their respective teacher-observer and learner-performer roles.

Ultimately, a dynamic assessment approach yields information about what a child is capable of doing, with some adult support or scaffolding so that a change in performance can occur. This approach is also more likely to answer the questions being asked by the family, primary health care provider, and educational case manager. Dynamic assessment leads to creating a profile of a child's strengths and challenges, identifying adaptations the child needs to be successful, determining ways the child can regulate learning, and establishing a foundation for developmentally and individually appropriate interventions (Lidz, 1987, 1991).

Questions of reliability and validity of ecological and dynamic approaches to assessment are important to address. Reliability is established through the natural inquiry and interdisciplinary nature of the approaches. More than one examiner, and usually a team, engages in asking questions, observing behavior, and interpreting the work to ensure that the decisions made are methodologically sound. Videotaping is used to provide opportunities for more than one team member to observe the child's strengths and challenges and comment on potential recommendations. In addition, the videotapes serve as potential teaching tools for family members and practitioners. Validity in ecological and dynamic assessments lies in both what is assessed and how that information is interpreted. Assessment teams must determine whether the information obtained is accurate and whether the way it was collected reflects the questions initially posed by the family and practitioners involved. Further, the assessment team must determine whether the information obtained will lead to an understanding of the child's impairment, involvement in expected activities, and participation in the larger community.

Role of Families and Practitioners in Assessment

There has been a paradigm shift over the past 10 years from the practitioner as expert to the practitioner as partner with families (Johnson & Lindschau, 1996; Prelock, Beatson, Contompasis, & Bishop, 1999; Shelton, Jeppson, & Johnson, 1987; Vincent, 1985). This shift in thinking values the expertise that both families and practitioners bring to service delivery. Several researchers have also suggested that assessment approaches that are family centered and interdisciplinary offer promising outcomes for meeting the needs of children with neurodevelopmental disabilities (Andrews, 1990; Brewer, McPherson, Magrab, & Hutchins, 1989; Diehl, 2003; Dunst, Trivette, & Deal, 1988; Roberts-DeGennaro, 1996; Shelton & Stepanek, 1994; Vig & Kaminer, 2003).

Effective teams are composed of individuals who are working on the same side to meet the needs of children with ASD and their families. Effective teams are also organized in their work together, setting agendas, establishing goals for their meetings, and developing action plans. For example, they might define and follow a particular team meeting agenda to ensure that their work is accomplished (see Figure 3.1). Effective teams are also committed to a joint purpose, sharing a common vision and goal. For example, they may have engaged in a visioning process like that of *Making Action Plans* (MAP; see O'Brien, Forest, Snow, & Hasbury, 1989), an IEP planning process like that of *Choosing Outcomes and Accommodations for Children* (COACH; Giangreco, Cloninger, & Iverson, 1998), or a creative problem-solving process (Giangreco, Cloninger, Dennis, & Edelman, 2000; Osborn, 1993; Parnes, 1985, 1988, 1992) to determine the direction of their work (see Chapter 8 for a discussion of each of these strategies). Effective teams share leadership and responsibility. For example, they may assign and carry out team member roles (see Table 3.1) to engage everyone in the work that needs to be done. The collaborative partnerships that develop among team members celebrate the varied background and expertise of individuals, including families, and agree that problem solving is best achieved through the joint efforts of the team.

There are, however, challenges with building successful community-based teams. Chapter 2 outlined the principles of family-centered care and the barriers often faced by families and practitioners as they work to establish meaningful partnerships. Strategies to manage barriers and shift thinking about how to engage team members in a more family-centered exchange were outlined. Some of the barriers facing teams in the assessment process include finding the time to plan as a team, scheduling sufficient time to gather the information needed, recognizing philosophical differences in assessment practices, and having different levels of team experience. Therefore, training that recognizes the role of team building in practice is critical for all members of the team, including families.

Most important, however, assessment teams must never lose sight of the role a family plays in a child's life. This is particularly important considering

Agenda for Team Meetings

Child and family: _____ Date: _____

Purpose of the meeting: _____

Members present: _____

Roles   **Team Meeting Norms**

Facilitator: _____

Recorder: _____

Timekeeper: _____

Processor: _____

Wellness provider: _____

	Suggested Time Spent on Item	**Person Responsible**
Agenda Items		
1.		
2.		
3.		
4.		
5.		

Action Plans

Activity	Person Responsible	Date To Be Accomplished

Agenda Building for Next Meeting

1. _____

2. _____

3. _____

4. _____

Processing _____

_____

Wellness _____

_____

FIGURE 3.1. Agenda format for team meetings.

TABLE 3.1

Team Meeting Roles

Key Roles

Facilitator: Leads the discussion; ensures that agenda is followed, including action planning; involves all team members.

Recorder: Keeps minutes and shares them with team members.

Timekeeper: Ensures that time limits are set for agenda items, keeps track of time on each item, and helps team renegotiate times for higher priority items.

Jargon buster: Listens for unfamiliar terminology and asks for clarification for the group.

Processor: Evaluates the meeting process, assesses success of agenda and use of roles, reflects on respectfulness of team members and whether discussions went well or were challenging, among other things.

Wellness provider: Offers a poem, reading, music, reflection, treat, or something else that ends the meeting on a high note.

Additional Roles

"But" watcher: Calls the group on the use of "yes, but" and helps group defer judgment.

Clarifier: Reflects on what is said to check accuracy and clarify an issue, question, or response.

Conflict acknowledger: Signals the group when conflict emerges and prompts the group to initiate resolution.

Encourager: Supports risk taking, offers new ideas, and keeps the group moving forward.

Equalizer: Ensures equal air time for all participants.

Keeper of the rudder: Keeps the group on topic.

Norm prompter: Ensures that the group abides by the agreed-upon rules for group behavior.

Praiser: Compliments participants for meeting a goal, demonstrating respect in conversations, or achieving success in problem solving.

Snack provider: Brings edibles to share with the group during meeting time.

Summarizer: Puts together what has been heard on a particular issue or topic.

the pervasive nature of ASD and the impact that social, communication, and behavioral challenges have not only on the child's daily functioning but also on the family's ability to be responsive to the child's needs. Winton (1996) explains that valued outcomes for working with families should include knowing their hopes and dreams, understanding their priorities and needs for assistance, considering their structure and routines, and recognizing their existing resources. It is also critical to recognize the impact of the family's culture, knowing that the particular role a child has is affected by the family's values and beliefs (Westby, 1990; Winton, 1996).

Assessment planning for children with ASD leads to desired outcomes when using a collaborative team approach that is interdisciplinary (recognizing the role of multiple perspectives), family centered (understanding the child in the context of family), culturally competent (knowing the values and beliefs that drive the family), and community based (identifying the most appropriate environment) (Beatson & Prelock, 2002; Prelock et al., 1999; Vig & Kaminer, 2003). Such an approach will maximize opportunities for successful communication and interaction among team members. Team members learn, plan, implement, evaluate, and make decisions together using a collaborative approach. Through trust and respect, risk taking and uncertainty, success and confidence, ongoing growth and expansion, and sharing, collaborative relationships are established and maintained (Bauer & Murphy, 1990).

An Interdisciplinary Assessment Model for Children with ASD

I have implemented the model for assessment that is presented in this section over the last 8 years as part of two federal- and state-funded training projects. These training projects, the Vermont Rural Autism Project (VT-RAP) mentioned in Chapter 2 and the Vermont Interdisciplinary Leadership Education for Health Professionals Program (VT-ILEHP), were designed specifically to incorporate best practice principles in collaborative, interdisciplinary, family-centered, and culturally competent care (see Beatson & Prelock, 2002, and Prelock et al., 1999, for more complete program descriptions). Although both projects were initiated through outside funding, the principles of practice and the lessons learned for developing community-based teams have sustainability and application to any assessment team committed to children with special needs and their families. The assessment model has incorporated an ecological, dynamic assessment framework that has been invaluable in understanding, supporting, and planning for children with ASD and their families. There are seven components or steps in the model: intake, preassessment planning meeting, community-based assessment, postassessment planning meeting, report writing, community-based follow-up meeting, and care coordination. Each of these components is described in detail below, with samples of assessment planning frameworks used for children with ASD and their families.

Intake

The intake team includes a family support parent and an assessment coordinator. The family support parent has direct experience as a parent of a child with ASD. The assessment team assigns an assessment coordinator as the primary person responsible for establishing a connection and maintaining communication with the family and the community-based team. The intake process includes several features intended to ensure that the information gathered is comprehensive and that the family and the community-based team play an integral role; these features include face-to-face or phone interviews, background information forms or questionnaires, and genograms and ecomaps. Each of these elements of the intake process is described below.

Interviews. A face-to-face interview is held with the family in a location of their choice. Selecting an environment that is comfortable and not associated with historically difficult situations is important (Westby, 1990). Their own home or that of another family member or friend is often the best choice. Families are encouraged to include a support person (family member or friend) in the process. During the interview, the intake team asks a series of questions that allow family members to share their stories, discuss the strengths of their child and family, identify unmet needs, and define what is working well and what is not working well. These questions might include the following:

- Tell me about what your child does that brings you joy.
- Tell me about your child's strengths.
- Tell me about the challenges you are most worried about.
- Previously, what have you been told about your child?
- How does what you have been told fit with what you know about your child?
- How would others describe your child's strengths?
- How would others describe your child's challenges?
- Tell me about your priorities for your child.
- Tell me about what you value most in your family.
- If you could have three questions addressed by the assessment team, what would they be?

Throughout the interview, the intake team attempts to assess the family's support networks, understand their values and beliefs, identify critical events in the family's life, and recognize family priorities (Winton, 1996). Other interview formats, such as the *Conversation Guide* developed by Turnbull and Turnbull (1996), can be used to support the intake process. The questions in that guide focus on family characteristics, interactions, functions, and life cycle.

Following the intake interview, the family support parent or the assessment coordinator contacts the family to address any questions that remain about the assessment process and to revisit the family's desired role on the assessment team. The contact also serves to assess the family's initial impression of their experience with the intake team. The intake team processes the intake interview, reflecting on the information obtained and their ability to begin to establish a family–professional partnership.

At least one member of the intake team also meets with the child's primary health care provider and educational case manager. These community-based team members are asked questions similar to those posed to the family. The goal is to begin to gather an overview of the child's strengths, challenges, and needs. The team also attempts to define clearly and prioritize the questions being asked, so that the assessment process is responsive to the identified needs for the child with ASD.

Questionnaires or Information Forms. It is important to gather some background information regarding the child suspected of or diagnosed with ASD. The use of a questionnaire or information form can provide at least a basic context for the intake interview and supports the team in making appropriate decisions regarding the kinds of observations and assessment tools that may be considered. For children with ASD, it is often useful to gather information in the key deficit areas of communication, social interaction, play, and behavior prior to the assessment. The *Caregiver Questionnaire* (Wetherby & Prizant, 1993) has been a particularly effective tool to obtain that information for young children. It probes a family's perspective on how their child communicates (both verbally and nonverbally), what the child understands, how he/she plays with toys and interacts with children and adults, and what emotions are expressed. It is family friendly and can be used as a framework for follow-up interviews with the family if there is a need to clarify written comments. A general information format, which specifies relevant medical, educational, developmental, and overall health history and concerns, is also valuable to the preassessment planning process (see Appendix 3.A for an example).

Genograms and Ecomaps. The development of a genogram (McGoldrick & Gerson, 1985; McGoldrick et al., 1999) and an ecomap (Hartman & Laird, 1983) occurs during the intake process in an effort to understand the child in the context of his or her family, and to map community resources and their availability to the child and family. Both tools are created in collaboration with the family. They are used to summarize the information that a family shares during an intake interview and to identify community and family resources.

A genogram is a format used for drawing a family tree that records information about family members and their relationships over at least three generations (see Figure 3.2 for an example). Genograms map family structure, record family information, and delineate family relationships. They provide an efficient summary, allowing someone unfamiliar with the family to quickly grasp key information. The use of a genogram supports team members' recollection of family members and patterns and events that have recurring significance in a family's ongoing care. Providers should develop and use the genogram with care and in collaboration with families, respecting their privacy and the sensitivity of the information that may be shared.

An ecomap is a paper-and-pencil simulation that maps a family's ecological system (see Figure 3.3 for an example). It provides a picture of the family within the environment. The examiner who chooses to use an ecomap as part of the assessment process should remain cognizant of the purpose of the family interview and determine whether the ecomap will be helpful to understanding the child with ASD and his or her family in a larger

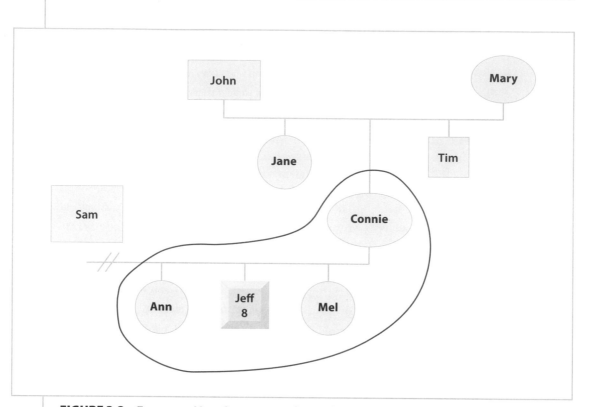

FIGURE 3.2. Genogram. *Note.* Squares = males, circles = females, horizonal lines = parents, vertical lines = children of parents, double slash = divorced parents, area circled = those living in the same household.

community context. The process of mapping family and community resources is ongoing. Although it begins at the intake interview with identification of current resources, resources may be added or eliminated following the actual assessment and intervention planning. Team members should think first about the family's current strengths and supports in the development of the ecomap. This should be followed by an examination of what resources might be missing, considering both needs and potentially untapped resources. Further, the ecomap can be used to examine conflicts between families and current or available resources. Because it displays a family's connection with the world and the energy flow of resources, it can be an effective tool for setting goals and planning actions.

Preassessment Planning Meeting

The second component in the assessment process is the preassessment planning meeting, which is facilitated by the assessment coordinator assigned to the particular family. Family members and their support persons, the primary health care provider, the educational case manager, and other core

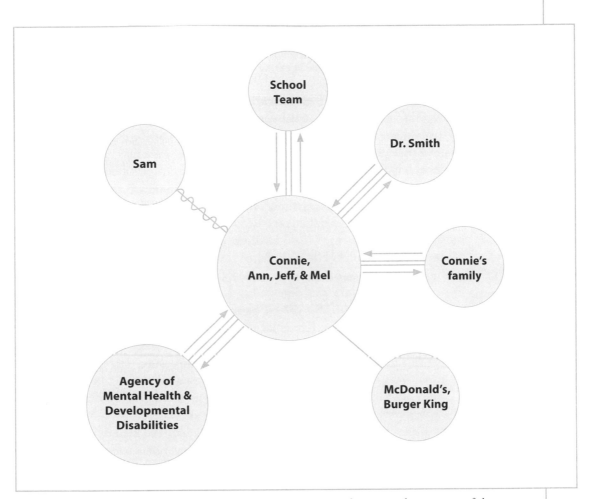

FIGURE 3.3. Ecomap. *Note.* Straight lines = strong connections, large wavy lines = stressful connections, arrows = source of energy flow.

team members are invited to participate in this planning meeting with the interdisciplinary assessment team members. The interdisciplinary team represents many disciplines, including developmental pediatrics, nursing, psychology, speech–language pathology, audiology, nutrition, occupational therapy, physical therapy, education, social work, family support, and public administration. Although not all of these team members participate in the actual assessment, their perspectives during planning ensure that a comprehensive view of the child's impairment, activity, and participation is obtained and that personal and environmental variables are considered as suggested by the ICF (WHO, 2001). Approximately 2 hours are allotted for the pre-assessment planning. Families and community-based team members are prepared ahead of time for this planning meeting because of the format used and the number of individuals involved. For families unable or choosing not to attend, a videotape of the meeting is made. There are three main features to the preassessment planning meeting: roles and rules for participation; presentation of intake information; and planning the assessment. Each of these features of the process is explained below.

Roles and Rules for Participation. Before presenting the intake information and planning the assessment, team members introduce themselves and establish roles for the meeting. Following a collaborative team process ensures that the work that needs to be done is accomplished and that all players have both an opportunity and a responsibility to participate. The assessment coordinator facilitates the meeting and assigns specific roles to team members, although team members are encouraged to volunteer for roles. Collaborative team roles that have been particularly helpful in the preassessment planning meetings include those of facilitator, recorder, timekeeper, jargon buster, equalizer, keeper of the rudder, norm prompter, processor, and wellness provider (see a description of roles in Table 3.1).

The team also establishes rules for sharing information and defines and agrees upon norms for the exchange that occurs among team members throughout the meeting. Examples of norms might include

- being respectful of families, children, and practitioners;
- using first names if that is comfortable for the family;
- using person-first language (e.g., child with autism versus autistic child);
- being respectful of and valuing different perspectives; and
- being respectful of time frames that have been set.

Presentation of Intake Information. During the preassessment planning meeting, the assessment coordinator shares the information collected from the intake interview with the team, both in written form (see Figure 3.4 for a sample) and through an oral presentation. The family's genogram and ecomap are presented to the group on large chart paper as a visual support to introduce the family to the other interdisciplinary assessment team members. The family's three key questions and priorities, as well as those of the primary health care provider and the educational case manager, are also shared with the group. If the child has an Individualized Education Program (IEP) or an Individualized Family Service Plan (IFSP), an IEP or IFSP at-a-glance (see Figure 3.4) is prepared and distributed to the team for review. Further, the child's strengths and challenges are identified, and relevant health, developmental, and educational histories are described. Team members read the prepared information prior to the assessment coordinator's oral presentation and ask questions for clarification as needed. If available, a brief videotape of the child to be assessed is presented.

Planning the Assessment. Using the intake information, all participants in the planning meeting begin to define those aspects of the child's development to be evaluated and the context in which the assessment is to occur. Team members consider at least three means of assessment to gather the

IFSP or IEP At-a-Glance

Child's name: _____   Date: _____

Location: _____   Observer: _____

IFSP or IEP Goals or Goal Areas	Accommodations	Observations

FIGURE 3.4. IFSP or IEP at-a-glance.

information that will lead to answering the questions that have been asked. The means considered include conducting interviews with key personnel, reviewing records, and observing and interacting with the child. The professional team members, in partnership with the family, determine the individuals who need to be interviewed and the types of questions they should be asked. They identify available records and specify the information to be reviewed. They make suggestions for specific observations of and interactions with the child. Team members are reminded by the assessment coordinator to consider how their suggestions will help to address the questions being asked.

As collaborators in the process, families should help choose the disciplines and family supports that are involved in the assessment, the contexts in which they want their child to be assessed, and the individuals they wish to have interviewed. Families may ask to have their children observed in child-care settings, at friends' houses, at local recreation facilities, in school settings (including the lunchroom), and on playgrounds. Individuals to be interviewed may include members of the immediate and extended family, teachers, individual aids, speech–language pathologists (SLPs), occupational therapists, physical therapists, siblings, and an array of health care providers (e.g., pediatrician, neurologist, nurse practitioner).

Through the preassessment planning meeting, an action plan for the actual assessment emerges. Families and community practitioners engage in discussion and develop a common language for describing the assessment plan and related actions in which they have an integral role. The team makes a tentative schedule for a visit to the child's home and community and assigns core team members to participate in the assessment. See Appendix 3.B for a sample preassessment planning meeting format.

Community-Based Assessment

Prior to the assessment, the assessment coordinator communicates with the family and the community-based team about the assessment process and what to expect when the team arrives. During the assessment, a family is typically involved in components such as interviews and completing checklists or rating scales. Families also participate in the assessment by observing their child alongside the assessment team or interacting with their child as team members gather data. This side-by-side participation ensures that families and practitioners share a common experience for describing the outcomes of the evaluation (Filer & Mahoney, 1996).

As noted earlier, the assessment process incorporates an ecological and dynamic assessment approach. Information is gathered from three major sources so that it can be triangulated, synthesized, and integrated to formulate responses to the key questions asked by the family, primary health care provider, and case manager. The three sources are those mentioned in the preassessment planning meeting: interviews, record reviews, and observations or interactions. Some strategies for obtaining the desired information through these sources are described below.

Interviews. Team members are assigned to interview family members and other practitioners using the questions brainstormed in the preassessment planning meeting. Examples of some of the questions that were developed for one child suspected of autism are presented in the preassessment planning meeting format in Appendix 3.B.

An effective interview requires the inclusion of several components. Westby (1990) suggests three ways for obtaining desired information in a culturally competent, family-centered manner: design questions that help to develop rapport; use questions that provide a description of what a family or individual is reporting; and word questions to get all the desired information. These approaches ensure that the families and practitioners being interviewed ask the questions they wish to have answered and that the assessment team gets an important perspective from those who are most often with the child (Westby, 2001).

To develop rapport with families and other interviewees, Westby (1990, 2001) describes four exploration strategies: using rapport-building statements and questions; restating what has been heard; asking for use and not meaning in what an interviewee reports; and avoiding asking why. The first strategy, using rapport-building statements, might involve providing a repeated explanation for the interview. For example, the interviewer might say the following to a parent who attended the preassessment planning meeting, "At our planning meeting last week, it was suggested that we talk about Jeremy's sleeping habits." For a teacher who was unable to attend the planning meeting, the interviewer might repeat the steps in the assessment planning process to provide a context. For example, the interviewer might say, "As I mentioned in our phone call to set up this interview, the family, Jeremy's case manager, and his family doctor met with our interdisciplinary team, and we came up with some questions we wanted to ask you about Jeremy's school day."

The second rapport-building strategy is restating what the interviewee says. For example, the interviewer might say to a parent, "I understand what you are saying about the packed schedule you have with Jeremy's appointments to the speech–language pathologist, the occupational therapist, and the physical therapist."

A third rapport-building strategy is asking for an example of use and not meaning in response to what has been said (Westby, 1990). For example, a parent might say something like, "Jeremy is really irritable when he comes home from school." The interviewer would respond by saying, "Tell me what Jeremy does when he is irritable." In this case, the interviewer is asking for a description rather than putting a parent on the defensive by asking a question like, "What do you mean by irritable?"

The final rapport-building strategy is avoiding the use of "why." Westby (2001) suggests that the use of "why" in an interview can be perceived as a judgment and often presumes a cause–effect relationship. Asking such a question also assumes that the interviewee knows why. It may serve to limit open and honest communication with the interviewee. For instance, in the above example if an interviewer asked, "Why do you think Jeremy is irritable?" the parent might interpret that as meaning that the parent should have a reason or explanation for the behavior. It might also suggest that the interviewer has the answer or that there is a clear cause–effect relationship. None of these scenarios is likely to be true, and each limits the opportunity for the interviewer to gather the needed information.

Following rapport building, the interviewer needs to gather as much descriptive information as possible to address the questions that have been posed. Using grand tour and mini tour questions is an effective strategy for gathering this descriptive information. A grand tour question probes descriptions of broad experiences, while a mini tour question probes descriptions of specific activities or events (Spradley, 1979). Within each of these, there are levels of question use that can refine the information obtained. For example, if it was determined at the preassessment planning meeting that one of the areas to be probed in the assessment interview with the family was greater discussion about their child's morning behavior, the interviewer might ask the following grand tour questions that can in turn be labeled *typical, specific,* and *guided*:

- What is Jeremy's typical morning like? (typical question that gets at how things usually are)
- Tell me about what you and Jeremy did this morning. (specific question that focuses on a recent or specific time frame)
- Next Monday morning, could I set up a time to visit with you and Jeremy as you do your usual thing in the morning? (guided question that asks for a "grand tour" of what is happening)

The interviewer could then follow with some mini tour questions:

- Describe a typical breakfast time with Jeremy. (typical question)
- Tell me about breakfast time this morning with Jeremy. (specific question)
- When I visit next Monday morning, why don't I come at breakfast time, so I can see how Jeremy interacts with you and eats his food. (guided question)

Following the grand and mini tour questions, the use of example, experience, and native language questions adds to the descriptive information regarding a particular child and family (Westby, 1990). An *example question* is more specific than the tour questions in that the interviewer takes an idea or experience and asks for a specific example (e.g., "Give me an example of what Jeremy does when he is being irritable at breakfast"). *Experience questions* ask the interviewee to relate an experience in a particular setting (e.g., "Tell me about some of your experiences with the speech–language pathologist"). *Native language questions* are used to ensure that the interviewer understands how words are being used. They can be either direct language questions (when the interviewer thinks someone is using a word for the interviewer's benefit) or hypothetical interaction questions (when the interviewer is trying to determine someone's understanding of information and how the person might usually talk about it) (Westby, 1990). For example,

- You mentioned that Jeremy doesn't pay attention because he has auditory processing difficulties. What other words would you use to describe "auditory processing difficulties"? (direct language question)
- Let's say your sister was here. How would you explain Jeremy's auditory processing difficulties to her? (hypothetical interaction question)

The third approach Westby (1990) describes for facilitating the flow of an interview in a culturally competent and family-centered manner has to do with the wording of questions. Westby recommends avoiding the use of problematic questions such as close-ended (e.g., "Are you happy with Jeremy's communication program?") versus open-ended (e.g., "What is your opinion of Jeremy's communication program?") questions; bombardment questions (a series of questions one after another as if grilling the interviewee); multiple questions within a single question (e.g., "When is Jeremy irritable, what do you do, and how does he respond?"); hidden agenda questions (e.g., "What do you think about putting Jeremy on a behavior management plan?"); and leading (e.g., "Why do you dislike what the SLP is doing with Jeremy?") versus neutral (e.g., "Tell me about your experiences with the SLP") questions (Westby, 1990, 2001). To increase the richness and depth of information gathered, Westby (1990) suggests using *presupposition questions*. For example, the interviewer might ask, "What is the most valuable part of working with Jeremy's educational team?" Lastly, Westby (1990) makes use of *prefatory statements* to alert the interviewee to the type of question coming next. Prefatory statements help interviewees to prepare their response, as can be seen in the examples below:

- We've been talking about Jeremy's irritability at breakfast. Now I'd like to ask you about the progress you have seen in his eating skills. (transition format: ends one topic and begins another)
- You said that Jeremy is now using a sipper cup and an adapted spoon to scoop food. Before we move on to his play, do you have any additional eating concerns? (summarizing transition format: closes a discussion through repetition and asks for clarification or additions)
- Let me ask you about the changes you have seen in Jeremy since he started preschool. How has he changed since entering preschool? (direct announcement format: uses preface statement about what is going to be asked)

The important elements to remember in the interview process are to know what information is needed, ask the right questions to get the information needed, and give appropriate feedback. Remembering these elements will help the interviewer to maintain control of the interview and develop an atmosphere of respectful communication.

Coonrod and Stone (2004) also suggest that in some situations, there may be a need for more specific questions directed at social communication behaviors during the assessment process. Often, parents of young children may not report the subtle social challenges that may be red flags for a diagnosis of autism. Coonrod and Stone found that parents of children with autism identified more deficits in the social and communicative behaviors of their children when they were asked specific questions about their children's current social behaviors.

Record Reviews. Knowing the questions that have been posed by the family, primary health care provider, and educational case manager, the team decides what records are to be reviewed, what specific information is needed, and who is going to review specific records. Most often, the assessment team is involved in reviewing school records, including IEPs and IFSPs, evaluation reports, progress notes, and report cards and samples of a child's work. They also review medical records, including outside evaluation reports and hearing, vision, and general health records. A format that can be used to review records during an assessment can be found in Figure 3.5.

Observations. The assessment team, in collaboration with the family and the community-based team, determines who will observe what part of the child's day, as well as what specific observations are to occur across settings. Observations usually occur in the home and at school, although for some children, additional settings such as childcare, after-school programs, and community sites are considered critical to gaining a comprehensive picture of the child's strengths and challenges. The family may also choose not to have an assessment team in their home. The family guides the assessment team in defining the most comfortable and valuable environments for gathering the needed information.

Both formal and informal protocols are used to assess those developmental domains and daily living skills that are most likely to provide the team with the information needed to answer the questions asked. In keeping with a functional, ecological approach to assessment, observation formats are sometimes created around a particular task or activity so that a child's performance, skill, or behavior can be evaluated in terms of what is expected or required in a particular activity. The team also identifies specific assessment tools to use, as appropriate, and interaction opportunities to be created between parents, siblings, teachers, peers, and assessment team members. Considering the core deficits reported for ASD, the following are usually

Record Review

Child's name: _____

Reviewer: _____

Date: _____

Record (e.g., medical evaluations, testing, grades, logs)	Date	Relevant Results (i.e., to assessment questions being asked)	Recommendations Made	Follow-up Needed (specify)

FIGURE 3.5. Format for record review.

identified in the preassessment planning meeting as areas in which observation or assessment is needed:

- intentional communication (e.g., behavioral regulation, joint attention, and social interaction, using both conventional and unconventional, verbal and nonverbal means);
- language understanding and use (verbal and nonverbal);
- interaction with both familiar and unfamiliar adults and peers;
- play across environments and play partners;
- sensory–motor abilities and needs;
- behavior and routines;
- attachment, temperament, attention, and memory;
- environments in which the child plays, interacts, and communicates; and
- other behaviors or issues, depending on the questions asked, such as potential seizure activity, medication concerns, toileting challenges, sleep problems, and nutrition issues.

A more complete description of ways to profile areas of concern for children with ASD during the assessment process can be found in Chapters 4, 5, 6, and 7, which examine communication, play, social–emotional development, and sensory–motor function in children with ASD.

If a question of diagnosis has been asked, the team uses the DSM–IV criteria to guide their observations as well as using one or more of the tools described in Chapter 1. For example, the *Autism Diagnostic Observation Schedule–Generic* (Lord, Rutter, DiLavore, & Risi, 1999) is often used to supplement the informal observations made. To gather multiple perspectives, teachers and parents are asked to complete the *Autism Behavior Checklist* (Krug, Arick, & Almond, 1993) or the *Gilliam Autism Rating Scale* (Gilliam, 1995). Further, the family and community team members participate with the assessment team in a review and discussion of the diagnostic criteria for autism. All team members identify what they have seen and what they know about a particular child's behavior and how that may or may not fit the specific DSM–IV criteria using the checklist presented in Chapter 1.

At the end of the assessment day, the assessment team meets to clarify their responsibilities for report writing, to determine timelines for task completion, and to evaluate the effectiveness with which they collaborated as a team and carried out the assessment plan. Team members write up their observations, interviews, and record reviews and pass that written documentation to the assessment coordinator, who uses the information to prepare the interdisciplinary report. Within a week following the assessment, the assessment coordinator makes contact with the family and the community-based team to reflect on what worked and what did not work during the assessment process, to answer questions that may have arisen, and to clarify any steps in the process. Family and community participation in the assessment and review of the day's events ensures that the information collected is representative of the child's skills and behaviors and that family–professional and interprofessional partnerships are maintained and enriched.

Postassessment Planning Meeting

Once the assessment is completed, the assessment coordinator works with the family and community team members to schedule a postassessment planning meeting with the assessment team. The process for this meeting is similar to that of the preassessment planning meeting, in that roles are assigned and rules and norms for participation are reviewed. As before, families and community team members are prepared for what is to occur during this meeting.

The assessment coordinator facilitates the meeting. The family's genogram and ecomap are reintroduced and updated to remind everyone of who the child is in the context of family and community. Questions originally asked by the family, primary health care provider, and educational case manager are reviewed, and similar questions are grouped into categories as they are in the preassessment planning meeting. Key observations related to the original assessment questions are presented to the team (see Appendix 3.C for an example). Following any updates to the observations reported, team members identify possible recommendations that meet the needs of the child and family. An effort is made to provide recommendations that address all three dimensions of the disablement framework described earlier in this chapter: impairment, activity, and participation. Open dialogue with all team members around these recommendations provides a common framework from which expectations for service delivery are drawn. In addition, this meeting allows for family participation in discussion and decision making around the variety of services that can be accessed to address the family's priorities. Throughout this postassessment brainstorming, team members are reminded to consider the total child in terms of the behaviors, situations, and contexts assessed; the interrelationships among the observations made; the information gathered; and the potential impact of the information obtained on the child's life and well-being.

Report Writing

The next step in the assessment process is the completion of a written report and the development of a resource notebook. The report is designed to answer the family's questions and provide recommendations based on information obtained through the assessment process and postassessment planning meeting. The assessment coordinator works hard to develop a cohesive, useful working draft, which is shared with the family first and then with the community team members for input. Together, all team members review the report's contents and collaboratively make modifications to ensure that the report satisfactorily answers the family's questions and addresses their needs. (See Figure 3.6 for a sample report format and Appendices 3.D and 3.E for samples of actual interdisciplinary reports, Sample Report A for a child already diagnosed with ASD and Sample Report B confirming a diagnosis of ASD.)

The assessment coordinator also develops a resource notebook for the family and the community team involved in providing services. The notebook contains the final report and related appendices, as well as several pieces of information perceived as important for informing and supporting the team. This resource information might include the most recent articles regarding the child's particular diagnosis or challenges, handouts on intervention strategies, contacts for health care and respite, assistance for funding augmentative and alternative communication devices, and tips on improving the child's environment (e.g., the sensory or acoustic environment). All materials included in the notebook consider the knowledge base and skills of the families and practitioners involved.

Community Follow-Up Meeting

As the assessment process nears its end, the assessment coordinator organizes and facilitates a community follow-up meeting. In this meeting, which is held in the child's community, the family, community team members, and members of the assessment team are brought together to discuss outcomes of the assessment, review recommendations made, and make action plans for implementing the recommendations. The format of the meeting follows the collaborative framework used for all the meetings in the process (i.e., establishing roles and rules for participation). For each question area, updates on the child's performance and behavior since the assessment are offered, additional changes to the report are made, and recommendations are reviewed. Team members then engage in action planning for each recommendation. A resource notebook is distributed to the family, the educational team, and the primary health care provider. This follow-up meeting in the community ensures that all members of the child's team share an understanding of the recommendations made and agree to the roles and responsibilities for implementation. As before, the assessment coordinator communicates with the family and the educational case manager within a week of this meeting to assess the effectiveness of the process, to determine whether individual needs were met, and to address further questions and concerns.

Care Coordination

The final step in the interdisciplinary assessment process is the provision of coordinated care for children with ASD and their families. Often, assessment teams provide a comprehensive evaluation and a report full of recommendations, yet the family and the community-based team are left on their

Interdisciplinary Consultation Summary

Child's name: _____ Date of birth: _____

Parents: _____ Chronological age: _____

Address: _____ School: _____

Phone: _____ Referral source: _____

Consultation date: _____

Interdisciplinary Team

Assessment coordinator _____

Family support _____

Developmental pediatrics _____

Speech–language _____

Psychology _____

Special education _____

Occupational therapy _____

Other team members _____

_____

Primary Health Care Provider

Name: _____

Address: _____

Phone: _____

Case Manager

Name: _____

Address: _____

Phone: _____

Referral Questions (No more than 3 to 5 key questions should be raised by the family, community providers, and primary health care provider.)

Family: _____

_____

_____

(continues)

FIGURE 3.6. Sample report format.

Community program or school: _____

_____

_____

Primary health care provider: _____

_____

_____

Background Information (Include child's age; family history, with genogram and ecomap as Appendix A; current placement and services as documented in an IEP or IFSP; and relevant medical history and medications being taken.)

_____

_____

Assessment Summary and Recommendations (Include a one-paragraph summary of the child, highlighting his or her strengths and identifying any unique diagnostic information and specific challenges.)

_____

_____

Action Planning (Include a plan for the coordination of care and implementation of the proposed recommendations.)

_____

_____

If you have any questions or comments regarding this report or the recommendations made, please don't hesitate to contact the assessment coordinator, _____,

at _____.

_____   _____
Assessment Coordinator   Developmental Pediatrics

_____   _____
Speech–Language   Psychology

_____   _____
Family Support Faculty   Special Education

_____
Occupational Therapy

FIGURE 3.6. *Continued.*

own to follow through and carry out a number of complex tasks that require coordinated efforts among several agencies and programs. The goal of care coordination is to support, not supplant, the efforts of in-place teams working to best meet the needs of children with ASD and their families. Following the completion of the community follow-up meeting, the assessment coordinator becomes a care coordinator, ensuring that the recommendations made and actions established are implemented in a timely and coordinated fashion. The care coordinator works with the family, the primary health care provider, and the educational case manager to understand the interrelationships among education, health, developmental services, and community and to facilitate both the establishment and maintenance of community and agency connections. The care coordinator also continues to model the collaborative team framework for learning, working, and making decisions together. Two to three hours of care coordination are offered weekly for a year following the interdisciplinary assessment, although some teams do not require that level of extended support.

Potential Limitations of the Community-Based Assessment Model

I have found that many teams work hard with families to make a difference in the lives of children with ASD. As is true of all situations, however, the interdisciplinary assessment process described in this chapter is not without limitations. It requires a commitment of time (nearly 20 hours of contact over an 8-week period) by both professionals involved in the care of a child with ASD and the child's family. The process assumes an expected level of collaboration among providers and the family. It also requires a commitment by the administration to take the necessary steps to improve programming for children with ASD. Further, team members must have a level of sophistication in the assessment process to ensure that the needs of children with ASD are comprehensively assessed, which may involve not only informal but also formal assessment approaches. Thus, it may be that this approach to assessment and program planning is not the most effective or efficient means for all teams attempting to serve children with ASD. The limitations of the community-based interdisciplinary assessment can be addressed, however, if team and family are willing to be creative and collaborative in defining and implementing those parts of the assessment process that will be most valuable in addressing the specific needs of a child with ASD.

Summary

In this chapter, a disablement framework has been proposed that can guide the assessment of children with ASD. An ecological and dynamic approach to assessment can enrich the information being gathered and support future intervention planning. The role of the family and the practitioners in assessment was described, and an interdisciplinary model for community-based assessment was presented. The following reiteration of the questions posed at the beginning of the chapter highlights the key points.

What components of a disablement framework should guide the assessment process for children with ASD?

Just as the ICD–10 is used worldwide to classify disorders like ASD, the ICF is a classification system that helps define the consequences of such health conditions. The disablement framework provided by the ICF describes three aspects of health that should be considered in both assessment and intervention planning for children with ASD. These three dimensions refer to the consequences individuals experience as a result of their condition at the body (impairment), person (activity), and society (participation) levels. When a condition such as ASD is diagnosed, a comprehensive assessment of the consequences of that diagnosis should include identifying the signs of the impairment, the alteration in performance of activities, and the disadvantage experienced relative to others.

How should ecological and dynamic assessment be incorporated into a functional evaluation process for children with ASD?

During assessment, it is important to obtain information not only about a child's skill levels, but also about the environments in which the child uses those skills (Haney & Cavallaro, 1996). This is the value of an ecological approach to assessment. It provides information about the opportunities that a child has to develop specific skills and the expectations for skill development to ensure successful participation in particular activities. A dynamic approach to assessment also provides the examiner with more functional information about a child. It requires structured and systematic observations across contexts and settings over a period of time. Dynamic assessment involves highly individualized interactions guided by intervention principles. Both approaches to assessment lead to more effective program planning because of the functional relevance of the information obtained.

What role do families and practitioners play in the assessment of children with ASD?

A shift in thinking has occurred in the last 10 years regarding the roles and relationships between and among families and professionals. This shift has moved the professional as expert to the professional as partner with families, recognizing the value and expertise of both parties. Effective assessment planning and implementation require input from those who know and understand the daily routines and behaviors of a child with or suspected of ASD, as well as those with experience identifying the core deficits of autism. Valued outcomes are achieved when both families and practitioners can collaborate in the effort to assess a child's strengths, challenges, and needs.

What are the components of an interdisciplinary, family-centered, and community-based assessment model for children with ASD?

The interdisciplinary assessment model described in this chapter incorporates best practice principles for family-centered care and ensures that the family is recognized as a partner in the assessment, with valued knowledge and expertise. As a constant and crucial component in the child's life, the family guides the assessment process. Other team members learn to listen and respond to the family's concerns and priorities, honor their cultural diversity, recognize their different methods of coping, and support their needs. This assessment model avoids the discrepancy that Filer and Mahoney (1996) found in their research between the services families wanted and what they were actually receiving. Further, the assessment model supports decision making for intervention that is both developmentally and individually appropriate for a particular child with ASD.

The model of assessment proposed in this chapter and implemented by my colleagues and me has led to collaboration among school teams, families, and consultants willing to spend increased time and effort to obtain a more comprehensive view of children with ASD. This is done so that effective programming can be developed. As with any assessment model, however, there are challenges to be faced. The first challenge is a paradigm shift toward family-centered practice. Team members need to recognize and trust families' knowledge and expertise. Families need to guide the assessment process through the questions they ask. Practitioners often struggle to bridge the gap between the needs of the child and family and the federal and state mandates that require appropriate but not the best possible services. The outcomes for the teams with whom I have worked over the last 8 years have been invaluable. Families taught my colleagues and me to trust them, their children, and what is known as best practice.

Sample Information Form for Children

Instructions

Please fill out this form in as much detail as possible. This information will be treated as confidential. If information is not available, please explain the reason so that we will know that the question has been considered. Please return this form as soon as possible prior to your appointment, so that we can consider this information.

Mail it to: _____

_____

_____

If you have questions about this form, you are encouraged to ask these at the scheduled intake interview and give the form to the assessment coordinator who has been assigned to manage the community assessment for you and your child. Thank you.

Identification Information

Child's name: _____ Sex: _____
              (First)   (Middle)   (Last)

Address: _____
        (Street)   (City, State)   (Zip)

Date of birth: _____ Place of birth: _____

Social Security #: _____ Referral source: _____

Child's primary physician: _____ Phone: _____

Address: _____

Medical diagnosis given (if known): _____

Name of person completing this form: _____

Relationship to child: _____

Family Information

Father's name: _____ Mother's name: _____

Age: _____ Age: _____

Living with family? _____ Living with family? _____

Occupation: _____ Occupation: _____

Education level: _____ Education level: _____

Social Security #: _____ Social Security #: _____

Phone: (H) _____ Phone: (H) _____

      (W) _____   (W) _____

(continues)

APPENDIX 3.A

With whom does the child live? (If other than own parents, give name, address, and phone #.)

_____

Brothers and sisters:
(Name) _____ (Age) _____ (Name) _____ (Age) _____

_____ _____ _____ _____

_____ _____ _____ _____

_____ _____ _____ _____

General Questions

Identify 3 to 5 key questions or concerns you would like addressed in this evaluation.

_____

_____

_____

_____

_____

Describe your concerns about your child's development (including social interaction, communication, play, language, and behavior).

_____

_____

_____

_____

List the people, agencies, or clinics you have consulted about your child's difficulties. Include such persons as pediatricians, psychologists, neurologists, speech–language pathologists, and so on.

Date   Name and address   What you were told

_____   _____   _____

_____   _____   _____

_____   _____   _____

Developmental History

Indicate at what age your child first performed the following:

_____ sit up alone	_____ walk alone	_____ say single words
_____ use sentences	_____ respond to his or her name	_____ understand simple words
_____ follow simple directions	_____ babble	_____ point
_____ coo	_____ become toilet trained	_____ sleep through the night
_____ dress self	_____ eat independently	

Has your child ever gained skills and then lost them in any developmental area (e.g., language, toileting, motor skills)?   ☐ Yes   ☐ No

If yes, please explain: _____

_____

(continues)

APPENDIX 3.A

Temperament

Check one of the 3 choices for each of the 9 items listed that best describes your child.

1. ☐ highly adaptable   ☐ variable adaptability   ☐ slow to adapt
2. ☐ usually active   ☐ variable activity level   ☐ usually active
3. ☐ usually distractible   ☐ variable distractibility   ☐ usually distractible
4. ☐ usually positive mood   ☐ variable mood   ☐ usually negative mood
5. ☐ intense responder   ☐ variable responder   ☐ mild responder
6. ☐ high threshold/tolerance   ☐ variable threshold/tolerance   ☐ low threshold/tolerance
7. ☐ usually persistent   ☐ variable persistence   ☐ usually nonpersistent
8. ☐ usually rhythmic*   ☐ variable rhythmicity   ☐ usually arhythmic
9. ☐ usually approachable   ☐ variable approachability   ☐ usually withdrawn

*Related to body functions—eating, sleeping, toileting.

Social Interaction

Does your child interact with other children?   ☐ Yes   ☐ No

Describe how your child interacts with other children: _____
_____
_____

Does your child interact with adults?   ☐ Yes   ☐ No

Describe how your child interacts with adults: _____
_____
_____

Play

Does your child prefer to play alone?   ☐ Yes   ☐ No

Describe how your child plays alone: _____
_____
_____

What games and toys does your child prefer? _____
_____

Describe how your child plays with toys: _____
_____
_____

Does your child play with other children?   ☐ Yes   ☐ No

If yes, describe how your child plays with other children: _____
_____
_____
_____

(continues)

APPENDIX 3.A

Interests and Behavior

Is your child easily upset?   ☐ Yes   ☐ No

What behaviors does your child typically exhibit when upset? _____

_____

_____

What triggers these behaviors? _____

_____

_____

When were the above behaviors first noticed? _____

By whom? _____

Has it ever changed in severity? Worsened _____   Improved _____

_____

What do you usually do when your child exhibits these behaviors? _____

_____

_____

Does your child demonstrate specific or perseverative interests in activites, objects, or topics of conversation?   ☐ Yes   ☐ No

If yes, please describe these specific interests: _____

_____

_____

Communication

Circle all statements that describe your child's communicative behavior:

a.   Has not yet started to talk.

b.   Was late in starting to talk.

c.   Is not developing speech as rapidly as expected.

d.   Does not talk very much.

e.   Is not making speech sounds correctly that are expected for age.

f.   People have trouble understanding the child.

g.   Tries hard and seems to want to communicate.

h.   Uses lots of gestures.

i.   Has an unusual voice quality (hoarse, harsh, whispery, etc.).

j.   Speech is too loud or too soft. (underline which)

k.   Pitch level is unusual (e.g., too high, too low).

l.   Hesitates or repeats sounds and words excessively.

Does your child have a means to indicate "yes" or "no"? If yes, please describe: _____

_____

_____

_____

(continues)

APPENDIX 3.A

Do you think your child can understand more than he or she can say?   ☐ Yes   ☐ No

If yes, please explain and give an example: _____

_____

_____

_____

Do you think your child gets frustrated when he or she cannot communicate effectively?   ☐ Yes   ☐ No

If yes, please explain: _____

_____

_____

_____

Describe your child's current means of communication. (Please be specific.) _____

_____

_____

Has your child's communication ever been evaluated?   ☐ Yes   ☐ No

If yes, please summarize the results of your child's most recent speech and language evaluation in terms of language comprehension, language production, and speech production: _____

_____

_____

_____

_____

Pregnancy History

Check any that apply.

Condition during pregnancy:

☐ drugs or medications   ☐ accidents   ☐ German measles
☐ alcohol   ☐ hepatitis   ☐ cigarettes
☐ toxemia   ☐ bleeding   ☐ anemia
☐ extreme nausea   ☐ Rh incompatibility   ☐ unusual fatigue
☐ emotional upset   ☐ high blood pressure

Birth History

Length of pregnancy? _____   How long was labor? _____   Was labor induced? _____

Was baby pre/postmature? _____   Cesarean delivery? _____   What was the birth weight? _____

Incubator? _____   Were any drugs used at all? _____   In need of oxygen? _____

At birth were any of the following noted?

☐ difficulty breathing   ☐ jaundice
☐ injuries   ☐ birth defects

Is there any other information about the mother or baby that may be pertinent? _____

_____

_____

(continues)

APPENDIX 3.A

Child's General Health

Check all that apply.

Feeding: ☐ Typical oral intake ☐ Feeding tube

General health: ☐ Good ☐ Average ☐ Fair ☐ Poor

Child's physical endurance: ☐ Good ☐ Average ☐ Fair ☐ Poor

Child has had the following:

☐ German measles	☐ mumps	☐ bronchitis
☐ high fever	☐ measles	☐ surgery
☐ chicken pox	☐ allergies	☐ CMV
☐ scarlet fever	☐ influenza	☐ adenoidectomy
☐ tonsillitis	☐ earaches	☐ tonsillectomy
☐ frequent colds	☐ asthma	☐ meningitis
☐ convulsions or seizures	☐ cleft lip or cleft palate	

State any physical handicaps: _____

Does your child take any medication? ☐ Yes ☐ No Please specify: _____

Hearing and Vision

1. Have you ever questioned your child's ability to hear normally? ☐ Yes ☐ No
   If yes, please explain why: _____
2. Has your child ever had his or her hearing tested? ☐ Yes ☐ No
   By whom? _____ When? _____
3. Has your child had ear infections? ☐ Yes ☐ No
   Which ear? _____ Age at first ear infection: _____
   Number of ear infections in first 12 months: _____
   Number of ear infections by age 2: _____
4. Has your child received medical attention for earaches or infections? ☐ Yes ☐ No
   Name of physician: _____
5. Did the ear infection resolve after first course of antibiotics? ☐ Yes ☐ No
6. Is your child's hearing the same from day to day? ☐ Yes ☐ No
   Please describe: _____

7. Has a doctor ever said your child has fluid in his or her ears? ☐ Yes ☐ No
8. Has your child ever had tubes placed in his or her ears? ☐ Yes ☐ No
9. Has your child had an ear infection within 3 months of this evaluation? ☐ Yes ☐ No
10. Have you ever questioned your child's ability to see normally? ☐ Yes ☐ No
11. Has your child's vision been tested? ☐ Yes ☐ No
    When? _____ Results: _____

Auditory Behavior

1. Which of the following is most typical of your child's ability to understand speech? (Circle one):
   a. Does not understand what is said.
   b. Understands very little of what is said.

(continues)

APPENDIX 3.A

   c. Understands what is said when the speaker gestures.

   d. Understands familiar statements or questions.

   e. Understands clearly everything that is said.

2. Does your child have difficulty determining which direction sound comes from?   ☐ Yes   ☐ No

3. Does your child favor one ear?   ☐ Right   ☐ Left

4. Is your child annoyed by a noisy environment?   ☐ Yes   ☐ No

5. Does your child seem to hear less well in noise?   ☐ Yes   ☐ No

Services

What services does your child currently receive? _____

_____

_____

_____

Service provider (e.g., speech–language pathologist)	Service (e.g., individual therapy)	How Long (e.g., 6 mos)	Frequency (e.g., twice a week)	Goals (e.g., increase utterance length; develop understanding of questions)

PLEASE COMPLETE THIS SECTION IF YOUR CHILD IS USING OR HAS USED AN AUGMENTATIVE COMMUNICATION SYSTEM.

When was an augmentative system introduced? _____

Describe all components of the system: _____

_____

Why was this particular system chosen for your child? _____

How long has your child been using the system? _____

Has your child used a different system in the past?   ☐ Yes   ☐ No

If yes, please describe the system: _____

_____

_____

(continues)

APPENDIX 3.A

If using a nonelectronic aid, how does your child indicate the elements he or she wishes to communicate?

☐ Finger ☐ Head stick ☐ Eye gaze ☐ Auditory scanning ☐ Other _____

If using an electronic aid, what type of switch or control mechanism is being used, and how does your child operate it? _____

Can your child match (check all those that apply):

☐ object to object ☐ object to photo ☐ object to picture
☐ object to drawing ☐ picture to photo ☐ picture to drawing

Check the items that your child can identify (by pointing or looking) with names:

☐ objects ☐ photos ☐ pictures ☐ line drawings ☐ written words

Other (please specify) _____

Can your child sequence or select two pictures to represent a thought or idea? ☐ Yes ☐ No

If yes, indicate the highest number of items he or she can sequence: _____

If signing, in your opinion, how adequate is your child's motor control? _____
_____

Has your child's speech improved since introduction of an augmentative aid? ☐ Yes ☐ No

Please explain: _____

Is this system used outside of therapy? ☐ Yes ☐ No

If so, where? _____

Does your child use his or her communication system to (check all those that apply):

☐ initiate communicative interaction ☐ ask questions ☐ respond to questions
☐ comment on past ☐ reject ☐ comment on future
☐ comment on present ☐ request people ☐ request objects
☐ request activities

Educational Information

Please complete for children in school.

Child's present school: _____ Grade: _____

Does your child attend day care? ☐ Yes ☐ No

If yes, where? _____

Did/does your child attend preschool? ☐ Yes ☐ No

If yes, where? _____

Did/does your child attend kindergarten? ☐ Yes ☐ No

If yes, where? _____

Please describe your child's classroom performance or participation in the classroom (if appropriate):

_____
_____
_____
_____

(continues)

APPENDIX 3.A

What are your child's most enjoyable subjects? _____

_____

_____

What are your child's least enjoyable subjects? _____

Grades repeated, if any: _____

Please describe your child's behavior in school: _____

_____

Does your child have difficulty in: ☐ Math ☐ Reading ☐ Writing

Does your child receive any special assistance or help at school? ☐ Yes ☐ No

If yes, please describe: _____

APPENDIX 3.A

Sample Preassessment Planning Meeting Format

Child's name: <u>Sammy Smith</u>

Date of birth: <u>7/17/01</u>   Chronological age: <u>3 years 6 months</u>

Family: <u>Mother, Father, Brother</u>

Address: <u>10 Main Street</u>

Phone: <u>555-1111</u>

Referral source: <u>Mike Davis, special educator</u>

Consultation dates: <u>1/15/05; 2/4/05; 2/11/05</u>

Interdisciplinary Team

Speech-language pathology   Psychology

Developmental pediatrics   Early childhood special education

Occupational therapy   Family support

Primary Health Care Provider

Case Manager

Child's Strengths

Loving   Adept at jumping and climbing

Caring   Strong

Attached to parents   Good sleeper

Recovers quickly from tantrums   Fun

Curious   Recognizes family members

Seeks engagement with adults

Child's Challenges

Aggressive and irritable   Gastrointestinal difficulty

Limited verbal language   Inflexible

Poor organization for getting what   Demanding

   he wants and needs   Limited play

Genogram

Presented on chart paper and reviewed.

(continues)

APPENDIX 3.B

Ecomap

Presented on chart paper and reviewed.

Background Information

Sammy Smith, a 3-year 6-month-old boy was referred for a Vermont Rural Autism assessment within his home and preschool environments. Sammy presently lives with his mother, father, and older brother. He currently attends play dates two afternoons per week with case manager, classroom teacher, physical therapist, and occupational therapist. He receives speech-language services three times a week from a speech-language pathologist, plus consultation for occupational therapy and physical therapy in his home environment. Family is awaiting approval of additional services (e.g., respite care, personal care, and flexible funding) through the county mental health program.

According to parental report, Sammy's pregnancy and birth history were unremarkable. He weighed 7 pounds 3 ounces at birth. Mother noted an unusual cry that sounded like a squeal.

Sammy experienced numerous health complications during his first year of life. He was diagnosed with hydrocephalus at 8 weeks, and a subsequent MRI showed partial agenesis of the inferior part of the cerebellar vermis and hydrocephalus. He was shunted on November 10, 2002.

Sammy also had a series of seizures at 6 months of age. He was treated with phenobarbital 30 mg, and seizures discontinued by March of 2003. A recent EEG showed no epileptiform discharges, although some concern persists about possible subtle seizure activity.

Sammy's health has been within normal limits, except for two ear infections by the age of 2. Parents questioned his hearing because of his inability to speak and respond when spoken to as a toddler. He also becomes annoyed by a noisy environment and appears to hear less well in noise. Hearing has been tested, and results are within normal limits. Parents noted that he sleeps excessively (11 hours at night and a 3-hour nap during the day) and has had several vomiting episodes/illnesses throughout his life.

Sammy's developmental history has not followed the typical pattern. In the past 6 months, he has begun making sounds and producing single words (e.g., "go," and "eee" for "delicious"). Mother believes that he does not understand what is said sometimes, but he will not indicate that he does not understand. He has not yet begun to talk and has an unusual voice quality. He tries hard to communicate and has begun to incorporate pointing into his communication. During the past few months, he has started taking an adult's hand, bringing the adult to where he wants to go. He'll express frustration by screaming and throwing himself onto the floor. Parents feel that he has some real behavioral issues. They believe that this may be because he has difficulty communicating. He has to be watched every minute, because he climbs on everything, unsafely, and constantly has things in his mouth. Parents also reported that transitions are extremely

(continues)

APPENDIX 3.B

difficult for him. He prefers to interact with adults on a one-on-one basis and does not play with other children. He loves picture books, peek-a-boo games, cars and trucks. He explores objects by mouthing them.

The purpose of the Vermont Rural Autism Project assessment is to assess Sammy's health, development, communicative functioning, and educational needs to establish an intervention plan to help develop self-care skills and to confirm a diagnosis of Autism Spectrum Disorder. Both parents would like to gain a clearer picture of what Sammy's development will be like, how he'll function later in life, whether he'll be independent, and what the future may hold.

Family's Questions

Based on face-to-face intake:

1. Does Sammy fall on the Autism Spectrum?
2. What kind of treatment programs would be most appropriate for Sammy and at what intensity?
3. What kind of prognosis can be made for him in the future? What would be appropriate goals to set for him? Will he be able to develop independent skills?
4. Will he be able to interact with other kids?
5. Will he understand danger (threats to life and limb)?

School's Questions

Based on face-to-face intake:

1. Does Sammy have ASD?
2. Are his digestive system and absorption system functioning properly?
3. Is medication a good or bad option for behavior management?
4. Will he always be texturally challenged when it comes to food?
5. Will he ever be able to formulate words correctly or speak so that others will understand him?
6. What can we do in his environment to help him make sense of the world, to better regulate himself, and to communicate his wants and needs more successfully?

Primary Care Provider's Questions

Based on phone conference intake:

1. What gastrointestinal, medical assessments would help answer why Sammy suffers from constipation, diarrhea, and stomach cramping?
2. How does Sammy interpret language?
3. Can a diagnosis of ASD be confirmed?

Current Agencies Involved

- County mental health
- Early Essential Education program

(continues)

APPENDIX 3.B

- Child Development Clinic
- Children with Special Health Needs
- Parent to Parent of Vermont

The Plan

Team arrives at home _____

Team arrives at playgroup _____

Team gathers to process _____

Directions to Home

Directions to Playgroup

Child's Schedule (sample)

Time	Activity
8:00–8:30 A.M.	Breakfast
8:30–11:00 A.M.	At home
11:00–11:30 A.M.	Lunch
11:30 A.M.–12:30 P.M.	Nap
12:30 P.M.–12:45 P.M.	Free time to play or read a story
12:45 P.M.–1:00 P.M.	Transport to play group
1:00–2:30 P.M.	Play group
2:30–2:45 P.M.	Transport home

Assessment Schedule (sample)

Who	What	When	Where
Developmental pediatrician (DP) and assessment coordinator (AC)	Review medical records: look at history of vomiting, gastrointestinal symptoms, shunt status, past seizure activity, brain X-rays)	Prior to assessment date	Office
AC and DP	Interview Sammy's neurologist and pediatrician	Prior to assessment date	Office/phone conference
SLP	Review previous speech-language evaluations and progress notes	Prior to assessment date	Office
Psychologist (PSYCH)	Review previous IFSP and current IEP	Prior to assessment	Office

(continues)

APPENDIX 3.B

Who	What	When	Where
OT	Review OT and PT records	Prior to assessment	Office
Early childhood special educator (ECSE)	Review nutrition records	Prior to assessment	Office
ECSE and SLP	Complete *Communication Symbolic Behavior Scales (CSBS)*	9:00–10:00 A.M.	Home
OT and PSYCH	Complete sensory profile	9:00–10:00 A.M.	Home
Family Support (FS) and AC	Interview parents & complete *Pediatric Evaluation of Disability Inventory (PEDI)*	10:00–11:00 A.M.	Home
DP and ECSE	Observe play	10:00–11:00 A.M.	Home
OT and SLP	Observe lunch	11:00–11:30 A.M.	Home
ECSE and PSYCH	Interview teacher	12:00–12:30 P.M.	School
FS and SLP	Interview paraprofessional	12:30–1:00 P.M.	School
OT and DP	Interview community OT and PT	12:30–1:00 P.M.	School
DP, ECSE, SLP, OT, and PSYCH	Observe and complete *Childhood Autism Rating Scale (CARS)*	1:00–2:15 P.M.	School
Entire team	Meet to process and complete DSM-IV	2:45–3:30 P.M.	School or home

Interview Questions (to be asked of everyone)

> What do you see as Sammy's strengths?
>
> What are his greatest challenges?
>
> What brings you joy in working with him?
>
> What is your greatest frustration in supporting his needs?
>
> If you could ask VT-RAP to address one question, what would that be?

Sample Questions for Parents and School Providers

Behavior

1. Describe a situation in which Sammy becomes aggressive.
2. When does this usually occur?
3. Who is he usually aggressive with?
4. What does he appear to be communicating?

(continues)

APPENDIX 3.B

Communication

5. Describe how Sammy lets you know he wants something.

6. Describe a situation in which Sammy indicates that he understands what has been said.

7. Describe a situation in which Sammy indicates that he doesn't understand.

Social Interaction and Play

8. Describe Sammy's interaction with siblings.

9. Describe Sammy's interactions with peers in a playgroup.

10. How does Sammy like to spend his time?

11. Describe the types of games and toys Sammy enjoys.

Sample Questions for Older Sibling

Social Interaction and Play

1. What do you like to do with your brother?

2. How do you get him to play with you?

Communication

3. How does your brother tell you what he wants?

4. How does he let you know he understands what you want?

5. What do you like most about your brother?

6. What do you wish was different about your brother?

Sample Questions for Pediatrician and Neurologist

Medical and Diagnostic

1. What is your understanding of Sammy's condition?

2. What medications have been prescribed and why?

3. What have been the effects of the medications used?

4. What worries you most about Sammy?

5. What type of intervention would you like to see to address his current and future needs?

Sample Questions for OT and PT

Sensory and Motor

1. Describe Sammy's current programming.

2. What is working and not working?

3. Describe his sensory challenges as you have observed them.

4. What sensory activities are invasive to him (e.g., toothbrushing, eating)?

5. What oral motor needs does he appear to have?

6. Describe any concerns with his motor planning.

7. Describe his ability to focus, shift attention, and regulate behavior.

(continues)

APPENDIX 3.B

Sample Questions for SLP and Teacher

Communication and Social Interaction

1. Describe what you believe Sammy understands in predictable versus unpredictable situations.

2. Describe how Sammy currently communicates his needs and wants.

3. Describe his interaction with adults and peers.

4. Describe his play.

Record Reviews (team members' list to review)

Medical records (MRI, neurology reports, pediatric follow-up; hearing report, vision report, growth charts)

IFSP

Draft IEP

Nutrition assessment with 3-day food recall

OT report and progress notes

PT report and progress notes

SLP report and progress notes

Assessment Tools

Checklist for Autism in Toddlers

DSM-IV Checklist

Childhood Autism Rating Scale

Sensory Profile

Communication Symbolic Behavior Scales

Pediatric Evaluation of Disability Inventory

Observations (team members to document throughout the assessment day)

Arousal level in different settings and activities

Ability to shift attention

Affect

Activity level

Ability to regulate behavior

Ability to establish joint attention

Social interaction with peers and adults (familiar and unfamiliar)

Imitation (verbal and nonverbal)

Use of vocalizations

Use of gestures

Play with objects

Motivators

Ability to follow routines

Flexibility in routines and activities

Response to challenging situations

Consistency of behavior across activities, settings, communication partners

APPENDIX 3.B

Sample of Follow-Up Planning

Questions Asked at Intake	Information from Observations, Interviews, Record Reviews of Child at the Assessment	Recommendations Brainstormed at Postassessment Planning Meeting
Category: Social Family question: How can social/pragmatic interventions be consistently and effectively implemented across school and home settings? School question: How do we provide appropriate social supports?	*Activity* • Provided with social supports primarily through adults. • Imitates models of interactions with peers and adults. • Responds well to adult intervention with visual and gestural modeling, prompting. • Initiates with a peer at recess to start a chase game. • Inconsistent social support provided on playground. • Best times for interactions are mornings. • Home/school provide daily information but missing work samples make it difficult to assess progress. *Participation* • Child wants to be one of the kids and is interested in what they are doing, especially at recess. • Multiple opportunities for child to interact; specifically at circle time, sharing, music, game time, physical education, and choice time. • No documentation of child's daily involvement in school activities or response of peers. • More interactive at home.	*Activity* • Scaffolding: Team to clarify the goals of scaffolding, videotape successful and unsuccessful examples of scaffolding, meet collaboratively to train and plan for how and when to scaffold. • Preteaching: Preteach games with emotional themes using social stories. *Participation* • Peer involvement: Train and model with peers ways to engage and sustain interactions in structured and unstructured settings at home and school.

(continues)

APPENDIX 3.C

Questions Asked at Intake	Information from Observations, Interviews, Record Reviews of Child at the Assessment	Recommendations Brainstormed at Postassessment Planning Meeting
Category: Communication Family and school question: How can we support communication and language development?	*Activity* • With increased verbal language, frustration decreases, which positively affects behavior. • Receives 90 minutes of child-directed speech–language programming weekly (three 30-minute sessions). • Scaffolding during therapy facilitates spontaneous verbal responses. • Daily supports are needed for communicative acts and social interactions to be successful. *Participation* • Staff training is done to carry over intervention strategies throughout day. • Modeling and prompting are continuously provided to increase opportunities for interaction and engagement in peer's play.	*Activity* • Preteaching *Participation* • Direct training of instructional assistant (IA) and teacher. • Share videos from home and school demonstrating successful communicative exchanges. • Set up environment to increase opportunities for communication. • Use peers as communication partners.
School question: What is the best means to communicate with child?	*Impairment* • Imitates spoken language. • Engages in parallel, functional, and some creative play. *Activity* • Responds to adult modeling, verbal questioning, and verbal and gestural prompting. • Responds to verbal scaffolding to facilitate verbal communication exchanges.	

(continues)

APPENDIX 3.C

Questions Asked at Intake	Information from Observations, Interviews, Record Reviews of Child at the Assessment	Recommendations Brainstormed at Postassessment Planning Meeting
	• Comprehends and responds verbally to pictured verbal cues. • Successful feedback provided verbally and tactily.	
Category: Program Planning School questions: How much should we expect from child? What are appropriate kindergarten goals for child? How do we encourage independent work and satisfaction with work? Primary health care provider questions: What additional information do we need on the child? How will his transition work?	*Impairment* • Limited communication and social interaction. • Difficulty with transition from home to school and breaks in routine. • Limited endurance. • $3\frac{1}{2}$- to 4-year-old fine motor skills. • Struggles completing gross-motor activities in physical education. • Destroys his work when it does not appear right to him. *Activity* • Limitations in communication, social interaction, and written tasks affect level of engagement in kindergarten curriculum. • Responds well to visual cues or supports and modeling. • Follows kindergarten routine with adult support. • Has learned most kindergarten routines. • When frustrated or fatigued other activities should be pursued by IA. • Breaks from school routine affect consistent performance and progress in curriculum. • Limited endurance affects ability to engage consistently.	*Impairment* • Build in nap time or regular rest time. *Activity* • Complete language-based curriculum analysis to determine expectations for students and potential breakdowns for child. • Initiate "priming" (i.e., practicing activities ahead of time) at home to reduce anxiety and increase likelihood of working independently. • Consider computer as a tool to engage child in participating and completing writing and art tasks. • Schedule regular meetings times to review and evaluate child's progress in the kindergarten curriculum. *Participation* • Have teachers and IAs for this year and next year attend intervention course in autism in the spring and participate in the summer Autism Institute.

(continues)

APPENDIX 3.C

Questions Asked at Intake	Information from Observations, Interviews, Record Reviews of Child at the Assessment	Recommendations Brainstormed at Postassessment Planning Meeting
	• Morning activities are more successful than afternoon activities.	
	• Asks an adult to do unfamiliar tasks, walks away from or destroys what he has done.	
	Participation	
	• Increased exposure to activities and tasks increases familiarization, which increases participation.	
Category: Behavior	*Impairment*	*Impairment*
School questions: How do we address aggressive behaviors toward others?	• Throws objects	• Have IA in close proximity to remove objects or obstruct attempts to lash out at other children.
	• Pinches other children	
How do we encourage or increase willingness to try new things, specifically things we already know are hard for him?	*Activity*	*Activity*
	• No formal behavior plan in place at home or school.	• Make accommodations around responsive classroom.
	• Time-out used during school when child is physical toward others; once in time-out, he is able to decide when to return to the activities he was removed from; firm tone of voice is used to let him know what he has done is not okay.	• Use home–school journal.
		• Develop a daily schedule board.
		• Acknowledge attempts at self-regulation.
		• Develop social stories to teach impulse control.
	• At home specific and consistent consequences are used to address his behavior; time-out, "no," and verbal warnings are used and are effective.	• Develop a written behavior plan:
		—Relate to IEP goals.
		—Take data.
		—Use school format.
	• At school, child is rewarded/motivated by books, kids, and recess.	—Use phrase "We don't do that" across settings.
		—Be clear about purpose of time-out.
	• At home, child is rewarded/motivated by computer, bath time, TV, books, and cooking.	—Be consistent across settings.

(continues)

APPENDIX 3.C

Questions Asked at Intake	Information from Observations, Interviews, Record Reviews of Child at the Assessment	Recommendations Brainstormed at Postassessment Planning Meeting
	Participation	*Participation*
	• Not permitted to attend assemblies or field trips.	• Use priming and social stories to prepare child for assembly and field trip participation.
		• Inform and train assembly and field trip monitors on ways to respond to child.

APPENDIX 3.C

Sample Report A
Interdisciplinary Consultation Summary

Child's name: __Jay Jones__   Date of birth: __7/17/00__

Parents: __Paul and Mary Jones__   Chronological age: __5 years 3 months__

Address: __21 Lilac Way__   School: __Mountain View Elementary__

Phone: __555-7777__   Referral source: __Martha Smith, MD__

Consultation date: __10/20/05__

Vermont Rural Autism Project Team

Assessment coordinator   Early childhood special education

Speech–language   Family support

Developmental pediatrics   Occupational therapy

Psychology

Primary Health Care Provider

Name: __Martha Smith, MD__

Address: __17 Main Street__

Phone: __555-2222__

Case Manager

Name: __Cynthia Marsh__

Address: __5 Mountain View Drive__

Phone: __555-4444__

Background Information

(Obtained from the Information Form for Children and the CSBS questionnaire)

Jay is a 5-year 3-month-old boy who lives with his parents, his 3-year 6-month-old sister, and his 18-month-old sister. Jay has a noticeably strong and unique bond with 3-year-old sister. Much of the parents' extended family are in close geographical proximity and offer support in a variety of ways. Jay's father works as a postal worker, and his mother works as an LPN at the local hospital. Jay has a medical diagnosis of Autism.

Jay's mother was hospitalized for approximately 1 month due to ruptured membranes before his birth. During that time, she was given Tributalean, antibiotics, and steroids. Labor was induced at 32 weeks. Jay weighed 5 pounds 6 ounces, and had Apgars of 7 and 9 at 1 and 5 minutes. He was jaundiced and received oxygen for 12 hours.

Jay's general health is now described as good with average physical endurance and low muscle tone. In the past, he has had frequent colds and pneumonia. His hearing has been questioned due to a behavior described as "zoning out." In October of 2002, hearing testing resulted in a referral to a developmental clinic. Neither fluid nor ear infections were reported. Currently, Jay understands most familiar statements

(continues)

APPENDIX 3.D

or questions, does not have difficulty determining which direction sound comes from, does not favor one ear, is not annoyed by a noisy environment, and does not seem to hear less well in noise. Vision appears to be normal, although it has not been formally tested.

Jay's developmental history is reported to include challenging behavior, delayed social interaction, poor coordination, and impulsivity. He was toilet trained at age 4 and can dress himself. He sat alone at 7 to 8 months and walked alone at 15 months. He used single words at 14 months and sentences at 4 years of age. Understanding of simple words began at 28 months.

Jay is described as getting along with other children, although he prefers to play alone. When he plays alone, he is observed to engage in a combination of scripted, creative, parallel, and pretend play. For example, he uses a castle with knights, and he likes to play with stuffed animals. He will act out video scenes with toys. When he plays with other children, particularly his sister, he likes chase games. He also creates houses and barns using couch cushions. He loves computer games, although he does not appear to understand the goals.

Family first noticed Jay's tendency to get upset easily at about 2 years of age. Typically, he would scream. This behavior would be triggered by the word "no" when he was being restricted from doing something. From 2 to 4 years of age, this behavior worsened, although it has since improved. Overall, difficult behaviors have improved. He is much less rigid in his routines.

Speech and language development did not occur at the expected rate. Jay's first words were late, and speech sound production was inaccurate. He used gestures and was reported to have an unusually high-pitched voice. Others have difficulty understanding him, although he tries hard to communicate. He attempts to answer yes and no questions. His receptive language is much better than his expressive language. He is able to understand gestures, words, phrases, and sentences. He understands names of people and pets, toys, food items, body parts, and action words. Currently, he communicates expressively using verbal language, although his sentences are described by the family as "broken." He also uses pointing, gestures, and sounds to communicate. His language continues to improve. He spoke his first sentence in December. When he needs help, he will use phrases such as "Help," "Come, need help," "Help, please," along with physically leading the person to his need. However, when objects are out of reach, he tends not to ask for assistance, which creates the need for constant intervention from parents. When he does not want something, he will verbalize, saying, "No," "Go away," or "No, not here," and sometimes he will scream or whine. To get others' attention he might say, "Come on, Mommy, come on," or "Put, put that phone away." If he wants someone to notice something, he will bring the object to show the person. When a person is entering or leaving a room, he often says, "Hello" or "Good-bye," sometimes with prompting and other times independently. He has been seen to slam the door while saying, "Go away." Upon being awakened in the morning, he tends to say, "Go away, Jay sleeping," or "Mommy, you go to your room" while pointing out of the room. He will cry or seek

(continues)

APPENDIX 3.D

comfort when he is upset or frustrated. Frustration can be seen when he screams, because the words don't come easily to him. Laughter and excitement show his happiness.

Jay loves to play social games with his family and people with whom he is familiar. He loves peek-a-boo and chase. He also wants his mom to engage in scripted play with him, such as acting out the computer game Frogger with stuffed frogs and playing with toy trucks. He is very happy during this play and uses names when playing; however, it was noted that he does not engage in the organized play required for participation in board games. He also loves books. He usually likes to look at them alone, yet he will now let his mom read to him. In the past, he would turn the pages quickly and not look at the words, but lately he has been pointing at the words and asking, "What's this say?"

In the past, Jay received services from an early education program. This center-based preschool provided him with 15 hours per week of direct services, including support from a special education teacher, speech-language pathologist, and occupational therapy and physical therapy consultants, as well as an individual aid. After the family moved, Jay participated in a public preschool for social opportunities with typical peers, and an individual aid provided most of the services. A special educator visited with him 1 hour per week, and he received 45 to 50 minutes per week of services from an SLP. Currently, he attends kindergarten, where he receives services from an instructional assistant, 90 minutes per week of direct therapy from the SLP, and OT consultation.

Jay's has the ability to learn academic information, yet the need exists to find the best style to nurture his abilities. His current communication goals involve social/pragmatic language skills and working on increasing his conversational language.

Assessment Summary and Recommendations

A variety of methods were used to assess the strengths and challenges of Jay and his home and school environments. These included record review, interviews with family members and community providers, and observations and direct interaction with Jay. [Summaries of the actual interviews, observations, and record reviews could be attached as appendices.] The questions raised by the family and community providers are organized by category. The results of the assessment are integrated from the observations made, interviews completed, and records reviewed to answer each question, with three to five priority recommendations offered under each category and set of questions.

Overall, Jay is enthusiastic, with strong visual learning skills. He has a unique interest in other children, which is both motivating and rewarding for him. During unstructured activities, specifically recess, he is eager to engage children in his play. He primarily communicates verbally and demonstrates strong receptive language skills. At this time, his verbal interactions are greater at home than at school. His preferred play materials and contexts include the computer, books, and playing with "kids." When he is involved in these activities or any others that he may enjoy, he becomes very expressive, both verbally and gesturally. He highly benefits from adult support to interact successfully and follow daily routines. He has been described as an affectionate child with a beautiful smile and a desire to relate.

Questions raised by the family and other team members can be categorized in the following areas: social interaction, communication, behavior/motivation, and program planning. Presented below is a summary response to the questions asked in each area, based on information obtained during the interdisciplinary assessment process, with key recommendations described.

Social Interaction

1. How can social/pragmatic interventions be consistently and effectively implemented across school and home settings?
2. How do we provide appropriate social supports?

Based on record reviews, interviews, and observations done both at home and at school, social interaction has been identified as an area in need of program development. It has also been determined that Jay is interested and eager to engage with others and is in need of consistent support in order to do that successfully. Currently, his social supports are adults. He responds well to verbal prompting by adults to interact with his peers, but this verbal scaffolding is inconsistent throughout his day. Also, when he does attempt to interact, it has been noted that his peers are often unsure of how to respond. In order to develop his social interaction skills, consistent programming across all environments is critical. Action plans on how to develop this programming are outlined below.

• *Scaffolding.* Clear and specific social interaction goals need to be identified and written into Jay's IEP. These goals need to be measurable and relevant to his everyday activities. Videotaped information needs to be obtained of his interactions with social supports in place. Video should be of both successful and unsuccessful interactions at home and at school. Successful interactions should be shared with all those involved in his programming. The purpose is to provide team members with models of verbal scaffolding that are effective when facilitating his social interactions. These models can and should be followed by all those involved in his program and throughout his daily routine. These videos should be used as training tools as well as assessment tools so that his skills are being observed on an ongoing basis and scaffolding can be altered as necessary. Furthermore, in order for all team members to be aware of his social interaction goals and the identified intervention strategies used to address them, regular team meetings should be held. The purpose of these meetings should be to collaborate on strategies for providing Jay with opportunities to interact and appropriate social supports to be used across settings. The meetings should also be used as a way to monitor his progress and to identify a progression of how to continue to develop his social interaction skills. The team can also incorporate the use of pivotal response intervention

(continues)

APPENDIX 3.D

(see Koegel, Koegel, Harrower, & Carter, 1999) to support the scaffolding of social interaction goals in Jay's school environment.

• *Peer training.* For Jay to have successful interactions, it is important for his communication partners to be aware of how to respond to his attempts. His peers need to be educated on how he communicates and how they can best respond in order to keep him engaged. Classroom teaching as well as teaching to individual peers that Jay has sought out should be done in both structured and unstructured activities. This might be done through a buddy system, for which students would be carefully and sensitively guided. Jay's peers should be provided with verbal models so that they, too, have an idea of how to verbally scaffold an interaction with him.

• *Preteaching.* To expand Jay's play and increase his opportunities for social interactions, it is important to model roles that he may take on in various social routines. Preteaching, including the use of social stories, should be used to script social interaction routines for him to follow. He should be provided with opportunities to follow modeled interactions on an individual basis. Once he is clear on how to follow these routines, he should be provided with opportunities to follow them in a group setting with peers. We also recommend that preteaching be done to provide him with instruction on games that include a variety of emotional themes.

Communication

1. How do we continue to support Jay's language development?
2. Does he require more speech and language intervention?
3. What is the best means to communicate with him?

Jay is a verbal communicator. He is talking in whole sentences and is participating verbally in group activities. He consistently demonstrates verbal initiation skills with peers and adults during unstructured activities. He can respond to verbal communications, appropriately demonstrating comprehension of spoken language. When he is able to verbalize his wants and needs, his frustration level decreases, which then positively affects his behavior. He responds extremely well to verbal prompting and modeling from adults. He needs to be provided with consistent support in the area of communication throughout his daily routine. We recommend that the model of how speech–language services are provided be modified so that Jay is consistently receiving opportunities to use and improve his verbal language skills. Suggestions of how best to meet this need are outlined below in three key categories.

• *Education and environment.* Jay's teacher and instructional assistant need to be educated by the speech–language pathologist on when and how to scaffold situations verbally so that Jay is required to use his verbal communication skills. Videotaping should be done of successful scaffolding to demonstrate for parents and school staff. We recommend that training of parents and staff occur so that Jay's kindergarten

(continues)

APPENDIX 3.D

environment can be arranged to set up frequent communication situations. For instance, preferred activities or materials might be placed out of his reach so that he needs to use his language to request them. This intervention strategy can be set up to occur throughout his school day and at home. In addition, both parents and school staff should be instructed on the consistent use of "wait time" to facilitate Jay's verbal initiations and responses.

• *Preteaching.* As discussed under "Social Interaction," we recommend preteaching to prime Jay for participation in a variety of communication exchanges. Prior to structured activities introduced in the classroom, he should be taught verbal scripts that will allow him to engage successfully in the activity. To support his success, he should also be taught rules for games, closings, openings, and other verbal responses related to the activity that's about to take place. Communication strategies to increase successful interactions with peers should also be pretaught. We recommend that Jay's home-school journal be formatted to include information that can be used to help in the preteaching process, specifically around classroom sharing and headline news.

• *Peer training.* We recommend that Jay's peers be trained on how to respond to his interactions, as stated. They should be provided with models of how to maintain a communication interaction with him. In addition, it is important to surround Jay with peers who use more verbal language. For example, at his snack table, provide him with a seating assignment that would expose him to numerous communication opportunities with good language models. Also, we suggest that a peer buddy participate in his structured language instruction.

Behavior/Motivation

1. How do we address Jay's aggressive behaviors toward others?
2. How do we encourage him to work independently and be satisfied with his own work?
3. How do we encourage and increase his willingness to try new things, specifically things we already know are hard for him?

Jay behaves aggressively when he is frustrated or is required to share both attention and materials. There is currently no formal behavior plan in place for him at home or at school. Time-out, "no," verbal consequences, and a firm tone of voice are used to address his behavior. When tasks or transitions are unfamiliar, he often refuses to try them or walks away. He responds well to visual cues and supports and modeling to follow daily routines. Once familiar with an activity or routine, he increases his participation overall. The following recommendations have been identified to improve the management of his behavior:

• *Preventive strategies.* Provide Jay with a daily picture board that represents the classroom schedule, including specials and services that are part of his individualized program. His behavior plan should be adjusted so that it builds on the school's policy of the responsive classroom. As a prevention strategy, it is

(continues)

APPENDIX 3.D

important to identify and acknowledge Jay's attempts to regulate his own behavior. For example, when he is able to ask for help when frustrated, as opposed to responding aggressively, verbal acknowledgment and praise should be given. Another prevention strategy is to recognize his possible motor limitations in completing projects. Projects can be modified for his partial participation so that he is successful. Also, the format recommended above for the home–school journal should include a section for information to be provided on his behaviors at home and at school. This information allows for the opportunity to identify social stories that can be used to assist him in successful interactions.

• *What to do when an aggressive behavior occurs.* We recommend that a formal written behavior plan be developed through the collaboration of parents and school staff. The plan should be related to Jay's IEP goals, which are measurable and reviewed on a regular basis. We suggest that the plan use phrases from home that Jay has heard his parents use and that he will frequently respond to. Therefore, when an aggressive behavior occurs, the adult responses will be consistent across home and school environments. It is also important that the formal behavior plan include any consequences that the school already has in place that Jay is able to relate to (e.g., thinking chair, time-out). When any consequences are used, whether at home or at school, it is imperative that Jay has a clear understanding of what the consequence means and why he is receiving it. For example, if his consequence is a time-out, team members need to be clear with him as to whether he is having a time-out because he has been aggressive toward another person or taking a break from an activity because he is noticeably frustrated. However the consequence is going to be used, it needs to be written out clearly in the plan, and it needs to be consistently implemented across all school and home settings.

Program Planning

1. How much should we expect from Jay?
2. What are appropriate kindergarten goals for him this year?

Jay is currently following the kindergarten routine with adult support. It is reported that when he becomes frustrated or fatigued, alternative activities are pursued by his instructional assistant. Morning activities have been identified as more successful for him than afternoon activities due to fatigue. His limited endurance affects his ability to engage consistently throughout the day. When he is away from school for a day or two, he is observed to have difficulty reestablishing himself into the daily routine. His difficulty with transitions and communication currently affects how much he engages in the kindergarten curriculum. Listed below are program recommendations intended to help parents and school staff provide for him so that he is working to his potential.

• *Scheduled team meetings.* Regularly scheduled team meetings should be established so that intervention strategies can be communicated across contexts and settings and used consistently across

(continues)

APPENDIX 3.D

all environments. Meetings should include all individuals involved in Jay's program. Meetings need to be scheduled at a time that is convenient for both school staff and family members.

- *Home–school journal.* As mentioned in the previous three categories, a home–school journal format should be established so that all target intervention areas can be commented on daily. This format should also allow for Jay's parents to be informed of his schedule from week to week.

- *Daily schedule.* A daily picture schedule should be developed and used consistently. Included in the schedule should be a designated time for Jay to rest in order to avoid fatigue. Also included in his schedule should be a time for speech–language teaching to be done when Jay is engaged in a motor activity. This will allow for teaching to occur at a time when he has been observed to be the most verbal. We recommend that speech–language support occur two to three times a week.

- *Curriculum.* The curriculum for kindergarten and first-grade students should be reviewed to identify areas that the team can appropriately target for Jay and, given his current skill level, expect him to master.

- *Transition planning.* A plan for Jay's transition from kindergarten to first grade should begin to be established. It is important that all those involved in his current program think about how to educate and prepare future team members on his needs as a student. The sooner this plan is in place, the smoother the transition will be. It is also recommended that a plan for summer programming be established. Again, the purpose is to identify and educate those who will be involved in Jay's program on his strengths as well as his challenges. We also recommend that a transition plan be put in place to cover any time that Jay's primary providers are unavailable (e.g., absence, maternity leave). This will allow programming to remain consistent regardless of who the provider may be.

- *Computer.* A computer should be available for Jay's use. The purpose is to provide him with a tool for early writing and art, as these have been identified as areas of frustration for him due to possible motor difficulties. The computer has also been identified as an area of high interest for Jay, which may help motivate him to participate in written activities.

If you have any questions or comments regarding this report or the recommendations made, please don't hesitate to contact the assessment coordinator.

Addendum

A follow-up meeting was held with the VT-RAP team, the family, and the school team on November 30, 2005. At that time, the team, including the family, made changes to the drafted assessment summary, discussed updated information on Jay, and developed action plans for implementing the recommendations.

(continues)

APPENDIX 3.D

The action plans are outlined below under each question/category that was targeted during the assessment process. Updates discussed at the follow-up meeting are also summarized.

Physical Therapy

Physical therapist (PT) saw Jay because he had been fitted for orthotics but won't wear them. PT provided recommendations for gym at school, but parents wonder if Jay needs direct service from a PT. Parents might consider a PT evaluation from a person with expertise in pediatrics and children with special health needs. Consultation from a PT might be considered once every 6 weeks. PT suggested that Jay have a sensory program in place on a daily basis.

Action Plan

1. OT will meet with parents and instructional assistant to set up a daily sensory program for Jay.
2. OT will also discuss a strength and endurance program.
3. Parents may wish to pursue further evaluation for strength and endurance through another PT.

Health

Mrs. Jones reported that Jay has a persistent cough and worries about pneumonia. She asked if the school nurse could listen to his lungs, since his primary health care provider is on vacation.

Action Plan

1. SLP will talk with the nurse upon return to school and ask her to listen to Jay's lungs.
2. Special educator will request reports/checklists from school psychologist to be given to parents and the VT-RAP team.

Speech–Language Programming

Transitioning Jay from SLP's caseload to a new SLP has been initiated. They have done therapy in the new SLP's room, and she has been present periodically to help him become more comfortable.

Recommendation Categories

Social Interaction Action Plans

1. Special educator, in collaboration with parents, will develop social storybook to prepare for Jay's transition to first grade.
2. Individual speech–language therapy will be used to prepare Jay for novel social interactions and to introduce social stories.
3. IA will have available a picture schedule for those daily activities in which Jay is participating.
4. Strategies will be brainstormed by the team to get video camera access at home and school.
5. Team will determine how often videotaping will be done.

(continues)

APPENDIX 3.D

Communication Action Plans

1. IA will attend Jay's individual speech–language therapy.
2. At their regular team meetings, team will begin to examine what aspect of the curriculum Jay is participating in, what modifications are being made or are needed, and how progress is being measured.

Behavior/Motivation Action Plan

1. Team members will talk about their understanding and use of time-out at home and school. Currently, Jay's mom uses a time-out clock, which seems to work. She has consistently used the phrase "time-out" so Jay is clear on expectations and behavioral consequences.
2. The school will work to maintain consistent use of the phrase and the environment for time-out. This should be different from "taking a break."
3. Mom would also like the team to map out the emotions that go with the behavior. The team will formalize the process for time-out versus taking a break at a team meeting.

Program Planning Action Plans

1. *Team meetings:* Special educator will schedule a team meeting to discuss a consistent schedule and agenda for meetings to ensure implementation of an effective program. This meeting will include the IA, SLP, OT, case manager, classroom teacher, and family.
2. *Home–school journal:* Special educator will format a framework for sharing information about Jay's day to be sent home. It will follow the format she recently shared with the family.
3. *Curriculum:* The team will review the language-based curriculum analysis (LBCA) to examine the curriculum expectations and the likely breakdowns, considering Jay's challenges, as well as modifications that could be considered. The VT-RAP team will provide the framework and an article explaining the LBCA process.

APPENDIX 3.D

Sample Report B
Interdisciplinary Consultation Summary

Child's name: _Sammy Smith_   Date of birth: _7/17/01_

Parents: _Darlene and Joe Smith_   Chronological age: _3 years 6 months_

Address: _10 Main Street_   School: _Catamount Preschool_

Phone: _555-1111_   Referral source: _Mike Davis, special educator_

Consultation date: _1/15/05, 2/4/05, 2/11/05_

Vermont Rural Autism Project Team

Assessment coordinator

Speech–language pathology

Developmental pediatrics

Psychology

Early childhood special education

Family support

Primary Health Care Provider

Name: _Steven Brown, MD_

Address: _5 Pine Street_

Phone: _555-3333_

Case Manager

Name: _Mike Davis_

Address: _2 Catamount Drive_

Phone: _555-8888_

Background Information

Sammy Smith, a 3-year 6-month-old boy was referred for a Vermont Rural Autism assessment within his home and preschool environments. Sammy presently lives with his mother, father, and older brother. He currently attends play dates two afternoons per week with case manager, classroom teacher, physical therapist, and occupational therapist. He receives speech–language services three times a week from a speech–language pathologist, plus consultation for occupational therapy and physical therapy in his home environment. Family is awaiting approval of additional services (e.g., respite care, personal care, and flexible funding) through the county mental health program.

According to parental report, Sammy's pregnancy and birth history were unremarkable. He weighed 7 pounds 3 ounces at birth. Mother noted an unusual cry that sounded like a squeal.

Sammy experienced numerous health complications during his first year of life. He was diagnosed with hydrocephalus at 8 weeks, and a subsequent MRI showed partial agenesis of the inferior part of the cerebellar vermis and hydrocephalus. He was shunted on November 10, 2002.

Sammy also had a series of seizures at 6 months of age. He was treated with phenobarbital 30 mg, and seizures discontinued by March of 2003. A recent EEG showed no epileptiform discharges, although some concern persists about possible subtle seizure activity.

(continues)

APPENDIX 3.E

Sammy's health has been within normal limits, except for two ear infections by the age of 2. Parents questioned his hearing because of his inability to speak and respond when spoken to as a toddler. He also becomes annoyed by a noisy environment and appears to hear less well in noise. Hearing has been tested, and results are within normal limits. Parents noted that he sleeps excessively (11 hours at night and a 3-hour nap during the day) and has had several vomiting episodes/illnesses throughout his life.

Sammy's developmental history has not followed the typical pattern. In the past 6 months, he has begun making sounds and producing single words (e.g., "go," and "eee" for "delicious"). Mrs. Smith believes that he does not understand what is said sometimes, but he will not indicate that he does not understand. He has not yet begun to talk and has an unusual voice quality. He tries hard to communicate and has begun to incorporate pointing into his communication. During the past few months, he has started taking an adult's hand, bringing the adult to where he wants to go. He'll express frustration by screaming and throwing himself onto the floor. Parents feel that he has some real behavioral issues. They believe that this may be because he has difficulty communicating. He has to be watched every minute, because he climbs on everything, unsafely, and constantly has things in his mouth. Parents also reported that transitions are extremely difficult for him. He prefers to interact with adults on a one-on-one basis and does not play with other children. He loves picture books, peek-a-boo games, cars and trucks. He explores objects by mouthing them.

The purpose of the Vermont Rural Autism Project assessment is to assess Sammy's health, development, communicative functioning, and educational needs to establish an intervention plan to help develop self-care skills and to confirm a diagnosis of Autism Spectrum Disorder. Both parents would like to gain a clearer picture of what Sammy's development will be like, how he'll function later in life, whether he'll be independent, and what the future may hold.

Assessment Summary and Recommendations

A variety of methods were used to assess the strengths and challenges of Sammy and his home and school environments. These included record review, interviews with family members and community providers, observations, and direct interaction with Sammy. [Summaries of the actual interviews, observations, and record review could be attached as appendices.] The questions raised by the family and by community providers are organized by category. The results of the assessment are integrated from the observations made, interviews completed, and records reviewed to answer each question. Priority recommendations are offered under each category and set of questions.

Sammy is a caring, loving 3-year-old who has a strong attachment to his parents. He is a keen observer, appears to have strong visual skills, and has a good memory for settings, recognizing people and toys. He knows what he likes and dislikes. He has good physical and motor skills and is adept at jumping and climbing. He loves repetitive play, routines, and block building. He has a contagious laugh. He is very methodical within his activities. Attention skills are inconsistent, but he can attend to a favorite movie for an extended

(continues)

APPENDIX 3.E

period. He will hide under his bed and in between pillows, and he will hug his mom to help himself calm down when he's overstimulated.

Sammy is challenged by limited communication skills. He is currently at the early linguistic stage of language development, using just a few single words (e.g., "go"). His use of these words is inconsistent. He has recently begun to indicate his wants and needs, mainly through nonverbal means, by manipulating an adult's hand or body and by reaching. He has limited use of other conventional gestures, though he is beginning to point. When he is frustrated or upset and unable to express his feelings verbally, he becomes aggressive toward his brother and will sometimes bite. His verbalizations are becoming more frequent and have intonation, which suggests that he is attempting to talk, though most of his babbling is difficult to understand. His comprehension level is unknown.

Sammy does not know how to organize himself or his environment to get what he wants and needs. He has many sensory challenges and is constantly active. He appears to have intermittent gastrointestinal and digestive difficulties, and his diet is rigid. He is not aware of safety issues and will run or climb onto unsafe structures.

Referral Questions

Several questions were raised by the parents and other team members, which are categorized in three areas: diagnosis, intervention, and prognosis; medical; and communication. A summary follows of the responses to the questions asked in each area, based on information obtained during the interdisciplinary assessment process, with key recommendations.

Diagnosis, Intervention, and Prognosis

1. Does Sammy fall on the Autism Spectrum?
2. What kind of treatment programs would be most appropriate for him and at what intensity?
3. What kind of prognosis can be made for him in the future? What would be appropriate goals to set for him? Will he be able to develop independent skills?

Based on record reviews, interviews, observations, and results of DSM–IV consultation and the *Childhood Autism Rating Scale* (CARS), the team has determined that Sammy currently meets the criteria for Autistic Disorder. He demonstrated marked impairment in the use of multiple nonverbal behaviors such as eye-to-eye gaze, facial expression, body postures, and gestures to regulate social interaction. It is important to note that he did demonstrate some eye-to-eye gaze when interacting with his mother. His spontaneous attempts to share enjoyment, interests, or achievements were restricted, but he occasionally demonstrated emotional reciprocity when things were working for him. He obtained a 37 out of 60 on the CARS, which placed him in the category for autism.

(continues)

APPENDIX 3.E

Sammy demonstrated little spoken language at the time of the assessment, and it was reported that he uses only about five words. He did not demonstrate any stereotyped or repetitive use of language, but he had a habit of putting items in his mouth. He lacked varied, spontaneous make-believe or social imitative play appropriate for his developmental level.

It should be noted that Sammy's scores have improved dramatically since the protocols were first used to make the diagnosis of Autism November 2, 2004. It is not uncommon for children on the Autism Spectrum to be at different points on the spectrum as they progress through different stages of development. Thus, this diagnosis is made with caution, recognizing that as Sammy acquires skills, he may stop meeting the criteria for a technical diagnosis at some point and then meet them again at another point. The criteria for his diagnosis should be reviewed annually. It should also be noted that he has physiological issues, which do have behavioral effects.

Sammy's prognosis is positive, considering the number of skills he has acquired in the past 6 months; his solid performance on motor, flexibility, and functional skills; and his strong attachment to both of his parents. Though it is impossible to predict exactly how his development will progress, his positive response to a variety of interventions indicates that improvement will continue and that he should continue to acquire functional and language skills.

Treatment Approaches

Three general approaches to the treatment of individuals with Autism have been described in the literature (Heflin & Simpson, 1998). The first is a relationship-based approach. Greenspan and Wieder's (1998, 2001) floor time approach, in which the adult establishes engagement, builds two-way communication with the child, shares meaning, and facilitates social-emotional thinking, is one example that has been used with young children on the Autism Spectrum. The benefit of using a relationship treatment approach is that many children with marked impairments in social interactions need to have an adult scaffold their social and emotional environment so that they can learn how to develop and use those skills.

A second approach to treatment is skill based. This approach includes specific methods or strategies that have been used to develop a particular skill or achieve a desired outcome in a child with Autism (e.g., Picture Exchange Communication System, or PECS (Bondy & Frost, 1994, 1998); social stories; applied behavioral analysis). The benefit of using a skill-based intervention approach is that skills can be explicitly taught and generalized into other environments over time.

The third intervention approach encompasses alternative strategies. This includes such things as specific diets and treatment affecting the sensory system (e.g., gluten-free diet, sensory integration, auditory integration). The potential benefit of these alternative strategies is indicated by case studies and anecdotal reports of gains in attention, focus, and desired behavior for some children with Autism.

(continues)

APPENDIX 3.E

Based on observations made and parental reports, it is thought that Sammy would benefit from a combination of treatment approaches.

Recommendations

1. Early intervention is recommended, but it is important to take into account what the family and child need. Sammy should receive intensive intervention for up to 20 to 30 hours weekly. This therapy should include relationship-based intervention (e.g., floor time techniques, as described by Greenspan and Wieder [1998, 2001]), skill-based intervention (e.g., discrete trial training, pivotal response techniques, joint action routines, and PECS), and alternative interventions (e.g., sensory based). These should focus on developing functional daily skills such as learning about safety, social interactions, and specific speech and language skills across environments.

2. Sammy should continue to attend and participate in preschool as part of his intervention program.

3. Occupational and physical therapy services should continue to be provided. They should include a sensory "diet" and sensory interventions that can be offered to Sammy several times a day across settings.

Medical

1. Are Sammy's digestive system and absorption system functioning properly?

2. What gastrointestinal medical assessments would help answer why he suffers from constipation, diarrhea, and stomach cramping?

3. Is medication a good or bad option for behavior management?

4. Will Sammy always be texturally challenged when it comes to food?

Based on interviews, record reviews, and observations, Sammy's overall health is good. It should be noted that he has physiological differences that may or may not be affecting some of his behavioral challenges and his gastrointestinal difficulties. Research has shown an association between Autism and cerebellar defects, and Autism and an enlargement of the fourth ventricle. Dandy-Walker malformation has also been known to have a range of delayed developments associated with it. Research studies have further shown that some children with shunts suffer chronic constipation, as the shunts drain spinal fluid from the ventricles into the abdomen. Pseudo-cysts may develop around the shunt and cause abdominal pain in approximately 5% of children who have been shunted. Sammy's stools are frequently coated with blood, according to parental report. Currently, he is drinking about 40 ounces of milk a day, with a low fiber intake, which may be contributing to his constipation.

(continues)

APPENDIX 3.E

Recommendations

1. It is suggested that follow-up occur with a neurologist to rule out problems associated with Sammy's shunt.
2. It is strongly recommended that Sammy have another GI evaluation and ultrasound to help determine the etiology of his gastrointestinal and constipation issues and to rule out celiac disease, even though it is not usually associated with constipation, and anemia, given his blood loss and the iron content in milk.
3. A specific bowel regime should be implemented to help control Sammy's constipation with the help of his primary care physician, Dr. Stafford.
4. Further assessment of Sammy's micronutrient intake should be addressed by the community nutritionist after his GI consultation.
5. Before his parents decide to consider a casein-free diet or other specialized diet, they are cautioned to check on the cause of his constipation.
6. Introduction of new foods or textures should be presented slowly with help from the OT. It is possible that Sammy may always be a "picky eater," along with a lot of other typically developing children.
7. Behavior medication is not recommended at this time. It is thought that once relationship-based, skill-based, and alternative treatments (sensory based) are implemented, Sammy's behaviors will become better regulated. Children without language often can't express their wants and needs, causing behavior difficulties. Stimulant medications have been known to increase seizures, and the effects of those medications on the development of the neurochemistry of the brain are unknown.

Communication

1. Will Sammy ever be able to formulate words correctly or speak so that others will understand him?
2. What can we do in his environment to help him make sense of the world, to better regulate himself, and to communicate his wants and needs more successfully?
3. How does Sammy interpret language?
4. Will he understand danger (threats to life and limb)?
5. Will he be able to interact with other kids?

Sammy's play and language skills are below those expected for children his age, based on record review, observations, and careful functional analysis of his play and language use through the *Communication and Symbolic Behavior Scales (CSBS)* and *Childhood Autism Rating Scale (CARS)*. Most of his scores on the CSBS fell within the 23rd to 32nd percentile for his age, placing him at the 12- to 15-month age level. He obtained a 37 out of 60 on the CARS, placing him with fellow children who have challenges related to Autism Spectrum Disorder. Since intervention was initiated 18 months ago, many new skills have emerged, such as pointing, requesting by reaching, and manipulation of an adult's hand. Sammy has acquired a few single-word approximations (e.g., "cracker," "go") and has used several multiple syllables, indicating an awareness

(continues)

APPENDIX 3.E

of the flow of language. He has also demonstrated a few instances of social interaction and joint attention. Nonetheless, these communication attempts are frequently muddled by lack of gaze shift between the object and the adult. Language comprehension is a particular area of concern, since Sammy responds to few simple directions without visual or contextual cues. He is at the initial stages of symbolic play. His attention span is usually fleeting but can last up to 10 minutes if he is highly engaged with a specific object (e.g., movie, car toys). He uses complex motor schemes (crumples, swings, tears, etc.) to accommodate the characteristics of particular objects. He also pays visual attention to objects and is able to manipulate them in an exploratory manner, such as turning them around and touching various protuberances on an object. He is an observant child, is beginning to respond to visual cues, enjoys social time with his parents, is interested in other children, and imitates actions within familiar routines. These strengths can be capitalized on to improve other communication and play skills.

Recommendations

1. A resource notebook will be compiled for the family and the preschool team that includes information about a sequence of developmental skills in the area of verbal communication, symbolic play, and social interactions, both for typically developing children and for children with Autism. Using these as milestones and comparing them with Sammy's developmental pattern will help answer questions about his prognosis.

2. An augmentative communication consultation (AAC) is suggested. Augmentative means of communication could be useful to Sammy to enhance his ability to express his wants and needs. They may also assist in his understanding of the world.

3. Continue using a total communication system at school and at home. The use of the Picture Exchange Communication System should be implemented at both home and school to provide Sammy with a method for requesting his wants through a communicative picture exchange with an adult communication partner. Research suggests that 67% of children with Autism who have successfully used PECS have begun using verbal language (Bondy & Frost, 1994, 1998). In addition, PECS includes a social component that will help support social interactions. It is designed so that it can be used across several contexts and with a variety of communication partners, including peers. It is also appropriate to begin PECS using photographs and objects, if pictures are too abstract for Sammy.

4. Scaffolding (supporting and facilitating expansion of a child's development step by step) a variety of situations across environments will help Sammy make sense of the world. This can be done by both adults and peers and will help to increase his communication and social skills.

(continues)

APPENDIX 3.E

5. It is highly recommended that the preschool and home environments use schedule boards throughout Sammy's day. This will help him to understand and recognize his routine and the transitions from one activity or event to the next.

Action Planning

To help the family and the preschool implement these recommendations, the RAP team will prepare a resource notebook for the family and the preschool team to be used with Sammy. The RAP team will also help implement the recommendations made in this report during the summer program. The RAP team will help the family develop schedule boards and visual cues to be used at home. In addition, the RAP team will help train family members to use PECS to help support and stimulate Sammy's verbal language. The RAP team will help the family and the preschool team decide how best to use a personal care attendant and respite funding. A follow-up meeting will occur on March 22, 2005, to assess implementation of the team's recommendations and follow through with other questions or concerns at that time.

If you have any questions or comments regarding this report or the recommendations made, please don't hesitate to contact the assessment coordinator.

Practice Opportunities

1. Reexamine how you carry out team meetings for children with ASD. Consider instituting the following:

   a. establish roles for each of your meetings,

   b. define rules and norms for participation in meetings and put them on chart paper for everyone to see and follow, and

   c. create an agenda format that consistently works for the team.

2. Complete a genogram and ecomap for a child with or suspected of ASD whom you are currently working with or will be involved in assessing. Use these tools to keep the team cognizant of the family context and of current and potential resources for supporting the child's and family's needs.

3. Brainstorm and identify three things you can do as an assessment team to ensure that families are an integral part of your assessment process. Include families in this brainstorming to get their perspective about reasonable ways they could and would like to be involved in the assessment process.

4. Using the WHO disablement framework described in this chapter, identify areas of assessment for a child with ASD that consider the three dimensions of impairment, activity, and participation.

5. During an interview with a family member regarding their child with or suspected of ASD, incorporate the use of grand tour and mini tour questions to get a clear understanding of a particular problem area.

Suggested Readings

Pena, E. D. (1996). Dynamic assessment: The model and its language applications. In K. N. Cole, P. S. Dale, & D. J. Thal (Eds.), *Assessment of communication and language* (pp. 281–307). Baltimore: Brookes.

In this chapter, Pena defines dynamic assessment and how that approach to assessment provides valuable information for intervention planning. Strategies for using that assessment approach in a valid and reliable manner are also discussed. Pena describes the specific role that dynamic assessment can and should have in examining a child's language understanding and use.

Prelock, P. A., Beatson, J., Contompasis, S., & Bishop, K. K. (1999). A model for family-centered interdisciplinary practice in the community. *Topics in Language Disorders, 19*, 36–51.

This article explains the key principles for interdisciplinary practice. Using child and family stories, a model for family-centered assessment is presented that has been field tested during interactions with several families that have children with special needs.

Westby, C. E. (1990). Ethnographic interviewing: Asking the right questions to the right people in the right ways. *Journal of Childhood Communication Disorders, 13,* 101–111.

This article describes the results of research related to question asking with different cultural groups. It defines the kinds of questions that lead to gaining the information needed through interviews. It also provides several examples of question-asking techniques that facilitate building rapport, open communication, trust, and respect.

Resources

Prelock, P. A. (1999). *Serving children with Autism Spectrum Disorders & their families: Strategies for assessment, treatment, & curriculum planning* (4-hour videotape and manual). ASHA Products, 800/498-6699, http://www.asha.org/shop

Wetherby, A. M., & Prizant, B. M. (1996). *Autism Spectrum Disorders: New service delivery models for nonverbal children* (2-hour audiotape and manual). ASHA Products, 800/498-6699, http://www.asha.org/shop

Glossary

Activity. One of the three dimensions of the ICF; refers to the whole person.

Dynamic assessment. Gathering structured and systematic observations within functional context-bound activities across several settings on an ongoing basis.

Ecological assessment. An approach to assessment that provides information about the environmental variables that influence a child's performance and the particular skills needed in specific contexts.

Ecomap. Paper-and-pencil simulation that maps a family's ecological system.

Genogram. Format used for drawing a family tree that records information about family members and their relationships over at least three generations.

Grand tour questions. Used in interviews to probe descriptions of broad experiences or events.

ICF. *International Classification of Functioning, Disability and Health;* revision of the *International Classification of Impairments, Disabilities and Handicaps;* a classification of disablement that defines the consequences of health condition across the dimensions of impairment, activity, and participation.

Impairment. One of the three dimensions of the ICF; refers to the body structure and function.

Medical model. View of disablement as person related, caused by a health condition that requires individual treatment.

Mini tour questions. Used in interviews to probe descriptions of specific activities or events.

Participation. One of the three dimensions of the ICF; refers to the individual's involvement in life activities on the societal level.

Social model. View of disablement that sees health conditions as society's problem, with a goal of integrating individuals with disabilities into society.

References

Andrews, A. B. (1990). Interdisciplinary and interorganizational collaboration. In G. Ginsberg, S. Khinduka, J. A. Hall, F. Ross-Sheriff, & A. Hartman (Eds.), *Encyclopedia of social work* (pp. 175–188). Silver Springs, MD: National Association of Social Work Press.

Bauer, A. M., & Murphy, E. S. (1990, Fall/Winter). Teachers, teacher educators, researchers, and students: Communities of learners. *HEARSAY: Journal of the Ohio Speech and Hearing Association,* pp. 88–90.

Beatson, J. E., & Prelock, P. A. (2002). The Vermont Rural Autism Project: Sharing experiences, shifting attitudes. *Focus on Autism & Other Developmental Disabilities, 17*(1), 48–54.

Bondy, A. S., & Frost, L. A. (1994). The Picture Exchange Communication System. *Focus on Autistic Behavior, 9*(3), 1–19.

Bondy, A. S., & Frost, L. A. (1998). The Picture Exchange Communication System. *Seminars in Speech and Language, 19*(4), 373–388.

Brewer, E. J., McPherson, M., Magrab, P. R., & Hutchins, V. L. (1989). Family-centered, community-based, coordinated care for children with special health care needs. *Pediatrics, 83,* 1055–1060.

Coonrod, E. E., & Stone, W. L. (2004). Early concerns of parents of children with autistic and nonautistic disorders. *Infants and Young Children, 17*(1), 258–268.

Diehl, S. F. (2003). The SLP's role in collaborative assessment and intervention for children with ASD. *Topics in Language Disorders, 23*(2), 95–115.

Dunst, C. J., Trivette, C. M., & Deal, A. (1988). *Enabling and empowering families.* Cambridge, MA: Brookline Books.

Feuerstein, R., Rand, Y., Jensen, M. R., Kaniel, S., & Tzuriel, D. (1987). Prerequisites for assessment of learning potential: The LPAD model. In C. S. Lidz (Ed.), *Dynamic assessment: An interactional approach to evaluating learning potential* (pp. 35–51). New York: Guilford Press.

Filer, J. D., & Mahoney, G. J. (1996). Collaboration between families and early intervention service providers. *Infants and Young Children, 9,* 22–30.

Giangreco, M. F., Cloninger, C. J., Dennis, R. E., & Edelman, S. W. (2000). Problem solving methods to facilitate inclusive education. In R. A. Villa & J. S. Thousand (Eds.), *Restructuring for caring and effective education: Piecing the puzzle together* (2nd ed., pp. 293–327). Baltimore: Brookes.

Giangreco, M. F., Cloninger, C. J., & Iverson, V. S. (1998). *Choosing outcomes and accommodations for children: A guide to educational planning for students with disabilities* (2nd ed.). Baltimore: Brookes.

Gilliam, J. E. (1995). *Gilliam Autism Rating Scale.* Austin, TX: PRO-ED.

Greenspan, S. I., & Wieder, S. (1998). *The child with special needs: Encouraging intellectual and emotional growth.* Reading, MA: Addison-Wesley.

Greenspan, S., & Wieder, S. (2001). *Floor time techniques and the DIR model: For children and families with special needs.* Bethesda, MD: ICDL Publications.

Haney, M., & Cavallaro, C. C. (1996). Using ecological assessment in daily program planning for children with disabilities in typical preschool settings. *Topics in Early Childhood Special Education, 16*(1), 66–81.

Hartman, A., & Laird, J. (1983). *Family-centered social work practice.* New York: Free Press.

Heflin, L. J., & Simpson, R. L. (1998). Interventions for children and youth with autism: Prudent choices in a world of exaggerated claims and empty promises. Part I: Intervention and treatment option review. *Focus on Autism and Other Developmental Disabilities, 13,* 194–211.

Johnson, A., & Lindschau, A. (1996). Staff attitudes toward parent participation in the care of children who are hospitalized. *Pediatric Nursing, 22,* 99–102.

Koegel, L. K., Koegel, R. L., Harrower, J. K., & Carter, C. M. (1999). Pivotal response intervention I: Overview of approach. *Journal of the Association of Persons with Severe Handicaps, 24,* 174–185.

Krug, D. A., Arick, J. R., & Almond, P. J. (1993). *Autism Behavior Checklist.* Austin, TX: PRO-ED.

Lidz, C. S. (1987). *Dynamic assessment: An interactional approach to evaluating learning potential.* New York: Guilford Press.

Lidz, C. S. (1991). *Practitioner's guide to dynamic assessment.* New York: Guilford Press.

Lord, C., & Risi, S. (2000). Early diagnosis in children with autism spectrum disorders. *Advocate, 33,* 23–26.

Lord, C., Rutter, M., DiLavore, P. C., & Risi, S. (1999). *Autism Diagnostic Observation Schedule–Generic.* Los Angeles: Western Psychological Services.

McGoldrick, M., & Gerson, R. (1985). *Genograms in family assessment.* New York: Norton.

McGoldrick, M., Gerson, R., & Shellenberger, S. (1999). *Genograms: Assessment and intervention* (2nd ed.). New York: Norton.

Notari-Syverson, A., & Losardo, A. (1996). Assessing children's language in meaningful contexts. In K. N. Cole, P. S. Dale, & D. J. Thal (Eds.), *Assessment of communication and language* (pp. 257–280). Baltimore: Brookes.

O'Brien, J., Forest, M., Snow, J., & Hasbury, D. (1989). *Action for inclusion.* Toronto, Ontario: Frontier College Press.

Osborn, A. F. (1993). *Applied imagination: Principles and procedures of creative problem solving* (3rd ed.). Buffalo, NY: Creative Education Foundation Press. (Original work published 1953)

Parnes, S. J. (1985). *A facilitating style of leadership.* Buffalo, NY: Bearly Limited in association with the Creative Education Foundation.

Parnes, S. J. (1988). *Visionizing: State-of-the-art processes for encouraging innovative excellence.* East Aurora, NY: D.O.K.

Parnes, S. J. (Ed.). (1992). *Source book for creative problem solving: A fifty year digest of proven innovation processes.* Buffalo, NY: Creative Education Foundation Press.

Pena, E. D. (1996). Dynamic assessment: The model and its language applications. In K. N. Cole, P. S. Dale, & D. J. Thal (Eds.), *Assessment of communication and language* (pp. 281–307). Baltimore: Brookes.

Prelock, P. A., Beatson, J., Contompasis, S., & Bishop, K. K. (1999). A model for family-centered interdisciplinary practice in the community. *Topics in Language Disorders, 19,* 36–51.

Roberts-DeGennaro, M. (1996). An interdisciplinary training model in the field of early intervention. *Social Work in Education, 18,* 20–29.

Schwartz, I. S., Boulware, G. L., McBride, B. J., & Sandall, S. R. (2001). Functional assessment strategies for young children with autism. *Focus on Autism and Other Developmental Disabilities, 16*(4), 222–227.

Shelton, T. L., Jeppson, E. S., & Johnson, B. H. (1987, September). Facilitation of parent/professional collaboration at all levels of health care. In T. L. Shelton, E. S. Jeppson,

& B. H. Johnson, *Family centered care for children with special health care needs* (pp. 3–8). Washington, DC: Association for the Care of Children's Health.

Shelton, T. L., & Stepanek, J. S. (1994, September). *Family-centered care for children needing specialized health and developmental services* (3rd ed.). Bethesda, MD: Association for the Care of Children's Health.

Spradley, J. (1979). *The ethnographic interview.* New York: Holt, Rinehart & Winston.

Turnbull, A. P., & Turnbull, H. R. (1996). Conversation guide. In A. P. Turnbull & H. R. Turnbull, *Families, professionals and exceptionality: A special partnership* (pp. 321–326). Englewood Cliffs, NJ: Prentice Hall.

Vig, S., & Kaminer, R. (2003). Comprehensive interdisciplinary evaluation as intervention for young children. *Infants & Young Children, 16*(4), 342–353.

Vincent, L. J. (1985). Family relationships. In L. J. Vincent, *Equals in this partnership: Parents of disabled and at-risk infants and toddlers speak to professionals* (pp. 33–41). Washington, DC: National Center for Clinical Infant Programs

Westby, C. E. (1990). Ethnographic interviewing: Asking the right questions to the right people in the right ways. *Journal of Childhood Communication Disorders, 13,* 101–111.

Westby, C. E. (2001, August). *New paradigms in assessment for children with autism spectrum disorders.* Presentation at the University of Nevada at Reno.

Wetherby, A. M., & Prizant, B. M. (1993). *Communication and Symbolic Behavior Scales.* Chicago: Riverside Press.

Winton, P. J. (1996). Understanding family concerns, priorities and resources. In P. J. McWilliam, P. J. Winton, & E. R. Crais (Eds.), *Practical strategies for family-centered intervention* (pp. 31–53). San Diego: Singular.

World Health Organization. (1999). *ICIDH-2: International Classification of Impairments, Disabilities and Handicaps.* Geneva, Switzerland: Author.

World Health Organization. (2001). *ICF: International Classification of Functioning, Disability and Health.* Geneva, Switzerland: Author.

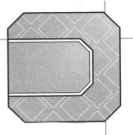

CHAPTER 4

Understanding and Assessing the Communication of Children with ASD

Patricia A. Prelock

QUESTIONS TO CONSIDER

In this chapter, you will be exposed to some of the theoretical perspectives that have been used to explain the language and communication impairments of children with autism spectrum disorders (ASD). You will also learn about the communication difficulties and pragmatic challenges that plague their ability to engage in reciprocal exchanges with their communicative partners. Profiles for assessing communication strengths and challenges will be highlighted in an effort to move you closer to an understanding of the critical connections between assessment and intervention planning. The disablement framework described in Chapter 3 will be applied to the assessment practices described for evaluating the communication skills of children and adolescents with ASD. Consider the following questions:

1. What theoretical frameworks are used to explain impairment in language and communication in children with ASD?

2. What early communication challenges are typical for children with ASD?

3. What pragmatic language challenges interfere with the ability of verbal children with ASD to engage in conversation?

4. How can communication profiles be used to assess the strengths and challenges of children with ASD in this core deficit area?

5. What areas of communication assessment should be considered across the three dimensions of the disablement framework?

Introduction

Impairment in communication is one of the core deficit areas historically associated with autism. In the *Diagnostic and Statistical Manual of Mental Disorders–Fourth Edition* (DSM–IV; American Psychiatric Association [APA], 1994) and its text revision (DSM–IV–TR; APA, 2000), communication impairment has been characterized in the following manner:

- delay in or lack of development of spoken language and gestures,
- impairment in the ability to initiate or maintain conversation,
- repetitive and idiosyncratic use of language, and
- lack of pretend play.

The central role that language and communication play in both diagnosis of and intervention for children with ASD highlights the critical role speech–language pathologists (SLPs) have in assessment. It also requires the SLP to collaborate with families and other practitioners in creating profiles of communication strengths and challenges for this population, as was discussed in Chapter 3. Further, it has been suggested that the long-term positive outcomes seen for individuals with ASD are predicted by the level of communicative competence they achieve (Garfin & Lord, 1986; McEachin, Smith, & Lovaas, 1993). It is important, therefore, to understand the communication challenges experienced by children with ASD and explore ways to effectively assess and support their needs in this area. This chapter will emphasize the descriptions of early language learning, gestural communication, and conversation that impair the ability of children and adolescents with ASD to participate fully in their home, school, and community. Aspects of imagination and play will be discussed separately in Chapter 5. Although individual chapters have been devoted to the assessment of communication, play, and social–emotional development (to be discussed in Chapter 6), it is important to recognize the interrelationships among each of these aspects of development that present challenges for children with ASD.

Theoretical Views of Language Impairment in Children with ASD

Some researchers have suggested that impairment in the development of theory of mind, which is often used to explain the social impairments in ASD, also provides a theoretical framework for explaining the language and communication impairments characteristic in ASD (Happe, 1993, 1994; Tager-Flusberg, 1993, 1996, 1997a, 1997b). Tager-Flusberg (1997a) believes that this theoretical framework can be used to explain what is and is not spared in the language of children with autism. For example, those children with ASD who develop functional language often have little difficulty with the form of language (i.e., phonology and syntax). However, their development of certain aspects of language use (i.e., pragmatics), requiring perspective taking or understanding the minds of others, is a frequent area of impairment. The failure to orient to social stimuli (Dawson, Meltzoff, Osterling, Rinaldi, & Brown, 1998) and the inability to make sense of the affective signaling in interactions, which were described in Chapter 1 as early and persistent indicators of the core deficits in ASD, are key components of communication development and perspective taking. Tager-Flusberg (1997a) suggests that the "disconnects" between language form and use in verbal children with ASD highlight the complexity among several neurocognitive mechanisms. These mechanisms involve processing linguistic information such as phonological and syntactic structures, developing conceptual structures such as semantics, and processing visual and vocal input in social contexts, as in pragmatics (Tager-Flusberg, 1997a).

In the past, researchers have also explained the acquisition of language in children with ASD as different from their typical peers (Menyuk & Quill, 1985). More recently, however, similarities in language acquisition have been observed, particularly in the development of language form (Tager-Flusberg et al., 1990). Tager-Flusberg and her colleagues found that although the development of language form was slower than that reported for children without autism, the order of and processes involved in the acquisition of syntactic and morphological structures were similar. In contrast, aspects of pragmatic language seem to be significantly delayed or fail to develop in children with ASD (Tager-Flusberg, 1997a). Thus, Tager-Flusberg proposes that a more appropriate view for understanding the language impairment seen in ASD is a dissociation between language form and use, as opposed to a deviance view. She also suggests that using a theory of mind framework for explaining the language and communication deficits identified for children with ASD supports a "connection between these aspects of autistic dysfunction and current neurobiological theories of autism" (Tager-Flusberg, 1996, p. 171).

Early Communication Challenges

Children with ASD exhibit early and persistent communication challenges (Wetherby, Prizant, & Schuler, 2000). In fact, nearly half of the children with ASD never develop speech or demonstrate limited speech and language development (Lord & Paul, 1997; Lotter, 1978). Comprehension of verbal and gestural communication is also poor for many children along the spectrum. Three specific areas of early communication challenge have been described for children with ASD, including the development of intentional communication, gesture use, and the use of unconventional verbal behavior (Camaioni, Perucchini, Muratori, & Milone, 1997; Mundy, Sigman, & Kasari, 1990; Peck & Schuler, 1987; Prizant, 1987; Prizant & Rydell, 1993; Wetherby & Prizant, 1996; Wetherby et al., 2000). Each of these warrants further discussion to aid in understanding the importance of early communication experiences and later language development in children with ASD. It is also important to recognize the heterogeneous nature and emergence of different communicative functions for children with ASD, and the potential for change in the type and degree of impairment over time (Camaioni et al., 1997).

Intentional Communication

A continuum of intentional communication development exists for children who are typically developing that begins preverbally and moves to a linguistic stage (Bates, 1976). A range of intentions have been described in the literature, from attention seeking, requesting, and greeting at the preverbal stage (Bates, Camaioni, & Volterra, 1975; Dore, 1974; Halliday, 1975; Roth & Spekman, 1984a, 1984b) to naming, commenting, and protesting at the single-word stage (Dale, 1980; Dore, 1974; Halliday, 1975; Roth & Spekman, 1984a, 1984b).

Three specific communication intentions emerge in children during their first year of life (Wetherby & Prizant, 1992). These are behavior regulation, social interaction, and joint attention. *Behavior regulation* is the use of specific acts to regulate or control the behavior of others for the purpose of obtaining something desirable. *Social interaction* involves children's use of specific acts to call attention to them, to greet another, or to sustain a social routine. *Joint attention* occurs when children initiate a communicative act that directs the attention of others for the purpose of sharing an event (Wetherby & Prizant, 1992). The communicative acts children with ASD use to signal intentional communication are more limited in function than has been reported for children who are typically developing. Unlike children who are typically developing and easily engage others in social interaction and joint attention, children on the autism spectrum generally use verbal or nonverbal means to regulate behavior to meet their immediate needs without developing the capacity for social interaction and joint attention (Wetherby, 1986).

The limited communicative functions reported for children with ASD compromise their opportunities for social engagement. In particular, deficits in the capacity for establishing joint attention highlight the lack of communication for social purposes described for children with ASD (Wetherby et al., 2000). Research suggests that joint attention emerges before words, is present in young children, predicts language development, and helps to coordinate attention between objects and people (Mundy et al., 1990; Wetherby & Prizant, 1992; Wetherby, Prizant, & Hutchinson, 1998; Wetherby et al., 2000). Further, failure to develop joint attention has been linked to limitations in play and in the development of peer relationships. Considering the critical role of joint attention in making early social and symbolic connections, it is an important target for both assessment and intervention.

Gesture Use

Gestures are used to convey information and provide a means for sharing affective experiences (Stone, Ousley, Yoder, Hogan, & Hepburn, 1997). Gestural communication develops early in children who are typically developing. This is not true of children with ASD (Buffington, Krantz, McClannahan, & Poulson, 1998; Camaioni et al., 1997; Mundy et al., 1990). In fact, children with ASD demonstrate a limited range of nonverbal behaviors (Baron-Cohen, 1988). They have been reported to use less frequent eye contact, decreased pointing to and showing of objects, and fewer gestures combined with meaningful vocalization. Curcio (1978) found that children with ASD seldom demonstrated "showing" gestures to call attention to themselves and gain the attention of another. Children with ASD have also been described as using less conventional gestures and exhibiting more primitive motoric gestures than their typical peers (Wetherby et al., 1998), as well as minimal to no expressive gestures (Stone & Caro-Martinez, 1990). In fact, the lack of gestures to establish joint attention has been identified as a predictor of language development in children with ASD (Mundy et al., 1990).

The ability to coordinate gestures with vocalizations appears to increase with age in children who are typically developing (Stone et al., 1997). In contrast, children with ASD have been reported to use a higher number of isolated gestures and a lower use of gesture plus vocalization in comparison to their typical peers (Wetherby et al., 1998). The ability to coordinate multiple nonverbal cues increases the salience and interpretation of a communicative act and increases the probability of responsiveness to the communicative attempt (Yoder, Warren, Kim, & Gazdag, 1994). Limitations in gesture use for children with ASD certainly compromise the quality of their meaningful communicative attempts.

Unconventional Verbal Behavior

Those children with ASD who are verbal often exhibit unconventional verbal behavior in the form of echolalia, perseverative speech, or excessive questioning (Prizant & Rydell, 1993). *Echolalia* is described as the repetition of exactly what is said or heard. The timing of the echoed response varies. It may be immediate, as in the following example of a 4-year-old with ASD:

FATHER: Give that to me, Joshua.
CHILD: Give that to me, Joshua.

Or the echolalia may be delayed, as in a 12-year-old saying, "Christopher, come on down," a phrase heard on a TV game show a week earlier. Children with ASD sometimes exhibit variations in echoic behaviors. This variation, known as *mitigated echolalia,* might involve a modification in the words used, the prosody of the utterance, or the context in which it occurs (Prizant,

1987). For example, if a child with ASD observes milk spilling on the kitchen floor and hears someone say, "Clean it up!" he might repeat this statement in another highly charged situation (i.e., child hears words in one situation and repeats those words in another similar situation). Mitigated echolalia also can be immediate or delayed. Prizant (1987) and Fay and Schuler (1980) suggest that it is best to consider echolalia on a continuum, as the actual repetitions made, the understanding demonstrated, and the intent of the repeated utterance vary for children on the spectrum at different points in time.

Although some researchers explain echolalia from a deficit perspective, others have attached meaning to echoic productions. At the very least, echolalia may serve a function to request, to label, or to maintain contact or take a turn with a potential communicative partner (Prizant, 1987; Prizant, Wetherby, & Rydell, 2000; Rydell & Prizant, 1995). It may also be a response to a highly aroused state, serve as an aid to comprehension, or help to regulate behavior. Prizant (1987) and Prizant and Rydell (1993) have defined several functional categories for immediate and delayed echolalia that have both interactive and noninteractive roles and can provide a framework for assessing this unconventional verbal behavior in children with ASD. Further, they have suggested that depending on the cognitive level of the individual with ASD, echolalia may be analyzed into more spontaneous and creative language forms or remain repetitive and inflexible as a memorized unit of language.

Perseverative speech is also frequently observed in verbal children with ASD (Prizant & Rydell, 1993). This type of speech is characterized by either imitated or self-generated utterances that are produced repeatedly by a child with ASD with no real evidence of intent. It has been related to an increase in arousal level, anxiety, or processing difficulties. For example, a child might say, "Come on down" repeatedly across settings after hearing it on a TV game show, with no real intent but seemingly related to heightened anxiety. In the following example, a 4½-year-old boy with autism exhibits perseverative speech in what seemed to be an unsuccessful attempt at answering a question by his mom, as well as a way to fill time as he waited for his dad to go to the market:

MOTHER: Daddy is coming back.
CHILD: Daddy, mommy, baby [as he looked to where his dad had gone and where his mom and baby brother were standing].
MOTHER: Who are you?
CHILD: Daddy, mommy, baby.
MOTHER: Taylor, what is your name?
CHILD: Daddy, mommy, baby. Father, mother, brother.
MOTHER: Very good, Taylor.
CHILD: Father, mother, brother [as he pointed to each].
MOTHER: Who are you?
CHILD: Father, mother, brother.

Kanner (1971), in his review of 11 children with autism who were first described in his 1943 study, provides an example of perseverative speech as a child finds a toy train in a closet, sets it up, and says many times as he connects and disconnects the cars: "More train—more train—more train" and then counts the train windows, "One, two windows, four windows, eight windows" (p. 133).

A third type of unconventional verbal behavior that is sometimes observed in children with ASD is *excessive questioning*. Often a child will repeatedly direct a question to a communicative partner with intent and an expectation of a response. These repeated questions usually occur following a response. Even though the answer has been provided, the child continues to ask the question, which raises the likelihood that there is a relationship to increased arousal level, anxiety, or processing difficulties. For example, a child might repeatedly say, "Jennifer coming?" in reference to a respite provider who is picking up the child with ASD after school, even though a teacher has repeatedly indicated that this would occur. Another example follows, as a 6-year-old girl with ASD questions her SLP:

> CHILD: Are you wearing a watch today?
>
> SLP: Yes, I am.
>
> CHILD: What time is it?
>
> SLP: 9:00 A.M. It is time for morning meeting.
>
> CHILD: Do you have a watch? What time is it?
>
> SLP: Do you remember what I said?
>
> CHILD: 9:00 A.M. Is it time for morning meeting? Do you have
>   a watch?

A third example is offered by Barron (2001), who describes how he used repetitive questions as a child with ASD to gain some sense of control in his life. He would repeatedly ask potential conversational partners if they had been to a particular state, and then would ask the same question about all 50 states. Once he completed that mantra of questions, he would cycle back and ask if the person had visited the capital of the state and so on.

Prizant and Rydell (1993) suggest that some excessive questioning and perseverative speech may be forms of echolalia that are facilitated by a communication partner's previous utterance or by a particular context. They also report that repeated questions and perseverative speech can be self-generated with little connection to previously heard utterances. Recognizing unconventional verbal behavior and then attempting to understand the purpose it may serve for particular children with ASD are important steps to more effective intervention planning for a child. We must identify those behaviors children with ASD use to indicate potential linguistic confusion or increasing anxiety in response to approaching a task or meeting an expectation. It may also be that some children with ASD require repeated input to map information as part of their preparation for engaging in or responding to a particular activity.

Pragmatic Challenges for Verbal Children with ASD

Over the last 30 years, researchers and practitioners have recognized the importance of considering the action component of language, or pragmatics (Bates, 1976; Dore, 1974; Ochs, 1979; Ochs & Schieffelin, 1979; Prutting, 1982; Prutting & Kirchner, 1983; Searle, 1969). *Pragmatics* is the use of language in social contexts. Searle (1969) has described language understanding and use as a speech act in which the speaker has a particular intent, the utterance selected to represent that intent has a particular meaning, and the listener interpreting the message infers a specific intent. How an individual uses words can change an event or activity and influence the direction of a conversation. Children who understand the rules for pragmatic language appropriately select the syntactic and semantic constructs needed to share their intent across a variety of contexts.

Pragmatic language difficulties have been reported as a significant area of weakness for children with ASD who have high cognitive skills, particularly children with Asperger disorder (Church, Alisanski, & Amanullah, 2000; Twachtman-Cullen, 1998). Several key features in the use of language for social purposes create problems for verbal children with ASD. These include paralinguistic features, extralinguistic features, linguistic features, and conversational features (Koegel, 1995; Twachtman, 1995; Twachtman-Cullen, 1998). Understanding each of these pragmatic components offers insight into the message and intentional communication of both the speaker and the listener in conversational exchanges. It is critical to assess these pragmatic components more carefully in the communication of children with ASD.

Paralinguistic Features

The skills speakers possess that manage their speech intelligibility and prosody are known as *paralinguistic features* of communication. Intelligible speech is critical to establishing communicative intent and maintaining listener engagement. Shriberg et al. (2001) found an increased prevalence of distortions in the speech of adolescents and adults with ASD in comparison to peers who were typically developing. They suggested that these speech distortions might indicate "a speaker's failure to attend to and/or allocate resources for fine-tuning speech production to match the model of the ambient linguistic community" (Shriberg et al., 2001, p. 1109).

The *prosody* or rhythm of speech involves intonation or an emphasis on particular words that can distinguish subtle word meanings, signal whether an interpretation should be literal or nonliteral, and add emotion. It has been reported that children with ASD often exhibit a monotone voice quality (Baltaxe & Simmons, 1985; Fay & Schuler, 1980). Many children with ASD fail to use appropriate pitch (inappropriately high or low), intensity (inappropriately loud or soft), and intonation (inappropriately flat or unusual) during conversation (Fay & Schuler, 1980; Lord & Paul, 1997). Shriberg and his colleagues (2001) completed a prosody–voice analysis with adolescents and adults with ASD compared to those without ASD and found significant differences in phrasing, stress, and nasal resonance. Individuals with ASD exhibited nonfluent phrasing, including sound, syllable, and word repetitions. They also placed emphatic stress within an utterance rather than marking stress grammatically or lexically and used speech that was inappropriately loud and high pitched. These features of pragmatic communication require attention to and understanding of how a change in pitch, intensity, or intonation can impact the intent of the message heard. Interpretation and use of prosodic information appear to be significant problems for children with ASD. Shriberg et al. (2001) recommend that speech–language pathologists at least screen verbal individuals with ASD for possible difficulties in prosody and voice, recognizing the potential impact of involvement in these areas on social and vocational adjustment.

Extralinguistic Features

The nonverbal components of pragmatic communication are called *extralinguistic features*. These include the use of gestures and body movements to aid communicative intent and the expression of feelings or emotions of an utterance in discourse. Children with ASD often lack the expected hand and arm movements, facial expressions and head nods (Ricks & Wing, 1975), and body posturing that are important in conversation. Mundy and Sigman (1989) reported that children with ASD send less clear affective messages with their facial expressions than children who are typically developing. Bieberich and Morgan (1998) also found that children with ASD exhibited less positive affect with their mothers when engaged in play than children with Down syndrome. This inability to coordinate movements and send appropriate affective signals during the reciprocal exchange that occurs in conversation and play seriously detracts from their ability to communicate intent and to make sense of the information they are taking in. Further, the reported difficulty of children with ASD in interpreting the meaning of facial expressions beyond the emotion of "happiness" has important implications for interacting in social contexts (Feldman, McGee, Mann, & Strain, 1993). For example, Barron (2001) described his difficulty as a child with ASD integrating the facial expressions of others and understanding the motivation behind those facial expressions. This deficit in a critical nonverbal component of pragmatic communication compromised his ability to relate to others.

Linguistic Features

Several linguistic features support successful engagement in social discourse. Most important, though, children must be able to use utterances that demonstrate what they know and understand about the listener. Children with ASD have significant challenges in two areas of linguistic intent. First, their ability to attend to their communicative partner so that an actual participatory exchange can occur is compromised. As was learned in Chapter 1, children with ASD have difficulty disengaging, orienting, and shifting attention (Harris, Courchesne, Townsend, Carper, & Lord, 1999; Townsend & Courchesne, 1994; Townsend et al., 1999). The *ability to disengage* allows communicators to respond to unexpected information that is not immediately within their attentional focus. *Orienting* allows communicators to focus on the location of information that is being presented, increasing the speed and accuracy of their processing. The *ability to shift attention* allows communicators to change their focus quickly from one source to another. Children with ASD appear to be slow to disengage and are often slow and inaccurate in their processing of both social and nonsocial information (Harris et al., 1999; Townsend et al., 1999). Further, because they are generally slow and inaccurate in their ability to shift attention between sights and sounds, children with ASD often miss important information. As an added challenge, Dawson and her colleagues (1998) found that the impairments they observed in the ability of children with ASD to orient to social stimuli (e.g., another person's eyes or facial expressions) may account for the lack of shared attention reported for this population. Therefore, it is not difficult to understand the problems children with ASD demonstrate in their ability to interpret incoming linguistic information (including all its paralinguistic and extralinguistic features). In addition, they are challenged to formulate an utterance that is responsive to what has been said and how it has been related, and that accurately interprets the intent of what has been communicated.

The second area of deficit in expressing linguistic intent lies in the actual linguistic skills children with ASD possess and use to express themselves. Often, their language is characterized by unconventional verbal behavior, as previously described, which fails to engage a communication partner. For example, the use of recurring linguistic forms that do not consider the linguistic information a communication partner provides is sure to terminate a conversation. Further, the quality and extent of a communicative exchange are influenced by the linguistic repertoire of the communicator. Children with ASD are limited in both the quantity and the quality of the linguistic information they can understand and express, particularly in the pragmatic (language use) aspects of language. The following example provided by one mother of a child with ASD is a clear example of the challenges her son and their family experienced when Eddy used the language he had to communicate a need in an unconventional way. In spite of Eddy's linguistic limitations, however, his family figured out how to meet his needs building on the language and intent he had.

It was Thursday afternoon, about 6 P.M., when Eddy came up to my husband, Brian, and me, and said, "I want Dr. Mike!" (Eddy's pediatrician). We said fine and put him in the car to take him to the local health center. Fortunately for us, the emergency room was open and Dr. Mike was there. I told him what was happening, so he waited in the hallway. Eddy did not acknowledge Dr. Mike, but walked right past him to the last waiting room. He entered the room, went over to the table, opened a jar, took out a Band-Aid, put it on a scratch on his leg, and said, "I want Dr. Mike." At that point, Dr. Mike and I remembered that Eddy had had a blood drawing the previous week in that same examining room, and Dr. Mike had put a Band-Aid on the site of the blood draw. He had wanted a Band-Aid for a cut, and this was the only way he knew how to ask. Over the next few weeks, we worked with Eddy to cue him to ask for a Band-Aid for a paper cut and a scraped knee. He finally started requesting a Band-Aid. About 2 months later, he had been quite grumpy most of the day. When putting him to bed, he asked for a Band-Aid. I gave him one, and he put it on his stomach. About 10 minutes later, he became very sick with a stomach flu. From this point, we have been able to teach him stomach ache, headache, and other ailments. He now can use his words and/or picture symbols to tell us about his illnesses.

Conversational Features

The verbal and nonverbal skills used by speakers during communicative interactions are important in monitoring the effectiveness of discourse as well as ensuring the flow of that discourse. Comprehension of specific speech acts and the ability to make judgments in the context of discourse also contribute to the success or failure of a communication exchange (Twachtman-Cullen, 1998).

The verbal aspects of communication that are important to successful conversational exchanges include the following:

- selecting, maintaining, and changing topics
- taking turns
- initiating topics of conversation
- responding to conversational topics presented by another
- knowing when and where not to pause, interrupt, or overlap
- giving feedback to the listener or the speaker
- providing responses contingent on those of the conversational partner
- using concise utterances
- knowing how much or how little to say

Each of these verbal skills in conversational exchanges contributes to the reciprocal nature of communication. Tager-Flusberg (1996) suggests that the tendency for children with ASD to restrict their language use for instrumental functions (e.g., requesting a desired object from an adult) limits their conversational abilities. Children with ASD appear to struggle with the discourse rules Grice (1975) proposed for successful conversational interaction. Frequently, verbal children with ASD are unable to judge conversational cues to tell when they have said too much (quantity), how important a specific comment is to the conversational topic (relevance), or whether they have been clear about the information conveyed (clarity) (Lord & Paul, 1997; Lord et al., 1989; Twachtman-Cullen, 1998). For example, Volden, Mulcahy, and Holdgrafer (1997) described the referential communication skills of adolescents and young adults with ASD and found their conversation to be more redundant, non–task related, and linguistically peculiar than that of a group of adolescents and young adults without ASD. These observed responses tended to interrupt the flow of discourse and led to more inefficient communication for the group of individuals with ASD. During a semistructured conversational exchange around vacation, friends, and school, Capps, Kehres, and Sigman (1998) found that children with ASD were able to sustain their dialogue but often failed to respond to questions and comments, and usually made less relevant contributions to the conversation than children with other developmental disorders.

There are also two important nonverbal aspects of successful conversational exchanges. The first, *eye gaze,* tells speakers that their conversational partners (i.e., the listeners) are attending and listening to what is being said. Effective eye gaze by the listener informs the speaker that the listener is interested in the information being shared. Eye gaze also tells listeners that their conversational partners (i.e., the speakers) are directing the information to them to hear and understand. Effective eye gaze by the speaker engages the listener in the conversational exchange. Snow, Hertzig, and Shapiro (1987) found that children with ASD direct less eye gaze to individuals during interactions. The second nonverbal aspect of conversation is *proximity,* or the use of space and body orientation. Recognizing a comfortable "talking" area during conversational exchanges is critical to the successful initiation and sustainability of social discourse.

In addition to the verbal and nonverbal aspects of reciprocal conversational exchanges, a level of comprehension is required to participate successfully in discourse. Specific areas of understanding may pose difficulties for children with ASD, including understanding the use of indirect requests, interpreting and responding to nonliteral language, and making presuppositions or assumptions about the listener's needs (Twachtman-Cullen, 1998). For example, a teacher might say to a student with ASD, "Kevin, there is a lot of noise coming from your group," and he would respond, "I know," instead of quieting down, which was the indirect intent of the teacher's utterance. Teenagers might be talking about someone who "kicked the bucket," and the peer with ASD would not understand that the nonliteral interpretation in that context is that someone has died. A student with ASD might explain something to his teacher about a boy named Tom who came over to his house, without identifying who Tom was, assuming the teacher knew that Tom was his cousin.

Children with ASD struggle in their ability to participate in the reciprocal nature of conversational exchanges. Their limited communication means may lead to more unconventional, inappropriate communication attempts (Wetherby et al., 1998). Failed attempts to communicate intent in conversation might lead to aggressive acts. In the example that follows, the preschool child with ASD became physically aggressive and began to scream when approached by his teacher, who did not initially understand what the child was trying to communicate:

TEACHER: Kevin, it's time to get ready to go outside on the playground [as she approached with a pair of boots].
CHILD: Screeches [and shakes head no].
TEACHER: You are almost done with the train. Once you put it away, I will help you with your boots.
CHILD: [Gets up from the table and throws himself on the floor]
TEACHER: [Approaches the child]
CHILD: [Attempts to slap the teacher]

This aggressive behavior continued for some time before the teacher realized that the child was upset because the boots she was bringing to him were not his. He did not have a conventional way to inform his communicative partner what was wrong and why he was so upset.

Less conventionally appropriate attention-seeking behaviors (e.g., pacing, yelling out) may also be used to initiate an exchange or at least get the attention of a potential communicative partner, as demonstrated in the following example.

A 4-year-old with ASD frequently raced around the learning areas in his preschool classroom. This pacing and bolting behavior continued for several weeks. Initially, the team interpreted this behavior as a result of his increased anxiety and arousal level in this new environment. Each time an adult approached him, he bolted from that person as well. Upon further observation and assessment, however, the SLP realized there was a pattern to the pacing and bolting behavior. She also noted some attempts by the child to touch or look at another child, or peer into the activity in which the children were engaged (e.g., making cookies or painting). When there was no response to the child's subtle and unconventional attempts to engage, he would bolt and try again in another area of the room.

Once these unconventional behaviors were interpreted as meaningful attempts to engage potential communicative partners, the child's initiation behaviors were shaped using peer-mediated intervention strategies (discussed in Chapter 10). Again, the importance of careful and critical assessment of the unconventional behaviors children with ASD demonstrate cannot be understated if effective intervention planning is to occur.

More able children might avoid conversational discourse altogether because they lack facility with the conversational features listed above. To a potential communicative partner, they may appear generally aloof or unapproachable for discourse. For example, a highly verbal teenager with ASD who lacks an understanding of the humor so often expressed by his peers might ignore their attempts to engage him because of his weak knowledge of this abstract form of language. The result is often a discontinuation of the peers' attempts to involve the adolescent with ASD.

Recognizing the bidirectional influence and general interdependence of language and social interaction makes it easier to understand the complexities of social communication that individuals with ASD so often experience. It is not difficult to see the social challenges brewing for children with ASD who have limited linguistic capacity and thus fewer opportunities to experience and participate in reciprocal social discourse. Lack of involvement in a sufficient number of quality interactions limits the ongoing feedback children with ASD can integrate into their scripts for social interaction. Children who have limited opportunities with typical language models lack the powerful linguistic input and feedback provided in that context that can be used in future social discourse encounters. In addition, when opportunities for conversation present themselves, breakdowns are likely. For example, children with ASD may fail to recognize the speaker's intent (e.g., in indirect requests), misinterpret the use of nonliteral or figurative language, or misunderstand the active and reciprocal roles of speaker and listener. Such breakdowns in conversation make it difficult for children with ASD to sustain their discourse with potential communication partners.

Other Language Challenges

Several other language problems are reported for verbal children with ASD that impact on their semantic understanding and linguistic performance (Landa, 2000). Difficulties in word choice and meaning exhibited by children with ASD often reflect an inflexible cognitive style, a need for control of the linguistic environment, and an attempt to make sense of the world. Some of the specific challenges described for individuals with ASD include the use of metaphoric language, literal meanings, gestalt processing, theme building, and inference making. Each of these language difficulties is explored more fully in the paragraphs that follow. It is important for professionals to understand the importance of both assessing the occurrences of these language challenges and making determinations about how best to ameliorate them through intervention planning.

Metaphoric Language

Although children with ASD have been observed to assign words to the same categories as other children, some use metaphoric language, in which they make associations that have private meanings (Lord & Paul, 1997; Twachtman, 1995; Twachtman-Cullen, 1998; Volden & Lord, 1991). For example, a child might say, "Help the alligator" to a teacher during math class, which seems out of context. With probing and help from the child, the teacher learns there is a tear in the child's math book that creates an image similar to a picture of an alligator the child saw in his science book earlier in the day. The child does not possess the linguistic skill to report his concern in a more conventional way, so he creates an association recycled from information previously seen, heard, or read. Twachtman-Cullen (1998, 2000) suggests that the use of inappropriate metaphoric language by verbal children with ASD is an indication of their poorly developed knowledge of the importance of sharing understanding in a social context. She also states that the inappropriate use of metaphors may be related to the lack of perspective taking that is reported for children with ASD. It would be important, then, to examine perspective taking more comprehensively in verbal children with ASD and define situations of metaphoric language use. In addition, Prizant (1987) indicated that metaphorical language may involve delayed echolalia, including variations of repeated utterances that have some creativity. If so, it would be important for families and practitioners to trace such utterances to determine their meaning. Considering the need for making sense and the cognitive inflexibility described for many children with ASD, the use of metaphors associated with private meanings is not surprising.

Literal Meanings

Responding to literal versus implied meanings also poses challenges for children with ASD (Landa, 2000; Twachtman, 1995). Consider the classroom context in which many instructions make assumptions about how a student will respond. For example, when a teacher asks her students to "sign your name" at the top of a paper, she would not expect students to write "your name," although that might be the literal interpretation the student with ASD makes. Similarly, the tendency of children with ASD to interpret information literally is reflective of a cognitive style that is inflexible even when the context suggests an alternative interpretation (Ozonoff & Miller, 1996; Twachtman-Cullen, 1998). Sean Barron, an adult who has described his early experiences with autism, remembers being very literal, rote, and concrete in his use of words (Barron, 2001). He has described how he compensated for his difficulty with imagination, concrete thinking, and relating by looking up words in the dictionary so that he would at least have a plethora of words to use. Kanner (1971) offers an example of literal interpretation in his review of 11 children with autism whom he first studied in 1943. Kanner provides this scenario of a 5½-year-old child asking his father about a picture he saw in an office:

> "When are they coming out of the picture and coming in here?" He was serious about this. His father said something about the pictures they have at home on the wall. John corrected his father: "We have them *near* the wall." (p. 137)

Gestalt Processing

Descriptions of early language development in children who are typically developing have proposed the occurrence of both an analytic and a gestalt processing style (Peters, 1977, 1983). Children exhibiting an analytic approach to early language learning are described as recognizing, analyzing, and producing individual words or parts of language (e.g., using nouns to label objects). In contrast, children demonstrating a more gestalt approach exhibit more conversational features (e.g., rising and falling intonation, producing multiple syllables without clearly marking individual words) and favor the use of "whole" units of language or phrases (e.g., "How are you?") in their early language learning. Peters (1977, 1983) even proposes a dual storage notion in which some "gestalts" that children learn and use can be analyzed further as the need arises, whereas others remain essentially unanalyzed language wholes. Nelson (1973) described a similar phenomenon in early language learning style differences in her explanation of referential and expressive language learners. She suggested that the two different learning styles eventually merge, and language growth moves forward.

Two perspectives have been shared on the child's use of a gestalt style of language learning (Duchan, 1994). One perspective, the deficit view, suggests that the use of such gestalts is not productive and that learners who use the gestalt approach may be less proficient language learners (Krashen & Scarcella, 1978; Prizant, 1983). Seeing gestalt processing from a deficit perspective assumes that children learn best through an "analytic" approach (Duchan, 1994). A second perspective is more competence based, indicating that a gestalt style is creative and productive for many children who use it (Landau & Gleitman, 1985; Peters, 1983).

The use of a gestalt processing style has been reported as a specific challenge for children with ASD (Prizant, 1983; Prizant & Schuler, 1987). Prizant (1987) has considered the occurrence of echolalia in children with ASD as a potentially extreme form of gestalt processing in which children process their language and experience as whole units rather than segmenting language into meaningful rule-based components. Duchan (1994) proposes that how professionals perceive gestalt learners should depend on the flexibility of the gestalts used and how they are understood and function for the gestalt language learner. Therefore, it would be important to more carefully examine the role of gestalts in children with ASD. The type of gestalts that may occur include single utterances, events, or discourse scripts that follow a routine (Duchan, 1994). A single-utterance routine might occur as follows: A child with ASD goes to touch a pizza that has just been placed on the table. Because it is very hot, his mother says, "Don't touch the pizza!" The child processes this unit of language as a whole and then applies it to similar situations. For example, the same child goes to the stove that is turned on for dinner and says, "Don't touch the pizza!" or the child sees his mom using a hot iron and says, "Don't touch the pizza!"

The use of some single-utterance gestalts might be likened to using immediate, delayed, or mitigated echolalia, as described earlier. What is important, though, is to determine whether the child has a means for breaking down the utterance. It may be that the use of mitigated echolalia reflects a growing awareness of how language might be used (Twachtman, 1995) even if that use is somewhat unconventional, as in the preceding example. Certainly, the child's use of "Don't touch the pizza!" in similar situations suggests he has an understanding of things or situations that are hot and should be avoided or not touched. He does not, however, have the linguistic flexibility to adjust the content of the utterance to describe the specific situations more accurately.

Assessment of gestalt processing should also consider the routines in events or discourse that children with ASD sometimes display. Again, children who are typically developing also exhibit some gestalt-like processing in familiar event (e.g., bedtime routine) or discourse (e.g., first learning to talk on the telephone) routines. Depending on the perspective taken and the flexibility within the gestalt, the use of such routines can be seen as productive or nonproductive. An event routine for a child with ASD might be similar to that of a child without ASD. However, it may be less flexible (e.g., a bedtime routine that requires only Mom to read a book and no one else; driving to see Grandma must follow the same roads without diversion). A discourse routine in which a child with ASD has memorized a script from a television program and uses it in response to questions about his favorite television show may limit the meaningfulness of his communication encounter. It would be important, then, to define the gestalts that do occur for children with ASD, determine whether they contain elements that are used elsewhere, assess what level of flexibility exists in their use, identify and determine the appropriateness of the contexts of their use, and describe how the gestalts function. Approaches to intervention addressing those gestalts that remain seemingly unanalyzed for children with ASD will be discussed in Chapter 9.

Theme Building

Language use in conversational exchanges is not just about introducing a topic. It often facilitates a cognitive process of theme building that individuals use to make sense of the world (Twachtman, 1995). The perseverative speech of children with ASD has been described as locking into a theme, whereas stimulus overselectivity has been described as reflecting a more rigid focus on a larger theme (Twachtman, 1995). An adolescent with ASD who will talk only about the players and scores of a regional baseball team and repeatedly names the team players and game scores has locked onto a theme. The young child who plays only with trains and fails to make connections with related vehicles is overfocused on the stimulus he has selected that has a particular motivating interest. The challenge in conversational exchanges is realized when the adolescent is unable to divert his attention to consider other activities or the young child limits his ability to learn and talk about other objects that can do similar and different things. For some children with ASD, themes that interfere with conversational discourse often satisfy a need for making sense. Consider the following example:

> An 8-year-old boy with ASD often engaged in conversation by explaining how to get from one place to another. His ability to map out trips across the state was detailed and accurate. Upon further probing of this ability, it became evident that the maps he created had a specific theme. The child's father worked in several towns across the state. The little boy was mapping out all these trips as a way to know how his father would get to his destination, where he would be, and how he would be returning.

In this example, the child used the creation of maps as a conversational theme that helped him to make sense of the world that was important to him.

The general tendency of verbal children with ASD to initiate topics of their particular interest without regard to the listener's interest indicates poor recognition of both the nonverbal and indirect verbal cues offered by listeners (Landa, 2000; Wing & Attwood, 1987). For some individuals with ASD, focusing on a topic of interest or theme is the only way to make sense of their world. In describing his attempts to eliminate the symptoms of autism, Barron (2001) explains the need to feel a sense of comfort, security, and control in his life. That need for control dictated his rigid, rhythmic pattern of speech early on and focused his speech on those themes or topics that he knew a lot about (e.g., states, numbers, chemical elements).

Inference Making

Children with ASD have sometimes been reported to have difficulty making judgments about the physical world based on information that is present at the time (Landa, 2000; Twachtman-Cullen, 1998). For example, if a student with ASD walks into a classroom and another student is placing birthday treats on everyone's desk in the room, the student with ASD might not make the logical connection—that is, that the student passing out the treats is celebrating her birthday with the class that day. This challenge in inference making is not surprising considering the reliance on cues that are usually indirect and socially determined. Twachtman-Cullen suggests difficulties in inferring might also be used to explain the preference for factual information frequently reported for individuals with ASD.

Some researchers have proposed that the inferring required in tasks with more complex humor, which is so difficult for people with ASD, may be explained by their rigid and concrete thinking process (Ozonoff & Miller, 1996). This rigidity causes the individual with ASD to focus on an initial interpretation and does not allow for a reinterpretation based on the context. Others have suggested that the abstract language challenges experienced by individuals with ASD are a result of an underlying deficit in ability to process complex information (Minshew, Goldstein, & Siegel, 1995). Barron (2001) has described rigidity in his own cognitive processing, stating that he could not take information that was learned in one situation and apply it in another situation. He also indicated some difficulty with complex information processing, describing "word islands" as words he knew and understood but whose meaningful contexts he could not process. It is clear that during assessment, practitioners should consider the ability of children with ASD to make inferences, and should identify those situations in which both successful and unsuccessful attempts at inference making affect communication, social interaction, and play.

Creating Profiles of Communication Strengths and Challenges

Once a diagnosis has been made, it is important to begin to develop a holistic and comprehensive view of children with ASD by profiling their communication strengths and challenges. This is particularly important if practitioners are to implement a developmentally and individually appropriate curriculum and have the information they need for prioritizing communication intervention goals (Wetherby et al., 2000).

There are several considerations as practitioners prepare to create a profile of a child's communication strengths and challenges. First, situations need to be designed that will foster observation of a child's attempts to communicate. Wetherby and her colleagues (Wetherby & Prizant, 1992, 1993; Wetherby et al., 1998; Wetherby et al., 2000) have suggested the use of communicative temptations (e.g., placing a desirable object in a closed container near a child) to assess a child's communication functions and means. A number of communicative temptations are described in the *Communication and Symbolic Behavior Scales* (CSBS; Wetherby & Prizant, 1993). The CSBS is a standardized assessment tool Wetherby and Prizant developed for young children, which has value in profiling the communication strengths and challenges of children with ASD who have no or limited verbal skills.

The second consideration is that practitioners must observe what the child does to communicate both nonverbally and verbally. Third, an assessment of joint attention should be made, including whether the child's shared attention is object or person focused. Fourth, the child's repertoire of gestures, sounds, and words should be defined. Fifth, it is critical to describe at what point the child's existing communication skills no longer meet his or her communication needs. Finally, a closer inspection of the child's echolalia or other unconventional verbal behavior should be completed.

Specific assessment strategies that can be used for determining the communication strengths and challenges of children with ASD who have no or limited verbal skills, those with unconventional verbal behavior, and those with verbal skills are described in the following sections.

Communication Assessment for Nonverbal Children with ASD

Clinical researchers have suggested three important preverbal areas to assess in all children but that have important implications for children with ASD (Bruner, 1981; McLean & Snyder-McLean, 1978; Wetherby & Prizant, 1993). First, practitioners must determine the presence of communication functions in the nonverbal behaviors of children with ASD. Wetherby (1986) and Wetherby and Prizant (1992, 1993) have offered descriptions of three categories of communicative function that should be assessed in children with ASD: behavior regulation, social interaction, and joint attention. A child can regulate the behavior of another by requesting objects or action. Attempts at social interaction would include requesting a social routine (e.g., peek-a-boo), seeking comfort or permission, calling out, greeting, and showing off (Wetherby & Prizant, 1992, 1993). Joint attention would involve "commenting" on objects or actions or requesting information.

The second preverbal area that is important to assess is the means used for communication across the three categories of communicative function. Wetherby and Prizant (1992, 1993) have described the use of contact and distal gestures, as well as vocalizations. In the preverbal child, contact gestures that have a communicative function might include showing, giving, and pushing where there is some contact with an object or a communication partner. Distal gestures that serve a communicative function include pointing, reaching, and waving. These gestures do not require actual physical contact with an object or a communication partner. Vocalizations in preverbal children can also potentially serve a communicative function. Therefore, practitioners should carefully assess the use of noises, crying, laughter, and sound productions, including syllable shapes and phonetically consistent forms, to establish some communicative connection.

A third area of assessment in preverbal children with ASD requires an examination of nonlinguistic comprehension. It is possible that some children with ASD who have no or limited verbal skills understand some of the nonverbal, situational, and paralinguistic cues used among communication partners. For example, practitioners would want to assess whether the child with ASD knows that pointing or looking (nonverbal cues) at an object or activity means that the communication partner should attend to it. The ability to respond to a situational cue like observing someone placing an object in a container and following along should likewise be assessed. Responses to paralinguistic cues should also be examined. For example, does the child with ASD understand that a loud voice accompanying an instruction might mean that a parent or teacher is angry?

The CSBS provides an effective framework for examining the communicative functions and means and nonlinguistic comprehension skills of children with ASD (Wetherby & Prizant, 1993). In my experience, although many children with ASD are unable to comply with the formal requirements of this tool, the actual framework is useful in creating a meaningful profile of the communication strengths and challenges of children with ASD.

Communication Assessment for Children with ASD Who Exhibit Unconventional Verbal Behavior

As previously discussed, Prizant (1987) and Prizant and Rydell (1993) describe three specific areas of unconventional verbal behavior that interfere with the communication success of children with ASD: echolalia, perseverative speech, and excessive questioning. Prizant and Rydell also suggest that unconventional verbal behavior seems to increase in situations with heightened cognitive and social demands. For example, adult communication partners who employ a highly directive interaction style place greater demands on the child with ASD because of their control of the social and learning environments and their expectations for specific responses. These social and cognitive demands to follow the communication partner's lead tax the child's processing and may lead to a more familiar, predictable response by the child with ASD (e.g., echolalia). In contrast, a more facilitative style follows the child's lead, placing fewer social and cognitive demands for responding on the child and yielding more social initiations and fewer echoic responses (Rydell & Mirenda, 1991).

Knowing the challenges that face children with ASD to comply with the cognitive and linguistic demands of their learning environments, it is important to understand unconventional verbal behavior as part of the strategies used by children on the spectrum to communicate their intent. A careful assessment of this behavior is needed if we are to understand not only their possible intentions but also the situations in which unconventional verbal behavior is likely to occur. Several factors should be considered in the assessment of unconventional verbal behavior (Prizant, 1987; Prizant & Rydell, 1993; Rydell & Prizant, 1995):

- situations of frequent occurrence (e.g., transitions; unstructured, unfamiliar, or difficult tasks; emotionally arousing activities; communication partner's style; complexity of linguistic input);

- antecedent events (e.g., what happens preceding the observed behavior);
- range of functions potentially served (e.g., labeling, requesting, greeting, commenting);
- interference with successful communication; and
- any progressive change in behavior.

It is important to obtain a complete history of the unconventional verbal behavior from the family, as well as from those who have the most consistent experience with the child. Observation of the behavior in a variety of contexts is also critical.

Other considerations for examining echolalic responses require attention to timing, context, and conversational role (Prizant, 1987). First, determine the latency of the response (e.g., Is the response time greater for more intentional forms?). Second, identify the impact of context (e.g., Does echolalia occur more in two-way or large group situations?). Finally, assess whether the echoic behavior is an initiation or a response. Figure 4.1 is a sample format that could be used to guide the assessment of unconventional verbal behavior in children with ASD so that a more complete communication profile could be developed.

Semantic Assessment in Verbal Children with ASD

Despite the production of often well-formed syntactic structures (e.g., gestalt or echolalic utterances), meaningfully expressing semantic relationships in socially appropriate ways is a particular challenge for children with ASD. Landa (2000) suggests that an assessment of semantic knowledge is critical for this population. She proposes that both receptive and expressive vocabulary be examined as well as the comprehension and production of a variety of semantic relationships, word categories, antonyms, synonyms, figurative language, inferencing, and prediction skills. Considering the tendency of verbal children with ASD to create their own metaphors to represent private meanings, as well as their overreliance on literal interpretation, careful analysis of word selection and responses to literal versus abstract language is critical across settings and communication contexts. Further, an assessment of narrative and discourse comprehension is important.

Semantic knowledge makes an important contribution to academic and social learning. It gives students access to the gist of what goes on in the classroom, as well as among peers. For children with ASD who are included in general education classrooms, an assessment of their semantic knowledge is crucial. Some of the formal tools that might be considered for determining particular areas of semantic strength and weakness are highlighted in Table 4.1. An observational framework for more carefully examining semantic understanding and use can be found in Figure 4.2.

(text continues on p. 191)

Assessment of Unconventional Verbal Behavior

Child's name: _____   Date: _____

Observer: _____   Location: _____

Unconventional Verbal Behavior (i.e., immediate or delayed echolalia, perseverative speech, excessive questions)	Context (e.g., task difficulty, transition, familiarity, partner style)	Antecedent Event (i.e., what happened just before)	Function Served (e.g., labeling, requesting, directing attention, commenting)	Response (i.e., successfully communicated intent; demonstrated comprehension)	Rigidity in Form and Function (e.g., any novel production or adjustment in form)

FIGURE 4.1. Assessment of unconventional verbal behavior.

TABLE 4.1

Selected Assessment Tools for Semantic Language

Test	Age range	Description	Reliability and Validity
Figurative Language Interpretation Test (Palmer, 1991)	9 to 16+ years (4th through 10th grades)	A norm-referenced diagnostic tool designed to assess a student's ability to comprehend figurative language, including • similes, • metaphors, • hyperbole, and • personification.	Inter item consistency: reliability coefficient of .84. Reliability across Forms A and B: .77 correlation. Construct validity: Correlated with reading total on the California Achievement Tests. Concurrent validity: Correlated with figures of speech from basal readers and trade books.
Language Processing Test–Revised (Richard & Hanner, 1995)	5 to 11 years	Assesses ability to organize information and make sense of what is heard; identifies breakdowns in processing that affect memory and word retrieval.	Test–retest reliability: .86 across ages for total test. Validity: Item–test correlations and differences between children with and without language impairments.
Test of Word Knowledge (Wiig & Secord, 1992)	5 to 17 years	Assesses semantic knowledge, both the understanding and the expression of the content or meaning of language. Two levels of word knowledge are assessed: Level 1—Referential and relational aspects • receptive vocabulary, • word opposites, • expressive vocabulary, and • word definitions. Level 2—Relational and metalinguistic aspects • synonyms, • figurative language, • word definitions, and • multiple contexts.	Content validity: The test content is clearly defined and supported by research. Construct validity: Correctly identified participants as language learning disordered (LLD) or non-LLD in comparison to several other tests making the same discrimination. Concurrent validity: Correlated with the *Clinical Evaluation of Language Fundamentals–Revised*. Internal consistency: Ranged from .86 to .96 for the total composite scores. Test–retest reliability: Higher for total scores (.94) than for subtest scores (.46–.96).

(continues)

TABLE 4.1 *Continued.*

Selected Assessment Tools for Semantic Language

Test	Age range	Description	Reliability and Validity
The Word Test 2: Elementary (Bowers, Huisingh, LoGiudice, & Orman, 2004)	7 to 11 years	Assesses the following aspects of semantic language: • association, • synonyms, • semantic absurdities, • antonyms, • definitions, and • multiple definitions.	Test–retest reliability: .93 for total test, with a range from .70 to .80 for subtests. Validity: Item–total test correlations; subtest intercorrelations; mean differences between individuals with and without language impairments.
The Word Test 2: Adolescent (Bowers, Huisingh, LoGiudice, & Orman, 2005)	12 through 17 years	Assesses the following aspects of semantic language: • brand names, • synonyms, • signs of the times, and • definitions.	Normed on over 1,600 students. Test–retest reliability: .91 across all ages. Validity: Large differences between students with and without language impairments.

Pragmatic Assessment in Verbal Children with ASD

Following the work of Bates (1976) and others suggesting that because language is learned and used in a social context, it should be studied in a social context, it is important for practitioners to consider this in their assessment of children suspected of pragmatic difficulties, particularly children with ASD. With its multifaceted and context-bound nature, an ecologically valid assessment of pragmatics is a difficult yet critical element for profiling the communication skills of children with ASD (Landa, 2000).

Many attempts have been made to incorporate what has been learned about pragmatics into an assessment framework for clinical use. In particular, Prutting and Kirchner (1983) created a speech act framework for examining pragmatics that extends the description of the utterance act from verbal information alone to nonverbal (e.g., physical proximity, body posture, gestures) and paralinguistic (e.g., intelligibility, prosody or intonation and stress patterns, message rate) information. This framework has value for the assessment of pragmatic language in verbal children with ASD, considering the challenges described earlier for paralinguistic, extralinguistic, linguistic, and conversational features of pragmatic language. Further, in the assessment of pragmatic language, practitioners must consider levels of analysis, assessment contexts, and the specific pragmatic parameters examined.

Assessment of Semantic Language in Children with ASD

Child's name: _____ Date: _____

Observer: _____ Location: _____

Semantic Parameters	Understanding	Use	Influence of Contextual Variables (including physical environment, props, adult or peer interaction style, prompts)
Word Categories			
Antonyms			
Synonyms			
Figurative Language • Metaphor • Simile • Idiom			
Inferences			
Atypical Semantic Behavior • Metaphoric language representing private meanings • Literal vs. abstract understanding			

FIGURE 4.2. Observational framework for examining semantic language in children with ASD.

Levels of Analysis. Roth and Spekman (1984a) described an organizational framework for examining pragmatic communication skills. They proposed three levels of analysis: communicative intentions, presupposition, and social organization of discourse. At the first level, the intent of a speaker's message (e.g., to comment on, acknowledge, or request information) should be assessed. Second-level analysis occurs when the communication focus is broadened to include not only the speaker's intent but also how that intent reflects the information needs of the listener. It requires an assessment of presupposition, or an individual's ability to infer the needs of a conversational partner. The third area of analysis deals with the ability to maintain or sustain a dialogue or conversation among partners through multiple turns. This last level of assessment focuses on the reciprocity in social discourse.

Assessment Contexts. To investigate fully the three levels of pragmatic analysis, the different contexts of interaction must be considered (Roth & Spekman, 1984a, 1984b). The physical environment, the communication skills of the conversational partners, and the channels used for feedback should be examined. These are the kinds of variables that will influence the message type and form, the information presupposed, and the conversational organization (Roth & Spekman, 1984a).

Social discourse, as well as the conversational exchanges that occur in the home and in educational settings, may be the most useful contexts in which to evaluate a child's pragmatic strengths and deficits. As an initial screening of the pragmatic language skills for children with ASD, parental and teacher input could provide useful information because parents and teachers observe children in social contexts throughout the day.

Pragmatic Parameter: Communicative Intentions. Both the intent of the speaker and the effect of that intent on the listener should be assessed in the communication of verbal children with ASD. It is important to know, too, that intent can be expressed in a variety of ways: through gestures (nonverbal), changes in intonation and emphatic stress (paralinguistic), and the actual words selected (linguistic). Intentional language at the multiword stage generally includes requesting information, responding to requests, and regulating conversational behavior (Dore, 1974, 1986; Roth & Spekman, 1984a).

The form of intentional communication can be examined by exploring the linguistic, paralinguistic, and other nonverbal means used to communicate a message. The use of different sentence types and the explicit nature of a communication utterance can be assessed to determine the different ways children with ASD might get what they want (e.g., by using directive forms). Further, the ability to recognize situations that require more indirect expression of intent (e.g., use of a polite form versus a directive) is important to examine, particularly for determining social success (Landa, 2000). Practitioners should attend to the flexible use of linguistic forms in children with ASD. Inflexible or rigid linguistic forms are likely to affect the child with

ASD in a negative way, leading to social isolation and limited cooperation from potential communicative partners (Landa, 2000).

Pragmatic Parameter: Presupposition. It is important to determine the ability of verbal children with ASD to understand their communication partners' perspectives. Speakers infer information about their listeners just as listeners infer the intentions of speakers (Roth & Spekman, 1984a). Affective and linguistically based prosodic cues frequently reported as inefficient in children with ASD (Baltaxe & Simmons, 1985; Fine, Bartolucci, Ginsberg, & Szatmari, 1991) challenge their ability to both recognize and understand the attitudes and intents of speakers—for example, when using jokes and sarcasm (Landa, 2000). In addition, the tendency of children with ASD to engage in conversations based on themes or areas of interest they have developed or inferences they have made about specific topics compromises their ability to attend to the nonverbal and indirect verbal cues displayed by their listeners (Landa, 2000). Such disregard for the listeners' relative level of interest leads to unsuccessful social encounters.

The following areas of assessment are likely to provide the practitioner with a greater understanding of the perspective taking of verbal children with ASD:

- topics children choose to talk about (e.g., examine tendency for theme building);
- their ability to comment versus add new information;
- their approach to representing new information;
- their use of vague or ambiguous messages;
- their ability to talk about items, events, or people that are present versus not present; and
- their ability to interpret indirect expressions (e.g., attend to inferences being made).

Social context variables must also be integrated to achieve perspective taking. Often, children with ASD have difficulty adjusting their language to the changing contexts typical for conversation (Landa, 2000). Therefore, the ability of children with ASD to talk differently to different conversational partners, depending on their age, ability level, and shared experiences, should be assessed. In addition, their appreciation of the communication requirements in conversations where their communication partner is present (e.g., face-to-face conversations) versus not present (e.g., telephone conversations) should be observed, as well as the discourse rules for home, school, and community.

Pragmatic Parameter: Social Organization of Discourse. The pragmatic skills necessary for assuming and interchanging the roles and responsibilities of speaker and listener require careful investigation for children with ASD. Practitioners need to observe children's talking time, their ability to take turns and initiate conversation, and their ability to engage in relevant conversations, providing on-topic comments, questions, and responses throughout a communication exchange. An assessment of conversational repairs should also be completed. Roth and Spekman (1984a, 1984b) suggest evaluating communication breakdown through an analysis of the cause, any attempt at repair, who initiates the repair, what repair strategy is selected, and the outcome of the repair attempt.

Organizing information within a conversational exchange requires providing some background early on. Often speakers will use words as cohesive devices to help the listener make connections between old and new information presented in discourse (Landa, 2000). The use of such devices decreases potential confusions that might occur in the use of referents that are not specifically defined. Deficits in reciprocal social communication appear to be a consistent challenge for children with ASD (Landa, 2000). The tendency to be associative and to build conversation around familiar topics and comfortable themes may cause children with ASD to make quick topic shifts. This limits their ability to develop a back-and-forth exchange with a potential communication partner. Therefore, practitioners should carefully assess the use of cohesive devices and topic shifting in children with ASD.

Some of the formal tools that might be considered for determining particular areas of pragmatic strength and weakness in children with ASD are highlighted in Table 4.2. An observational framework for more carefully examining pragmatic understanding and use can be found in Figure 4.3.

Communication Assessment Across Impairment, Activity, and Participation

Communication assessment that addresses the ICF dimensions of disability (as described in Chapter 3) takes multiple forms, including record review, interview, observation in clinical or natural environments, and the use of standardized and nonstandardized tools appropriate for the age of the child and the experience of the examiner. It is important that assessments in this area of deficit for children with ASD consider all three dimensions of disability—impairment, activity, and participation—in light of personal and environmental contextual factors. This ensures that interventions developed and planned for a child with ASD will be responsive to each of the levels. Table 4.3 describes the dimensions of disability proposed by the World Health Organization (2001) and the relevant communication assessment areas for children with ASD.

Record Review

A current and historical perspective on the communication development and performance of children with or suspected of ASD is an important component of the assessment process. The development of communication plays

(*text continues on p. 199*)

TABLE 4.2

Selected Assessment Tools for Pragmatic Language

Test	Age range	Description	Reliability and Validity
Test of Pragmatic Skills–Revised (Shulman, 1986)	3 through 8 years	Using 4 different tasks and examiner probes in a play-based format, this tool attempts to elicit the following conversational intentions: • answering, • informing, • naming, • rejecting, • requesting, • reasoning, • closing, and • calling.	Normative raw score data is provided for the individual tasks and the test composite across six age groups; no specific reliability and validity data are reported.
Test of Pragmatic Language (Phelps-Terasaki & Phelps-Gunn, 1992)	5 through 13 years	Using pictures to establish a social context, this tool assesses a child's use of pragmatic language, including abstraction, topic selection and use, speech acts, visual–gestural cues.	Internal consistency: .82 average across age groups. Interscorer reliability: .99. Content validity: Model created to construct and control test item selection. Concurrent validity: Measured against teacher ratings of pragmatic skills and yielded a coefficient of .82. Construct validity: Ability measured was shown to be differentiated by age and related to spoken language and school achievement.
Test of Problem Solving–Adolescent Version (Zachman, Barrett, Huisingh, Orman, & Blagden, 1991)	12.0 through 17 years (7th through 12th grades)	Using spoken stimuli, children's critical thinking is assessed, including • clarifying, • analyzing, • generalizing solutions, • evaluating, and • affective thinking.	Test–retest and internal consistency measures revealed highly satisfactory reliability across age level for the total test. Internal consistency and contrasted groups validity measures indicated acceptable levels of item consistency and an ability to differentiate subjects with language disorders.

(continues)

TABLE 4.2 *Continued.*

Selected Assessment Tools for Pragmatic Language

Test	Age range	Description	Reliability and Validity
Test of Problem Solving–Revised Elementary Version (Bowers, Barrett, Huisingh, Orman, & LoGiudice, 1994)	6 through 11 years	Employing photographs of familiar contexts and probing questions, this tool assesses a child's ability to • explain inferences, • determine causes, • understand and respond to "why" questions, • determine solutions, and • consider ways to avoid problems. It also includes a teacher checklist for rating student's classroom problem-solving behavior.	Test–retest and internal consistency measures revealed highly satisfactory reliability across age level for the total test. Internal consistency and contrasted groups validity measures indicated acceptable levels of item consistency and an ability to differentiate subjects with language disorders from subjects developing language normally.
Test of Language Competence–Expanded (Wiig & Secord, 1989)	Level 1: 5 to 9 years (preschool and early elementary-age children) Level 2: 9 to 18+ years (older children and adolescents)	As a measure of language competence and metalinguistic ability, this tool assesses a child's understanding of • ambiguous sentences, • making inferences, • recreating speech acts, and • figurative language.	Content validity: The test content is clearly defined and supported by research. Concurrent validity: Moderately with the *Test of Adolescent Language,* the *Test of Language Development–2,* the *Clinical Evaluation of Language Fundamentals–Revised,* and the *Peabody Picture Vocabulary Test–Revised.* Construct validity: Moderate correlations among subtests. Internal consistency reliability: Composite reliabilities for Level 1 are .86 to .92 and for Level 2, .75 to .82. Test–retest reliability: Moderate to high stability.
Evaluating Communicative Competence: A Functional Pragmatic Procedure–Revised Edition (Simon, 1986)	4th through 12th grades	The tasks on this tool probe the auditory processing, metalinguistic, and expressive skills that are critical to successful classroom performance.	Provides a pragmatic model for expressive communicative competence and for encouraging functional flexibility; no reliability or validity data are reported.

Assessment of Pragmatic Language in Children with ASD

Child's name: _____ Date: _____

Observer: _____ Location: _____

Pragmatic Parameters	Understanding	Use	Influence of Contextual Variables (including physical environment, props, adult or peer interaction style, prompts)
Paralinguistic Features • Intelligibility • Prosody • Resonance • Vocal pitch • Vocal intensity			
Extralinguistic Features • Gestures • Facial expressions • Proximity			
Conversational Features • Attention shifting • Pausing • Concise language • Speaker role • Listener role			
Communication Intentions • Directive forms • Polite forms • Indirect forms			

(continues)

FIGURE 4.3. Observational framework for examining pragmatic language in children with ASD.

Pragmatic Parameters	Understanding	Use	**Influence of Contextual Variables (including physical environment, props, adult or peer interaction style, prompts)**
Presupposition • Representing old information • Representing new information • Vague or ambiguous messages • Inferences			
Social Organization of Discourse • Topic initiation • Topic maintenance • Topic change • Turn taking • Contingent responses • Communication breakdown and re-pair			

FIGURE 4.3. *Continued.*

a role in early and differential diagnosis (see Chapter 1), and some clinical researchers have identified the following communication markers as clear discriminators of ASD at 2 years of age (Lord, 1995):

- Fewer than five meaningful words
- Cessation of talking after saying three or more meaningful words
- Saying no meaningful words
- Poor understanding of words out of context
- Lack of attention to voice
- Failure to demonstrate joint attention

Practitioners should carefully examine early reports and records of communication development, as well as changes in development, to identify any

TABLE 4.3

Dimensions of Disability and Aspects of Communication To Be Assessed in Children with ASD

Impairment: Function and Structure at the Body Level	Activity: Performance at the Person Level	Participation: Involvement at the Societal Level
• Voice (e.g., intensity, pitch, inflection, rate) • Speech intelligibility • Gestural understanding and use • Facial expression understanding and use • Intentional communication (e.g., behavior regulation, social interaction, joint attention) • Pragmatics (e.g., presupposition, social discourse) • Semantics (e.g., word understanding and use, figurative language, abstract terms) • Syntax, phonology, and morphology • Hearing	Quality and quantity of skill performance; what child can and cannot do in everyday activities: • simple activities (e.g., communicate basic needs; respond to basic requests); and • complex activities (e.g., engage in a conversation with peers and adults; take on speaker and listener roles; read and write; understand oral and written instructions).	Compared to the standard or norm for participation of other children without disabilities, participation in typical activities: • school, • home, • church, • restaurants, • recreational programs, • friendships, • other community activities or programs, and • work.

Context

- Personal: Age, gender, health conditions, past and current experiences, educational level, fitness, lifestyle, habits, coping styles, or other personal–social characteristics.
- Environmental: Societal attitudes, cultural norms, laws, educational systems, architectural characteristics, or other environmental conditions.

indication of regression in the use of language. Further, a history of auditory responsiveness should be gathered, including documentation of valid and reliable hearing testing.

Interview

As highlighted in Chapter 3, interviewing is an important component of the assessment process and has a critical role in obtaining valuable information about a child's understanding and use of communication. Interviews should be conducted with those individuals who have had a consistent opportunity to observe a child's communication attempts and to engage as a communication partner across environments. Watson, Lord, Schaffer, and Schopler (1989) developed a *Home Assessment Interview* as part of the spontaneous communication curriculum for the Treatment and Education of Autistic and

Related Communication Handicapped Children (TEACCH) at the University of North Carolina at Chapel Hill. This interview format is designed to obtain information about the purposes or functions of communication that families describe for their children with ASD, the semantic categories and words used by the children, the contexts for communication, and the form communication takes.

Recognizing the value of parents and primary caregivers, Peck and Schuler (1987) designed an informal interview process, the *Communication Interview,* to identify the communicative means and functions used by children with ASD and other severe disabilities in the context of their interactions with their caregivers. Practitioners are guided through the interview process by "What if" questions that reflect common contexts for communication (e.g., What if _____ wants an adult to sit near? What if _____ wants an object that's out of reach?). The interviewer then codes the specific means used by the child per parental report.

A sample format for completing a home or school communication assessment interview for children with ASD can be found in Appendix 4A.

Observation

To gather relevant information that will guide a practitioner to intervention planning, it is important to observe communication and social interactions during spontaneous exchanges in a variety of environments. A number of different approaches are described in the research literature. Hobson and Lee (1998) suggest that behavior be systematically observed in socially significant settings with familiar and unfamiliar adults. They found that children, adolescents, and adults with ASD were less likely than people without ASD to spontaneously greet an unfamiliar adult using an utterance, nod, or smile, and that eye-to-face contact was also limited. Further, the combination of eye-to-face contact with a smile and verbalization did not occur even after prompts were given, as compared to children, adolescents, and adults with mental retardation (Hobson & Lee, 1998). Snow and colleagues (1987) also found that children with ASD show less eye gaze and positive affect with unfamiliar adults. Considering the contexts for observing communication, Volden and Lord (1991) noted that semistructured communication exchanges (e.g., describing a poster) were difficult for children with ASD. Knowing the potential communication strengths and challenges experienced by children with ASD across a variety of situations, observations should be made in the following contexts:

- with familiar and unfamiliar adults,
- with familiar and unfamiliar peers,
- in structured and unstructured situations,
- in small and large groups, and
- at home, at school, and in the community.

Quill (1995) suggests that if one of the goals of communication assessment is to identify relationships between children's communicative behavior and that of their communication partners, then a child's skills must be observed within a meaningful context. She goes on to state that an analysis of social communicative interactions requires systematic classification of behavior in both natural and contrived situations. This is needed to determine when interactions occur, what is communicated during interactions, how the individual child communicates, and what characteristics of the context and the communication partner affect the child's ability to communicate (Quill, 1995).

Finnerty and Quill (1991) created a *Communicative Means–Function Questionnaire* to describe how children with ASD communicate functionally. This questionnaire focuses on the kinds of opportunities children have to initiate communication, as well as on those contexts that appear to be the most motivating for communication to occur (Quill, 1995). The *Communicative Means–Function Questionnaire* serves to identify how children with ASD communicate, for what purposes they communicate, and in what contexts they communicate. Another example of an observation format used to assess the communicative means of children with ASD is the *Request for Assistance Protocol* (Peck & Schuler, 1987). In this protocol, the practitioner sets up a situation in which the child must solve a problem (e.g., requesting assistance to open a clear plastic container that holds an object of interest and cannot be easily opened). The observer then codes whatever communicative behavior the child initiates. The goal throughout this protocol is to answer the question "What communicative behaviors does the student use to get assistance?" (Peck & Schuler, 1987).

For practitioners interested in an ecologically based communication assessment of young children, Wilcox (1988) recommends an assessment of four parameters (communication mode, use, effectiveness, and needs) across activities, settings, and communication partners. Her *Assessment Worksheet* is used to determine the ecological sensitivity of a practitioner's communication assessment. Wilcox states, "Although communication modes, per se, can be examined independently, a more meaningful picture of communication abilities is drawn when modes are considered in conjunction with their use during communicative interactions" (Wilcox, 1988, p. 2).

Efforts have been made to observe more effectively the social communication of children with ASD in the context of interaction. For example, Quill (1995) developed an *Interaction Analysis* to code the responses children with ASD make to adult or peer messages in spontaneous interactions. The *Interaction Analysis* can be used to assess the relationships between the characteristics of the communication partner and the social communication competence of the child being observed. This framework for analyzing interaction helps practitioners to recognize partner features that both enhance and hinder a child's communicative competence.

Peck and Schuler (1987) also developed an observational framework, the *Social Interaction Observation Guide,* for assessing the social communication skills of children with ASD in the context of interaction. This framework assesses the child's ability to initiate, respond to, maintain, or terminate social interactions. As opposed to quantifying the rate of particular interactive responses, this guide is used to describe actual behavior and define the contextual variables that affect the child's social interactions.

Based on what we have learned about the social discourse needs of children with ASD to be successful communication partners, practitioners should sample social communication behavior by designing opportunities for observing the following:

- initiating interactions;
- responding to attempts at interaction;
- requesting information from a communicative partner;
- commenting on an activity or event or during an interaction;
- following routines;
- providing or offering information; and
- understanding requests or expectations for performance.

Within the observations made to gain information about the communication skills of a child with ASD, it would also be useful to identify the contextual supports that aided the child's communication attempts. This might include a description of the environmental arrangement (how the environment is set up), the props used, and the level of prompting needed.

Standardized and Nonstandardized Tools

The use of standardized and nonstandardized tools may be useful in gathering specific information about the communication strengths and needs of children with ASD. For young children or those with limited verbal skills, the *Communication Symbolic Behavior Scales* (Wetherby & Prizant, 1993) is a valuable standardized norm-referenced tool. It uses communication temptations within a semistructured play sequence to assess children's communication functions (behavior regulation, social interaction, and joint attention), communication means (gestural, vocal, and verbal), reciprocity, social/affective signaling, and symbolic behavior. It is normed for typical children from birth to 2 years old and is appropriate for assessing children up to 8 years old who perform developmentally at a much younger age.

The *MacArthur Communicative Development Inventories* (CDI; Fenson et al., 1993) are also appropriate for use with very young children in the early stages of language development. The CDI is a norm-referenced tool that taps the knowledge of parents and offers an efficient and valid strategy for assessing early language. There are two components to the inventory. One part of the inventory, "Words and Gestures," is designed for 8- to 16-month-olds and yields information for vocabulary comprehension and production and gesture use. The second part of the inventory, "Words and Sentences," is designed for 16- to 30-month-olds and generates information for vocabulary production and several aspects of grammatical development, including mean length of utterance and sentence complexity. Both portions of the CDI have been used by clinicians and researchers in the assessment of children with developmental disabilities.

Another appropriate assessment tool for early identification of communication difficulties, as well as other developmental skills, is the *Ages and Stages Questionnaires* (ASQ; Squires, Potter, & Bricker, 1995). The ASQ is a parent-completed questionnaire designed to provide periodic developmental screening for infants and children with potential developmental problems. It includes 11 questionnaires that are completed by parents when their child is 4, 8, 12, 16, 20, 24, 30, 36, and 48 months old, with optional forms for 6 and 18 months. There are 30 developmental items in each questionnaire across five areas: communication, gross motor, fine motor, problem solving, and personal–social. Parents indicate whether their child performs a particular behavior and whether it occurs only occasionally. Practitioners convert parental responses to points, which translate into values that are compared to available cutoff points. The advantage of this screening tool is the value held for parental input and the flexibility it has for use in a variety of settings across disciplines.

A nonstandardized communication tool, *Evaluating Acquired Skills in Communication* (EASIC; Riley, 1991), has been used to inventory the communication skills of preschool children with ASD. The EASIC assesses five levels of relevant communication in preschool children: prelanguage, receptive (simple comprehension); expressive (emerging communication modes); receptive (complex comprehension); and expressive (semantic, syntactic, morphologic, and pragmatic skills). Children's responses are evaluated qualitatively during assessment across six performance levels: spontaneous, cued, imitated, manipulated, no response, or inappropriate response. Practitioners judge whether a skill has been accomplished, is still emerging, or has not yet developed, based on the child's ability to demonstrate that skill spontaneously, in response to a cue, or only when imitating or manipulating. The value of this tool is the opportunity to qualify children's performance beyond a correct versus incorrect response.

Project TEACCH (Watson et al., 1989) also designed a *Communication Assessment* for obtaining and analyzing a communication sample that leads to setting and prioritizing intervention goals for children with ASD and other developmental disabilities. The assessment involves taking a communication sample, during which a practitioner identifies what a child says or does, describes the context (e.g., with teacher, parents, siblings, peers), determines the function served (e.g., request, get attention, comment, express feelings), and specifies the semantic category (e.g., object, action, location). Once the communication sample is analyzed, a *Communication Assessment Summary* is completed that includes information gathered from both home and school and evaluates whether the skills observed are strong, emerging, or not yet observed.

Bishop (1998) created the *Children's Communication Checklist* (CCC) as an alternative to standardized language tests that fail to look at the qualitative aspects of a child's communication impairment, particularly in the area of pragmatics. The checklist is composed of nine subscales that look at speech, syntax, inappropriate initiation, coherence, stereotyped conversation, use of context, rapport, social relationships, and interests. A pragmatic composite is derived from ratings on the inappropriate initiation, coherence, stereotyped conversation, use of context, and rapport subscales. Bishop found that both teachers and SLPs reliably rate pragmatic aspects of communication difficulty in children 7 to 9 years of age and that the pragmatic composite discriminates children with semantic–pragmatic disorders (those most often on the autism spectrum) from those with other types of language impairment.

Although not an exhaustive list and not specifically designed only for young children with ASD, the assessment tools mentioned here have value in supporting practitioners in their efforts to identify formally communication difficulties. They also provide a means for observing change in communication skills over time.

Summary

This chapter has discussed the language and communication impairments frequently described for children with ASD. Several strategies have been outlined for assessing communication and pragmatic language difficulties in this population, including creating profiles of communication strengths and challenges. The summary that follows refers to the questions at the beginning of the chapter and highlights key points.

What theoretical frameworks are used to explain impairment in language and communication in children with ASD?

Tager-Flusberg (1996, 1997a) has suggested that the language impairment seen in children with ASD can be explained as a disconnect between language form and use, rather than a deviance in the development of language. Tager-Flusberg and others use a "theory of mind" to further explain the specific deficits in communication described for this population. Although language form (e.g., syntax) may be delayed, it is relatively intact in children with ASD, whereas language use (e.g., pragmatics) and the aspects of language requiring perspective taking and understanding the thoughts and ideas of others are more impaired.

What early communication challenges are typical for children with ASD?

Wetherby and Prizant (1992, 1993) describe several challenging areas of early communication for children with ASD. The development of intentional communication in such children is generally characterized by behavior regulation, with weaker development of social interaction and limited emergence of joint attention. Gesture use is also limited, and pointing often is delayed or never develops. The understanding and use of facial expression, including eye gaze, is also poorly developed in young children with ASD. Often, when verbal behavior does emerge, it takes on several unconventional forms.

Children with ASD have been described as using echolalia, perseverative speech, and excessive questioning in their early language production.

What pragmatic language challenges interfere with the ability of verbal children with ASD to engage in conversation?

Several features in the use of language for social purposes create problems for verbal children with ASD. These include paralinguistic features (the prosody and intelligibility of speech), extralinguistic features (gestures and body movement), linguistic features (attention to communication partner and available linguistic forms), and conversational features (topic selection and maintenance, changing topics, turn taking, contingent responding, initiating, etc.). Children and adolescents with ASD will demonstrate variation in the range and degree of pragmatic language challenge they experience. In addition, they may develop their own, less conventional strategies for managing the several purposes language can serve. For example, children with ASD have been reported to use metaphors with private meanings, interpret what they hear literally, and create conversations around their own themes or special topics of interest. Assessment requires practitioners to be aware of the continuum of pragmatic difficulties that are likely to plague children and adolescents with ASD and to understand the contextual and personal variables that will influence the effect of these difficulties.

How can communication profiles be used to assess the strengths and challenges of children with ASD in this core deficit area?

Wetherby and her colleagues (Wetherby & Prizant, 1992, 1993; Wetherby et al., 1998; Wetherby et al., 2000) support the notion of developing a holistic and comprehensive view of young children with ASD by profiling their communication strengths and challenges. Communication profiling is an important preintervention step that can be used by practitioners to prioritize communication intervention goals. There are several considerations for creating a profile of a child's communication strengths and challenges. Situations need to be designed to foster observation of attempts to communicate. Practitioners must observe what the child does to communicate both nonverbally and verbally. Joint attention should be assessed, and a child's repertoire of gestures, sounds, and words should be defined. Unconventional verbal behavior should be carefully examined. Most important, practitioners will need to define when children's communication skills no longer meet their needs.

Profiling the communication strengths and challenges of verbal children and adolescents with ASD requires close inspection of their pragmatic language. Past research examining the pragmatic language development of children with and without language impairment suggests the need for a comprehensive analysis across a variety of environmental contexts and communication partners. Roth and Spekman (1984a, 1984b) offer a useful organizational framework for assessing pragmatic skills in children, which includes an analysis of communicative intention, presupposition, and the social organization of discourse. This framework has value in profiling the pragmatic language skills of verbal children and adolescents with ASD. The literature also supports an examination of language use across a variety of settings, contexts, and communication partners.

What areas of communication assessment should be considered across the three dimensions of the disablement framework?

Communication assessment should address all three areas of disability impairment, activity, and participation—as described by the World Health Organization (2001). Practitioners can use record reviews, interviews, observations in clinical or natural environments, and standardized and non-standardized tools to describe areas of impairment in communication. A more comprehensive evaluation of communication impairment, in light of its impact on the ability of children and adolescents with ASD both to engage in a variety of daily activities important for learning and living and to participate fully in their community, is critical. Personal and contextual factors should also be considered in this assessment. Assessment that considers the three dimensions of the disablement framework ensures that the interventions developed and planned for children and adolescents with ASD will be responsive to their actual needs.

Communication Assessment Interview

Child: _____ Interviewee: _____

Date: _____ Interviewer: _____

Communication Use

1. In what situations does _____ communicate with you? Please give examples.

2. If _____ wants something, what does he/she do to let you know? (behavior regulation: requesting an action or object)

3. How do you know _____ does not want something or does not want to do something? (behavior regulation: protesting)

4. If _____ wants your attention, what does he/she do? (social interaction: getting attention)

5. How does _____ greet someone? (social interaction: greeting)

6. How does _____ let you know he/she wants to continue an action, event, or interaction? (social interaction: requesting a social routine)

7. How does _____ share interesting experiences with you or others? (joint attention: commenting on information)

8. Please describe those situations, if any, in which _____ asks you or others a question to obtain information. (joint attention: seeking information)

9. Please describe those situations, if any, in which _____ offers information about something that is not present and that you or others don't know about. (joint attention: giving or offering information)

10. Please describe those situations in which _____ currently does not communicate with you or others and say why you think that is.

(continues)

APPENDIX 4.A

Communication Form

1. Describe the gestures (e.g., pointing, showing, waving, giving, nodding) you have observed _____ using and the situations in which they have occurred.

2. Describe the facial expressions (e.g., smiling, frowning, squinting) you have observed _____ using and the situations in which they have occurred.

3. Give some examples of the sounds, words, and sentences (depending on language level of child) you have observed _____ using and describe the situations in which these have occurred.

4. Describe any other means of communication you have observed _____ using and describe the situations in which this has occurred.

5. Give an example of _____ using any of the following and describe the situations in which each has occurred:
   a. echolalia
   b. repetitive questions
   c. perseverative speech

6. What other forms of communication (e.g., pictures, signs, symbols, written words), if any, does _____ use and in what situations?

7. When _____ speaks, how easy is it for you to understand what he/she has said?

   Not at all   Rarely   Sometimes   Frequently   Always

8. When _____ speaks, how easy is it for someone who is less familiar with his/her speech to understand what he/she has said?

   Not at all   Rarely   Sometimes   Frequently   Always

9. How would you describe the tone (pitch and loudness) of _____'s voice?

   Inappropriate   Rarely   Sometimes   Frequently   Always
                        Appropriate   Appropriate   Appropriate   Appropriate

   Please explain: _____

10. How would you describe the rhythm (rate and prosody) of _____'s voice?

   Inappropriate   Rarely   Sometimes   Frequently   Always
                        Appropriate   Appropriate   Appropriate   Appropriate

   Please explain: _____

(continues)

APPENDIX 4.A

Communication Content

1. What are some examples of the types of words _____ understands?

2. What are some examples of the types of words (e.g., action words, object words, feeling words, descriptive words) _____ uses when communicating?

3. How would you describe _____'s understanding of words? (receptive vocabulary)

   Poor   Fair   Adequate   Very Good   Excellent

   Please explain: _____

4. How would you describe _____'s use of words? (expressive vocabulary)

   Poor   Fair   Adequate   Very Good   Excellent

   Please explain: _____

5. Give an example of _____'s understanding of any of the following:
   a. metaphor
   b. idiomatic expression
   c. inference

6. Give an example of _____'s misunderstanding of any of the following:
   a. metaphor
   b. idiomatic expression
   c. inference

7. Give an example of _____'s appropriate use of any of the following:
   a. metaphor
   b. idiomatic expression
   c. inference

8. Give an example of _____'s inappropriate use of any of the following:
   a. metaphor
   b. idiomatic expression
   c. inference

9. What specific topics, if any, does _____ show a particular interest in and talk a lot about?

10. Please explain those situations, if any, in which _____ has difficulty finding the right word(s) to explain what he/she means?

APPENDIX 4.A

Practice Opportunities

1. Observe a verbal child with ASD at home and in school using the assessment format for examining unconventional verbal behavior (Figure 4.1). Identify any instances of echolalia, perseverative speech, or excessive questioning. Describe the context, what immediately preceded the unconventional verbal behavior, the possible function served by the behavior, and the response elicited. Determine the rigidity or flexibility in the unconventional verbal behavior observed.

2. Create a communication profile for a young child with ASD that considers the child's early intentional communication behaviors, including the functions served and the means used.

3. As a team, determine what standard tools would be most effective for assessing the semantic language of a verbal child or adolescent with ASD.

4. Develop a profile for a child or adolescent with ASD that describes both the child's strengths and challenges in the paralinguistic, extralinguistic, linguistic, and conversational features of pragmatic language.

Suggested Readings

Landa, R. (2000). Social language use in Asperger syndrome and high-functioning autism. In A. Klin, F. R. Volkmar, & S. S. Sparrow (Eds.), *Asperger syndrome* (pp. 125–155). New York: Guilford Press.

This chapter comprehensively describes the areas of pragmatic language use important to understanding verbal children with ASD. Landa provides a description of what is expected in the normal development of communicative intentions, presupposition, and discourse, as well as what might be observed in those same areas for children with ASD. The author recommends both formal and informal means for assessing the pragmatic skills of children with ASD and offers some guidelines for intervention.

Peck, C. A., & Schuler, A. L. (1987). Assessment of social/communicative behavior for students with autism and severe handicaps: The importance of asking the right question. In T. Layton (Ed.), *Language and treatment of autistic and developmentally disordered children* (pp. 35–62). Springfield, IL: Charles C Thomas.

This chapter clearly defines the limitations of traditional assessment methods when examining the social communication behavior of children with ASD. It offers several protocols for completing observations that are rich in information and contextually valid. The authors also provide an explanation of those contextual and environmental variables (e.g., adult interaction style, peer characteristics, situational characteristics) that are likely to affect the social communication of children with ASD and related disorders.

Wetherby, A. M., Prizant, B. M., & Hutchinson, T. A. (1998). Communicative, social/affective, and symbolic profiles of young children with autism and pervasive developmental disorders. *American Journal of Speech–Language Pathology, 7,* 79–91.

Based on clinically applied research, this article provides a framework in which to create communication profiles for children with ASD. The authors effectively characterize the early behaviors critical to communication success over time in children with ASD.

Resources

Early Communication Assessments

Fenson, L., Dale, P. S., Reznick, J. S., Thal, D., Bates, E., Hartung, J. P., et. al. (1993). *MacArthur Communicative Development Inventories: User's guide and technical manual.* San Diego: Singular.

Riley, A. M. (1991). *Evaluating Acquired Skills in Communication–Revised.* San Antonio, TX: Psychological Corp.

Squires, J., Potter, L., & Bricker, D. (1995). *The ASQ user's guide for the Ages & Stages Questionnaires: A parent-completed, child-monitoring system.* Baltimore: Brookes.

Wetherby, A. M., & Prizant, B. M. (1993). *Communication and Symbolic Behavior Scales manual.* Chicago: Riverside Press.

Prosody–Voice Assessments

Shriberg, L. D., Kwiatkowski, J., & Rasmussen, C. (1990). *The Prosody–Voice Screening Profile.* Tucson, AZ: Communication Skills Builders.

Semantic Assessments

Boehm, A. E. (1986). *Boehm Test of Basic Concepts–Preschool version.* San Antonio, TX: Psychological Corp.

Boehm, A. E. (1986). *Boehm Test of Basic Concepts–Revised.* San Antonio, TX: Psychological Corp.

Bracken, B. A. (1986). *Bracken Basic Concept Scale.* San Antonio, TX: Psychological Corp.

Brownell, R. (1987). *Receptive One-Word Picture Vocabulary Test–Upper Extension.* Novato, CA: Academic Therapy Publications.

Dunn, L., & Dunn, L. (1997). *Peabody Picture Vocabulary Test–III.* Circle Pines, MN: American Guidance Service.

Edmonston, N., & Thane, N. L. (1988). *Test of Relational Concepts.* Austin, TX: PRO-ED.

Gardner, M. F. (2000). *Receptive One-Word Picture Vocabulary Test–2000 Edition.* Austin, TX: PRO-ED.

Gardner, M. F. (2000). *Expressive One-Word Picture Vocabulary Test–2000 Edition.* Austin, TX: PRO-ED.

Huisingh, R., Barrett, M., Zachman, L., Blagden, C., & Orman, J. (1989). *The Word Test–Revised Elementary.* East Moline, IL: LinguiSystems.

Richard, G. J., & Hanner, M. A. (1985). *Language Processing Test–Revised*. East Moline, IL: LinguiSystems.

Wiig, E. H., & Secord, W. (1992). *Test of Word Knowledge*. San Antonio, TX: Psychological Corp.

Williams, K. T. (1997). *Expressive Vocabulary Test*. Circle Pines, MN: American Guidance Service.

Zachman, L., Huisingh, R., Barrett, C., Orman, J., & Blagden, C. (1990). *The Word Test–Adolescent*. East Moline, IL: LinguiSystems.

Pragmatic Assessments

Barrett, M., Zachman, L., & Huisingh, R. (1988). *Assessing semantic skills through everyday themes*. East Moline, IL: LinguiSystems.

Bowers, L., Barret, M., Huisingh, R., Orman, J., & LoGiudice, C. (1994). *Test of Problem Solving–Revised Elementary*. East Moline, IL: LinguiSystems.

Phelps-Teraski, D., & Phelps-Gunn, T. (1992). *Test of Pragmatic Language*. San Antonio, TX: Psychological Corp.

Shulman, B. B. (1986). *Test of Pragmatic Skills–Revised*. Tucson, AZ: Communication Skill Builders.

Simon, C. S. (1986). *Evaluating Communicative Competence: A Functional Pragmatic Procedure–Revised Edition*. Tucson, AZ: Communication Skill Builders.

Wiig, E. H., & Secord, W. (1989). *Test of Language Competence–Expanded Edition*. San Antonio, TX: Psychological Corp.

Glossary

Affect. The emotion component of communication.

Analytic processing. Recognizing, analyzing, and producing individual words or parts of language.

Behavior regulation. Intentional communication acts used to regulate or control the behavior of others for the purpose of obtaining something desirable.

Delayed echolalia. Delay in the repetition of what has been said or heard.

Extralinguistic features. Gestures and body movement used to signal intentional communication.

Gestalt processing. Processing language and experience as "whole units" rather than segmenting language into meaningful rule-based components.

Immediate echolalia. Immediate repetition of what has been said or heard.

Joint attention. Intentional communication acts used to direct the attention of others for the purpose of sharing an event.

Metaphorical language. Making associations that have private meanings.

Mitigated echolalia. Can be immediate or delayed and involves variation in the repetition in the form of a modification in the words used, the prosody of the utterance, or the context in which it occurs.

Overselectivity. Rigid focus on a theme or topic of interest.

Paralinguistic features. A component of pragmatics involving the prosody and intelligibility of speech.

Perseverative speech. Imitated or self-generated utterances that are produced repeatedly without evidence of intent.

Pragmatics. The use of language in social contexts.

Prosody. Rhythm of speech involving intonation and the emphasis on particular words that signals meaning or adds emotion.

Semantics. The meaning component of language.

Social interaction. Intentional communication acts used to call attention, to greet another, or to sustain a social routine.

References

American Psychiatric Association. (1994). *Diagnostic and statistical manual of mental disorders* (4th ed.). Washington, DC: Author.

American Psychiatric Association. (2000). *Diagnostic and statistical manual of mental disorders* (4th ed. text rev.). Washington, DC: Author.

Baltaxe, C. M., & Simmons, J. Q. (1985). Prosodic development in normal and autistic children. In E. Schopler & G. Mesibov (Eds.), *Communication problems in autism* (pp. 95–126). New York: Plenum Press.

Baron-Cohen, S. (1988). Social and pragmatic deficits in autism: Cognitive or affective? *Journal of Autism and Developmental Disorders, 18*(3), 379–402.

Barron, S. (2001, November). *Consumers' views on autism.* Paper presented at the American Speech–Language–Hearing Association Convention, New Orleans, LA.

Bates, E. (1976). *Language and context: The acquisition of pragmatics.* San Diego: Academic Press.

Bates, E., Camaioni, L., & Volterra, V. (1975). The acquisition of performatives prior to speech. *Merrill-Palmer Quarterly, 21,* 205–226.

Bieberich, A. A., & Morgan, S. B. (1998). Brief report: Affective expression in children with autism or Down syndrome. *Journal of Autism and Developmental Disorders, 28*(4), 333–338.

Bishop, D. V. M. (1998). Development of the Children's Communication Checklist (CCC): A method for assessing qualitative aspects of communicative impairment in children. *Journal of Child Psychology and Psychiatry, 39*(6), 879–891.

Bowers, L., Barrett, M., Huisingh, R., Orman, J., & LoGiudice, C. (1994). *Test of Problem Solving–Revised Elementary Version.* East Moline, IL: LinguiSystems.

Bowers, L., Huisingh, R., LoGiudice, C., & Orman, J. (2004). *The Word Test 2: Elementary.* East Moline, IL: LinguiSystems.

Bowers, L., Huisingh, R., LoGiudice, C., & Orman, J. (2005). *The Word Test 2: Adolescent.* East Moline, IL: LinguiSystems.

Bruner, J. S. (1981). The ontogenesis of speech acts. *Journal of Child Language, 2,* 1–19.

Buffington, D. M., Krantz, P. J., McClannahan, L. E., & Poulson, C. L. (1998). Procedures for teaching appropriate gestural communication skills to children with autism. *Journal of Autism and Developmental Disorders, 28,* 535–545.

Camaioni, L., Perucchini, P., Muratori, F., & Milone, A. (1997). Brief report: A longitudinal examination of the communicative gestures deficit in young children with autism. *Journal of Autism and Developmental Disorders, 27*(6), 715–725.

Capps, L., Kehres, J., & Sigman, M. (1998). Conversational abilities among children with autism and children with developmental delays. *The International Journal of Research and Practice, 2,* 325–344.

Church, C., Alisanski, S., & Amanullah, S. (2000). The social, behavioral, and academic experiences of children with Asperger syndrome. *Focus on Autism and Other Developmental Disabilities, 15*(1), 12–20.

Curcio, F. (1978). Sensorimotor functioning and communication in mute autistic children. *Journal of Autism and Childhood Schizophrenia, 3,* 281–292.

Dale, P. S. (1980). Is early pragmatic development measurable? *Journal of Child Language, 8,* 1–12.

Dawson, G., Meltzoff, A. N., Osterling, J., Rinaldi, J., & Brown, E. (1998). Children with autism fail to orient to naturally occurring social stimuli. *Journal of Autism and Developmental Disorders, 28*(6), 479–485.

Dore, J. (1974). A pragmatic description of early language development. *Journal of Psycholinguistic Research, 4,* 343–350.

Dore, J. (1986). The development of conversational competence. In R. Schiefelbusch (Ed.), *Language competence: Assessment and intervention* (pp. 3–60). San Diego: College-Hill Press.

Duchan, J. F. (1994). Intervention principles for gestalt-style learners. In J. F. Duchan, L. E. Hewitt, & R. M. Sonnenmeier (Eds.), *Pragmatics: From theory to practice* (pp. 149–163). Englewood Cliffs, NJ: Prentice Hall.

Fay, W., & Schuler, A. L. (1980). *Emerging language in autistic children.* Baltimore: University Park Press.

Feldman, R. S., McGee, G. G., Mann, L., & Strain, P. (1993). Nonverbal affective decoding ability in children with autism and in typical preschoolers. *Journal of Early Intervention, 17*(4), 341–350.

Fenson, L., Dale, P. S., Reznick, J. S., Thal, D., Bates, E., Hartung, J. P., et al. (1993). *MacArthur Communicative Development Inventories: User's guide and technical manual.* San Diego: Singular.

Fine, J., Bartolucci, G., Ginsberg, G., & Szatmari, P. (1991). The use of intonation to communicate in subjects with pervasive developmental disorders. *Journal of Child Psychology and Psychiatry, 32,* 771–882.

Finnerty, J., & Quill, K. A. (1991). *The communication analyzer.* Lexington, MA: Educational Software Research.

Garfin, D., & Lord, C. (1986). Communication as a social problem in autism. In E. Schopler & G. Mesibov (Eds.), *Social behavior in autism* (pp. 237–261). New York: Plenum Press.

Grice, P. (1975). Logic and conversation. In J. Cole & P. Morgan (Eds.), *Syntax and semantics: Speech acts* (pp. 41–59). New York: Academic Press.

Halliday, M. (1975). *Learning how to mean.* London: Edward Arnold.

Happe, F. (1993). Communicative competence and theory of mind in autism: A test of relevance theory. *Cognition, 48,* 101–119.

Happe, F. (1994). An advanced test of theory of mind: Understanding of story characters' thoughts and feelings by able autistic, mentally handicapped and normal children and adults. *Journal of Autism and Developmental Disorders, 24,* 129–154.

Harris, N. S., Courchesne, E., Townsend, J., Carper, R. A., & Lord, C. (1999). Neuroanatomic contributions to slowed orienting of attention in children with autism. *Cognitive Brain Research, 8,* 61–71.

Hobson, R. P., & Lee, A. (1998). Hello and goodbye: A study of social engagement in autism. *Journal of Autism and Developmental Disorders, 28*(2), 117–127.

Kanner, L. (1971). Follow-up study of eleven autistic children originally reported in 1943. *Journal of Autism and Childhood Schizophrenia, 1*(2), 119–145.

Koegel, R. (1995). Communication and language intervention. In R. L. Koegel & L. K. Koegel (Eds.), *Teaching children with autism: Strategies for initiating positive interactions and improving learning opportunities* (pp. 17–32). Baltimore: Brookes.

Krashen, S., & Scarcella, R. (1978). On routines and patterns in language acquisition and performance. *Language Learning, 28,* 283–300.

Landa, R. (2000). Social language use in Asperger syndrome and high-functioning autism. In A. Klin, F. R. Volkmar, & S. S. Sparrow (Eds.), *Asperger syndrome* (pp. 125–155). New York: Guilford Press.

Landau, B., & Gleitman, L. (1985). *Language and experience: Evidence from the blind child.* Cambridge, MA: Harvard University Press.

Lord, C. (1995). Follow-up of two-year-olds referred for possible autism. *Journal of Child Psychology and Psychiatry, 36,* 1365–1382.

Lord, C., & Paul, R. (1997). Language and communication in autism. In D. Cohen & F. Volkmar (Eds.), *Handbook of autism and pervasive developmental disorders* (2nd ed., pp. 195–225). New York: Wiley.

Lord, C., Rutter, M., Goode, S., Heemsbergen, J., Jordan, H., Mawhood, L., et al. (1989). Autism diagnostic observation schedule: A standardized observation of communicative and social behavior. *Journal of Autism and Developmental Disorders, 19,* 185–212.

Lotter, V. (1978). Follow-up studies. In M. Rutter & E. Schopler (Eds.), *Autism: A reappraisal of concepts and treatment* (pp. 475–496). New York: Plenum Press.

McEachin, J. J., Smith, T., & Lovaas, O. I. (1993). Long-term outcome for children with autism who received early intensive behavioral treatment. *American Journal on Mental Retardation, 97,* 359–372.

McLean, J., & Snyder-McLean, L. (1978). *A transactional approach to early language training: Derivation of a model system.* Columbus, OH: Charles Merrill.

Menyuk, P., & Quill, K. (1985). Semantic problems in autistic children. In E. Schopler & G. Mesibov (Eds.), *Communication problems in autism* (pp. 127–146). New York: Plenum Press.

Minshew, N. J., Goldstein, G., & Siegel, D. J. (1995). Speech and language in high-functioning autistic individuals. *Neuropsychology, 9,* 255–261.

Mundy, P., & Sigman, M. (1989). Specifying the nature of the social impairment in autism. In G. Dawson (Ed.), *Autism: Nature, diagnosis and treatment* (pp. 3–21). New York: Guilford Press.

Mundy, P., Sigman, M., & Kasari, C. (1990). A longitudinal study of joint attention and language development in autistic children. *Journal of Autism and Developmental Disorders, 20*(1), 115–128.

Nelson, K. (1973). Structure and strategy in learning how to talk. *Monographs of the Society for Research in Child Development, 38*(149).

Ochs, E. (1979). Introduction: What child language can contribute to pragmatics. In E. Ochs & B. B. Schieffelin (Eds.), *Developmental pragmatics* (pp. 1–17). New York: Academic Press.

Ochs, E., & Schieffelin, B. (1979). *Developmental pragmatics.* New York: Academic Press.

Ozonoff, S., & Miller, J. (1996). An exploration of right hemisphere contributions to the pragmatic impairments of autism. *Brain and Language, 52,* 411–434.

Palmer, B. C. (1991). *Figurative Language Interpretation Test.* Novato, CA: Academic Therapy Publications.

Peck, C. A., & Schuler, A. L. (1987). Assessment of social/communicative behavior for students with autism and severe handicaps: The importance of asking the right question.

In T. Layton (Ed.), *Language and treatment of autistic and developmentally disordered children* (pp. 35–62). Springfield, IL: Charles C Thomas.

Peters, A. (1977). Language learning strategies: Does the whole equal the sum of the parts? *Language, 53,* 560–573.

Peters, A. (1983). *The units of language acquisition.* New York: Cambridge University Press.

Phelps-Terasaki, D., & Phelps-Gunn, T. (1992). *Test of Pragmatic Language.* Austin, TX: PRO-ED.

Prizant, B. M. (1983). Language acquisition and the communicative behavior in autism: Toward an understanding of the "whole" of it. *Journal of Speech and Hearing Disorders, 48,* 296–307.

Prizant, B. M. (1987). Theoretical and clinical implications of echolalic behavior in autism. In T. Layton (Ed.), *Language and treatment of autistic and developmentally disordered children* (pp. 65–88). Springfield, IL: Charles C Thomas.

Prizant, B. M., & Rydell, P. J. (1993). Assessment and intervention considerations for unconventional verbal behavior. In S. F. Warren & J. Reichle (Series Eds.) & J. Reichle & D. Wacker (Vol. Eds.), *Communication and language intervention series: Vol. 3. Communicative alternatives to challenging behavior: Integrating functional assessment and intervention strategies* (pp. 263–297). Baltimore: Brookes.

Prizant, B. M., & Schuler, A. (1987). Facilitating communication: Theoretical foundations. In D. Cohen & A. Donnellan (Eds.), *Handbook of autism and pervasive developmental disorders* (pp. 289–300). New York: Wiley.

Prizant, B. M., Wetherby, A. M., & Rydell, P. J. (2000). Communication intervention issues for young children with autism spectrum disorders. In A. M. Wetherby & B. M. Prizant (Eds.), *Autism spectrum disorders: A transactional developmental perspective* (pp. 193–224). Baltimore: Brookes.

Prutting, C. (1982). Pragmatics as social competence. *Journal of Speech and Hearing Disorders, 47,* 123–133.

Prutting, C., & Kirchner, D. M. (1983). Applied pragmatics. In T. M. Gallagher & C. A. Prutting (Eds.), *Pragmatic assessment and intervention issues in language* (pp. 29–64). San Diego: College-Hill Press.

Quill, K. A. (1995). Enhancing children's social communication interactions. In K. A. Quill (Ed.), *Teaching children with autism: Strategies to enhance communication and socialization* (pp. 163–189). New York: Delmar.

Richard, G. J., & Hanner, M. A. (1995). *Language Processing Test–Revised.* Austin, TX: PRO-ED.

Ricks, D., & Wing, L. (1975). Language, communication, and the use of symbols in normal and autistic children. *Journal of Autism and Childhood Schizophrenia, 5,* 191–220.

Riley, A. M. (1991). *Evaluating Acquired Skills in Communication–Revised.* Tucson, AZ: Communication Skill Builders.

Roth, F. P., & Spekman, N. J. (1984a). Assessing the pragmatic abilities of children: Part 1. Organizational framework and assessment parameters. *Journal of Speech and Hearing Disorders, 49,* 2–11.

Roth, F. P., & Spekman, N. J. (1984b). Assessing the pragmatic abilities of children: Part 2. Guidelines, considerations, and specific evaluation procedures. *Journal of Speech and Hearing Disorders, 49,* 12–17.

Rydell, P. J., & Mirenda, P. (1991). The effects of two levels of linguistic constraint on echolalia and generative language production in children with autism. *Journal of Autism and Developmental Disorders, 21,* 131–157.

Rydell, P. J., & Prizant, B. M. (1995). Assessment and intervention strategies for children who use echolalia. In K. A. Quill (Ed.), *Teaching children with autism: Strategies to enhance communication and socialization* (pp. 105–132). New York: Delmar.

Searle, J. (1969). *Speech acts: An essay in the philosophy of language.* Cambridge, MA: Harvard University Press.

Shriberg, L. D., Paul, R., McSweeny, J. L., Klin, A., Cohen, D. J., & Volkmar, F. R. (2001). Speech and prosody characteristics of adolescents and adults with high functioning autism and Asperger syndrome. *Journal of Speech, Language, and Hearing Research, 44*(5), 1097–1115.

Shulman, B. S. (1986). *Test of Pragmatic Skills–Revised.* Tucson, AZ: Communication Skill Builders.

Simon, C. S. (1986). *Evaluating Communicative Competence: A Functional Pragmatic Procedure–Revised Edition.* Tuscson, AZ: Communication Skill Builders.

Snow, M. E., Hertzig, M. E., & Shapiro, T. (1987). Expressions of emotion in young autistic children. *Journal of the American Academy of Child and Adolescent Psychiatry, 27,* 647–655.

Squires, J., Potter, L., & Bricker, D. (1995). *The ASQ user's guide for the Ages and Stages Questionnaires: A parent-completed, child-monitoring system.* Baltimore: Brookes.

Stone, W. L., & Caro-Martinez, L. (1990). Naturalistic observations of spontaneous communication in autisitc children. *Journal of Autism and Developmental Disorders, 20,* 513–522.

Stone, W. L., Ousley, O. Y., Yoder, P. J., Hogan, K. L., & Hepburn, S. L. (1997). Nonverbal communication in two and three year old children with autism. *Journal of Autism and Developmental Disorders, 27*(6), 677–696.

Tager-Flusberg, H. (1993). What language reveals about the understanding of mind in children with autism. In S. Baron-Cohen, H. Tager-Flusberg, & D. J. Cohen (Eds.), *Understanding other minds: Perspectives from autism* (pp. 138–157). Oxford, England: Oxford University Press.

Tager-Flusberg, H. (1996). Brief report: Current theory and research on language and communication in autism. *Journal of Autism and Developmental Disorders, 26*(2), 169–172.

Tager-Flusberg, H. (1997a). Perspectives on language and communication in autism. In D. J. Cohen & F. R. Volkmar (Eds.), *Handbook of autism and pervasive developmental disorders* (2nd ed., pp. 894–900). New York: Wiley.

Tager-Flusberg, H. (1997b). The role of theory of mind in language acquisition: Contributions from the study of autism. In L. Adamson & M. A. Romski (Eds.), *Research on communication and language disorders: Contributions to theories of language development* (pp. 133–158). Baltimore: Brookes.

Tager-Flusberg, H., Calkins, S., Nolin, T., Baumberger, T., Anderson, M., & Chadwick-Dias, A. (1990). A longitudinal study of language acquisition in autistic and Down syndrome children. *Journal of Autism and Developmental Disorders, 20,* 1–21.

Townsend, J., & Courchesne, E. (1994). Parietal damage and narrow "spotlight" spatial attention. *Journal of Cognitive Neuroscience, 6,* 220–232.

Townsend, J., Courchesne, E., Singer-Harris, N., Covington, J., Westerfield, M., Lyden, P., et al. (1999). Spational attention deficits in patients with acquired or developmental cerebellar abnormality. *Journal of Neuroscience, 19,* 5632–5642.

Twachtman, D. (1995). Methods to enhance communication in verbal children. In K. A. Quill (Ed.), *Teaching children with autism: Strategies to enhance communication and socialization* (pp. 133–162). Albany, NY: Delmar.

Twachtman-Cullen, D. (1998). Language and communication in high-functioning autism and Asperger syndrome. In E. Schopler, G. Mesibov, & L. J. Kunce (Eds.), *Asperger syndrome or high functioning autism?* (pp. 199–225). New York: Plenum Press.

Twachtman-Cullen, D. (2000). More able children with autism spectrum disorders: Socio-communicative challenges and guidelines for enhancing abilities. In A. M. Wetherby & B. M. Prizant (Eds.), *Autism spectrum disorders: A transactional developmental perspective* (pp. 225–249). Baltimore: Brookes.

Volden, J., & Lord, C. (1991). Neologisms and idiosyncratic language in autistic speakers. *Journal of Autism and Developmental Disorders, 21,* 109–130.

Volden, J., Mulcahy, R. F., & Holdgrafer, G. (1997). Pragmatic language disorder and perspective taking in autistic speakers. *Applied Psycholinguistics, 18,* 181–198.

Watson, L. R., Lord, C., Schaffer, B., & Schopler, E. (1989). *Teaching spontaneous communication to autistic and developmentally handicapped children.* New York: Irvington.

Wetherby, A. M. (1986). Ontogeny of communicative functions in autism. *Journal of Autism and Developmental Disorders, 16,* 295–319.

Wetherby, A. M., & Prizant, B. M. (1992). Profiling young children's communicative competence. In S. F. Warren & J. Reichle (Series & Vol. Eds.), *Communication and language intervention series: Vol. 1. Causes and effects in communication and language intervention* (pp. 217–253). Baltimore: Brookes.

Wetherby, A. M., & Prizant, B. M. (1993). *Communication and Symbolic Behavior Scales manual.* Chicago: Riverside Press.

Wetherby, A. M., & Prizant, B. M. (1996). *Autism spectrum disorders: New service delivery models for nonverbal young children.* ASHA Teleconference. Rockville, MD: American Speech-Language-Hearing Association.

Wetherby, A. M., Prizant, B. M., & Hutchinson, T. A. (1998). Communicative, social/affective, and symbolic profiles of young children with autism and pervasive developmental disorders. *American Journal of Speech–Language Pathology, 7,* 79–91.

Wetherby, A. M., Prizant, B. M., & Schuler, A. L. (2000). Understanding the nature of communication and language impairments. In A. M. Wetherby & B. M. Prizant (Eds.), *Autism spectrum disorders: A transactional developmental perspective* (pp. 109–141). Baltimore: Brookes.

Wiig, E., & Secord, W. (1989). *Test of Language Competence–Expanded.* San Antonio, TX. Psychological Corp.

Wiig, E. H., & Secord, W. (1992). *Test of Word Knowledge.* San Antonio, TX: Psychological Corp.

Wilcox, M. J. (1988). Designing an ecologically-based communication assessment. *The Clinical Connection, 3*(1), 1–4.

Wing, L., & Attwood, A. (1987). Syndromes of autism and atypical development. In D. J. Cohen & A. M. Donnellan (Eds.), *Handbook of autism and pervasive developmental disorders* (pp. 3–19). New York: Wiley.

World Health Organization. (2001). *International classification of functioning, disability and health.* Geneva, Switzerland: Author.

Yoder, P. J., Warren, S. F., Kim, K., & Gazdag, G. (1994). Facilitating prelinguistic communication skills in very young children with developmental disabilities II: Systematic replication and extension. *Journal of Speech and Hearing Research, 37,* 841–851.

Zachman, L., Barrett, M., Huisingh, R., Orman, J., & Blagden, C. (1991). *Test of Problem Solving–Adolescent Version.* East Moline, IL: LinguiSystems.

CHAPTER 5

Understanding and Assessing the Play of Children with ASD

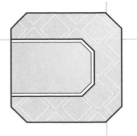

Patricia A. Prelock

QUESTIONS TO CONSIDER

In this chapter, principles of early play development will be identified, and definitions of play will be provided. You will discover some of the interrelationships that have been identified to explain the development of play, language, and cognition in children and the implications these interrelationships have for children with autism spectrum disorders (ASD). You will learn about the challenges in play development that affect the ability of children with ASD to engage in a range of play activities. Strategies for observing and profiling play will be discussed as part of assessment, leading to intervention planning and goal setting. The disablement framework described in Chapter 3 will be applied to this aspect of assessment for children and adolescents with ASD. As you read this chapter on play assessment, consider the following questions:

1. What principles guide early play development, and how is play defined?

2. What are the relationships among play, language, and cognition that have implications for children with ASD?

3. What are the challenges in play reported for children with ASD?

4. How can play profiles be used to assess the strengths and challenges of children with ASD in this core deficit area?

5. What areas of play assessment should be considered across the three dimensions of the disablement framework?

Introduction

Several theoretical perspectives have been influential in our understanding of play. Two theorists in particular, Piaget (1962) and Vygotsky (1978), have described the central role of play in the overall development of children. Piaget's constructivist view suggests that play is an intrinsically motivated and self-initiated activity that supports the acquisition of different ways of thinking and behaving (Wolfberg, 1999). Children achieve satisfaction and joy in the independent experience of constructing their knowledge through actions on objects and within events.

Although Vygotsky shares Piaget's recognition of play as part of a child's developing symbolic function, he conceptualizes play as a more social activity, in which a child represents behavior characterized by rules and imagination. This Vygotskian, or sociocultural, view suggests that a child in play constructs and transforms shared meanings and skills, values, and beliefs inherent in his or her culture (Wolfberg, 1999). Vygotsky further defines a "zone of proximal development" created by play. This zone is "the distance between the child's developmental level as determined by independent problem solving and the level of potential development as determined through problem solving under adult guidance or in collaboration with more capable peers" (1978, p. 86).

It seems that children's play development is socially connected to adult scaffolding, which supports the children's ongoing experiences and learning. A social-constructivist view seems to best explain my experience with the development of play—that is, children construct their knowledge through their experience with objects, actions, and events, sharing the meaning, values, and beliefs of a familiar social context. For children with ASD, the construction of knowledge may be limited or constrained in form and content because of their difficulty connecting with the social context. The use of adult support becomes highly important if children with ASD are to expand their experiences and increase their learning.

Impairment in play is described as part of the communication deficit defined for autism in the *Diagnostic and Statistical Manual of Mental Disorders–Fourth Edition* (DSM–IV; American Psychiatric Association [APA], 1994) and its text revision (DSM–IV–TR; APA, 2000). Specifically, "lack of pretend play" has been characterized as having a central role in the diagnosis of and intervention with children with ASD. It is important to recognize the interrelationships between play, language and communication, and social development, as mentioned in Chapter 4. However, this entire chapter is devoted to the assessment of play in children with ASD so that practitioners can understand the powerful role that play has in the overall development and social success of this population.

Principles of Play Development

Play is an ongoing, complex area of exploration influenced by culture, history, and religion (Sutton-Smith & Kelly-Byrne, 1984). It has been a difficult area to define because of the variable theoretical orientations described in the literature and the heterogeneous nature of play (Wolery & Bailey, 1989). It is not time, age, setting, or form specific.

Some basic characteristics or principles of play have been identified, however. Play is voluntary, pleasurable, and intrinsically motivated; it requires active engagement and is flexible and nonliteral (Burghardt, 1984; Garvey, 1990; King, 1986; Sutton-Smith & Kelly-Byrne, 1984; Weininger & Daniel, 1992; Wolfberg, 1995, 1999). Children are active learners who explore their world to make sense of it. Early on, children use their motor learning (reaching out, pulling up, moving around, seeking stimulation) to figure out actively what is happening in the world. This learning is also affected by environmental variables, such as the context in which the exploration takes place and the stresses experienced by children during their active learning.

Children also learn through physical experience, social interaction, and reflection. They have a powerful need to make sense of everything they encounter through manipulation, smell, taste, and performing actions on objects. Children use their own activities to construct and reconstruct their understanding of their world. Further, they need feedback from the physical and social environments to either confirm or challenge their understanding of the world.

Some have made a distinction between early exploration and play, suggesting that children learn how to use the information they gather through exploration in their actual manipulation of objects or situations in play (Hutt, 1979; Nourot, Scales, Van Hoorn, & Almy, 1987). Others believe play begins the moment a child is able to take an object in hand and bring it to the mouth or before the eyes (McCune, 1986). Whether making a distinction between exploration and play is important or not, it is valuable to consider the ways in which play has been classified and the importance of symbolic or pretend play in assessment.

Classifications of Play

Whatever perspective is held for describing the nature of play, it is important to understand the different ways that play has been categorized. Notions of play taxonomies or stages of play provide a useful framework for play assessment. For example, Parten (1932) classified play in the context of social participation. She defined six types of play:

- unoccupied (no real evidence of play other than standing, sitting, moving around others);

- onlooker (watching other children play, possibly talking and providing suggestions without engaging in the play);
- solitary (independent play with toys, with no effort to engage with other children);
- parallel (independent play alongside or among other children);
- associative (engaged in common activities and interests with other children, although loosely organized); and
- cooperative (organized with other children around a particular purpose involving making something, dramatizing a situation, or playing a game).

Piaget (1962) described three sequences or stages of play, which begin with sensorimotor practice play in the first year of life, move to symbolic play in the second year of life, and then to games with rules by the fourth year of life. Smilansky (1968) also proposed sequences of play, indicating that one stage of play would predominate at any given time, although overlap was likely. She defined four play stages, three of which mirrored those proposed by Piaget:

- functional—simple motor activities, including repetitious manipulations (similar to Piaget's sensorimotor practice play in year 1);
- constructive—sustained creative activity around a simple theme;
- dramatic—also described as symbolic, an accumulation of the skills and experience from the previous stages, with increased social awareness (similar to Piaget's symbolic play in year 2); and
- games with rules—play organized around rules and requiring a child's ability to adjust (similar to Piaget's games with rules in year 4).

Based on their observations of 40 infants, Belsky and Most (1981) developed a play sequence that recognized the relationship between play and exploration in very young children. Twelve different stages were defined in their study, several of which shared the characteristics specified by Piaget (1962) and Smilansky (1968). These stages included:

- mouthing (indiscriminate),
- simple manipulation (visually guided and lasting at least 5 seconds),
- functional (visually guided with information gained),
- relational (relating play materials in unexpected ways),
- functional–relational (relating play materials in expected ways),
- enactive naming (unconfirmed pretense activity like holding a phone to the ear without making talking sounds),
- pretend self (pretense behavior related to self like drinking from an empty cup), and
- pretend other (pretense behavior related to others like having a doll drink from an empty cup).

McCune (1986) classified play into two broad categories, sensorimotor exploration and pretend play. She further classified pretend play into several subcategories, including presymbolic schemes, self-pretend, decentered pretend, pretend play combinations, and planned pretend. Her subcategories of pretend play were similar to those proposed by Belsky and Most (1981). A *presymbolic scheme* involves a young child's first meaningful encounter with objects. The action is the meaning held for the child, since the child is not able at that point to represent meaning. In *self-pretend*, a child is aware of "pretend," but the activity focus is the child's body. When pretend is extended beyond the child, it is known as *decentered pretend play*. Once several actors or receivers of action occur, the activity is a *pretend play combination*. The final subcategory of pretend, *planned pretend play*, exists when a child indicates that the activity was preplanned. That level of play also requires symbolic identification of one object with another.

Symbolic or Pretend Play

The classification of play as symbolic or involving pretense is of particular interest in the assessment of children with ASD, because a lack of pretend play has been suggested as part of the core deficit (APA, 1994, 2000; Wetherby & Prizant, 1992, 1993). Symbolic play is referred to by several terms, including *pretend (pretense) play, representational play,* and *sociodramatic play.* The common element is the expectation that a child is representing or substituting objects in play (Belsky & Most, 1981; Bergen, 1988; Piaget, 1962; Wetherby, 1992). Leslie (1987), however, proposes two less traditional expectations. The first is that symbolic play involves *primary representation,* in which a child codes objects or events as they are. The second involves *meta-representation,* in which a child recodes the primary representation. At the very least, pretend play is a reflection of children's ability to manipulate their external world through symbols or representations made internally. A suspension of reality allows children to treat objects as if they were something else.

It is generally agreed that symbolic or pretend play begins during the second year of life, around 14 to 19 months of age (Bates, O'Connell, & Shore, 1987; Belsky & Most, 1981; Bergen, 1988; Fewell & Kaminski, 1988; McCune, 1986; Piaget, 1962; Wetherby, 1992). A shift or progression toward pretense becomes evident at about 12 months, beginning with object decontextualization and moving to self–other relationships, object substitutions, and sequential combinations (Bergen, 1988). Early on, pretend play is described as more solitary play, in which children substitute realistic pretend objects for the actual objects. With advancement in pretend play, the social context becomes more important than the representation of objects (Saltz & Saltz, 1986). Even further advancement leads to the development of fictional characters and situations, as is characteristic of sociodramatic play. In that context, rules are established based on the roles that are assigned and assumed. The rules typical of pretend play provide an internal consistency to the play that supports problem solving.

Examples of pretend play are frequently observed in preschool classrooms as children use a variety of play materials and props in different activities. Some of these activities might include

- make believe (child takes on characteristics of an object or person and acts out a sequence);
- exploration of an object;
- creation of stories supported by graphic representations using art materials;
- use of construction material to support a pretend theme or action sequence;
- manipulation of buildings and people as the environment and characters for a story;
- implementation of a sequence of events or actions that are related to one another, as in dramatic play; and
- implementation of more complex schemes sustained for longer periods, involving several children negotiating a narrative play scene with established rules, as in sociodramatic play.

The preschool environment is an obvious context in which to assess not only the opportunities for pretend play but also those play activities in which children engage. It is a setting for highly imaginative play among peers, which supports the development of children's social competence (Singer & Singer, 1990; Wolfberg, 1999). Through play, children are able to express intimacy and affection toward their peers and begin to establish friendships (Hartup & Sancilio, 1986).

Little research has been done on the development of play as children approach middle childhood, although children are thought to abandon make-believe for somewhat more complex play experiences around that time (Piaget, 1962; Wolfberg, 1999). The opportunity for pretend play is often limited in elementary school, where organized sports and games with rules are substituted. But the desire to pretend is sustained through children's individual fantasies, imaginary characters, and dramatic play with miniatures, dolls, and peers (Wolfberg, 1999). The establishment of friendships and associations with particular peer groups becomes a priority during this time.

Relationships Among Play, Language, and Cognition

Play is an important medium for the intellectual, linguistic, emotional, and social development of children (Fewell & Kaminski, 1988; Wolfberg, 1999).

More important, there also appears to be a developmental sequence characteristic of play that parallels that of language and cognitive development (Bates et al., 1987; Fewell & Kaminski, 1988).

Wetherby (1992) describes progressive levels of play comparable to the major stages of language development. Under the age of 12 months, children are exploring objects and performing actions on those objects at the same time that intentional communication is developing. Around 12 to 18 months of age, when children are using realistic objects directed toward self and combining two objects in play, their first words appear. At 18 to 24 months, children are using realistic objects directed toward others and demonstrate single-action schemes with several objects and receivers of actions, combining at least four objects (Bates et al., 1987; Wetherby, 1992). It is at this time that word combinations are observed. During the transition from 2 to 4 years, children begin to use objects symbolically and engage in related action schemes combining four to six objects and pretending without props. Linguistically, this is a time when children exhibit sentence grammar. By the time children reach age 4, they are engaging in sociodramatic play, taking on roles and cooperating with others, as they develop their skills in discourse.

Westby (1980, 1988) highlights similar parallels in the development of play and language, describing 10 stages of play and associated linguistic skills. These parallels are presented below:

- Stage I (9–12 months), appropriate toy use—no true language; some communicative intent and joint attention
- Stage II (13–17 months), purposeful toy exploration, multiple motor schemes—first words are variable and context dependent (e.g., saying "swing" when sitting on a swing but not when seeing it); communicative functions increase
- Stage III (17–19 months), symbolic play directed toward self, such as pretending to drink from a cup—true verbal communication; using words with several functional and semantic relationships
- Stage IV (19–22 months), play moves beyond the child, such as feeding a doll—word combinations; expanding semantic relationships
- Stage V (24 months), routine and familiar events or experiences are represented in play—functional and semantic relationships appear in short phrases and sentences
- Stage VI (30 months), less familiar events or experiences are represented in play using realistic props—responding to wh-questions, using wh-question forms (excluding "why") at the beginning of sentences
- Stage VII (36 months), play themes combined into episodes with multiple schemes—use of past tense and future verbs
- Stage VIII (36–42 months), play is less dependent on realistic props; includes scripts that have been observed but not experienced— vocabulary expansion; use of dialogue and indirect requests

- Stage IX (42–48 months), play themes are more organized and elaborate—use of modals and conjunctions; appropriate response to "why" questions
- Stage X (60 months), play themes include events never observed or experienced; play is planned and monitored—use of relational terms like *when, first, next*

More recently, Westby (2000) redefined her developmental play scale to include two phases, presymbolic and symbolic. In the presymbolic phase, there are two levels roughly commensurate with Stages I and II of her original *Symbolic Play Scale Checklist* (Westby, 1980). In the symbolic phase, there are eight levels relatively paralleling Stages III through X in the original scale. Westby continues to refine her description of the development of symbolic play, specifying the props, themes, organization, roles, and language used in play and highlighting the form, content, and function of language (Patterson & Westby, 1998; Westby, 2000). The framework for examining play and language that Westby describes has valuable implications for assessment.

The theoretical relationship between play and language has at its foundation the work of Piaget and Vygotsky (G. Fein, 1979). It is clear that these theorists shared some assumptions about development. For example, both saw mental development as constructed and organized through a sequence of qualitative changes in experience. They also recognized the role of symbolic play in preschool language, literacy, and art activities (Berk & Winsler, 1995). Differences are evident, however, in the influence they assigned to biological and cultural factors. G. Fein (1979) described those differences as stemming from Vygotsky's belief that symbolic play reduced the tension between unrealizable desires and substitutes for gratification and Piaget's view of symbolic play as a consolidation of past experience. Vygotsky also believed language had an important referential function in play; Piaget saw a minor role for language in play, suggesting that language and play are independent of one another in both development and use. Thus, although there is support for a relationship that suggests play contributes to the development of language, the parallels are not exact. Further, play and language can and do operate independently of each other. Nevertheless, it is important for practitioners to consider potential relationships between play and language in their assessment of individual children with ASD. Such relationships may provide some insight into intervention strategies that can support the children's play, language, and social interaction.

Considering the relationship of play to cognition, play helps children recognize that objects have functions other than those originally intended. That recognition facilitates children's ability to solve problems, imagine, and create (Libby, Powell, Messer, & Jordan, 1998). The flexibility and creativity characteristic of play foster innovation in how children think and problem solve. Pretend play, in particular, helps children to think differently about objects, supporting their ability to generalize their learning and to develop more abstract conceptual relationships.

Piaget's constructivist view of development recognized the role of children's self-regulated and independent play in the construction of knowledge (Piaget, 1962; Van Hoorn, Nourot, Scales, & Alward, 1993). Through children's self-effort and initiative, they learn to modify what they know and how they interpret their experiences. Vygotsky's view—that every function occurs first at a social level and then at an individual level (Van Hoorn et al., 1993; Vygotsky, 1978)—adds to the understanding of the development of play and its role in cognition. Consistent with Vygotsky's notion of the "zone of proximal development," play with capable peers stretches children's learning. Play experiences lead to more ideas, enhanced associations, and greater opportunities to make logical connections.

Challenges in Play for Children with ASD

Reflecting on the core deficits and behavioral symptoms often reported for children with ASD, it is not difficult to understand the challenges this population experiences in using play to support their language and learning. The transactional nature of play includes an expectation of joint attention and contingent responding (Wolfberg, 1999). In addition, a certain social finesse is required when children are planning, coordinating, and cooperating within group play activities. These expectations for participating in the play experience place children with ASD at a great disadvantage. Particular areas of challenge exist in the principles of play and in the development of symbolic play and creativity or imagination in children with ASD. Several views are offered in the literature to explain the play impairment in autism.

Applying the Principles of Play to Children with ASD

As stated earlier in this chapter, play is voluntary, pleasurable, and intrinsically motivated for most children. Repeated experiences and familiarity with objects, routines, and events increase the pleasure of and motivation for playing in those contexts. For children with ASD, who often limit their novel experiences and have difficulty initiating across contexts, the pleasurable, voluntary, and motivating aspects of play may not be realized. Motivation in play might also be dictated by the predictable, repetitive nature of activities that do not require shifts in attention or abstract or symbolic connections. Further, it may be difficult to recognize the pleasure children with ASD do experience in play activities because of their poorly developed affective signaling.

In addition to the voluntary, pleasurable, and motivating aspects, other principles define children's play as flexible, nonliteral, and requiring active engagement—characteristics that are frequently absent in children with ASD (Wolfberg, 1999). Given the opportunity to play freely, children who have ASD are most likely to isolate themselves socially and exhibit repetitive or stereotypic actions on objects with few variations (Wing, Gould, Yeates, & Brierly, 1977). Lack of flexibility and a tendency toward isolation in play are evident in the following example of a 4-year-old boy with ASD:

> Mark was playing with a small train that he pushed around a small round track over and over again. When peers or adults approached him, he moved the train set closer and closer to a corner of the room where no one else could interfere with his play with the train. When an adult attempted to add a variation to his play by placing a character in one of the cars for a ride, he removed the character and said, "No!"

Children with ASD tend to play less and exhibit less diverse functional play. They also demonstrate less elaborate functional play and fewer actions than do other children with and without a variety of disabilities (McDonough, Stahmer, Schreibman, & Thompson, 1997; Riguet, Taylor, Benaroya, & Klein, 1981; Stone, Lemanek, Fishel, Fernandez, & Altemeier, 1990; Ungerer & Sigman, 1981; Williams, Reddy, & Costall, 2001). An example of less elaborate and diverse functional play is shown in the following example of Brian, a 5-year-old boy with ASD:

> Brian was in a kindergarten classroom composed of children with and without disabilities. The teacher had set up a sociodramatic play area that was a house with a kitchen and living room. As the other children engaged in a variety of dramatic play episodes, taking on roles as Mom, Dad, Baby, or Sibling, Brian stood near the kitchen set. He placed a spoon in each of the cups that were on the table. When given a baby doll to feed, he pushed the doll aside.

The perspective of individuals with autism is also informative about why they might exhibit particular play behaviors. Barron (2001), an adult who has described his life experiences with autism, characterized his early play as being less diverse and elaborate, isolating, and serving a functional need. His actions on objects and tendency to manipulate objects in a certain way were attempts to gain comfort, control, and security in his life. It seems important, then, for practitioners not only to observe play and its context during assessment, but also to determine the possible function the play may serve for the child with ASD.

Challenges in Symbolic Play and Creativity or Imagination in Children with ASD

Children with ASD are also described as specifically impaired in their symbolic play (Baron-Cohen, 1987; Charman et al., 1997; Libby et al., 1998; Riguet et al., 1981; Rutherford & Rogers, 2003; Stone et al., 1990; Ungerer & Sigman, 1981; Wulff, 1985). Studies in symbolic play in autism, however, are plagued with methodological problems, particularly related to the matching of groups, the definitions of symbolic play, and the conditions under which play is assessed (Jarrold, Boucher, & Smith, 1993). Some research investigating ways to elicit, teach, or model play in children with ASD indicates that a capacity for symbolic play that is not spontaneously exhibited may exist in this population (Charman & Baron-Cohen, 1997; Jarrold et al., 1993; Lewis & Boucher, 1988; McDonough et al., 1997; Riguet et al., 1981). Children with ASD appear to have an understanding of the notion of pretense similar to that of children without ASD (Jarrold, Smith, Boucher, & Harris, 1994). Further, research indicates that more formal or structured assessments of play may yield better performance in children with ASD than assessments under spontaneous conditions (McDonough et al., 1997; Ungerer & Sigman, 1981). Consider the following example of play behavior in Carla, a 4½-year-old with ASD in an integrated preschool classroom:

> The sociodramatic play area was designed to represent a doctor's office. There were also a kitchen set and a dollhouse in close proximity. While most of the children were engaged in a variety of sociodramatic play episodes related to a visit to the "doctor's office," Carla stood on the outside of the group near the dollhouse. She typically took the people characters and slid them off the roof of the dollhouse. When an adult approached, she looked and then continued having the people characters climb to the top of the roof and slide off. The adult took one of the people characters to the front door of the house and knocked on the door, asking if anyone was home. Carla opened the door, and when the adult asked, "Can I come in?" Carla said "Yes!" The dialogue continued as the adult modeled the character sitting on the couch. Carla then brought one of the characters she had been sliding off the roof to sit on a chair that was next to the couch.

Although Carla initially had a less diverse and more perseverative interaction with the objects of play, increased variation in use of the objects and in type of play occurred following the modeling and prompting strategies of the adult play partner.

Creativity, a frequently reported deficit of children with ASD, requires an ability to generate novel representations through various manipulations of images (Craig & Baron-Cohen, 1999). In three experiments examining the imagination and creativity of children with autism and Asperger syndrome, Craig and Baron-Cohen found that children with ASD can generate novel changes to objects but do so to a lesser extent than children without ASD. Additionally, these novel changes are based more in reality than in imagination. In the following example, Carla (the little girl with ASD described in the previous example) shows some creativity in her ability to imagine a different way to use a particular play object, although it is reality based:

> Carla removed the roof from the dollhouse. She set it on the floor and slid over it just as she had done with the wooden characters previously.

She then turned the roof upside down. She stepped into it and rocked it back and forth while calling it a "boat."

The experimental results on creativity in children with ASD reported by Craig and Baron-Cohen (1999) suggest important connections to theory of mind (the ability to understand another's perspective) and, thus, to social understanding and communication. Rutherford and Rogers (2003) confirm connections between deficits in pretend play and theory of mind for children with ASD. The creativity and imagination component of ASD, however, requires further research.

Explanations for Impairment in Play in Children with ASD

Jarrold et al. (1993) summarized several hypotheses to explain the play impairment in autism, based on an assimilation of the methodological concerns and the experimental evidence gained through play research in children with ASD. The broad categories include a deficit in competence, performance, or both. Meta-representational and social impairments are used to explain the competence deficit. From a meta-representational perspective, children with ASD are perceived to lack the symbol system necessary to form second-order representations and solve problems that require an understanding of the mental state of others (Brook & Bowler, 1992). Children with ASD may either fail to develop theory of mind, for which symbolic play is an important prerequisite, or take longer to reach that capacity than other children of a similar developmental age (Baron-Cohen, 1989). The explanation that children with ASD fail to develop theory of mind falls short, however, when one considers their ability to demonstrate play in more structured situations (Jarrold et al., 1993). From a social impairment perspective, the argument is that the failure to engage in social situations and the inability to form social-affective relationships, as well as a poorly coordinated representation of self and others, impair symbolic play development (D. Fein, Pennington, Markowitz, Braverman, & Waterhouse, 1986; Rogers & Pennington, 1991). This account suggests differences in the level of impairment for physical and social pretends (Jarrold et al., 1993).

Jarrold and colleagues (1993) describe a motivational, central executive and generative impairment to explain a specific performance deficit in the play of children with ASD. Some clinical researchers suggest that reduced interest in play, poor task completion, and difficulty generalizing skills hint at a lack of motivation in children with ASD (Koegel & Mentis, 1985; Lord, 1985). Although evidence to support that view is lacking, it could explain positive changes noted in play following intervention. Difficulty carrying out volitional acts and decreased saliency of mental schemas versus physical reality indicate a central executive impairment in the development of symbolic play (Lewis & Boucher, 1988; Russell, Mauthner, Sharpe, & Tidswell, 1991). Similar to the central executive impairment, the generative impairment indicates difficulties for children with ASD in the creation of internal representations, even without the interference of external actions like perseverations. The repetitive, stereotypic nature of play, the lack of spontaneous play, and the ability to respond to prompted play reported for children with ASD support both a central executive impairment and a generative impairment view (Jarrold et al., 1993; McDonough et al., 1997).

It may be that the deficits in symbolic play described for children with ASD have both competence and performance components. The combination view hypothesizes that children with ASD have later developing symbol systems (competence) that are poorly used (performance) (Jarrold et al., 1993). The implications are that symbolic play would be affected in spontaneous contexts for those children who have developed a symbol system and that children who have yet to develop a symbol system are less likely to benefit from elicited or instructed contexts (Jarrold et al., 1993). Given the variation in communication profiles for children with ASD and the relationships between language and play, assessment needs to consider the potential interactions and create contexts in which both play competence and play performance can be assessed. It is also important to assess the generalization of play skills across contexts, given the rigid, more gestalt-like learning style of children with ASD, as discussed in Chapter 4.

Creating Profiles of Play Strengths and Challenges

Preparation for intervention around play requires a clear understanding of both the knowledge and the execution of play that children with ASD exhibit. There are several considerations for practitioners as they develop play profiles for children with ASD. First, a child's understanding of the world must be defined. This can be done through observation by practitioners who can identify the interactions among play, language, and social cognition and describe the strategies children use to problem solve. Second, a clear understanding of the child's ability to explore and experiment with objects is needed. Practitioners must be able to describe how children with ASD learn about the physical properties of objects, the range of strategies they use for exploration (e.g., tactile, visual, auditory), and their attempts to combine strategies in their exploration and experimentation. Third, a child's learning through play is affected by environmental variables. Therefore, practitioners must know the environment and the stresses characteristic of that environment that are likely to affect the play competence and performance of a child with ASD. Fourth, children with ASD often lack the social competence to establish a mutual play focus with peers and may not be able to communicate their play interests or interpret those of others (Wolfberg, 1999). Practitioners must carefully observe the opportunities for peer play and the impact of the social context on the play of children with ASD. Finally, the play of children with ASD may be different in structured and unstructured situations.

Research suggests that symbolic play, in particular, may be facilitated under prompted or modeled conditions (Charman & Baron-Cohen, 1997; Jarrold et al., 1993; Lewis & Boucher, 1988; McDonough et al., 1997; Riguet et al., 1981; Wolfberg, 1999). Therefore, practitioners need to observe spontaneous play, as well as play that is elicited through prompting or modeling.

Profiling the play strengths and challenges of children with ASD requires practitioners to ask at least the following questions:

- In what ways does this child use objects?
- In what ways does this child explore objects?
- How does language affect this child's play?
- How does the social context affect this child's play?
- How does this child's independent play look in comparison to peer play?
- Does this child's play look different in structured versus unstructured situations?
- What happens when play is prompted or modeled?
- What might happen if the context was changed?
- Have the duration and contexts of observation been sufficient to create a valid profile of this child's play behavior?

These questions guide practitioners in their pursuit of learning what children with ASD know about their world through play.

Play Assessment Across Impairment, Activity, and Participation

Play assessment is useful for learning how children play with practitioners versus how they play in their own world. Play assessment that addresses the ICF (World Health Organization [WHO], 2001) dimensions of disability (as described in Chapter 3) takes multiple forms, including record review, interview, observation in structured or natural environments, and the use of formal assessment tools appropriate for the age of the child. It is important that assessment in this area of deficit for children with ASD consider all three dimensions of disability—impairment, activity, and participation—in light of personal and environmental contextual factors. This ensures that interventions developed and planned for a child with ASD will be responsive to each of the levels. Table 5.1 describes the dimensions of disability proposed by the WHO and the relevant play assessment areas for children with ASD.

Record Review

A current and historical perspective on the play development and performance of children with or suspected of having ASD is an important component of the assessment process. The development of play has a role in early

TABLE 5.1

Dimensions of Disability and Aspects of Play To Be Assessed in Children with ASD

Impairment: Function and Structure at the Body Level	Activity: Performance at the Person Level	Participation: Involvement at the Societal Level
• Motivation • Joint attention • Understanding of use of objects and actions • Functional use of objects and actions • Understanding of symbolic use of objects and actions • Symbolic use of objects and actions • Pretend with self • Pretend with others • Variation in the use of objects • Variation in actions performed on objects • Flexibility in play themes • Social competence • Theory of mind • Understanding and use of nonliteral language • Negotiation	Quality and quantity of skill performance; what child can and cannot do in everyday activities: • simple activities (e.g., independent play with objects or toys, filling and emptying containers, block building, running on the playground, climbing, throwing a ball) in structured and unstructured situations; and • complex activities (e.g., board games, organized sports, drama, role playing, storytelling, drawing, writing, constructing, dialoguing) in structured and unstructured situations.	Compared to the standard or norm for participation of other children without disabilities, participation in typical activities: • school, • home, • play dates and overnights, • recreational programs, • sports programs, • friendships, and • other community activities or programs.

Context

- Personal: Age, gender, other health conditions, past and current experiences, educational level, fitness, lifestyle, habits, coping styles, or other personal–social characteristics.
- Environmental: Societal attitudes, cultural norms, laws, educational systems, architectural characteristics, or other environmental conditions.

and differential diagnosis (see Chapter 1). The lack of symbolic play development early on raises concerns (Baron-Cohen, Allen, & Gillberg, 1992; Baron-Cohen et al., 1996). Practitioners should carefully examine early reports and records of play development, as well as changes in development following intervention. Documentation of children's early play experiences is also critical.

Interview

As mentioned in Chapter 3, interviewing is an important component of the assessment process, and it has a critical role for obtaining valuable information about a child's play competence and performance. Interviews should be conducted with those individuals (e.g., parents and teachers) who have had a consistent opportunity to observe a child's play and know how a child engages in play with a variety of partners across multiple environments. Further, it is important to have an understanding of the child's early social play experiences with other children.

A sample format for completing a home or school play assessment interview for children with ASD can be found in Figure 5.1. Both grand and mini tour questions (as described in Chapter 3) are identified to facilitate gathering information about a child's play through general descriptions and specific examples.

Observation

To gather relevant information that will guide a practitioner in intervention planning, it is important to observe play during both elicited and spontaneous conditions. Research suggests that the potential for play in children with ASD might not be realized in unstructured contexts and that play can be elicited in more prompted or modeled conditions (see Jarrold et al., 1993, for a review). Therefore, it is important to assess play across several contexts. Further, the practitioner needs to observe long enough to have an accurate picture of the behavior.

Due to the potential play strengths and challenges experienced by children with ASD across a variety of situations, observations should be made in the following contexts:

- in elicited contexts, through prompting or modeling,
- in unstructured situations,
- in independent play,
- in peer play, and
- at home, at school, and in the community.

The observer must carefully examine the symbolic, social, and language dimensions of play to begin defining the steps that may facilitate play performance.

Wolfberg (1995) developed a framework for observing play, noting that many play-based assessments fail to consider more subtle and individual variations in the play of children with ASD. Typically, play-based assessments follow a linear process, examining play from simple to complex activities. That approach fails to consider the dissociations in development reported for children with ASD, however. Wolfberg's framework for observing play includes both a symbolic and a social dimension. She recommends that the practitioner identify the play of children with ASD across four categories in the symbolic dimension:

- no interaction (no play with toys; self-stimulatory actions that do not involve toys);

Play Assessment Interview

Child's name: _____ Date: _____

Interviewee: _____ Interviewer: _____

Grand Tour Questions

I'd like to talk about _____ play experiences.

1. Tell me, in general, how _____ plays: _____

   _____

   _____

   _____

   _____

   Probes: with objects: _____

   with siblings or peers: _____

   in structured situations: _____

   in unstructured situations: _____

   with familiar toys: _____

   in predictable activities: _____

   with new toys: _____

   in new activities: _____

2. Yesterday, at this time, did _____ play? Tell me what happened.

   _____

   _____

   _____

   _____

Mini Tour Questions

You gave me a general description of _____ play. Now I'd like to talk about it more specifically.

1. Tell me about who _____ plays with and how they play: _____

   _____

(continues)

FIGURE 5.1. Play assessment interview.

2. Tell me about what kinds of things _____ plays with and how _____ plays with them:

_____

3. Tell me about what _____ does when _____ plays: _____

_____

4. Tell me about how long _____ plays: _____

_____

5. Tell me about what _____ says when _____ plays: _____

_____

6. Tell me what you think _____ is feeling when _____ plays: _____

_____

7. Tell me how you know that _____ is having fun when _____ plays: _____

_____

8. Tell me what you think makes _____ excited or happy when _____ plays:

_____

9. Is there anything that bothers _____ when he plays with _____?

_____

10. Tell me what you think motivates _____ to play with _____?

_____

FIGURE 5.1. *Continued.*

- manipulation of toys (including a motivation to control the physical world and an interest in unconventional exploration);
- functional play (using toys in conventional ways with delays in imitation); and
- symbolic play (pretending to be someone or to do something).

Wolfberg also describes four categories in the social dimension that the practitioner should consider:

- isolation (children are essentially unaware of others, occupying themselves by watching situations of interest or playing alone);
- orientation (children are aware of others by looking at them or their play but not entering the play activity);
- parallel (simultaneous use of play space as peers with some imitation and showing but generally independent play); and

- common focus (engagement in and attention to play activities with one or more peers).

Taking the time to observe the play of children with ASD, including reflecting on the symbolic and social dimensions of play they exhibit, provides practitioners with an enhanced understanding of the children's individual strengths and challenges in this aspect of development.

Two observation tools, the *Play Preference Inventory* and the *Profile of Individual Play Characteristics*, have been created by Wolfberg (1995) to facilitate the recording and evaluation of observations made of children with ASD and peers without ASD. The *Play Preference Inventory* records all the children's (both novice and expert players') play preferences, including preferred materials, themes, playmates, interactions on objects, and activities. It is used to identify shared patterns of play interests for an entire play group. The *Profile of Individual Play Characteristics* more carefully examines the play preferences of the novice player. It provides an opportunity to identify the symbolic and social dimensions of play exhibited by children with ASD, as well as their communicative functions and means and their individual play preferences.

Another useful framework for observing play in children with ASD is proposed by Howlin, Baron-Cohen, and Hadwin (1999). Their framework requires analyzing videotaped observations. They describe five types of play that are similar to Wolfberg's (1995) symbolic dimensions of play:

- sensory motor play (simple manipulation of toys);
- emerging functional play (conventional use of toys but without pretense);
- established functional play (conventional use of toys without pretense that occurs more than three times in a 10-minute interval);
- emerging pretend play (object substitution, attribution of pretend properties, and use of imaginary objects or events); and
- established pretend play (spontaneous use of three or more examples of object substitution, attribution of pretend properties, or use of imaginary objects or events).

Although Howlin and colleagues define levels of functional and pretend play to a greater extent than Wolfberg (1995) does, they do not specifically propose identifying the social dimensions of play in children with ASD.

Observations by teachers who interact with children in play on a daily basis can contribute much to understanding the play behavior of children with ASD. Teachers can use a *Play Observation Diary* (Van Hoorn et al., 1993) to record children's spontaneous and guided play and to identify the learning (e.g., science play) and social (e.g., small group) contexts in which the play occurs. Documentation through this diary format allows teachers, families, and other practitioners to review the levels of play a child is engaged in and to identify the changes occurring over time. This type of assessment is a powerful intervention planning tool.

It is important for practitioners and family members to recognize the potential role of the environment in understanding and observing the play exhibited by children with ASD. Comprehensive play assessment involves a careful and reflective look at the environment in which a child has opportunities for play. Several questions should be asked:

- What is the climate for play in this environment?
- How is play accepted and encouraged?
- What opportunities are there to incorporate make-believe into interactions with peers?
- How is pretend play encouraged?
- How adequate is the space for play?
- What materials are provided to enhance pretend play?
- How much time is given for pretend play in this environment?

Answers to these questions guide the practitioner or family member in determining some environmental changes extrinsic to the child with ASD that may be needed to support the development and use of play.

Assessment Tools

Assessment in the context of play has several benefits (Linder, 1993). First, it provides a measure of a child's behavior that is both reliable (what one observes will be similar from time one to time two) and valid (what one observes is relevant to what one is interested in). Second, it is holistic, in that the child is seen as an integrated being across several developmental domains simultaneously. A functional picture is provided that considers motivation, interaction patterns, and learning style. Third, play-based assessment accommodates each child's unique characteristics. That is, children are able to move at their own pace, practitioners can follow their lead, there is no need for establishing a basal or ceiling, and there is little negative impact on self-esteem. Fourth, it is strength-based, looking at what children can do instead of what they cannot do. Fifth, this type of assessment involves those who know the child best and actively engages family members. Sixth, play-based assessment ensures that useful information will be gained for children typically described as "untestable." Finally, it creates a comfortable, unobtrusive environment for children, their families, and the practitioners who are involved in the assessment.

Several play-based assessment tools have been used to evaluate the play of children with ASD. Linder's (1993) *Transdisciplinary Play-Based Assessment* (TPBA) is a particularly dynamic assessment model that considers the total child and requires practitioners to share information and roles across disciplines. The TPBA provides a flexible structure for assessing developmental skills in young children that considers the individual needs of children by changing event sequences, participants, and content. The format is especially responsive to the play characteristics of children with ASD who have generally less organized play with fewer play sequences, more interest in objects and functional play than symbolic and peer play, and more rigid play themes and interests. The TPBA examines six developmental play levels from 6 months to 6 years:

- birth to 24 months—exploratory play
- 9 to 24 months—functional play
- 24+ months—constructive play
- 21 to 72 months—symbolic play
- 36+ months—rough-and-tumble play
- 60+ months—games with rules

The TPBA involves a number of participants. The parents act as informants and often participate in the play. A parent facilitator informs parents about the TPBA process and supports their involvement. The play facilitator follows the child's lead to obtain a spontaneous and interactive sample of play behavior. Other team members observe and document behaviors and cue the play facilitator to perform specific tasks so that all aspects of development are probed.

Six phases of assessment are designed in the TPBA to probe cognition, communication, sensory–motor, and social–emotional development in the context of play (Linder, 1993). The role of the players is defined for each phase, so that opportunities to probe all aspects of play, language, and learning are provided. Play is facilitated through both structured and unstructured tasks, as well as child-to-child and parent-to-parent interactions. Observation worksheets and an outline of observation guidelines across domains of learning are included with the TPBA manual.

Westby's (1980) *Symbolic Play Scale Checklist* is another assessment tool that can be used to examine not only the play of children with ASD but also the relevant language observed at each stage of play. As described earlier, Westby defines 10 stages of play that can be observed in children from 9 months to 5 years of age. This checklist is accompanied by an observation form that identifies the type of play observed along both social (onlooking, solitary, parallel, associative, cooperative) and symbolic (practice, symbolic imitative, symbolic spontaneous, game) dimensions of play.

In 1988, Westby refined her original checklist and developed the *Symbolic Play Scale* to include an evaluation of the props used in play; the content represented; the organization of the play script; the roles the child and others take on; and the language form, content, and function represented in play. As practitioners evaluate a child's play using Westby's framework, the questions outlined in Figure 5.2 may be useful probes to guide the assessment.

The *Autism Diagnostic Observation Schedule–Generic* (ADOS–G; Lord, Rutter, DiLavore, & Risi, 1999), a commonly used diagnostic tool described in Chapter 1, assesses specific information about a child's play and probes elements of imagination and creativity. Although typically used as a diagnostic

Play Assessment

Child's name: _____ Date: _____

Observer: _____ Location: _____

Questions To Guide Play Assessment	Yes	No	Comments and Examples (explain how the child demonstrates observed behaviors)
Decontextualization—dependency of the child on a realistic prop: • Does the child require a realistic prop to engage in play? • Does the child substitute one object for another? • Does the child use language to prepare the play scene?			
Theme—familiarity of the child with the content of the play: • Has the child previously experienced these events on a daily basis? • Has the child previously experienced these events on a periodic basis? • Has the child seen or read about these events but not personally experienced them?			
Organization—ability to organize and plan play: • Does the child fail to organize play and include unrelated activities? • Does the child incorporate sequences of temporally related activities? • Does the child plan activities prior to beginning play?			
Self–Other Relationships—ability to define roles, feelings, and beliefs of self and others: • Does the child relate "pretend" only to himself or herself?			

(continues)

FIGURE 5.2. Questions to guide play assessment.

Questions To Guide Play Assessment	Yes	No	Comments and Examples (explain how the child demonstrates observed behaviors)
Self–Other Relationships (*continued*) • Does the child pretend to take on familiar roles (e.g., mommy, daddy, baby brother or sister)? • Does the child give voice to dolls and puppets in play? • Does the child use multiple roles for a single character (father, brother, son, fireman)?			
Communication—ability to use a variety of language functions and gestures in play: • Does the child use language to meet a need in play? • Does the child use language to describe activities? • Does the child use language to report or narrate what is going on in play? • Does the child use language to solve problems or predict in play?			

FIGURE 5.2. *Continued.*

measure for children through adults suspected of having autism, its structured and semistructured interaction format makes it an appropriate instrument for learning about and probing a child's play and imagination.

Although this is not an exhaustive list, and not specifically designed for children with ASD, the assessment tools mentioned here have value in supporting practitioners in their effort to identify formally the play strengths and challenges for this population. They also provide a means for observing change in development over time.

Summary

This chapter has discussed the development of play and the deficits in specific areas of play frequently described for children with ASD. The principles that guide play development; the relationships that exist among aspects of play, language, and cognition; and ways practitioners might approach a meaningful play assessment have been described. The following paragraphs refer to the questions at the beginning of the chapter and highlight key points one should be familiar with when assessing play in children with ASD.

What principles guide early play development, and how is play defined?

Several principles guide the play of children. Play is voluntary and occurs spontaneously. It is fun and provides pleasure, often accompanied by signs of positive affect (Wolfberg, 1995). Intrinsically motivated, play seldom requires external demands or rewards to occur. Play actively engages children in a chosen activity. It is also characterized by a flexible and nonliteral nature that allows children to manage the unexpected, to change the rules, and to imagine something different. Each of these principles poses particular challenges for children with ASD.

Several classifications are used to describe the play of children who are developing in a typical manner. Both symbolic and social dimensions and a range of interaction with objects and other people, from simple manipulation to highly complex pretending, characterize children's play.

What are the relationships among play, language, and cognition that have implications for children with ASD?

Play is a natural vehicle for examining how children understand, think about, and learn from their experiences. It has been described as an important medium for the intellectual, linguistic, emotional, and social development of children (Fewell & Kaminski, 1988; Wolfberg, 1999). It also follows a developmental sequence that seems to parallel that of language and cognitive development (Bates et al., 1987; Fewell & Kaminski, 1988). The specific relationships between play and language are complex. Although there is support for the idea that play contributes to the development of language, the parallels are not exact. Play and language also operate independently of each other.

The relationship of play to cognition is supported in children's early exploration and manipulation of objects and their later representation of objects and actions in pretend play. Play helps children recognize that objects have functions other than those originally intended, which facilitates problem solving, imagination, and creativity (Libby et al., 1998). Pretend play, in particular, supports children's ability to think differently about objects, to generalize their learning, and to develop more abstract conceptual relationships.

What are the challenges in play reported for children with ASD?

Children with ASD often isolate themselves socially and exhibit repetitive or stereotypic actions in their play with objects, using fewer variations (Wing et al., 1977). They tend to play less often and exhibit less diverse and elaborate functional play (McDonough et al., 1997; Riguet et al., 1981; Stone et al., 1990; Ungerer & Sigman, 1981; Williams et al., 2001). Children with ASD are also described as specifically impaired in their symbolic play, although they may be responsive to elicited or prompted symbolic play. Given the difficulties that children with ASD have with a variety of play activities, they might not act on play materials without a cue, external facilitation, or instruction. This makes access to play and expansion of play skills difficult.

How can play profiles be used to assess the strengths and challenges of children with ASD in this core deficit area?

To accurately assess play in children with ASD, practitioners must first possess an understanding of the typical stages of play development and the variables that affect a child's ability to perform in a particular context. An assessment of play must account for diversity in children's cultural, linguistic, and family backgrounds and individual differences in interests and behavioral style (Van Hoorn et al., 1993). In their development of play profiles for children with ASD, practitioners must define children's understanding of their world, observe their ability to explore and experiment with objects and play with peers, understand how their play is affected by environmental variables, and assess play in both structured and unstructured situations.

What areas of play assessment should be considered across the three dimensions of the disablement framework?

Play assessment should address all three areas of disability—impairment, activity, and participation—as described by the World Health Organization (2001). Practitioners can use records review, interviews, observations, and a variety of assessment tools to describe the play of children with ASD. It is critical to engage in a holistic play assessment of children along the spectrum if practitioners are to support them to participate fully in their community. Factors both intrinsic and extrinsic to the individual child must also be considered. Play assessment following the disablement framework ensures that interventions designed to enhance play in children with ASD will be responsive to their actual needs.

Practice Opportunities

1. Create a profile of the strengths and challenges in play noted for a child with ASD.

2. Using one of the observation or assessment tools described in this chapter, define the following:

   - symbolic level of play observed
   - social level of play observed
   - language accompanying the play observed

3. Ask the teacher of a child with ASD to complete a play observation diary, and use that information to help in intervention planning.

4. Probe the play of a child with ASD in both structured and unstructured situations to determine whether his or her capacity for play is enhanced by modeling, prompting, or direct instruction.

Suggested Readings

Jarrold, C., Boucher, J., & Smith, P. (1993). Symbolic play in autism: A review. *Journal of Autism and Developmental Disorders, 23*(2), 281–307.

This review article examines the research that has attempted to define the nature of the deficit in play experienced by children with ASD. The authors make a case for specific challenges in spontaneous symbolic and functional play for children with autism. Interestingly, however, the research also indicates the potential or capacity for symbolic play in children with ASD when prompted or instructed.

Wolfberg, P. (1995). Enhancing children's play. In K. A. Quill (Ed.), *Teaching children with autism: Strategies to enhance communication and socialization* (pp. 193–218). Albany, NY: Delmar.

In this chapter, Wolfberg defines the principles inherent in play that may pose particular challenges for children with ASD. She also describes play that is characteristic of early and middle childhood. In addition, she identifies the variations in play that have been observed for children with ASD and develops a framework for observing both the symbolic and social dimensions of play.

Wolfberg, P. J. (1999). *Play and imagination in children with autism.* New York: Teachers College Press, Columbia University.

This book describes the role of play in typical development and offers perspectives on the play of children with autism. Using ethnographic child stories, Wolfberg establishes an understanding of the play culture that emerges for children along the spectrum. She ends the book with valuable theory-to-practice implications.

Resources

Fantuzzo, J., Sutton-Smith, B., Coolahan, K., Manz, P., Canning, S., & Debnam, D. (1995). Assessment of preschool play interaction behaviors in young low-income children: Penn Interactive Peer Play Scale. *Early Childhood Research Quarterly, 10,* 111.

Linder, T. W. (1993). *Transdisciplinary play-based assessment: A functional approach to working with young children* (Rev. ed.). Baltimore: Brookes.

Lowe, M., & Costello, A. J. (1976). *The Symbolic Play Test.* Berkshire, England: NFER-Nelson.

Rogers, S. J. (1986). *Play Observation Scale.* Denver: University of Colorado Health Sciences.

Rubin, K. H. (1984). *Play Observation Scale* (Rev.). Waterloo, Ontario: University of Waterloo.

Westby, C. E. (1980). *Symbolic Play Checklist.* Assessment of cognitive and language abilities through play. *Language, Speech and Hearing Services in the Schools, 11,* 154–168.

Westby, C. E. (1988). *Symbolic Play Scale.* Children's play: Reflections of social competence. *Seminars in Speech and Language, 9,* 1–13.

Westby, C. E. (1991). A scale for assessing development in children's play. In C. E. Scharfer, K. Gitlin, & A. Sandgrun (Eds.), *Play diagnosis and assessment* (pp. 131–161). New York: Wiley.

Glossary

Associative play. Play that is loosely organized around shared interests, materials, or activities.

Cooperative play. Play that is sustained and complex, including common goals and a variety of roles among players.

Decentration. In pretend, moving from self to other as agent.

Decontextualization. In pretend, moving away from using real objects.

Functional play. Play that includes appropriate use of an object or the conventional association of two or more objects.

Game. Play that includes understanding of rule-governed behavior.

Onlooking. Observing but not participating in play.

Parallel. Play among children using similar materials but with no interaction.

Practice play. Play involving fine-motor (e.g., stringing beads, putting together puzzles) and gross-motor (e.g., running, bike riding) activities.

Solitary play. Playing alone.

Symbolic imitative play. Pretend play initiated or guided by another.

Symbolic/pretend play. Play behavior that is nonliteral, acting as if something is the case when in reality it is not.

Symbolic spontaneous play. Pretend play that a child initiates on his or her own.

References

American Psychiatric Association. (1994). *Diagnostic and statistical manual of mental disorders* (4th ed.). Washington, DC: Author.

American Psychiatric Association. (2000). *Diagnostic and statistical manual of mental disorders* (4th ed., text rev.). Washington, DC: Author.

Baron-Cohen, S. (1987). Autism and symbolic play. *British Journal of Developmental Psychology, 5,* 139–148.

Baron-Cohen, S. (1989). The autistic child's theory of mind: A case of specific developmental delay. *Journal of Child Psychology and Psychiatry, 30,* 285–297.

Baron-Cohen, S., Allen, J., & Gillberg, C. (1992). Can autism be detected at 18 months? The needle, the haystack, and the CHAT. *British Journal of Psychiatry, 161,* 839–843.

Baron-Cohen, S., Cox, A., Baird, G., Swettenham, J., Nightingale, N., Morgan, K., et al. (1996). Psychological markers in the detection of autism in infancy in a large population. *British Journal of Psychiatry, 168,* 138–163.

Barron, S. (2001, November). *Consumers' views on autism.* Paper presented at the American Speech–Language–Hearing Association Convention, New Orleans, LA.

Bates, E., O'Connell, B., & Shore, C. (1987). Language and communication in infancy. In J. Osofsky (Ed.), *Handbook of infant development* (pp. 149–203). New York: Wiley.

Belsky, J., & Most, R. (1981). From exploration to play: A cross-sectional study of infant free play behavior. *Developmental Psychology, 17,* 630–639.

Bergen, D. (1988). Stages of play development. In D. Bergen (Ed.), *Play as a medium for learning and development* (pp. 49–66). Portsmouth, NH: Heinemann.

Berk, L., & Winsler, A. (1995). *Scaffolding children's learning: Vygotsky and early childhood education*. Washington, DC: National Association for the Education of Young Children.

Brook, S. L., & Bowler, D. M. (1992). Autism by another name? Semantic and pragmatic impairments in children. *Journal of Autism and Developmental Disorders, 22*(1), 61–81.

Burghardt, G. (1984). On the origins of play. In P. Smith (Ed.), *Play in animals and humans* (pp. 5–41). New York: Basil Blackwell.

Charman, T., & Baron-Cohen, S. (1997). Brief report: Prompted play in autism. *Journal of Autism and Developmental Disorders, 27*(3), 325–332.

Charman, T., Swettenham, J., Baron-Cohen, S., Cox, A., Baird, G., & Drew, A. (1997). Infants with autism: An investigation of empathy, pretend play, joint attention, and imitation. *Developmental Psychology, 33*(5), 781–789.

Craig, J., & Baron-Cohen, S. (1999). Creativity and imagination in autism and Asperger syndrome. *Journal of Autism and Developmental Disorders, 29*(4), 319–326.

Fein, D., Pennington, B., Markowitz, P., Braverman, M., & Waterhouse, L. (1986). Toward a neuropsychological model of infantile autism: Are the social defects primary? *Journal of the American Academy of Child Psychiatry, 25*, 198–212.

Fein, G. (1979). Echoes from the nursery: Piaget, Vygotsky, and the relationship between language and play. *New Directions for Child Development, 6*, 1–14.

Fewell, R., & Kaminski, R. (1988). Play skills development and instruction for young children with handicaps. In S. Odom & M. Karnes (Eds.), *Early intervention for infants and children with handicaps* (pp. 149–158). Baltimore: Brookes.

Garvey, C. (1990). *Play*. Cambridge, MA: Harvard University Press.

Hartup, W. W., & Sancilio, M. F. (1986). Children's friendships. In E. Schopler & G. B. Mesibov (Eds.), *Social behavior in autism* (pp. 61–80). New York: Plenum Press.

Howlin, P., Baron-Cohen, S., & Hadwin, J. (1999). *Teaching children with autism to mindread*. New York: Wiley.

Hutt, C. (1979). Exploration and play. In B. Sutton-Smith (Ed.), *Play and learning* (pp. 174–194). New York: Gardner Press.

Jarrold, C., Boucher, J., & Smith, P. (1993). Symbolic play in autism: A review. *Journal of Autism and Developmental Disorders, 23*(2), 281–307.

Jarrold, C., Smith, P., Boucher, J., & Harris, P. (1994). Comprehension of pretense in children with autism. *Journal of Autism and Developmental Disorders, 24*, 433–456.

King, N. (1986). Play and the culture of childhood. In G. Fein & M. Rivkin (Eds.), *The young child at play* (pp. 29–41). Washington, DC: National Association for the Education of Young Children.

Koegel, R. L., & Mentis, M. (1985). Motivation in childhood autism: Can they or won't they? *Journal of Child Psychology and Psychiatry, 26*, 185–191.

Leslie, A. M. (1987). Pretence and representation: The origins of "theory of mind." *Psychological Review, 94*, 412–426.

Lewis, V., & Boucher, J. (1988). Spontaneous, instructed and elicited play in relatively able autistic children. *British Journal of Developmental Psychology, 6*, 325–339.

Libby, S., Powell, S., Messer, D., & Jordan, R. (1998). Spontaneous play in children with autism: A reappraisal. *Journal of Autism and Developmental Disorders, 28*, 487–497.

Linder, T. W. (1993). *Transdisciplinary play-based assessment: A functional approach to working with young children* (Rev. ed.). Baltimore: Brookes.

Lord, C. (1985). Autism and the comprehension of language. In E. Schopler & G. B. Mesibov (Eds.), *Communication problems in autism* (pp. 257–281). New York: Plenum Press.

Lord, C., Rutter, M., DiLavore, P. C., & Risi, S. (1999). *Autism Diagnostic Observation Schedule–Generic (ADOS–G)*. Los Angeles: Western Psychological Services.

McCune, L. (1986). Symbolic development in normal and atypical infants. In G. Fein & M. Rivkin (Eds.), *The young child at play* (pp. 45–61). Washington, DC: National Association for the Education of Young Children.

McDonough, L., Stahmer, A., Schreibman, L., & Thompson, S. J. (1997). Deficits, delays, and distractions: An evaluation of symbolic play and memory in children with autism. *Development and Psychopathology, 9,* 17–41.

Nourot, P. M., Scales, B., Van Hoorn, J., & Almy, M. (1987). *Looking at children's play.* New York: Teachers College Press.

Parten, M. B. (1932). Social participation among preschool children. *Journal of Abnormal Psychology, 27,* 243–269.

Patterson, J., & Westby, C. E. (1998). The development of play. In B. Shulman & W. Haynes (Eds.), *Communicative development: Foundations, processes, and clinical application* (pp. 135–163). Baltimore: Brookes.

Piaget, J. (1962). *Play, dreams, and imitation in childhood.* New York: Norton.

Riguet, C. B., Taylor, N. D., Benaroya, S., & Klein, L. S. (1981). Symbolic play in autistic, Down's, and normal children of equivalent mental age. *Journal of Autism and Developmental Disorders, 11*(4), 439–448.

Rogers, S. J., & Pennington, B. F. (1991). A theoretical approach to the deficits in infantile autism. *Development and Psychopathology, 3,* 137–162.

Russell, J., Mauthner, N., Sharpe, S., & Tidswell, T. (1991). The "windows task" as a measure of strategic deception in preschoolers and autistic subjects. *British Journal of Developmental Psychology, 9,* 331–349.

Rutherford, M. D., & Rogers, S. J. (2003). Cognitive underpinnings of pretend play in autism. *Journal of Autism and Developmental Disorders, 33*(23), 289–302.

Saltz, R., & Saltz, E. (1986). Pretend play training and its outcomes. In G. Fein & M. Rivkin (Eds.), *The young child at play* (pp. 155–173). Washington, DC: National Association for the Education of Young Children.

Singer, D. G., & Singer, J. L. (1990). *The house of make-believe.* Cambridge, MA: Harvard University Press.

Smilansky, S. (1968). *The effects of sociodramatic play on disadvantaged preschool children.* New York: Wiley.

Stone, W. L., Lemanek, K. L., Fishel, P. T., Fernandez, M. C., & Altemeier, W. A. (1990). Play and imitation skills in the diagnosis of autism in young children. *Pediatrics, 86,* 267–272.

Sutton-Smith, B., & Kelly-Byrne, D. (1984). The idealization of play. In P. Smith (Ed.), *Play in animals and humans* (pp. 305–321). New York: Basil Blackwell.

Ungerer, J. A., & Sigman, M. (1981). Symbolic play and language comprehension in autistic children. *Journal of the American Academy of Child Psychiatry, 20,* 318–337.

Van Hoorn, J., Nourot, P. M., Scales, B., & Alward, K. (1993). *Play at the center of the curriculum.* New York: Macmillan.

Vygotsky, L. S. (1978). *Mind in society: The development of higher psychological processes.* Cambridge, MA: Harvard University Press.

Weininger, O., & Daniel, S. (1992). *Playing to learn.* Springfield, IL: Charles C Thomas.

Westby, C. E. (1980). Assessment of cognitive and language abilities through play. *Language, Speech, and Hearing Services in Schools, 11,* 154–168.

Westby, C. E. (1988). Children's play: Reflections of social competence. *Seminars in Speech and Language, 9,* 1–13.

Westby, C. E. (2000). A scale for assessing development in children's play. In K. Gitlin-Weiner, A. Sandgrun, & C. Schaefer (Eds.), *Play diagnosis and assessment* (pp. 135–163). New York: Wiley.

Wetherby, A. (1992). *Communication and language intervention for preschool children.* Buffalo, NY: EDUCOM Associates.

Wetherby, A. M., & Prizant, B. M. (1992). Profiling young children's communicative competence. In S. F. Warren & J. Reichle (Eds.), *Communication and language intervention series: Vol. 1. Causes and effects in communication and language intervention* (pp. 217–253). Baltimore: Brookes.

Wetherby, A. M., & Prizant, B. M. (1993). *Communication and Symbolic Behavior Scales manual.* Chicago: Riverside Press.

Williams, E., Reddy, V., & Costall, A. (2001). Taking a closer look at functional play in children with autism. *Journal of Autism and Developmental Disorders, 31*(1), 67–77.

Wing, L., Gould, J., Yeates, S. R., & Brierly, L. M. (1977). Symbolic play in severely mentally retarded and autistic children. *Journal of Child Psychology and Psychiatry, 18,* 167–178.

Wolery, M., & Bailey, D. (1989). Assessing play skills. In D. Bailey & M. Wolery (Eds.), *Assessing infants and preschoolers with handicaps* (pp. 429–446). Columbus, OH: Merrill.

Wolfberg, P. (1995). Enhancing children's play. In K. Quill (Ed.), *Teaching children with autism* (pp. 193–218). New York: Delmar.

Wolfberg, P. (1999). *Play and imagination in children with autism.* New York: Teachers College Press.

World Health Organization. (2001). *ICF: International classification of functioning, disability and health.* Geneva, Switzerland: Author.

Wulff, S. B. (1985). The symbolic and object play of children with autism: A review. *Journal of Autism and Developmental Disorders, 15,* 139–148.

Understanding and Assessing the Social–Emotional Development of Children with ASD

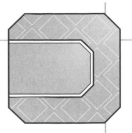

Patricia A. Prelock and Amy Ducker

QUESTIONS TO CONSIDER

In this chapter, you will learn about differences in the social–emotional development of children with autism spectrum disorders (ASD), compared to children with other disabilities and without disabilities. How the interactions among social–emotional development, communication, and play are affected by poorly developed joint attention, facial expression and gesture use, theory of mind, and executive function will be emphasized. Methods for assessing the strengths and challenges of social–emotional development in children with ASD will be highlighted to facilitate an understanding of the role assessment has in intervention planning. The disablement framework described in Chapter 3, and applied to assessment practices in communication (Chapter 4) and play (Chapter 5), will also be applied to the assessment practices described for evaluating the social–emotional development of children and adolescents with ASD. As you read this chapter, consider the following questions:

1. In what ways does the social–emotional development of children with ASD differ, qualitatively and quantitatively, from that of typically developing peers and peers with other disabilities?

2. How are specific impairments in joint attention, facial expression and gesture, theory of mind, and executive function related to the core social impairment described for children with ASD?

3. How are arousal and attention affected in children on the spectrum, and what is the relationship between these characteristics and overall social development?

4. What should practitioners consider when creating a profile of social–emotional strengths and challenges for children with ASD?

5. What areas of social–emotional assessment should be examined across the three dimensions of the disablement framework?

Introduction

Differences in social–emotional development, and social interaction in particular, are frequently cited as one of the most salient features of individuals with an autism spectrum disorder (Lord, 1993; Volkmar, 1987; Volkmar & Klin, 1990). In fact, the social impairment so clearly described by Kanner (1943) in his original work has remained the key area of deficit and pervasive challenge for individuals with autism. In the current chapter, an attempt is made to address key questions about social–emotional development in children with autism by identifying specific areas of impairment and distinguishing the social development of children with autism from that of both their typically developing peers and peers with other developmental disabilities. Further, information is provided about how to assess children's strengths and challenges in this area of development, in order to aid families and teams in diagnosis and program planning.

Social functioning is one of the three identified areas of impairment used to determine the appropriateness of a diagnosis on the autism spectrum. Specifically, in the *Diagnostic and Statistical Manual of Mental Disorders–Fourth Edition* (DSM–IV; American Psychiatric Association [APA], 1994) and its text revision (DSM–IV–TR; APA, 2000), social impairment has been characterized in the following manner:

- marked impairment in the use of multiple nonverbal behaviors such as eye-to-eye gaze, facial expression, body postures, and gestures to regulate social interaction;
- failure to develop peer relationships appropriate to developmental level;
- lack of spontaneous seeking to share enjoyment, interests, or achievements with other people (e.g., by a lack of showing, bringing, or pointing out objects of interest); and
- lack of social or emotional reciprocity.

The failure to develop peer relationships can look different in children depending on their age. In younger children, it is typically manifested by a limited interest in developing friendships or interacting with peers. Among older children, there is often an interest in developing social relationships, but a lack of social conventions hinders relationship development. Further, instead of the back-and-forth or give-and-take that characterizes most successful social interactions, children with ASD typically prefer solitary games or activities. When they do involve others in interaction, they commonly view or use others as tools to accomplish a personal goal or pursue an individual interest.

Although these and other features of social–emotional functioning have been identified as some of the central or core features of autism and critical to its diagnosis, the social–emotional development of children with ASD is not fixed. Rather, it is characterized by quantitative and qualitative differences in development, and continuity and change over time (Sigman & Norman, 1999; Sigman & Ruskin, 1999). The notions of developmental differences, continuity, and change represent important advances from earlier characterizations of children with ASD that described a socially isolated and withdrawn child with little interest or skill in interacting with others, as a constant, lifelong feature. Currently, it is understood that social skills emerge over time and at varying degrees for children with ASD. Despite such developmental advances, however, social interaction tends to occur less frequently and remain somewhat impaired and highly challenging throughout life for most individuals with ASD (Church, Alisanski, & Amanullah, 2000; Mundy & Sigman, 1989; Volkmar, 1987; Volkmar & Cohen, 1985; Volkmar & Klin, 1990).

Further, important research on social–emotional functioning in children with ASD suggests that impairment in social interaction during infancy and early childhood is one of the most powerful and accurate predictors of a later diagnosis of ASD (Lord, 1993; Siegel, Vulocevic, Elliott, & Kramer, 1989; Volkmar, Carter, Sparrow, & Cicchetti, 1993). Likewise, achievement in the area of social–emotional development and attainment of key social skills have been identified as two of the strongest predictors of developmental outcomes for individuals with autism and other developmental disorders. Clearly, there is a significant need for understanding and accurately assessing this aspect of an individual's functioning.

Social–Emotional Development

Social–emotional development refers to a child's capacity to "experience and express a variety of emotional states, to regulate emotional arousal, to establish secure and positive relationships, and to develop a sense of self as distinct from others" (Prizant & Wetherby, 1990, p. 1). To fully understand the social–emotional development of children with ASD, it is important to first understand the typical course in this developmental area. In this section, the normative course of social development is defined, and ways in which that developmental pattern is different for children with ASD are identified. Wherever possible, attention is drawn to the ways that social development of children with autism is distinct from that of children with developmental delays or other disabilities, as that information is particularly important to assist with differential diagnosis.

Social–Emotional Development in Children Without Disabilities

Neurotypically developing infants are born with certain preferences and skills that suggest they are socially motivated from the earliest days of life.

Examples of these early signs include preferences for the human voice and face over other objects and sounds and an ability to orient themselves toward their parents (DeCasper & Fifer, 1980; Mayes, Cohen, & Klin, 1993; Morton & Johnson, 1991; Olson & Sherman, 1983). Within the first few months of infancy, it is apparent that babies have social goals (e.g., maintaining contact with or receiving attention from a caregiver).

Social interaction begins in early infancy when children use facial expression, eye contact, and a social smile to interact with key members (most commonly adults) in their environment. As early as 3 months of age, infants are capable of distinguishing between different emotions in others' facial expressions (Ludemann, 1991), and they display a capacity to help regulate some of their own emotions through head turning and gaze aversion when they become overaroused or uncomfortable. Later, infants and young children incorporate other strategies for self-regulation, such as approaching and withdrawing from stimuli, depending on their arousal level.

Over the course of the first year of life, infants learn to differentiate their caregivers from other individuals in their environment, and they demonstrate a preference for or bond with caregivers, commonly referred to as an attachment (Bowlby, 1969). Infants will use preferred caregivers as a "safe base," often remaining in close physical proximity to those individuals when exploring their environment and seeking comfort or contact following a threat or separation. Further, typically developing children will look to their caregivers and read their facial expressions to both appraise uncertain situations and share emotions (such as surprise and delight).

While children's earliest social relationships involve parents and other primary caregivers, very young children also demonstrate interest in peers. In the first year of life, children will reach for other children and direct looks, vocalizations, and smiles in the direction of another infant (Brownell & Brown, 1992). Although the majority of infants' interest and play initiatives during the first year of life are directed toward the exploration of objects, simple imitation of both peer and adult behavior can be observed during that period.

By the second year of life, children demonstrate an increased tendency to coordinate their behavior with others in their environment, and by toddlerhood, children are often actively engaging in parallel play, in which they play near others, in a similar manner, but with limited interaction. As children develop, this type of play is often expanded to include the sharing of materials and commenting on behavior. Throughout the preschool years, children increasingly demonstrate less of this parallel and associative play and begin to engage in more cooperative play, in which they share goals and coordinate their actions with peers. Children's social goals are more numerous and complex and become more focused on others and less egocentric over time. Children also become more skilled at coordinating and cooperating with adults as well as peers during their play (Brownell & Carriger, 1990), and their ability to imitate the actions of others improves. Although evidence suggests that children begin to demonstrate rudimentary perspective-taking skills (taking on the view of another) as early as age 2, perspective taking, which is vital to cooperating and coordinating behavior, more fully develops through early childhood and helps facilitate social interaction among peers. As perspective-taking skills improve, so does children's ability to read, interpret, and adjust their own behavior to the facial expressions and body language of others.

The earliest forms of friendships typically appear during the toddler and preschool period (Brownell & Brown, 1992) and initially are a function of proximity and play interests. The basis and characteristics of children's friendships, change throughout childhood and adolescence, as qualities such as trust, assistance, intimacy, and loyalty become increasingly valued among social partners.

Social–Emotional Development in Children with ASD

Retrospective parental report and videotape review of children later diagnosed with ASD, as well as some prospective studies, suggest differences in the social–emotional development of children with ASD compared to typically developing peers during the first year of life (Adrien, 1991; Bernabei, Camaioni, & Levi, 1998; Charman et al., 1997; Gillberg et al., 1990; Osterling & Dawson, 1994). Some of the early features noted to characterize social–emotional development in infancy for children later diagnosed with ASD include a lack of reciprocal eye contact, an infrequent or absence of social smile, and less interest in the human face, in comparison to their typically developing peers. These features also distinguish very young children with ASD from peers with other developmental disabilities (Lord, 2000). Early in childhood, children with ASD often appear to receive less pleasure from physical contact, such as being picked up or held by a caregiver, and are less likely to reach for or seek physical comfort from their parents (Klin, Volkmar, & Sparrow, 1992). Despite this apparent lack of interest in social interaction with adults, children with ASD will form attachments to caregivers. These attachments develop more slowly, however, compared to those of both typically developing peers and peers with developmental delays or disabilities other than autism (Sigman & Mundy, 1989). Children with ASD look at others in their environment less frequently and less consistently respond to their own name. Unresponsiveness to name is a specific trait that differentiates autism from other disability categories (Lord, 2000). Further, the marked preference for objects over social interaction distinguishes children with ASD from both typically developing peers and peers with other developmental delays or disabilities.

During the period when typically developing children become increasingly interested and involved in social interaction, in general, children with ASD appear to remain socially isolated and continue to prefer engagement in primarily solitary activities. They tend to display a more limited range of facial and body expressions and have difficulty both reading others and, more specifically, taking the perspective of a potential social partner (Volkmar &

Cohen, 1985). The absence of spontaneous offering to share and comfort, and of seeking to share enjoyment, is markedly different in comparison to typically developing peers and peers with other developmental delays (Lord, 2000). Cooperative play is uncommon, even among those children on the autism spectrum who do display an interest in developing peer relationships. Throughout childhood, social relationships with adults, rather than peers, appear to be both more common and more highly preferred by children with ASD.

Adolescence may mark a period of increased interest in social relationships for individuals with autism (APA, 2000; Bolick, 2001). However, one challenge that frequently appears when adolescents with ASD pursue social relationships is a difficulty with the reciprocal social exchanges that characterize social interaction. Further, adolescents with ASD often remain focused on their own interests and pursuits, which can be particularly problematic during adolescence, when relationships are typically based on mutual support and sharing and emotional connectedness.

Key Areas of Impairment

From the previous overview of social–emotional development in both typically developing children and children on the autism spectrum, it is apparent that children with ASD demonstrate generalized social differences in a variety of social skills and behaviors. Research has identified several components of social–emotional development in which children with ASD are reported to demonstrate specific challenges, suggesting that impairment in those areas (e.g., joint attention, face perception and emotion recognition, gesture and imitation, theory of mind, executive function) might help to explain their overall social functioning. In the following sections, these components will be explained and the impact of these areas of challenge on social interaction will be outlined.

Joint Attention

As described in Chapters 1 and 4, *joint attention* refers to the ability to use gesture, body language, facial expression, or verbal communication such as commenting or labeling to direct another's attention to or share interest in objects or events and their properties. Research indicates that impairment in joint attention emerges early, usually before the development of words in typically developing children (Mundy, Sigman, & Kasari, 1994; Wetherby, Prizant, & Hutchinson, 1998). In fact, lack of joint attention may be one of the earliest indicators of autism in very young children, suggesting that failure to develop this skill could potentially influence the development of other social–emotional skills.

Charman and colleagues (1997) described the failure of the 20-month-old infants with autism they observed to establish joint attention through social gaze. Mundy (1995) considers deficits in joint attention as responsible for the social-approach challenges children with ASD often experience. His view suggests that the social–emotional function served by joint attention allows children the information and experience required for social–cognitive development. Roeyers, van Oost, and Bothuyne (1998) concur and add that the deficit in joint attention observed in their study appeared to be an autism-specific deficit that is important to the development of theory of mind. Most recently, Travis, Sigman, and Ruskin (2001) found that the group of verbally able children with ASD they studied were less able to initiate joint attention and showed less empathy and concern, which significantly impaired their social interactions as compared to children with other developmental delays.

Social-orienting impairments in children with ASD have also been related to deficits in joint or shared attention. Dawson, Meltzoff, Osterling, Rinaldi, and Brown (1998) proposed that the inability to share attention with others, which requires a rapid shift in attention between stimuli, may be due more to the nature of the stimuli than to a poorly developed ability to shift attention. Their hypothesis is important, as poor attention to social stimuli may limit opportunities for engagement in early social experiences.

Dawson and her colleagues (1998) examined the ability of children with ASD, children with Down syndrome, and typical children matched for language and cognitive ability to orient to familiar social stimuli (hand clapping and calling child's name) and nonsocial stimuli (playing with a musical jack-in-the-box and shaking a rattle). They also investigated the relationship of attention to social stimuli and shared attention (following another's gaze and declarative pointing). Their results indicated that children with ASD show a general orienting impairment that is more severe for social stimuli when compared to the children with Down syndrome and those who were typically developing. The relationship between shared attention and orienting to social, as opposed to nonsocial, stimuli is also strong. The results support the theory that deficits in shared attention may derive from a basic failure to attend to social stimuli selectively, like the eyes or facial expressions of another person (Dawson et al., 1998). If, in fact, the lack of gaze or attention to social stimuli is characteristic of children with ASD early on, their inability to integrate important interpersonal information would compromise the later development of reciprocal communication (Volkmar, Carter, Grossman, & Klin, 1997).

Face Perception and Emotion Recognition

One element of face perception is the ability to recognize or distinguish "self" from "nonself," also known as self-recognition. Although some have reported impairment in self-recognition to be a primary feature of autism, others have found some evidence of self-recognition in children with ASD (Mundy & Sigman, 1989). For example, Dawson and McKissick (1984) found that children with ASD smiled at their mirror images as often as children without ASD yet failed to display some of the coy or self-conscious affect noted for the children without ASD. It seems that children with ASD possess a visual self-recognition, but their affective response differs from that of their typical peers. Further, research suggests that deficits in the vocal, gestural, and facial expression of affect may be a primary impairment in autism (Mundy & Sigman, 1989).

Another element of face perception in children with ASD is inability to recognize the faces of others. The research interest in face perception is the perceived importance of facial processing to early social engagement (Klin et al., 1999). Early work in face perception in autism investigated the ability of adolescents and young adults with autism to recognize their peers (Langdell, 1978). Although the individuals with autism could identify their peers, they appeared to rely on the lower parts of the face (the mouth) as opposed to the usual approach of attending to the eyes or upper part of the face. Over the years, research in the face perception of individuals with autism, however, has been equivocal. Some have found significant deficits (Boucher & Lewis, 1992), and others have not (Celani, Battacchi, & Arcidiacono, 1999). Further, little correlation has been found between IQ and face recognition in individuals with autism as compared to individuals with other disabilities, suggesting that face perception may not be related to overall cognitive function in individuals with autism (Klin et al., 1999).

To examine further the issue of face perception in autism, Klin and his colleagues (1999) studied younger children with autism, a relatively unresearched group in this area. They used a normed test of face recognition to address the confounding methodological issues of previous research. Their results indicated significant impairments in the face perception of children with autism but not of children with pervasive developmental disorder—not otherwise specified (PDD-NOS), compared to children with mental retardation and language disorders matched for chronological, verbal, and nonverbal mental age. Klin and colleagues also found little correlation between face recognition in autism and general cognitive ability, as had been previously reported.

To summarize, although face recognition deficits reported for older children and young adults with autism are inconclusive, peculiarities in facial processing have been consistently identified. Klin and his colleagues (1999) speculate that older children may develop ways to compensate for their earlier challenges in facial processing, so that they can perform accurately on identity tasks, although they display qualitative differences in their ability to integrate the available social information.

Emotion recognition involves the ability to understand affective facial expression, which was discussed in detail in Chapter 4 as an extralinguistic feature that challenges effective pragmatic communication in children with ASD. Two types of cognitive processing have been used to describe emotion recognition through facial expressions: analytic and holistic. *Analytic processing* involves perception of the individual properties of facial expression, which allows inferences to be made. In contrast, *holistic processing* involves a gestalt perception of facial expression and understanding of emotional meaning (Celani et al., 1999). Recognition of these contrasting approaches is important in the selection of methods used to assess emotion recognition. Specifically, the type of task, either sorting or matching, may influence the observed results. For example, in a typical sorting task, individuals are asked to pair pictures of people that vary in gender, age, facial expression, and type of hat; in a typical matching task, individuals are asked to match objects, faces by identity, or faces by expression.

In their study comparing children with autism to children with Down syndrome and children without disabilities matched for verbal mental age, Celani and colleagues (1999) addressed the potential influences of different processing approaches and types of tasks. They used a delayed matching task, in which children were expected to match faces based on the emotions being expressed (e.g., happy, sad) or based on identity (i.e., emotionally neutral faces). In contrast to previous studies, which usually presented the target and sample pictures simultaneously, Celani and colleagues briefly presented the target and then displayed the sample pictures for children to choose from. They also used a sorting-by-preference task in which children were asked to evaluate the pleasantness of faces (i.e., the same face with either a neutral or a happy expression) or agreeable and disagreeable situations with no people represented. Their results indicated that children with autism were more impaired in their ability to match and sort faces by emotional expression than in their ability to match and sort faces by identity and agreeable or disagreeable situations, as compared to both children with Down syndrome and children without disabilities. In summary, this research suggests that children with autism display specific difficulties in their emotion recognition, characterized by their qualitatively different evaluations of the emotional meaning of facial expressions.

The debate regarding deficits in emotion recognition for children with ASD, however, continues. Gepner, Deruelle, and Grynfeltt (2001) studied the influence of motion on the ability of children with autism to recognize emotional expressions (joy, sadness, surprise, and disgust) and nonemotional expressions (e.g., pronouncing vowels, tongue protrusion) using videotaped sequences of a still face, a dynamic face, and a strobe face. The performance of the children with autism was not significantly worse than that of children without disabilities, matched for gender and developmental level. Further, in contrast to previous research, peculiarities in the processing of emotional expression were not observed. However, Gepner and colleagues did make two incidental observations that may have implications for facilitating the recognition of facial expressions. First, the children with autism were highly interested in the video setup and presentation of the facial stimuli. Second, the dynamic face presentation led to imitation of the facial expressions by many of the children with autism. Gepner and his colleagues speculate that the video clips may appear more ecologically valid than photographs to children with autism but elicit less overarousal than is seen in real life. Practitioners may want to consider the value of video use in the education of children with autism.

Just as Klin and colleagues (1999) did not find children with PDD-NOS to be impaired in their face perception ability, Serra, Jackson, van Geert, and

Minderaa (1998) did not find impairments in emotion recognition for this population. When given sufficient time, children with PDD-NOS and normal intelligence processed simple emotional stimuli as effectively as children without disabilities. Additional research is certainly warranted in this area as the processing of more complex emotional expressions and the rate at which children must react and respond to emotion recognition are considered.

Gesture and Imitation

As described in Chapter 4, gestures convey important social information and provide a means for sharing affective experiences. Children with ASD demonstrate a limited range of gestures, however, including less frequent pointing to and showing of objects and fewer gestures combined with meaningful vocalization (Baron-Cohen, 1988). The gestural acts generally produced by children with ASD serve a request function. The use of gestures to comment on or indicate awareness of an object's presence or the occurrence of an action is more impaired (Curcio, 1978; Wetherby & Prutting, 1984). In addition, minimal expressive gestures are reported for children with ASD (Stone & Caro-Martinez, 1990). The lack of gesture use to comment or indicate compromises the ability of children with ASD to share experiences with others and to recognize and respond to the emotional expression of potential social interaction partners.

An imitation deficit has also been suggested as a characteristic of individuals with autism (Rogers, Bennetto, McEvoy, & Pennington, 1996; Rogers & Pennington, 1991; Smith & Bryson, 1998; Stone, Lemanek, Fishel, Fernandez, & Altemeier, 1990). Imitation requires an ability to match internal states to the behaviors of others. It may be the "motor" for developing an understanding of others' mental states (Roeyers et al., 1998). Impaired imitation ability can hinder affective, social, and communicative development. Some have described the imitation deficits in children with ASD as primary, resulting from an underlying executive function deficit (Rogers & Pennington, 1991). The executive function theory can be used to explain imitation deficits because imitation requires the development of a plan for body movement that must be kept in working memory during its execution while competing factors are managed (Rogers et al., 1996). Others propose that imitation deficits are secondary to an underlying symbolic deficit (Baron-Cohen, 1988). The symbolic or meta-representational theory suggests the presence of a cognitive process that allows for the formation of representations necessary to understand the beliefs and intentions of others and to engage in symbolic play. An imitation deficit, then, would be a result of a child's inability to represent information symbolically.

To test these competing theories, Rogers and her colleagues (1996) examined imitation and pantomime in adolescents with ASD who had high cognitive skills and a comparison group of children with mixed diagnoses. The results provided additional support for the existence of imitation deficits in children with ASD. However, the researchers found no support for the symbolic deficit hypothesis; the children with ASD did not perform differentially worse on meaningful tasks (those with symbolic content) than on nonmeaningful tasks (those with nonsymbolic content). Partial support for the executive function hypothesis was found, in that group differences were either not seen or seldom seen on motor and memory control tasks. These results argue against deficits in motor initiation, basic motor coordination, and visual recognition memory that might be predicted by the executive function theory (Rogers et al., 1996).

Theory of Mind

The knowledge of one's own mind is achieved through direct inspection of what one knows about what one thinks and what one actually does think. One's knowledge of others' minds is a complex task that requires an ability to infer or reason based on analogies one can make about how others might perceive or think about a particular situation. There is some question of whether this "mind understanding" exists in children with ASD.

Baron-Cohen, Leslie, and Frith (1985) suggested that individuals with autism lack a "theory of mind," or the ability to recognize the mental state of others as well as self, so that predictions and explanations of action can occur. Baron-Cohen (1995) also proposed four mechanisms to explain the basis for engagement in children and their formation of mental states: Intentionality Detector, Eye-Direction Detector, Shared Attention Mechanism, and Theory of Mind Mechanism. The Intentionality Detector interprets others' mental states that are directed at achieving a particular goal or desire. For many children with ASD, the ability to detect intention can be relatively intact, although not all aspects of complex mental states or intentions may be understood. The Eye-Direction Detector identifies the presence of eye motion, computing what the eyes are directed to and reading the mental state based on an inference about what the eyes are perceiving. The ability to determine the focus of eye movement also seems to be relatively normal for children with ASD. Neither the Intentionality nor the Eye-Direction Detector, however, enables children to recognize when both they and others are attending to the same event or object. That is the job of the Shared Attention Mechanism, which links the two detectors so children can recognize that they and others are similarly focused. This shared-attention function is critical to the ability of children to communicate about shared realities (Westby, 1998). Children with ASD often exhibit impairments in their ability to establish shared attention.

The Theory of Mind Mechanism, then, serves a critical role in creating inferences about a full range of mental states (e.g., pretending, deceiving, guessing, thinking) that might be represented and how they are related to the behaviors or actions observed. Children with ASD have difficulty making inferences about what others might be thinking, feeling, or believing about particular objects, actions, or events. For example, when a false-belief task was given to children with ASD, 80% answered incorrectly, whereas most 4-year-olds without ASD and 86% of children with Down syndrome answered correctly (Baron-Cohen et al., 1985). This false-belief task, known as the Sally-and-Ann task, constitutes a less complex approach to mental representation; performance on this task provides a powerful example of the inability of children with ASD to take on the perspective of another. In this task, one girl hides a marble in one of two containers while another girl watches. When the girl who is watching leaves, the first girl changes the hiding place. The question for the child in the study is whether the girl who left will know where the marble is when she returns. Those children who understand that the returning girl was not privy to the change provide the correct answer. For most children with ASD, however, the perspective they take is their own. The marble has been moved, it has a new location, and the returning girl will know that.

Baron-Cohen, Tager-Flusberg, and Cohen (1993) comprehensively review the research on theory of mind that has converged from a variety of experimental paradigms, and Baron-Cohen and Swettenham (1997) summarize those results as follows for children with ASD:

- They fail to differentiate between the physical properties of objects and thoughts about those objects.
- They understand brain functions (physical movement, actions) but not mind functions (thinking, dreaming, deceiving).
- They have difficulty distinguishing between what an object looks like and what it really is.
- They fail first-order false-belief tasks (knowing or perceiving what someone else knows).
- They fail tests assessing that seeing leads to knowing.
- They have poor recognition of mental state words (e.g., know, think, imagine).
- They have a decreased use of mental state words.
- Their pretend play is impaired.
- Their understanding of complex causes of emotions (such as beliefs) is impaired.
- They have difficulty discriminating between thinking and wanting through facial expressions by focusing on the eyes.
- They have difficulty distinguishing between accidental and intentional behaviors or events.
- They are unable to deceive.
- They have poor understanding of nonliteral language such as metaphors, irony, and sarcasm.
- They have difficulty with several aspects of pragmatics.

The review of past research presents strong evidence for a theory of mind deficit in children with ASD.

Greater complexity in theory of mind testing has also been initiated, moving from "look questions" (e.g., Sally-and-Ann task) to "think questions" (e.g., Mary thinks John thinks …) to more carefully assess the potential deficit in mentalizing, or representing mental states. Some are raising questions, however, about what ability theory of mind tasks actually reflect and whether performance on particular tasks is just an artifact of the tasks. Researchers also question if theory of mind is part of the core impairment in autism, because not all individuals with ASD fail false-belief tasks. For example, some children perform as well as typical peers on first-order false-belief tasks. Baron-Cohen (1989) points out, however, that performance on second-order belief tasks (predicting what one person thinks another person is thinking) is usually less accurate. Individuals who do pass these second-order belief tasks usually have higher cognitive and linguistic skills than those children with ASD who do not pass them, but many still have difficulty explaining their answers to the belief questions (Bowler, 1992) and more often provide irrelevant or incorrect responses in their explanations (Bauminger & Kasari, 1999).

The impairment in theory of mind has been related to primary deficits in joint attention (Mundy, Sigman, & Kasari, 1993). Joint attention requires the development of affect and the ability of a child and another person to share or coordinate their attention to an object or event. The emergence of a deficit in joint attention often seen in children with ASD occurs at the same time they are experiencing difficulty in their functional play skills. Concurrently, the ability to self-regulate or manage arousal level affected by stimulation is often associated with atypical affective responses (Dawson & Lewy, 1989). The development of representational skills is associated with a delay in functional play skills leading to deficits in concrete operations (Yirmiya, Sigman, Kasari, & Mundy, 1992). Thus, the child with ASD has difficulty understanding the social value that is signaled through affect and the ability to share others' experiences.

The development of specific social and cognitive skills is related to opportunities for shared experiences that give information about the world. In the context of joint attention, the maturing infant perceives another's affective signals and associates them with his or her own affect. Therefore, a disturbance in joint attention may be related to an inability to compare one's own affect with the affect of others. This lack of integration of affect and cognition may contribute to the challenges of developing a theory of mind.

Executive Function

Another area of cognitive function that has been identified as impaired in children with ASD is executive function (Ozonoff, Pennington, & Rogers, 1991). Executive function is a sort of goal-directed overseer of behavior that incorporates the mental processes needed to control actions (Twachtman-Cullen, 2000). It allows individuals to shift their attention with flexibility and to solve problems in an organized, strategic manner. Impairments in this area of cognitive function may result in ineffective planning, poor impulse control, inflexibility in thought and action, and poor working memory (Baron-Cohen & Swettenham, 1997; Twachtman-Cullen, 2000). The behavioral manifestations of these impairments for children with ASD may include rigidity or inflexibility, inability to delay gratification or inhibit inappropriate responses, repetitive behaviors, difficulty with transitions, poor self-regulation, and poor organization. Challenges in executive function and theory of mind converge to affect critical thinking skills, so that children with ASD struggle to sustain their attention and to manage declarative knowledge important for drawing conclusions, making inferences, and reasoning to solve problems (Twachtman-Cullen, 2000). Specifically, children with ASD are challenged by executive tasks because they fail to verbally encode the rules that function as reminders for successful completion of a particular task (Russell, Jarrold, & Hood, 1999).

Notably, executive function deficits are reported for several other disorder groups, suggesting that a deficit in theory of mind could occur with executive dysfunction but would not necessarily be fully explained by it. Further, the importance of an executive function hypothesis in autism is its potential to explain the frequent reports of repetitive and perseverative behaviors in this population that cannot be explained by a deficit in theory of mind (Baron-Cohen & Swettenham, 1997). More recent research, however, challenges the executive dysfunction theory in younger children with autism (Griffith, Pennington, Wehner, & Rogers, 1999).

Impact of Deficits in Arousal and Attention

Related deficits in children with ASD that have implications for developing attachments, emotional expression, and the coordination of affective expression are arousal modulation and attention (Dawson & Lewy, 1989). Typically, highly predictable stimuli fail to elicit an orienting response, whereas intense and unpredictable stimuli elicit more aversive responses. Research suggests that response thresholds for children with ASD may be lower than expected for unpredictable stimuli, resulting in a narrow range for acceptable stimulation. This narrow range could have selective effects on an individual's social processing (Dawson & Lewy, 1989). For example, objects are usually characterized by physical properties, and the actions related to objects are predictable. In contrast, the goals, feelings, and actions that characterize people and their actions are not always predictable. It may be the more complex, novel, and unpredictable nature of people that challenges children with ASD to make sense of the stimulation they receive from other people. The impact on social–emotional development is the distortion of information being processed that is important to establishing early emotional connections and interpreting and coordinating emotional and affective expressions.

The degree of social withdrawal and inattentiveness in children with ASD might also relate to level of familiarity with a potential social partner. Familiar social partners might be less stimulating because their behaviors are more predictable. Lord and Magill (1989) offer support for this hypothesis in their study of children's day camp experiences; children with ASD increased their social interaction with peers at day camp over time.

Children with ASD have also been described as failing to attend to social stimuli and responding more frequently with negative affect in social interactions (Dawson & Lewy, 1989). Further, coordination of affective expressions is challenged when one member of a social interaction has very different attentional and emotional responses than the other. Failure to attend to and respond to a shared interest or pleasure will certainly interfere with the ability of children with ASD to share the social experience and learn ways to coordinate the affective expressions associated with that experience. This challenge continues as children with ASD are unable to sustain their attention to face-to-face interactions.

Creating Profiles of Social–Emotional Development

Impairments in the area of social–emotional development are central to the understanding of autism. Further, social development and strengths and challenges in the area of social interaction can vary significantly among children with ASD over time. Therefore, it is essential that a comprehensive assessment of children's social and emotional strengths and challenges be obtained. In the paragraphs that follow, specific areas to profile in the social and emotional development and behavior of children with ASD are highlighted. Strategies for examining social development using behaviors identified as pivotal to responsive interaction and friendship building are provided. A framework for assessing emotional development in children with ASD is also presented. Although aspects of social and emotional assessment are separated here for clarity, it is important that families and practitioners recognize the relationships between them and the interrelationships with communication and play. Also, as part of the assessment and program planning process, an examination of strengths and challenges in the area of social and emotional development and behavior should be repeated regularly to evaluate a child's ongoing progress and the effectiveness of intervention.

Profiling Social Development and Behavior

The degree of social impairment reported for children with ASD is often more severe in the first 5 years of life. As children with ASD grow older, they exhibit some gains in social responsiveness, moving from generally aloof to more responsive but still different (Mundy & Sigman, 1989). Familiarity and predictability increase the likelihood that the child with ASD will be responsive to some level of relationship building. Understanding the social development of children with ASD requires careful examination of their joint attention, imitation, social responsiveness, pivotal response behaviors, peer interactions and friendship behaviors, theory of mind, and executive function.

Joint Attention. As previously discussed, deficits in joint attention can negatively impact opportunities for sharing early social experiences that influence later social development. Prizant and Meyer (1993) suggested several considerations to practitioners for assessing joint attention in children. The following are some key questions practitioners might ask as they are investigating the presence or absence of joint attention in children with ASD:

- Does the child observe other children's or adults' activities?
- Does the child follow others' visual line of regard?
- Does the child communicate (verbally or nonverbally) to establish joint attention by commenting and providing or requesting information?
- Does the child respond to the signals of others to establish shared attention?

Imitation. Although imitation is not a consistent deficit reported for children with ASD, it is important to examine a child's ability to imitate in the context of social experiences. Therefore, practitioners need to look for imitation of actions, vocalizations, and verbalizations (Prizant & Meyer, 1993). Any evidence of the child's social orientation, as might be seen through gaze checking, affect sharing, or communicating verbally, should be noted when they accompany these imitations.

Social Responsiveness. Reciprocal social behavior suggests that children can engage and take turns with others in social interactions in emotionally appropriate ways (Constantino, Przybeck, Friesen, & Todd, 2000). It requires children to be "cognizant of the emotional and interpersonal cues of others, to be aware of others' perceptions or reactions to his or her own behaviors, and to be capable of emotional development" (Constantino et al., 2000, p. 2). The requirements for achieving reciprocal social behavior relate strongly to the challenge children with ASD face in their efforts to be socially responsive. For example, children with ASD are less likely to greet using spontaneous verbal and nonverbal gestures and may not establish eye contact when they are greeted (Hobson & Lee, 1998). An assessment of social responsiveness requires practitioners to consider several social behaviors that characterize the social impairment in children with ASD:

- attempts to avoid interaction,
- responds selectively to social opportunities,
- responds differently in complex environments,
- reacts to different levels of stimulation, and
- avoids social encounters in unfamiliar or unpredictable contexts.

Children with ASD do respond to others who have made active attempts to engage them, however. They also demonstrate attachment, seeking close proximity to their caregivers as opposed to adults they do not know (Mundy & Sigman, 1989; Sigman & Ungerer, 1984; Sigman, Ungerer, Mundy, & Sherman, 1987). When profiling social responsiveness in children with ASD, then, it is just as important to define their strengths as their challenges in this area. Practitioners should look for attempts by children with ASD to engage with other children and consider the social context, including the environment, its predictability and familiarity, the interactive partners, and the level of stimulation.

Researchers have found differences in both the manner and frequency with which children with ASD initiate interactions. For example, Hauck, Fein, Waterhouse, and Feinstein (1995) found differences in the initiations of children with ASD compared to those with developmental disabilities when interacting with adults and peers. The type of initiations that characterized a routine or play episode also influenced interactions with social partners. Hauck and colleagues reported that children with ASD increased their engagement in routines and more frequently monitored the social environment when placed in proximity to their peers. It was also discussed in Chapter 4 that social initiation is a significant challenge for children with ASD because of their limited or unconventional communicative means and the limited range of communicative partners they pursue. Difficulty initiating in social contexts further compromises the ability of children with ASD to be socially responsive. Therefore, assessment requires practitioners to consider the current means children use to initiate and determine the success of initiations in social contexts. Further, a child's social communicative interactions should be examined in a variety of contexts with familiar communication partners to establish features of the interaction that enhance the child's social communicative competence (Quill, 1995). Assessment that considers more authentic observations of children's interactions in the contexts described here is most likely to lead to meaningful goals and effective intervention.

Constantino and colleagues (2000) developed a *Social Reciprocity Scale* (SRS) to profile the reciprocal social behaviors often reported as missing in children with ASD. Using parent and teacher input, the SRS assesses several behaviors in each of the seven categories listed below:

- recognition of social cues,
- interpretation of social cues,
- response to social cues,
- tendency to engage socially,
- core autistic features (restricted or stereotyped patterns of behavior),
- language deficits (qualitative impairment in communication), and
- miscellaneous symptoms (frequently associated with ASD).

For each of the 65 items assessed across the seven categories, the respondent rates the behavior of a particular child as *not true* (0), *sometimes true* (1), *often true* (2), or *almost always true* (3) during the past 6 months. The SRS may be useful to practitioners interested in tracking the social development of children with ASD.

Pivotal Response Behaviors. Pivotal response behaviors have been identified in the literature as important intervention targets for children with ASD, because there is an assumption that targeting a pivotal behavior will have greater impact or broader effects on several other behaviors (L. K. Koegel, Koegel, Harrower, & Carter, 1999; R. L. Koegel & Koegel, 1996). The Koegels and their colleagues report such broad effects (L. K. Koegel, Koegel, & Carter, 1998; L. K. Koegel, Koegel, Shoshan, & McNerney, 1999). Five of these pivotal response behaviors have been identified as playing a significant role in the social, emotional, and language competence of children with ASD: motivation, self-regulation, initiation, empathy, and social interaction. During the assessment process, practitioners need to identify motivators for children with ASD. This should include an examination of both real and potential intrinsic motivators (e.g., individual interests or themes, wanting to please, wanting to connect or have a friend, completing a task) and extrinsic motivators (e.g., objects, activities, events, specific people). R. L. Koegel and Koegel (2001) describe *motivation* as a particularly important pivotal response behavior to identify and then facilitate because of the tendency for children with ASD to exhibit learned helplessness and to be given fewer opportunities to demonstrate what they know. Social motivation might also be seen in children's preference to be alone or in the proximity of others; their attempts to bring attention to themselves; their response to social games and routines; their tendency to orient visually and shift their gaze to connect with others; and their attempts to direct the acts of others (Prizant & Meyer, 1993). The lack of motivation to interact socially because of language limitations or confusion interpreting the affective signaling of interaction partners helps to explain the impact this pivotal response behavior has on social development.

Self-regulation is another pivotal response behavior requiring assessment in children with ASD. Families and practitioners need to consider the ability of children with ASD to monitor their own behavior. There seem to be four important areas that require some level of self-management in children with ASD: arousal (level of alertness), attention (sustained focus), affect (emotional response), and activity (level of movement appropriate for the situation) (Bolick, 2001). An inability to monitor and regulate self in these areas compromises opportunities for sustained social encounters important to social development.

A third pivotal area is *initiation*. This has been a long reported area of challenge for children with ASD. Failure to initiate leads to numerous missed opportunities for social engagement. Profiling this pivotal area requires practitioners to consider unconventional attempts to initiate, as well as environmental opportunities for initiation to occur.

Also important as a pivotal area of development is *empathy*. Empathy requires an understanding of the perspective and emotion of others and an ability to share that understanding. Deficits in perspective taking and theory of mind, as well as language limitations reported for children with ASD, make this important to assess. It is likely that some children with ASD do have empathy but do not have the language they need to express or share their empathetic feelings. It would be important to profile more subtle and nonverbal expressions of empathy in this population. For example, early demonstration of empathy developing might be seen in children's attachments and emotional expressions. Practitioners should consider the following questions in their observations:

- Are caregivers used for security or emotional support?
- Do older children with ASD use other adults for security or emotional support?
- What emotions do children display through their facial expressions?
- Are children's facial expressions appropriate to the situation?
- Do children appropriately respond to others' facial expressions?

As children grow older, observations should be made of the concern children demonstrate for others and attempts they make to comfort someone who is hurt or upset (Prizant & Meyer, 1993).

The last pivotal area important to profile in children with ASD is *social interaction*. Children with ASD should be observed in several different contexts to identify those situations in which social interaction is more or less likely to occur. For example, children with ASD might pursue interactions with caregivers more than with strangers (Mundy & Sigman, 1989; Sigman & Ungerer, 1984; Sigman et al., 1987), with adults more than with peers (Baltaxe & Simmons, 1983; Lord & Magill, 1989), in structured more than unstructured situations, and in environments with less complexity (Baron-Cohen, 1987; Jarrold, Boucher, & Smith, 1993; Lewis & Boucher, 1988). Therefore, practitioners should observe and profile the social interaction of children with ASD in the following situations:

- with familiar and unfamiliar adults,
- with familiar and unfamiliar peers,
- in structured and unstructured situations, and
- in small and large groups.

A framework for assessing these five pivotal response behaviors in children with ASD is displayed in Figure 6.1. This framework requires practitioners to identify the context in which the pivotal behavior occurs, to describe what is observed using actual examples, and to suggest potential interventions for capitalizing on a particular strength or managing a particular weakness.

Peer Interactions and Friendship Behaviors. Effective social behavior with peers is a critical part of early social development and a powerful predictor of independence and the formation of adult relationships later in life (Brown, Odom, & Holcombe, 1996; Guralnick, 1992; Strain, 2001). Specifically, social connections are a critical influence in the development

Assessment of Pivotal Response Behaviors

Child's name: _____   Date: _____

Observer: _____   Location: _____

Pivotal Behaviors	Context	Describe Observations (include examples)	Intervention Suggestions
Motivation • Extrinsic motivators • Intrinsic motivators			
Self-Regulation • Arousal • Attention • Affect • Activity			
Self-Initiation			
Empathy			
Social Interaction			

FIGURE 6.1. Assessment of pivotal response behaviors.

of positive friendships. Unfortunately, children with ASD spend less time interacting with peers than do children without disabilities and those with other disabilities. Lord and Magill (1989) offer three major reasons to account for the lower rate of interaction: lack of opportunity, lack of familiarity and experience, and lack of the needed social skills. Depending on the educational philosophy and culture of a school program, children with autism may be isolated from their typical peers, so there is limited opportunity, and perhaps no real goal, to establish time for peer interaction. When there is an opportunity to interact, the ability of children with ASD to capitalize on that opportunity may be compromised by their general lack of experience with peers in a variety of social contexts. The role of social skills in interactions is a bit more complex. It may be that the failure of children with ASD to use gestures, eye contact, and language for social purpose results in decreased interaction, but the reverse may also be true. Decreased opportunity for social interaction may limit the contexts in which children with ASD can use the social communication skills they possess (Lord & Magill, 1989).

Related to the pivotal response behaviors described by R. L. Koegel and Koegel (1996, 2001), there are key social behaviors identified and supported at the preschool level that have long-term developmental significance (Strain & Hoyson, 2000) and should be examined. Those specifically related to the development of peer friendships include the ability to share, show affection, suggest play ideas, assist others, sustain encounters, and engage in reciprocal interactions (Strain, 1983, 2001; Tremblay, Strain, Hendrickson, & Shores, 1981). These behaviors support the development of peer acceptance and the establishment of friendships within peer groups. An assessment of these friendship behaviors, beginning in the preschool years, when peer interaction increases its prominence, is important to determining those challenges children with ASD are already experiencing in relationships and potential targets for intervention. A framework for assessing these friendship behaviors in young children is shown in Figure 6.2. This framework allows practitioners to examine the context in which the behaviors may or may not occur, provide real examples, and suggest interventions to facilitate the behaviors in the future. This format can also be used to observe and evaluate the friendship behaviors demonstrated by potential peer buddies, who later can be taught facilitating techniques to engage children with ASD.

As children become school age, they form deeper relationships, with a focus on increased sensitivity to others and a desire for peer acceptance (Goldstein & Morgan, 2002). The perspective-taking challenges reported for children with ASD compromise their ability to decrease the egocentric approach characteristic of their interactions. When adolescence approaches and a desire for more interpersonal intimacy is pursued, children must be able to explore their identities, beliefs, and aspirations through discussion and problem solving (Goldstein & Morgan, 2002). The linguistic challenges identified for children with ASD, particularly in their understanding and use of complex language forms, literal versus abstract meanings, and other pragmatic behaviors, indicate that opportunities for successful exploration with peers are likely to be limited.

Assessment of Friendship Behaviors

Child's name: _____   Date: _____

Observer: _____   Location: _____

Friendship Behaviors (Strain, 2001)	Context	Describe Observations (include examples)	Intervention Suggestions
Sharing			
Showing Affection			
Suggesting Play Ideas			
Assisting Others			
Sustaining Encounters			
Engaging in Reciprocal Social Interaction			

FIGURE 6.2. Assessment of friendship behaviors. *Note.* Can be used to assess children with ASD as well as typical peers who may serve as possible "peer" coaches for children with ASD.

At all ages, the opportunity to engage in a variety of social contexts is critical to the development of the social skills and competencies necessary for relationship building (Buhrmester & Furman, 1986). Unfortunately, the core impairments that define autism place children with ASD at risk of having limited opportunities to experience those social exchanges so important to achieving social competence. Therefore, practitioners should also assess the opportunities to engage with peers that have been and continue to be provided to children with ASD.

Although it is labor intensive, collecting information from a variety of sources, within different settings, and using multiple methods is critical to an assessment of children's social competence with peers. Brown and his colleagues (1996) described a system for observing children's social interactions that may be useful to practitioners interested in defining the social goals children have established and the behavioral strategies they use to achieve their goals. Careful assessment of these components of interaction and the achieved outcomes provides valuable information for intervention planning. It is important for observers to differentiate between social behavior (individual action of one child directed to another), social interaction (reciprocal exchange among two or more children), social goals (intended outcomes), and behavioral strategies (social behaviors used to achieve goals) (Brown et al., 1996). The *System for Observation of Children's Social Interactions* provides a framework in which to assess 15 behavioral strategies used by children to achieve 12 different social goals. It also considers an evaluation of the outcome of the social interaction, indicating whether a child successfully accomplishes or fails to accomplish the apparent purpose of the interaction (Brown et al., 1996).

Quill (2000) described a process for profiling the social and communication skills of children with autism that inventories the children's social and communication behaviors across several contexts. Quill and her colleagues provide the *Assessment of Social and Communication Skills for Children with Autism* as one tool that can be used to guide a team's understanding of the child with autism, foster a discussion about the child's core deficits, and promote educational planning (Quill, Bracken, & Fair, 2000).

The *Social Skills Rating System* (SSRS; Gresham & Elliot, 1990) offers a different option for gathering information on the social behavior in children with special needs, particularly those with autism. The SSRS examines social skills that can affect the relationships between students and teachers, peer acceptance, and academic competence by using a series of rating forms completed by parents, teachers, and students. The assessment results are then linked to intervention planning, including social goal development. This standardized, norm-referenced assessment tool examines three domains (social skills, problem behaviors, and academic competence) and includes several subscales within each domain. For example, there are five social skills subscales, including cooperation (helping others, sharing, complying), assertion (initiating), responsibility (communicating with adults and having regard for work and property), empathy (concern and respect for others' feelings), and self-control (response to situations with and without conflict).

Each social behavior is rated on its frequency of occurrence, as well as its importance to success. Three problem behavior subdomains (externalizing, internalizing, and hyperactivity) are examined, and five academic competence behaviors (reading, mathematics, motivation, parental support, and general cognitive function) are reviewed. The results of the ratings then guide practitioners to consider the social strengths of a child and his or her challenges in both acquiring skills that are absent and considered important and performing skills that are inconsistently present and seen as critically important. The SSRS provides an integrated assessment of the social skills of children from preschool through high school, with and without disabilities, that is valid and reliable and leads logically to intervention planning for social skills training, using operant, social learning, and cognitive behavioral approaches.

Theory of Mind. Impairments in theory of mind described earlier in the chapter present several challenges for children with ASD. Some of these challenges include difficulty in the following:

- inferring mental states,
- predicting behavior,
- adjusting one's own behavior to accommodate a particular situation,
- establishing joint attention,
- taking turns and creating communicative circles,
- playing symbolically,
- recognizing and understanding emotions,
- using pragmatic language skills,
- recognizing character goals in stories,
- recognizing false beliefs, and
- understanding deception.

Practitioners need to consider these challenges in the assessment of children with ASD, because they are likely to affect not only the children's social encounters but their learning experiences as well. And because differential performance is reported for children of varying ages and cognitive abilities, assessment should consider a range of tasks that assess both first-order and second-order beliefs and the ability to provide explanations for answers given. The *Theory of Mind Test* is one example of a valid and reliable instrument that can be used to assess various aspects of theory of mind (Muris et al., 1999). Other tools are listed in the resource section at the end of this chapter.

A critical aspect of the theory of mind challenges experienced by children with ASD is their difficulty taking on the perspective of others or recognizing that others have points of view that may differ from their own. Geller (1989) identifies three areas practitioners should consider in their assessment of perspective taking in children with ASD. The first is *perceptual understanding,* which involves a child's ability to determine what another person sees and how it is seen when the person is in a different location.

A lack of perceptual understanding is seen in the behavior of an 8-year-old child with ASD in the following example.

It is Valentine's Day, and at the end of the day the teacher allows all the children to pass out their valentines to their classmates. Jarret, an 8-year-old boy with ASD and strong cognitive and verbal skills, proceeds to shout out to his peers their names and state that he has their valentines. Jarret is unsure why Amy, a fellow classmate, doesn't come over when he shouts from across the room: "Hey, Amy, here's your valentine." He is unaware that Amy and others are delivering their valentines individually to their friends.

The second area is *cognitive perspective taking,* which involves a child's ability to understand that others may have different ideas or intentions. For example, a child with ASD saying, "Fix Florida" to his teacher assumes that the teacher understands the unusual metaphor the child has created. The child had fallen on the playground and had a scrape that looked like the state of Florida on the map they had reviewed earlier in the day in geography class.

The final area of perspective taking important to assess is *linguistic,* or the ability of the child to adjust the form, content, and purpose of an utterance to fit the needs of the situation. An example is whether the child is able to shift from listener to speaker and use demonstrative forms like "I" and "you" appropriately.

The ability to recognize that others have thoughts and feelings that may differ has significance for functional communication and the success or failure of a variety of social encounters. Consider the child with ASD who believes the teacher does not like him because she does not always call on him when he raises his hand to answer in class, or the adolescent with ASD talking about answers on a TV game show as if his communicative partner had been there and knew the questions that were asked.

Aspects of theory of mind and perspective taking may evolve over time, so it is crucial to use knowledgeable informants in your assessment. As discussed in Chapter 2 and reinforced throughout the chapters focusing on assessment, parents are integral to the assessment process. Their knowledge of their children's developing theory of mind is an important contribution to assessment, as shown in the following example shared by a parent of an 8-year-old boy (Seth) with autism who is certainly developing a theory of mind.

A close friend of the family had died. Seth and his sister were asking questions about death and dying, so the parents had their pastor over to help explain these difficult concepts. One night as Seth was saying his prayers, he added the name of the friend who died. This surprised Seth's mom because Seth follows a pretty rigid routine, and he always repeated the same bedtime prayers. So she asked, "Why are you praying for Marshall?" Seth responded, "I want him to be happy."

Executive Function. Although the results of research investigating executive function impairment as central to autism are equivocal, there is sufficient evidence of the need to be aware of the potential challenges in planning, impulse control, and problem solving that may characterize the behavior of children with ASD, particularly older children. Practitioners should assess the flexibility with which children with ASD approach tasks and investigate their ability to transition from one task to another, inhibit inappropriate responses, develop a plan for completing tasks, and monitor their own behavior.

Profiling Emotional Development and Behavior

Greenspan and Wieder (1998) provide a useful model for examining the strengths and challenges in the emotional development and behavior of children with ASD that interacts with the development of communication and play. They theorize that by examining how children take in, process, and respond to information from their environment, practitioners can identify the underlying aspects of children's difficulties and develop a treatment plan to address those difficulties. They also believe that the information children integrate and attempt to regulate contributes to their social–emotional development. A reason for caution in considering this model as an explanation of emotional development is the lack of empirical evidence for its application to children with ASD. The developmental focus of the model, however, warrants discussion.

Using a developmental–structuralist approach, Greenspan describes six phases of emotional development in young children (Greenspan, 1992, 1998; Greenspan, DeGangi, & Wieder, 2001). The uniqueness of Greenspan's approach rests with his focus on levels and organizations of experience in which the practitioner learns to attend not only to what a young child is demonstrating but also to what the child is not demonstrating. Further, caregiver behaviors across the six phases are considered in his assessment process, because caregivers make a critical contribution to the organization of children's experiences.

Each of the six phases of emotional development builds upon the others, helping children to develop a sense of self (Greenspan & Wieder, 1998). The first phase is *self-regulation*, or the ability to take an interest in the world and take control of one's emotions and feelings. This homeostasis usually occurs between birth and 3 months. Self-regulation is an essential building block for emotional, social, and intellectual growth. The ability of children with ASD to regulate their emotional thinking influences the competence and success of their social encounters. When children exhibit a harmonious or balanced interest in the world, they have achieved internal regulation. If an infant is overly excitable or apathetic, then unregulated behavior is indicated.

The second phase of emotional development is *intimacy,* or the ability to form a relationship with others. This level of engagement generally occurs between 2 and 7 months and leads to rich emotional investments with primary caregivers; when engagement is lacking, the infant may have little involvement in the animate world (Greenspan, 1992; Greenspan et al., 2001). Once children recognize and learn that people are nurturing, they begin to trust them. This trust may facilitate the motivation of children with ASD to engage in reciprocal social exchanges.

Two-way communication represents the third phase of emotional development. Children learn early on that when they smile at Mom or Dad, their smile is likely to be returned. In fact, such purposeful communication may occur between 3 and 10 months (Greenspan, 1992; Greenspan et al., 2001). Greenspan refers to these early attempts at communicating and interacting as circles of communication. For example, when a child looks for something with his eyes, he is opening a circle of communication. The parent who responds by looking back is building on the child's action. If the child then responds by turning away, the child is closing the circle (Greenspan, 1998). As the interactions become more complex, children learn to communicate with gestures and eventually words. They also begin to understand the intentions of others. The development of two-way communication facilitates the development of intentionality. Children gain a sense of who they are, which helps them see the logic of the world. When their communicative behavior and affective responses with caregivers are more random or rigid and stereotyped, which are often characteristic of children with ASD, however, children challenge caregivers to attend to a range of more unexpected affective responses (Greenspan, 1992; Greenspan et al., 2001). Greenspan believes mastery of this phase of emotional development is critical to communicative interaction, leading to an increase in both number and complexity of the circles of communication that occur.

The fourth phase of emotional development is the *ability to establish complex communication* and use gestures to put together a series of complex thoughts and actions for deliberate problem-solving situations. Children as early as 9 to 18 months of age link gestures into complicated responses, as evident in the following example: A child runs to the door when his dad arrives home, puts up his arms to be lifted and kissed by his dad, and then tickles his dad under the chin (Greenspan, 1998). These gestures serve as the child's "vocabulary" for expressing wishes, helping the child to communicate complicated thoughts. Children learn to arrange their thoughts in a logical order and to comprehend the sequence of behaviors displayed by others. They are gaining a complex sense of self. This complexity of thinking and communicating is facilitated by increased opportunities for opening and closing circles of communication. The challenges reported for children with ASD in their understanding and use of gestures place them at particular risk of having difficulties in their thinking and problem solving. Their behavior and emotions may be more fragmented and stereotyped, requiring caregivers to honor children's initiative and independence while helping them to organize their thinking and associated affective components (Greenspan, 1992; Greenspan et al., 2001).

The *ability to create emotional ideas* is the fifth phase of emotional development that Greenspan (1992) describes. Play soon evolves into complex fantasy play where children use scenes (e.g., a fort made of blocks) to express feelings and ideas (e.g., good guys vs. bad guys). Children also begin to use words to express needs and wants and over time are able to build a dialogue into their play. Through play and expansion of their lexicons, they learn that symbols are meaningful. Every symbol relates to a feeling, activity, or object. Children learn to manipulate ideas and use them to meet their needs through their circles of communication. Once children have mastered the ability to manipulate symbols, they move forward in their ability to communicate (Greenspan, 1998). Again, the limitations in symbolic play, perspective taking, and pragmatic language reported for children with ASD challenge their ability to respond to and create new ideas.

The final phase of emotional development is the *ability to bridge emotional ideas* so that they become logical and realistic. Children learn to put logical thoughts and ideas together and begin to describe their feelings, as opposed to acting them out. They learn to share their emotions in play settings and begin to understand the concepts of time and space in an emotional way. Mastery of this milestone suggests that children understand emotional thinking and that over time they are able to integrate their life experiences into their sense of self and their ability to problem solve. With the challenges in joint attention, symbolic play, and abstract thinking, children with ASD are likely to have difficulty connecting ideas and the associated emotions in a manner that is both logical and meaningful to them, as well as to other social partners.

The final two phases of emotional development described involve a period of forming and elaborating internal representations, gaining cognitive insight, and differentiating self from others that generally occurs between 18 and 48 months of age. Children with ASD often display concrete thinking, a narrow and rigid view of self and others, and difficulty with impulse control and mood stabilization (Greenspan, 1992; Greenspan et al., 2001). Responsive caregivers learn to adjust to the emotional ups and downs and changing dependency needs of the child with ASD. They encourage symbolic understanding across variable affective domains and facilitate limit setting and reality orientation (Greenspan, 1992; Greenspan et al., 2001).

Thus, children with ASD are more susceptible to unsuccessful interactions than children without disabilities, because of their underdeveloped social and emotional skills. Greenspan's (1992) framework for emotional development provides a vehicle for explaining the challenges children with ASD encounter in their interactions with their communication partners. Typically, children without disabilities conform to the expectations adults set for them as they progress through the six phases of emotional development. In contrast, children with ASD usually rely on their interaction partners to make sense of the world, as they have not yet mastered the emotional skills critical to the development of competent social communicative interactions. How potential communication partners view the world becomes an important variable in their ability to interact successfully with children and advance children's understanding and use of their social–emotional skills (Willard & Schuler, 1987). When a communication partner begins to understand the social–emotional strengths and challenges of a child with ASD, he or she can usually facilitate more effective two-way communication. Preconceived notions of the child's ability can also restrict the development of a child's social–emotional skills (Greenspan & Wieder, 1998).

Greenspan and his colleagues (Greenspan, 1992; Greenspan et al., 2001) developed the *Functional Emotional Assessment Scale* (FEAS) as a descriptive tool that practitioners can use to profile the emotional and social development of children with ASD and related disabilities. The FEAS is a criterion-referenced measure that has both a clinical and a research version. The clinical version is intended to facilitate a practitioner's thinking for evaluating children's observed emotional, social, and developmental capacities from 3 to 48 months of age in a systematic way. A 5-point rating scale is used to identify the capacity for a particular behavior and includes *not present* (0), *fleetingly present* (1), *intermittently present* (2), *present most of the time* (3), and *present all of the time in all circumstances* (4). The FEAS assesses young children's regulation of and interest in the world through an examination of primary emotional behaviors (e.g., interest in sensations, ability to calm self); emotional range reflecting both sensory–motor and affective capacities (e.g., looking, listening, smiling, tolerance of touch); and selected capacities in motor, sensory, cognitive, and language abilities. General infant tendencies that are constitutionally and maturationally based (e.g., ability to calm self; to focus attention; to enjoy sensory experiences involving sights, sounds, and movement) and caregiver tendencies that facilitate or hinder social–emotional behavior (e.g., ability to comfort, to engage, and to encourage the child to move forward developmentally) are also documented.

Greenspan et al. (2001) recommend that practitioners observe a child's emotional and developmental capacities for at least 15 to 20 minutes while the child is freely interacting with a caregiver. This can be followed by a similar interaction between the child and the practitioner. Greenspan and his colleagues provide several ideas for facilitating meaningful observations of the six aspects of the child's emotional development, as presented in the following paragraphs. Examiners are encouraged to make adjustments in their approach to facilitating behaviors when they are assessing the emotional capacities of an older child.

Self-Regulation and Interest in the World. Practitioners are encouraged to examine the child's ability to attend, be calm, experience sensation across sensory modalities with regulatory control, and organize motor movements. For example, the examiner might make different sounds, varying pitch and intensity, and observe the child's reaction, both positive and negative. The same might be done for assessing response to touch (e.g., by stroking the child's arm or face using light and firm touches) and smell (e.g., by placing cologne on a finger and placing the finger under the child's nose). The child could be gently moved or lifted in different directions with varying speeds to observe level of pleasure or dislike. The examiner might display funny faces from a distance and gradually move closer or shine a flashlight on his or her own face to facilitate a reaction.

Forming Relationships. When assessing intimacy or relationship building and engagement, the practitioner is investigating the child's ability to take an interest, to show pleasure, and to seek warmth and pleasure in communicating and relating with another person. To do this, the examiner might find a strategic position near the child and use a variety of facial expressions and inviting sounds or gestures (e.g., moving face back and forth or side to side, putting a favorite toy on his or her own head) and observe any evidence of relating, such as a smile or responsive movement. The examiner's approach to the child should always be respectful—moving slowly, waiting patiently, and sensitively responding to evidence of discomfort or uneasiness.

Two-Way Communication. Assessing two-way purposeful communication will allow the practitioner to determine the child's ability to initiate with and respond to gestures, including smiling, vocalizing, pointing, reaching out, and exchanging and searching for desired toys. The examiner must create opportunities for interaction, such as offering the child a preferred toy and then asking for it back. The examiner might use exaggerated or animated gestures to take a favorite toy and hide it (e.g., in a pocket or under something) and then respond to the child's facial expressions, sounds, or motor gestures. The examiner's task is to provide numerous opportunities for interaction.

Complex Communication, Organization, Problem Solving, and Internalization. The practitioner is encouraged to explore the child's initiations and responses in a chain of purposeful interactions used to negotiate emotional themes such as anger, curiosity, closeness, and independence (Greenspan & Wieder, 2001). The examiner has several options to elicit pretend play that can lead a child to open and close several circles in a row. For example, pretending to talk on a telephone might be introduced, in which a back-and-forth conversation is developed, with the child and examiner taking turns. A similar back-and-forth exchange might be developed by exchanging silly hats or pretending to be a horse or other animal a child might try to ride or imitate. The child's interests and the examiner's ability to improvise and support whatever complex interactions evolve often determine the opportunities for complex communication, increased organization, meaningful problem solving, and internalization of behavioral and emotional patterns.

Emotional Ideas. A child's assessment of emotional ideas or representational capacity requires the practitioner to consider how a child initiates play and symbolic communication to convey intentions, wishes, or feelings. To do this, the examiner must elicit opportunities for symbolic play by engaging the child around toys such as action figures, dolls, a toy house, vehicles, and kitchen utensils to observe what the child actually does with the toys. The task for the examiner is to add objects and verbalizations to the child's play to create some drama. The examiner may substitute other items or play scenarios, as long as they successfully lead the child to initiate a pretend play sequence (Greenspan & Wieder, 2001).

Building Logical Bridges Between Ideas and Emotional Thinking. Assessment of the last phase of emotional development involves examining a child's representational differentiation, including the child's ability to connect pretend sequences (e.g., making action figures play together, one action figure starts a fight, and the other walks away) and symbolic communication (e.g., "I don't like airplanes because they make loud noises") in a logical manner, and ability to connect visual–spatial concepts (e.g., building something with several connected parts). The examiner creates play opportunities similar to those described under "Emotional Ideas" but enhances those play scenarios with the mention of other feelings or by posing questions that require some logical reasoning. For example, when a child initiates a play sequence involving two action figures who then begin to fight, the examiner might ask, "Why are they fighting?" or "What happened?" The examiner would then look for logical connections in the child's responses. To explore the child's ability for spatial reasoning and reasoning about the physical properties of the world, the examiner might hide objects of interest in plain view of the child and then increase the complexity of the displacements (e.g., hiding a toy in a container that is placed in a second container). The examiner might also create an obstacle course or a mazelike structure with the object being retrieval of a favorite toy (Greenspan & Wieder, 2001).

Greenspan and Wieder (2001) have also developed a FEAS developmental growth chart and questionnaire for observing and monitoring a child's development. Both practitioners and family members can use the chart as a visual tool to identify the milestones a child has achieved and the age at which they were achieved. It also can be used to identify the milestones yet to be developed compared with what might be expected for a child exhibiting typical development, including accelerated progress, slower progress, and developmental problems. The questionnaire lists several questions under each developmental milestone to capture areas in which the child is progressing as well as facing challenges. The answer to all the questions under each milestone must be yes to indicate mastery. For example, under two-way purposeful communication, caregivers should be able to answer yes to the following questions for a 9-month-old (Greenspan & Wieder, 2001, p. 120):

- Is your baby able to show what he/she wants by reaching for or pointing at something, reaching out to be picked up, or making purposeful special noises?
- Does your baby respond to people talking or playing with him/her by making sounds, faces, initiating gestures (reaching), etc.?

A research version of the FEAS is also available to clinical researchers who wish to evaluate a child's functional emotional development. It is designed for children ages 7 months to 4 years, broken up into six age groups: 7 to 9 months, 10 to 12 months, 13 to 18 months, 19 to 24 months, 25 to 36 months, and 36 to 48 months. The sampling group included 197 children with typical development, 190 children with regulatory disorders, 41 children with pervasive developmental disorders, and 40 children from families with complex problems including drug exposure. The assessment takes place in the home, in approximately 15 to 30 minutes. The examiner observes the caregiver interacting with the child and then determines a need for the child and examiner to interact. The research version has two parts that are scored, one for the child and one for the caregiver. The caregiver's interaction is scored to provide information on the caregiver's ability to support the child's emotional development and play. Each capacity assessed across the six phases of emotional development is given a score of 0 (*behavior not observed or only briefly observed and skill not mastered*), 1 (*behavior present some of the time and skill partially mastered*), or 2 (*behavior present consistently and skill mastered*). Validity studies have been completed for the research version to assess construct validity (ability to discriminate between normal and clinical populations), decision validity (accuracy of scores in classifying children as typical, at risk, or delayed), and concurrent validity (comparing scores with other measures of attention and sensory processing) (DeGangi & Greenspan, 2001). The FEAS is recommended as one component of a comprehensive assessment of a child. Some of the strengths of the research version include its systematic and comprehensive approach to observation of the targeted behaviors, its theoretical foundation in relevant domains of social–emotional development, its use with children on the autism spectrum and ability to differentiate children with autism from those with other regulatory disorders, and its interobserver reliability (DeGangi & Greenspan, 2001). Although useful for children with autism between 2 and 4 years of age, the FEAS may be less useful for differentiating developmental capacities of younger children (under 2 years) suspected of autism.

Social–Emotional Assessment Across Impairment, Activity, and Participation

An assessment of social–emotional development and behavior provides important information about how children with ASD understand the social and emotional behaviors of others, as well as how they use social–emotional information to participate in tasks and interact with others. Social–emotional assessment that addresses the World Health Organization (WHO's; 2001) dimensions of disability (as described in Chapter 3) uses multiple forms, including record review, interview, observation in structured or natural environments, and formal assessment tools. It is important that assessment in this area of deficit for children with ASD consider all three dimensions of disability—impairment, activity, and participation—in light of personal and environmental contextual factors, as suggested for communication assessment (see Chapter 4) and play assessment (see Chapter 5). Comprehensive assessment ensures that program planning and specific interventions implemented for a child with ASD will be responsive to each of the disability dimensions. Table 6.1 describes the dimensions of disability proposed by the WHO and the relevant social–emotional assessment areas for children with ASD.

TABLE 6.1

Dimensions of Disability and Aspects of Social–Emotional Function To Be Assessed in Children with ASD

Impairment: Function and Structure at the Body Level	Activity: Performance at the Person Level	Participation: Involvement at the Societal Level
Social Behaviors • Eye gaze • Social smile • Face perception • Joint attention • Initiation • Social gestures • Imitation • Theory of mind • Executive function • Motivation **Emotional Behaviors** • Attachment • Emotion recognition • Self-regulation **Related Areas** • Arousal • Attention	Quality and quantity of skill performance; what child can and cannot do in everyday activities: • Simple activities, including recognizing and responding to a look or facial expression; using gestures to greet, comment, or share information; imitating gestures, vocalizations, actions, or verbalizations; responding to social initiations by adults or peers; and establishing attachments; and • Complex activities, including using a variety of facial expressions appropriate to the situation; initiating connections with adults or peers; understanding the perspectives of others; planning and completing tasks; inhibiting inappropriate responses; engaging in problem solving; managing transitions; demonstrating emotions appropriate to the situation; recognizing and responding to the emotions of others; regulating emotions appropriate to the situation; sustaining focus during social encounters; and modulating arousal level in social contexts.	Compared to the standard or norm for participation of other children without disabilities, participation in typical activities: • family outings or events, • play dates, • recreational activities, • community programs, • extracurricular school activities, • friendships, • church activities, • school events, and • work.

Context

• Personal: Age, gender, other health conditions, past and current experiences, educational level, fitness, lifestyle, habits, coping styles, or other personal–social characteristics.

• Environmental: Societal attitudes, cultural norms, laws, educational systems, architectural characteristics, or other environmental conditions.

Record Review

A current and historical perspective on the development of imitation, gesture use, facial expression, and reciprocity in children with or suspected of ASD is a critical component of the assessment process. Impairments in social interaction play a primary role in early and differential diagnosis (see Chapter 1). Specifically, a lack of social responsiveness and limited interest in others are red flags and early markers for ASD (APA, 2000; Baron-Cohen, Allen, & Gillberg, 1992; Lord & Risi, 2000; Osterling & Dawson, 1994). Practitioners should carefully examine early reports and records of social–emotional development, as well as changes in development following intervention. Documentation of children's early social experiences is also critical.

Interview

As described in Chapter 3, interviewing is an important component of the assessment process. It has a valuable role in obtaining critical information about a child's social competence. Interviews should be conducted with those individuals (e.g., teachers, family members, peers) who have had a consistent opportunity to observe a child's social–emotional development or participate in social encounters with the child. Teachers have multiple opportunities to observe social interactions and emotional responses, and family members have a unique perspective for reporting on social interactions and emotional responses occurring in environments that teachers seldom have an opportunity to observe (Kaczmarek, 2002). Over time, peers become valuable reporters of what they perceive as the critical social skills of other children. Therefore, the interview should seek out information that highlights the impact of different environmental contexts on the child's motivation and ability to respond, initiate, self-regulate, demonstrate empathy, and interact socially with familiar and unfamiliar adults and peers. Further, it is important to have an understanding of the child's early social experiences, particularly with other children.

The *Autism Diagnostic Interview–Revised* (ADI–R; Lord, Rutter, & LeCouteur, 1994), as mentioned in Chapter 1, is a formal tool for interviewing primary caregivers using a semistructured format. It is primarily used to assist clinicians in determining the appropriateness of an autism diagnosis and focuses on the three defined areas consistent with the diagnostic criteria for autism: reciprocal social interaction; language and communication; and repetitive, restricted, and stereotyped behavior. Several specific elements of social–emotional development are assessed within this interview: interest in others; friendship development; elements of reciprocity, including greeting, emotional sharing, offering, and seeking comfort; and social language use. For practitioners adequately trained in the use of the ADI–R, this interview format provides insight into some key areas of potential strengths and identified challenges in the social–emotional development of children with ASD.

Observation

Perhaps the most important part of any assessment of social–emotional functioning in children with ASD is an observation of their social tendencies, behavioral style, and emotional responses in real-life situations. There are several reasons this is an important component of the assessment process. Perhaps most important, the structured assessment format may lead practitioners to either over- or underestimate the child's social interaction ability. For example, the anxiety and unfamiliarity that often accompany formal testing may inhibit the child's performance. Further, the language used to explain formal testing procedures may make it difficult for children with ASD to understand and respond to the questions asked or the tasks posed. In contrast, the structure formal assessments provide may be easier and more comfortable for some children with ASD to participate in than social interactions in another setting, particularly those in which the child is required to initiate interactions. Observations of a child at home, at school, and in the community allow for consideration of naturally occurring social interactions, consideration of the environment in which those interactions occur, the opportunity to explore differences in interactions between children versus adults, and the use of emotional expression in realistic and appropriate situations.

Observers should look for social preferences including social activities versus inanimate objects or solitary activities, preferred social partners, initiations versus responses to initiations by others, the use of language during social interactions, examples of reciprocity, and indications that the child seems aware of social conventions. It is important to note what systems in addition to language the child possesses to manage social situations, such as the use of eye contact, gesture, body language, and facial expression. Observers should also be alert to the impact of arousal level and attention span on children's social behavior. Observations over an extended period of time are essential so that the observer can witness children in a variety of emotion-evoking situations that provide opportunities to view their style of emotional expression, their responses to the emotions and feelings of others, and their strategies for emotional regulation and coping.

Another useful step in observational assessment is to structure some play interactions. This might include play with certain types of toys, such as puppets or action figures, or asking children to engage in drawing tasks, all of which allow for exploration of more advanced social–affective skills such as role playing, perspective taking, and responses to particular emotions and situations. This type of assessment can be particularly useful in program planning. In contrast to more naturally occurring observations, which provide good evidence of children's current social functioning, structured play interactions provide insight into the skills children with ASD might be capable of when their interactions are supported and opportunities for social interaction and emotional expression are facilitated.

Standardized Tools

Because of the central role of social characteristics in the diagnosis of autism, a number of the currently used diagnostic assessments provide important and useful information about a child's specific social characteristics. These assessment instruments also give practitioners an opportunity to observe the social performance of children with ASD during more structured tasks.

A widely used diagnostic tool that can be repeatedly administered to examine change over time is the *Childhood Autism Rating Scale* (CARS; Schopler, Reichler, & Rochen-Renner, 1988). This rating scale consists of 15 areas of observed behavior that are scored on a 4-point continuum ranging from *normal* to *severely abnormal* behavior. Although the scale is typically completed by clinicians following a period of observation, it has also been scored by parents and teachers and administered to parents as an interview. Of particular interest to the assessment of children's social and emotional development, the CARS includes scales that explore an individual's level of impairment in human relationships, imitation, and the expression of affect.

The *Autism Diagnostic Observation Schedule–Generic* (ADOS–G; Lord, Rutter, DiLavore, & Risi, 1999) is a commonly used diagnostic tool that is well regarded for both the breadth of information it provides and its appropriateness for use with a wide age range of individuals with varying communication skills. As described in Chapter 1, the ADOS–G is a standardized assessment instrument that uses a structured and semistructured observation, interview, and interaction format. This tool is appropriate for use with children as young as 2 years of age through adulthood. The ADOS–G is designed to help determine whether a diagnosis on the autism spectrum is appropriate, and it provides specific information about a child's (or adult's) communication, social interaction, and play. Behaviors and responses in the following areas of social interaction are coded as part of the scoring system:

- use of gesture,
- facial expression,
- smiling and eye contact,
- presence of shared enjoyment and joint attention,
- frequency of social initiations,
- quality of social overtures and responses, and
- aspects of reciprocal social communication.

In addition, when used with older children (preadolescent and adolescent), this measure is one of the few that also specifically assesses elements of emotional development, including understanding of feelings, expression of empathy for others, and insight into the nature of social relationships. Although the summary score generated from this assessment method determines whether a child meets a cutoff for an autism diagnosis, the information obtained about social and emotional development is invaluable in identifying specific areas of strength and challenge.

The *Autism Behavior Checklist* (ABC), a component of the *Autism Screening Instrument for Educational Planning* (Krug, Arick, & Almond, 1993), is used both in the diagnosis of autism and in program planning and can be completed by both parents and classroom teachers. It contains 57 items or behaviors relating to five content areas, including relating and social interaction. Unlike many of the diagnostic instruments discussed above, an advantage of the ABC is that it can be administered repeatedly to document progress or change over time in aspects of social functioning that are central to reported symptoms of autism.

Several assessment instruments not designed specifically for use with individuals with autism but commonly used to obtain information about children and adults with developmental disabilities provide insight into elements of children's social–emotional development. The most well known and widely used is the *Vineland Adaptive Behavior Scales* (VABS; Sparrow, Balla, & Cicchetti, 1984). The VABS is completed through an interview with primary caregivers and is appropriate for children from birth through adulthood. It assesses three areas of functional behavior: communication, daily living skills, and socialization. A motor skills scale is also available for children under age 5 years. The socialization scale includes three subscales, including interpersonal relationships, play and leisure time, and coping skills, an important component of social–emotional development frequently overlooked in other measures. Specific items address friendships, understanding of social conventions, emotional expression, and social interests. In addition, there is a supplementary maladaptive behavior scale that some practitioners find useful in identifying particular behaviors that interfere with social functioning. As a norm- and age-referenced tool, the VABS provides both level of impairment and age equivalents. Recently, supplementary norms for use with individuals with autism have been developed (Carter et al., 1998).

The *Achenbach System of Empirically Based Assessment* (ASEBA; Achenbach & Rescorla, 2000), with its preschool forms and profiles, as well as the forms for children and youth, offers practitioners a way to determine the similarities and differences in how children function under different conditions with different interactive partners. Within the ASEBA there is a *Child Behavior Checklist* for ages 1½ to 5 years as well as ages 6 to 18 years that is completed by parents and other primary caregivers who see the child in the home setting. There is also a *Caregiver–Teacher Report Form* for younger children and a *Teacher Report Form* for older children, a *Language Development Survey* (LDS) for children 1½ to 5 years old, and a *Youth Self Report* for students 11 to 18 years old. The *Child Behavior Checklist* examines both internalizing problems (e.g., emotionally reactive, anxious or depressed, having somatic complaints, or withdrawn) and externalizing problems (involving conflicts with others and performance expectations), as well as sleep problems, important to understanding a child's social–emotional development. There are also DSM–oriented scales available for scoring the preschool forms of the ASEBA, in which the practitioner can look at responses in relation to the DSM criteria for affective, anxiety, pervasive developmental, attention, or oppositional defiant problems. Similar interpretations are available for the *Caregiver–Teacher Report Form.* With an ethnoculturally diverse normative sample and high marks in test–retest reliability, as well as content- and criterion-related validity, the ASEBA appears to be a potentially useful instrument for periodic reassessment of performance change across externalizing and internalizing behaviors in children with ASD. This assessment approach could provide important insights from a variety of informants on the ability of children with ASD to function across settings and partners.

Given the importance of social–emotional development in children with ASD, there is a relative dearth of assessment tools that specifically focus on social–emotional skills. For this reason, it may be useful to include in the assessment process a social skills assessment not specific to autism, such as the *Social Skills Rating System* (SSRS; Gresham & Elliot, 1990) described earlier. The measure purports to tap essential elements of social competence in children 3 to 18 years of age, suggesting that socially competent children need certain key social skills. Those who possess these identified skills should demonstrate fewer problem behaviors that might interfere with social competence. The SSRS has been standardized on a sample of over 4,000 children, and norms are available for both boys and girls. The measure has both good internal consistency and test–retest reliability, as well as strong content, construct, and concurrent validity (Gresham & Elliot, 1990). Parent, teacher, and student versions of the scale are available. The SSRS yields two summary scores: a standardized social skills score and a standardized problem behavior score. A measure such as the SSRS can be useful in helping to determine the level of a child's social impairment relative to peers. However, a primary reason for including an instrument such as the SSRS in an assessment of a child with ASD is that it serves as a reminder of the social skills that are particularly important during key developmental periods. A strong understanding of what social skills are expected of their typically developing peers helps remind practitioners of what social skills to focus on when supporting children with ASD.

Summary

Differences in social–emotional development and, in particular, social interaction are frequently cited as one of the most salient features of individuals with an autism spectrum disorder (Lord, 1993; Volkmar, 1987; Volkmar & Klin, 1990). This chapter has discussed the social and emotional impairments most often described for children with ASD. Key areas of impairment have also been identified that interfere with the ability of a child with ASD to engage in meaningful and sustaining social relationships. This chapter proposed aspects to consider when developing profiles of social and emotional strengths and challenges and presented potential means of assessment. The following paragraphs refer to the questions at the beginning of the chapter and highlight those points you should be familiar with when assessing social and emotional skills in children with ASD.

In what ways does the social–emotional development of children with ASD differ, qualitatively and quantitatively, from that of typically developing peers and peers with other disabilities?

One of the most salient features of autism is the difficulty reported in social–emotional development, specifically social interaction. Early on, children with autism are described as lacking reciprocal eye contact, failing to exhibit a social smile, and showing less interest in the human face compared to children without disabilities and children with other developmental disabilities. They appear to obtain less pleasure from physical contact and display less interest in social interaction with adults than do comparison groups, although they often form attachments with their primary caregivers. As they move through childhood, children with ASD remain essentially isolated, preferring solitary activities. In adolescence, they may have more interest in social experiences but lack the necessary social conventions to capitalize on available opportunities.

How are specific impairments in joint attention, facial expression and gesture, theory of mind, and executive function related to the core social impairment described for children with ASD?

A failure to develop joint attention is a powerful early indicator of autism and has been speculated to hinder the development of other social–emotional skills. It has been specifically identified as responsible for the social approach challenges that children with ASD often experience. Further, the failure to develop a social gaze or social orienting response compromises the ability of children with ASD to achieve shared attention around an object, action, or event. Some researchers have suggested, however, that this may be a function of the type of stimuli being attended to. It has also been suggested that impairment in joint attention may relate to the inability of children with ASD to compare their own affect with that of others, contributing to difficulties in theory of mind development.

Although some researchers have reported that children with ASD have difficulty recognizing their own faces, others have found evidence of self-recognition in children with ASD. Another consideration in the face perception abilities of children with ASD is their recognition of others' faces. Generally, studies of face recognition in individuals with autism are inconclusive; however, peculiarities in facial processing have been consistently identified.

Research has indicated that children with ASD lack the use of gestures to comment or indicate, which compromises their ability to share experiences with others, including recognizing and responding to the emotional expression of their interaction partners. Imitation deficits have also been reported as characteristic of children with ASD. The importance of imitation to social and emotional development is the role it has in matching internal states to the behavior of others.

Two specific cognitive functions have been identified as impaired in children with ASD: theory of mind and executive function. Theory of mind is the ability to recognize the mental state of others as well as self, so that predictions can be made about the actions observed. Baron-Cohen (1995) proposed four mechanisms to explain the basis for engagement in children and their formation of mental states. The Intentionality and Eye-Direction Detectors work together to facilitate the connections made by the Shared Attention Mechanism. The Theory of Mind Mechanism then facilitates the creation of inferences about mental states such as pretending, believing, deceiving, and guessing. There is strong support in the literature for a theory of mind deficit in children with ASD and a relationship of that deficit to early deficits in joint attention. It is important to note, however, that some children and adolescents with ASD and higher cognitive abilities perform well on theory of mind tasks, although they continue to demonstrate significant social impairment. Research needs to continue to examine the role of theory of mind as one potential explanation of the social deficits in autism.

Executive function oversees goal-directed behavior and employs the mental processes (e.g., problem solving, organizing and planning, cognitive flexibility) that are needed to control one's actions. Impairments sometimes reported for children and adolescents with ASD include ineffective planning, poor impulse control, inflexibility in thought and action, and poor working memory.

How are arousal and attention affected in children on the spectrum, and what is the relationship between these characteristics and overall social development?

Arousal modulation and attention deficits in children with ASD affect the development of attachment, emotional expression, and coordination of affective expression. Difficulty in these areas often distorts the information being processed, which is critical to making early emotional connections and coordinating feelings with expressions of those feelings. More specifically, failure to attend or respond to a shared interest will interfere with the ability of children with ASD to share social experiences and sustain face-to-face interactions.

What should practitioners consider when creating a profile of social–emotional strengths and challenges for children with ASD?

A comprehensive profile of the strengths and challenges observed for children with ASD requires a careful look at key areas of impairment identified in the literature. Practitioners should establish whether or not a child demonstrates joint attention and in what contexts that shared attention occurs. A child's reciprocal social behavior and general social responsiveness should also be examined. Those behaviors identified as pivotal to enhancing social and communicative responsiveness (e.g., self-initiation, motivation, self-regulation, empathy, and social interaction) should be observed and probed. Evidence of behaviors important to developing and sustaining social relationships (e.g., sharing, showing affection, suggesting ideas) should also be examined. The presence or absence of theory of mind should be determined, including an assessment of perceptual, cognitive, and linguistic perspective taking. In addition, more executive function behaviors, such as planning, flexibility, and impulse control, should be noted. Finally, a child's achievement of the six milestones of emotional development (i.e., self-regulation and interest in the world, intimacy, two-way communication, complex communication, emotional ideas, and emotional thinking) should be evaluated.

What areas of social–emotional assessment should be examined across the three dimensions of the disablement framework?

Assessment of the social and emotional skills of children with ASD should address all three areas of disability—impairment, activity, and participation—as described by the WHO (2001). As described in the previous two chapters, practitioners can use record reviews, interviews, observations in natural settings, structured play situations, and standardized assessment tools to define and better understand the social and emotional impairment in children with ASD. A comprehensive investigation of social and emotional impairment is needed. The informational value of this assessment is significant in helping practitioners to understand and eventually support the ability of children and adolescents with ASD to participate fully in their communities.

Practice Opportunities

1. Observe a child with ASD at home and in school using the assessment format for examining pivotal response behaviors (Figure 6.1). Describe instances of self-initiation, motivation, self-regulation, empathy, and social interaction. For each observation made, note potential strategies that could be incorporated in the child's intervention program to build on those pivotal behaviors.

2. Create a profile of perspective taking demonstrated by a child or adolescent with ASD.

3. As a team, assess the friendship behaviors currently exhibited by a child with ASD and a child without ASD who might serve as a potential peer for initiating social interaction.

4. Using Greenspan's six milestones in emotional development, assess the emotional skills of a child with ASD, describing those skills that have been mastered, are emerging, and are yet to be observed.

Suggested Readings

Baron-Cohen, S., & Swettenham, J. (1997). Theory of mind in autism: Its relationship to executive function and central coherence. In D. J. Cohen & F. R. Volkmar (Eds.),

Handbook of autism and pervasive developmental disorders (2nd ed., pp. 880–893). New York: Wiley.

This chapter highlights the research in theory of mind, making a case for the significance of this impairment in children with ASD. It also offers explanations for differences found in research with children of varying ages and ability levels. In addition, the authors define the relationship between theory of mind and executive function, recognizing a possible co-occurrence of these deficits in some children with ASD.

Baron-Cohen, S., Tager-Flusberg, H., & Cohen, D. J. (Eds.). (1993). *Understanding other minds: Perspectives from autism.* Oxford, England: Oxford University Press.

This edited book presents a comprehensive look at the research in theory of mind and the implications for understanding this social impairment in children with ASD. The research in theory of mind is reviewed carefully across several different experimental paradigms.

Resources

Assessment of Social Behavior

Achenbach, T. M. (1991). *Manual for the Child Behavior Checklist/4–18 and 1991 Profile.* Burlington: University of Vermont, Department of Psychiatry.

Beckman, P. J., & Lieber, J. (1994). The Social Strategy Rating Scale: An approach to evaluating social competence. *Journal of Early Intervention, 18,* 1–11.

Blagden, C. M., & McConnell, N. L. (1985). *Interpersonal Language Skills Assessment.* East Moline, IL: LinguiSystems.

Constantino, J. N., Przybeck, T., Friesen, D., & Todd, R. D. (2000). Reciprocal social behavior in children with and without pervasive development disorders. *Developmental and Behavioral Pediatrics, 21*(1), 2–11.

Freedman, B. J., Rosenthal, L., Donahoe, C. P., Schlundt, D. G., & McFall, R. M. (1978). A social behavioral analysis of social skills deficits in delinquent and nondelinquent adolescent boys. *Journal of Counseling and Clinical Psychology, 46,* 1448–1462.

Ghuman, J. K., Freund, L., Reiss, A., Serwint, J., & Folstein, S. (1998). Early detection of social interaction problems: Development of a social interaction instrument in young children. *Developmental and Behavioral Pediatrics, 19,* 411–419.

Gresham, F. M., & Elliot, S. N. (1990). *Social Skills Rating System.* Circle Pines, MN: American Guidance Service.

Hughes, J. N., Boodoo, G., Alcala, J., Maggio, M. C., Moore, L., & Villapando, R. (1989). Validation of a role play measure of children's social skills. *Journal of Abnormal Child Psychology, 17,* 633–646.

Luteijn, E. F., Jackson, A. E., Volkmar, F. R., & Minderaa, R. B. (1998). The development of the Children's Social Behavior Questionnaire: Preliminary data. *Journal of Autism and Developmental Disorders, 28,* 559–565.

Matson, J. L. (1989). *The Matson Evaluation of Social Skills with Youngsters.* Orland Park, IL: International Diagnostic Systems.

Merrell, K. W. (1994). *Preschool and Kindergarten Behavior Scales.* Brandon, VT: Clinical Psychology Publishing.

Quay, H. C., & Peterson, D. R. (1983). *Revised Behavior Problems Checklist.* Los Angeles: Western Psychological Services.

Schopler, E., Reichler, R. J., Bashford, A., Lansing, M., & Marcus, L. (1990). *Individualized assessment and treatment for autistic and developmentally disabled children: Vol. I. Psycho-Educational Profile–Revised* (PEP–R). Baltimore: University Park Press.

Schopler, E., Reichler, R. J., & Rochen-Renner, B. (1988). *Childhood Autism Rating Scale.* Los Angeles: Western Psychological Services.

Selman, R. L., & Byrne, D. F. (1974). A structural–developmental analysis of levels of role taking in middle childhood. *Child Development, 45,* 803–806.

Williamson, D. A., Moody, S. C., Granberry, S. W., Letherman, V. R., & Blouin, D. C. (1983). Criterion-related validity of a role-play social skills test for children. *Behavior Therapy, 14,* 466–481.

Taxonomies for Assessing Social–Communication Skills

Brown, W. H., Odom, S. L., & Holcombe, A. (1996). Observational assessment of young children's social behavior with peers. *Early Childhood Research Quarterly, 11,* 19–40.

Goldstein, H., Kaczmarek, L., Pennington, R., & Shafer, K. (1992). Peer-mediated intervention: Attending to, commenting on, and acknowledging the behavior of preschoolers with autism. *Journal of Applied Behavior Analysis, 25,* 289–305.

Guralnick, M., & Groom, J. M. (1985). Correlates of peer-related social competence of developmentally delayed preschool children. *American Journal of Mental Deficiency, 90,* 140–150.

Kohler, F. W., & Strain, P. S. (1997). Procedures for assessing and increasing social interaction. In N. N. Singh (Ed.), *Prevention and treatment of severe behavior problems: Models and methods in developmental disabilities* (pp. 49–59). Pacific Grove, CA: Brooks/Cole Thomson Learning.

Assessment of Executive Functions

Diamond, A. (1991). Neuropsychological insights into the meaning of object concept development. In S. Carey & R. Gelman (Eds.), *The epigenesis of mind: Essays on biology and knowledge* (pp. 67–110). Hillsdale, NJ: Erlbaum.

Heaton, R. K. (1981). *The Wisconsin Card Sorting Test manual.* Odessa, FL: Psychological Assessment Resources.

Perret, E. (1974). The left frontal lobe of man and the suppression of habitual responses in verbal categorical behaviour. *Neuropsychologia, 12*(3), 323–330.

Reynolds, C. R., & Bigler, E. D. (1994). *Test of Memory and Learning.* Austin, TX: PRO-ED.

Shallice, T. (1982). Specific impairments of planning. *Philosophical Transactions of the Royal Society of London, B298,* 199–209.

Assessment of Theory of Mind

Baron-Cohen, S. (1989). Are autistic children behaviorists? An examination of their mental–physical and appearance–reality distinctions. *Journal of Autism and Developmental Disorders, 19,* 579–600.

Baron-Cohen, S., Leslie, A., & Frith, U. (1985). Does the autistic child have a "theory of mind"? *Cognition, 21,* 37–46.

Baron-Cohen, S., Leslie, A. M., & Frith, U. (1986). Mechanical, behavioral and intentional understanding of picture stories in autistic children. *British Journal of Developmental Psychology, 4,* 113–125.

Heavy, L., Phillips, W., Baron-Cohen, S., & Rutter, M. (2000). The Awkward Moments Test: A naturalistic measure of social understanding in autism. *Journal of Autism and Developmental Disorders, 30*(2), 225–236.

Hogrefe, G. J., Wimmer, H., & Perner, J. (1986). Ignorance versus false belief: A developmental lag in attribution of epistemic states. *Child Development, 57,* 567–582.

Muris, P., Steerneman, P., Meesters, C., Merckelbach, H., Horselenberg, R., van den Hogen, T., et al. (1999). The TOM Test: A new instrument for assessing theory of mind in normal children and children with pervasive developmental disorders. *Journal of Autism and Developmental Disorders, 29,* 67–80.

Perner, J., Frith, U., Leslie, A. M., & Leekam, S. R. (1989). Exploration of the autistic child's theory of mind: Knowledge, belief and communication. *Child Development, 60,* 689–700.

Perner, J., & Wimmer, H. (1985). "John thinks that Mary thinks that …" Attribution of second order beliefs by 5–10 year old children. *Journal of Experimental Child Psychology, 39,* 437–471.

Steerneman, P. (1994). *Theory of Mind Screening Scale.* Apeldoorn, Holland: Garant.

Vijtigschild, W., Berger, H. J. C., & van Spaendonck, J. A. S. (1969). *Social Interpretation Test.* Amsterdam: Swets & Zeitlinger.

Assessment of Emotional Behavior

Greenspan, S. (1992). *The Functional Emotional Assessment Scale.* In S. Greenspan, *Infancy and early childhood: The practice of clinical assessment and intervention with emotional and developmental challenges.* New York: Teachers College Press.

Spence, S. (1980). *Test of Perception of Emotion from Facial Expressions and Test of Perception of Emotion from Posture Cues.* In S. Spence, *Social skills training with children and adolescents: A counselor's manual.* Windsor, England: NFER-Nelson.

Glossary

Affect. Emotion shown through vocalizations, facial expressions, posture, and gestures.

Executive function. Mental processes needed to control actions and oversee goal-directed behavior.

Eye-Direction Detector. Mechanism that identifies the movement of eyes toward an object, action, or person.

First-order theory of mind tasks. Tasks that reveal whether the individual is able to perceive the predictable thoughts of another person.

Friendship. Mutual liking between two children.

Intentionality Detector. Mechanism that reads the intention or mental state of others.

Joint attention. The ability to use gesture, body language, facial expression, or verbal communication, such as commenting or labeling, to direct another's attention to or share interest in objects or events and their properties.

Learned helplessness. Thinking and acting as if one cannot do something, when in fact one can.

Line of regard. The direction of another's gaze.

Mentalizing. Representing mental states.

Peer acceptance. Extent to which children are liked and accepted by each other.

Reciprocal social behavior. Engaging and taking turns in social interactions that are emotionally appropriate.

Referential looking. Looking back and forth between a person and an interesting object or event.

Second-order theory of mind tasks. Tasks that reveal whether the individual is able to perceive the predictable thoughts of another person about what a third person knows.

Self-recognition. Distinguishing between "self" and "nonself" or discriminating a change in one's mirror image.

Self-regulation. Taking an interest in the world and taking control of one's emotions and feelings.

Shared Attention Mechanism. Mechanism that links the Intentionality and Eye-Direction Detectors so that connections can be made about who is sharing their attention to what.

Social behavior. Individual action of one child directed to another (e.g., gesturing, responding to a question).

Social competence. The knowledge, skills, and behaviors needed to meet social expectations at any point in development, including initiating, developing, and maintaining relationships.

Social goals. Intended outcomes of a social interaction.

Social interaction. Reciprocal exchange among two or more children.

Theory of mind. Recognizing the mental state of others as well as self so that predictions and explanations of action can occur.

Theory of mind mechanism. Mechanism that represents knowledge states (e.g., believing, pretending, deceiving) and infers the relationship between those mental states and actions.

References

Achenbach, T. M., & Rescorla, L. A. (2000). *Achenbach System of Empirically Based Assessment preschool forms & profiles.* Burlington: University of Vermont.

Adrien, J. (1991). Autism and family home movies: Preliminary findings. *Journal of Autism and Developmental Disorders, 21,* 43–49.

American Psychiatric Association. (1994). *Diagnostic and statistical manual of mental disorders* (4th ed.). Washington, DC: Author.

American Psychiatric Association. (2000). *Diagnostic and statistical manual of mental disorders* (4th ed., text rev.). Washington, DC: Author.

Baltaxe, C. A., & Simmons, J. Q. (1983). Communication deficits in the adolescent and adult autistic. *Seminars in Speech and Language, 4,* 27–42.

Baron-Cohen, S. (1987). Autism and symbolic play. *British Journal of Developmental Psychology, 5,* 139–148.

Baron-Cohen, S. (1988). Social and pragmatic deficits in autism: Cognitive or affective? *Journal of Autism and Developmental Disorders, 18,* 379–402.

Baron-Cohen, S. (1989). The autistic child's theory of mind: A case of specific developmental delay. *Journal of Child Psychology and Psychiatry, 30,* 285–297.

Baron-Cohen, S. (1995). *Mindblindness.* Cambridge, MA: MIT Press.

Baron-Cohen, S., Allen, J., & Gillberg, C. (1992). Can autism be detected at 18 months? The needle, the haystack, and the CHAT. *British Journal of Psychiatry, 161,* 839–843.

Baron-Cohen, S., Leslie, A., & Frith, U. (1985). Does the autistic child have a "theory of mind"? *Cognition, 21,* 37–46.

Baron-Cohen, S., & Swettenham, J. (1997). Theory of mind in autism: Its relationship to executive function and central coherence. In D. J. Cohen & F. R. Volkmar (Eds.), *Handbook of autism and pervasive developmental disorders* (2nd ed., pp. 880–893). New York: Wiley.

Baron-Cohen, S., Tager-Flusberg, H., & Cohen, D. J. (Eds.). (1993). *Understanding other minds: Perspectives from autism.* Oxford, England: Oxford University Press.

Bauminger, N., & Kasari, C. (1999). Brief report: Theory of mind in high-functioning children with autism. *Journal of Autism and Developmental Disorders, 29*(1), 81–86.

Bernabei, P., Camaioni, L., & Levi, G. (1998). An evaluation of early development in children with autism and pervasive developmental disorders from home movies: Preliminary findings. *Autism, 2*(3), 243–258.

Bolick, T. (2001). *Asperger syndrome and adolescence: Helping preteens and teens get ready for the real world.* Gloucester, MA: Fair Winds Press.

Boucher, J., & Lewis, V. (1992). Unfamiliar face recognition in relatively able autistic children. *Journal of Child Psychology and Psychiatry and Applied Disciplines, 33*(5), 843–859.

Bowlby, J. (1969). *Attachment and loss: Vol. 1. Attachment.* London: Hogarth Press.

Bowler, D. M. (1992). "Theory of mind" in Asperger's syndrome. *Journal of Child Psychology and Psychiatry, 33,* 877–893.

Brown, W. H., Odom, S. L., & Holcombe, A. (1996). Observational assessment of young children's social behavior with peers. *Early Childhood Research Quarterly, 11,* 19–40.

Brownell, C. A., & Brown, E. (1992). Peers and play in infants and toddlers. In V. B. VanHasselt & M. Hersen (Eds.), *Handbook of social development: A lifespan perspective* (pp. 183–200). New York: Plenum Press.

Brownell, C. A., & Carriger, M. S. (1990). Changes in cooperation and self–other differentiation during the second year. *Child Development, 61,* 1164–1174.

Buhrmester, D., & Furman, W. (1986). The changing functions of friends in childhood: A neo-Sullivan perspective. In V. J. Derlega & B. A. Winstead (Eds.), *Friendship and social interaction* (pp. 41–62). New York: Springer-Verlag.

Carter, A. S., Volkmar, F. R., Sparrow, S. S., Wang, J. J., Lord, C., Dawson, G., et al. (1998). The Vineland Adaptive Behavior Scales: Supplementary norms for individuals with autism. *Journal of Autism and Developmental Disorders, 28*(4), 287–302.

Celani, G., Battacchi, M. W., & Arcidiacono, L. (1999). The understanding of the emotional meaning of facial expressions in people with autism. *Journal of Autism and Developmental Disorders, 29,* 57–66.

Charman, T., Swettenham, J., Baron-Cohen, S., Cox, A. Baird, G., & Drew, A. (1997). Infants with autism: An investigation of empathy, pretend play, joint attention and imitation. *Developmental Psychology, 33*(5), 781–789.

Church, C., Alisanski, S., & Amanullah, S. (2000). The social, behavioral, and academic experiences of children with Asperger syndrome. *Focus on Autism and Other Developmental Disabilities, 15*(1), 12–20.

Constantino, J. N., Przybeck, T., Friesen, D., & Todd, R. D. (2000). Reciprocal social behavior in children with and without pervasive development disorders. *Developmental and Behavioral Pediatrics, 21*(1), 2–11.

Curcio, F. (1978). Sensorimotor functioning and communication in mute autistic children. *Journal of Autism and Childhood Schizophrenia, 2,* 264–287.

Dawson, G., & Lewy, A. (1989). Arousal, attention, and the socioemotional impairments of individuals with autism. In G. Dawson (Ed.), *Autism: Nature, diagnosis and treatment* (pp. 49–74). New York: Guilford Press.

Dawson, G., & McKissick, F. (1984). Self-recognition in autistic children. *Journal of Autism and Developmental Disorders, 14,* 383–394.

Dawson, G., Meltzoff, A. N., Osterling, J., Rinaldi, J., & Brown, E. (1998). Children with autism fail to orient to naturally occurring social stimuli. *Journal of Autism and Developmental Disorders, 28*(6), 479–485.

DeCasper, A., & Fifer, W. (1980). Of human bonding: Newborns prefer their mothers' voices. *Science, 171,* 1174–1176.

DeGangi, G., & Greenspan, S. I. (2001). Research applications of the Functional Emotional Assessment Scale. In S. I. Greenspan, G. DeGangi, & S. Wieder (Eds.), *The Functional Emotional Assessment Scale (FEAS) for Infancy and Early Childhood* (pp. 131–247). Bethesda, MD: Interdisciplinary Council on Developmental and Learning Disorders.

Geller, E. (1989). The assessment of perspective taking skills. *Seminars in Speech and Language, 10,* 28–41.

Gepner, B., Deruelle, C., & Grynfeltt, S. (2001). Motion and emotion: A novel approach to the study of face processing by young autistic children. *Journal of Autism and Developmental Disorders, 31*(1), 37–45.

Gillberg, C., Ehlers, S., Schaumann, H., Jakobson, G., Dahlgren, S. O., Lindbolm, R., et al. (1990). Autism under age 3 years: A clinical study of 28 cases referred for autistic symptoms in infancy. *Journal of Child Psychology and Psychiatry, 31,* 921–934.

Goldstein, H., & Morgan, L. (2002). Social interaction and models of friendship development. In H. Goldstein, L. A. Kaczmarek, & K. M. English (Eds.), *Promoting social communication: Children with developmental disabilities from birth to adolescence* (pp. 5–25). Baltimore: Brookes.

Greenspan, S. I. (1992). The basic model: The influence of regulatory and experiential factors on the six organizational levels of experience. In S. I. Greenspan, *Infancy and early childhood: The practice of clinical assessment and intervention with emotional and developmental challenges* (pp. 3–28). New York: Teachers College Press.

Greenspan, S. I. (1998). Guidance for constructing clinical practice guidelines for developmental and learning disorders: Knowledge-based vs. evidence-based approaches. *The Journal of Developmental and Learning Disorders, 2,* 171–215.

Greenspan, S. I., DeGangi, G., & Wieder, S. (2001). Theoretical and clinical perspectives on emotional functioning in infancy and early childhood. In S. I. Greenspan, G. DeGangi, & S. Wieder (Eds.), *The Functional Emotional Assessment Scale (FEAS) for Infancy and Early Childhood* (pp. 1–72). Bethesda, MD: Interdisciplinary Council on Developmental and Learning Disorders.

Greenspan, S., & Wieder, S. (1998). *The child with special needs: Encouraging intellectual and emotional growth.* Reading, MA: Addison-Wesley.

Greenspan, S. I., & Wieder, S. (2001). The clinical application of the Functional Emotional Assessment Scale. In S. I. Greenspan, G. DeGangi, & S. Wieder (Eds.), *The Functional Emotional Assessment Scale (FEAS) for Infancy and Early Childhood* (pp. 73–129). Bethesda, MD: Interdisciplinary Council on Developmental and Learning Disorders.

Gresham, F. M., & Elliot, S. N. (1990). *Social Skills Rating System.* Circle Pines, MN: American Guidance Service.

Griffith, E. G., Pennington, B. F., Wehner, E. A., & Rogers, S. J. (1999). Executive functions in young children with autism. *Child Development, 70*(4), 817–832.

Guralnick, M. J. (1992). A hierarchical model for understanding children's peer-related social competence. In S. L. Odom, S. R. McConnell, & M. A. McEvoy (Eds.), *Social competence of young children with disabilities: Issues and strategies for intervention* (pp. 37–64). Baltimore: Brookes.

Hauck, M., Fein, D., Waterhouse, L., & Feinstein, C. (1995). Social initiations by autistic children to adults and other children. *Journal of Autism and Developmental Disorders, 25*(6), 579–595.

Hobson, R. P., & Lee, A. (1998). Hello and goodbye: A study of social engagement in autism. *Journal of Autism and Developmental Disorders, 28*(2), 117–127.

Jarrold, C., Boucher, J., & Smith, P. (1993). Symbolic play in autism: A review. *Journal of Autism and Developmental Disorders, 23*(2), 281–307.

Kaczmarek, L. A. (2002). Assessment of social-communicative competence: An interdisciplinary model. In H. Goldstein, L. A. Kaczmarek, & K. M. English (Eds.), *Promoting social communication: Children with developmental disabilities from birth to adolescence* (pp. 55–115). Baltimore: Brookes.

Kanner, L. (1943). Autistic disturbances of affective contact. *Nervous Child, 2,* 217–250.

Klin, A., Sparrow, S. S., de Bildt, A., Cicchetti, D. V., Cohen, D. J., & Volkmar, F. R. (1999). A normed study of face recognition in autism and related disorders. *Journal of Autism and Developmental Disorders, 29*(6), 499–508.

Klin, A., Volkmar, F. R., & Sparrow, S. (1992). Autistic social dysfunction: Some limitations of the theory of mind hypothesis. *Journal of Child Psychology and Psychiatry, 33,* 861–876.

Koegel, L. K., Koegel, R. L., & Carter, C. M. (1998). Pivotal responses and the natural language paradigm. *Seminars in Speech & Language, 19,* 355–372.

Koegel, L. K., Koegel, R. L., Harrower, J. K., & Carter, C. M. (1999). Pivotal response intervention I: Overview of approach. *Journal of the Association of Individuals with Severe Handicaps, 24,* 174–185.

Koegel, L. K., Koegel, R. L., Shoshan, Y., & McNerney, E. (1999). Pivotal response intervention II: Preliminary long-term outcome data. *Journal of the Association of Individuals with Severe Handicaps, 24,* 186–198.

Koegel, R. L., & Koegel, L. K. (1996). *Teaching children with autism: Strategies for initiating positive interactions and improving learning opportunities.* Baltimore: Brookes.

Koegel, R. L., & Koegel, L. K. (2001, November). *Improving socialization, behavior and communication in children with autism and Asperger's syndrome.* Paper presented at the annual convention of the American Speech-Language-Hearing Association, New Orleans, LA.

Krug, D. A., Arick, J. R., & Almond, P. J. (1993). *Autism Screening Instrument for Educational Planning.* Austin, TX: PRO-ED.

Langdell, T. (1978). Recognition of faces: An approach to the study of autism. *Journal of Child Psychology and Psychiatry, 19,* 255–268.

Lewis, V., & Boucher, J. (1988). Spontaneous, instructed and elicited play in relatively able autistic children. *British Journal of Developmental Psychology, 6,* 325–339.

Lord, C. (1993). The complexity of social behavior in autism. In S. Baron-Cohen, H. Tager-Flusberg, & D. Cohen (Eds.), *Understanding other minds: Perspectives from autism* (pp. 292–316). Oxford, England: Oxford University Press.

Lord, C. (2000). Autism spectrum disorders and ADHD. In P. J. Accardo & T. A. Blondis (Eds.), *Attention deficits and hyperactivity in children and adults* (pp. 401–417). New York: Marcel Decker.

Lord, C., & Magill, J. (1989). Methodological and theoretical issues in studying peer-directed behavior in autism. In G. Dawson (Ed.), *Autism: Nature, diagnosis and treatment* (pp. 326–345). New York: Guilford Press.

Lord, C., & Risi, S. (2000). Early diagnosis in children with autism spectrum disorders. *Advocate, 33,* 23 26.

Lord, C., Rutter, M., DiLavore, P. C., & Risi, S. (1999). *Autism Diagnostic Observation Schedule–Generic.* Los Angeles: Western Psychological Services.

Lord, C., Rutter, M., & LeCouteur, A. (1994). Autism Diagnostic Interview–Revised: A revised version of a diagnostic interview for caregivers of individuals with possible pervasive developmental disorders. *Journal of Autism and Developmental Disorders, 24*(5), 659–685.

Ludemann, P. M. (1991). Generalized discrimination of positive facial expressions by seven- and ten-month-old infants. *Child Development, 62,* 55–67.

Mayes, L., Cohen, D., & Klin, A. (1993). Desire and fantasy: A psychoanalytic perspective on theory of mind and autism. In S. Baron-Cohen, H. Tager-Flusberg, & D. Cohen (Eds.), *Understanding other minds: Perspectives from autism* (pp. 450–464). Oxford, England: Oxford University Press.

Morton, J., & Johnson, M. H. (1991). CONSPEC and CONLERN: A two-process theory of infant face recognition. *Psychological Review, 98,* 164–181.

Mundy, P. (1995). Joint attention and social–emotional approach behavior in children with autism. *Development and Psychopathology, 7,* 63–82.

Mundy, P., & Sigman, M. (1989). Specifying the nature of the social impairment in autism. In G. Dawson (Ed.), *Autism: Nature, diagnosis, and treatment* (pp. 3–21). New York: Guilford Press.

Mundy, P., Sigman, M., & Kasari, C. (1993). The theory of mind and joint attention deficits in autism. In S. Baron-Cohen, H. Tager-Flusberg, & D. Cohen (Eds.), *Understanding other minds: Perspectives from autism* (pp. 181–203). Oxford, England: Oxford University Press.

Mundy, P., Sigman, M., & Kasari, C. (1994). Joint attention, developmental level and symptom presentation in autism. *Development and Psychopathology, 6,* 389–401.

Muris, P., Steerneman, P., Meesters, C., Merckelbach, H., Horselenberg, R., van den Hogen, T., et. al. (1999). The TOM Test: A new instrument for assessing theory of mind in normal children and children with pervasive developmental disorders. *Journal of Autism and Developmental Disorders, 29,* 67–80.

Olson, G., & Sherman, T. (1983). Attention, learning and memory in infants. In M. M. Haith & J. J. Campos (Eds.), *Infancy and developmental psychology* (Vol. 2, pp. 117–134). New York: Wiley.

Osterling, J., & Dawson, G. (1994). Early recognition of children with autism: A study of first birthday home videotapes. *Journal of Autism and Developmental Disorders, 24,* 247–257.

Ozonoff, S., Pennington, B. F., & Rogers, S. J. (1991). Executive function deficits in high-functioning autistic individuals: Relationship to theory of mind. *Journal of Child Psychology and Psychiatry, 32*(7), 1081–1105.

Prizant, B. M., & Meyer, E. C. (1993). Socioemotional aspects of language and social–communication disorders in young children and their families. *American Journal of Speech–Language Pathology, 3,* 56–71.

Prizant, B. M., & Wetherby, A. M. (1990). Toward an integrated view of early language and communication development and socioemotional development. *Topics in Language Disorders, 10,* 1–16.

Quill, K. A. (1995). Enhancing children's social–communicative interactions. In K. A. Quill (Ed.), *Teaching children with autism: Strategies to enhance communication and socialization* (pp. 163–189). New York: Delmar.

Quill, K. A. (2000). *Do–watch–listen–say: Social and communication intervention for children with autism.* Baltimore: Brookes.

Quill, K. A., Bracken, K. N., & Fair, M. E. (2000). Assessment of social and communication skills for children with autism. In K. A. Quill (Ed.), *Do–watch–listen–say: Social and communication intervention for children with autism* (pp. 54–69). Baltimore: Brookes.

Roeyers, H., van Oost, P., & Bothuyne, S. (1998). Immediate imitation and joint attention in young children with autism. *Development and Psychopathology, 10,* 441–450.

Rogers, S. J., Bennetto, L., McEvoy, R., & Pennington, B. F. (1996). Imitation and pantomime in high-functioning adolescents with autism spectrum disorders. *Child Development, 67,* 2060–2073.

Rogers, S. J., & Pennington, B. F. (1991). A theoretical approach to the deficits in infantile autism. *Development and Psychopathology, 3,* 137–163.

Russell, J., Jarrold, C., & Hood, B. (1999). Two intact executive capacities in children with autism: Implications for the core executive dysfunctions in the disorder. *Journal of Autism and Developmental Disorders, 29*(2), 103–112.

Schopler, E., Reichler, R. J., & Rochen-Renner, B. (1988). *Childhood Autism Rating Scale.* Los Angeles: Western Psychological Services.

Serra, M., Jackson, A. E., van Geert, P. L. C., & Minderaa, R. B. (1998). Brief report: Interpretation of facial expressions, postures, and gestures in children with pervasive developmental disorder not otherwise specified. *Journal of Autism and Developmental Disorders, 28*(3), 257–263.

Siegel, B., Vulocevic, J., Elliott, G. R., & Kramer, H. C. (1989). The use of signal detection theory to assess DSM–III–R criteria for autistic disorder. *Journal of the American Academy of Child and Adolescent Psychiatry, 28,* 542–548.

Sigman, M., & Mundy, P. (1989). Social attachments in autistic children. *Journal of Child Psychiatry, 28,* 74–81.

Sigman, M., & Norman, K. (1999). Continuity and change in the development of children with autism. In S. H. Broman & J. M. Fletcher (Eds.), *The changing nervous system: Neurobehavioral consequences of early brain disorders* (pp. 274–291). New York: Oxford University Press.

Sigman, M., & Ruskin, E. (1999). Continuity and change in the social competence of children with autism, Down syndrome, and developmental delays. *Monographs of the Society for Research in Child Development, 64*(1), 1–114.

Sigman, M., & Ungerer, J. (1984). Attachment behaviors in autistic children. *Journal of Autism and Developmental Disorders, 14,* 231–244.

Sigman, M., Ungerer, J., Mundy, P., & Sherman, T. (1987). Cognition in autistic children. In D. Cohen, A. Donnellan, & R. Paul (Eds.), *Handbook of autism and atypical developmental disorders* (pp. 103–120). New York: Wiley.

Smith, I., & Bryson, S. E. (1998). Gesture imitation in autism 1: Nonsymbolic postures and sequences. *Cognitive Neuropsychology, 15*(6–8), 747–770.

Sparrow, S., Balla, D., & Cicchetti, D. (1984). *Vineland Adaptive Behavior Scales.* Circle Pines, MN: American Guidance Service.

Stone, W. L., & Caro-Martinez, L. M. (1990). Naturalistic observations of spontaneous communication in autism children. *Journal of Autism and Developmental Disorders, 20,* 437–454.

Stone, W. L., Lemanek, K. L., Fishel, P. T., Fernandez, M. C., & Altemeier, W. A. (1990). Play and imitation skills in the diagnosis of autism in young children. *Pediatrics, 86,* 267–272.

Strain, P. S. (1983). Identification of social skill curriculum targets for severely handicapped children in mainstreamed preschools. *Applied Research in Mental Retardation, 4,* 369–382.

Strain, P. S. (2001, June). *Teaching and evaluating peer mediated intervention.* Presentation at the annual Vermont Rural Autism Project Summer Institute, Burlington, VT.

Strain, P. S., & Hoyson, M. (2000). The need for longitudinal, intensive social skill intervention: LEAP outcomes for children with autism. *Topics in Early Childhood Special Education, 20*(2), 116–122.

Travis, L., Sigman, M., & Ruskin, E. (2001). Links between social understanding and social behavior in verbally able children with autism. *Journal of Autism and Developmental Disorders, 31*(2), 119–130.

Tremblay, A., Strain, P. S., Hendrickson, J. M., & Shores, R. E. (1981). Social interactions of normal preschool children: Using normative data for subject and target behavior selection. *Behavior Modification, 5*, 237–253.

Twachtman-Cullen, D. (2000). More able children with autism spectrum disorders: Socio-communicative challenges and guidelines for enhancing abilities. In A. M. Wetherby & B. M. Prizant (Eds.), *Autism spectrum disorders: A transactional developmental approach* (pp. 225–249). Baltimore: Brookes.

Volkmar, F. R. (1987). Social development. In D. J. Cohen & A. M. Donnellan (Eds.), *Handbook of autism and pervasive developmental disorders* (pp. 41–60). New York: Wiley.

Volkmar, F. R., Carter, A., Grossman, J., & Klin, A. (1997). Social development in autism. In F. R. Volkmar & D. J. Cohen (Eds.), *Handbook of autism and pervasive developmental disorders* (2nd ed., pp. 173–194). New York: Wiley.

Volkmar, F., Carter, A., Sparrow, S. S., & Cicchetti, D. V. (1993). Quantifying social development in autism. *Journal of Child and Adolescent Psychiatry, 32*, 627–632.

Volkmar, F. R., & Cohen, D. J. (1985). A first person account of the experience of infantile autism by Tony W. *Journal of Autism and Developmental Disorders, 15*, 47–54.

Volkmar, F. R., & Klin, A. (1990). Social development in autism: Historical and clinical perspectives. In S. Baron-Cohen, H. Tager-Flusberg, & D. Cohen (Eds.), *Understanding other minds: Perspectives from autism* (pp. 40–55). Oxford, England: Oxford University Press.

Westby, C. E. (1998). Social–emotional bases of communicative development. In W. O. Haynes & B. B. Shulman (Eds.), *Communication development: Foundations, processes, and clinical applications* (pp. 167–204). Baltimore: Williams & Wilkins.

Wetherby, A. M., Prizant, B. M., & Hutchinson, T. A. (1998). Communicative, social/affective, and symbolic profiles of young children with autism and pervasive developmental disorders. *American Journal of Speech–Language Pathology, 7*, 79–91.

Wetherby, A. M., & Prutting, C. A. (1984). Profiles of communicative and cognitive–social abilities in autistic children. *Journal of Speech and Hearing Research, 27*, 364–377.

Willard, C. T., & Schuler, A. L. (1987). Social transaction: A vehicle for intervention in autism. In T. Layton (Ed.), *Language and treatment of autistic and developmentally disordered children* (pp. 265–289). Springfield, IL: Charles C Thomas.

World Health Organization. (2001). *ICIDH–2: International classification of functioning, disability and health.* Geneva, Switzerland: Author.

Yirmiya, N., Sigman, M. D., Kasari, C., & Mundy, P. (1992). Empathy and cognition in high functioning children with autism. *Child Development, 63*, 150–160.

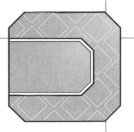

CHAPTER 7

Sensory and Motor Considerations in the Assessment of Children with ASD

Ruth Dennis, Susan Edelman, and Patricia A. Prelock

QUESTIONS TO CONSIDER

This chapter considers the range of sensory, motor, and functional characteristics associated with individuals who experience autism spectrum disorders (ASD). You are asked to consider three questions emphasizing how assessment practices can make a difference in the lives of children with ASD:

1. Are sensory and motor characteristics of children with ASD specific to the diagnosis?

2. Can sensory and motor characteristics be considered separately?

3. How do assumptions about the origin and function of sensory and motor differences affect the tools, strategies, and approaches used in assessment and intervention?

Introduction

Parents, therapists, and teachers can provide many examples of sensory and motor differences associated with ASD. They often describe behaviors that reflect unusual preferences or sensitivities to sounds, tastes, textures, touch, visual avoidance, or tactile defensiveness. Atypical motor performance or movements might include hand flapping; spinning; jumping; ritualistic play with objects; difficulty of motor planning; and a range of manipulation, balance, and coordination abilities. They also describe functional movement activities and sequences that are challenging for some children, including difficulty speaking, writing, dressing, playing with toys, learning to use the toilet, and adapting to changes in routine or environments. Some children with ASD demonstrate none of those characteristics, however, and some children without the label do demonstrate one or more of those characteristics. Many of these same sensory and motor behaviors are seen in children of various ages with and without a range of neurodevelopmental disabilities (Koegel & Koegel, 1995). Even when children exhibit the same sensory or motor characteristic, they may demonstrate it inconsistently or to a different degree (Anzalone & Williamson, 2000). For example, a number of children show atypical responses to texture in foods, but some may appear hypersensitive and others hyposensitive. An individual child's response may be inconsistent from day to day or minute to minute. It is important to keep variation in mind while exploring the literature's description of sensory and motor characteristics in children with ASD.

Descriptions of Sensory and Motor Characteristics in ASD

The relationship between sensory and motor behaviors and the diagnosis of ASD has been discussed since Kanner first described autism in 1943. Much of the current literature related to ASD attempts to identify children who are affected by autism, to examine the most beneficial intervention approaches, and to increase acceptance and understanding of the unique experiences of persons living with autism. Descriptions of children who show a range of common sensory and motor characteristics are included in the diagnostic, definitional, and professional literature, as well as in a growing number of personal accounts of those who live with autism.

Diagnostic Literature

Although efforts are under way to identify genetic or physiological characteristics that are indicative of ASD and to distinguish subtypes within the population, there is no known physical, genetic, or molecular marker that defines ASD, as discussed in Chapter 1. The diagnosis continues to be made based on the presence or absence of certain observed or described behavioral characteristics. The early diagnostic literature, however, contained specific references to sensory and motor characteristics of autism. Kanner (1943), in his original descriptions, noted a failure to assume or initiate an anticipatory posture in children he studied. The current diagnostic literature references sensory and motor characteristics in more general terms. For example, the *Diagnostic and Statistical Manual of Mental Disorders–Fourth Edition* (American Psychiatric Association, 1994) refers to "abnormal responses to sensory stimuli" and to "stereotypic and repetitive motor behavior (e.g., hand or finger flapping or twisting or complex whole body movements)" as behaviors that might be observed. The World Health Organization (WHO; 1993) also describes restrictive and repetitive behaviors or interests, which broadly considered might suggest atypical sensory processing and motor responses.

Standardized behavioral assessments used by both researchers and clinicians to distinguish children with ASD from children with other developmental disorders include specific sensory and motor items (Lord & McGee, 2001). Descriptive screening and assessment tools have also included sensory and motor behaviors. Some of these include the *Checklist for Autism in Toddlers* (CHAT; Baron-Cohen, Allen, & Gillberg, 1992), the *Australian Scale for Asperger's Syndrome* (Garnett & Attwood, 1998), and the *Modified Checklist for Autism in Toddlers* (Robins, Fein, Barton, & Green, 2001) presented in Chapter 1.

Definitional Literature

The 1997 Amendments to the Individuals with Disabilities Education Act (IDEA) defines those children who would be eligible to receive special education services under the categorical definition of autism. The IDEA definition mentions sensory and motor behaviors such as "engagement in repetitive activities and stereotyped movements, resistance to environmental change or change in daily routines, and unusual responses to sensory experiences" [Section 300.7 (c)(i)(ii)]. The Autism Society of America (2001) describes more specific sensory and motor characteristics of autism—that is, disturbances in the rate of appearances of physical, social, and language skills and abnormal responses to sensations: "Any one or a combination of senses or responses are affected: sight, hearing, touch, balance, smell, taste, reaction to pain, and the way a child holds his or her body."

Professional Literature

While the core characteristics of ASD—that is, deficits in social interactions and communication skills, accompanied by restrictive and repetitive behaviors or interests (Klinger & Dawson, 1996)—are critical to the diagnosis, there is much discussion in the professional literature regarding the importance of associated characteristics, including atypical sensory or motor behaviors. Sensory and motor differences are described in most children with ASD but may be variable over the course of the child's development (Anzalone & Williamson, 2000; Lord & Risi, 2000; Scott, Clark, & Brady, 2000; Wetherby & Prizant, 2000). There has been a great deal of attention to the sensory challenges of children with ASD, including difficulty with sensory registration, hypersensitivity, hyposensitivity, poor sensory modulation, and stimulus overselectivity. These characteristics are noted to frequently involve more than one sense. Based on retrospective studies and parental histories, it has been suggested that sensory-related behaviors are early indicators of ASD, often predating the diagnosis of ASD (Anzalone & Williamson, 2000). It has also been suggested that sensory differences in persons with ASD particularly affect social and communication skills such as the ability to orient to social stimuli or engage in social gaze, shared attention, motor imitation, and play (Anzalone & Williamson, 2000; Klinger & Dawson, 1996; Osterling & Dawson, 1994). Greenspan and Wieder (1997) hypothesize that sensory modulation difficulties may explain the self-absorbed behaviors typical of autism. There appear to be distinct sensory reactivity profiles in children with ASD, which should be explored further to provide a framework for understanding differences between groups of children (Williamson, Anzalone, & Hanft, 2000). There is no evidence, however, of a consistent developmental expression of sensory or motor differences among children diagnosed with ASD.

Aside from descriptions of stereotypic behaviors, such as, hand flapping, tapping, rocking, swinging, and repetitive actions on preferred objects, motor issues have not been as well documented in the literature of ASD. Stereotypic movements are typically observed by age 3, and usually after delays in social and communication skills have been suspected (Lord & Risi, 2000). Precursors to these movements might be seen earlier, but the more classic features of stereotyped mannerisms are typically observed between 3 and 5 years of age. It has been suggested that for some children these repetitive or self-stimulatory behaviors may serve a useful purpose, such as allowing them to meet the physical, perceptual, or emotional demands of their environment—in essence, helping them to regulate their sensory systems (Baranek, Foster, & Berkson, 1997; Hill & Leary, 1993). Other motor issues commonly noted in children with ASD include delays in skill development, overactivity, low muscle tone, apraxia or dyspraxia, and clumsiness (Anzalone & Williamson, 2000; Filipek et al., 2000; Trevarthen, Aitken, Papoudi, & Robert, 1998).

There is less literature documenting the development of gross, fine, and oral motor skills in children with ASD. It has been suggested, however, that early differences in the quality of motor performance in very young children may be a powerful indicator of autism. Retrospective studies of children at age 4 to 6 months who were later diagnosed with autism reveal early movement differences that vary from child to child and can be seen in the shape of the mouth and in some of the motor milestones, including lying, righting reactions, sitting, crawling, and walking (Teitelbaum, Teitelbaum, Nye, Fryman, & Maurere, 1998). Generally, gross motor skills are reported to develop within the anticipated time frame and may be an area of relative strength for children with ASD. If gross motor skills are delayed, they are usually less delayed than social and communication skills (Lord & McGee, 2001). Fine motor skills may be more delayed than gross motor skills but are also variable. Some children are proficient in manipulation and dexterity, but their interests may be restricted to specific activities and their skills generalize poorly to novel materials. Oral motor characteristics noted in eating and speech production are similarly variable.

A number of authors describe deficits in praxis, the ability to learn new motor skills or use skills in novel environments. Praxis difficulties can influence gross, fine and oral motor performance, communication, and other behaviors (Biklen, 1990; Donnellan & Leary, 1995). Three components of praxis may be problematic for children with ASD: formulating goals (deciding why there is a need to move); motor planning (solving the problem of how to move); and execution (actually carrying out the move) (Anzalone & Williams, 2000). The quality of voluntary movement may also be problematic. Hill and Leary (1993) described how difficulties controlling voluntary movement, including starting, stopping, executing, continuing, combining, and switching, can adversely affect a range of behaviors. They proposed that these difficulties may impede the ability to assume adaptive postures and engage in specific voluntary actions and may interfere with the smooth flow of speech, thought, perceptions, emotions, and memories.

Sensory and motor differences referenced in the professional literature are not described as unique to ASD. They have been described for children with vision or hearing loss, attention-deficit/hyperactivity disorder, Down syndrome, schizophrenia, attachment disorders, developmental coordination disorder, and post-traumatic stress disorder (Klinger & Dawson, 1996; Osofsky, 1995; Trevarthen et al., 1998; P. H. Wilson & McKenzie, 1998). These same characteristics have also been described, perhaps to a lesser extent, in persons without disabilities under certain conditions (e.g., sensory deprivation, space travel, drug therapy, sexual or physical abuse). What is unique to ASD is the expression of these characteristics before age 3 and the impact that these differences have on the course of individual child development.

Personal Accounts

Growing numbers of people who live with ASD have shared their childhood experiences of sensory and motor phenomena that, in many cases, have continued in various forms into their adult life (Barron & Barron, 1992; Grandin, 1996). Although these individuals have unique stories to tell, they commonly relate differences in perception of sound, vision, touch, taste, and smell, as well as kinesthetic and proprioceptive sensations. Sue Rubin

(2000) is a young woman with autism who has shared an enlightening description of her experiences. She described her difficulty with movement and the misunderstandings that difficulty can create in others:

> I often cannot control my body and make jerky weird movements. I know some people with autism are agile but research by Martha Leary and David Hill show movement disturbances are very common in autism. I believe the problem is with purposeful movement. Sadly we cannot even move from one place to another when we want to. We compensate by going where a movement takes us and actually use our weird movements to get where we want to go. For example, when I want to move from one area on the keyboard to another I will jerk and have my hand land where I want it to…. Movement disorders makes it appear that we don't understand what is being asked or we are being noncompliant…. My proprioceptive and vestibular senses are quite a mess. I cannot regulate how fast or slow I am moving, so I often hold on to another person…. I also have poor balance so holding on helps. Basically I have no idea where parts of my body are. I think this might affect my ability to tell when I am sick. I can't feel where I feel pain when I do. I just know I feel lousy. (Rubin, 2000, ¶ 4)

The impact of motor planning difficulties on conscious thought becomes clearer from reading Sue's description:

> Movement also means movement in thought. For example, when the eye doctor asked me to put my chin on a machine, I put my eye on it because I was still thinking eye. My awful echolalia is also an example of movement of thought. I say a word or sound and am unable to switch it off or change to a different sound. Obsessive compulsive behavior is also an example of a movement problem. I sadly get stuck with certain thoughts and actions. (Rubin, 2000, ¶ 5)

Each sense seems to have its own problematic features of reception and interpretation. Sue describes her experience of sensory distortion in general: "Loads of sensory information is distorted when it comes into my brain. I am able to receive sensory information normally sometimes so I can recognize when it is abnormal." She further describes her understanding and experiences of specific sensory systems:

> My sense of hearing is most problematic for me. Sometimes my sense of hearing is very acute. When an audiologist tested my hearing she said my right ear heard sounds at the extremes of the test. She asked if I heard sounds [that] other people don't. I think I do. Sometimes I can hear people talking in another room. The audiologist said I pass sounds from my right to my left ear because the right one is so sensitive. I am also very sensitive to loud sounds. When we are in a crowded noisy place like London Airport I make a loud sound to block out the noise. The surrounding sounds get lower. That is assuming I am in a place

where I can yell. If I'm in the synagogue and it's noisy I can wade through for quite a while. (Rubin, 2000, ¶ 6)

Touch is problematic for me. I am both hyper- and hyposensitive to touch. My sense of touch becomes very awfully hyposensitive when I am sick or upset. Last month I couldn't feel my ear hurting even when it perforated and bled. The doctor said this was not normal. I also couldn't feel pain when I pulled out a handful of hair. Getting some feeling in my body becomes essential so I turn to self-abuse. Head banging is my method right now but I am trying to extinguish that because my future lies in my ability to express my intellect. It would be ironic if I caused myself to become mentally retarded because of head banging. I am also hypersensitive to pain. Sometimes I feel pain when I shouldn't. For example, I hate to brush my teeth. I love nice white teeth but I actually am in pain when my teeth are brushed. Touch can also be calming for me. I love to have a friend or my mother gently stroke my arm. I also feel good when my hands are touching plastic. I often walk around carrying a plastic spoon. I know it is dumb looking but I need the spoon to relax me. (Rubin, 2000, ¶ 7)

My sense of sight is not normal . . . I do see pages of books in pieces. I glance at the page because I see it quickly. I then put the pieces together in my mind. I understand all the words and can answer questions about the material on the page, but I don't read each word or go down the page line by line. I don't know how I do this. My sense of sight becomes overloaded in places like libraries and supermarkets. I have forced myself to tolerate both because I need to shop and do research for school, but I still don't like those environments. My vision never shuts off, but I do look away to avoid the emotions attached to looking at people. I need to work on looking at people when they are talking to me. (Rubin, 2000, ¶ 8)

Taste and smell are not areas that Sue describes as particularly problematic. She does note, however, that she has definite preferences related to food textures. Finally, she describes the overlay emotions have on her sensory processing and motor performance:

Each of my senses works well at times, but emotions prevent them from working sometimes. Basically emotions mess up my sensory systems. I am able to function as well as I do only by controlling my emotions. . . . Being scared is a common feeling for me. I am often afraid of losing control, which then makes losing control happen. Fear always accompanies me. I cannot control my body and am always afraid of what I may do or say. I often run away instead of sitting down. I mask this by running to the bathroom even though I don't really have to go there. I can usually get where I want to go on the second or third try. I am also afraid of what might come out of my mouth. While I am visiting someone I often say "go home" even if I don't want to leave. Having an opportunity to type a message helps this. Although my reactions to emotions are inappropriate I can identify which ones they are. I am able to understand what emotions other people are experiencing too. In fact, I am so good at knowing how another person feels, that I get sucked up in their emotions. I am actually experiencing their feelings. I think this is why an awful cycle begins when a staff person gets upset with my behavior. We feed off each other and escalate the emotional level. (Rubin, 2000, ¶ 10)

Sue's personal account opens the doors to understanding what it might be like for other individuals affected by autism.

In summary, a review of the diagnostic, definitional, and professional literature, as well as the personal accounts of persons living with ASD, leads one to conclude that although a range of sensory and motor differences are experienced by children with ASD, no set of characteristics is seminal to the diagnosis. However, a variety of sensory and motor behaviors are hypothesized to underlie critical differences in communication, social interaction, and behavior noted in and by persons with ASD.

Relationships Between Sensory and Motor Characteristics

Professionals make assumptions about the sensory experience of young children by observing their behaviors that most often involve motor or movement responses. Exploring two different conceptual models of sensory and motor functioning can enhance practitioners' understanding of the complex relationship between sensory and motor performance. The neuromaturational model of central nervous system (CNS) functioning has been the dominant model in the literature for over 50 years and is supported by research based in the neurosciences. A more recent dynamic systems model has added to the understanding of the complexity of human behavior and is based on analysis of adaptive movement responses and growing information about brain development. Both the neuromaturational and dynamic systems models offer ways to conceptualize the relationship between sensory and motor characteristics in all children and, for the purposes of this chapter, in children with ASD. While reading the following discussion, however, one should proceed cautiously, as there is limited to no research to support, for example, the connections between sensory function and emotional development in children with ASD.

Neuromaturational Model

The neuromaturational model describes the function of the CNS—that is, the brain and spinal cord—and the changes in function that occur over the course of typical development. It further supports the developmental approach to assessment and intervention that has historically dominated the analysis of sensory and motor differences in children. The model relies on research generated through animal and human autopsy and surgical and electroencephalogram (EEG) studies. More recent neuroimaging techniques that show the live brain at rest and at work—computerized axial tomography (CAT), positron emission tomography (PET), functional magnetic resonance imaging (FMRI), magnetoencephalography (MEG), and blood oxygenation level–dependent (BOLD) contrast—have furthered the understanding of where, and in what sequences, sensory and motor information is processed and generated in the CNS. These procedures may someday contribute to assessment of ASD but are currently used primarily in research.

The neuromaturational model describes hierarchical levels of CNS functioning, from lower levels of the spinal cord and brain stem through midbrain structures to the cerebrum, which is involved in attention, memory, and voluntary motor activity. The outermost cerebral layer, the cortex, is considered to be the highest level of the CNS and the locus of executive function or mental control processes for handling complex information (Lyon & Krasnegor, 1996). Lower levels of the CNS are thought to be responsible for integration of sensory input and simple reflex movement responses. The hierarchical view suggests that as the CNS matures, it becomes capable of interrupting or changing unconscious processes to ensure more adaptive responses. This ability to control and adapt responses is an essential component of praxis—that is, the planning, initiating, and learning of new motor skills. Praxis, or motor planning, problems are often associated with ASD.

The maturational aspect of the model is attributed to the sequential development of myelin within the CNS, which renders individual neurons and groups of neurons optimally functional. Myelin, a mucopolysaccharide sheathing, is laid down along neuronal axons in a fairly predictable pattern and sequence in development. At birth, myelin is most obvious at the spinal cord and brain stem levels of the CNS, so that neurons in those areas function most efficiently. This is reflected in behaviors and skills typically observed in newborns, such as in control of vital functions, oral reflexes, efficient feeding patterns, and reflex gross and fine motor responses. After birth, the process of myelinization extends up through higher levels of the brain and down through lower levels of the spinal cord, resulting in predictable patterns of motor skill development: development of head control, shoulder stability, arm movement, reach, grasp, release, rolling, crawling, sitting, creeping, standing, and walking. As the myelinization process progresses, reflex and primitive movement patterns gradually become incorporated into adaptive responses, voluntary movements, and skills. While myelinization progresses most rapidly during the first 2 years of life, myelin continues to develop into adolescence. Typically occurring bursts of myelinization have been correlated with periods of cognitive development, as well as motor skill acquisition, noted in normal development. The neuromaturational model suggests that one can assess functioning at various levels of the CNS by observing developmental milestones and comparing them to observations in other children of the same age. It further suggests that sensory or motor differences in development are the result of atypical nervous system functioning.

The functional unit of the neuromaturational model is the neuron, which has been the focus of both genetic and neuroanatomical research studies related to ASD. Genetic research, including chromosomal analysis and inheritance studies, seeks to identify genes or gene sequences that code for specific proteins that ultimately influence the development or function of neurons (Ingram et al., 2000; Rutter, 2000). Neuroanatomical studies in autism similarly seek to identify differences that may exist in the form and function of brain structures that are composed of many neurons (Bauman & Kemper, 1994; Critchley et al., 2000).

The neuromaturational model of sensory–motor functioning is conceptualized in the context of the relationship among four critical components: sensory input, central nervous system integration, motor response, and feedback. Understanding the relationships among these components is important because concerns in each of these areas have been reported for children with ASD. Figure 7.1 depicts the critical components of sensory–motor functioning and areas of concern in ASD.

Sensory Input. Sensory input is generated by stimulation of sensory receptors and transmitted via peripheral nerves or cranial nerves to the CNS. Receptors are typically categorized by the source of the sensory input to which they respond. The exteroceptive receptors respond to information from the outside world and are typically considered the five senses: vision, hearing, taste, smell, and touch. The proprioceptive receptors are deep touch or pressure receptors that respond to input from intermediate body structures, including muscles, tendons, ligaments, joints, and bones, and from tactile receptors in the vestibular apparatus of the inner ear stimulated by movement and gravity. Proprioceptive input is important in the interpretation and regulation of movement, and it contributes to the development of spatial awareness, body scheme, balance, and equilibrium responses. The interoceptive receptors are located in the innermost body structures and affect the regulation of vital systems and maintenance of homeostasis in the body. Interoceptors are located in the capillaries, alveoli, and gut and provide information to regulate circulation, respiration, and digestion, as well as other functions. We are usually unaware of interoceptive input, except in the case of pain, when it takes priority.

Sensory input concerns related to children with ASD are similar to those of other children. It is important to determine whether the sensory receptors are intact, particularly those of vision and hearing, as well as touch and pain receptors, which are more difficult to assess. Dimensions of sensory input such as intensity, location, and duration also need to be considered. Sensory input may vary in a range from low to high intensity, near to distant proximity to the person, and phasic to constant duration for each sensory modality (Anzalone & Williamson, 2000). Various types, qualities, and ranges of sensory input may be problematic for individual children.

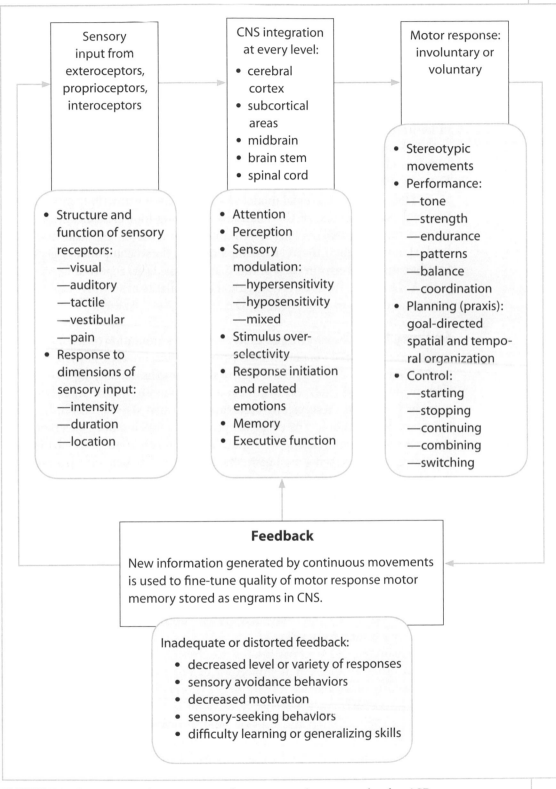

FIGURE 7.1. Components of sensory–motor functioning and concerns related to ASD.

CNS Integration. Information from all receptors is received simultaneously and continuously, and it is the role of the CNS to help interpret, prioritize, and use input to generate adaptive responses, including motor responses. Integration of sensory input occurs at all levels of the CNS within specific structures or clusters of neurons that serve a designated function. Some sensory information from the body is transmitted to the spinal column, where it is immediately integrated and an automatic unconscious motor response, or reflex, is generated. An example of spinal-level integration is the deep tendon reflex that results in an automatic muscular response that extends the knee after the patellar tendon receives a quick stretch. Other sensory information from the body and primary sense organs enters the CNS via peripheral, cranial, or autonomic nerves and is transported to higher brain centers via the dorsal pathways of the spinal column or directly to lower brain centers.

A number of interrelated CNS structures contribute to both the interpretation of sensory input and the generation of motor responses. Figure 7.2 depicts the CNS hierarchical levels and the structures involved in integration at each level. At all levels, the most important or relevant stimuli are discriminated from ongoing or background information. At higher levels, current input is compared with past experiences to create conscious awareness and memories. Sensory information is initially processed in the reticular activating system (RAS), which includes parts of the pons and medulla at the brain stem level and the cerebellum. The RAS regulates the amount and flow of sensory input and is responsible for regulating levels of alertness and attention. The midbrain level relays information from the RAS to higher cerebral levels and is also responsible for integrating specific automatic responses such as visual and auditory reflexes. Sensory information reaches the cerebral level first through lower subcortical structures and finally reaches the cortex. Information from exteroceptors is transmitted to the thalamus, and information from proprioceptors is transmitted first to the hypothalamus, where it is further sorted. Both of these structures then relay sensory messages to other subcortical structures, from the cerebellum (for interpretation of spatial, temporal, and movement qualities of input), to the amygdala (for interpretation of emotional content), to the hippocampus (for identification and categorization of input), to the corpus callosum (for sharing information between the two sides of the brain), and finally to the cerebral cortex (for conscious awareness, memory, and generation of voluntary movement responses). Specific areas of the cerebral cortex process, store, and further integrate unique types of sensory information and play a role in generating motor responses. For example, the parietal lobe, which contains the primary sensory strip, serves a role in the interpretation of touch, pain, temperature, and information related to the body's position in space. The frontal lobe further integrates touch, taste, sight, and emotional components. It contains the primary motor strip that generates voluntary movement responses, controlling movement on the opposite side of the body. The occipital lobe deals with integration of visual and proprioceptive input. The temporal lobe is where auditory input is processed and stored as memory.

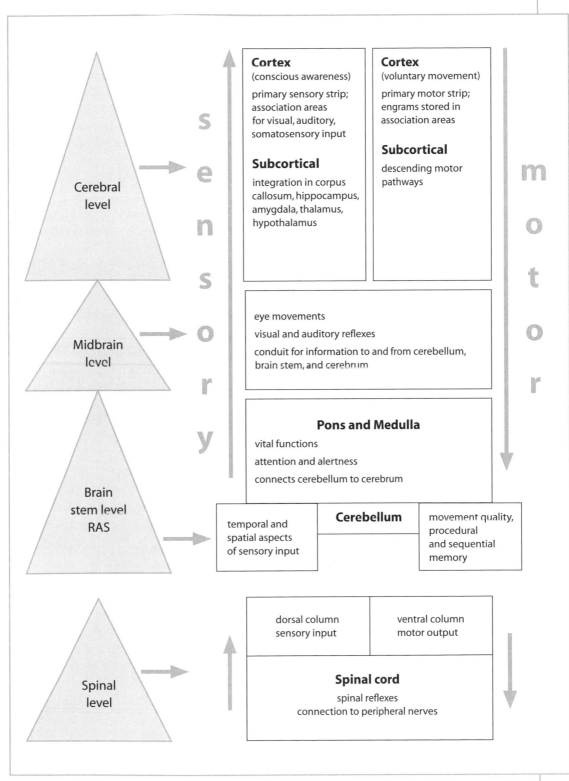

FIGURE 7.2. Hierarchical levels of CNS sensory and motor functioning. RAS = reticular activating system.

Another important aspect of CNS integration is the hypothesized relationship between sensory input and emotions (Kientz & Dunn, 1997). Many of the same structures involved in interpreting sensory information for the purpose of generating motor responses also play a role in generating emotional responses. The amygdala compares sensory information received from the thalamus with its own stored emotional memory and with other areas where short- and long-term memory are stored, including the hippocampus. If sensory input is not recognized as safe, the amygdala will trigger the hypothalamus, which in turn sends hormonal messages to endocrine glands that signal the fight-or-flight response. When sensory information is disorganized or unpredictable, it can be perceived as threatening and can stimulate emotional as well as physical responses. Physical changes in the body may include increased levels of adrenaline and cortisol in the blood, resulting in muscle contractions and changes in heart rate and blood pressure. Emotional responses may be expressed as pleasure, fear, panic, or anxiety. These physical and emotional responses that result from sensory processing problems can have an indirect but broad impact on homeostatic functions typically regulated by the hypothalamus, including sleep, appetite, and aggressive behavior. Regulation difficulties in these areas can, in turn, further influence the emotions and behaviors of children (Sylvester, 1995; Wolfe, 2001).

Concerns related to CNS integration are frequently described in the literature of ASD. A distinction between sensory perception and sensory modulation difficulties is made (Williamson et al., 2000). Sensory perception is an unconscious integration function that can range from simple perception of sight, sound, touch, taste, and smell to higher-level perceptual skills such as visual–spatial perception, auditory processing, figure–ground discrimination, and visual memory. Sensory perception problems can affect attention and learning and tend to be fairly consistent over time. Sensory modulation deficits, however, seem to be a primary concern for children with ASD and may span a continuum from poor registration to sensory defensiveness (Anzalone & Williamson, 2000; Dunn, 1999; Kientz & Dunn, 1997; Koegel & Koegel, 1995; Waitling, Dietz, & White, 2000). Sensory modulation is the ability to generate responses that are appropriately graded to incoming sensory stimuli, so there is neither an underreaction nor an overreaction to incoming sensory information (Parham & Mailloux, 1996). There is a tendency for sensory modulation difficulties to fluctuate between extremes on the continuum over time.

Hypersensitivity and hyposensitivity to sensory input can be indicators of sensory modulation problems in children with ASD. A child who demonstrates hypersensitivity may respond to lower than normal amounts of sensory input. If the environment presents complex cues, the child who is hypersensitive may need to focus on specific aspects of input and ignore others. This is particularly true of complex stimuli such as the human face. As a way of compensating for sensory hypersensitivity, a child may demonstrate overselectivity to certain less confusing attributes of a complex situation. In contrast, a child who is hyposensitive may have a higher than normal threshold for sensory input, with a subsequent craving for increased levels of input

(Grandin & Scariano, 1996; Scott et al., 2000). A child might also demonstrate both hyper- and hyposensitivity in different sensory modalities. For example, a child can be hypersensitive to sound, becoming distressed with certain frequencies or noises. At the same time, he or she may be hyposensitive to proprioceptive or vestibular input and seek additional input through motor behaviors such as jumping, hugging, or spinning.

Specific sensory profiles have been proposed that distinguish between groups of children with sensory modulation disorders, including children with ASD (Anzalone & Williamson, 2000). These sensory profiles include a hyperreactivity profile, in which children tend to have a low sensory threshold; a hyporeactivity profile, in which there is a high threshold for sensory input; and a mixed pattern, in which there is hypersensitivity in specific modalities, usually vision and hearing, and hyposensitivity in others. Anzalone and Williamson (2000) suggest that each profile is expressed differently in four behavioral characteristics that affect learning and skill development: (a) arousal, the ability to maintain an alert state; (b) attention, the ability to focus on relevant sensory information for an adequate amount of time; (c) affect, the emotional response to sensory input; and (d) action, the ability to engage in goal-directed motor activity.

Motor Response. The third critical component of sensory–motor functioning is the motor response. Some motor responses are generated unconsciously at lower levels of the spinal cord and brain and remain essentially automatic. A voluntary motor response, involved in praxis, is goal directed and generated in the primary motor strip of the cortex. Motor neurons transmit messages down through lower levels of the brain, cross over to the opposite side of the body in the brain stem, and connect with motor neurons in the ventral column of the spinal cord. As motor messages descend through CNS levels, they make multiple connections with subcortical brain structures that refine the quality of movement. For example, connections with the cerebellum influence sequencing and timing of movement and result in coordinated balance and equilibrium responses. Motor messages eventually exit the spinal column through the peripheral nerves, where they connect with individual muscle fibers at the motor end plate. Characteristics of muscles, tendons, ligaments, and bones of the musculoskeletal system further affect the directional movement of body parts, muscle tone, force, and strength.

In addition to concerns about stereotypic movements, motor concerns related to children with ASD include problems with performance, praxis, and control (Donnellan & Leary, 1995). Motor performance problems are seen in atypical muscle tone, posture, strength, endurance, patterns of movement, balance, and coordination. They can interfere with the development of age-appropriate gross, fine, and oral motor skills such as mobility, positioning, reach, grasp, manipulation, eating, and speaking. Problems in motor planning are commonly described in children with ASD (Dunn, 1996; Lord & McGee, 2001; Williamson et al., 2000). Effective motor planning involves voluntary initiation of movement toward a cognitively generated goal and spatial and temporal synchronization of movement based on body scheme. *Body scheme* is an unconscious stored memory or awareness of one's own body supported by the integration of tactile, movement, and proprioceptive sensory input. The term *apraxia* is used to refer to difficulty in the generation, timing, and sequencing of voluntary movement responses when learning new skills or when performing previously demonstrated skills in a new context. Children with ASD are believed to be able to learn to perform specific functional tasks given opportunities for repeated practice but often have difficulty generalizing them to new settings. Motor control problems include difficulties with starting, stopping, executing, continuing, combining, and switching between motor behaviors, as mentioned earlier in the chapter (Donnellan & Leary, 1995). Motor control difficulties in children with ASD can affect their ability to initiate movement in a timely manner, inhibit stereotypic movements or repetitive behaviors, finish tasks, combine movements, imitate the actions of others, or attend to sensory and movement activities simultaneously.

Feedback. The final component of the sensory–motor system is the feedback mechanism generated by each movement. Contracting and relaxing muscles used in movement and changes in postures and joint positions generate new and continuous sensory input. This input is fed back into the sensory–motor system as new sensory information. It is once again processed and interpreted in the structures of the CNS at a rate so fast that one cannot be consciously aware of it. Feedback contributes to the development of body scheme in the young child, facilitates the adaptation of movement qualities, and supports the development of skilled performance through trial-and-error learning. With practice, successful motor patterns are encoded in specific neuronal pathways called engrams. *Engrams* are efficient, practiced neural sequences and patterns of motor behaviors stored in subcortical association areas of the brain. They are the basis of automatic movement and can be tapped as needed for goal-directed motor performance. For example, a child initially thinks about writing his name, concentrating and planning each stroke of each letter. With practice and feedback, a pattern or neural circuit for name writing becomes encoded as an engram. The engram can eventually be accessed without cortical attention to each stroke. Most adults can think about the check they are signing without concentrating on how to form each letter of their name. Without feedback, every motor movement would have to be planned over and over again, which would require much more energy than an automatic movement pattern.

Children with ASD often display performance problems that could be associated with inaccurate feedback. When sensory information that results from a child's actions is perceived inaccurately or distorted, the child may react by shutting down and not responding to specific input. Overselectivity to a narrow range of environmental input can also be reinforced. When inadequate sensory input is generated, self-stimulatory or even self-abusive behaviors may develop and be used to provide needed input. One of the greatest concerns about inadequate feedback from motor activities is decreased motivation for engaging in activities. If a child's performance is inadequate or unsuccessful in his environment over time, or requires extraordinary amounts of energy because of motor planning difficulties, there may ultimately be a decrease in the level and variety of responses that the child is able or willing to demonstrate. Children with ASD may be distressed by changes in routines or sensory characteristics of specific materials or settings and unable to respond in a flexible way to changes in motor demands. They could develop a range of interfering behaviors that allow them to avoid new activities, specific settings, people, or tasks, and they may resist activities that interrupt their own predictable routines or self-stimulatory behaviors (Koegel & Koegel, 1995).

In summary, the neuromaturational model is useful in exploring the relationship between sensory and motor characteristics of children with autism. Specifically, it explains the sequential relationship and critical components of sensory motor functioning; it describes the roles played by CNS structures in the processing of sensory information and motor planning; and it supports the developmental approach used in many sensory and motor assessments. Further, the neuromaturational model increases the understanding and appreciation of biologically based research related to physiological differences in autism, including differences in the number and structure of neurons and the size and characteristics of the cerebrum, amygdala, corpus callosum, and hippocampus (Baron-Cohen et al., 2000; Bauman & Kemper, 1994; Cook, 1996; Critchley et al., 2000; Hardan, Minshew, & Keshaven, 2000; Hendren, DeBacker, & Pandina, 2000; Townsend et al., 2001). Although the growing research related to biological characteristics of ASD supports the hypothesis that the function and structures of specific areas of the CNS involved in sensory and motor functioning are suspected areas of difference in children with ASD, it is not clear what such differences might mean to an individual child whose nervous system is relatively plastic. Many questions also remain regarding the impact of the individual child's unique sensory and motor experiences.

Dynamic Systems Model

In recent decades, assumptions of the neuromaturational model have been questioned, and a new dynamic systems model has emerged. This model is based on a theory first described by Thelan, Kelso, and Fogel (1987) and is reflective of more contemporary ideas about brain functioning and motor development (Campbell, 1994). It seeks to address several questions that are relevant to ASD:

- How can professionals account for the tremendously adaptive and dynamic capabilities of young children?

- If reflex integration and skill development are programmed to follow a fairly predictable sequence and timing, why does their expression vary greatly among children without neurologic impairment?
- Can the expression of early motor behaviors be changed by factors other than maturation, such as altered internal states, practice, or change in environmental characteristics?
- Can cultural differences that drive child rearing practices influence the neurodevelopmental picture?

The dynamic systems model has emerged in response to these questions and from related research in a number of fields that address human behavior and human development, including movement science, neurophysiology, and psychology. The idea that brain function is analogous to a static computer with sequential inputs, information processing, and outputs is replaced by a view of the brain as an ecosystem of interdependent and interrelated components that ebb and flow together. This model recognizes the immense complexity of the functions of many systems, internal and external, working together in symbiotic ways, and the importance of both nature and nurture in developing child behavior.

More recent brain development theories are reflective of the dynamic systems model, which expands concepts of the neuromaturational model by emphasizing that structure and unique environments and experiences affect the function of an individual child's brain. Recent research has suggested that overlapping phases of neural development affect learning and skill acquisition during childhood. These phases include new neuron development before and after birth; neuron migration to specific functional areas; neural synapse proliferation and pruning; and the development of supportive brain tissue around nerve cells, which includes but is not limited to myelin. Studies have indicated that sensory neurons have patterns of rapid synaptic growth in the first year, followed by gradual pruning or refinement into adolescence that results in more precisely organized sensory and motor patterns. An individual child's environment that stimulates use of neural pathways affects all phases of neural development and the chemical nature of neural transmission, including sensitivity to specific sensory inputs. This new research suggests that the child's brain remodels itself in response to the environment and experience. Remodeling is responsible for the unique variations in child development that are now seen as more the rule than the exception. Appreciation of the importance of experience on brain development has led researchers to focus on those environmental experiences that support optimal brain function (e.g., adequate nutrition, enriched environments, and certain qualities of early caregiving), as well as those experiences that can have negative impacts on development (e.g., stress, anemia, prenatal alcohol exposure, prematurity, infections, and nutritional or emotional deprivation). Questions remain about periods of time when the brain may be most sensitive to specific internal or external experiences, and about the ability of the child's system to recover from insults and build organized neural systems that can guide sensory and motor development (Shonkoff & Phillips, 2000).

Applying the dynamic systems model to the study of movement and motor learning, Heriza (1991) and others have described the organization of movement as a responsive and interactive process among three components: the individual (internal systems), the task or activity in which the person engages, and the characteristics of the environment. In this view, motor performance is determined not only by neurological and musculoskeletal integrity, but by cognitive variables as well, including aspects of memory, reasoning, and judgment. Application of the model enables one to consider the interrelationships of the components that occur at any point in time, and the contribution of each to the adaptability of children as they learn and use new skills. An individual child's motor response is more variable than one might predict when considering any of the components separately. New behaviors that emerge are dependent not only on neurological characteristics of the child, but also on the interaction of other characteristics and past experiences of the child, the task, and the environment. This model suggests that motor behaviors are not simply the product of accurate sensory integration, but are the child's most adaptive response possible at a given time and in a given context (Piper & Darrah, 1994).

The neuromaturational and dynamic systems models differ in several ways (see Table 7.1). First, the view of neural functioning differs. The neuromaturational model views the CNS as a separate system that is responsible for integrating sensory input and directing motor output. Performance varies because of maturational or structural characteristics of the CNS. The dynamic systems model views the brain as a changing system, one that guides behavior in response to the external and internal environment and the experiences of the child. Second, the emphasis on feedback as a primary mechanism for learning in the neuromaturational model is shifted to a consideration of the importance of feed-forward information in the dynamic systems model. This is represented in the anticipation and planning that is incorporated in matching a response to a specific situation. Third, the models differ in the way sensory and motor neural pathways are related to each other. The neuromaturational model discusses the hierarchical pathways for movement and the encoding of movement patterns in the brain as engrams. Voluntary and automatic movement signals are transmitted from the cortex along motor pathways, while feedback follows sensory pathways. In the dynamic systems model, a confluence of systems creates responses and self-corrects as part of the act. Sensory and motor impulses are nested within each other, without separate and distinct functions, so that movement and sensory perception are interconnected and neither operates in isolation. Fourth, the models differ in the way they interpret differences in performance. The neuromaturational model describes motor deficits that are attributed to CNS dysfunction and result in delayed development of age-appropriate skills or abnormal qualities of movement. In contrast, the dynamic systems model

TABLE 7.1

Comparison of Features of the Neuromaturational and Dynamic Systems Models

Neuromaturational Model	Dynamic Systems Model
Neural functioning: CNS is a separate and static system; performance is dependent on structural and functional characteristics of CNS.	*Neural functioning:* CNS is a changing system; performance is dependent on interaction between internal (including CNS) and external environments, the nature of the task, and the unique experiences of the individual.
Feedback information is primary mechanism for learning.	*Feed-forward* information (anticipatory and planning) is important in generating the appropriate response in a specific situation.
Separate pathways: Movement patterns that are encoded as motor engrams in brain, that are activated cortically and follow motor pathways; feedback follows sensory pathways.	*Nested pathways:* Sensory and motor responses are nested within each other without separate and distinct functions.
Differences in performance: Explained in terms of deficits in CNS maturation and organization; CNS dysfunction results in delayed development or abnormal movement qualities.	*Differences in performance:* Viewed as variability in ways of adapting; differences are attributed to the individual's best attempt to compensate to achieve function.

views the same differences as variability in the individual's best attempt to compensate and achieve function in a given context, emphasizing the ability of the child to both change and respond to new experiences and changes in environment.

The dynamic systems model contributes a new dimension to the understanding of sensory and motor concerns related to children with ASD. For example, the role of anticipatory strategies in planning functional motor tasks can be appreciated in their effect on performance of tasks that are familiar versus those that may be novel or unfamiliar. In this view, the preference and need for routine expressed by many children with ASD may be a logical adaptation strategy rather than a peculiarity. The overlay of emotion, whether positive or negative, becomes an equally contributing factor or variable in sensory motor functioning. "Nonfunctional" behaviors can be seen as functional in regulating, calming, or facilitating selective attention. The dynamic systems model presents a broader view of sensory motor functioning in children with ASD and supports the consideration of a wider range of assessment avenues. The neuromaturational characteristics of the child are only a piece of the picture that influences skill development. Cognitive and psychological factors, the nature of the task, previous experience, and the characteristics of the physical and social environment are all important and can be accommodated for, modified, or adapted in order to improve sensory motor functioning and functional performance for children with ASD.

Assumptions About Sensory–Motor Functioning and Implications for Assessment and Intervention

Assumptions about the importance and prevalence of sensory and motor differences in children with ASD will affect the scope of assessment for either diagnostic or intervention purposes. A number of these assumptions have been discussed in response to the first two questions considered in this chapter. If practitioners agree with the assumption proposed in the literature that sensory and motor functioning has an important impact on the core deficits of ASD, a child's performance in those areas should be assessed. While there have been few studies of the sensory and motor characteristics of children with autism, and no longitudinal studies, the prevalence of both sensory and motor differences are reported as possible early signs of ASD that may have implications for diagnosis, assessment, and early intervention (Lord & McGee, 2001; Waitling et al., 2000). Similarly, assumptions about the complex neurological relationship between sensory and motor systems, the importance of the unique experiences of the child, and the influence of environment and the nature of the task lead to a recognition that sensory functioning and motor functioning are essentially interconnected. Neither area can be assessed in isolation. These assumptions ultimately influence the interpretation of assessment results for an individual child with ASD.

Assessment practices can be further influenced by assumptions about disability in general—that is, whether differences are viewed from a deficit or a strengths perspective (Saleeby, 1996). A deficit perspective typically dominates clinical assessment processes and assumes that a difference, when attached to a disability label, is a challenge that needs to be overcome or corrected through intervention. The focus of assessment is on the child and the identification of pathology, problems, abnormalities, and disorders that interfere with "normal" functioning, as supported by the neuromaturational model. A deficit perspective of assessment often engenders intervention strategies that are problem focused and aimed at "fixing" the child. In contrast, the strengths perspective suggests that each child is unique and that assessment should rely on the child's interpretation of his experiences and on the identification of the child's capacities and resources. This perspective does not imply that the sensory–motor challenges and specific limitations of children with ASD should be ignored, but it reminds practitioners to focus on issues identified as important to the child and family, and on how an individual child can "get on" with life. Assessment from a strengths perspective involves the identification of supports the child and family might use to further their participation in typical activities. A strengths perspective would lead practitioners to consider whether the unique sensory and motor characteristics of children with ASD might serve a useful function for the child, and whether they might represent an avenue of potential strength when the environment is appropriately supportive.

As described in Chapter 3, the World Health Organization (WHO) has developed and refined a sociomedical model of disability that incorporates elements of both the traditional deficit perspective and the strengths perspective (Verbrugge & Jette, 1994). The most recent version of the model, the *International Classification of Functioning, Disability and Health* (ICF) describes dimensions of disability (impairment, activity, and participation) that are affected by contextual factors (WHO, 2001). Sensory–motor assessments of children with ASD can be guided by these dimensions in the hope of developing a common understanding of assessment results and an international language useful for both researchers and practitioners. Table 7.2 describes the dimensions of disability proposed by the WHO and relevant assessment areas for children with ASD. The table separates activity and participation, as these dimensions were described in the earlier version of the ICF (WHO, 1999, 2001).

Dimensions of Disability and Aspects of Sensory–Motor Function To Be Assessed in Children with ASD

Dimensions of disability, including impairment, activity, participation, and contextual factors that should be considered in the assessment of children with ASD are described in the following paragraphs. Specific suggestions for assessment in each of these areas are provided.

Impairment. The impairment dimension refers to function and structure at the body level. Impairments represent some difference from the norm and are detectable by others, by the person, or by indirect observation or clinical tests and can be scaled in terms of severity. This dimension can be expanded to include cellular or molecular differences in functioning, with an appreciation that some impairments may result in others. At the impairment level, assessments of sensory–motor performance would include gathering information about the structure and functioning of sensory receptors and components of the musculoskeletal system. It would also consider general health and possible diseases, injuries, or congenital conditions that could affect sensory–motor function. It might include a visual exam, hearing test, laboratory studies, or nutritional assessment. Hyper- or hyposensitivity to particular sensory input should be assessed at this level, as well as the child's ability to modulate sensory input for the purpose of attention and planning adaptive responses. Motor assessment in this dimension would include attention to joint range of motion and muscle strength, coordination, balance, posture, and tone. Although the information is not typically used by clinicians, researchers may assess anatomical, physiological, or chemical differences in cells or neural structures at the impairment level.

Activity. The activity dimension considers the whole person, rather than cells, organs, or systems of the body. Sensory–motor assessments at this level

TABLE 7.2
Dimensions of Disability and Aspects of Sensory–Motor
Function To Be Assessed in Children with ASD

Impairment: Function and Structure at the Body Level	Activity: Performance at the Person Level	Participation: Involvement at the Societal Level
Sensory • Sensory receptors • Vision • Hearing • Hyper- or hyposensitivity to sensory input • Sensory modulation • Sensory perception	Quality and quantity of skill performance; what child can and cannot do in everyday activities: • simple activities (e.g., mobility, posture, reach, grasp, eating); and • complex activities (e.g., self-care, play, handwriting, speech, job performance, manipulation).	Compared to the standard or norm for participation of other children without disabilities, participation in typical activities: • school, • church, • public facilities and programs, • recreation, • social experiences and friendships, and • work.
Motor • Musculoskeletal system • Joint range of motion • Muscle strength • Coordination, balance, tone		
Development and Health • General health • Developmental history and risk factors • Nutrition • Possible diseases, injuries, congenital conditions, medications • Laboratory studies (EEG, lead levels, genetic studies) • Anatomic, physiological, or chemical differences in neural structures or functioning		

Context
- Personal: Age, gender, other health conditions, past and current experiences, educational level, fitness, lifestyle, habits, coping styles, or other personal–social characteristics.
- Environmental: Societal attitudes, cultural norms, laws, educational systems, architectural characteristics, or other environmental conditions.

attend to the everyday life activities and tasks expected of the child. These activities can range from simple to complicated, may depend on the age of the child, and should be described in terms of what a child can and cannot do. How a child actually performs an activity may or may not be related to impairments. In this dimension, an activity limitation can reflect a difference in quality or quantity of skill performance and can be scaled by the extent of difficulty or the level of assistance required in performing the skill. Assessments can explore behaviors that are simple or complex. For example, one may assess simple behaviors such as reach, grasp, posture, mobility, swallowing, and breathing, as well as the performance of more complex manipulations, such as handwriting, self-care, play, work, leisure, and speech skills. Use of assistive devices that minimize limitations can be considered when assessing activity-level skills. Most clinicians assess children with ASD in this dimension, employing a range of informal and formal strategies that support their own observations of functional skills or the reports of those who know the child well.

Participation. The participation dimension refers to the child's involvement in life activities on the societal level. It includes the consequences of impairment and disability and how they might hinder that involvement because of internal or external physical, social, or attitudinal factors. Participation or restrictions can be assessed by comparing the standard or norm for participation of children without disability. Assessment in this dimension is, therefore, relative to what is observed or expected for other children in the same context and culture. Restrictions in participation can occur even when a child does not have an impairment or disability, sometimes as a result of a social stigma associated with a diagnosis or other personal characteristic. Sensory and motor assessments of children have historically focused on impairment- and activity-level dimensions and have only recently begun to attend to participation issues.

Contextual Factors. All three dimensions of the ICF are affected by contextual factors through which the disablement process occurs. These factors are either environmental or personal. Environmental factors are outside or "extrinsic" to the child and might include societal attitudes, cultural norms, laws, educational systems, or architectural characteristics. Personal factors are specific or "intrinsic" to the child and might include age, gender, other health conditions, past and current experiences, education, fitness, lifestyle, habits, and coping styles. Appreciation of the contextual factors that influence how children perceive both physical and social aspects of their lives adds depth to assessment results. Contextual factors enlarge the scope of assessments beyond a traditional deficit focus and toward a more individual, holistic, and dynamic view of a child's experience.

Considerations for Assessment

The assessment of the sensory–motor functioning of children with ASD requires the involvement of interdisciplinary team members, including family members and professionals trained and experienced in sensory–motor assessment approaches. Whenever possible, teams should include the child's perception of his own experience in the assessment. It is also important for the team to explore the assumptions that guide the assessment approaches and that underlie the assessment strategies selected. Assessments based on the assumptions of the neuromaturational model reflect a more deficit-oriented perspective that focuses on problem identification and leads to interventions for skill development that are developmental or remedial. Assessments that reflect the assumptions of the dynamic systems model and a strengths-oriented perspective will view ability and disability more holistically and focus on interventions that include adaptations and accommodations that can support participation. We believe that a dynamic systems model provides the greatest opportunities for capitalizing on the strengths of children with ASD and ensuring their full participation in society.

Sensory–motor assessments that address the ICF dimensions of disability take multiple forms, including record review, interview, observation in clinical and natural environments, and use of specific standardized and nonstandardized tools appropriate for the age of the child and the experience of the examiner. It is important that such assessments consider all three dimensions of disability—impairment, activity, and participation—in light of personal and environmental contextual factors. This ensures that interventions that are developed and planned for a child with ASD will be responsive to each of the levels, as appropriate.

Record Review

A review of medical, service, and educational records can provide information related to the sensory–motor functioning of children with ASD across dimensions of impairment, ability or disability, and participation and can provide contextual information as well. Medical and developmental records provide information about early risk factors, birth history, age of acquisition and loss of milestones, history of illnesses such as ear infections, results of visual examinations, past and current medications, and early nutrition and eating habits. The American Academy of Pediatrics (AAP) has endorsed practice parameters for the screening and diagnosis of autism developed by the American Academy of Neurology and the Child Neurology Society (Filipek et al., 2000), which remind health-care providers that any child with delayed development should have ongoing developmental surveillance. In addition, children with communication or social delays should have formal audiological evaluations. Other laboratory tests might also be considered for children suspected of having ASD, including lead level testing for children who mouth objects, EEGs, genetic testing, and neuroimaging. The AAP recommends specific autism screening assessments, many of which include sensory and motor items, such as the *Checklist for Autism in Toddlers* (Baron Cohen et al., 1992), mentioned earlier in this chapter. Careful review of medical records from the pediatrician and other specialists can provide important information related to sensory–motor functioning. In addition, review of service plans such as the Individualized Family Service Plan (IFSP) for children ages 0 to 3 and the Individualized Education Program (IEP) for children ages 3 to 21 can provide information about family concerns and priorities; child characteristics and skills; services, interventions, and accommodations that have been provided; the setting where the child has received services; and outcomes related to sensory and motor performance.

Interviews

Structured and unstructured interviews, some of which are standardized and others of which are individualized, can also provide important information related to the sensory–motor functioning of children with ASD across all dimensions. Initial intake interviews can be used to focus subsequent assessment activities on questions related to sensory–motor behaviors that are relevant to the family, health-care providers, and service providers. It is important to interview the child when possible, as well as family members and others who know the child well. Interviews should seek to identify both areas of strength and perceived challenges experienced by the child and his caregivers. Interview information can be used to better understand contextual factors, including the family constellation and relationships (the genogram, as described in Chapter 3) and the supports available to the child and family in their community (the ecomap, also in Chapter 3). Valuable information about sensory and motor activities or limitations can be obtained by asking about typical daily self-care, play, school, and childcare routines and associated performance strengths or challenges. Interviews can address participation issues by exploring physical and social characteristics of the child's environment and supports, accommodations, and adaptations that are perceived as effective. Some interviews have been structured and standardized and are discussed in the standardized assessment section.

Observations

There are both formal and informal observational guides that can be used in clinical or natural contexts to assess sensory–motor performance across all dimensions. Since children with ASD typically have difficulty performing in new or unfamiliar settings, observations in natural environments are critical in assessment. Ecological assessments focus on observations of a child's activities and behaviors, as well as on the nature of the task and factors in the environment that affect performance and participation. An ecological observation can be used to compare what the child does with what other children in the same setting do or are expected to do. An ecological observation can specifically assess sensory and motor factors by including a task analysis of the sensory and motor requirements of specific routines and activities that are problematic for a child.

Dunn (1996) has developed an example of a task analysis that focuses on the tactile, vestibular, proprioceptive, auditory, and other sensory characteristics of the task, as well as on the motor requirements needed for successful performance, including muscle tone, physical capacity, movements, postural control, and essential skills such as looking, reaching, manipulation, and oral skills. Hall (1993) has developed a more general observational guide for sensory–motor development, which focuses on observations of general appearance and movement, muscle tone, strength and endurance, reactivity to sensory input, attention span, stationary positions, mobility, prehension, and manipulation. Greenspan and Wieder (2001) have developed a rating scale to monitor the sensory processing and motor planning capacities of older children and adults via a series of questions that can be asked of either the individual or the individual's caregiver. The rating scale provides a framework for guiding, organizing, and rating observations of regulatory capacities such as sensory modulation, auditory processing, visual–spatial processing, and motor planning. Kientz and Miller (1999) have developed questions to guide classroom observations of children with autism that address child characteristics; requirements of the task; and characteristics of the environment, including physical, social, and cultural characteristics. *Pre-Feeding Skills–2* (Morris & Klein, 2000) is a nonstandardized observation of oral motor functioning from birth through adolescence. This tool contains information about normal development of eating and feeding (e.g., observational guides for assessing reflexes, sensory issues, oral motor skills, and eating behaviors). It includes parent questionnaires about eating and drinking, as well. There are many standardized observation tools related to sensory–motor functioning, but none is designed specifically for children with ASD.

Standardized Assessments

Selecting a standardized tool to assess sensory–motor functioning in children with ASD can be difficult because of the variety of unique communication and social interaction characteristics of the children. Many traditional sensory–motor assessments require that the child be able to respond to verbal instructions or imitate the performance of the evaluator, skills that are to some degree problematic for most children with autism. With an appreciation that children with ASD share common sensory–motor characteristics with some other children, with and without disabilities, a number of standardized measures can be useful in supporting observations and interview information reported by clinicians and others who are familiar with the child. The selection of standardized tools needs to be individualized to match the communication and interaction skills of the child with ASD.

Williamson and colleagues (2000) have reviewed standardized assessments that address sensory processing, praxis, neuromotor processes, gross motor function, fine motor function, and oral motor function for all children. Their compilation of descriptions of assessment tools is available online at the Web site of the Interdisciplinary Council on Developmental and Learning Disorders (http://www.icdl.com) or in printed format and serves as a resource for selecting tools that might be appropriate for children with ASD at different ages. Law and her collaborators (1999) have compiled a resource for practitioners who seek to match their pediatric assessment tools to the ICF proposed dimensions of disablement. They provide an interactive process for clinicians and teams to make decisions about appropriate measures by selecting from available measures according to specific relevant attributes. An interactive CD enables practitioners to select measures according to the team's consideration of important questions related to assessment attributes, including the following:

- For what purpose (evaluative, descriptive, predictive) are the measures used?
- Which dimensions would you like to have an impact on (impairment, or organic systems; abilities or limitations; participation or environment or context)?
- Where do you want to have an impact (e.g., home, school, community)?
- Whose perspective (client, caregiver, service provider) is used to gather information?
- Are the measures individualized or standardized?
- For what age are the measures appropriate?

Drawing from over 125 critically reviewed pediatric assessments, this program identifies tools appropriate to the set of specific attributes described by the team and provides descriptive information about each tool, validity and reliability information, related articles about the measure, and source information.

It is not the purpose of this chapter to include similar reviews of available tools that assess sensory–motor function in children. Rather, we focus on examples of standardized assessments that may be useful for many children with ASD in light of their core deficits in communication and social interaction and in relation to dimensions of disability proposed by the ICF. Assessments that use interviews and observations and do not require verbal instructions are generally more appropriate for children with ASD. Ecological observation approaches in natural environments typically reveal the child's optimal performance. It should be noted that many criterion-referenced or norm-referenced sensory and motor assessments that do not involve protocols for verbal instructions or imitation are standardized for populations of children who are preverbal or under the age of 3. They would not be valid measures for children ages 3 and above, when the diagnosis of ASD most often occurs.

Examples of standardized assessments of sensory and motor functioning in the dimension of impairment include both interview and observational instruments. The *Sensorimotor History Questionnaire for Preschoolers* (DeGangi & Balzer-Martin, 2000) is a parent or caregiver interview questionnaire validated for 3- and 4-year-olds that explores self-regulation, sensory processing of touch, movement, and emotional and motor maturity. The *Sensory Profile* (Dunn, 1999) is a caregiver interview questionnaire most appropriate for children 5 to 7 years of age. This profile measures sensory processing, sensory modulation, and behavioral and emotional responses, including thresholds for response. There is a short screening form, as well as a longer interview form. Although normed on typically developing children, the *Sensory Profile* has been used to examine the performance of children with ASD relative to children without ASD and with other disabilities, including ADHD (Waitling et al., 2000). The *Developmental Coordination Disorder Questionnaire* (B. Wilson, Kaplan, Crawford, Campbell, & Dewey, 2000) is designed to identify children with developmental coordination disorder, which, by definition, does not include children with autism. Because many children with ASD demonstrate coordination problems, this tool can be helpful in exploring areas addressed in the interview (e.g., control during movement, fine motor and handwriting skill, gross motor planning, and general coordination). This instrument is available for research purposes and has been described in the literature (B. Wilson et al., 2000).

Many observational tools in the impairment dimension also assess the activities, or limitation, dimension. The *Peabody Motor Development Scales–Second Edition* (Folio & Fewell, 2000) is a standardized test that measures gross motor and fine motor functioning, including reflexes, balance, locomotion, grasp, hand use, eye–hand coordination, and manual dexterity. It was originally designed for children with motor impairments ages 0 to 5 years, or children working within that age level. Although there are specific verbal and physical cues for the test items, directions can be adapted so that it may be appropriate for some children with ASD who can follow simple verbal commands or imitate actions. The *Gross Motor Function Measure* (Russell et al., 1990) was originally designed for children with cerebral palsy. It assesses postures, movements, and transitions and may be appropriate for children with more significant motor impairment. The *Alberta Infant Motor Scale* (Piper & Darrah, 1994) is an observation tool administered in natural environments to children 0 to 18 months of age who have gross motor delays or older children who are functioning below the 18-month level. It involves minimal handling of children and contains observations in various positions (e.g., floor lying, sitting, and standing) that assess weight bearing, posture, and antigravity movements. The *Motor-Free Visual Perception Test–Revised* (Colarusso & Hammill, 1996) is a norm-referenced test for children without disabilities, 4 to 11 years old, that assesses visual–motor skills without drawing or copying requirements. Children must be able to follow directions to point to matching designs or pictures that involve visual discrimination, figure–ground, visual closure, and visual memory items.

Some standardized measures that assess the activity dimension also address the participation dimension. The *Pediatric Evaluation of Disability Inventory* (Haley, Coster, Ludlow, Haltiwanger, & Andrellos, 1992) is a caregiver questionnaire that assesses functional skills for children 6 months through 7½ years but may be used for individual comparison of progress for older children who have skills within that age range. It measures self-care, mobility, and social function performance; the level of caregiver assistance needed to perform those functions; and the level of modifications (i.e., environmental adaptations or equipment) that may be used. It measures the child's capacity to perform functional activities, not actual observed performance, with or without modifications, as reported by caregivers or parents. This tool has been normed on a large population of children, including children with disabilities, and is appropriate for most children with ASD.

The *School Function Assessment* (Coster, Deeney, Haltiwanger, & Haley, 1998) is an interview questionnaire that can be completed by a number of adults familiar with a child's performance at school from kindergarten through sixth grade. It addresses levels of participation in major school settings and activity related to performance of specific physical and cognitive–behavioral tasks. It addresses areas such as mobility around school environments, using school materials, interacting with others, following school rules, communicating needs, manipulation, use of materials, eating and drinking, hygiene, clothing management, stair and computer use, and written work. The assessment also notes modifications that may be used by the child to perform activities, including architectural, behavioral, instructional, and positioning modifications. The results are summarized in a functional profile that illustrates the relationship between participation, tasks, and child performance.

There are no standardized assessments of sensory–motor functioning that are specific to children with ASD. The deficits of ASD, and the variability in those deficits, can make it difficult to identify standardized measures that may be appropriate. In selecting standardized sensory and motor assessments for children with ASD, it is important to identify the relevant questions of team members and to individualize assessment strategies, include multiple sources of information, and focus on functional performance in natural environments. It is also important to report abilities as well as limitations and to develop interventions that maximize individual strengths. Although sensory and motor impairments may be described by some standardized assessment approaches, there is not a clear understanding of how interventions focused on impairments can effectively improve functional performance for children with ASD. There is support for intervention that focuses on the practice of functional skills in routine and natural environments.

Summary

Considering the three questions posed at the beginning of the chapter, reiterated in the following paragraphs, you should have an increased understanding of the way sensory and motor behaviors affect the core deficits in ASD, the relationship between sensory and motor functioning, and the assumptions that guide decisions about the assessment strategies and tools one can use to learn more about sensory and motor functioning.

Are sensory and motor characteristics of children with ASD specific to the diagnosis?

Currently, no sensory or motor characteristics are specific to all children with ASD. However, sensory and motor behaviors may underlie some of the impairments seen in communication, social interaction, and behavior difficulties so often reported in children with ASD. The range of differences in sensory and motor function associated with ASD, and also present in other groups of people with and without disabilities, may be clarified as more advanced biological and physiological frameworks evolve to describe "typical" and "atypical" sensory and motor functioning.

Can sensory and motor characteristics be considered separately?

Conceptual models of sensory and motor functioning were explored in this chapter to examine the complex relationships between sensory and motor performance. The dominant approach used to explain sensory and motor functioning has been the neuromaturational model. It describes the hierarchical levels of CNS from a structural and functional perspective, supports a developmental approach to assessment and intervention, and underlies research initiatives intended to identify genetic or structural differences in the brains of persons with ASD. The neuromaturational model is largely deficit based. In contrast, the dynamic systems model suggests that there are more factors contributing to sensory and motor functioning than neurologic integrity. This model describes the interactions among variables such as the unique experiences of the individual child, the nature of the task, and the environmental context, which includes the individual's internal and external states. It is strength based, recognizing that individual differences contribute to variability in adaptive responses. Since sensory and motor behaviors appear to be interconnected rather than isolated responses, it is important to consider sensory and motor factors together. Both must be viewed in the context of other environmental and task characteristics in order to explain how children with ASD might be responding in particular situations at particular points in time.

How do assumptions about the origin and function of sensory and motor differences affect the tools, strategies, and approaches used in assessment and intervention?

Although a growing body of literature discusses the sensory–motor characteristics of children with ASD, no formal sensory or motor assessments have been developed specifically for this population. This is reflective of the variability in characteristics among children with ASD and the fact that sensory–motor characteristics have not been seen as core indicators of the diagnosis. The broad impact of sensory–motor functioning on the development, functional activities, and participation of children with ASD does, however, merit attention in assessment. Assessment of sensory–motor functioning should involve the collaboration of multidisciplinary team members including parents and professionals knowledgeable about sensory, gross, fine, and oral motor areas. The child's own perceptions should be included in assessment when possible, as well as those of others who know the child well. Teams should employ a number of assessment strategies, including record review, observations, and interviews and consider the use of selected standardized measures when appropriate. The team should explore the assumptions that guide their assessment strategies and consider the best approach to answering their assessment questions. They should be aware of whether their various approaches reflect the assumptions of the neuromaturational model, which focuses on identification of deficits and problems and supports interventions that are developmental or remedial, or the assumptions of the dynamic systems model, which focuses on the strengths of the child and family and the supports they need to support participation. Teams might choose to combine approaches based on differing assumptions in order to address individualized assessment questions.

Practitioners are reminded that the participation dimension has too often been neglected in the clinical and research literature related to sensory–motor characteristics of children with and without ASD. Assessment in the dimensions of disablement and contextual factors proposed by the ICF will provide information about the kinds of adaptations, accommodations, and supports needed to enhance the quality of life for children with ASD and their families. If the goal is to support children with ASD to live as members of their communities and families, attend school, and work and play with others, practitioners need to assess children in those environments. Practitioners also need to tailor supports and interventions to promote both skill development and participation in the activities and settings that are important to children with ASD and with the people who are important to them.

Practice Opportunities

1. Select one child with ASD you have been working with and describe the sensory and motor characteristics that appear to affect the core deficit areas of communication, social interaction, play, and behavior. Ask the family to do the same. Share the information collected among team members, including the family. Compare and integrate the input from all team members to create a descriptive sensory–motor profile for the child.

2. Select areas of assessment in the impairment, activity, and participation dimensions of the ICF and determine those tools and environmental contexts you will use to complete a functional assessment of the child's sensory and motor functioning.

3. Complete a task analysis of the sensory and motor requirements of a specific routine at home, in school, and in the community for one child with ASD. Determine any breakdowns in sensory or motor functioning

while the child attempts to participate in the routines analyzed. Brainstorm with your team ways to support the child's success in meeting the sensory and motor requirements across the three contexts.

4. Develop a framework for sensory and motor profiling for an individual child with ASD that can be used to identify both the child's strengths and challenges in each of the critical components of sensory and motor functioning.

Suggested Readings

Anzalone, M. E., & Williamson, G. G. (2000). Sensory processing and motor performance in autism spectrum disorders. In A. M. Wetherby & B. M. Prizant (Eds.), *Autism spectrum disorders: A transactional developmental perspective* (pp. 143–166). Baltimore: Brookes.

This chapter describes sensory integration and the four A's of behavior: arousal, attention, affect, and action. It also provides guidelines for assessment and intervention related to specific challenges in sensory and motor functioning.

Donnellan, A. M., & Leary, M. R. (1995). *Movement differences and diversity in autism/ mental retardation: Appreciating and accommodating people with communication and behavioral challenges.* Madison, WI: DRI Press.

This book explores the impact of motor differences on communication and behavior and challenges some assumptions about autism and the abilities of people labeled autistic or mentally retarded. The authors describe a variety of movement difficulties that can interfere with effective action and interaction, movements, postures, speech, images, thoughts, perceptions, memories, and emotions. The authors suggest that people with autism use a constellation of adaptations or accommodations in order to function in light of their movement difficulties.

Grandin, T. (1996). *Thinking in pictures.* New York: Bantam Doubleday Dell.

This autobiography of Temple Grandin, an adult with autism, provides a powerful description of her sensory experiences. She highlights the sensory input that was most challenging to her and the strategies she used to manage the problems created for her when she did not receive enough or experienced too much sensory input.

Kranowitz, C. S. (1998). *The out-of-sync child: Recognizing and coping with sensory integration dysfunction.* New York: Berkley Publishing Group.

A clearly written book that explains the sensory dysfunction so often experienced by children with ASD, ADHD, LLD, and other related neurodevelopmental disabilities. The book also provides practical suggestions for parents in support of their children's sensory needs.

Myles, B. S., Cook, K. T., Miller, N. E., Rinner, L., & Robbins, L. A. (2000). *Asperger syndrome and sensory issues: Practical solutions for making sense of the world.* Shawnee Mission, KA: Autism Asperger Publishing.

This well-written book provides an overview of sensory functioning and the challenges of children with ASD, particularly Asperger syndrome. It provides suggestions for parents to determine the sensory characteristics of their child, how they may affect functioning either positively or negatively, how to interpret their child's actions or reactions, and what can be done to help.

Resources

Observational Tools

Dunn, W. (1996). The sensorimotor systems: A framework for assessment and intervention. In F. P. Orlove & D. Sobsey (Eds.), *Educating children with multiple disabilities: A transdisciplinary approach* (3rd ed., pp. 35–78). Baltimore: Brookes.

Task analysis forms that focus on sensory and motor components of tasks.

Hall, S. (1993). Observation guideline for sensorimotor development. In J. Case-Smith (Ed.), *Pediatric occupational therapy and early intervention* (pp. 369–375). Boston: Andover Medical Publishers.

A general observational guide for sensory–motor development.

Kientz, M., & Miller, H. (1999). Classroom evaluation of the child with autism. *School System Special Interest Section Quarterly, 6*(1), 1–4.

Questions to guide classroom observations of children with autism.

Morris, S., & Klein, M. (2000). *Pre-feeding skills* (2nd ed.). San Antonio, TX: Therapy Skill Builders.

A nonstandardized tool for observation of oral motor functioning and eating behaviors, which uses questionnaires to obtain parents' perceptions of prefeeding skills.

Standardized Assessments

Adolescent Sensory Profile (Brown & Dunn, 2002). Self-questionnaire used for students 11 years and older to evaluate sensory processing patterns and effects on daily performance. Results generate an individualized profile across four areas: low registration, sensory sensitivity, sensation seeking, and sensation avoiding.

Alberta Infant Motor Scale (Piper & Darrah, 1994). Examination of motor skills conducted in natural environments for children 0 to 18 months old who have gross motor delays or older children who are functioning below the 18-month level. May be appropriate for young children with ASD or those with low-level motor skills.

Developmental Coordination Disorder Questionnaire (B. Wilson et al., 2000). A parent questionnaire to measure gross motor skills and identify children with Developmental Coordination Disorder (DCD), which, by definition, does not include children with autism. Available from the authors at Alberta Children's Hospital Research Center, Calgary, Alberta, T2T 5C7 Canada.

Motor-Free Visual Perception Test–Revised (Colarusso & Hammill, 1996). A norm-referenced test for children 4 to 11 years old that assesses visual–motor skills without drawing or copying requirements.

Peabody Motor Development Scales–Second Edition (Folio & Fewell, 2000). A developmental scale that measures gross motor and fine motor functioning for children ages 0 to 5 years. Although specific verbal and physical cues for the test items are given, directions can be adapted for some children with ASD.

Pediatric Evaluation of Disability Inventory (Haley et al., 1992). A questionnaire for care-givers to assess functional skills for children ages 6 months through 7½ years, but may be used for individual comparison of progress for older children who have skills within that age range. Tool has been normed on typical populations, including children with disabilities, and is appropriate for most children with ASD.

School Function Assessment (Coster et al., 1998). A questionnaire that can be completed by a number of adults familiar with a child's performance at school from kindergarten through sixth grade; used to assess levels of participation in major school settings and the child's ability to perform specific physical and cognitive–behavioral tasks.

Sensorimotor History Questionnaire for Preschoolers (DeGangi & Balzer-Martin, 2000). Parent or caregiver interview questionnaire validated for 3- to 4-year-olds. Available in ICDL Clinical Practice Guidelines online or in printed form (see "Books Online").

Sensory Profile (Dunn, 1999). A caregiver interview questionnaire most appropriate for children 5 to 7 years of age. Includes a short screening form, as well as a longer interview form. Has been used to examine the performance of children with ASD relative to children with other disabilities, including ADHD.

Resources Online

CanChild of McMaster University in Ontario provides up-to-date short reviews of literature and reports on topics of interest in pediatrics and developmental disabilities. Go to www.fhs.mcmaster.ca/canchild, click on "Browse by Subject," and then go to "Sensory Integration."

ICF, *International Classification of Functioning, Disability and Health Final Draft*, developed by the World Health Organization, http://www.who.int/icidh

Practice Parameter: Screening and Diagnosis of Autism. The American Academy of Pediatrics endorsed these guidelines, as proposed by the American Academy of Neurology and Child Neurology Society, http://www.aap.org/policy/autism.html

Sensory Integration International. The history of sensory integration, research, and selected publication abstracts, http://www.sensoryint.com

Sensory Resources, LLC, http://www.sensoryresources.com, 888/357-5867.

Therafin Corporation, http://www.therafin.com, 800/843-7234. The Squeeze Machine by Temple Grandin.

Books Online, in CD Interactive Format, or in Hard Copy

Interdisciplinary Council on Developmental and Learning Disorders. (2000). *The ICDL Clinical Practice Guidelines.* Bethesda, MD: ICDL.

Available for viewing and downloading at http://www.icdl.com/ICDL guidelines/toc.htm or call 301/656-2667. Contains chapters that describe approaches to sensory–motor assessment for children with disabilities and specifically review many standardized assessments.

Law, M., King, G., MacKinnon, E., Russel, D., Murphy, C., Hurley, P., et al. (1999). *All about outcomes: An educational program to help you understand, evaluate, and choose pediatric outcome measures, Version 1.0.* Thorofare, NJ: Slack.

Interactive CD for review of outcome approaches and measures for children, aligned with ICF. Review or order at http://www.slackbooks.com

Lord, C., & McGee, J. (Eds.). (2001). *Educating children with autism.* Washington, DC: National Academy Press.

> To order and for online viewing, go to http://www.nap.edu

Shonkoff, J., & Phillips, D. A. (Eds.). (2000). *From neurons to neighborhoods: The science of early childhood development.* Washington, DC: National Academy Press.

> To order and for online viewing, go to http://www.nap.edu

Books

Bogdashina, O. (2003). *Sensory perceptual issues in autism and Asperger syndrome.* New York: Jessica Kingsley.

Huebner, R. A. (2000). *Autism: A sensorimotor approach to management.* Austin, TX: PRO-ED.

Trott, M. C., Laurel, M., & Windeck, S. L. (1993). *SenseAbilities: Understanding sensory integration.* Tucson, AZ: Therapy Skill Builders.

Williamson, G. G., & Anzalone, M. (2001). *Sensory integration and self-regulation in infants and toddlers: Helping very young children interact with their environment.* Bethesda, MD: Zero to Three.

Glossary

Action. Goal-directed motor activity.

Affect. Emotional response to sensory input.

Apraxia. Difficulty in the generation, timing, and sequencing of voluntary movement responses in the performance of new skills or previously demonstrated skills in a new context.

Arousal. An alert state.

Attention. Focus on relevant sensory information for an adequate amount of time.

Deficit perspective. View of an individual's difference as a challenge that needs to be overcome or "corrected."

Dynamic systems model. Describes the function of the brain as an ecosystem of interdependent and interrelated components that ebb and flow together.

Engrams. Efficient, practiced, and automatic movement neural sequences and patterns that can be tapped as needed for motor performance.

Exteroceptive receptors. Sensory receptors used to respond to information from the outside world; includes the five senses—vision, hearing, taste, smell, and touch.

Hypersensitivity. A response to lower than normal amounts of sensory input.

Hyposensitivity. A response to higher than normal amounts of sensory input.

Impairment. One of the dimensions of the ICF; refers to body function and structure.

Interoceptive receptors. Sensory receptors located in the innermost body structures that contribute to the regulation of vital systems and maintenance of homeostasis in the body.

Motor planning. Voluntary initiation of movement toward a cognitively generated goal, and spatial and temporal synchronization of movement based on body scheme.

Myelin. Mucopolysaccharide sheath that coats the axons of neurons.

Neuromaturational model. Describes the function of the central nervous system and the changes in function that occur with typical maturation.

Primary motor strip. Area of the frontal cortex responsible for generating voluntary movement of muscles and patterns of movement on the opposite side of the body.

Proprioceptive receptors. Sensory receptors used to respond to information from intermediate body structures (e.g., muscles, tendons, ligaments, joints, bones) and tactile receptors in the vestibular apparatus of the inner ear that respond to movement and gravity.

Sensory modulation. Ability to generate responses that are appropriately graded to incoming sensory stimuli, so there is neither an underreaction nor an overreaction to incoming sensory information.

Sensory perception. Unconscious central nervous system integration that ranges from simple perception of sight, sounds, touch, taste, and smell to higher-level perceptual skills such as visual–spatial perception, figure–ground discrimination, and visual memory.

Sensory registration. Ability to become alert or attend to incoming sensory information.

Stimulus overselectivity. Limited response to specific sensory input or aspects of input, while ignoring other related sensory dimensions.

Strengths perspective. View of an individual's difference as unique and serving a useful function.

References

American Psychiatric Association. (1994). *Diagnostic and statistical manual of mental disorders* (4th ed.). Washington, DC: Author.

Anzalone, M. E., & Williamson, G. G. (2000). Sensory processing and motor performance in autism spectrum disorders. In A. M. Wetherby & B. M. Prizant (Eds.), *Autism spectrum disorders: A transactional developmental perspective* (pp. 143–166). Baltimore: Brookes.

Autism Society of America. (2001). *What is autism?* Retrieved April 27, 2005, from http://www.autism-society.org

Baranek, G. T., Foster, L. G., & Berkson, G. (1997). Tactile defensive and stereotyped behaviors. *American Journal of Occupational Therapy, 51,* 91–95.

Baron-Cohen, S., Allen, J., & Gillberg, C. (1992). Can autism be detected at 18 months? The needle, the haystack, and the CHAT. *British Journal of Psychiatry, 161,* 839–843.

Baron-Cohen, S., Ring, H. A., Bullmore, E. T., Wheelwright, S., Ashwin, C., & Williams, S. C. (2000). The amygdala theory of autism. *Neuroscience & Behavioral Reviews, 24,* 355–364.

Barron, J., & Barron, S. (1992). *There's a boy in here.* New York: Simon & Schuster.

Bauman, M. L., & Kemper, T. L. (Eds.). (1994). *The neurobiology of autism.* Baltimore: Johns Hopkins University Press.

Biklen, D. (1990). Communication unbound: Autism and praxis. *Harvard Educational Review, 60,* 291–314.

Brown, C., & Dunn, W. (2002). *Adolescent/Adult Sensory Profile.* San Antonio, TX: Psychological Corp.

Campbell, S. (1994). The child's development of functional movement. In S. Campbell (Ed.), *Physical therapy for children* (pp. 3–37). Philadelphia: W.B. Saunders.

Colarusso, R. R., & Hammill, D. D. (1996). *Motor-Free Visual Perception Test–Revised Manual.* Novato, CA: Academic Therapy Publications.

Cook, E. H. (1996). Brief report: Pathophysiology of autism: Neurochemistry. *Journal of Autism and Developmental Disorders, 26,* 221–225.

Coster, W., Deeney, T., Haltiwanger, J., & Haley, S. (1998). *School Function Assessment.* San Antonio, TX: Psychological Corp.

Critchley, H. D., Daly, E. M., Bullmore, E. T., Williams, S. C., VanAmelsvoort, T., Robertson, D. M., et al. (2000). The functional neuroanatomy of social behavior: Changes in cerebral blood flow when people with autistic disorder process facial expressions. *Brain, 123*(11), 2003–2012.

DeGangi, G. A., & Balzer-Martin, L. A. (2000). Sensorimotor History Questionnaire for Preschoolers. In ICDL Clinical Practice Guidelines Workgroup (Eds.), *The Interdisciplinary Council on Developmental and Learning Disorders (ICDL) clinical practice guidelines: Refining the standards of care for infants, children and families with special needs* (pp. 181–184). Bethesda, MD: ICDL.

Donnellan, A., & Leary, M. (1995). The upending experience. In A. Donnellan & M. Leary, *Movement differences and diversity in autism/mental retardation: Appreciating and accommodating people with communication and behavioral challenges* (pp. 11–34). Madison, WI: DRI Press.

Dunn, W. (1996). The sensorimotor systems: A framework for assessment and intervention. In F. P. Orlove & D. Sobsey (Eds.), *Educating children with multiple disabilities: A transdisciplinary approach* (3rd ed., pp. 35–78). Baltimore: Brookes.

Dunn, W. (1999). *Sensory Profile: User's manual.* San Antonio, TX: Psychological Corp.

Filipek, P. A., Accardo, P. J., Ashwal, S., Baranek, G. T., Cook, E. H., Dawson, G., et al. (2000). Practice parameter: Screening and diagnosis of autism: Report of the Quality Standards Committee of the American Academy of Neurology and the Child Neurology Society. *Neurology, 55*, 468–479.

Folio, M. R., & Fewell, R. R. (2000). *Peabody Motor Development Scales* (2nd ed.). Austin, TX: PRO-ED.

Garnett, M. S., & Attwood, A. J. (1998). The Australian Scale for Asperger's Syndrome. In T. Attwood (Ed.), *Asperger's syndrome: A guide for parents and professionals* (pp. 17–19). Philadelphia: Jessica Kingsley.

Grandin, T. (1996). *Thinking in pictures.* New York: Bantam Doubleday Dell.

Grandin, T., & Scariano, M. M. (1996). *Emergence: Labeled autistic.* New York: Warner Books.

Greenspan, S., & Wieder, S. (1997). Developmental patterns and outcomes in infants and children with disorders in relating and communicating: A chart review of 200 cases of children with autism spectrum diagnosis. *Journal of Developmental and Learning Disorders, 1*, 87–141.

Greenspan, S. I., & Wieder, S. (2001). The clinical application of the Functional Emotional Assessment Scale. In S. I. Greenspan, G. DeGangi, & S. Wieder (Eds.), *The Functional Emotional Assessment Scale (FEAS) for infancy and early childhood* (pp. 73–129). Bethesda, MD: Interdisciplinary Council on Developmental and Learning Disorders.

Haley, S. M., Coster, W. J., Ludlow, L. H., Haltiwanger, J. T., & Andrellos, P. J. (1992). *Pediatric Evaluation of Disability Inventory (PEDI), Version 1: Development, standardization and administration manual.* Boston: PEDI Research Group, New England Medical Center Hospitals.

Hall, S. (1993). Observation guideline for sensorimotor development. In J. Case-Smith (Ed.), *Pediatric occupational therapy and early intervention* (pp. 369–375). Boston: Andover Medical Publishers.

Hardan, A. Y., Minshew, N. J., & Keshaven, M. S. (2000). Corpus callosum size in autism. *Neurology, 55*, 1033–1036.

Hendren, R. L., DeBacker, I., & Pandina, G. J. (2000). Review of neuroimaging studies of child and adolescent psychiatric disorders from the past 10 years. *Journal of the American Academy of Child and Adolescent Psychiatry, 39,* 815–828.

Heriza, C. B. (1991). Motor development: Traditional and contemporary theories. In M. J. Lister (Ed.), *Contemporary management of motor control problems. Proceedings of the II Step Conference* (pp. 99–126). Alexandria, VA: Foundation for Physical Therapy.

Hill, D., & Leary, M. (1993). *Movement disturbance: A clue to hidden competencies in persons diagnosed with autism and other developmental disabilities.* Madison, WI: DRI Press.

Individuals with Disabilities Education Act Amendments of 1997, 20 U.S.C. § 1401.

Ingram, J., Stodgell, C., Hyman, S., Figlewicz, D., Weitkamp, L., & Rodier, P. (2000). Discovery of allelic variants HOXA1 and HOXB1: Genetic susceptibility to autism spectrum disorders. *Teratology, 62,* 393–405.

Kanner, L. (1943). Inborn disturbances of affective contact. *Nervous Child, 2,* 217–250.

Kientz, M. A., & Dunn, W. (1997). A comparison of the performance of children with and without autism on the Sensory Profile. *American Journal of Occupational Therapy, 51*(7), 530–537.

Kientz, M. A., & Miller, H. (1999). Classroom evaluation of the child with autism. *School System Special Interest Section Quarterly, 6*(1), 1–4.

Klinger, L. G., & Dawson, G. (1996). Autistic disorder. In E. Mash & R. Barkley (Eds.), *Child psychopathology* (pp. 311–339). New York: Guilford Press.

Koegel, R., & Koegel, L. K. (1995). *Teaching children with autism: Strategies for positive interactions and improving learning opportunities.* Baltimore: Brookes.

Law, M., King, G., MacKinnon, E., Russel, D., Murphy, C., Hurley, P., et al. (1999). *All about outcomes: An educational program to help you understand, evaluate, and choose pediatric outcome measures, Version 1.0.* Thorofare, NJ: Slack.

Lord, C., & McGee, J. (Eds.). (2001). *Educating children with autism.* Washington, DC: National Academy Press.

Lord, C., & Risi, S. (2000). Early diagnosis in children with autism spectrum disorders. *Advocate, 33,* 23–26.

Lyon, G. R., & Krasnegor, N. A. (1996). *Attention, memory, and executive function.* Baltimore: Brookes.

Morris, S., & Klein, M. (2000). *Pre-feeding skills* (2nd ed.). San Antonio, TX: Therapy Skill Builders.

Osofsky, J. D. (1995). The effects of the exposure to violence on young children. *American Psychologist, 50,* 782–788.

Osterling, J., & Dawson, G. (1994). Early recognition of children with autism: A study of first birthday home videotapes. *Journal of Autism and Developmental Disorders, 24,* 247–258.

Parham, L. D., & Mailloux, Z. (1996). Sensory integration. In J. Case-Smith, A. S. Allen, & P. N. Pratt (Eds.), *Occupational therapy for children* (3rd ed., pp. 307–356). St. Louis, MO: Mosby.

Piper, M., & Darrah, J. (1994). *Alberta Infant Motor Scale: Motor assessment of the developing infant.* Philadelphia: W.B. Saunders.

Robins, D. L., Fein, D., Barton, M. L., & Green, J. A. (2001). The Modified Checklist for Autism in Toddlers: An initial study investigating the early detection of autism and pervasive developmental disorders. *Journal of Autism and Developmental Disorders, 31*(2), 131–144.

Rubin, S. (2000, February 22). Sue Rubin's experience with inclusion: "I was seen as a competent person." Newsletter posted to the FEATNews mailing list. Retrieved July 15, 2005, from http://www.feat.org/scripts/wa.exe?A2=ind0002d&L=featnews&D=1&O=D&P=59

Russell, D., Rosenbaum, P., Gowland, C., Hardy, S., Lane, M., McGavin, H., et al. (1990). *Gross Motor Function Measure: A measure of gross motor function in cerebral palsy.* Hamilton, Ontario: Children's Developmental Rehabilitation Programme, McMaster University.

Rutter, M. (2000). Genetic studies of autism: From the 1970s into the millennium. *Journal of Abnormal Child Psychology, 28,* 3–14.

Saleeby, D. (1996). The strengths perspective in social work practice: Extensions and cautions. *Social Work, 41,* 296–305.

Scott, J., Clark, C., & Brady, M. (2000). *Students with autism: Characteristics and instructional programming for special educators.* San Diego: Singular.

Shonkoff, J., & Phillips, D. A. (Eds.). (2000). *From neurons to neighborhoods: The science of early childhood development.* Washington, DC: National Academy Press.

Sylvester, R. (1995). *A celebration of neurons: An educator's guide to the human brain.* Alexandria, VA: Association for Supervision and Curriculum Development.

Teitelbaum, P., Teitelbaum, O., Nye, J., Fryman, J., & Maurere, R. G. (1998). Movement analysis in infancy may be useful for early diagnosis of autism. *Journal of Neuroscience, 95*(23), 13982–13987.

Thelan, E., Kelso, J. A. S., & Fogel, A. (1987). Self-organizing systems and infant motor development. *Developmental Review, 7,* 39–65.

Townsend, J., Westerfield, M., Leaver, E., Makeig, S., Jung, T., Pierce, K., et al. (2001). Event-related brain response abnormalities in autism: Evidence for impaired cerebello-frontal spatial attention networks. *Cognitive Brain Research, 11,* 127–145.

Trevarthen, C., Aitken, K., Papoudi, D., & Robert, J. (1998). *Children with autism: Diagnosis and intervention to meet their needs.* Bristol, PA: Jessica Kingsley.

Verbrugge, L. M., & Jette, A. M. (1994). The disablement process. *Social Science Medicine, 38,* 1–14.

Waitling, R. L., Dietz, J., & White, O. (2000). Comparison of Sensory Profile scores of young children with and without autism spectrum disorders. *American Journal of Occupational Therapy, 55,* 416–423.

Wetherby, A. M., & Prizant, B. M. (2000). Introduction to autism spectrum disorders. In A. M. Wetherby & B. M. Prizant (Eds.), *Autism spectrum disorders: A transactional developmental perspective* (pp. 1–11). Baltimore: Brookes.

Williamson, G. G., Anzalone, M. E., & Hanft, B. E. (2000). Assessment of sensory processing, praxis and motor performance. In ICDL Clinical Practice Guidelines Workgroup (Eds.), *The Interdisciplinary Council on Developmental and Learning Disorders (ICDL) clinical practice guidelines: Refining the standards of care for infants, children and families with special needs* (pp. 155–184). Bethesda, MD: ICDL.

Wilson, B., Kaplan, B., Crawford, S., Campbell, D., & Dewey, D. (2000). Reliability and validity of a parent questionnaire on childhood motor skills. *American Journal of Occupational Therapy, 20*(54), 484–493.

Wilson, P. H., & McKenzie, B. E. (1998). Information processing deficits associated with developmental coordination disorder: A meta analysis of research findings. *Journal of Child Psychology & Psychiatry, 39,* 829–840.

Wolfe, P. (2001). *Brain matters: Translating research into classroom practice.* Alexandria, VA: Association for Supervision and Curriculum Development.

World Health Organization. (1993). *ICD–10: Classifications of mental and behavioral disorders*. Geneva, Switzerland: Author.

World Health Organization. (1999). *ICIDH–2: International classification of impairment, disability and handicap*. Geneva, Switzerland: Author.

World Health Organization. (2001). *ICF: International classification of functioning, disability and health*. Geneva, Switzerland: Author.

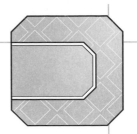

PART 2

Intervention

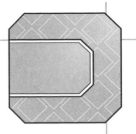

Making Intervention Decisions To Better Serve Children with ASD and Their Families

Patricia A. Prelock

QUESTIONS TO CONSIDER

In this chapter, you will be exposed to some of the conceptual frameworks that have been proposed to address the programming needs of children with autism spectrum disorders (ASD), as well as strategies that have been used to support practitioners and providers in making intervention decisions. You will also learn a process for establishing meaningful goals, determining related service needs, evaluating nonstandard intervention practices, and analyzing the curriculum to support intervention planning. As you read this chapter on making intervention decisions, consider the following questions:

1. What philosophies drive current interventions and programming for children with ASD?

2. How can families and practitioners effectively support the intervention needs of children with ASD?

3. What are some strategies for difficult decision making?

4. What considerations should be given to nonstandard interventions for children with ASD?

5. How can curriculum analysis be incorporated into intervention planning for children with ASD across the core deficit areas?

Introduction

Clinical researchers generally agree that children with autism spectrum disorders require early intervention, intensive instruction, planned teaching opportunities, and adult support (National Research Council, 2001). Planning for an individual child's program also requires the involvement of families; the establishment of goals for intervention; and the use of psychosocial, pharmacological, and related interventions that have empirical evidence of effectiveness (American Academy of Child & Adolescent Psychiatry, 1999). Differences in philosophies and approaches to intervention, however, have led to confusion and frustration for families and practitioners. Some interventions are guided by what is known about neurotypical development, whereas other interventions are nondevelopmental in their treatment approach. To effectively engage in a discussion of intervention, practitioners need to be able to evaluate claims of effectiveness and recognize principles of best practice. They also need to explain clearly the available intervention approaches, including the advantages and disadvantages, to families who are making these difficult decisions. Further, the intervention selected must be matched to the individual needs of the child with ASD.

Perspectives on Current Interventions

Several frameworks have been used to view interventions for children with ASD. For example, Heflin and Simpson (1998) categorize interventions in four ways. The first category includes *relationship-based interventions*. These interventions attempt to facilitate a child's attachment, affect, or relatedness. Floor time (Greenspan & Wieder, 1998) is one example of a relationship-based intervention (see Chapter 11 for a more complete description) because of its focus on facilitating the emotional development of children through playful interactions with adults and peers to establish attachments, two-way communication, and emotional thinking. The second category comprises *skill-based interventions*. Intervention approaches included in this category support the development of specific skills. For example, the Picture Exchange Communication System (PECS; Frost & Bondy, 1994) teaches the use of functional requests by exchanging a picture for a desired item or action (see Chapter 9 for a more complete description of PECS). The third category includes *physiologically oriented interventions*. These focus on how information is received and processed by the brain and ways for making necessary adjustments. This category of interventions includes sensory and auditory integration and psychopharmacologic and dietary treatments. The final category is *programs that combine intervention approaches* that address all aspects of a child's behavior. Project TEACCH (Watson, Lord, Schaffer, & Schopler, 1989) is an intervention program that combines several approaches, such as the use of visual supports, joint action routines, structured teaching, and various applied behavioral analysis (ABA) strategies to support communication, interaction, activities of daily living, and independence.

Rogers's (1998) framework includes two intervention categories: focal treatments and comprehensive programs. Similar to skill-based interventions, *focal treatments* address specific learning needs. The use of peer mediation (Strain, Kohler, & Goldstein, 1996) to facilitate social interaction is one example of a focal treatment (see Chapter 11 for a more complete description of peer mediation). In contrast, *comprehensive programs* are designed to reduce impairment across several ability areas and improve long-term outcomes. For example, Project TEACCH (Watson et al., 1989), described by Heflin and Simpson (1998) as a combined approach, is seen by Rogers (1998) as an intensive intervention program designed to facilitate the language and behavior of children over time.

A third framework used to describe interventions is based on a continuum of intervention approaches from traditional behavioral to more pragmatic developmental (Prizant & Wetherby, 1998). Prizant and Wetherby place discreet trial learning (Lovaas, 1987), representing a traditional behavioral approach, on one end of the continuum. Discreet trial learning uses a highly prescribed teaching structure that focuses on skill development during individual instruction. Criteria for correct responses are predetermined. Floor time (Greenspan & Wieder, 1998) is at the other end of the continuum. Floor time represents a more developmental approach, emphasizing initiation, spontaneity, following a child's lead, and using natural contexts to support development. A "middle ground" has also been proposed. Prizant and Wetherby (1998) note that more contemporary behavioral approaches provide choices, share control of teaching opportunities, and use child-preferred activities and materials. Important differences remain, however, in the incorporation of developmental research, the emphasis on eliciting specific behaviors, the type of data collected, and the recognition of interrelationships between social–emotional and communication development (Prizant & Wetherby, 1998).

Intervention Efficacy and Effectiveness

Practitioners who serve children with ASD and their families have a responsibility to be informed about the available interventions and to evaluate them critically. Intervention should be considered along two dimensions: (a) *efficacy,* or the ability of an intervention to change behavior in a specific disorder area in a clinical research setting, and (b) *effectiveness,* or the ability of the intervention to work in a real-world setting (Chorpita et al., 2002). Discrepancies certainly exist between what is known about particular interventions applied to children with ASD and how that knowledge is put into practice (Dawson & Osterling, 1997; Gresham, Beebe-Frankenberger, & MacMillan, 1999; National Research Council, 2001). Clinical researchers and practitioners often disagree about the content, type, and intensity of services that are described as affecting positive change in children with ASD (Kasari, 2002). Practitioners need to consider several principles when evaluating available interventions and making recommendations to families. Prizant and Rubin (1999) share some caveats practitioners should be aware of as they read the literature and collaborate with team members to make intervention decisions for children with ASD:

- No single approach should be the primary or only recommendation.
- Comparisons have not been made between the available interventions.
- Benefits are variable for individual children.
- Design problems plague the research (e.g., participant description, uncontrolled variables, vaguely defined treatment procedures).
- Intervention emphasis has been narrowly defined to include child outcomes while failing to consider the valued outcomes of families.
- No clear method is used to determine intervention intensity.
- Overlapping methods exist across interventions.
- Communication and social–emotional development outcomes in natural contexts are often excluded.
- Limited consideration is given to what is known about child development and a child's developmental level.
- Some interventions fail to address the core deficits in autism.
- The process for evaluating valued outcomes over time is poorly defined.

Chorpita and colleagues (2002) offer a specific framework within which practitioners can examine the interventions being considered for a child with ASD. Using efficacy criteria for empirically supported interventions, they propose a five-level system with important implications for treatments applied to children with ASD. Level 1 interventions are considered "well-established treatments" based on four specific criteria:

1. Either two or more examples exist in the literature of between-group designs that lead to better performance than a placebo or other treatment or demonstrate effects equivalent to an established treatment with adequate statistical power; *or* a large series of case studies have been done with strong experimental designs comparing one intervention to another.
2. Treatment manuals exist for the experimental procedures.
3. Participant samples are clearly defined.
4. Two or more researchers have reported significant effects.

Level 2 interventions are considered "probably efficacious treatments" because they meet *one* of the following three criteria:

1. Intervention is found to be superior to a control group in at least two studies reported in the literature.

2. One example exists in the literature of a between-group design that leads to better performance than a placebo or other treatment or demonstrates effects equivalent to an established treatment with adequate statistical power.

3. A small series of case studies have been done with clear partici-pant description, strong experimental designs, and use of proce-dural manuals for intervention compared to a placebo or other intervention.

Level 3, described by Chorpita and colleagues as "possible efficacious treat-ments," requires *one* of the following criteria:

1. One example exists in the literature of a between-group design that leads to better performance than a placebo or other treatment or demonstrates effects equivalent to an established treatment with adequate statistical power.

2. A small series of case studies have been done with clear participant and treatment description, strong experimental designs, two or more researchers reporting similar effects, and comparison to a placebo or other intervention.

Level 4 is described as "unsupported treatments," while Level 5 specifies "pos-sibly harmful treatments" because at least a single study has demonstrated harmful effects (Chorpita et al., 2002, p. 169).

In addition to proposing efficacy criteria, Chorpita and colleagues (2002) identified parameters for determining treatment effectiveness. Three general categories of effectiveness were defined (feasibility, generalizability, and cost and benefit), under which several variables to be considered were listed and operationally defined. In the area of *feasibility,* both compliance (or the percentage of children who were maintained throughout a treatment study) and trainability (the degree to which a particular training level was required and the availability of an intervention manual) were assessed. An evaluation of *generalizability* considered several parameters, including age, gender, ethnicity, interventionist training, frequency of contact, duration of treatment, format for intervention, setting in which intervention was deliv-ered, and robustness of the outcomes (e.g., low [specialized setting] to high [no specialized setting and more than one team and protocol demonstrating positive results]). *Cost and benefit* considered the level of training and num-ber of contact hours required and the resulting size of the effect.

The results of the analysis of interventions for autism using the effi-cacy and effectiveness parameters Chorpita and colleagues (2002) proposed yielded six areas of treatment to review: auditory integration training, dis-crete trial training, functional communication training and applied behav-ioral analysis, play school program, caregiver-based intervention program, and the TEACCH program. They based their analysis on Rogers's (1998) comprehensive and focal treatments and considered only published research that included a "placebo control, an alternative treatment condition, or a waitlist control" (Chorpita et al., 2002, p. 174). Their results were disappointing but consistent with previous reports of intervention effectiveness in autism. They found no support for the efficacy of comprehensive treatments (e.g., discrete trial training) because of the inability to rule out other explanations for changes in behavior. It was unclear whether the positive results reported were due to intervention or selection procedures, development, unclear diagnosis, or factors unrelated to the intervention. They did find support, however, for some focal treatments (e.g., functional communication training and applied behavioral analysis and caregiver-based intervention). Functional communication training has been used to teach children with autism communication strategies, such as requesting to reduce their involvement in inappropriate behaviors. Applied behavioral analysis has been used to teach new skills or eliminate undesirable behaviors in children with autism. Both of these focal treatments were supported at Level 3, in which single-subject experimental designs involving alternative intervention conditions led to treatment effects as a result of a specific aspect of intervention. Caregiver-based intervention, in which parents are supported in their ability to parent their child with autism, was also seen at Level 3, based on one study with an alternative treatment condition. An evaluation of effectiveness also yielded positive results for functional communication training and applied behavioral analysis in that these interventions could be generalized to children across age levels and gender, used by a variety of interventionists, and implemented in school settings. These treatments also were high in duration and led to quick results. Although effect size could not be determined because of design variability across studies, practitioners reported positive changes in children's behavior. Caregiver-based intervention also yielded high compliance rates and moderate positive effects on parents' knowledge of autism and distress rates.

The application of Chorpita and colleagues' (2002) framework for determining the efficacy and effectiveness of interventions applied to children with autism suggests a need for ongoing research that considers the treatment parameters presented in this discussion. Practitioners also have a responsibility as members of a team supporting the programming of children with ASD to examine carefully the literature on available interventions and apply efficacy and effectiveness parameters such as those described here.

Researchers are also challenged to define more clearly the interventions targeted in treatment studies and to measure change more reliably. Components of treatment (e.g., group vs. individual), comparisons with other treatments as well as control groups, documentation of procedures and fidelity checks on implementation of the treatment, randomization and matching procedures, sample size, participant characteristics, and outcome measures are all critical considerations in treatment research designs (Kasari, 2002). Further, studies should focus on those valued outcomes (e.g., imitation, attention, engagement, play) often identified for children with ASD (Wolery & Garfinkle, 2002).

Best Practice Considerations

The National Research Council (2001) suggests that services for children with ASD should be immediate, involve approximately 25 hours a week of intervention, and occur throughout the year. The American Academy of Child & Adolescent Psychiatry (1999) adds that intervention planning for children and adolescents with ASD requires collaborative planning and goal setting with families and practitioners, an assessment of available resources, a clear understanding of the individual characteristics of the child with ASD that are likely to have an impact on the intervention program, and the use of empirically based interventions.

Intervention initiated between the ages of 2 and 4 years leads to greater gains for children with autism than intervention that is delayed (Fenske, Zalenski, Krantz, & McClannahan, 1985; Lovaas & Smith, 1988). Further, children with autism appear to respond more rapidly to early intervention than children with other severe developmental delays (Rogers, 1996). Research suggests that the most positive outcomes reported for young children with autism are a result of intensive treatment for 15 or more hours a week, low child-to-adult ratios, and sustained treatment for a period of 1 to 2 years (Rogers, 1996). During intervention, the child with ASD should be engaged in developmentally appropriate, systematically planned, and individually defined activities that are responsive to the child's identified goals (National Research Council, 2001).

Clinical researchers have also proposed some guidelines or principles for best practice (Freeman, 1997; Prelock, 2001; Prizant & Rubin, 1999; Strain, Wolery, & Izeman, 1998). Freeman (1997) offers several suggestions that can support best practice in intervention decision making:

- Approach treatments with a clear, pragmatic perspective.
- Select treatments that support quality of life and do no harm.
- Consider the cultural values and priorities of the family.
- Have a method for assessing intervention effectiveness.
- Be aware of your own philosophical bias.

Prizant and Rubin (1999) suggest that practitioners match the individual needs of children with ASD to their developmental level, consider what is known about child development, and ensure that the intervention selected addresses the core deficits in autism. They also highlight the importance of evaluating the consistency between the valued outcomes identified for an individual child with ASD and the process used to achieve those outcomes. It is also critical that practitioners understand the derivation of the interventions being considered to support the social, communication, and learning needs of children with ASD.

Strain and his colleagues (1998) offer several promising practices to guide the decision making of administrators and educational teams designing services for children with ASD. These practices are drawn from empirically supported service delivery models that differ in philosophy and practice but share some critical dimensions. First, programming should ensure regular and planned interactions among peers without disabilities. Second, thoughtful planning, execution, and evaluation should characterize instruction. Third, intervention should be commensurate with an individual child's needs. Fourth, services should be implemented across contexts including settings, activities, and people. Fifth, a scope and sequence for instruction across all developmental domains should be provided. Sixth, it is critical to initiate intervention as soon as possible. Finally, positive, proactive strategies should be incorporated in the educational program to address the challenging behaviors often exhibited by children with ASD. These promising practices can serve as a guide for team decision making regarding the need for and allocation of resources.

Programming Needs

A child with ASD has significant difficulties that will require intensive and ongoing intervention to ensure progress and prevent regression in communication and behavior. The pervasive nature of the child's language disorder and behavior challenges requires extended day programming in an environment familiar to the child with a script the child understands and staff with whom the child has been successful in establishing two-way communication and joint attention.

Families play a critical role in the development of services for their child with ASD. Collaborative partnerships between families and providers during the assessment process were discussed in Chapter 3. Such collaboration must also occur during intervention decision making and planning. True partnerships require careful attention to mutual expectations for involvement and acceptance and recognition of and respect for each other's expertise (Wehman, 1998). When planning intervention for children with ASD, the team should consider the role and success of families in the implementation process (Anderson, Avery, DiPietro, Edwards, & Christian, 1987).

Summer services should be commensurate with the programming supports the child receives during the school year. Further, if it is clear that a child with ASD will regress over the summer without services, summer programming is a mandate of the child's Individualized Education Program (IEP). Often, however, the same programs that are provided during the academic school year are not available in the summer. It is important, then, for the family and school team to brainstorm a creative plan for supporting the child's needs that can meet the child's IEP goals and decrease the likelihood of regression in performance. Often school districts have summer programs in which children with ASD can participate, but it is important that whatever program is selected be individualized for each child.

Several elements have been identified as critical to ensuring successful programming for children who demonstrate the unique profile of behaviors that a child along the autism spectrum exhibits. These have been reported in the literature (Dawson & Osterling, 1997), as well as through anecdotal evidence provided by families and professionals working with children with significant communication, behavior, and social interaction difficulties. These elements include the following:

- a curriculum with content that supports attention, opportunities for imitation, comprehensive use of language, appropriate play with toys, social interaction with adults and peers, and support for motor planning and sensory input as needed;
- a highly supportive teaching environment and opportunities to generalize skills with decreased adult support;
- a need for predictability and routines;
- a functional approach to managing behavior that demonstrates an understanding of why the behavior may be occurring and what skills need to be developed to handle the behavior;
- a plan for implementing transition;
- a way to involve families; and
- a program of intense intervention, recognizing that most successful programs provide 20 to 40 hours per week, depending on the child's needs, and involve parents as collaborators to carry over intervention in the home.

Powers (1992) also describes some considerations for programming following his review of several early intervention programs for children with ASD that were implementing best practice. He suggests that programs should use structured treatment following the principles of applied behavior analysis, engage parents, start intervention early, provide intensive treatment, ensure ways to generalize information learned, establish a curriculum that emphasizes both communication and social skills, and offer opportunities to engage with peers in inclusive settings.

Hurth, Shaw, Izeman, Whaley, and Rogers (1999) reviewed seven programs identified as effective in supporting young children with ASD. Similar to other clinical researchers, they found that an early start is a priority, as is individualization of services. In addition, programs should provide systematic, planned teaching opportunities and a specialized curriculum that incorporates sustained engagement and family involvement.

Iovannone, Dunlap, Huber, and Kincaid (2003) considered the core components reported in the literature as responsible for the success of early intervention programs for children with ASD and applied them to programs developed for elementary and older school-age children with ASD. They proposed the integration of six core components for establishing a comprehensive instructional program for students with ASD and their families.

- individualized supports and services—match practices, services and supports to a student's unique profile through the IEP process (e.g., consider child and family preferences, focus on strengths, identify weaknesses that require support);

- systematic instruction—plan carefully, identify valid goals, define instructional procedures, evaluate effectiveness, and adjust instruction appropriately;
- structured learning environment—make sure the curriculum is clear to both students and staff (e.g., schedule of activities, choices);
- specialized curriculum content—focus on social engagement, initiation of and responding to social bids, and appropriate recreational and leisure skills;
- functional approach to problem behavior—focus on replacing problem behavior with appropriate or "replacement" behavior; and
- family involvement—establish parent–professional collaboration that is consistent across instructional settings.

Determining the number of hours needed to support a child with significant needs often presents a challenge to families and providers. Intensity of intervention is really different for individual children and should consider the child's social–emotional, motor, communication, and cognitive needs as well as his attention, temperament, and family supports. Teams are also encouraged to carefully consider developing an evaluation plan that will help determine the effectiveness of intervention and the valued outcomes obtained for the type and intensity of service provided.

Program evaluation addresses two fundamental issues: the quality of the process to achieve the identified goals and the actual progress children make toward achieving their goals. An intervention program for children with ASD needs to provide valid and reliable information from multiple sources across a range of services (Oren & Ogletree, 2000). *Goal attainment scaling* (GAS; Kiresuk, Smith, & Cardillo, 1994) is one strategy teams might consider as a method for measuring outcomes toward goal achievement for children with ASD. It requires the collection of data from multiple sources and identifies the areas in which goals should be written. It also develops criteria for predicting goal attainment using a continuum for proposed success—from the most favorable outcome thought likely (+2) to the most unfavorable outcome thought likely (−2)—and scores outcomes for each goal area in a standardized way (Kiresuk & Sherman, 1968). The value of GAS in program evaluation is that it allows practitioners to analyze critical components of an educational plan, and it informs all members of the team regarding the progress a child is making toward meeting the identified goals.

Visioning and Planning for Effective Intervention

It is important that families who have children with ASD and the practitioners who serve them take advantage of available strategies for long-term intervention planning that supports building a common vision. Making Action Plans (MAPS) is an effective planning tool for outlining where an individual with a disability wants to go and the path to be followed to get there (Forest & Pearpoint, 1992a, 1992b; Furney, 1994; O'Brien, Forest, Snow, & Hasbury, 1989; Vandercook, York, & Forest, 1989). The MAPS process, which comes from personal futures planning (Mount & Zwernik, 1988), emphasizes an individual's dreams; promotes self-advocacy; and responds to the needs, preferences, and interests of the individual. It supports the IEP writing and transition process because of the holistic approach it takes in understanding and considering all aspects of an individual's current situation and future goals. It also provides a structure within which a team can initiate the difficult challenge of long-term planning (Furney, 1994). The information gathering that occurs through the process leads to visioning for the individual's future.

I have frequently recommended and used the MAPS process with teams who were struggling with their program planning for children with ASD of all ages. It has served as an impetus for building and repairing relationships among families and practitioners who were initially unable to articulate a common vision for a child. The process builds on the creativity of the team, including the child with ASD.

In preparation for MAPS, team members determine a comfortable location and time in which the visioning process can take place. Those in attendance include the individual for whom the MAPS is being developed and his or her parents or guardians as well as other family members. Teachers, administrators, friends, and the primary health care provider might also be invited to participate in the meeting. Roles are assigned to the participants to ensure that a productive and effective meeting occurs. A facilitator, someone familiar with the process, is selected to guide the team through the process. A recorder is assigned to write or draw the ideas that are offered during each step of the process. A timekeeper manages the time for each step, ensuring that all the steps of the process are completed within an agreed-upon time period. At the completion of each step, a team member is assigned to integrate and summarize the key points for the group. Often a snack provider is assigned prior to the meeting, so that food can be brought to celebrate the event.

Five steps have been described for the MAPS process (Furney, 1994). In the first step, group participants share a "history" of the individual. This includes describing the individual's background, including relevant home, school, and community events. The second step provides an opportunity for the team to "dream" or create a vision of those things the individual and team see happening in the individual's future. The dreams can be immediate or long term. Participants generally brainstorm a vision for 1, 5, and 10 years into the future. Step 3 requires participants to identify their "fears" or their concerns or worries about things that could stand in the way of the individual achieving his or her dreams. In Step 4 the participants create a description of who the individual is. Participants identify the individual's likes, skills, strengths, favorite activities, and friends. In the final step, a list of needs is identified. These are the things that need to happen to ensure that the individual's dreams are realized. The information shared in this step can often be used to support development of the individual's IEP.

The MAPS process leads to a number of valued outcomes for the participants. I have seen the impact of these outcomes for children with ASD, their families, and their other team members. A culminating outcome is a shared vision by all team members. For example, members of the school team of a child with Rett's disorder had frustrations about the child's inconsistent attendance at school and had decreased their expectations for performance over time because of their understanding of her potential. A MAPS was completed in the child's home with family, members of the school team, and the child's primary health care provider. It included an honest sharing of fears for the child's future, including health, feeding, and mortality concerns, and the parents' choice to treasure moments at home. It also was used to increase all participants' understanding of the child's strengths and to share reports of positive health outcomes for girls with Rett's who have close medical follow-up and educational teams who are innovative in their approach to sustained engagement, mobility, communication, and learning. The team finally shared a vision of who this child was and what they all hoped would be achieved for her future.

The MAPS process also leads to tremendous family support, as well as the development of an individual support plan, which occurred in the previous example. Ultimately, MAPS leads to a team that commits itself to working collaboratively to meet the needs of the individual. The little girl with Rett's disorder finally had a team who understood who she was and what she could achieve if all members of the team collaborated to make it happen.

Another tool that has been used to examine a student's educational program and identify strategies for implementing the program in general education settings is the Choosing Outcomes and Accommodations for Children (COACH) process (Giangreco, Cloninger, & Iverson, 1998). Like the MAPS process, this research-based planning tool was designed to facilitate collaboration between families and practitioners. In addition, it was specifically created to help teams develop effective IEPs and avoid the deficits rampant in IEPs that are unfocused and not individualized. COACH can be used for any student with a disability. I have found it to be an effective tool for supporting the programming needs of children with ASD.

The COACH process is grounded in several principles that have important meaning for developing educational plans for children with ASD. First, it links curriculum with valued life outcomes. Through research, Giangreco and colleagues (1998) identified five outcomes most valued by families. These included being safe and healthy, having a home, establishing meaningful relationships, having choices and control, and creating opportunities for meaningful activities across environments. Pursuing valued life outcomes is a critical aspect of a child's education, and through the COACH process, a team examines what a child's current status is and what the family would like it to be.

Another principle guiding the COACH process is that families are seen as the cornerstone of education planning (Giangreco et al., 1998). They certainly have the greatest interest in seeing their children learn and usually are the only constant in the child's life. As described in Chapter 2, it is important that families are approached in culturally sensitive ways and are respected for the positive influence they can have on their children's education. Since families must live with the outcomes educational teams decide are important, they should have a primary role in the educational planning process. Families of children with ASD have an incredible fund of knowledge about their children and offer tremendous insight into their learning needs.

Collaborative teaming is also a critical principle of the COACH process. This requires a clear identification of who the team members are and making sure they share a vision for the child. Because the team will be implementing the educational program in line with the valued outcomes identified through the COACH process, teamwork is critical. The importance of coordination among service providers is another guiding principle of the process. Since COACH focuses on learning outcomes, specific therapy goals are not emphasized. Instead, team members create discipline-free goals. Together, they determine the particular behaviors or learning outcomes expected for a child and identify the general supports that will be used to help the child achieve the desired behaviors. Selected learning outcomes are drawn from the broader valued life outcomes identified by families. Coordination among team members ensures that the intention of the educational goals that are eventually developed for the IEP are understood by all members of the team.

Problem-solving methods (described later in this chapter) also guide the COACH process. Giangreco and his colleagues (1998) suggest that using problem-solving strategies can improve the effectiveness of educational planning. Problem solving provides an alternative to asking open-ended questions that often result in insufficient family input. It also provides a systematic way to collect facts, clarify any challenges that arise, and consider alternative approaches. Problem solving offers team members opportunities to approach educational planning from multiple perspectives before making decisions about what intervention plan is most likely to address the child's learning outcomes.

There are several components to the actual COACH process. The manual includes a preparation checklist, a framework for interviewing families that leads to determining IEP priorities, and a method for developing learning outcomes in the form of annual goals and short-term objectives. The process can be particularly useful in planning educational programs for children with ASD because of its family-centered emphasis, its collaborative approach to goal setting, and its recognition of valued life outcomes.

Strategies for Difficult Decision Making

Making intervention decisions is a difficult task for families of children with ASD and the practitioners who work hard to meet their needs. Guidelines have been proposed for facilitating decisions about interventions for children with ASD (Freeman, 1997; Nickel, 1996). As teams face intervention decisions, the following guidelines should be considered:

- Approach all treatments with a clear, pragmatic perspective.
- Determine the goals you are trying to meet and base your intervention selections on the treatments most likely to meet those goals.
- Select treatments that support an individual's quality of life and do not harm the individual or family.
- Consider the cultural priorities and values of the family when proposing various interventions.
- Be aware of which treatments recognize that all individuals may not respond to the proposed intervention in the same way, as opposed to treatments that suggest all individuals will benefit.
- Consider an eclectic approach to treatment, and be aware of programs that encourage the use of several treatments to serve the needs of individuals with autism.
- Use assessment information to help determine which treatment approaches respond to the needs of the individual with autism.
- Select treatment approaches that include procedures for evaluating whether the treatment is appropriate and effective for a particular child.
- Be aware of your philosophical bias when considering different treatments for autism, and listen to those with autism to help you determine what might work.

Freeman (1997) offers additional questions team members should raise as they work through the difficulty of making intervention decisions for children with ASD—for example, If the treatment fails, how will it affect the child and family? Who has the treatment been tested on? How can the treatment be integrated into the child's current program? And how will you know whether the treatment is working?

Creative Problem Solving

As mentioned in the previous discussion of strategies for visioning and educational planning, problem solving is a useful method for gaining varied perspectives related to educational planning, as well as addressing the difficulties teams encounter when making intervention decisions. The complexity of intervention choices and needs for children with ASD requires a systematic approach to problem solving.

Often teams experience blocks to creativity when thrown into the midst of challenging situations. Thousand (1995) describes several blocks that interfere with creative thinking, including perceptual blocks (e.g., having stereotypes of how things should be done), cultural blocks (e.g., favoring tradition over change), emotional blocks (e.g., being afraid of taking risks), and linguistic blocks (e.g., having no common language). Creative problem solving requires team members to think about the "what if" possibilities, to be optimistic, to alternate between divergent and convergent thinking, and to brainstorm ideas by deferring judgment, breaking down the problem, forming new mental connections, and generally thinking "outside the box" (Giangreco, Cloninger, Dennis, & Edelman, 1994, 2000). Team members who are able to call on their senses and emotions to consider alternative solutions to problems can make a difference in the educational planning and implementation of intervention for children with ASD.

A creative problem-solving process has been described by Osborn (1953, 1993) and Parnes (1981, 1985, 1988, 1992, 1997) that can be applied to challenging situations teams face in making difficult program planning and intervention decisions for children with ASD. Team members should be aware, however, that developing creativity is a lifelong process and requires more than just learning steps to a process; it requires a creative attitude (Parnes, 1985, 1988). Cycling through a creative problem-solving process helps to foster a creative attitude that becomes part of a practitioner's toolkit in addressing daily challenges with a particular child or system of service.

Six basic steps or stages define the Osborn–Parnes creative problem-solving process. In my experience, the process has evolved as an effective strategy for supporting teams faced with challenges in implementing interventions in the school setting for children with ASD. I have also recommended the process as a strategy for managing different perspectives among team members, including families, regarding approaches to intervention and outcome measurement. In the first step, *objective finding* is required of team members. This means participants sharpen their ability to observe, capitalizing on all their senses and perceptions to explore new possibilities (Giangreco, Cloninger, et al., 1994, 2000). The process begins with divergent thinking, considering possible problems to solve, and then leads to convergent thinking, focusing on a particular challenge or problem that requires resolution. During this step, roles are assigned (e.g., facilitator, recorder, timekeeper, jargon buster, equalizer, keeper of the rudder—see descriptions in Chapter 3), and team members share high-priority issues for which support is needed (Giangreco, Cloninger, et al., 1994).

The second step requires team members to engage in *fact finding*. Team members identify all possible facts related to the identified problem. If the issue raised in Step 1 is clear and small enough (e.g., the type of augmentative device selected to support the communication of a child with ASD and limited verbal skills), the team spends time exploring the facts around the issue. This step is quick-paced and demands listing just the facts. Team members might use basic questions such as who, what, when, where, how, and why to guide their thinking (Giangreco, Cloninger, et al., 1994, 2000). For example, the team finds out what is and is not the current state of affairs for using a communication device (e.g., whether a device has been used in the past, what other communication strategies have been introduced, and what challenges have been met with different communication systems). Team members identify the facts that are most relevant to the specific challenge they have identified (Giangreco et al., 2000).

If the issue is unclear and too big (e.g., should the child go on to middle school), the team engages in Step 3, *problem finding*. During problem finding, team members restate the issues in many different ways, using the phrase: "In what ways might we ..." (Giangreco, Cloninger, et al., 1994, 2000). The goal is to clarify the problem by defining it in new ways and determining what the team hopes to accomplish. This is an important step in problem solving, because clearly defined challenges are most likely to lead to creative and thoughtful solutions (Giangreco, Cloninger, et al., 1994).

Step 4 engages the team in *idea finding*. The purpose of this stage of the process is to generate as many ideas or potential solutions as possible without making judgments. Team members are encouraged to have fun and consider possibilities beyond the norm. A recorder is selected, and chart paper is labeled with a phrase like "We could ...." The rules for brainstorming are implemented: No team member is permitted to say, "Yes, but" when an idea is presented; there is no evaluation of ideas; and team members rapidly fire ideas for 5 minutes (Giangreco, Cloninger, et al., 1994, 2000; Osborn, 1953; Parnes, 1992). To broaden possible perspectives during this creative exercise, team members are encouraged to change roles after approximately 5 minutes. This means that one discipline takes on the role of another discipline, or a practitioner takes on the role of a family member or the child with ASD. Another 2 to 5 minutes of brainstorming occurs, in which the team generates additional ideas. The facilitator then helps team members to cluster those ideas that are related, paraphrase them, eliminate redundancies, and agree on the categories that emerge.

Solution finding is the fifth step in the creative problem-solving process. In this step of the process, team members collaboratively determine what makes a good idea, selecting from those ideas generated in Step 4. The team also defines the criteria for evaluating these ideas. Team members begin with divergent thinking, considering a number of possible criteria for evaluating the proposed ideas, and then move to convergent thinking, agreeing on a subset of criteria for evaluating the ideas (Giangreco, Cloninger, et al., 1994, 2000). A recorder is selected who labels chart paper, "Will the idea ...?" or "A good idea is one that ..." as a probe to support the brainstorming process of the team members. Team members working to problem-solve around intervention planning for a child with ASD might ask the following questions or make the following statements:

Will the idea ...	meet the needs of the child with ASD?
	be possible for the team to implement?
	involve the family of the child with ASD?
A good idea is one ...	that can be completed in the required time frame.
	that will lead to measurable outcomes for the child with ASD.

The team may choose different strategies to work through the solution-finding process. If the team chooses to engage in informal consensus building, each team member would comment on the potential solutions or ideas (which are numbered) and state something like "I like solution or idea #_____ because it meets _____ criteria" or "I don't think solution or idea #_____ is a good choice because is goes against _____ criteria" (Thousand, 1995). Another strategy would be to have team members individually rate each solution or idea with a plus or minus sign and record and sum the ratings, selecting those solutions or ideas that receive the highest ratings.

Acceptance finding is the final step in the creative problem-solving process. During this step, team members make plans to overcome the potential barriers to solutions or ideas that hold promise (Giangreco, Cloninger, et al., 1994, 2000). They discuss strategies to manage the identified challenges and pose questions such as the following:

- Who needs to be involved?
- Who might get in the way?
- What resources are necessary?
- What scheduling changes are necessary?
- When should we get started?
- When should the task be completed?
- Where will we find the resources we need?
- How should we respond if things don't go as planned?

Team members then identify the steps they need to take to implement the solutions or ideas that have been selected. Action planning includes what activities need to be completed in what order, how success will be defined for each, the person responsible, and the start date.

The creative problem-solving process described here has an important role for practitioners and families working to manage complex intervention programs for children with ASD. Hopefully, teams will capitalize on this strategy and others to support creative efforts to address the behavioral, communication, and social needs of children with ASD, as well as the planning, communication, and implementation challenges often faced by teams serving this population.

Mediating Conflict

Unfortunately, intervention planning and implementation for children with ASD is often plagued with problems. Complexity of needs, limited resources, poor understanding of intervention practices, and the individual nature of autism lead to expected and unexpected conflicts. Learning to problem-solve during a time of conflict is particularly challenging and requires team members to possess some understanding of the steps involved in decision making around problems. First, the problem must be clearly defined. Second, additional information may need to be gathered if team members feel that they do not have sufficient information to make a decision. Third, some potential options for managing the problem must be conceived. Fourth, an option is selected and implemented. Finally, the response to the option is monitored to determine whether the desired results have been achieved. In some situations, teams initiate a creative problem-solving process like the one just described. In other situations, however, internal conflict may already exist within a team, making it nearly impossible to engage in a successful creative problem-solving effort.

For those teams experiencing conflict, it is important to evaluate what might be at the root of the conflict. Team members may have conflicting aims, or tension may exist between comfortable and uncomfortable solutions. Often teams feel the pressure of time or fear undesirable results. Certainly, problem solving in and of itself is frustrating, because it is not easy. It requires a commitment to resolution, compromise, and redefining what individuals value most.

A useful framework for resolving conflict that I often employ in challenging situations is a *mediation model* (Lahar, 1996). In this model, team members learn to move away from a position framework (i.e., inclusive vs. individual intervention) to a more interest-based framework (i.e., a combination program that addresses interests shared by both positions). When teams engage in interest-based mediation, more creative, alternative solutions are likely.

To apply a mediation framework to conflict resolution, team members must first determine the different positions being expressed. Once the positions are defined, the specific interests of each position are identified, and interests shared by both positions are highlighted. Decision making is then based on the shared or common interests of the opposing views, often requiring the establishment of a new position. If, for some reason, a new interest-based position cannot be determined, team members have the option of agreeing to a compromise. Sometimes a compromise is acceptable to speed up a solution or to maintain the security of a relationship. Compromise may also be acceptable if some version of the "other" position can meet most of the valued interests of both parties. Certainly, an interest-based framework for mediating conflict provides a more creative and satisfying solution than a compromise that will require giving up certain interests. Figures 8.1, 8.2, and 8.3 present an example of application of the mediation framework for a family and school team members who shared different positions on program planning that were adjusted to a new position once the interests shared by both were identified.

Making Related Services Decisions

Coordinating educational support services for children with ASD is a frequently encountered task for teams designing intervention programs for those children. An array of related service providers come into the homes and classrooms of children with ASD. Some of these providers appear to have clearly defined goals and have developed these goals as part of a team process. Other providers have been added to the educational program without a clear understanding of their role or how they can and should coordi-

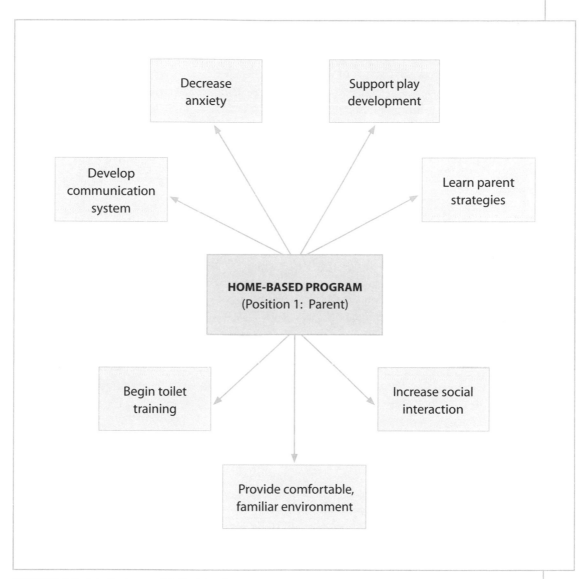

FIGURE 8.1. Mediation model: Position 1.

nate their efforts. The Vermont Interdependent Services Team Approach (VISTA) offers one way to think about and operationalize the tenets of collaboration while making related services decisions for students with disabilities (Giangreco, 1996). I encourage teams to pursue the use of this process in making related services decisions for children with ASD. It has value in supporting teams in making some of the most difficult decisions they are likely to encounter as they try to determine who should be providing what service, how often, and in what context. The VISTA process and the level of collaboration required of the participants are described in the paragraphs that follow.

Giangreco (1996) describes several practice problems that are characteristic of educational planning for children with ASD when the input from

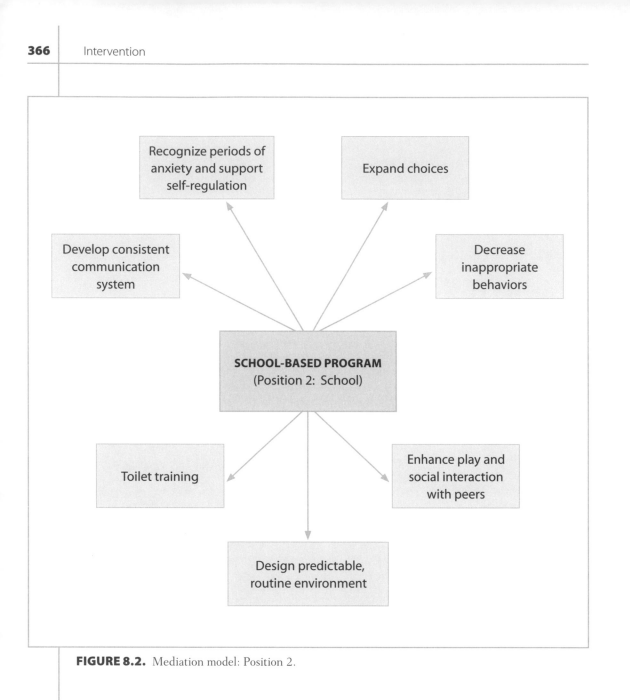

FIGURE 8.2. Mediation model: Position 2.

a related services professional is not integrated with the input from family, teachers, and other support professionals. These problems, which indicate a need for the collaboration characteristic of the VISTA process, include such practice issues as service fragmentation, disorganized teams, and discipline-specific decision making. Fragmentation often results when there is a failure to share the educational relevance and necessity of support services. For example, Giangreco, Edelman, and Dennis (1991) found that professionals and parents across the United States made decisions about need, frequency, and model of service delivery before knowing the goals on a student's IEP. Giangreco and colleagues also found that the IEPs of students with multiple disabilities included different goals for different professional disciplines

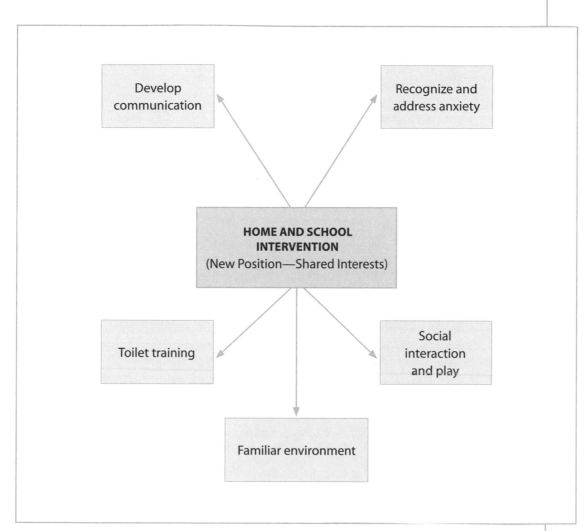

FIGURE 8.3. Mediation model: New position.

(Giangreco, Dennis, Edelman, & Cloninger, 1994). Confusion results when teams are disorganized and members have ambiguous roles and goals for the services they provide. The literature suggests that related service providers favor retaining control over discipline-specific decisions, whereas educators and families favor consensus building (Giangreco, 1990). Further, professionals hold different views regarding the use of integrated services in early childhood programs (McWilliam & Bailey, 1994).

Historically, service delivery models used in occupational and physical therapy favored decision making from a single discipline perspective (Carr, 1989; Effgen, 1984; Farley, Sarracino, & Howard, 1991; Hall, Robertson, & Turner, 1992). Yet many functions of educational team members overlap (Giangreco & Eichinger, 1991). Several questions need to be considered as teams initiate the decision-making process for related services intervention (Giangreco, 1996):

- What is the role of each team member?
- Do team members share an understanding of their roles?
- How do team members think about educationally relevant and necessary related services?
- Who makes the decisions about support services?
- How does the team coordinate assessment, planning, decision making, implementation, and evaluation?
- How could the team be better coordinated?

Giangreco (1996) offers 10 guidelines to teams participating in the VISTA process as they consider the manner in which they make intervention decisions about related service providers, including speech–language pathologists (SLPs). First, he suggests establishing and maintaining a collaborative team. The team should be composed of all those affected by team decisions and may include those with ongoing involvement (core members), those with less frequent involvement (extended members), and those focused on specific issues (situational members). Team members need to develop a shared framework and pursue common goals for the child with ASD.

The second guideline requires teams to define the components of the child's educational program. Giangreco (1996) suggests that these components should include priority learning outcomes that are individual, family determined, and discipline free. Some examples of priority learning outcomes for children with ASD might be health, meaningful social relationships, communicating needs and wants, making choices, and independence. To ensure that the child with ASD experiences a broad-based curriculum, additional learning outcomes (e.g., language arts, math, science, physical education) that extend the previously identified priority outcomes might be selected by the team. General supports that provide children with ASD with access to and participation in inclusive settings (e.g., teaching others about the augmentative communication device the child uses in the classroom) should also be identified.

Understanding the interactions among program, placement, and services is the third guideline for supporting team decision making. Educational placement is determined after educational components are identified but before services are determined, whereas related services are determined after both the educational program components and placement have been determined. So teams providing service to children with ASD should ask themselves the following question: Have we made service decisions before identifying the child's educational program components and placement?

Giangreco (1996) proposes a fourth guideline: that teams use a value system to guide their decision making that can be phrased "Only as special as necessary." He raises some concerns about previously held value systems that have guided practice, such as "More is better," suggesting that the *quantity* of what is done has greater value than the *quality* of what is done.

Giangreco's tenet accounts for children's individual concerns and acknowledges the contribution of various disciplines but avoids well-intentioned overservice. More service than is necessary has the potential of decreasing time for children with ASD to participate with their typical peers. It may disrupt the acquisition, practice, or generalization of important educational skills and can cause inequity in the use of scarce resources. Overservice often overwhelms families with the involvement of a large number of professionals and may create unnecessary dependency. Certainly, it complicates team communication and coordination.

A fifth guideline is to determine the functions of service providers and how they are interrelated (Giangreco, 1996). All team members should be clear about the contribution of each support person to the team and the child's educational plan. Support personnel may develop adaptations or identify equipment to aid the child's access to full participation, facilitate the transfer of information and skills to others, or serve as a resource and support to family. Clarifying individual functions and roles allows the team to understand the interrelationships in service provision and provides an opportunity to clarify roles to ensure a shared framework. A critical step for the team, however, is to explore the gaps, overlaps, and contradictions that may exist between the identified functions of service providers and the goals of the child's educational program (Giangreco, 1996).

The team now considers a sixth principle: Apply essential criteria (i.e., educational relevance and necessity) when making service recommendations. For example, if increasing a child's meaningful social interactions is an identified component of his or her educational program, service by an SLP who is developing the child's response to peer initiations is relevant. Giangreco (1996) recommends that teams establish educational necessity by using four criteria: whether the absence of service interferes with children's access to or participation in their educational program; whether the service represents an overlap, contradiction, or gap; whether both the provider and the benefactor of the service agree that the service is needed; and whether the service can generalize to other contexts without direct involvement of the service provider.

Establishing a consensus on who has the authority for decision making is the seventh principle (Giangreco, 1996). Two methods are often used during decision making, both of which have drawbacks. The first method is *autocratic,* in which a specific service provider retains authority for determining whether and how a service should be provided. The challenges with this method are potential judgment errors and fragmented services. The second method is a *democratic* approach, in which every team member has a say and those in the majority determine the services. Challenges exist with this method as well, in that polarization among team members can occur, dissenting opinions are devalued, and parents are outnumbered (Giangreco, 1996). A possible solution to the problems of these two methods is the use of consensus decision making. Building consensus requires time, effort, skill in group processes, an ability to understand the perspectives of others, and sharing a framework of best practice. Like the first two methods, it has a disadvantage when decisions are being made, as team members may defer to the "expert" in a particular discipline without truly understanding a specific recommendation made by the service provider.

The eighth principle Giangreco (1996) proposes is matching the mode and frequency of service provision to the functions served. That is, team members must be sure that the role or function defined for the service provider actually matches the identified service need. Team members need to consider the benefits of combining direct and indirect services, such as individual therapy sessions with the speech–language pathologist and consultation by the speech–language pathologist to the teacher and paraprofessionals regarding facilitation of social interaction among peers for a child with ASD. This may mean learning to effectively and efficiently apply indirect services that are educationally relevant when the direct support of an individual service provider is not required. It is important, though, that the decision to employ indirect services not reflect staff shortages.

Determining the location of the least restrictive educational environment and defining strategies for service provision are the critical goals established in the ninth principle (Giangreco, 1996). Although isolated settings and highly specialized strategies can be restrictive and intrusive, providing service in the classroom is not always the most appropriate option, particularly for children with ASD. Team members should consider some basic tenets as they define the primary intervention settings and strategies for children with ASD. Services should be socially acceptable, minimally intrusive, and evaluated to determine effectiveness and should consider peer perceptions while a child's privacy, dignity, and preferences are respected (Giangreco, 1996).

The final principle that Giangreco (1996) proposes to guide the decision-making process for service provision is to engage in ongoing implementation and evaluation of the support services provided. Effectiveness should be evaluated in the context of the specific components in a child's educational program that the proposed services are intended to address. Regular assessment of support service success should be completed. Certainly, success should consider the impact on valued life outcomes. Parents of children with disabilities have identified valued life outcomes that teams should consider in their planning for children with ASD. These include health and safety, networks of meaningful relationships, opportunities to make choices, interesting places to go and meaningful activities, having a home, opportunities for lifelong learning, and contributing to the community (Giangreco, Cloninger, Dennis, & Edelman, 1993).

I encourage team members to consider applying the VISTA process to their educational program planning for children with ASD. The principles highlighted by Giangreco (1996) provide a meaningful framework within which teams can define and redefine their roles and functions, ask the questions they need to ask about the educational relevance of the services they provide, consider the necessity of what they do, and evaluate the valued outcomes they hope to achieve. It is a process in which all members of the team collaborate to determine the most effective and efficient service decisions for children with special needs, including children with ASD, and their families.

Considerations for Nonstandard Interventions

Conventional treatments applied to children with ASD most often include intensive, coordinated programming in special education with a plan for behavior management and developmentally appropriate strategies (Levy & Hyman, 2002). Some less conventional treatments, known as nonstandard therapies or complementary and alternative medicine (CAM), have sparked parents' interest in helping their children with ASD. Nonstandard therapies or CAM are controversial therapies that are not consistent with medical research; however, they may be thought to be beneficial for some children (Nickel, 1996; Starrett, 1996). A variety of nonstandard therapies have been used in the treatment of autism (Heflin & Simpson, 1998). It is important, therefore, to be familiar with these nonstandard interventions and to consider their potential benefit or harm.

Nonstandard therapies have been described in several ways. Starrett (1996) has divided these therapies into dietary treatments, neurophysiologic retraining, and "other." Dietary treatments (e.g., megavitamins, food allergy analysis, Feingold diet, sucrose elimination) involve modifying a child's diet to change behavior. Improvements in speech, eye contact, social behavior, and attention span are often reported, although methodological flaws plague the available research. Neurophysiologic retraining (e.g., patterning, sensory integration, optometric training, and auditory training) involves using certain motor patterns or stimulating certain sensory inputs to improve central nervous system function (Starrett, 1996). Although a frequently used intervention for children with ASD, the effectiveness of sensory integration has not been supported in the scientific literature. Some have reported auditory training to reduce hearing hypersensitivity in children with ASD and to improve attention span and behavior, whereas others have noted little to no significant changes (Gerlach, 1993). The third category of "other" is used by Starrett (1996) to include controversial interventions (e.g., anti–motion sickness, chiropractic, antifungals, facilitated communication, and secretin injections) not covered in the first two categories.

Levy and Hyman (2002) also describe different types of complementary or alternative treatments, dividing them into biologic and nonbiologic. Biologic treatments (e.g., vitamin supplements, medications, antibiotics, antifungals, diet, chelation or mercury detoxification) can be bought over the counter or managed by a physician. Nonbiologic treatments (e.g., auditory integration, facilitated communication, craniosacral manipulation, interactive metronome) are usually considered to be new or expanded approaches to existing interventions that are administered by a therapist or the family.

The complementary or alternative treatments Levy and Hyman describe have some overlap with those nonstandard therapies presented by Starrett (1996), although they focus more on the biologic nature of the intervention and on who administers it (physician or other interventionist).

Little is known about why families choose nonstandard therapies and what their experiences have been in using them in the treatment of their children with ASD. The available research has reported, however, that families often choose nonstandard treatments or CAM in their effort to provide a comprehensive intervention plan for their children with a variety of disabilities (Golden, 1984; Levy & Hyman, 2002; Masland, 1984; Smith, Groen, & Wynn, 2000; Starrett, 1996). For example, Smith and colleagues (2000) surveyed families of children with ASD about interventions they were using, and over half reported the use of sensory integration (56%), elimination diets (50%), and vitamin supplements (61%). In a pilot study investigating the use of nonstandard therapies, families were surveyed regarding their reasons for initiating and terminating nonstandard therapies and their feelings about the importance of having specific information on the therapies used (Schneiderman & Prelock, 2000). Results indicated that sensory integration was the most common therapy used (87%), followed by auditory training (33%), megavitamins (29%), and chiropractic care and allergy avoidance (21%). Most families reported a desire to have research to support the selection of a nonstandard therapy, with 57% indicating a strong desire, although many indicated that they relied on word of mouth as a basis for whether or not to use a particular therapy. The survey indicated that having more information from both physicians and other parents about nonstandard therapies would be most helpful to families as they are deciding which nonstandard therapies to consider (Schneiderman & Prelock, 2000).

Although reports of nonstandard therapies indicate their limited success, parents continue to use them. It is important for practitioners to understand why parents choose to use a therapy that may be time consuming and yield little effect. Even though there are risks involved and doubts about the effectiveness of nonstandard therapies, their use can be understood in the context of families responding to the strong literature support for early intervention (Dawson & Osterling, 1997). Some families may choose a nonstandard therapy because they are disappointed in the results of a conventional therapy. Media reports highlighting a story of a therapy helping one child also may influence a parent's decision to try a nonstandard therapy. Such stories create interest in the therapy, even if no scientific research supports the benefit to other children (Starrett, 1996).

It is important to know what type of information families need to make their intervention decisions. Because any therapy may be a risk to a child, families must not only be informed of the available interventions but also learn to evaluate critically the validity of any proposed treatment (Levy & Hyman, 2002). Further, practitioners must understand the difficult choices families face when attempting to provide intervention for their children with ASD. Families have valuable insight about the potential effectiveness of a therapy because of the changes they can observe. It is critical that their perspective and insight be valued in the intervention decision-making process. Pediatricians, in particular, have been advised to be supportive of families during this process, while offering careful interpretation of treatment claims with little empirical support or peer review and closely watching the well-being of the child (American Academy of Pediatrics, 2001). Families and practitioners should have the information they need to make informed, potentially life-changing decisions for children with ASD.

Because the practice of nonstandard and complementary or alternative therapies is prevalent in intervention planning for children with ASD, it seems critical that team members consider a framework for making intervention decisions involving potentially controversial practices (Prelock, 2002). Based on a general protocol for considering controversial intervention practices proposed by Duchan, Calculator, Sonnenmeier, Diehl, and Cumley (2001), I offer several guidelines for families and practitioners involved in intervention decision making for children with ASD.

Practitioners must first identify sources of potential controversy in the interventions being considered. This involves investigating whether the intervention has a sound theoretical foundation, sufficient outcome data, and technical reports or position statements associated with it. After gathering and integrating this information, practitioners must determine whether the potential strengths and benefits of the intervention exceed the weaknesses and risks.

Examining how a particular intervention overlaps with established practices is also critical. Interventions for children with ASD should be intensive; be individualized; address core deficits in social interaction, communication, and behavior; be easily incorporated with other interventions; and meet the priority goals established by a team (National Research Council, 2001; Prelock, 2001, 2002; Prizant & Rubin, 1999).

If an intervention has been defined as nontraditional, controversial, or experimental, informed consent should be obtained from the person with ASD or from a guardian. Obtaining informed consent would require practitioners to provide an oral and written explanation of the proposed intervention, the controversy surrounding the intervention, reported benefits and risks, the existence of any validation studies, and possible alternative interventions. Families should be included in all decisions about any intervention being proposed for their children. They should have the opportunity, at any time, to refuse or terminate a controversial intervention (Duchan et al., 2001).

Selecting an intervention that has defined procedures for implementation is critical. As a controversial or nonstandard intervention is being considered, benefits and risks should be considered individually for each child and family, and a process should exist for evaluating the implementation and effectiveness of the intervention. Team members might also provide an explanation of why a particular intervention is appropriate for a specific child. For example, a particular intervention might be described in the literature as particularly appropriate to children with ASD who have high cognitive skills or those with limited verbal communication. A monitoring system for assessing procedural reliability and ongoing progress also should be in place. Most important, the intervention should be responsive to the long-term priority goals defined for the child.

The training necessary to implement a particular intervention is also an important consideration in the decision-making process. Team members need to find out whether necessary training is available, as well as who needs the training. Basic competencies for implementing the intervention also should be defined.

When considering the implementation of a controversial or nonstandard practice, it is particularly important to ensure that a process has been established for documenting and evaluating intervention outcomes. This means that team members must define a consistent data collection process that can assess performance over time in a variety of structured and unstructured contexts. The data collection process establishes a research basis for comparing the proposed intervention outcomes with previously reported results, noting similarities and differences.

Finally, all team members must prepare for the challenges they are likely to face when engaged in intervention decision making around nonstandard treatments. It is important to learn and apply principles of mediation and conflict resolution (described earlier in this chapter) to avoid contentious situations. Practitioners should be well informed in the application of mediation and conflict resolution, as well as the due process mechanisms used to develop programs for children with disabilities. Figure 8.4 is a checklist team members might use to evaluate controversial or nonstandard practices that are being considered as potential interventions for a child with ASD.

Curriculum Analysis and Intervention Planning

Service delivery in school-based settings has been refocused and redefined over the last 10 years, particularly for SLPs who provide services to children with a variety of communication disorders (Prelock, 1997). An area of assessment and intervention planning that has relevance for meeting the educational programming needs of children with ASD is language-based curriculum analysis (LBCA). To ensure that students with ASD have access to the educational curriculum of their peers, a process for systematically reviewing the curriculum, including identifying demands and expectations, defining potential breakdowns, and brainstorming modifications is needed. A collaborative process has been proposed for completing an LBCA in response to the needs of children with communication disorders in educational settings (Prelock, Miller, & Reed, 1993). LBCA helps a team to evaluate academic content from a language perspective and facilitates intervention

(*text continues on p. 378*)

Checklist for Considering Nonstandard or Controversial Practices

Questions to be answered for: _____ (intervention)	Yes (Y) No (N) Don't Know (DK)	What additional information is needed?	Who will gather the information?	When will it be done?	How are the child's priority short- and long-term goals addressed?	What is the evidence of potential benefit for the child?	What is the evidence of potential risk for the child?
Theoretical foundation							
Outcome data							
Technical reports and position statements							
Intensive							
Individualized							
Addresses social interaction							

(continues)

FIGURE 8.4. Checklist for considering nonstandard or controversial practices.

Questions to be answered for: (intervention)	Yes (Y) No (N) Don't Know (DK)	What additional information is needed?	Who will gather the information?	When will it be done?	How are the child's priority short- and long-term goals addressed?	What is the evidence of potential benefit for the child?	What is the evidence of potential risk for the child?
Addresses communication							
Addresses behavior, specified interests, play							
Reported risks							
Reported benefits							
Procedures clearly explained							
Systematic data collection process							

(continues)

FIGURE 8.4. *Continued.*

Questions to be answered for: ___ (intervention)	Yes (Y) No (N) Don't Know (DK)	What additional information is needed?	Who will gather the information?	When will it be done?	How are the child's priority short- and long-term goals addressed?	What is the evidence of potential benefit for the child?	What is the evidence of potential risk for the child?
Requires training							
Training available							
Trained personnel available							
Requires informed consent							
Other appropriate interventions are available							

FIGURE 8.4. *Continued.*

planning around the challenges in language and communication a student is likely to encounter in the classroom. This process has specific application to children with ASD who have a range of communicative and cognitive abilities. Two different frameworks are provided for completing an LBCA.

The LBCA framework recommended for younger children who have ASD and those who have limited verbal and cognitive abilities is presented in Appendix 8.A. It requires team members, including the family, SLP, and general and special education teachers, to meet to define an area of the curriculum a child is to be taught for a period of time. The team then determines what the child brings to the curriculum that will both facilitate and hinder his or her ability to participate fully in the curriculum. There are four steps for the team members to consider. For each step, the team considers the challenges or core deficit areas that often characterize young children with ASD—that is, communication, social interaction, play, and sensory deficits. In the first step, however, the team is required to consider not just the child's needs but also his or her strengths in each of these areas. Teams often fail to recognize that there are relative strengths in each deficit area that can be built upon and supported within the curriculum. The team, therefore, collaborates to identify the child's strengths and needs in communication (both verbal and nonverbal), social interaction (with both peers and adults), play (with objects and play partners), and sensory (across all modalities) skills. If another key challenge area exists (e.g., behavior), the team can specify strengths and needs in that area, as well.

The second step requires the team to consider the general expectations or curriculum requirements in communication, social interaction, play, and sensory skills for any student participating in the general education curriculum. This is done to ensure that team members clearly understand what a preschool teacher, for example, expects of all his or her students in each of the areas, as well as how the specific curriculum being implemented taps each of these areas. Capitalizing on his or her knowledge of child development across domain areas, the early childhood or general education teacher has a critical role in this discussion.

Next, the team must determine those expectations or requirements in the curriculum and the learning environment that are likely to be problematic for the child with ASD. Again, the team reviews these expectations or requirements across the areas of communication, social interaction, play, and sensory skills, considering the child's strengths and needs identified in the first step.

The final step in the process requires the team to brainstorm appropriate modifications in the curriculum or environment and determine those intervention strategies most likely to support the child's individual needs. Again, the team makes its determinations based on its review of the four targeted areas of strength and need (i.e., communication, social interaction, play, and sensory skills) for each child with ASD. Practitioners who have used this curriculum analysis format have found it to be a valuable framework for defining the specific issues facing young children in an educational setting and selecting strategies to modify the environment and build into the curriculum to facilitate access and success for the child with ASD (Prelock, 1997; Prelock et al., 1993).

LBCA for school-age children with ASD who are being served in integrated settings requires a comprehensive examination of a particular content area that considers both the curriculum and the communication objectives needed to successfully manage the academic information presented in the classroom (Prelock, 1997; Prelock et al., 1993). The framework proposed here is an adaptation of an earlier format (Prelock et al., 1993) devised for children with language disorders or language learning disabilities to support student success in listening, speaking, reading, and writing (see Appendix 8.B). This approach to intervention planning allows team members to understand the demands of the curriculum to which students are exposed. It also prepares the team for effectively meeting the overall communication needs of students with ASD in the general education setting. There are four components to the analysis: (a) stating the objectives, (b) reviewing requirements, (c) evaluating student needs, and (d) making modifications.

Stating Objectives

The first component in the curriculum analysis is to define the curriculum objectives expected of all students learning a specific content area within a specified time period. It is important that team members consider the curriculum objectives in terms of "units" of information or material to be covered over a predetermined time period. The time period covered is determined by the teacher's assessment of the knowledge needed to understand specific material or to gain competence in a particular area. Prelock and colleagues (1993) found that it is unreasonable to expect teams to consider all the curriculum objectives to be covered in a content area, such as science, for the entire school year. They found that teachers and SLPs were more effective in their curriculum analysis for children with language disorders when there was a defined period of time and amount of content to be covered. When making a determination of the objectives to be addressed in a curriculum analysis, it is recommended that team members emphasize the following:

- evidence of students' confusion with content area concept development;
- learning outcomes that are prerequisites for later learning; and
- standards or benchmarks for performance required by the school district.

The IEPs of students with ASD guide determination of the language learning and social communication objectives that are emphasized in the context of the curriculum objectives. Consider an example of a fourth grader with ASD in science class. For 4 weeks, the students will be learning about electricity. The team decides to complete an LBCA in that content area because of the student's motivation for learning and specific interest in it. The teacher has defined the curriculum objectives as follows: (a) students will identify conductors of electricity and explain why particular items are conductors of electricity; (b) students will understand and explain a parallel circuit; and (c) students will understand and explain a series circuit. The SLP identifies the targeted language learning objectives from the student's IEP: (a) to increase the student's ability to find the right word to explain a concept or answer a question in science class and (b) to increase the student's understanding of abstract terms as they relate to concepts presented during the science curriculum. The social communication objectives include (a) increasing the student's ability to complete a task in collaboration with peers during small group science projects using a social script and (b) increasing the student's ability to state his feeling when upset by a peer's comment.

Reviewing Requirements

During this component of the LBCA, the team determines the language demands of the classroom instruction, the textbook, and related materials used for the content area. The team examines the vocabulary demands, the ways students are expected to demonstrate their comprehension, the oral and written language expectations, and the social discourse requirements. Vocabulary knowledge is an essential component for learning as it lays the foundation for the ideas being developed in a content area (Prelock, 1997). Both prerequisite vocabulary (knowledge the teacher expects students to have to begin with) and new vocabulary (information that will be introduced) are identified. For example, prerequisite vocabulary in fourth-grade science might include words like *socket, electricity, circuit, demonstrate,* and *explain.* New vocabulary might include words such as *outlet, conductor, insulator, series circuit, parallel circuit,* and *invention.* The teacher also identifies any items in the LBCA sections (see Appendix 8.B) for comprehension (e.g., following oral and written directions), oral expression (e.g., defining vocabulary, answering questions, and explaining answers), written expression (e.g., making outlines, writing in complete sentences, writing research reports), and social discourse (e.g., acknowledging others' comments, waiting for a turn, attending to nonverbal cues in conversation) that students are expected to do to demonstrate their knowledge and skill. These items are not exhaustive but represent the more typical approaches used to demonstrate students' knowledge and skill. Teachers can add items at any time, based on the unique and creative activities used in their classrooms.

Evaluating Needs

The third component of the LBCA requires the team to define areas that require support for the student with ASD to be able to meet the curriculum objectives. To determine these vocabulary, language, and social discourse needs, the SLP asks specific questions about the student's knowledge and his or her application of that knowledge (Prelock, 1997). For example, has the student with ASD mastered the prerequisite vocabulary? Are there potential linguistic confusions in the new vocabulary? If the student does not have the required prerequisite vocabulary, intervention planning should ensure that he or she could successfully access the science curriculum. Possible problems for the student with ASD in learning the new vocabulary might be related to semantic confusions (e.g., multiple-meaning words such as *conductor*), syntactic confusions (e.g., *series* could be a noun, as in "sports series," or an adjective, as in "series circuit"), or phonological confusions (e.g., *circuit, electric,* and *electricity* require different sound productions for the letter *c*). In addition, the team examines the language comprehension, oral and written expression, and social discourse demands of the classroom curriculum and identifies those components most likely to be problematic for the student with ASD (e.g., answering questions, writing explanations, acknowledging others' comments).

Making Modifications

The final component in the LBCA process provides the team with an opportunity to brainstorm changes in the way the curriculum is presented that are sensitive to the vocabulary, language, and social communication needs of the student with ASD. To facilitate prerequisite vocabulary knowledge, some preteaching might occur in therapy with the SLP, or a science dictionary with words, pictures, and definitions might be created to support the student's understanding of the terms. Priming (preparing or rehearsing prior to instruction; see Chapter 9), visual cues, and concrete experiences might be used to support the student's learning of new vocabulary. Comprehension might be supported through demonstration of how to complete a task or activity or by teaching the student to underline or number the steps in a direction. Teaching word-finding strategies and using open-ended sentences could facilitate the student's oral expression, while computer use and scripts for outlines and papers could support written expression. To address pragmatic and social discourse challenges in the classroom, the team might teach specific roles in small-group interactions, use social stories or video modeling (see Chapters 9 and 11) to remind the student of social conventions, and use comic strip conversations (see Chapter 11) to help the student recognize different perspectives in challenging interactions.

LBCA Advantages

LBCA has a number of advantages for implementing a collaborative model of service delivery in an integrated setting (Prelock, 1997). First, student performance objectives drive intervention planning in the content areas. Second, increased awareness of the classroom language demands prompt teachers to respond more specifically to the challenges students with ASD often face in academic settings. Third, knowing the language and social communication strengths and challenges of students with ASD prior to their learning in an academic area helps team members predict areas of difficulty and address them directly. Finally, brainstorming modifications increases the team's preparedness for addressing the students' needs within the classroom setting.

Summary

In this chapter, you have learned a great deal about intervention decision making to support the needs of children with ASD and their families. It is becoming clear to families and practitioners that gaps exist in what is known about intervention outcomes and choices made in educational planning for children with ASD. You have also been exposed to several strategies for visioning, planning, and problem solving around educational planning for children with ASD. The following paragraphs refer to the questions at the beginning of the chapter and highlight key points you should be familiar with as you embark on the challenges of selecting interventions that address the priority goals established for children with ASD in collaboration with their families and the practitioners who support them.

What philosophies drive current interventions and programming for children with ASD?

Researchers and clinicians are now faced with several tasks if the intervention and educational programming needs of children with ASD are to be met. Scientific rigor must be a priority in the design of treatment protocols. Practitioners must emphasize the need for implementing evidence-based practice. All those involved in intervention planning for children with ASD must recognize that gains in treatment programs are often related to cognitive strength and that no specific intervention program has been identified as more or less successful than another. The current charge for practitioners, researchers, and families is to collaborate in their efforts to make a difference in the valued outcomes for individual children with ASD.

How can families and practitioners effectively support the intervention needs of children with ASD?

This chapter has presented several strategies that can be used to support the development of a student's IEP and ensure that children with ASD and their families have an opportunity to dream about and plan for their futures. MAPS (Vandercook et al., 1989) is one planning strategy that promotes self-advocacy and responds to the individual's needs, preferences, and interests. It supports the IEP writing and transition process, considering all aspects of an individual's current situation and future goals. COACH (Giangreco et al., 1998) is another strategy for guiding the educational planning process, one that is driven by the family's identification of valued life outcomes. Both of these strategies require a collaborative effort among families and practitioners committed to a shared vision for the child with ASD.

What are some strategies for difficult decision making?

Children with ASD often require intensive, long-term support and extensive resources, along with a clear understanding of their individual needs. Unfortunately, practitioners often lack the training or support to implement effective programs for them. This chapter presented three strategies that can be used to facilitate decision making. First, teams can follow the six steps of a creative problem-solving process to address specific problems that arise in service delivery, managing a particular behavior, or addressing a systems challenge. Second, the VISTA process (Giangreco, 1996) provides a series of guidelines to help teams determine what related services are relevant and necessary. Last, the chapter described a way to mediate conflict that moves from a position to an interest-based approach, focusing on shared interests to define a new position.

What considerations should be given to nonstandard interventions for children with ASD?

Parents continue to use nonstandard therapies, in spite of reports of limited success. Practitioners have a responsibility to understand why parents may choose a particular controversial therapy and to inform them of potential risks, while recognizing their interest in the reported benefits. It is also important to know what information families need to have if they are to make informed decisions. A framework for evaluating controversial or nonstandard intervention practices has been presented that may be useful to teams and, in particular, to families as they consider a variety of intervention approaches that may or may not have evidence for their effectiveness.

How can curriculum analysis be incorporated into intervention planning for children with ASD across the core deficit areas?

LBCA leads teams to intervention planning that is responsive to a particular content or subject area for students with ASD in an integrated setting. This systematic process addresses the curriculum challenges children with ASD often face when placed in inclusionary settings without sufficient assessment of their language learning and social communication needs. LBCA requires collaboration among teachers and SLPs to identify vocabulary, language comprehension, oral and written expression, and social communication requirements in general education settings, as well as the potential challenges in each of these areas for the student with ASD. Once potential areas of challenge have been clearly identified for a particular curriculum area, team members can brainstorm modifications to facilitate the student's access to the general education curriculum.

Curriculum Analysis for Young Children with ASD and Individuals with ASD Who Exhibit Limited Verbal and Cognitive Skills

Team members: _____ Date: _____

_____ Child: _____

_____

STEP 1: Identify the child's or individual's strengths and needs in the following areas:

	Strengths	Needs
Communication (verbal and nonverbal)		
Social interaction (with adults and peers)		
Play (with objects and play partners)		
Sensory (across all modalities)		
Other		

STEP 2: Specify requirements or expectations in the curriculum or environment for the following areas:

Communication (verbal and nonverbal)

Social interaction (with adults and peers)

Play (with objects and play partners)

Sensory (across all modalities)

Other

(continues)

APPENDIX 8.A

STEP 3: Determine those requirements or expectations in the curriculum or environment that are likely to be problematic for the child or individual with ASD in the following areas:

Communication (verbal and nonverbal)

Social interaction (with adults and peers)

Play (with objects and play partners)

Sensory (across all modalities)

Other

STEP 4: Determine appropriate modifications in the curriculum or environment and identify intervention strategies most likely to support the child's or individual's needs in the following areas:

	Curricular or Environmental Modifications	Intervention Strategies
Communication (verbal and nonverbal)		
Social interaction (with adults and peers)		
Play (with objects and play partners)		
Sensory (across all modalities)		
Other		

APPENDIX 8.A

Language-Based Curriculum Analysis for Schoolchildren and Adolescents with ASD

Subject Area: _____ Grade: _____

Teacher: _____ SLP: _____

School: _____ Date: _____

Number of Students: _____ Textbook: _____

Supplementary Materials: _____

_____

_____

Part I: State Objectives

Curriculum objectives emphasized for the content or subject area:

Language learning objectives emphasized for the student with ASD:

Social communication objectives emphasized for the student with ASD:

Part II: Review Vocabulary, and Language and Social Communication Requirements

A. Vocabulary Review

   1. Identify prerequisite vocabulary for achieving stated objectives:

   2. List new vocabulary to be introduced:

B. Language and Social Communication Requirements Review

   1. Comprehension. Students must demonstrate comprehension by (please check all that apply):

☐ pointing or showing   ☐ following oral directions

☐ ordering or sequencing pictures/words/   ☐ role playing
    sentences/numbers

☐ demonstrating directions   ☐ circling/drawing/ringing

☐ manipulating objects   ☐ answering questions

☐ following written directions

☐ other (please specify): _____

(continues)

APPENDIX 8.B

2. Oral Expression. Student must express self orally by (please check all that apply):

☐ defining vocabulary   ☐ storytelling   ☐ reading

☐ reciting known information   ☐ talking in complete sentences   ☐ answering questions

☐ clarifying responses   ☐ explaining answers   ☐ asking questions

☐ other (please specify): _____

3. Written Expression. Students must express self in written form by (please check all that apply):

☐ tracing numbers/letters/words   ☐ copying numbers/letters/words

☐ writing numbers/letters   ☐ filling in sentences

☐ spelling words   ☐ writing complete sentences

☐ making outlines   ☐ writing book reports

☐ writing stories   ☐ writing explanations

☐ writing equations/formulas   ☐ writing research reports

☐ other (please specify): _____

4. Pragmatics and Social Discourse. Students must express self and respond to others in conversation and social interaction by (please check all that apply):

☐ initiating topics   ☐ asking questions

☐ shifting topics   ☐ responding to questions

☐ closing a conversation   ☐ taking turns in conversation

☐ attending to the speaker   ☐ commenting

☐ asking for information   ☐ waiting for a turn to respond

☐ using vocal inflection with meaning   ☐ attending to nonverbal cues in conversation

☐ acknowledging the comments or topics of others   ☐ recognizing communication breakdown

☐ following scripts/routines during school/classroom   ☐ recognizing appropriate physical positioning activities

☐ understanding another's intent or perspective

☐ other (please specify): _____

Part III: Evaluate Needs for Vocabulary, and for Language and Social Communication Requirements

A. Vocabulary Needs Evaluation

1. Does the student have the prerequisite vocabulary?

☐ Yes   ☐ No (If no, specify vocabulary student lacks)

2. What semantic confusions are likely with the vocabulary to be introduced (e.g., concrete vs. abstract; figurative language such as metaphors; synonyms)?

3. What syntactic confusions are likely with the new vocabulary (e.g., words that function as both nouns and verbs)?

(continues)

    APPENDIX 8.B

4. What phonological confusions are likely with the new vocabulary (e.g., homophones, multisyllabic words)?

B. Language and Social Communication Requirements Needs Evaluation

1. Comprehension. Which of the requirements identified in Part II B.1 are likely to be difficult for the student with ASD?

2. Oral Expression. Which of the requirements identified in Part II B.2 are likely to be difficult for the student with ASD?

3. Written Expression. Which of the requirements identified in Part II B.3 are likely to be difficult for the student with ASD?

4. Pragmatics and Social Discourse. Which of the requirements identified in Part II B.4 are likely to be difficult for the student with ASD?

Part IV: Make Modifications

A. Modifications To Meet Vocabulary Needs

1. Ways to establish prerequisite vocabulary:

2. Ways to introduce new vocabulary:

B. Modifications To Meet Language and Social Communication Needs

1. Ways to address comprehension:

2. Ways to address oral expression:

3. Ways to address written expression:

4. Ways to address pragmatics and social discourse:

Practice Opportunities

1. Identify a possible problem that requires some creativity in determining a solution for addressing a specific intervention need for a child with ASD. Apply the creative problem-solving process to come to consensus about a solution.

2. Select one nonstandard intervention practice and apply those questions raised in Figure 8.4 to the use of that practice with one child with ASD.

3. Initiate a language-based curriculum analysis for one student with ASD, using either Appendix 8.A or Appendix 8.B, depending on the cognitive and verbal ability of the student, to increase his or her access to material in one academic content area.

4. Review the 10 principles described for VISTA and determine how effectively and efficiently your team provides support services that are educationally relevant and necessary for one student with ASD.

Suggested Readings

Chorpita, B. F., Yim, L. M., Donkervoet, J. C., Arensdorf, A., Amundsen, M. J., McGee, C., et al. (2002). Toward large-scale implementation of empirically supported treatments for children: A review and observations by the Hawaii Empirical Basis to Services Task Force. *Clinical Psychology: Science & Practice, 9*(2), 165–190.

This article describes the findings of a state panel in pursuit of a method for examining the efficacy and effectiveness of treatments reported for a number of childhood disorders including autistic disorder. The authors provide a methodology for establishing efficacy criteria for empirically supported treatments, as well as a description of parameters to consider in determining effectiveness.

Heflin, L. J., & Simpson, R. L. (1998). Interventions for children and youth with autism: Prudent choices in a world of exaggerated claims and empty promises. Part I: Intervention and treatment option review. *Focus on Autism and Other Developmental Disabilities, 13,* 194–211.

This article presents an overview of the available treatments often considered in the program planning for children with autism spectrum disorders. The authors provide a framework within which to consider the treatments and the areas of deficit likely to be supported within each intervention approach.

Seroussi, K. (2000). *Unraveling the mystery of autism and pervasive developmental disorder: A mother's story of research and recovery* New York: Simon & Schuster.

This personal story highlights what a family learns through carefully researching the literature and attempting treatments that seemed to meet the needs of their son. It provides a detailed approach to removing dairy and gluten from the diet of a child with ASD, developing special recipes to meet a child's nutritional needs, and identifying the key players in autism research. The goal throughout the discussion is to reduce the symptoms so often reported for children with ASD. This story provides an important example of the application of complementary and alternative therapies that remain controversial in the treatment of autism spectrum disorders.

Resources

Cohen, S. (1998). *Targeting autism: What we know, don't know and can do to help young children with autism and related disorders.* Los Angeles: University of California Press.

Cumine, V., Leach, J., & Stevenson, G. (1998). *Asperger syndrome: A practical guide for teachers.* London: David Fulton.

Freeman, S., & Drake, L. (1996). *Teach me language: A language manual for children with autism, Asperger's syndrome and related developmental disorders.* Austin, TX: PRO-ED.

Fullerton, A., Stratton, J., Coyne, P., & Gray, C. (1996). *Higher functioning adolescents and young adults with autism: A teacher's guide.* Austin, TX: PRO-ED.

Gabriels, R., & Hill, D. E. (2002). *Autism—From research to individualized practice.* Philadelphia: Jessica Kingsley.

Handleman, J. S., & Harris, S. L. (2000). *Preschool education programs for children with autism* (2nd ed.). Austin, TX: PRO-ED.

Harris, S. L., & Handleman, J. S. (1994). *Preschool programs for children with autism.* Austin, TX: PRO-ED.

Harris, S. L., & Weiss, M. J. (1998). *Right from the start: Behavioral intervention for young children with autism—A guide for parents and professionals.* Bethesda, MD: Woodbine House.

Holmes, D. L. (1998). *Autism through the lifespan: The Eden Model.* Bethesda, MD: Woodbine House.

Lehman, J. F., & Klaw, R. (2001). *From goals to data and back again: Adding backbone to developmental intervention for children with autism.* Pittsburgh, PA: KidAccess.

Lovaas, O. I. (1981). *Teaching developmentally disabled children: The me book.* Austin, TX: PRO-ED.

Lovaas, O. I. (2002). *Teaching individuals with developmental delays: Basic intervention techniques.* Austin, TX: PRO-ED.

Maurice, C., Green, G., & Foxx, R. (2001). *Making a difference: Behavioral intervention for autism.* Austin, TX: PRO-ED.

Maurice, C., Green, G., & Luce, S. C. (1996). *Behavioral intervention for young children with autism: A manual for parents and professionals.* Austin, TX: PRO-ED.

McConnell, K., & Ryser, G. (2000). *Practical ideas that really work for students with autism spectrum disorders.* Austin, TX: PRO-ED.

Murray-Slutsky, C., & Paris, B. (2000). *Exploring the spectrum of autism and pervasive developmental disorders: Intervention strategies.* Austin, TX: PRO-ED.

Scheuermann, B., & Webber, J. (2002). *Autism: Teaching does make a difference.* Belmont, CA: Wadsworth/Thomson Learning.

Simons, J., & Oishi, S. (1987). *The hidden child: The Linwood method for reaching the autistic child.* Bethesda, MD: Woodbine House.

Simpson, R. L., & Myles, B. S. (1998). *Educating children and youth with autism: Strategies for effective practice.* Austin, TX: PRO-ED.

Stewart, K. (2002). *Helping a child with nonverbal learning disorder or Asperger's syndrome: A parent's guide.* Oakland, CA: New Harbinger.

Waterhouse, S. (1999). *A positive approach to autism.* Philadelphia: Jessica Kingsley.

Watson, L. R., Lord, C., Schaffer, B., & Schopler, E. (1989). *Teaching spontaneous communication to autistic and developmentally handicapped children.* Austin, TX: PRO-ED.

Glossary

Autocratic. Individual authority over decision making.

COACH. Choosing Outcomes and Accommodations for Children, a process for identifying priority outcomes for children with disabilities and guiding the individual education planning process.

Consensus building. Achieving general agreement.

Convergent thinking. Identifying the most rational result or solution when problem solving.

Democratic. Decision-making process in which each person votes and the majority rules.

Divergent thinking. Identifying a variety of possible solutions when problem solving.

Effectiveness. The ability of intervention to work in a real-world setting.

Efficacy. The ability of intervention to change behavior in a specific disorder area in a clinical research setting.

MAPS. Making Action Plans, a visioning process for future personal planning for individuals with disabilities.

VISTA. Vermont Interdependent Services Team Approach, a process for determining which support services are educationally relevant and necessary.

References

American Academy of Child & Adolescent Psychiatry. (1999). Practice parameters for the assessment and treatment of children with autism and other pervasive developmental disorders. *Journal of the American Academy of Child & Adolescent Psychiatry, 38*(Suppl.), 32S–54S.

American Academy of Pediatrics, Committee on Children with Disabilities. (2001). Counseling families who choose complementary and alternative medicine for their child with chronic illness or disability. *Pediatrics, 107*(3), 598–601.

Anderson, S. R., Avery, D. L., DiPietro, E. K., Edwards, G. L., & Christian, W. P. (1987). Intensive home-based early intervention with autistic children. *Education and Treatment of Children, 10*(4), 352–366.

Carr, S. H. (1989). Louisiana's criteria of eligibility for occupational therapy services in the public school system. *American Journal of Occupational Therapy, 43*(8), 503–508.

Chorpita, B. F., Yim, L. M., Donkervoet, J. C., Arensdorf, A., Amundsen, M. J., McGee, C., et al. (2002). Toward large-scale implementation of empirically supported treatments for children: A review and observations by the Hawaii Empirical Basis to Services Task Force. *Clinical Psychology: Science and Practice, 9*(2), 165–190.

Dawson, G., & Osterling, J. (1997). Early intervention in autism. In M. J. Guralnick (Ed.), *The effectiveness of early intervention* (pp. 307–326). Baltimore: Brookes.

Duchan, J. F., Calculator, S., Sonnenmeier, R., Diehl, S., & Cumley, C. D. (2001). A framework for managing controversial practices. *Language, Speech, and Hearing Services in Schools, 32*(3), 133–141.

Effgen, S. K. (1984). Determining school therapy caseloads based upon severity of needs for services. *Totline, 10*(2), 16–17.

Farley, S., Sarracino, T., & Howard, P. (1991). Development of a treatment rating in school systems: Service determination through objective measurement. *American Journal of Occupational Therapy, 45*(10), 898–906.

Fenske, E. C., Zalenski, S., Krantz, P. J., & McClannahan, L. E. (1985). Age at intervention and treatment outcome for autistic children in a comprehensive intervention program. *Analysis and Intervention in Developmental Disabilities, 5*, 49–58.

Forest, M., & Pearpoint, J. (1992a). MAPS: Action planning. In J. Pearpoint, M. Forest, & J. Snow (Eds.), *The inclusion papers: Strategies to make inclusion work* (pp. 52–56). Toronto, Ontario: Inclusion Press.

Forest, M., & Pearpoint, J. (1992b). Putting all kids on the MAP. *Educational Leadership, 50*(2), 26–31.

Freeman, B. J. (1997). Guidelines for evaluating intervention programs for children with autism. *Journal of Autism and Developmental Disorders, 27*, 641–650.

Frost, L., & Bondy, A. (1994). *The Picture Exchange Communication System training manual.* Cherry Hill, NJ: Pyramid Educational Consultants.

Furney, K. S. (1994). *Making dreams happen: How to facilitate the MAPS process. A manual using a personal futures planning model to develop IEP/transition plans.* Burlington: Vermont's Transition Systems Change Project.

Gerlach, E. K. (1993). *Autism treatment guide.* Eugene, OR: Four Leaf Press.

Giangreco, M. F. (1990). Making related service decisions for students with severe disabilities: Roles, criteria, and authority. *Journal of the Association for Persons with Severe Handicaps, 15*(1), 22–31.

Giangreco, M. F. (1996). *Vermont Interdependent Services Team Approach: A guide to coordinating educational support services.* Baltimore: Brookes.

Giangreco, M. F., Cloninger, C. J., Dennis, R. E., & Edelman, S. W. (1993). National expert validation of COACH: Congruence with exemplary practice and suggestions for improvement. *Journal of the Association for Persons with Severe Handicaps, 18*(2), 109–120.

Giangreco, M. F., Cloninger, C. J., Dennis, R. E., & Edelman, S. W. (1994). Problem-solving methods to facilitate inclusive education. In J. S. Thousand, R. A. Villa, & A. I. Nevin (Eds.), *Creativity and collaborative learning* (pp. 321–346). Baltimore: Brookes.

Giangreco, M. F., Cloninger, C. J., Dennis, R. E., & Edelman, S. W. (2000). Problem-solving methods to facilitate inclusive education. In R. A. Villa & J. S. Thousand (Eds.), *Restructuring for caring and effective education: Piecing the puzzle together* (pp. 293–327). Baltimore: Brookes.

Giangreco, M. F., Cloninger, C. J., & Iverson, V. S. (1998). *Choosing Outcomes and Accommodations for Children: A guide to educational planning for students with disabilities* (2nd ed.). Baltimore: Brookes.

Giangreco, M. F., Dennis, R. E., Edelman, S. W., & Cloninger, C. (1994). Dressing your IEPs for the general education climate: Analysis of IEP goals and objectives for students with multiple disabilities. *Remedial and Special Education, 15*(5), 288–296.

Giangreco, M., Edelman, S., & Dennis, R. (1991). Common professional practices that interfere with the integrated delivery of related services. *Remedial & Special Education, 12*, 16–24.

Giangreco, M. F., & Eichinger, J. (1991). Related services and the transdisciplinary approach: A parent/professional training module. In M. Anketell, E. J. Bailey, J. Houghton, A. O'Dea, B. Utley, & D. Wickham (Eds.), *A series of training modules for educating children and youth with dual sensory and multiple impairments* (pp. 1–66). Monmouth, OR: Teaching Research Publications.

Golden, G. S. (1984). Controversial therapies. *Pediatric Clinics of North America, 31,* 459–469.

Greenspan, S. I., & Wieder, S. (1998). *The child with special needs: Encouraging intellectual and emotional growth.* Reading, MA: Addison-Wesley.

Gresham, F. M., Beebe-Frankenberger, M. E., & MacMillan, D. L. (1999). A selective review of treatments for children with autism: Description and methodological considerations. *School Psychology Review, 28,* 559–575.

Hall, L., Robertson, W., & Turner, M. (1992). Clinical reasoning process for service provision in the public schools. *American Journal of Occupational Therapy, 46*(10), 927–936.

Heflin, L. J., & Simpson, R. L. (1998). Interventions for children and youth with autism: Prudent choices in a world of exaggerated claims and empty promises. Part I: Intervention and treatment option review. *Focus on Autism and Other Developmental Disabilities, 13,* 194–211.

Hurth, J., Shaw, E., Izeman, S. G., Whaley, K., & Rogers, S. J. (1999). Areas of agreement about effective practices among programs serving young children with autism spectrum disorders. *Infants and Young Children, 12*(2), 17–26.

Iovannone, R., Dunlap, G., Huber, H., & Kincaid, D. (2003). Effective educational practices for students with autism spectrum disorders. *Focus on Autism and Other Developmental Disabilities, 18*(3), 150–165.

Kasari, C. (2002). Assessing change in early intervention programs for children with autism. *Journal of Autism and Developmental Disorders, 32*(5), 447–462.

Kiresuk, T., & Sherman, R. (1968). Goal attainment scaling: A general method for evaluating comprehensive community mental health programs. *Community Mental Health Journal, 4,* 443–453.

Kiresuk, T., Smith, A., & Cardillo, J. (1994). *Goal attainment scaling: Application, theory, and measurement.* Hillsdale, NJ: Erlbaum.

Lahar, S. (1996, October). *Conflict resolution using a mediation framework.* Presentation for the Vermont Interdisciplinary Leadership Education for Health Professionals Program, Burlington.

Levy, S. E., & Hyman, S. L. (2002). Alternative/complementary approaches to treatment of children with autistic spectrum disorders. *Infants and Young Children, 14*(3), 33–42.

Lovaas, O. I. (1987). Behavioral treatment and normal educational and intellectual functioning in young autistic children. *Journal of Consulting and Clinical Psychology, 55,* 3–9.

Lovaas, O. I., & Smith, T. (1988). Intensive behavioral treatment for young autistic children. In B. B. Lahey & A. E. Kazdin (Eds.), *Advances in clinical child psychology* (pp. 285–324). New York: Plenum Press.

Masland, R. L. (1984). Unproven methods of treatment. *Pediatrics, 37,* 713–714.

McWilliam, R. A., & Bailey, D. B. (1994). Predictors of service-delivery models in center-based early intervention. *Exceptional Children, 61*(1), 56–71.

Mount, B., & Zwernik, K. (1988). *It's never too early, it's never too late: A booklet about personal futures planning.* St. Paul, MN: Metropolitan Council.

National Research Council. (2001). *Educating children with autism.* Committee on Educational Interventions for Children with Autism. Division of Behavioral and Social Sciences and Education. Washington, DC: National Academy Press.

Nickel, R. E. (1996). Controversial therapies for young children with developmental disabilities. *Infants and Young Children, 8*(4), 29–40.

O'Brien, J., Forest, M., Snow, J., & Hasbury, D. (1989). *Action for Inclusion.* Toronto, Ontario: Frontier College Press.

Oren, T., & Ogletree, B. T. (2000). Program evaluation in classrooms for students with autism: Student outcomes and program processes. *Focus on Autism and Other Developmental Disabilities, 15*(3), 170–175.

Osborn, A. (1953). *Applied imagination: Principles and procedures of creative thinking.* Buffalo, NY: Charles Scribner's Sons.

Osborn, A. (1993). *Applied imagination: Principles and procedures of creative thinking* (3rd rev. ed.). Buffalo, NY: Creative Education Foundation Press.

Parnes, S. J. (1981). *The magic of your mind.* Buffalo, NY: Creative Education Foundation in association with Bearly Limited.

Parnes, S. J. (1985). *A facilitating style of leadership.* Buffalo, NY: Bearly Limited in association with Creative Education Foundation.

Parnes, S. J. (1988). *Visionizing: State-of-the-art processes for encouraging innovative excellence.* East Aurora, NY: D.O.K.

Parnes, S. J. (1992). *Source book for creative problem solving: A fifty-year digest of proven innovation processes.* Buffalo, NY: Creative Education Foundation Press.

Parnes, S. J. (1997). *Optimize the magic of your mind.* Buffalo, NY: Creative Education Foundation Press.

Powers, M. D. (1992). Early intervention in children with autism. In D. E. Burkell (Eds.), *Autism: Identification, education and treatment* (pp. 225–252). Hillsdale, NJ: Erlbaum.

Prelock, P. A. (1997). Language-based curriculum analysis: A collaborative assessment and intervention process. *Journal of Children's Communication Development, 19*(1), 35–42.

Prelock, P. A. (2001, September). Understanding autism spectrum disorders and the roles of SLPs and audiologists in service delivery. *Asha Leader, 6*(17), 4–7.

Prelock, P. A. (2002, June). Interventions for children with autism spectrum disorders: Making decisions based on the evidence. *Perspectives on Language Learning and Education, 9*(2), 3–7.

Prelock, P. A., Miller, B. L., & Reed, N. L. (1993). *Working with the classroom curriculum: A guide for analysis and use in speech therapy.* Tucson, AZ: Communication Skill Builders.

Prizant, B. M., & Rubin, E. (1999). Contemporary issues in interventions for autism spectrum disorders: A commentary. *Journal of the Association for Persons with Severe Handicaps, 24,* 199–208.

Prizant, B. M., & Wetherby, A. M. (1998). Understanding the continuum of discrete-trial traditional behavioral to social–pragmatic developmental approaches in communication enhancement for young children with autism/PDD. *Seminars in Speech and Language, 19,* 329–352.

Rogers, S. J. (1996). Brief report: Early intervention in autism. *Journal of Autism and Developmental Disorders, 26*(2), 243–246.

Rogers, S. J. (1998). Empirically supported comprehensive treatments for young children with autism. *Journal of Clinical Child Psychology, 27,* 168–179.

Schneiderman, R. P., & Prelock, P. A. (2000). *Parents' perception of nonstandard therapies in the treatment of autism.* Unpublished manuscript, University of Vermont, Burlington.

Smith, T., Groen, A. D., & Wynn, J. W. (2000). Randomized trial of intensive early intervention for children with pervasive developmental disorders. *American Journal of Mental Retardation, 105,* 269–285.

Starrett, A. (1996). Nonstandard therapies in developmental disabilities. In A. J. Capute & P. J. Accardo (Eds.), *Developmental disabilities in infancy and childhood: Vol. 1. Neurodevelopmental diagnosis and treatment* (2nd ed., pp. 593–608). Baltimore: Brookes.

Strain, P. S., Kohler, F. W., & Goldstein, H. (1996). Learning experiences ... An alternative program: Peer mediated interventions for young children with autism. In E. Hibbs & P. Jensen (Eds.), *Psychosocial treatments for child and adolescent disorders: Empirically based strategies for clinical practice* (pp. 573–586). Washington, DC. American Psychological Association.

Strain, P. S., Wolery, M., & Izeman, S. (1998, Winter). Considerations for administrators in the design of service options for young children with autism and their families. *Young Exceptional Children,* pp. 8–16.

Thousand, J. S. (1995, October). *Creative problem solving.* Presentation for the Vermont Interdisciplinary Leadership Education for Health Professionals Program, Burlington.

Vandercook, T., York, J., & Forest, M. (1989). The McGill Action Planning System (MAPS): A strategy for building the vision. *Journal of the Association for Persons with Severe Handicaps, 14*(3), 205–215.

Watson, L. R., Lord, C., Schaffer, B., & Schopler, E. (1989). *Teaching spontaneous communication to autistic and developmentally handicapped children* (TEACCH). New York: Irvington.

Wehman, T. (1998). Family-centered early intervention services: Factors contributing to increased parent involvement and participation. *Focus on Autism and Other Developmental Disabilities, 13*(2), 80–86.

Wolery, M., & Garfinkle, A N. (2002). Measure in intervention research with young children who have autism. *Journal of Autism and Developmental Disorders, 32*(5), 463–478.

CHAPTER 9

Interventions To Support the Communication of Children with ASD

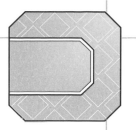

Patricia A. Prelock

QUESTIONS TO CONSIDER

In this chapter, you will be exposed to a variety of interventions that have been used to support the communications skills of children with autism spectrum disorders (ASD) who possess a range of verbal ability. The interventions selected for presentation here are those for which there is some evidence of effectiveness and that have been reported as valuable strategies for children with ASD. While reading this chapter, consider the following questions:

1. What strategies are effective for supporting the communication skills of children with ASD who have limited verbal capacity?

2. What interventions might be used to support the communication skills of verbal children with ASD?

3. How is unconventional verbal behavior addressed in children with ASD?

4. What strategies might be used to expand the conversational abilities of children with ASD?

5. How might the communication skills of children with ASD be supported in the home?

Introduction

As discussed in Chapter 8, there are several perspectives for conceptualizing the available interventions for children with ASD, including those emphasizing the development of relationships, those teaching a specific skill or skill set, and those with a physiological orientation (e.g., medication, nutrition supplements, sensory integration).

Much of what is presented in this chapter highlights teaching skills that will support the child's developing language and communication abilities. These teaching skills are developed through the relationships established between the child and the interventionist or primary caregivers and through adjustments within the environment and between communication partners.

Many of the strategies discussed in this chapter may also support social interaction, play, and building relationships with adults and peers, just as the social interaction and play strategies discussed in Chapters 10 and 11 will also support communication development.

Much of communication intervention for children with disabilities, including children with ASD, has its roots in behavioral principles (Brown & Murray, 2002). Most speech–language pathologists (SLPs) recognize the powerful role of applied behavior analysis (ABA) principles and strategies (e.g., prompting, modeling, differential reinforcement) in facilitating and generalizing communication skills across settings and partners.

To address the social–pragmatic deficits that are primary areas of concern for children with ASD, ABA has evolved and many components of the social–pragmatic developmental approaches have been integrated into traditional behavioral approaches to create more contemporary ABA interventions. Natural language paradigm interventions (described later in the chapter) and, specifically, pivotal response training (described in Chapter 11) are examples of such contemporary ABA interventions (Prizant & Wetherby, 1998).

This chapter provides a range of approaches to support the communication of children with ASD. It discusses interventions that facilitate the communication abilities of children with limited to no verbal skills (e.g., augmentative communication, visual supports, the Picture Exchange Communication System, joint action routines, minimal speech, proximal communication) and children who are verbal (e.g., natural language interventions, milieu teaching, time delay, modeling, video modeling, scripting). In addition, the chapter discusses ways to manage unconventional verbal behaviors and strategies for expanding the language and communication repertoires of children with ASD. All intervention approaches described are considered in light of their value to children with ASD, including the methods' perceived and documented effectiveness.

Interventions for Supporting Limited Verbal Skills

Communication is a vital skill for learning and establishing connections with others. Many children with ASD, however, have minimal or no verbal skills, which limits their opportunities for play, socialization, and learning. Some children may create less conventional ways to communicate their wants and needs, in some cases substituting undesirable behaviors to communicate intent. Therefore, it is critical that practitioners attend to the communication needs of children with ASD who have limited verbal capacity and find an approach that facilitates their ability to communicate intent. In the following sections, several strategies are offered using tools such as augmentative communication, visual supports, and the Picture Exchange Communication System (Frost & Bondy, 1994, 2002), as well as approaches such as minimal speech and proximal communication. Each of these is described with an emphasis on the goals that could be addressed using the intervention, the specific value the intervention has for children with ASD, and the available evidence regarding the effectiveness of the intervention. I selected these strategies because I have seen their use lead to positive outcomes for children and adolescents with ASD.

Augmentative Communication Strategies and Visual Supports

Visual supports are used for children with ASD to prompt joint attention, establish conversational referents, promote recall, enhance attention to and understanding of social messages, increase comprehension of language concepts, and facilitate communicative intent and social initiation (Johnston, Nelson, Evans, & Palazolo, 2003). Augmentative and alternative communication (AAC) techniques are often selected for children with ASD to either supplement or serve as a primary means for communication because of the verbal challenges many of them face. It is important to remember that the use of augmentative communication does not suggest that verbal communication is no longer a goal or focus for intervention. Rather, augmentative communication strategies are just added supports to ensure that children with limited verbal communication skills have immediate access to a meaningful system in which to communicate their intent.

AAC techniques fall under two primary types: aided and unaided. Aided communication requires the use of devices like communication books or voice output communication aids, whereas unaided communication requires no equipment external to the individual and instead incorporates signs, gestures, and pantomime (Mirenda, 2003). Total communication (involving speech and manual signing) is also a strategy frequently employed to support the functional communication of children with ASD.

Mirenda and Schuler (1988) describe several strategies used to elicit gestures and vocalizations in children with ASD who are nonverbal, such as establishing routines and then violating them, allowing the child some control over the interactions. One strategy the interventionist might consider for children with ASD who are essentially nonverbal and exhibit a unique gestural system is to create a gesture dictionary. Included in the dictionary would be a description (and possibly a photo) of each gesture the child uses, an explanation of what it means, and guidance on what should be done when the child uses that gesture. Gesture dictionaries facilitate communication with team members and identify areas of possible instruction for the child. Mirenda and Schuler stress that the implementation of AAC approaches does not mean that oral speech production is ignored. Rather, the goal becomes providing the child with a viable means of communicating. They discuss several factors that should be taken into account when implementing an AAC system. These include offering immediate feedback, providing community instruction, capitalizing on the child's visual–spatial strengths, recognizing any motor constraints, selecting an appropriate level of technology, considering the listener's requirements, and understanding the child's communication needs. Several AAC systems have been used for supporting the communication of children with ASD. System selection is individualized and based on the communication needs and desires of the children and their families. One method found to be particularly effective for this population is the Picture Exchange Communication System, described in greater detail following this general discussion of AAC intervention methods.

Intervention Goals. Three major goal areas might be the focus for supporting the communication skills of children with ASD using AAC and other visual supports: teaching the child to become a better communication partner; creating an environment that lessens the child's communication, social, and behavioral difficulties; and developing skills that support the child's participation (Hodgdon, 1995, 1999). In the first goal area, the team needs to capitalize on the visual strengths of children with ASD and increase the visibility of communication by using objects, pictures, written language, and other AAC devices to support communication, while limiting the "talk" of the verbal communication partner. In the second goal area, the team might develop visual tools that support giving information to a child with ASD. Often, children with ASD exhibit challenging behaviors because they do not understand what is expected of them. Goal setting needs to include ways to give information to and provide structure for children, so they can follow routines and increase their understanding of a communication. The third goal area requires the team to find ways to focus the attention of the child with ASD, to help the child manage transitions, to provide opportunities for the child to make choices, and to help the child accept changes to routines (Hodgdon, 1995, 1999). The strategic and effective use of visual supports and other AAC devices helps the educational team to address each of these goal areas.

Value for Children with ASD. Children with autism are particularly responsive to visual supports because of their strengths in visual–spatial organization and their ability to learn language "gestalts." Visual–spatial communication (e.g., drawings, pictures, written words) offers repeated opportunities for individuals with ASD to see the stimuli and matches the gestalt processing style often reported for this population (Beukelman & Mirenda, 1992). It helps to organize information for individuals with ASD, who typically take in or process information in a nonsequential way. Further, many individuals with ASD have an interest in or particular skill with literacy, and AAC strategies include a strong literacy component. Individuals with ASD also require predictability and respond to objects more easily than to people. AAC devices are predictable, have a structure that can be learned in steps, and do not require interaction. Unaided communication, such as manual signs, is most often used as one part of a total communication program for individuals with ASD. Signs and even gestures are less transient than verbal productions, and they can be easily prompted. Aided communication, including both low- and high-tech devices, is also responsive to the visual–spatial strengths of individuals with ASD. Electronic devices are usually considered when communication between individuals with ASD and their communication partners would benefit from printed or voice output (Beukelman & Mirenda, 1992).

Efficacy. Efficacy in the use of AAC is generally described within the context of communication behavior changes, as well as generalization (Schlosser & Braun, 1994). Two different kinds of generalization (stimulus and response) are usually emphasized in efficacy training. *Stimulus generalization* requires transferring what has been learned to stimulus conditions where training has not occurred. For example, a child with ASD could use an AAC system to communicate his desire to watch a specific video both at school (where training occurred) and at home (where training did not occur), or with the SLP (a trained communication partner) and then with a teacher (an untrained communication partner). *Response generalization,* on the other hand, describes behavior changes "that occur in one class of responses when another class of responses is manipulated through training" (Schlosser & Braun, 1994, p. 209). For example, a child with ASD may be taught how to request milk for lunch using his AAC system and then use that device to request a sandwich without specific training to do so. Although children can be taught to use AAC systems effectively, generalization has been somewhat elusive (Schlosser & Lee, 2000). Therefore, shifts in strategy use, such as greater emphasis on communication partner training, have attempted to elicit changes in communication behavior that are generalized and long lasting.

Johnston and colleagues (2003) investigated the use of visual symbols for gaining entrance into play situations, increasing spoken language, and decreasing problem behavior for three young boys (51–63 months of age) with ASD. Intervention consisted of four steps: establishing communication opportunities, modeling by a peer or teacher, guidance using a least-to-most prompting hierarchy, and natural consequences for correct responses. Results indicated a significant increase in the percentage of correct, unprompted use of visual symbols (0%–20% at baseline vs. 87%–100% during maintenance) for all three children. Verbal language increased and off-task behaviors decreased for each of the children. Visual supports have been effectively used to facilitate transitions for students with autism, decreasing the need for teacher commands and physical prompts (Dettmer, Simpson, Myles, & Ganz, 2000). Further, visual cues such as written prompts and pictorial cues have improved the social communication of children with ASD (Krantz & McClannahan, 1998). AAC systems have also been used effectively to establish social communication interactions between children with disabilities and their typical peers in the classroom setting (M. Carter & Maxwell, 1998).

Teachers in one study were taught interventions to replace prelinguistic behaviors with alternative forms of functional communication (Keen, Sigafoos, & Woodyatt, 2001). Four children with ASD (3–7 years of age) were the focus of the study. They exhibited communicative functions (e.g., greeting, requesting, choice making, turn taking) using prelinguistic means (looking, reaching) prior to the teacher intervention. Teachers were provided inservice training, consultation, and feedback on ways to acknowledge, encourage, and respond to replacement forms (e.g., waving, pointing, tapping the teacher's hand, signing) that the children used in place of their prelinguistic behaviors. Results indicated that the teacher training was effective in supporting the children's alternative forms of communication, which were more meaningful to their communication partners.

Following her review of the research on the use of AAC techniques, including total communication (i.e., signs, symbols, and oral communication), Mirenda (2003) suggested that a child with autism benefits from total communication if the child has adequate fine motor skills. Some results suggest aided AAC approaches are easier to learn and use than total communication, although the findings are mixed. The potential of aided systems to facilitate spoken language has been reported by several researchers (Charlop-Christy, Carpenter, Le, LeBlanc, & Kellet, 2002; Frost & Bondy, 2002; Schwartz, Garfinkle, & Bauer, 1998). Both aided approaches and manual signs have the potential to facilitate the development of spoken language in children with ASD. Mirenda states, however, that "decision making related to AAC interventions for individuals with autism is a complex and challenging endeavor" and that "the ultimate measure of a successful intervention is the extent to which it results in functional, unprompted communication across environments and people" (p. 212).

A review of interventions incorporating sign language for children with ASD indicates faster and greater vocabulary learning, particularly for those with limited communication abilities (Goldstein, 2002). Speech alone is not as helpful, especially for students with ASD who have weak verbal imitation skills. Overall, total communication appears to be an appropriate intervention approach to support the receptive and expressive vocabulary development in individuals with ASD.

Picture Exchange Communication System

The Picture Exchange Communication System (PECS) was originally developed at the Delaware Autism Institute for children with ASD and other sociocommunicative disorders who exhibited no functional communication (Frost & Bondy, 1994). The aim of PECS is to teach functional communication within a social context (e.g., requesting) using inherent nonsocial rewards (e.g., getting the item requested), because children with ASD are typically not socially motivated (Bondy & Frost, 1994, 2001). Bondy (2001) defines functional communication as that which "involves behavior (defined in form by the community) directed to another person who in turn provides related direct or social rewards" (p. 127). PECS was designed to circumvent problems associated with traditional language remediation programs such as sign language, picture pointing, and enhancing speech production. These problems include (a) prerequisite attending and motor and verbal imitation skills; (b) requiring pointing as a means to access the communication system despite frequent difficulties with finger pointing; (c) needing a listener to see the pointing or sign; (d) limited communication partners; and (e) initiation (Bondy, 2001; Bondy & Frost, 1994, 1998, 2001; Frost & Bondy, 1994).

Bondy and Frost (1998) believe that an effective communication training system should be grounded in some basic principles such as using effective reinforcers through the application of request situations rather than labeling situations; beginning with spontaneous communication; avoiding prompt dependency; and not requiring extensive training prior to the initiation of the system. The PECS system, created to espouse these principles, consists of six phases (Bondy & Frost, 1994):

> Phase I: Teaching the Physically Assisted Exchange
> Phase II: Expanding Spontaneity
> Phase III: Simultaneous Discrimination of Pictures
> Phase IV: Building Sentence Structure
> Phase V: Responding to "What do you want?"
> Phase VI: Commenting in Response to Questions

Prior to implementation, a reinforcer assessment is completed. This consists of determining whether items are *highly preferred, preferred,* or *nonpreferred* by probing a child's choices on five to eight items and requesting input from the child's parents (Frost & Bondy, 1994). Following the reinforcer assessment, Phase I is initiated. This phase requires two trainers, one to receive the child's picture and one to provide, at least initially, hand-over-hand assistance. The goal of Phase I is to have the child spontaneously pick up a picture of a highly preferred item from a communication board, reach toward the trainer, and release the picture into the trainer's open hand (Frost & Bondy, 1994). In Phase II, the distances between the child and the communication board and the child and the trainer are increased. The primary objective of Phase II is to expand spontaneity through increasing communicative persistence, so that the child goes to his communication board, removes a picture, finds the trainer, and releases the picture into the trainer's hand (Bondy & Frost, 1998; Frost & Bondy, 1994). Phase III teaches the child to discriminate between pictures. The child requests a desired item by going to his communication board, selecting the correct picture from an array, moving to the communication partner, and releasing the picture into the partner's hand (Frost & Bondy, 1994). Phase IV teaches the child to make a request using the carrier phrase "I want." In this phase, the child selects the desired picture and places it on a sentence strip next to a picture depicting "I want ____" to complete the phrase. The child then gives the entire sentence strip to the communication partner.

The child is taught to respond to the question "What do you want?" in Phase V, using delayed prompting. At the end of Phase V, the child is expected to spontaneously request desired items and answer the "What do you want?" question throughout his or her daily activities. The final phase, Phase VI, teaches communicative functions like labeling and naming by requiring the child to respond to different questions (e.g., "What do you see?" "What do you have?") using carrier phrases (e.g., "I see ____." I have ____."). The child is taught to respond to the communication partner's questions related to a particular referent, such as holding an egg and asking, "What do you see?" with the expectation that the child will select the correct picture for the item and create a sentence strip that says, "I see egg."

Beyond Phase VI, children are taught a variety of language concepts (e.g., location, verb concepts, attributes) using the basic PECS principles. Throughout the training phases of PECS, a variety of teaching procedures that fall into the category of ABA are used. These include fading of physical prompts with backward chaining, incidental training, shaping, discrete trials, delayed prompting, and discrimination training (Bondy & Frost, 1994). Functional spontaneous communication, however, remains the priority goal.

Frost and Bondy (2002) updated the PECS by broadening their view on the importance of establishing a foundation for communication training through systematic structuring of the learning environment. This environment includes school, home, and the community. They describe this "big picture" view as the Pyramid Approach to Education, emphasizing "functional activities and communication, powerful reinforcers and behavior intervention plans" (p. vii).

Intervention Goals. Frost and Bondy (2002) provide several examples of goals and objectives that follow their PECS training protocol. They emphasize the importance of establishing educational objectives that are functional and can be taught and used not only in the school setting but also in the home and community. They support the use of functional activities that can lead to independence, as well as real materials in real situations to teach all concepts. Goals drawn from PECS serve two broad communication functions: directive (e.g., requesting, demanding, commanding) and social (e.g., commenting, describing, naming) consequences. Goals are also established for the procedures associated with each phase of the training. Frost and Bondy (2002) provide a series of objectives used to address these goals, which include defining current levels of performance and the criteria for achieving each objective. Objectives are included for following directions, transitioning between activities, and following a visual schedule.

Value for Children with ASD. PECS was designed to address some of the problems associated with other, traditional, language training programs, including the need for prerequisite skills (e.g., motor imitation, visual attention), prompt dependency, and difficulty obtaining a listener's attention. Bondy and Frost (2001) state that "many traditional programs fail to consider the importance, from the child's perspective, of the potential outcomes of engaging in a communicative exchange" (p. 727). PECS does not require prerequisite skills prior to initiation of the training and is designed to facilitate spontaneous communication in the child, avoiding prompt dependency (Frost & Bondy, 1994, 2002). It was developed for children with autism who have little to no speech and are not reaping the social rewards of functional communication. Bondy and Frost (2001) have also found pictures to be beneficial in telling children with ASD what activity and reinforcers are coming next and how to wait for a desired action or object.

Webb (2000) describes PECS as a "catalyst" for the development of children's communicative competence, "as it facilitates their understanding of what communication is for and how to communicate effectively with others to get their needs met" (p. 38). It capitalizes on the visual strengths of children with ASD. Because it is difficult for them to shift attention and understand rapidly fading sequences of linguistic and social events, children with ASD benefit from the concrete nature of a visually based system (Quill, 1997). Further, the positive effects of learning a meaningful way to communicate wants and needs can decrease aggressive behavior (Frea, Arnold, & Vittimberga, 2001).

Efficacy. Bondy and Frost (1994) discuss the importance of speech acquisition as the preferred modality of communication and describe their observations that children using PECS will often develop speech without direct speech training. They present a case study of a 36-month-old boy with autism who is nonverbal and began using speech in conjunction with PECS during the 4th month of intervention at Phase VI. They also describe seven children with autism who displayed similar patterns of acquisition following PECS training. These children initially were nonverbal, exhibited rapid development of picture use through PECS, developed speech while using PECS, and eventually used speech as their sole means of communication. In addition, Bondy and Frost report on their observations of 66 preschool children who used PECS for at least a year. Twenty-five of the children used a combination of speech and pictures or a printed system, whereas 41 used speech alone. Bondy and Frost report that, of all the children who have been trained to use PECS in their program, 76% have developed speech and either use it as their sole communication modality or augment it with a picture-based system.

Kravitz, Kamps, Kemmerer, and Potucek (2002) examined the frequency of spontaneous language (verbal and pictorial) and the duration of social interactions with peers for one 6-year-old child with autism using PECS. Following baseline, at which the child was observed in play situations with a communication board and symbols available but not prompted, two treatment conditions were implemented. One consisted of Phases I, II, and III of PECS training and the other consisted of PECS training plus social intervention for the target child and her peers. Following PECS implementation, the child's total frequency of spontaneous language use (pictures and pictures plus verbalizations) increased across settings. Duration of social interaction with peers increased in only one setting (i.e., journal time). The authors hypothesized that limited peers in the home environment and lack of close proximity during free play may have contributed to little increase in social interaction in those settings. It was also impossible to determine whether changes following the introduction of PECS were attributable solely to PECS or were prompted by the additional social intervention. The use of PECS to facilitate increased social communication requires further research.

Liddle (2001) examined the use of the PECS with 20 children with autism and other learning difficulties and found that all but one of the children learned to use PECS to make a request, and 11 children learned to use sentence strips after 4 to 15 months of training. In addition, 9 of the 20 children had increased their verbalizations following the introduction of PECS, 7 of them using words.

Schwartz and colleagues (1998) describe two studies examining the efficacy of PECS use for children with severe disabilities. In the first experiment, they examined the rate of acquisition of functional communication using PECS for 31 children (3–6 years of age), 16 of whom had been diagnosed with autism or pervasive developmental disorder (PDD) and had limited communication skills. Training was conducted in the children's classrooms. Results indicated that all 31 children learned to communicate with various partners within an average of 14 months (a range of 3–28 months). In the second experiment, Schwartz and colleagues examined the effects of PECS training on the overall communication abilities of 18 of the children who participated in the first experiment. Training was again conducted in the children's classrooms, and data were collected at free time and snack time. Language samples were gathered to determine the communicative forms (e.g., gestures, vocalizations, manual signs, PECS exchanges, verbal productions) and functions (e.g., requests, comments, protests, responses) the children used. Results indicated that 8 of the 18 children were subsequently identified as talkers (with five or more words spoken in free time), and 10 were identified as nontalkers (with fewer than five words spoken in free time). It was also found that training in one communicative function (e.g., requesting) led to increased use of other functions (e.g., commenting, responding) that were not specifically trained. Overall, the children demonstrated increased communicative functions across settings, regardless of their verbal output. The authors hypothesized that focusing on requesting and persistence may influence acquisition of other communicative functions and support generalization.

Webb (2000) describes the use of PECS with six children (55–70 months), five of whom were diagnosed with autism and exhibited varying expressive language abilities, ranging from no speech to an ability to use sign and label. Before introducing PECS, Webb used a combination of strategies to support the communication of the children, including speech, signing, music, photographs, pictures, symbols, objects, and words. There were no significant gains, and the children were prompt dependent. The children learned to use the system (through Phase VI) within 6 months, using between 112 and 160 pictures. In addition, all six children exhibited gains in spoken language, producing between 36 and 145 words, both with and without use of the pictures. Webb also reports success in the use of PECS to facilitate social interaction, stating that the children increased their eye contact and use of each other's names. She states that "the deficits in joint attention and social affect which often characterize children with an ASD and which were present before PECS, have been lessened and replaced by pointing out and commenting on events [and] seeking out a communicative partner" (p. 38). Other researchers also report the rapid acquisition of the PECS system and development of speech in conjunction with PECS (Bondy & Frost, 1994, 1998; Charlop-Christy et al., 2002; Liddle, 2001; Schwartz et al., 1998).

Simon, Whitehair, and Toll (1996) report the successful implementation of PECS with a 14-year-old boy with autism who had been using facilitated communication (FC) as a primary mode of communication. The researchers assessed the efficacy of FC compared to PECS. The student was required to remove an object from a paper bag and then communicate what the object was to a naive partner in another room. Results indicated that the student's preferred communication modality was PECS and that he was 90% to 100% accurate in his message delivery.

Bondy and Frost (1993) describe the process of training educated staff to use PECS in Lima, Peru. The training included both individual support and all-day workshops. Follow-up data a year after staff training indicated that staff members were successful in introducing PECS to their students, "resulting in a higher rate of communicative initiations by these students" (p. 127). Thus, there is strong support for the use of PECS in supporting the communication skills of children with ASD.

Joint Action Routines

Joint action routines involve two or more individuals engaged in an activity that occurs within a familiar or well-established home (e.g., breakfast) or school (e.g., morning circle) routine. The routine has a logical, predictable sequence or structure for taking turns (Snyder-McLean, Solomonson,

McLean, & Sack, 1984). For example, at home, a child with ASD could help his mom set the table for breakfast. She would give him some items he needs and hold others back for him to request. She might ask him such questions as who will be eating or how many plates or cups or spoons he needs. In a routine at school, the child might be engaged in throwing and catching a ball with a peer, initiating the routine with a predictable movement or gesture, and responding to the movement or gesture of a peer.

The theme or purpose of a joint action routine is meaningful and recognizable to the participants. Three general types of routines may be designed for intervention: routines with a specified product or outcome (e.g., making cookies, setting the table); routines developed around a story line or theme (e.g., shopping at a department store); and routines involving cooperative turn taking (e.g., peek-a-boo, playing a game). The use of joint action routines requires some manipulation of the environment to increase a child's social and communicative responses. The nature of the activity and the materials used should set up opportunities for mutual attention and participation. At least two definable and predictable roles should be assigned (e.g., speaker and listener or doctor and patient) with opportunities for the child with ASD to learn and practice multiple roles. The sequence of steps in the activity should be predictable, based on the theme or outcome of the routine, and children should be able to anticipate when to take their turns (Wetherby, 1992). Repetition is an important aspect of the routine, allowing children to take many turns to gain an understanding of their role. Variation—violating a step or interrupting a routine—provides opportunities for novel language learning and interaction.

Intervention Goals. Intervention should focus on establishing joint attention and interaction among communication partners. It should also consider goals to support a child's negotiation skills with a communication partner. Joint action routines are ideal for implementing goals around spontaneous requesting, protesting, and commenting. They can also be used to facilitate a child's particular language forms and functions, as well as the development of turn taking, choice making, and discourse skills (Duchan & Weitzner-Lin, 1987).

Value for Children with ASD. The use of joint action routines is particularly valuable for children with ASD because the routines can be designed around the interests and motivating activities of the child. Joint action routines also require establishing joint attention, which is a critical need of children with ASD. Because the routines have clear beginnings and endings with a predictable structure, children with ASD are supported in their need to know what is going to happen, how it is going to happen, and what they are expected to do. Further, joint action routines support the child in creating some basic event knowledge that will facilitate language learning across settings and communication partners. Joint action routines provide a "context for learning how to communicate meaningfully" (Prizant, Wetherby, & Rydell, 2000, p. 203).

Efficacy. Joint action routines can be used to enhance the language and desired social responses of children with disabilities, including those with ASD. These routines are often used to stimulate language in the classroom setting (Snyder-McLean et al., 1984). The logical, predictable sequence of the routines and the focus on establishing joint attention have a strong foundation in the early literature on supporting language development in children with significant disabilities (McLean & Snyder-McLean, 1978).

Minimal Speech and Proximal Communication

Potter and Whittaker (2001) developed the minimal speech and proximal communication approach for children with minimal verbal output. This approach is founded on some basic beliefs: first, that children with limited verbal communication can and do communicate; second, that children need to be taught to communicate spontaneously for a variety of purposes in everyday routines; third, that environmental and social factors affect communication, including how adults talk and interact, the number and type of communication opportunities available, what kind of prompting occurs, the systems used to teach communication, and the communicator's motivation; and fourth, that communication is enhanced when integrated strategies are used. Potter and Whittaker proposed a "capacity model" to facilitate the social and communication potential of children by enabling the environment to take full advantage of the strengths they possess.

The minimal speech approach requires the interventionist to use conceptually simple speech (one to three words) in combination with nonverbal ways of interacting. Potter and Whittaker (2001) describe children with ASD as having difficulty comprehending and suggest that distress and anxiety set in when there is too much speech during adult attempts at interaction. Therefore, an initial goal for the interventionist is to interact with the child with as little speech as possible. For example, if an adult is prompting a child to get ready to go out for recess, the typical verbal prompt might sound something like, "Come on, George, let's go out. Get your coat on. It's time to go out." In a minimal speech approach, the adult might prompt the child by approaching George, gaining his attention, showing him a picture of the playground, and saying, "Coat" slowly and with emphasis.

As part of the minimal speech approach, proximal communication is emphasized to "enable" children's communication. The goal is to engage children with ASD "in playful and pleasurable nonverbal interaction to develop their early social communication skills" (Potter & Whittaker, 2001, p. 62). This goal is based on the recognition that children with ASD bring strengths to their communication experience. For example, they might reach for or look at adults after being tickled and move into close proximity following a pleasurable rough-and-tumble play activity.

There are several key elements to proximal communication. First, the interventionist expects to communicate intentionally by following the child's lead and interests. Next, the interventionist minimizes his or her use of speech during a session. Minimizing speech is followed by incorporating physically engaging and motivating activities such as tickling and rough-and-tumble play appropriate to the child's physical and developmental level into the intervention. The interventionist then alternates an "active burst phase" with a "passive pause phase" during interaction attempts. To illustrate, the following example is provided:

Active burst phase:
Interventionist exaggerates facial expressions, vocalizations, and physical responses during the tickling event.

Passive pause phase:
Interventionist remains quiet, watches the child, and responds to the child's attempt to communicate.

Potter and Whittaker suggest that it is important to have a notable contrast between the active and passive phases. In addition, the interventionist must decide what targeted or key communication responses are expected of the child. In the previous example, is the child expected to look at, reach for, or vocalize to the interventionist? When the child demonstrates the targeted response, the active burst phase is resumed. The child's responses are shaped by gradually increasing the pause phase. Another element of the proximal communication approach requires the interventionist to adopt a position lower than the child's eye level. The interventionist also imitates the child's vocalization and uses delayed echoing of the child's productions to elicit imitation. Another element requires concentrating on establishing interpersonal interactions with the child, possibly using large equipment on which active play can take place. Finally, the interventionist is encouraged to imitate the child's movements or actions to vary the interaction. Although the minimal speech and proximal communication approach may be difficult to sustain for a typical intervention session, I believe it is valuable as a warm-up strategy for the first 5 or 10 minutes of an intervention experience with a child with ASD who exhibits minimal verbal output and connection with others.

Intervention Goals. Several skills are emphasized in the minimal speech and proximal communication approach that can serve as intervention goals for the child with ASD who is essentially nonverbal or produces limited speech. These include intentionality, social timing, spontaneous communication, turn taking, social anticipation, communicative use of eye gaze, vocalizations and gestures, reciprocity, and joint attention. Each of these communication skills is an appropriate intervention goal for children with ASD who exhibit minimal verbal and communicative output.

Value for Children with ASD. The minimal speech and proximal communication approach to facilitating communication in children with ASD who exhibit minimal to no verbal communication recognizes the strengths of this population and builds on those strengths through active engagement and no immediate expectation for verbal communication. Potter and Whittaker's (2001) approach to intervention emphasizes a meaningful context, uses a structured and consistent sequence of support, breaks down tasks into steps that can be managed by both the child and the interventionist, and provides social support for the child's communication attempts. It also incorporates flexibility into the intervention, so that the interventionist's response to a child's communication focuses on the child's capacity. Further, consideration is given to the role of the environment in enabling or hindering communication, so that the responsibility for successful spontaneous communication is not just the child's problem.

Efficacy. In their work with 18 children with ASD (with a mean age of 4½ years), Potter and Whittaker (2001) found that the minimal speech and proximal communication approach led to more spontaneous communication and increased social responsiveness. In a videotaped review of a range of daily school activities over a 2- to 4-month period, they recorded the children's spontaneous communication, interviewed the children's teachers and speech–language pathologists, reviewed school reports, and periodically used assessment tools. Spontaneous communication was defined as communication that was intentional and not prompted. They employed Wetherby and Prizant's (1989) criteria for determining intentionality (i.e., alternating eye gaze between the goal and the listener, persistent signaling or changing the signal until the goal is achieved, waiting for a response, and showing satisfaction or dissatisfaction depending on whether the goal is met). Their results indicated that the children's communication rates and quality were independent of age and severity of autism and that spontaneous communication was related to creating a communication environment. Further, a majority of the children's communications served as requests or protests, and communications were most often directed toward the adults. Children used both physical manipulation and reenactment of a desired outcome to convey their intents, as well as some pointing and multipointing (pointing more than once following a sequence in which they attempted to communicate their message) (Potter & Whittaker, 1997). Spontaneous communication was also greatest during individual intervention sessions with the child, although small group sessions (with three to four children) in which the interventionist employed a variety of strategies to enable communication showed high rates of spontaneity.

Whittaker and Reynolds (2000) used aspects of the proximal communication approach in a study in which hand signaling was taught to four boys with ASD and significant learning challenges (with a mean age of 5 years 9 months). They explored the frequency of the boys' intentional hand signaling during proximal communication intervention with active burst and passive pause phases and found that all four boys increased their unprompted intentional hand signaling with the adult interventionist.

Interventions for Supporting Verbal Skills

As children with ASD who exhibit limited oral communication gain important skills through visual supports and alternative means, some may begin to develop oral communication. Further, some children with ASD can communicate verbally but require additional support and opportunities to develop their oral communication skills across communicative partners and settings. In the sections that follow, the reader will learn about natural language paradigm intervention and milieu language teaching, as well as specific strategies such as time delay, modeling, video modeling, and scripting, all of which are frequently used to enhance the effectiveness with which children with ASD can learn and use their communication skills.

Natural Language Paradigm Intervention and Milieu Teaching

Natural language paradigm intervention, also called natural language intervention, normalized teaching, and natural environment training, falls into the category of contemporary ABA approaches. It was designed to integrate aspects of more discrete trial programs (e.g., Lovaas, 1981) with naturalistic programs, such as pivotal response training (L. K. Koegel, Koegel, & Carter, 1998), and milieu or incidental teaching (Hart & Risley, 1982; Kaiser, Alpert, & Warren, 1987). Although discrete trial language programs appear to support quick acquisition of target behaviors, they are less effective in seeing the gains generalized. Natural language intervention promotes generalization, although learning targets may be acquired at a slower pace, because it is implemented in nonclinical settings. The implementation of natural language intervention also requires a clear plan; its success will be limited if practitioners employ this method with the expectation that children with ASD will learn incidentally without an emphasis on the particular goals that address their core areas of deficit.

Delprato (2001) suggests that when natural language intervention is properly conducted, the casual observer should not be able to tell that anything special is going on. Child-preferred materials are used, but systematic teaching, using behavioral principles such as stimulus control, natural consequences, and motivation, is incorporated into the natural environment to address the targeted language goals.

Natural language intervention also considers the context (e.g., environment, communication partners) and structure (e.g., one-to-one support, small group, large group) in which instruction takes place for increasing verbal behavior (Harris & Delmolino, 2002; Sundberg & Partington, 1998). Learning occurs in the context of naturally occurring interactions that are responsive to a child's interest, motivation, and choice. A variety of child-preferred activities are provided because children seem to learn more quickly if activities are selected and varied following their interests. Tasks the child has already mastered are interspersed with novel activities because this typically leads to improved responding, increased affect, increased happiness, and higher interest (R. L. Koegel, O'Dell, & Koegel, 1987).

To teach language, the interventionist incorporates multiple naturally occurring examples or targets into the natural environment. Language targets are explicitly prompted following a brief delay to give the child an opportunity to respond without a verbal prompt. Direct, natural consequences are used. For example, if the target verbal behavior is to have the child make a request, the interventionist might place a jar with an item of interest inside to facilitate the request. In the natural language paradigm, children are also reinforced for their communication attempts, as this increases their responsiveness and positive affect (R. L. Koegel et al., 1987). Language is taught within natural interactions, such as turn taking (the exchange that occurs between a listener and a speaker) and shared control of the conversation (sharing the topic of conversation and the types of communicative acts that occur), and through choosing the objects and activities that are used in play or learning tasks.

Milieu language teaching is an intervention approach that incorporates the principles of the natural language paradigm and specifies key teaching strategies to be used in the natural environment when facilitating language. Four specific techniques are usually incorporated into this natural language paradigm approach: child-directed modeling, mand modeling, time delay, and incidental teaching (Kaiser et al., 1987). Although two of these techniques, child-directed modeling and time delay, are described in greater detail in subsequent sections of the chapter, because of their broad application across intervention approaches for supporting the language of children with ASD, all four are discussed here as they relate to milieu teaching to facilitate functional communication in natural settings.

Child-directed modeling is a fundamental component of the milieu teaching approach. It involves focusing on a child's interest to establish joint attention, much like the earlier interventions discussed for children with limited verbal skills. It then requires the interventionist to provide a verbal model related to the child's interest (Kaiser et al., 1987). For example, the child with ASD might like to listen to tapes on a tape recorder, so the interventionist models the following to facilitate the child's request: "Say, 'Push the button.'" If the child responds by saying, "Push the button," that response receives immediate praise (e.g., "That was nice asking, Stephen") and is then expanded (e.g., "I'll push the button on the tape recorder") while the request is satisfied. If the child provides an incorrect response (e.g., "My tape") or a partial response (e.g., "Button"), a corrective model is provided (e.g., "Push the button"). If the child responds correctly then, the interventionist praises him or her, provides an expanded language model, and satisfies the request. If the child responds incorrectly to the corrective model (e.g., "Push"), corrective feedback is provided (e.g., "You want me to push the button"), and then the request is satisfied.

Mand-model procedures also focus on the child's interest and establish joint attention prior to presenting a verbal mand (or verbal instruction or request) (Kaiser et al., 1987). They support the generalization of language skills from more traditional individual teaching sessions to the classroom setting. For example, if a child approaches an object of interest (e.g., a train), the teacher might mand (or verbally instruct) the child to describe the object (e.g., "Tell me what you see"). The teacher praises a correct response and provides the object, produces a model to imitate if the child provides an incorrect response, or prompts the child to produce a more complex response (e.g., "Tell me what you see in a whole sentence"). Mand-model instruction is planned and initiated by the adult but incorporates the child's interest (Kaiser et al., 1987).

Time delay procedures are incorporated into a child's language training when the child is likely to require some level of assistance or desires specific materials, but it involves establishing stimuli other than verbal models and mands that might be used to cue a child's response. Providing pauses that increase in duration before providing a verbal model or cue characterizes the time delay approach. The delay in assistance supports the child's ability to learn what environmental cues (e.g., presence of an object or communication partner, location of an activity) can be used to facilitate an appropriate response. For example, a bus driver might wait to open the door of the school bus when arriving at a child's house until the child requests it (e.g., "Open the door, please").

Incidental teaching is typically the fourth procedure of milieu teaching. Its focus is to build more elaborate language use to facilitate conversation around a variety of topics (Kaiser et al., 1987). The interventionist arranges the environment to encourage the child's requests for interesting materials or help engaging in a desired activity. This is often accomplished by placing highly motivating or reinforcing items in the child's view but out of reach. Usually, a child will engage an adult either verbally or nonverbally to obtain the desired item or activity. The adult then responds by modeling, manding, or delaying to obtain a more complex or elaborated verbal production (Kaiser et al., 1987). The child is provided with the desired reinforcing item when an appropriate response is produced; the adult also repeats and expands on the child's response, providing a complex language model. This process is highlighted in the following example:

STEPHEN: [Pointing to a red train among three others that are blue, green, and yellow] Train. (*initiation*)

TEACHER: Tell me which one you want. (*mand*)

STEPHEN: Red one. (*correct response*)

TEACHER: Here you are, Stephen. You like the red train. I am glad you told me. Do you think Billy will like this blue train? (*natural consequence, expansion*)

STEPHEN: [Noding his head] He likes blue.

Arranging the environment is a critical component in implementing a milieu language teaching program so that child requests can be set up and specific teaching procedures applied (Kaiser et al., 1987). Interventionists must be familiar with basic behavioral techniques, including shaping, prompting, fading, and differential reinforcement, and be able to identify what a child is attending to, follow the child's lead, establish joint attention, and use the desired or motivating object or activity as the focus for teaching. Milieu teaching also requires data collection and evaluation to determine effectiveness. It can be used as a primary language intervention approach or in combination with other individual teaching approaches to support language learning for the child with ASD.

Intervention Goals. Educational teams will want to create opportunities systematically throughout the day in which children with ASD learn to make choices, take turns, and respond to language models. Goals around choice making should ensure that the choices are valid and reasonable; children are given sufficient information to make wise choices; choices are consistently and immediately responded to; and the consequences are natural, safe, and logical (McCormick, Jolivette, & Ridgley, 2003). Goals for turn taking should involve teaching the child to take turns with an adult or peer, talking about and playing with a preferred toy, or interacting within a motivating instructional activity. Goals for language within a natural language paradigm intervention should consider ways to model language and facilitate imitation across preferred items or activities that expand the child's understanding and use of language. For example, if a child's preferred play item is a train, the practitioner might model, "The train goes fast" and then "The train goes slow" and even expand it to "The train goes under the bridge." Other exemplars might be introduced to model similar actions, such as "The car goes fast" or "The big bus goes under the bridge."

Goals for using milieu language teaching involve teaching functional communication. Practitioners should select language forms that are functional for a particular child in a frequently occurring situation. They also need to consider teaching a linguistic form to address an important function like greeting or requesting. These functional language forms are usually determined by interviewing caregivers and other adults important in the child's life, as well as by observing the child in a variety of settings and noting the kinds of interactions the child is expected to participate in (e.g., greeting the teacher upon arrival to school, asking to go to the bathroom, requesting instructional materials). Goals using child-directed modeling might include increasing imitation abilities, developing a basic vocabulary, establishing turn taking, and engaging in conversation (Kaiser et al., 1987). Generally, the interventionist is attempting to increase the child's intelligibility and to teach more complex language forms. In the mand-model teaching procedures, goals might include establishing joint attention (such as topic selection) to support increased verbalization, teach turn taking, and train responding to verbal requests or instructions across a variety of cues (Kaiser et al., 1987). Mand-model teaching procedures are often used to teach more complex or higher-level conversational skills. Time delay is often used to teach initiation, whereas incidental teaching is used to train complex language forms.

Value for Children with ASD. More normalized language interventions, such as those in the natural language paradigm that incorporate incidental learning, natural reinforcers, choice making, and pivotal responses, are reported as significantly more effective than discrete trial training for teaching language to young children with ASD (see Delprato, 2001, for a review). The child's initiations through attending to a stimulus or demonstrating a particular want guide the teaching episodes. Instruction is carried out in a variety of places using multiple stimuli within a play setting. This approach to intervention allows the child to make choices that positively affect his or her social and behavioral responses across contexts (McCormick et al., 2003). Choice making, in particular, creates opportunities for children to use their communication, social, cognitive, and motor abilities and increases opportunities for independence. It offers children the opportunity to engage in decision making and involves engagement around preferred learning activities and materials (McCormick et al., 2003).

There are several advantages to using milieu teaching for children with ASD. Many of the language skills learned using incidental teaching strategies are easily generalized. Milieu teaching focuses on children's selected interests and follows their lead. Instruction can be delivered by a variety of potential communication partners, including parents, teachers, and peers. It can also be implemented across settings (e.g., home, school, and community).

Efficacy. Children with ASD are reported to increase their language skills and decrease their inappropriate behavior using the natural language teaching paradigm (Delprato, 2001; R. L. Koegel, Koegel, & Surrant, 1992; Sundberg & Partington, 1998). Research also suggests that capitalizing on teaching opportunities when the child has sustained attention to a target or intentionally communicates about a target leads to greater noun acquisition than when the child's attention is intrusively gained (Yoder, Kaiser, Alpert, & Fischer, 1993). R. L. Koegel et al. (1987) used a natural language teaching paradigm and incorporated pivotal response training (see Chapter 11) to teach imitative responses in two nonverbal children with ASD (4 and 5 years of age). They found that children with ASD increased both their imitative and their spontaneous utterances and generalized those responses to adults and settings that were not the focus of training. R. L. Koegel, O'Dell, and Dunlap (1988) successfully used reinforced attempts to facilitate the speech production and affective behavior of nonverbal children with ASD. Koegel and his colleagues also used the natural language paradigm to teach speech intelligibility to five children with ASD (R. L. Koegel, Camarata, Koegel, Ben-Tall, & Smith, 1998). They found that incorporating a systematic approach to instruction using motivating targets in a naturalistic context aided children's improved speech production. C. M. Carter (2001) investigated the effects of making choices during language intervention on the social play, pragmatic behaviors, language development, and disruptive behaviors of three children with ASD (5–7 years of age). In a choice and no-choice condition within natural language intervention using play, Carter found that providing opportunities for making choices in play during language intervention led to an increase in social play and pragmatic behaviors and a decrease in disruptive behaviors.

R. L. Koegel and colleagues (1998) used child-preferred activities and naturally occurring reinforcers to facilitate question asking in three children with ASD (3–5 years of age). They found that the children learned question use related to items they could not label previously and generalized their learning to ask about novel items that carried over into their home setting. Jahr (2001) investigated the ability of five children with ASD to answer questions using multiple exemplars. Results indicated that children with ASD were able to respond to novel questions in complete sentences following the use of multiple exemplars.

Speech–language pathologists have incorporated milieu teaching procedures, including time-delay and mand-model procedures, in their training of teachers to support the communication of eight children with ASD and other severe disabilities (Dyer, Williams, & Luce, 1991). Dyer and her colleagues provide descriptive data supporting the use of this approach to teacher training to make positive communication gains for children within the classroom setting.

McGee, Krantz, and McClannahan (1985) used incidental teaching to facilitate the use of prepositions in three children with ASD (6, 8, and 11 years of age). They found rates and levels of acquisition of prepositions similar to those of a more discrete trial training approach, but generalized preposition use favored the incidental teaching procedure. The children used prepositions in an untrained setting and generalized their use to untrained positions. McGee, Almeida, Sulzer-Azaroff, and Feldman (1992) also used incidental teaching to facilitate reciprocal peer interactions in three boys with ASD and three typical peers. They provided peer tutor training in an incidental teaching interaction (e.g., waiting for a child with ASD to initiate a request for a toy, asking the child to label the toy, giving the child the toy when it was labeled, and praising the child). They found that peer incidental teaching was effective in promoting peer interactions and that the interactions were maintained when teacher support was faded.

Delprato (2001) reviewed eight studies that evaluated the effectiveness of normalized teaching. He found that all eight supported the effectiveness of natural language teaching procedures when analyzing language criterion responses. Natural language teaching was found to be more effective in addressing language goals than the discrete trial (analog) format of intervention.

Time Delay

Time delay involves inserting a delay between the presentation of a target language response (e.g., a response to a question that was asked or a comment about an observed action) and a prompted response (e.g., the response the child expects). Time delay can be used in two ways: graduated or constant. *Graduated time delay* provides no extra time between modeling a target response and expecting the child to imitate that response at first but gradually increases the time between the model and the targeted response. For example, if the interventionist is teaching a child with autism to say "Hi" as a greeting when they first see each other in the classroom in the morning, the interventionist would establish eye contact with the child and then immediately provide a model (e.g., say, "Hi") for the child to imitate (Charlop-Christy & Kelso, 1997). Once the child consistently imitates the model, the interventionist gradually increases the time between establishing eye contact and modeling "Hi" from 2 seconds to 4, 6, 8, and then 10 seconds. Ten seconds is considered an appropriate interval within which to expect a response (Charlop-Christy & Kelso, 1997). The child is expected to reliably use the greeting after a 2-second delay before moving to 4 seconds and so on. *Constant time delay* might also be incorporated into the intervention plan for a child with ASD. In this situation, the interventionist starts with a 10-second time delay before modeling and prompting the child's expected response. With experience using constant time delay, a child with ASD will learn to respond.

When deciding which approach to take in using time delay, Charlop-Christy and Kelso (1997) recommend using graduated time delay for children with little spontaneous speech and when teaching more abstract communication (i.e., where a physical representation of the communication is not evident). If the child possesses a good deal of verbal communication and the communication target is more concrete (e.g., requesting a drink the child can see), however, then constant time delay is appropriate. Charlop-Christy and Kelso report that they use graduated time delay for teaching new responses to children with ASD and constant time delay for communication responses that are considered easier for the child.

Intervention Goals. Time delay is an intervention procedure designed to increase spontaneous speech. Several goals around enhancing spontaneous communication might be developed using the time delay procedure. These include increasing requests for desired items (e.g., "I want milk"), settings (e.g., "I want to go home"), activities (e.g., "I want to play ball"), and needs (e.g., "I want to go potty"); expressing a feeling (e.g., "I'm happy"); providing a greeting (e.g., "Hi"); and initiating an interaction (e.g., "Let's sing") or a conversation (e.g., "What did you see at the movies?") (Charlop-Christy & Kelso, 1997). Time delay might also be used when the team would like to move the child from using more imitative speech in communication with adults and peers to using more spontaneous speech across communication partners and settings.

Value for Children with ASD. Time delay is a valuable intervention strategy for children with ASD because it teaches communication without a verbal prompt. Essentially, the stimulus control moves from the verbal model (e.g., "I want milk") to the actual referent (i.e., a carton of milk) (Charlop-Christy & Kelso, 1997). This strategy provides children with ASD with increased freedom in making requests based on their own wants and needs, as opposed to an adult trying to predict what the child might want or need. Time delay works particularly well for teaching spontaneous greetings and for other times when a child wishes to initiate communication with an adult or peer partner.

Efficacy. Research suggests that using time delay increases the spontaneous speech of children with ASD (Charlop & Trasowech, 1991). Children can also learn appropriate greetings across situations and communicative partners using "small talk" following the time delay procedure.

Charlop, Schreibman, and Thibodeau (1985) examined generalization of spontaneous verbal responding across settings, people, situations, and novel stimuli for children with ASD using the time delay procedure. The researchers were interested in increasing the use of spontaneous requests or mands, as opposed to having children just imitate an immediate verbal model. First, a child's ability to spontaneously name the objects used in the task was determined; once that was established, a model for requesting was provided (e.g., "I want cookie" with the cookie present). A time delay was inserted, however, between providing the model and presenting the object in hopes that the child would spontaneously label without need of the verbal model. Once this spontaneous use of requests or mands was established, the researchers investigated generalization to the child's spontaneous speech. Results indicated that the children were able to spontaneously mand or request objects and generalize that ability to requests across settings and stimuli.

Ingenmey and Van Houten (1991) investigated the use of time delay to promote spontaneous speech in a child with ASD. In this single case study, the child was taught to describe his actions while playing with his cars and drawing pictures. Prior to implementation of the time delay procedure, imitation was the intervention strategy used to support the child's utterances. Time delay was introduced to increase the likelihood that he would transfer his ability to imitate targeted responses to using more spontaneous speech. Generalization across settings and behaviors was examined, and follow-up assessment was used to evaluate the child's maintenance of his newly learned communication behaviors. Results revealed that the use of time delay increased his spontaneous speech on trained items, with generalization to untrained stimuli across settings. At a 4-month follow-up, the child's spontaneous speech remained consistent during car play but decreased during drawing.

Matson, Sevin, Box, Francis, and Sevin (1993) used graduated time delay and visual cue fading to facilitate the self-initiated language (e.g., hello, excuse me, thank you, play with me) of three children with ASD and mental retardation (4 and 5 years of age). They found that both strategies were effective in increasing the children's self-initiated language responses. Taylor and Harris (1995) used time delay to teach three children with ASD (5 to 9 years of age) to use the question form "What's that?" The children were taught to use this question form when they were presented with new stimuli during an instructional task using gradual time delay. This was followed by an assessment of their ability to use the same question to learn labels. The children were then taught to use the question in a less structured situation (e.g., during a walk at school). All three children with ASD learned to use the question form across the three experimental tasks using time delay.

Modeling

Modeling, also known as observational learning, involves one person observing another person engaged in a particular activity. Observers learn to engage in a particular behavior because they have watched someone else perform that behavior. As an intervention strategy, modeling is used to facilitate a child's attention to desired target behaviors. The assumption is that the observer (e.g., the child with ASD) creates a mental representation of the behavior observed and therefore has the knowledge needed to perform that behavior (Charlop-Christy & Kelso, 1997). However, many variables dictate whether an individual will choose to engage in the behavior that has been modeled. Early research in this area suggests that an observer is most likely to engage in a modeled behavior when the model is reinforced for the behavior (Bandura, 1965). Also, the number of times the model is observed and how similar the model and observer are may be influencing factors.

Two types of modeling strategies are typically used for children with ASD: *in vivo, or live, modeling* (in which a person in the child's environment serves as the model) and *video modeling* (in which a model is videotaped engaging in a particular behavior). Because of the noted value of video modeling for supporting the needs of children with ASD, it is discussed in detail in the following section. The focus of this section is on in vivo modeling.

Children have many opportunities in their environment to observe individuals such as their parents, siblings, teachers, and peers engage in a variety of activities and model numerous behaviors. To support the observational learning of children with ASD, in vivo modeling is used to demonstrate a specific behavior, which the child imitates. Providing models of target behavior shows the child what kind of response is expected and reinforced in a particular situation.

When using in vivo modeling as an intervention strategy, interventionists should be sure the child with ASD is attending to the actions being modeled. Modeled behaviors should be clear and exaggerated (Charlop-Christy & Kelso, 1997). For example, if modeling a verbal behavior, the interventionist would speak clearly and in a loud enough voice to maintain the child's attention and would present the models at a slightly slower pace than normal without lending an unusual quality to the modeled productions. When presenting verbal models, it is also important to model only the words the child is expected to say.

Intervention Goals. As an intervention strategy, in vivo modeling can be used to support several learning goals for children with ASD—specifically, communication and social communication skills important to their day-to-day functions. Intervention goals supported by in vivo modeling might include increasing the appropriateness of a child's vocal intensity, pitch, and rate or increasing the complexity of language productions. In vivo modeling can also be used to support the child's ability to ask and respond to questions, initiate interactions or communication exchanges, and comment in a conversation. Further, concept knowledge and vocabulary development can be enhanced using in vivo modeling.

Value for Children with ASD. In vivo modeling provides multiple opportunities for children to observe, hear, and learn a particular behavior. These repeated opportunities for learning support the child with ASD, who often has difficulty attending, shifting attention between different communication partners, and focusing on what is relevant in a communication exchange or learning environment. Further, the use of in vivo modeling has important implications for children with ASD who are included in educational settings with their typical peers, where significant learning opportunities occur naturally by watching and imitating what other children say and do (Charlop-Christy, Le, & Freeman, 2000).

Efficacy. The use of adult models has been less successful than the use of peer models in effecting change in target responses for children with ASD. One 10 year-old girl with autism increased her language skills and improved the appropriateness of her vocal volume following observation of a typical peer model (Coleman & Stedman, 1974). Following the use of typical peer models, children with autism who demonstrated high cognitive skills learned their colors, shapes, and location words (e.g., *on, under*) (Egel, Richman, & Koegel, 1981). Children with autism have also been used as peer models to support the observational learning of children with autism. Charlop, Schreibman, and Tyron (1983) found that four children with autism and low cognitive skills (4–14 years of age) could be taught receptive labeling following observation of their peer models who had autism, were similar in age, and had demonstrated understanding of the targeted receptive labels with 100% accuracy. The target child with autism sat next to a peer model, who responded appropriately to the object requests by the experimenter and received a food reinforcer and verbal praise for correct responses. Following 20 trials of the modeled receptive labeling tasks, the target child was assessed to determine what had been learned. This condition was paired with a no-modeling condition for learning labels receptively. Generalization was tested in a new setting with an unfamiliar experimenter. Although all four children learned the receptive labels in both the modeling and no-modeling conditions, fewer learning trials were required and generalization was greater for the receptive labels learned in the in vivo modeling condition.

Video Modeling

Video modeling capitalizes on the effectiveness of observational learning by supporting children in watching the behavior of another and then using what was observed in their own interactions, language use, play, or daily self-care routines. It requires an individual to watch a video of adults or children talking or playing with one another or performing a particular task, during which time they are modeling targeted behaviors such as conversational scripts, self-help skills, greetings, and labeling. Video modeling helps focus the attention of the child with ASD on the relevant stimuli in the video. With practice and rehearsal, the child begins to retain and display the targeted language and behavior modeled in the video. Repeated viewings of the video also support the child's ability to learn the specific vocabulary associated with targeted situations. Through video modeling, children with ASD begin to understand the roles and responsibilities people might take on in particular situations; it provides the children with opportunities to exhibit perspective taking. Video modeling also fosters the ability of children with ASD to generalize the information they have learned in a video modeling session into all aspects of their daily life (Shipley-Benamou, Lutzker, & Taubman, 2002). It is a useful tool for working with children with ASD who have difficulty managing anxiety-producing situations. Video modeling can give the child an opportunity to become familiar with the anxiety-producing situation and to learn appropriate ways to respond. Helping a child become familiar with situations before they take place will facilitate the child's ability to feel prepared and confident when confronted with certain "unknown" situations.

There are several steps to consider when implementing video modeling. When designing a video model for a specific child, it is important to consider a motivating theme in the conversation or play that is being modeled. Depending on the focal point for the video, the camera might be strategically located to present a facial expression, or it might just show an actor's hands carrying out a particular task or activity. When teaching a child certain facial expressions and feelings, it is a good idea to "pause" the video when one of the actors exhibits that expression. This helps the child to clearly see the expression and fosters discussion around what the person viewed might be feeling. If necessary, the child's attention can be prompted by the practitioner saying something like "Watch the TV" or "Look." Following the video viewing, the practitioner could say something like "Okay, your turn" or "Now you do it, just like on TV" (Charlop-Christy & Kelso, 1997, p. 44).

Following each video modeling session, it is important to debrief with the child, reviewing what was seen and heard, identifying any new language heard, and noting the prosody and emotional expression of the models (Charlop & Milstein, 1989). It is also important to talk about possible variations of events, so the child with ASD has opportunities for flexible learning and thinking. When a child is in the process of learning a targeted behavior and the associated skills, it is important to encourage and reinforce his or her attempts to demonstrate the behavior that has been modeled. If a child has difficulty attending to the video, the instructor can show only the important parts, rewind to review important parts, or show the entire video again.

Many issues arise in using video modeling for a child with autism. The parents and the teachers of the child participating in video modeling need to understand the model and the script that the child is being supported to learn. If a parent or teacher is unaware of a particular script, the script is unlikely to be supported when the child attempts to make generalized connections across settings.

Charlop-Christy (2004) makes the following recommendations for developing a video and using video modeling as an intervention strategy to support the learning of a child with ASD. First, the team needs to select and define the behavior they wish to develop or enhance. The behavior should be operationally defined, so that is it measurable, observable, and specific to the individual with ASD. For example, a conversation goal to increase the number of turns in an exchange with a peer will be different for different children. Next, a task analysis is completed, in which the steps for the video model are itemized. For example, if teaching greeting, the team decides exactly what needs to occur (e.g., someone needs to say hello, child needs to respond). The team should observe same-age peers to decide what the appropriate greeting might be (e.g., hi, hey, or hello) and what the expectation is for facial expression or eye contact (e.g., approximate looking at the communication partner's face). It is valuable for the team to observe a greeting or whatever target script has been identified for children who are typically developing (e.g., a greeting on the playground or in the hallway). The team needs to determine who says hello first. Each step should be presented slowly and exaggerated while the actors are looking into the camera for the child to see. Typically, scripts for the video are short (usually three lines each for the child with ASD and the communication partner), so there is a reciprocal communication exchange. Input from parents, teachers, and the child should guide the development of the video models. At least two observations of the video should occur before the child's acquisition of learning is assessed. Charlop-Christy (2004) suggests that the child should demonstrate the target behavior about 75% to 80% of the time before acquisition is considered to have taken place.

Anyone can be an actor in the video. It appears that adults are just as effective as children, and they are usually easier to teach the content of the script and to present the action at a slowed pace (Charlop-Christy, 2004). Although the child with ASD can be an actor as well, self-modeling is not as useful if the child is engaging in inappropriate behavior on the videotape. The script needs to be rehearsed a few times before filming; the relevant information is acted out in an exaggerated manner and in slow motion. Charlop-Christy reports that children with ASD respond to stimuli that are exaggerated or emphasized and that grab their attention. For example, if creating a script for greeting using video modeling, the practitioner might begin by showing two individuals walking toward one another. One person would stop and look at the other person, turn to the camera and say, "Hi, Sam," and then look back at the other person. The other person would then turn to the camera and say, "Hi" and then look back. Both individuals would then walk away. Thus, the video highlights the behaviors the child is expected to learn.

The video director needs to remember several things, such as making sure the actors speak clearly and slowly, exaggerate the target behaviors, face the camera, and are clearly distinguishable. It is best not to have distractors in the video and to make sure the background is focused on the relevant cues.

Intervention Goals. Several goals can be developed around the use of video modeling to support the conversational skills of children with autism. The team identifies the goal, defines the script to achieve the goal, analyzes the steps for carrying out the script, and determines how the video is to be made. Communication goals that might be a focus for video modeling include greeting, naming or labeling, responding to questions, asking questions, and participating in a back-and-forth conversational exchange around a specified topic, among others.

Value for Children with ASD. Several explanations have been given for the value of video modeling for children with ASD. Many children with ASD have rote memory strengths, which makes remembering the target language or play behaviors a reasonable expectation. Verbal children with ASD are often echolalic. Watching video models and hearing language and social interaction targets may facilitate the use of delayed echolalia, which can be meaningful in similar contexts for the child with ASD. Often, watching a video is a favorite and motivating activity for the child with ASD (Charlop-Christy & Daneshvar, 2003; Charlop-Christy et al., 2000). For children who are highly verbal, text from the video can be included at the bottom of the video screen. Visual and auditory distractions are minimal with video modeling (Charlop-Christy & Kelso, 1997). A contained spatial area is used to focus on the relevant information; therefore, the critical information is always present. This is in contrast to the more transient information and the complexity of information when viewing activities live. In addition, in video modeling, the camera can zoom in on the relevant stimuli or cues for a target behavior. This is particularly helpful for children with problems of overselectivity because their selective focus is directed toward relevant versus irrelevant cues (Charlop-Christy & Daneshvar, 2003). Video modeling also capitalizes on the visual strengths reported for individuals with ASD. The salience of the visual model persists, in contrast to the transient nature of auditory input. Using video also provides opportunities to stop the tape and focus on the most important aspects of the content and behavior being modeled. Further, video modeling has broad application not only to supporting the development of communication and conversational scripts but also to facilitating play, social interaction, and knowledge of daily routines and self-care tasks.

An important benefit of video modeling is that it helps children to generalize what they have learned from the video into all environments in their daily life (Charlop & Walsh, 1986). In addition, it is a convenient way to create natural settings with a desired scene that can be viewed repeatedly (Charlop-Christy et al., 2000).

Video modeling appears to be appropriate across the lifespan for individuals with ASD. Charlop-Christy (2004) describes using this strategy with children as young as 4 years of age through older adults. She reports that most children successfully learn the targeted behaviors within just a few trials. If a child has not learned the targeted behaviors after about 16 viewings of the video, Charlop-Christy would consider a different approach to intervention.

Efficacy. Several studies have discussed the importance and effectiveness of video modeling for children with ASD in supporting their language use and perspective taking. Dowrick and colleagues were among the first to demonstrate the effectiveness of video modeling in supporting the skill development of children with a variety of disabilities (Dowrick & Dove, 1980; Dowrick & Hood, 1981; Dowrick & Raeburn, 1995). Charlop-Christy and her colleagues have successfully applied this intervention strategy to children with ASD (Charlop & Milstein, 1989; Charlop-Christy & Daneshvar, 2003; Charlop-Christy et al., 2000; LeBlanc et al., 2003).

Charlop and Milstein (1989) demonstrated increased question-asking ability and an ability to maintain conversation for three children with autism (6–7 years of age) who viewed a video of two familiar adults talking about toys of interest using five conversational scripts. Each modeled conversation had four lines for the conversational partner and three for the child, so that the last question was answered. During the 45-second videotape, the adults faced the camera, held the toys of interest, and took turns talking. Results indicated that not only did the children acquire conversational speech following video modeling but they also generalized this conversational skill to other settings, people, and topics of conversation, with maintenance observed at a 15-month follow-up. Further, the children exhibited increased question asking and spontaneous variation in their responses, with their parents reporting changes in conversational ability as well.

Charlop-Christy and her colleagues (2000) examined the effectiveness of video modeling compared to in vivo modeling for teaching skills to five children with autism of varying cognitive ability (7–11 years of age). The children watched familiar adults model several behaviors, depending on the specific targets for each child, including spontaneous greetings (e.g., hello, how are you; goodbye, see you later), conversational speech, independent play (e.g., car wash, coloring), cooperative play (e.g., card games), social play (e.g., red rover; number tag), oral comprehension following story reading (e.g., when, where, why, what questions), labeling of emotions depicted in pictures (e.g., happy or sad; tired or afraid), and self-help skills (e.g., teeth brushing, face washing). Procedures for both the live and video conditions were modeled in a similar manner, with slow, exaggerated demonstrations and reminders to the children to attend when necessary. The researchers also measured cost efficiency, including the time to train the adult models and the time used for the live models and for making the videos. Results indicated that video modeling led to faster skill acquisition and better generalization across settings, persons, and stimuli than in vivo modeling. Further, the time and cost of in vivo modeling was greater than that of video modeling.

Sherer et al. (2001) found that self (children watching themselves) versus other (children watching other children or adults) video modeling were equally effective in increasing children's ability to respond to questions and then ask questions in conversation with adults and peers. Sherer and colleagues suggest, as did Charlop-Christy and her colleagues (2000), that "other" video modeling may be easier to prepare and more cost effective.

Charlop-Christy and Daneshvar (2003) also reported success teaching three boys with autism (6–9 years of age) first-order false-belief tasks (similar to the Sally-and-Ann task). Instructional videos were viewed for five different perspective-taking tasks except for two untrained variations used to assess generalization. Familiar adults performed the tasks on video, stating the correct responses for each task. The adults clearly explained their problem-solving strategies to come up with the correct answers and demonstrated enthusiasm as they repeated the responses. Results indicated that perspective taking can be taught successfully to children with autism in an efficient and effective manner using video modeling, with both stimulus and response generalization occurring (Charlop-Christy & Daneshvar, 2003). LeBlanc and colleagues (2003) also successfully taught perspective taking to children with autism using video modeling and reinforcement. Three boys with autism, 7 to 13 years of age, viewed a video of an adult correctly completing perspective-taking tasks. For example, one task involved a puppet putting a treasure in one of two treasure chests. The puppet may or may not have left footprints as a clue to where the treasure was placed. The task required someone who left the room prior to the final hiding place to determine where the treasure was hidden. The video of this scenario focused on important details like zooming in on the footprints of the puppet and having the model explain that the person looked in the first chest where the footprints led because it was a clue. Then the correct response was provided, explaining that the person did not know when he or she left the room that the puppet changed the location and did not leave footprints. Immediately following the viewing of the correct response, the video was stopped and the children responded to perspective-taking questions. Correct responses were reinforced with tangible motivators.

Charlop-Christy, Carpenter, and Dennis (2004) used video modeling to facilitate the ability of three children with autism (5–11 years of age) to learn verbal comments, facial expressions, gestures, and intonation during play. They used a multiple baseline design. The results indicated that the children significantly increased their appropriate responses following video modeling, with two of the children achieving criterion across the four target responses with only three video presentations, and the third achieving criterion after four presentations. The rapid acquisition supports the results of previous research on video modeling and was explained as a result of the focus on relevant cues, the motivation that comes with watching videos for children with ASD, and its association with play and less structured teaching activities (Charlop-Christy et al., 2004). The results also support the training of multiple social behaviors at the same time through video modeling. Generalization occurred, as well, and was explained as a result of the use of multiple facilitators, using a variety of toys and activities. The usefulness of this intervention strategy for teaching social communication behaviors in children with ASD who exhibit lower cognitive abilities is unknown, however. Further, long-term generalization of the behaviors has not been followed. The authors suggest that additional research might consider including children with limited verbal abilities and lower cognitive skills to determine the effectiveness of video modeling for that population of children with ASD (Charlop-Christy et al., 2004).

Scripting

Children engaged in early routines (e.g., taking a bath, getting ready for bed) develop an understanding of predictable sequences of events (what happens first, second), knowledge about the language used at particular points in the event (what is said or talked about), knowledge about the roles of the participants (who does or says what), and an understanding of the reciprocal nature of the roles within the events (what to do as a listener or responder vs. speaker or initiator). Participation in daily events such as these facilitates learning about the world and making sense of new events or experiences (Sonnenmeier, 1994). Further, repeated experiences help to create a more generalized notion of an event. Sometimes events share similar components or have different versions, while at other times they do not proceed as expected. The ability to make comparisons and contrasts among these events or experiences is critical to establishing valuable event knowledge. Over time, children learn to develop a plan or schema for representing or organizing information they experience. A plan or schema is then created for a particular event that specifies the actions, actors, and props; this is called a *script*. Specific aspects of a script that remain constant and can be identified and taught are called a *routine*.

Knowledge of scripts helps to form a conceptual representation for experiences. Scripts organize an individual's knowledge (including thoughts, feelings, and language related to the events) and provide a structure for initiating and maintaining conversation. They also describe culturally defined events. Scripts are typically hierarchical and often have subscripts. For example, the script for going on a trip includes subscripts like determining where to go, how to get there, what to take, how to pack, and what to do when you get there. Scripts are also culturally defined, in that children often learn scripts not only through observation but also through adult guidance (Goodman, Duchan, & Sonnenmeier, 1994). Using scripts in daily life facilitates the ability to communicate functionally and socially.

Intervention for developing script knowledge involves providing perceptual supports (e.g., relevant objects) to represent relevant aspects of an event. The goal is to create a social context for learning so that the knowledge base is shared among the participants. Scripts follow a logical sequence, have a clear beginning point, identify the roles of the participants, and specify the response expectations. Scripted intervention often incorporates joint action routines (Snyder-McLean et al., 1984), as discussed earlier. It uses frameworks to enhance aspects of language such as form (syntax) and function (pragmatics) (Duchan & Weitzner-Lin, 1987).

When developing scripts to support the language and communication of children with ASD, practitioners should consider the following questions: (a) How should the event or script be organized? (b) What are the roles of the participants? (c) What perspectives will the participants need to understand? and (d) What are the language requirements for the different roles? Answers to these questions will guide the practitioner in creating scripts that are meaningful and responsive to the expectations for language performance.

Sonnenmeier (1994) describes the use of play to teach event or script knowledge to children. She recommends setting up the environment with the appropriate props and then introducing the focus of the play, asking children what they know about the particular event (e.g., doctor's office). The adult then models one version of the event, emphasizing a single aspect. For example, doctor's office might be broken down into three parts: getting ready to go, being at the office, and leaving to return home. The role modeled is the "patient" role. Once the adult models the event and the particular role of focus, the targeted child practices that role in the context of the play event. Other roles (e.g., doctor, nurse) are assigned to children without disabilities who are participating in the play script. Once all roles are assigned, the children act out the script. Over time, roles are switched and the script is reenacted. Sonnenmeier recommends that a child might initially be assigned the roles he or she is most likely to experience (e.g., patient). Eventually, the child is taught the less familiar roles so he or she can learn how to take different perspectives in a situation. Because perspective taking is likely to be an area of breakdown for the child with ASD, intervention might begin by first engaging the child in using the available materials. Once the child is engaged, redirection to the peers' actions and utterances is provided. Signed cues are also used to encourage the child to comment on actions or the routine.

The next intervention challenge is when to fade the adult model and cues, as the ultimate goal is to have the children with ASD spontaneously interact within the script and in other generalized situations. Script fading is one technique that may be used. This strategy involves removing sections of a written script from the intervention setting until no written cue remains. Children are responsible, however, for demonstrating the targeted language or social behavior based on their repeated experience.

Intervention Goals. In general, the use of scripts in language intervention for children with ASD is aimed at expanding their mental event representations, so that they can better express themselves in day-to-day routines (Sonnenmeier, 1994). There are a number of ways scripts can be used to support language intervention goals. The practitioner can use scripting to develop the child's understanding of pretend roles and the ability to follow and participate in an event sequence. Goals might also be established for using vocabulary relevant to the scripted events and for initiating requests to a peer to obtain desired items. In addition, the intervention goals might consider increasing the child's ability to participate in a joint activity with a peer, to direct language to the peer, and to use multiple-word phrases to comment (Sonnenmeier, 1994).

When developing intervention goals for older children and adolescents with ASD, the practitioner needs to investigate the students' knowledge of classroom scripts (e.g., routines for arrival and departure, getting lunch, requesting help, reviewing assignments) that have been suggested for other students with language impairment (Creaghead, 1991). A series of questions can be posed to assess their knowledge such as:

- What are the rules for classroom behavior?
- What are the rules for cafeteria behavior?
- How do you know when the teacher wants you to talk or answer a question in class?
- How do you know when the teacher wants you to listen and not talk?
- How do you know when you can ask the teacher for help?
- What tells you that the teacher is giving instructions to complete a particular task?
- How do you know when the teacher is telling the class something important?
- What does your teacher do to let you know you can ask for help?

An assessment of students' event knowledge of classroom routines and expected behavior can lead the practitioner to clear intervention goals that will support the students' language understanding and use in the classroom or broader school setting.

Value for Children with ASD. One of the advantages of using scripts for children with ASD is that the structure of the script can represent familiar social experiences using contextually appropriate language. Children with ASD may have less experience with daily routines than their typically developing peers, often because of their challenging behaviors. Providing intervention that scripts language helps children with ASD make sense of the world around them and aids their regulation of challenging social–emotional behaviors. In addition, adult-facilitated scripting exposes children to language models in a context that allows for varied language production and not just modeled imitation (Krantz & McClannahan, 1998). Applying scripts to events and routines during play or therapy, in the classroom or at home, gives children with ASD opportunities to experience activities about which they have little knowledge.

Efficacy. Research suggests that knowledge of scripts may be an area of particular difficulty for children and adolescents with autism. Loveland and Tunali (1991) compared the ability of individuals with ASD to respond to conversational social scripts with that of individuals with Down syndrome. Two social scripts were used: a tea party and the distressed account of a stolen wallet. Results indicated that individuals with ASD were less likely to respond verbally to the stolen wallet script than to the tea party script. With modeling, however, Loveland and Tunali demonstrated that individuals with ASD did learn to respond to the stolen wallet script. It appears that individuals with ASD may have knowledge of some aspects of subscripts but need help to establish socially appropriate responses.

In a more recent study, the ability of 12 children with ASD to retell a script for typical routines (e.g., how to shop at a supermarket, how to make a cake, how to celebrate a birthday) was examined in comparison to that of a group of typically developing children matched by mental age (Trillingsgaard, 1999). Results indicated that only half of the scripts the children with ASD generated contained the minimum criteria for simple scripts applied by this study. Volden and Johnston (1999) also compared 24 children and adolescents with ASD to 37 typically developing children in their ability to demonstrate basic script knowledge. They found that children and adolescents with ASD possess basic script understanding, but their difficulties in expressing these scripts are related to their deficits in expressive communication. It seems apparent that script training is essential for children and adolescents with ASD if they are to order events logically and be able to talk about them; these are key requirements for successful social communication.

Scripts have been used successfully in language intervention, with generalized use to untrained situations. Goldstein, Wickstrom, Hoyson, Jamieson, and Odom (1988) used scripts involving sociodramatic themes to teach preschool children with and without disabilities. Roles were taught, practiced, and exchanged. Scripts were designed with flexibility, allowing productions that varied from the targeted utterances. Goldstein and colleagues found improvements in functional social communication during structured play settings, with an increase in theme-related untrained utterances for all the children. Goldstein and Cisar (1992) demonstrated more frequent theme-related social behavior for children with disabilities after being taught a sociodramatic script for playtime. Scripted behavior generalized to a different time and setting.

Sarokoff, Taylor, and Poulson (2001) demonstrated that children with ASD increased their use of scripted statements following script-based intervention. Two children with ASD (8 and 9 years of age) were taught to engage in conversation using embedded text (e.g., "Let's eat our snacks") to talk about snack items or video games (Sarokoff et al., 2001, p. 82). Each script included six or seven conversational statements about an item. The children were seated across from each other during the intervention and could eat their snacks only when instructed to do so by the script. Gestural prompts were provided when needed to facilitate attention to the script. The script was gradually removed from the treatment environment until all that remained was the stimulus item. The children learned the scripted statements and were able to generalize those statements to other snack items with new peers.

Krantz and McClannahan (1998) used script fading to teach three boys with ASD (4–5 years of age). The intervention facilitated the children's unscripted interactions in untrained activities. Krantz and McClannahan note that adult rather than peer interaction was an effective context for intervention because teachers are more apt to communicate with the children at their language level, as well as to make comments regarding the children's interests.

TEACCH Language and Communication Curriculum

Division TEACCH (Treatment and Education of Autistic and Related Communication-Handicapped Children), a statewide program serving children with ASD and their families in North Carolina, has designed a language and communication curriculum that is valuable for developing spontaneous communication in children with ASD (Watson, 1985; Watson, Lord, Schaffer, & Schopler, 1989). There are five key components to the curriculum: the functions or purposes of communication; the contexts or settings in which communication takes place; the semantic categories or meanings the child expresses; the words or units (e.g., words, signs, gestures) of communication the child uses; and the communication forms or modes (e.g., signs, symbols, speech) (Watson et al., 1989). Each of these components is described briefly in the paragraphs that follow.

Communicative function typically refers to the purpose or intent of communicating. The TEACCH curriculum emphasizes six communicative functions that are assessed and used for intervention planning: getting attention, requesting, rejecting or refusing, commenting, seeking information, and expressing feelings (Watson et al., 1989, p. 13). Often, children with ASD are restricted in their ability to communicate for a variety of purposes; therefore, an important intervention goal is to teach them multiple communicative functions.

Contexts include those situations in which individuals communicate. They vary for individual children but may include several places and people. For example, places where the child with ASD might have an opportunity to communicate include school, home, the grocery store, a favorite department store, Sunday school, and favorite restaurants. People with whom the child might communicate include parents, other relatives, friends, teachers, peers, store clerks, strangers, and employers. Context has an important role in transition from home to school, so curriculum planning must consider developing carefully planned processes that can be implemented across settings and people. Teaching activities must also be planned and implemented in a variety of contexts, including structured and unstructured settings (Watson et al., 1989).

Semantic categories refer to word meanings that are used to communicate an idea or concept. Early concepts that children express include actions (e.g., swing, walk, run), agents or the person acting, objects or the thing that is acted on (e.g., Daddy pushed the car), and location of the objects (e.g., Daddy pushed the car on the floor). To communicate effectively about a variety of experiences encountered in day-to-day activities, children must learn how to communicate using a range of semantic categories (Watson et al., 1989).

The *words component* of the curriculum is broader than just spoken words in that signs, written words, gestures, pictures, and any other unit of communication are considered. The focus is on teaching new words to expand the child's communicative vocabulary. The quantity, though, is less important than the quality of words learned that can be used across several contexts in meaningful ways.

Form provides the structure for communication and refers to the mode or system of communication that a child uses to express intent (Watson et al., 1989). A child's form may begin with presymbolic communication like motor acts and then move to the use of gestures and picture board communication. This may be followed by more symbolic communication such as sign language, spoken language, and word boards. Watson and her colleagues caution interventionists not to sacrifice communicative functions and meanings to increase utterance length and complexity in their intervention planning.

The TEACCH curriculum provides an observational assessment tool for examining a child's spontaneous communication skills and a method for analyzing the communication sample. Suggestions for identifying program goals and prioritizing those goals are provided. Parents are incorporated into the assessment and intervention planning process, as their perspectives on their child's spontaneous communication are critical. Teaching objectives are defined, and teaching strategies to address those objectives are presented. Intervention strategies typically involve incidental teaching, engineering the environment, shaping the child's communicative behaviors, and providing natural consequences (Watson et al., 1989). Criteria are established for reaching objectives, and progress is monitored through consistent data collection. Both individual and group teaching strategies are employed.

Outcomes for children and adults who have participated in the TEACCH program are typically measured by the low rate of institutionalization (less than 8%) and documented positive changes after the first few years of participation (Lord & Schopler, 1994). Higher academic achievement has been reported for some students from TEACCH who had higher cognitive abilities (Venter, Lord, & Schopler, 1992). Follow-up studies have also looked at the course of autism for young children seen at TEACCH during their preschool years and found increases in IQ scores (Lord & Schopler, 1989). A primary component of the TEACCH model, however, is the recognition that children with ASD are individuals, that they are part of a unique community and family, and that they should be prepared for their future independence.

Managing Unconventional Verbal Behavior

Often children with ASD use unconventional verbal behavior in their communicative interactions with adults and peers. Since this is a frequent occurrence in many children with ASD, it is important that practitioners consider ways to manage the behavior, so the child's communication attempts can be honored and more meaningful interactions can occur. The primary goal is to increase the child's flexibility in communicating, using meaningful phrases and sentences while decreasing the use of echolalic speech in interactions with the child's family members and teachers in both structured and unstructured interactions. Some early work in this area suggested that echolalic responses could be shaped through the use of time delay and prompt fading, leading to an increase in more appropriate verbal imitation, including spontaneous labeling and expanded utterances (Risley & Wolf, 1967).

In general, interventions for reducing unconventional verbal behavior such as echolalia should be positive and supportive. Such behavior should never be punished because it is often socially motivated and functional, and it may represent a transition phase for the child to move ahead in conventional communication. Ways that students with echolalia can be supported will require both creative and sensitive responses. To begin, the child may need some reassurance, as descriptions of unconventional verbal behaviors such as echolalia (described in Chapter 4) indicate that increased anxiety or frustration is often associated with them. Making statements such as "I can see that you are trying to tell me something; let me see if I can figure it out" might help (Kluth, 2003, p. 113).

Prizant and Rydell (1993) offer additional strategies the team might consider to reduce unconventional verbal behavior, in particular, echolalia. First, team members should simplify their language input, using utterances only one to two words longer than the child's utterances. For example, if a child is using three- to four-word utterances, the language input provided to the child might range from four to five words. To support the child's comprehension of the language input, the content might refer to objects and relationships observed within the child's home and school environments. Second, the child's communication partners should respond to the child's *presumed* intent, as demonstrated in this example about Sam and his dad:

> DAD: Do you want cookies?
> SAM: Do you want cookies?"
> DAD: [Assuming intent is yes, Dad says to Mom] Sam wants cookies."

Third, the communicative partner can attempt to relate the child's utterances to actions or objects of interest. For example, if Sam is repeating,

"Sam want jack-in-the-box," his communication partner could point to and touch the jack-in-the-box and then say, "Sam, let's turn the handle on the box." Fourth, to support the correct use of pronouns, a frequent problem in echolalic speech, peer models (see Chapters 10 and 11) or video modeling (described earlier in this chapter) might be used. For example, Sam might be involved in observing his peers model the correct use of pronouns in their connected speech in structured play at his preschool. A fifth strategy might involve modifying the situation. If a particular situation is known to increase the anxiety of a child with ASD and potentially increase the child's use of unconventional verbal behavior like echolalia or incessant questioning, the goal would be to reduce the anxiety as much as possible. For example, if Sam is learning a new task and new tasks create anxiety for him, the task might be broken down into steps, simplifying the parts. Another strategy might be to prepare the child with ASD for a particular event that is likely to be challenging or create an emotional response. A disruption in routine or a transition to another activity may increase a child's emotional response, so it is important to create ways to inform and prepare the child. For example, when Sam is at his preschool and is expected to move from one activity to another when he is not yet finished with a particular task, giving him prompted reminders and a visual cue such as a visual schedule or a script that shows him what is to happen next could be helpful. A final strategy would be to provide relevant language opportunities as often as possible. For example, if Sam is likely to imitate language models when he is highly motivated, it is useful to create times throughout his day at home and school to give him choices and ask him to make decisions about what he wants to eat or what activity he would like to engage in. This way, the practitioner could capitalize on Sam's ability to "borrow" language structures, but in meaningful contexts.

Hetzroni and Tannous (2004) investigated the effects of a computer-based intervention program to decrease the unconventional verbal behaviors (e.g., delayed echolalia, immediate echolalia, irrelevant speech) of five children with ASD (7–12 years of age). They developed a software program that generated questions and answers around play, eating, and hygiene routines. Children were able to choose desired activities (e.g., "I want to play ball with you") depicted on the computer screen following a question (e.g., "What would you like to play?") and then watch a short animation of their selection (p. 112). Results revealed that the children's practice with the computer-based intervention led to a decrease in immediate and delayed echolalia and irrelevant speech and an increase in more relevant communication and initiations. In addition, the children transferred their learning to the classroom environment.

Expanding Conversational Abilities of Children with ASD

Children with ASD often fail to respond to questions and comments during informal conversation and seldom offer novel, relevant contributions or personal narratives (Capps, Kehres, & Sigman, 1998). The ability to participate in a conversation, however, is critical to the social success of children and adolescents with ASD. Therefore, intervention should incorporate strategies that promote their conversational abilities. Capps and her colleagues suggest that interventionists should identify and develop communication environments that can support the involvement of children with ASD in meaningful conversation. Strategies might include combining forced-choice questions with more open-ended questions. Outlining sequences of questions or providing a script for a series of questions that can be used in conversational exchanges may be valuable. Facilitating the ability to construct personal narratives should also be an intervention goal (Capps et al., 1998). Children with ASD who can organize their experiences in a series of sequenced events may be more apt to respond to questions in conversation related to a recall of those personal experiences or events, thus spurring an elaborated conversation with another.

Adolescents with ASD were taught to make both positive (e.g., "Isn't this fun?" "Great play.") and negative (e.g., "That's not fair, let's start over." "It's time to show your card.") assertions in the natural contexts of playing a ball game and a card game using modeling and reinforcement (McGee, Krantz, & McClannahan, 1984, p. 323). McGee and colleagues found that adolescents can learn conversational skills such as assertions, and generalize and maintain them, when taught in environments where the skills are actually needed.

As practitioners consider ways to expand the use of language for children and adolescents with ASD, several additional strategies are offered. Barrier games, in which one child (the sender) directs a second child (the receiver) to act on specific items while separated from seeing them, provide an excellent opportunity for refining conversational skills and facilitating complex language use. Because the children have different perspectives on what they see, they must provide more precise language instructions to facilitate the activity's success. The receiving child might be trying to recreate a drawing or a geometric design that is seen and being described by the sending child. Or the receiving child might be engaged in matching or selecting a picture from several choices that matches the picture the sending child is describing.

There are several advantages to using this strategy to develop the conversational language skills of children with ASD. First, the children learn to use their language to direct others' behavior. Second, they must be able to offer meaningful repair strategies when their communication partner is confused or does not understand the instruction to recreate or match a targeted item. Third, they develop increased knowledge of a variety of language concepts. Fourth, they have an opportunity to expand their conversational skills in the context of communicative interactions with a peer.

Freeman and Dake (1997) describe several strategies that can be used to establish topics in conversation and create scripts to guide a personal narrative about an experience for children and adolescents with ASD. Using a written script to identify the topic and making a probing remark such as

"Tell me something about [the topic]" can facilitate ongoing conversations. Additional prompts might include:

- Tell me something else about _____.
- Tell me about where you find it.
- Tell me about the shape.
- Tell me about the size.
- Tell me about the color.
- Tell me what it does.

To maintain conversational skills, Freeman and Dake (1997) suggest that children and adolescents with ASD may need to learn a script so they can make sense of their world and the topics their peers wish to discuss. For example, in preparation for discussing a movie, the following conversation script might be helpful:

- Did you see _____?
- Wasn't it cool when _____?
- What part did you like?
- Remember the part about _____?
- I liked it when _____.
- The best part was _____.

Producing reciprocal verbal comments also increases familiarity and ease with asking, answering, and commenting on what another says or does. To illustrate, see the following practice example:

I like to eat spaghetti.
I like to eat _____.
I like to go to the movies.
I like to go to _____.

I have a ball. (can use pictures or objects)
I have a _____.

I have brown hair.
I have _____.
I have blue eyes.
I have _____.

Using contingent statements is also important in developing conversational elaboration. The practitioner might type something and then have the student type, as in the following example:

CHILD SAYS:
    I like to eat ice cream.

THERAPIST RESPONDS:

Ice cream is cold.

THERAPIST ASKS A QUESTION:

What kind of ice cream do you like?

CHILD RESPONDS:

I like chocolate. What do you like?

THERAPIST ANSWERS:

I like vanilla with hot fudge on top. Do you like any sauce on your ice cream?

CHILD RESPONDS:

I like it plain. What else do you eat?

Students with ASD can create a generic script with a column for questions that can be asked and a column for comments that can be made about any particular topic. A conversation game spinner with question forms on the spinner could also be used to prompt students to answer who, what, where, when, and why.

Asking questions is a challenging area for children and adolescents with ASD, as it requires initiating a conversational topic that requires a response if reciprocity is to be established. The use of questions can begin at a very simple level and progress to more complex conversational exchanges. A series of self-initiated queries might be used to start. For example, to induce a child to ask, "What's that?" the practitioner might place highly desirable objects in an opaque bag and prompt the child to ask the question. To facilitate "Where is it?" the practitioner could hide the highly desirable objects in specific locations (in, on, under, or behind something) and prompt the child to ask the question. If promoting the use of "Whose is it?" the practitioner could bring items from the child's home that are of particular interest to the child and prompt the child to ask the question. To teach the use of "What happened?" the practitioner could use pop-up books of interest to provide the stimulus. The adult would manipulate the tabs in the book that perform the action, prompt the child to ask the question, and then describe and perform the action.

Supporting Communication and Language Intervention in the Home

Families play a critical role in the communication intervention for their children with ASD. Because of the number of hours of daily contact parents have with their children, much of the responsibility for language facilitation rests on their shoulders (Harris & Boyle, 1985). Most successful training programs for children with ASD and many interventions discussed throughout this book have a training component for parents and recognize the importance of their involvement to achieve generalized learning of communication concepts in the home setting. In the sections that follow, two particular approaches to supporting the language and communication of children using family members as interventionists are highlighted. The *Affect-Based Language Curriculum* supports the development of language through pleasurable reciprocal exchanges between the child with ASD and the child's parents. The *More Than Words* approach supports parents' understanding of what communication is, how it might be compromised in their children with ASD, and what strategies might be used in the home setting to facilitate meaningful communication.

Affect-Based Language Curriculum

The *Affect-Based Language Curriculum* (ABLC) is an intensive program designed for practitioners and families to support the development of communication and language skills that children are expected to master by a particular age (Greenspan & Lewis, 2002). The development of imitation and pragmatic, receptive, and expressive language is supported through pleasurable reciprocal exchanges. Greenspan and Lewis believe that engagement and affect facilitate the development of language. A significant feature of this curriculum "is its focus on the foundations of language which are embedded in early relationships and preverbal affective exchanges" (p. 8). There is a focus on developing basic language elements (e.g., phonology, syntax, semantics), but the curriculum also emphasizes abstract thinking and supporting the child's ability for inferential and creative thinking.

The ABLC contains several steps: sensory preparation, systematic instruction, applied floor time, floor time, oral motor work, and augmentative communication. In the first step, the team considers the child's sensory and motor system to create activities around sensory preferences. The second step emphasizes language goals around sound and word production developed in the context of applied floor time (Step 3), in which language goals are practiced in spontaneous interactions. In Step 4, floor time is used to create dynamic interactions in which the practitioner or parent follows the child's lead to facilitate attention, two-way communication, and problem solving. Oral motor skills are used to facilitate sound and word formation in Step 5, and visual supports are used to augment communication in Step 6.

Intervention Goals. There are four major areas of instruction in the ABLC: engagement, coregulated reciprocal interactions, and pragmatics; imitation; receptive language; and expressive language. Remembering that affect facilitates learning, the first major area focuses on several goals such as forming a pleasurable relationship with the child with ASD (engagement); establishing reciprocal exchanges using a range of gestures, vocalizations, and verbalizations (coregulated reciprocal interactions); and teaching the child to comment, report, greet, and maintain conversation (pragmatics). The second core area is designed to support imitation, with a goal of helping children with ASD to look at what others do and copy what they see. Goals for the third area, receptive language, include teaching the child to understand what is being said when introduced to new concepts. The final area, expressive language, focuses on teaching children to connect words to form sentences, respond to questions, and create new words.

Value for Children with ASD. Many children with ASD have significant language challenges that require ongoing support. Greenspan and Lewis (2002) report that the ABLC is especially useful for this population because it is systematic, intensive, and responsive to the core language deficits characteristic of children with ASD. It also takes advantage of the value of "structure and dynamic affective interaction" and keeps "the child as affectively engaged and interactive (a continuous flow of back-and-forth affective interactions) as possible" (p. 10).

Efficacy. Greenspan and Lewis (2002) provide several case studies to demonstrate the effective use of the ABLC for children with special needs and specifically children with ASD. Each of the steps outlined for the curriculum includes guidelines, teaching strategies, and an explanation of implementation for individual children. Skill areas are identified, systematic instructional goals are provided, and data sheets are used to define mastery (i.e., a skill is demonstrated during a semistructured thematic activity and occurs in a problem-solving context) and describe continuous flow (i.e., pleasurable contact is maintained for a minimum of three to four back-and-forth exchanges). There is no experimental research at this time, however, to support the effectiveness of this curricular approach to communication and language for children with ASD.

More Than Words

More Than Words—The Hanen Program for Parents of Children with ASD is designed to help families support the communication and social skills of their children with ASD (Sussman, 1999). Parents learn that their children's ability to communicate depends on being able to pay attention; find enjoyment in two-way communication; understand and imitate what others say and do; interact with people and have fun doing it; practice what they learn; and have structure, repetition, and predictability in their daily activities. Parents learn several things about how their children communicate, including what their children like and dislike, how their children communicate what they like and dislike, and how their children make sensory connections to the world. The program also supports parents' understanding of what communication is, what learning styles their children demonstrate, and what function their children's communication serves. Parents learn to recognize their children's communication stage and how to affect their children's communication.

Intervention Goals. The *More Than Words* program has parents focus on four major goals for supporting the communication of their children with ASD. The first goal is to help the children learn to interact with their parents and other people (Sussman, 1999). Parents learn that their children can find enjoyment in doing things with them, can understand that they have an effect on their parents, and can learn that communication is a two-way endeavor. The second goal is to support the children to communicate in new ways. Parents find ways to help their children communicate, such as using pictures, hand signs, pointing, or a combination of methods. A third goal is to teach the children to communicate for new reasons. Parents learn to help their children communicate intentionally by setting up situations in which the children need to make requests to get what they want. The final intervention goal is to help the children understand the connection between what is being said and what is happening. Parents learn to make sure that what they say is meaningful to their children. So children are exposed to words that match what is important to them in their daily life (Sussman, 1999). Parents are encouraged to focus on their children's preferences or interests and their children's learning style to achieve these four basic goals, in consideration of their children's stage of communication development.

Value for Children with ASD. *More Than Words* is particularly appropriate for supporting children with ASD in the home setting. It is based on what parents know about their children and honors the critical and constant role parents have in the lives of their children. It recognizes the special challenges children with ASD often face, including unique learning styles and sensory preferences that can interfere with communication and interaction. The program builds on children's interests, interprets what they say and do as intentional, encourages imitation, and insists on being a part of what the children are doing. Thus, the parents learn to follow their child's lead in a meaningful way to support two-way communication, which leads to turn taking and sustained interaction (Sussman, 1999).

Efficacy. Like many programs designed for children with ASD, *More Than Words* is responsive to the core deficits characteristic of this population, particularly the identified communication challenges. The program is clearly designed and provides numerous examples and opportunities for parents to practice what they learn in the context of everyday activities with their child. Intervention strategies are based in good practice that has been supported in the literature. For example, caregivers have been successfully taught to embed teaching strategies (e.g., modeling, imitation, reinforcement, time delay) similar to those used in the *More Than Words* program in daily routines to improve communication (Woods, Kashinath, & Goldstein, 2004). The program has no specific data, however, to support its effectiveness.

Summary

In this chapter, you learned about several interventions that have been used to support the communication needs of children with ASD. The literature suggests that intervention approaches that are both structured and functional are most effective in supporting the communication needs of children with ASD (Ogletree & Oren, 1998). In addition, the primary goal in developing early communication skills should be to develop communicative intent in ways that are interpretable between communicative partners. Table 9.1 provides a sample of some specific functional communication goals and possible strategies to support those goals for children with ASD. The summary below refers to the questions at the beginning of the chapter and highlights key points that will allow the practitioner to approach communication intervention for children with ASD in both a practical and an innovative way.

What strategies are effective for supporting the communication skills of children with ASD who have limited verbal capacity?

An intervention plan should ensure that children with ASD have the tools and skills they need to communicate effectively. For children with ASD who have limited verbal skills, aided communication has clear advantages, in that a variety of communication partners can be accessed; also, it requires visual–spatial processing, which is a strength for many individuals with ASD (Light, Roberts, DiMarco, & Greiner, 1998). PECS is one example of an augmentative communication tool that has been particularly effective in supporting the communication needs of children with ASD. It emphasizes important communicative functions, provides opportunities for choice making and independent communication, and supports the development of verbal communication in many children with ASD. The minimal speech and proximal communication approach also supports the development of verbal communication in children with limited oral communication skills by establishing engagement through physical play and limited speech, followed by shaping oral productions through motivating activities.

What interventions might be used to support the communication skills of verbal children with ASD?

There are several aspects of natural learning environments that support the communication of children with ASD. These include the child's interests, the setting, the type of activity used, the role of the interventionist, and the outcomes achieved (Roper & Dunst, 2003). This chapter discussed the value of several intervention strategies that have been drawn from the principles of applied behavior analysis but can be used to support generalized communication in natural contexts. Some of these strategies include time delay, in vivo modeling, video modeling, and scripting. They have been successfully applied in teaching language and communication to children and adolescents with ASD.

How is unconventional verbal behavior addressed in children with ASD?

Prizant and Rydell (1993) offer several considerations that address the challenges that unconventional verbal behavior (UVB) place on the communicative abilities of children with ASD. Because UVB often occurs in periods of heightened anxiety or stress, confusion, and transition, the practitioner is encouraged to employ the following: simplify language input; respond to

TABLE 9.1

Sample Communication Goals and Possible Strategies
To Support Those Goals for Children with ASD

Sample Goal	Possible Strategies
To increase the use of flexible, meaningful phrases and sentences and decrease the use of echolalic speech in interactions with family members and teachers, moving from structured routines to unstructured interactions.	*Managing echolalic speech* (Prizant & Rydell, 1993) EXAMPLE: The team will simplify the linguistic input given to the child and will relate that input to objects and relationships observed in the environment at home and at school. The team will respond to the child's communicative intent; relate utterances to actions or objects; support the use of correct pronouns; modify the situation; prepare the child for a new activity, event, or transition; and provide relevant language.
To increase the child's ability to use oral language, gestures, and facial expressions to establish joint attention with adults and peers, moving from structured to unstructured events at home and at school.	*Joint action routines* (Snyder-McLean, Solomonson, McLean, & Sack, 1984) EXAMPLE: School team and parents will use familiar or well-established routines at home (e.g., lunch) and at school (e.g., morning circle) that have a logical, predictable sequence to support the child's ability to take turns, make requests, and respond to requests. *Time delay* (Charlop & Trasowech, 1991) EXAMPLE: Team members will insert a delay between the presentation of a target language response (e.g., responding to a question that has been asked or making a comment about an observed action) and a prompted response (e.g., giving a child the response that is expected). *Incidental teaching* (Hart & Risley, 1982; Kaiser, Alpert, & Warren, 1987) EXAMPLE: In the childcare setting, the care provider will place materials out of reach to require the child to make requests for assistance and will model the appropriate language to make such requests.
To increase the child's ability to communicate experiences using meaningful language from home to school and school to home.	*Creating visual bridges* (Hodgdon, 1999) EXAMPLE: The SLP will design a variety of visual supports using words, pictures, or objects to support the child's ability to communicate about his or her experiences at home and at school. *Reciprocal book reading* EXAMPLE: Patterned literature, predictable books, and books with a script or clearly defined sequence of events will be used to expose the child to a variety of experiences and language forms through storytelling; this will provide the child with some modeled support for sharing his or her own stories and experiences.

the child's presumed communicative intent; relate the child's utterances to actions or objects of interest; support correct use of pronouns; modify the situation to increase the child's comfort with a task or activity; prepare the child for a particular event prior to its occurrence; and provide relevant language opportunities throughout the day.

What strategies might be used to expand the conversational abilities of children with ASD?

Once children and adolescents with ASD have successfully established a consistent communication system, efforts must be made to expand their language use so they can engage in reciprocal conversations with peers and adults. The interventionist may provide conversational scripts or written prompts to guide question asking. Goals should focus on responding to and asking questions, offering comments, using contingent verbal statements, and making assertions. Tables 9.2 and 9.3 list some strategies for teams working to improve the speaking and listening skills and support the language use of children and adolescents with ASD.

How might the communication skills of children with ASD be supported in the home?

Families are key partners in planning and implementing interventions for their children with ASD. Parents spend a significant amount of direct contact time with their children and are logical choices for teaching intervention strategies for supporting communication. Both the *Affect-Based Language Curriculum* and the *More Than Words* program engage parents in intervention, guiding them through the developmental process of language learning and supporting their natural opportunities to engage their children in meaningful communication.

Practice Opportunities

1. Identify a child with ASD who exhibits limited verbal communication skills and determine what visual supports might facilitate the child's communication attempts at home and at school.

2. Create a joint action routine for a child with ASD that will facilitate the child's initiation of requests during a play activity with a peer.

3. Identify an important language skill for a child with ASD and develop a script to be used in video modeling.

4. As a team, determine how you will engineer the classroom and home environments for a child with ASD so that the child's interests and motivators are evident, systematic instruction occurs on a targeted language skill within the natural environment, and natural consequences occur.

TABLE 9.2

Tips for Improving Listening and Speaking Skills in Children and Adolescents with ASD

1. It is important to increase students' awareness of their role in communication exchanges. They must develop an understanding of speaker–listener roles if they are to succeed in classroom communication. Teachers in collaboration with speech–language pathologists might develop a communication skills unit for implementation in the classroom. The communication skills unit should include the following:

   - specification of the problem listening behaviors in the classroom;
   - specification of the problem speaking behaviors in the classroom;
   - determination of curriculum goals that require skill in listening and speaking in the classroom setting;
   - identification of the key vocabulary that students should understand (e.g., communication, listener, speaker); and
   - identification of the behaviors associated with the key vocabulary, e.g.,
     —Communication: oral, written, gestural, facial, and body language;
     —Listener: looking at speaker, thinking about what is being said, not interrupting, etc.;
     —Speaker: looking at listeners, talking loud enough to be heard, using vocal expression, staying on topic, etc.

2. Use visual charts with both print and symbols to specify the listening and speaking behaviors expected in a particular setting.

3. Demonstrate both successful and unsuccessful listening and speaking skills in a variety of situations for a variety of purposes through role playing. Debrief with the students about what made the interactions successful or unsuccessful, identifying what listening and speaking skills contributed to or hindered the communication exchange. Brainstorm alternative listening and speaking behaviors in those situations where communication was unsuccessful.

4. Brainstorm with students the different ways messages can be communicated. Using a web or network drawing, divide the different kinds of communication mentioned into verbal, print, and gestural modes.

5. Help students to monitor their comprehension of messages heard in communication exchanges. Consider the following potential hindrances to successful communication:

   - acoustic signal of the message (e.g., not loud enough);
   - rate of the message (e.g., excessively fast);
   - ambiguity of the message (e.g., not enough information provided); and
   - complexity of the message (e.g., too much information given at once).

Suggested Readings

Potter, C., & Whittaker, C. (2001). *Enabling communication in children with autism.* Philadelphia: Jessica Kingsley.

This book reports the results of 2 years of research completed with children with ASD in five special schools in the United Kingdom. The authors describe a communication approach that builds the strengths of children with limited or no verbal speech. They found that factors within the environment and not just within the child affected the rate and quality of the children's spontaneous communication. Numerous practical examples are provided to

TABLE 9.3

Tips for Supporting Language Use in Children and Adolescents with ASD

1. Teach turn taking through natural interactions about shared interests.

2. Model appropriate verbal and nonverbal strategies for

   - initiating a greeting,
   - introducing a topic of conversation,
   - maintaining a topic of conversation, and
   - terminating a conversation.

3. Use videotape review to demonstrate different ways to engage in conversations.

4. Use students' strengths to create motivating activities that promote social language (e.g., Play Station or Nintendo Club, Science Club, Building Club).

5. Review the students' social environments to cue them in on information they might miss or misinterpret.

6. Create barrier games in which one student (the sender) directs a second student (the receiver) to act on specific items while separated from seeing the identical items. This activity requires precise language instructions and can facilitate

   - the use of language to direct others' behavior,
   - the use of meaningful repair strategies,
   - the development of concept knowledge, and
   - the development of communicative interactions.

7. Have students give directions to another to facilitate their explicit language use (e.g., directions to their home or to a special event).

describe the minimal speech approach and proximal communication intervention they used successfully with children affected by autism.

Sussman, F. (1999). *More than words: Helping parents promote communication and social skills in children with autism spectrum disorders.* Toronto, Ontario: Hanen Centre.

This resource is appropriate for parents who wish to develop the communication skills of their children with ASD. The strategies are drawn from current research and are used in naturalistic contexts. The content emphasized includes learning about a child's communication; setting goals; following the child's lead; taking turns; connecting through people games; understanding what is said; using visuals, music, books, and toys; and making friends.

Resources

Pragmatics

Developing the functional use of language is critical for communication success. Practitioners may wish to consider using some of the following resources to help facilitate the pragmatic language skills of children with ASD.

The tools and strategies listed here include ways to improve conversational language, social reasoning, and general listening and speaking skills.

Anderson-Wood, L., & Smith, B. R. *Working with pragmatics: A practical guide to promoting communicative confidence.* Eau Claire, WI: Thinking Publications.

This is a pragmatics-based guidebook to enhance knowledge of how speech and language are used appropriately in context. It is appropriate to use with preschoolers through adults. Some of the key components included in this resource are systematic ways to develop pragmatic skills, measures for diagnosis and assessment, an outline of pragmatic characteristics, numerous intervention activities, an annotated bibliography, and reproducible assessment and profiling forms.

Arick, J. R., Loos, L., Falco, R., & Krug, D. A. *The STAR Program: Strategies for teaching based on autism research: Levels I, II, and III.* Austin, TX: PRO-ED.

This comprehensive program, based on the critical skills emphasized by the National Research Council (2001), supports the development of receptive and expressive language, functional routines, social interaction, play skills, and preacademic and academic skills. The authors include lesson plans and ways to document and assess performance. Level I is used for those students with limited verbal skills who require support in understanding basic concepts, following simple commands, and engaging in independent constructive play. Level II emphasizes strategies for children using single words who need support for following two-step commands, using words to make requests, answering wh-questions, and playing interactively. Level III is selected for children who use two or more words and require support to expand their vocabulary and language, follow and participate in complex routines, and play interactively with peers.

Bernarding, M. B. *Exploring pragmatic language: Games for practice.* Austin, TX: PRO-ED.

This instructional manual and game materials are used to support the development of a variety of pragmatic skills for students from 6 to 14 years of age. The pragmatic language activities provide opportunities for students to describe, compare, and contrast pictures, as well as ask and answer questions, tell stories, and give directions. Further, students gain experience in drawing conclusions and making inferences.

Bliss, L. S. *Pragmatic language intervention: Interactive activities.* Eau Claire, WI: Thinking Publications.

Several functional and interactive activities are included in this resource to teach children between the ages of 4 and 15 years where and when communication skills are used. Procedures for each activity are clearly outlined, targeting a specific linguistic structure or pragmatic behavior in a naturalistic context.

Deal, J. E., & Hanuscin, L. *Barrier games for better communication.* Austin, TX: PRO-ED.

This instructional manual and accompanying games are used to help students from 5 to 9 years give relevant, accurate, and specific information in interactions. Further, the games provide opportunities for students to request information, give directions, and ask for clarification.

Hess, L. J. *Face to face: Facilitating adolescent conversational experiences.* Austin, TX: PRO-ED.

Using role playing and modeling, this manual and video can be used to help adolescents, 12 to 19 years old, learn effective conversational skills. It supports the learning of speaker and listener roles, as well as ways to initiate and maintain conversation. The particular pragmatic discourse skills emphasized include negotiation, persuasion, providing relevant and accurate information, and greeting.

Hoskins, B. *Conversations: A framework for language intervention.* Eau Claire, WI: Thinking Publications.

This tool emphasizes a natural way to support students' communication skill development—through conversation. Used for students 11 to 18 years of age and effective for supporting language critical to successful classroom interaction, the following conversational "moves" are targeted: introducing topics, maintaining topics, extending topics, changing topics, requesting clarification, and responding to requests for clarification.

Ketter, C., & Hesse, J. *The question: Colorful conversation starters.* Eau Claire, WI: Thinking Publications.

Two hundred questions are provided for developing students' higher-level thinking skills. It is appropriate for children age 10 through adults. The questions provide opportunities for students to use appropriate and complex sentence structure, slang and humor, and storytelling.

Koski, P. S. *Autism & PDD picture stories & language activities.* Austin, TX: PRO-ED.

Sequenced picture stories, routine, repetition, and structure are elements of this resource. Students learn to describe stories, predict, retell and sequence events, answer yes–no questions, and act out each story. The five content areas include the four seasons and one on animals.

Mattes, L. J., & Eddo, D. *Adventures in pragmatic problem solving.* Oceanside, CA: Academic Communication Associates.

Short stories and thinking activities are used to help children, ages 5 through 10, develop problem-solving strategies for communicating in challenging situations. Skills developed include verbalizing solutions for problems, identifying causes of problems, identifying consequences of behavior, and recognizing the viewpoints of others.

Mayo, P., & Waldo, P. *Scripting: Social communication for adolescents.* Eau Claire, WI: Thinking Publications.

Scripts are provided for 53 social communication skills that pose challenges for adolescents. Two different scripts are provided for each skill, one demonstrating the appropriate use of the skill and the other demonstrating inappropriate use of the skill. Through role playing and planned dialogue, students identify what was done or said that was inappropriate and make suggestions for changing the script.

Paul, R. *Pragmatic activities for language intervention: Semantics, syntax, and emerging literacy.* Austin, TX: PRO-ED.

In this resource, conversational language lessons are provided through role playing, arts and crafts, puppetry, and other means. Using scripts, the activities presented control linguistic input so that the language elicited is appropriate to the context. Appropriate for students 2 to 12 years of age; three developmentally structured sections are provided: for young children, ways to facilitate early word meaning; for preschoolers, ways to facilitate the language form and content they need for communication and school readiness; and for older children, ways to facilitate the transition from oral to written language and learn the complexities of later language understanding and use. As part of each lesson, goals, stimuli, feedback, developmental stage, needed props, scripted procedures, and variations of activities are provided.

Plourde, L. *Clas: Classroom listening and speaking—Early childhood.* Austin, TX: PRO-ED.

Focused on supporting the listening and speaking skills of young children, 2 to 6 years of age, this program uses thematic units to engage children actively in learning.

Plourde, L. *Clas: Classroom listening and speaking–Preschool.* Austin, TX: PRO-ED.

Targeting 3- to 5-year-olds, this program has developed both weekly classroom activities and home-based activities to support listening and speaking skills across 11 themes familiar to young children.

Schreiber, L., & McKinley, N. *Daily communication: Strategies for adolescents with language disorders (2nd ed.).* Eau Claire, WI: Thinking Publications.

Developed for students in Grades 7 through 12, this manual emphasizes learning strategies to enhance student skills in the following areas: listening, question asking, conversational skills, nonverbal communication, survival language, problem solving, and study skills. The activities provided can be used in small or large groups, can be adapted to students' individual ability levels, and highlight the use of communication strategies in daily life.

Schuchardt, P. R. *SITuation COMmunication.* Oceanside, CA: Academic Communication Associates.

Appropriate for children ages 8 through 15, this manual includes activities designed for effective problem solving and interacting with others in social situations. Specific skills that are highlighted include recognizing the communication needs of others; expressing feelings and points of view while respecting the points of view of others; reacting to and expressing criticism; giving explanations; asking appropriate questions; and knowing when to speak.

Sonders, S. A. *Giggle time: Establishing the social connection: A program to develop the communication skills of children with autism.* Philadelphia: Jessica Kingsley.

This guide offers practical strategies to support the communication skills of young children with autism. The activities are appropriate for both home and school. Some of the topics include turn taking, initiation, verbal play, and preconversational speech.

Semantics

Understanding the meaning of language is critical for communication success. Practitioners may wish to consider using some of the following resources to help facilitate the semantic skills of children with ASD. The tools and strategies listed here include ways to improve understanding and use of multiple-meaning words, figurative language, and vocabulary concepts.

Auslin, M. S. *Idiom workbook series.* Austin, TX: PRO-ED.

Targeted for students with a reading level of at least third grade, seven workbooks are included that present idioms within a written context followed by exercises to review the definition and support comprehension and application to students' experiences.

Flowers, T. *Activities for developing pre-skill concepts in children with autism.* Austin, TX: PRO-ED.

> Practical activities for classroom use to support children with autism in the following areas: auditory development, concept development, social development, speech and language development, and visual and motor development. Activities are appropriate for all ages and support educators in determining what the goals of the activities are, how the activities should be implemented, and what materials are needed for each activity.

Gorman-Gard, K. A. *Figurative language.* Eau Claire, WI: Thinking Publications.

> Designed for students 10 years of age and older, this activity book offers ways to support the comprehension and production of common figurative language forms. The author provides a pre- and posttest format and sample IEP goals. The figurative language forms emphasized include idioms, proverbs, multiple-meaning words, riddles and jokes, metaphors and similes, slang, and clichés.

Hamersky, J. *Cartoon cut-ups: Teaching figurative language & humor.* Eau Claire, WI: Thinking Publications.

> Used to teach 8- to 18-year-olds humor and figurative language, this activity book includes two sets of reproducible cartoons. One set of cartoons has the captions included so that the student can focus on the language that makes the cartoon funny. The second set of cartoons does not include the captions, so that these can be used to highlight facial expression, body language, and other environmental components contributing to the humor. The components of humor emphasized include idiomatic expressions, metaphors and similes, jokes and riddles, proverbs, and multiple-meaning words.

Hamersky, J. *Vocabulary maps: Strategies for developing word meanings.* Eau Claire, WI: Thinking Publications.

> This strategy-based approach to vocabulary development is most appropriate for students in Grades 6 through 12. Students are taught ways to organize words and relate word meanings so that they can learn, retain, integrate, and use newly learned words in meaningful contexts. Five organizational strategies are emphasized, including attribute web, multiple-meaning tree, semantic continuum, Venn diagram, and associated word format.

Kipping, P., & Gemmer, T. *Figurative language cards.* Austin, TX: PRO-ED.

> Four decks of cards are provided that foster students' comprehension of the meaning of figurative language, including idioms, proverbs, similes, metaphors, and clichés. The activities are appropriate for children and adolescents with language impairments.

Koski, P. S. *Autism & PDD: Early intervention.* East Moline, IL: LinguiSystems.

> Appropriate for supporting the language development of young children (ages 1–3 years) with autism and PDD, a set of five books are used to support children's understanding of concepts such as turn taking, following directions, and vocabulary. Using picture cards, children listen to and act out simple stories related to playing, getting dressed, eating and drinking, being healthy, and singing.

Lattyak, J., & Dedrick, S. *Multiple word meanings.* Austin, TX: PRO-ED.

> Appropriate for elementary students, this program is designed to support children's understanding of words that have more than one meaning. The program includes objectives and standards for teachers that can be individualized for students.

Mulstay-Muratore, L. *Autism & PDD: Abstract concepts–Levels 1 and 2.* East Moline, IL: LinguiSystems.

Using pictures to support children's connections between concrete and abstract language, these books facilitate children's ability to understand and answer wh-questions. Two levels are included, one for children ages 3 to 5 and the second for children ages 5 to 9. The content emphasized within the two levels includes helping children to describe feelings and to ask questions such as "What happened?" "What did you do?" "When?" "Why?" "What do you need?" "What should?" and "What if?"

Rea-Rosenberger, S. *Workbook for synonyms, homonyms, and antonyms.* Austin, TX: PRO-ED.

Appropriate for students 8 to 14 years of age, this workbook includes activities for choosing word pairs, completing sentences, matching words to definitions, unscrambling words, rhyming riddles, and completing crossword puzzles.

Reese, P. B., & Challenner, N. C. *Autism & PDD concept development.* East Moline, IL: LinguiSystems.

This set of six books uses visual cues to help children ages 3 to 8 years develop language emphasizing attributes, categories, and descriptions. The concepts presented cross several themes, including animals, clothing, food, household items, toys and entertainment, and transportation.

Spector, C. C. *Saying one thing, meaning another: Activities for clarifying ambiguous language.* Eau Claire, WI: Thinking Publications.

The activities included in this tool attempt to help students 10 years of age and older to analyze the ambiguous language frequently encountered in academic material, in social contexts, and in job settings. The author has put together a collection of words, phrases, and sentences that are ambiguous to facilitate the learning of idiomatic expressions and humor. Specifically, the activity book includes multiple-meaning words (e.g., homophones and homographs); multiple-meaning phrases (e.g., idioms and proverbs); sentences with stress changes (e.g., riddles); and sentences with double meanings (e.g., sarcasm, indirect requests, irony, polite evasions).

Sterling-Orth, A., Thurs, S. A., Radichel, T. J., McKinley, N. L., & Schreiber, L. R. *Working out with semantics.* Eau Claire, WI: Thinking Publications.

A number of flexible activities are included to support children's understanding and use of description, sequences, concepts, comparison, part–whole relationships, and categories. The activities are appropriate for children ages 5 to 10 years.

Visual Supports

The use of visual supports can be critical to the communication success of children with ASD. Practitioners may wish to consider using some of the following resources to help facilitate their use.

Bondy, A., & Frost, L. *A picture's worth: PECS and other visual communication strategies in autism.* Bethesda, MD: Woodbine House.

This book examines the use of nonverbal communication strategies for children with ASD of all ages and comprehensively defines the Picture Exchange Communication System.

McClannahan, L. E., & Krantz, P. J. *Activity schedules for children with autism: Teaching independent behavior.* Bethesda, MD: Woodbine House.

This resource provides both parents and practitioners with strategies for developing activity schedules, which are sets of pictures or words that cue children to engage in a series of activities. The book offers suggestions for assessing children's readiness to use the material, how to prepare the schedules, and how to evaluate progress.

Wiig, E., & Wilson, C. *Map it out: Visual tools for thinking, organizing & communicating.* Eau Claire, WI: Thinking Publications.

Appropriate for students in Grades 1 through 12, this resource provides maps for teachers to guide students' responses in the area of critical thinking. Four general language areas are supported, including semantics (meaning and content), pragmatics (context), text comprehension, and school knowledge and study skills.

Glossary

Antecedent. Event that occurs prior to a behavior, providing an opportunity to intervene or change an undesired behavior before it occurs.

Applied behavior analysis procedures. Strategies derived from the principles of behavior that are systematically applied to increase socially appropriate behavior in meaningful contexts.

Backstepping. Error correction procedure in which a prompter takes a child back in the sequence of trained behaviors to the last step completed correctly and then provides assistance to complete the sequence.

Backward chaining. Teaching a sequence of behaviors by reinforcing mastery of the last step, followed by the next to the last step, and so forth.

Consequence. Event that follows a behavior and determines whether that behavior occurs again.

Delayed prompting. Pairing a prompt with the natural cue that should control the target behavior; presenting the natural cue and after a predetermined time presenting the helping prompt if the desired behavior has not been exhibited.

Differential reinforcement. Greater reinforcement of one response over another.

Discrete trial teaching. Teaching technique that breaks down skills into smaller parts, teaching one skill at a time until the skill is mastered, using prompting, reinforcement, and one-on-one teaching.

Extinction. Withholding reinforcement to reduce the occurrence of a behavior.

Mand. Verbal instruction or request.

Milieu teaching. Natural language intervention technique emphasizing the teaching of functional communication skills in social contexts.

Modeling. When used in language instruction, providing examples of targeted verbalizations.

Multipointing. Pointing more than once following a sequence to communicate a message.

Prompts. Verbal, gestural, or physical stimuli used to produce a target behavior.

Reinforcement. A stimulus that is a consequence of a particular behavior and increases the likelihood that that behavior will occur again.

Response generalization. The occurrence of a response in a category other than the one in which training was received.

Responses. Behaviors that can be observed and measured and occur following a particular stimulus.

Routine. Specific aspects of scripts that remain constant and can be identified and taught.

Schema. A plan for representing and organizing information.

Script. A schema for a particular event that specifies the actions, actors, and props.

Script fading. Removing sections of a written script until no written cue remains.

Shaping. Reinforcing behavior that is closer to the target behavior than the behavior displayed previously.

Stimulus. An activity, event, or object that occurs within the environment and serves as an antecedent or consequence.

Stimulus control. Control over a particular behavior by a stimulus or cue.

Stimulus generalization. Transfer of learned behaviors to stimulus conditions different from those in which training occurred.

Two-person prompting (also **errorless learning**). Prompting in which one trainer interacts with the child while another physically prompts from behind without interacting; physical prompter gradually fades prompts using backward chaining.

References

Bandura, A. (1965). Influence of models' reinforcement contingencies on the acquisition of imitative responses. *Journal of Personality and Social Psychology, 1,* 589–595.

Beukelman, D., & Mirenda, P. (1992). *Augmentative and alternative communication: Management of severe communication disorders in children and adults.* Baltimore: Brookes.

Bondy, A. (2001). PECS: Potential benefits and risks. *The Behavior Analyst Today, 2,* 127–132.

Bondy, A. S., & Frost, L. A. (1993). Mands across the water: A report on the application of the Picture Exchange Communication System in Peru. *The Behavior Analyst, 16*(1), 123–128.

Bondy, A. S., & Frost, L. A. (1994). The Picture Exchange Communication System. *Focus on Autistic Behavior, 9*(3), 1–19.

Bondy, A. S., & Frost, L. A. (1998). The Picture Exchange Communication System. *Seminars in Speech and Language, 19*(4), 373–388.

Bondy, A. S., & Frost, L. A. (2001). The Picture Exchange Communication System. *Behavior Modification, 25*(5), 725–744.

Brown, J., & Murray, D. (2002). Communication-based behavioral interventions for children with autism spectrum disorder. *Perspectives on Language Learning and Education, 9*(2), 8–13.

Capps, L., Kehres, J., & Sigman, M. (1998). Conversational abilities among children with autism and children with developmental delays. *The International Journal of Research and Practice, 2,* 325–344.

Carter, C. M. (2001). Using choice with game play to increase language skills and interactive behaviors in children with autism. *Journal of Positive Behavior Interventions, 3*(3), 131–151.

Carter, M., & Maxwell, K. (1998). Promoting interaction with children using augmentative communication through a peer-directed intervention. *International Journal of Disability, Development and Education, 45*(1), 75–96.

Charlop, M. H., & Milstein, J. P. (1989). Teaching autistic children conversational speech using video modeling. *Journal of Applied Behavioral Analysis, 22*, 275–285.

Charlop, M., Schreibman, L., & Thibodeau, M. (1985). Increasing spontaneous verbal responding in autistic children using a time delay procedure. *Journal of Applied Behavior Analysis, 18*, 155–166.

Charlop, M. H., Schreibman, L., & Tyron, A. S. (1983). Learning through observation: The effects of peer modeling on acquisition and generalization in autistic children. *Journal of Abnormal Child Psychology, 11*(3), 355–366.

Charlop, M. H., & Trasowech, J. E. (1991). Increasing autistic children's daily spontaneous speech. *Journal of Applied Behavioral Analysis, 24*, 747–761.

Charlop, M. H., & Walsh, M. E. (1986). Increasing autistic children's spontaneous verbalizations of affection: An assessment of time delay and peer modeling procedures. *Journal of Applied Behavior Analysis, 19*, 307–314.

Charlop-Christy, M. H. (2004, June). *Using video modeling to teach perspective taking to children with autism.* Presentation at the annual Vermont Summer Autism Institute, Burlington.

Charlop-Christy, M. H., Carpenter, M. H., & Dennis, B. (2004). *Teaching socially expressive behaviors to children with autism.* Unpublished manuscript, Claremont McKenna College, Claremont, CA.

Charlop-Christy, M. H., Carpenter, M., Le, L., LeBlanc, L. A., & Kellet, K. (2002). Using the Picture Exchange Communication System (PECS) with children with autism: Assessment of PECS acquisition, speech, social–communicative behavior, and problem behavior. *Journal of Applied Behavior Analysis, 35*(3), 213–231.

Charlop-Christy, M. H., & Daneshvar, S. (2003). Using video modeling to teach perspective taking to children with autism. *Journal of Positive Behavior Interventions, 5*(1), 12.

Charlop-Christy, M. H., & Kelso, S. E. (1997). *How to treat the child with autism.* Claremont, CA: Author.

Charlop-Christy, M. H., Le, L., & Freeman, K. A. (2000). A comparison of video modeling with in vivo modeling for teaching children with autism. *Journal of Autism and Developmental Disorders, 30*(6), 537–552.

Coleman, S. L., & Stedman, J. M. (1974). Use of a peer model in language training in an echolalic child. *Journal of Behavior Therapy and Experimental Psychiatry, 5*, 275–279.

Creaghead, N. A. (1991). Classroom interactional analysis/script analysis. *Best Practices in School Speech–Language Pathology, 2*, 65–72.

Delprato, D. J. (2001). Comparisons of discrete trial teaching and normalized behavioral language intervention for young children with autism. *Journal of Autism and Developmental Disorders, 31*, 315–325.

Dettmer, S., Simpson, R. L., Myles, B. S., & Ganz, J. B. (2000). The use of visual supports to facilitate transitions of students with autism. *Focus on Autism and Other Developmental Disabilities, 15*(3), 163–169.

Dowrick, P. W., & Dove, C. (1980). The use of self-modeling to improve the swimming performance of spina bifida children. *Journal of Applied Behavior Analysis, 13*, 51–56

Dowrick, P. W., & Hood, M. (1981). Comparison of self-modeling and small cash incentives in a sheltered workshop. *Journal of Applied Psychology, 66*, 394–397.

Dowrick, P. W., & Raeburn, J. M. (1995). Self-modeling: Rapid skill training for children with physical disabilities. *Journal of Developmental and Physical Disabilities, 7*, 25–37.

Duchan, J. F., & Weitzner-Lin, B. (1987). Nurturant–naturalistic language intervention for language-impaired children: Implications for planning lessons and tracking progress. *Asha, 29,* 45–49.

Dyer, K., Williams, L., & Luce, S. C. (1991). Training teachers to use naturalistic communication strategies in classrooms for students with autism and other severe handicaps. *Language, Speech, and Hearing Services in Schools, 22,* 313–321.

Egel, A. L., Richman, G., & Koegel, R. L. (1981). Normal peer models and autistic children's learning. *Journal of Applied Behavior Analysis, 14,* 3–12.

Frea, W. D., Arnold, C. L., & Vittimberga, G. L. (2001). A demonstration of the effects of augmentative communication on the extreme aggressive behavior of a child with autism within an integrated preschool setting. *Journal of Positive Behavior Interventions, 3*(4), 194–198.

Freeman, S., & Dake, L. (1997). *Teach me language: A manual for children with autism, Asperger's syndrome and related developmental disorders.* Langley, British Columbia: SKF Books.

Frost, L., & Bondy, A. (1994). *The Picture Exchange Communication System Training Manual.* Cherry Hill, NJ: Pyramid Educational Consultants.

Frost, L. A., & Bondy, A. S. (2002). *The Picture Exchange Communication System Training Manual* (2nd ed.). Newark, DE: Pyramid Educational Products.

Goldstein, H. (2002). Communication intervention for children with autism: A review of treatment efficacy. *Journal of Autism and Developmental Disorders, 32,* 373–396.

Goldstein, H., & Cisar, C. (1992). Promoting interaction during sociodramatic play: Teaching scripts to typical preschoolers and classmates with disabilities. *Journal of Applied Behavior Analysis, 25*(2), 265–280.

Goldstein, H., Wickstrom, S., Hoyson, M., Jamieson, B., & Odom, S. L. (1988). Effects of sociodramatic script training on social and communicative interaction. *Education and Treatment of Children, 11*(2), 97–117.

Goodman, G., Duchan, J., & Sonnenmeier, R. (1994). Children's development of scriptal knowledge. In J. Duchan, L. Hewitt, & R. Sonnenmeier (Eds.), *Pragmatics: From theory to practice* (pp. 120–133). Englewood Cliffs, NJ: Prentice Hall.

Greenspan, S. I., & Lewis, D. (2002). *The affect-based language curriculum (ABLC): An intensive program for families, therapists and teachers.* Bethesda, MD: Interdisciplinary Council on Developmental and Learning Disorders.

Harris, S. L., & Boyle, T. D. (1985). Parents as language trainers of children with autism. In E. Schopler & G. B. Mesibov (Eds.), *Communication problems in autism* (pp. 207–227). New York: Plenum Press.

Harris, S. L., & Delmolino, L. (2002). Applied behavior analysis: Its application in the treatment of autism and related disorders in young children. *Infants and Young Children, 14*(3), 11–17.

Hart, B., & Risley, T. R. (1982). *How to use incidental teaching for elaborating language.* Lawrence, KS: H & H Enterprises.

Hetzroni, O. E., & Tannous, J. (2004). Effects of a computer-based intervention program on the communicative functions of children with autism. *Journal of Autism and Developmental Disorders, 34*(2), 95–113.

Hodgdon, L. A. (1995). *Visual strategies for improving communication: Practical supports for school and home.* Troy, MI: Quirk Roberts.

Hodgdon, L. A. (1999). *Solving behavior problems in autism: Improving communication with visual strategies.* Troy, MI: Quirk Roberts.

Ingenmey, R., & Van Houten, R. (1991). Using time delay to promote spontaneous speech in an autistic child. *Journal of Applied Behavior Analysis, 24,* 591–596.

Jahr, E. (2001). Teaching children with autism to answer novel wh-questions by utilizing a multiple exemplar strategy. *Research in Developmental Disabilities, 22,* 407–423.

Johnston, S., Nelson, C., Evans, J., & Palazolo, K. (2003). The use of visual supports in teaching young children with autism spectrum disorder to initiate interactions. *Augmentative and Alternative Communication, 19*(2), 86–103.

Kaiser, A. P., Alpert, C. L., & Warren, S. F. (1987). Teaching functional language: Strategies for language intervention. In M. E. Snell (Ed.), *Systematic instruction for persons with severe handicaps* (pp. 247–271). Columbus, OH: Charles Merrill.

Keen, D., Sigafoos, J., & Woodyatt, G. (2001). Replacing prelinguistic behaviors with functional communication. *Journal of Autism and Developmental Disorders, 31*(4), 385–398.

Kluth, P. (2003). *"You're going to love this kid!" Teaching students with autism in the classroom.* Baltimore: Brookes.

Koegel, L. K., Camarata, S. M., Valdez-Menchaca, M., & Koegel, R. L. (1998). Setting generalization of question-asking by children with autism. *American Journal on Mental Retardation, 102*(4), 346–357.

Koegel, L. K., Koegel, R. L., & Carter, C. M. (1998). Pivotal response training and the natural language paradigm. *Seminars in Speech and Language, 19,* 355–372.

Koegel, R. L., Camarata, S., Koegel, L. K., Ben-Tall, A., & Smith, A. E. (1998). Increasing speech intelligibility in children with autism. *Journal of Autism and Developmental Disorders, 28,* 241–251.

Koegel, R. L., Koegel, L. K., & Surrant, A. (1992). Language intervention and disruptive behavior in preschool children with autism. *Journal of Autism and Developmental Disorders, 22,* 141–153.

Koegel, R. L., O'Dell, M. C., & Dunlap, G. (1988). Producing speech use in nonverbal autistic children by reinforcing attempts. *Journal of Autism and Developmental Disorders, 18,* 525–538.

Koegel, R. L., O'Dell, M. C., & Koegel, L. K. (1987). A natural language teaching paradigm for nonverbal autistic children. *Journal of Autism and Developmental Disorders, 17,* 187–200.

Krantz, P., & McClannahan, L. (1998). Social interaction skills for children with autism: A script-fading procedure for beginning readers. *Journal of Applied Behavior Analysis, 31,* 191–202.

Kravitz, T. R., Kamps, D. M., Kemmerer, K., & Potucek, J. (2002). Brief report: Increasing communication skills for an elementary-aged student with autism using the Picture Exchange Communication System. *Journal of Autism and Developmental Disorders, 32*(3), 225–230.

LeBlanc, L. A., Coates, A. M., Daneshvar, S., Charlop-Christy, M. H., Morris, C., & Lancaster, B. M. (2003). Using video modeling and reinforcement to teach perspective-taking skills to children with autism. *Journal of Applied Behavior Analysis, 36,* 253–257.

Liddle, K. (2001). Implementing the Picture Exchange Communication System (PECS). *International Journal of Language and Communication Disorders, 36,* 391–395.

Light, J. C., Roberts, B., DiMarco, R., & Greiner, N. (1998). Augmentative and alternative communication to support receptive and expressive communication for people with autism. *Journal of Communication Disorders, 31,* 153–180.

Lord, C., & Schopler, E. (1989). Stability of assessment results of autistic and nonautistic language impaired children from preschool years to early school age. *Journal of Child Psychology and Psychiatry, 30,* 575–590.

Lord, C., & Schopler, E. (1994). TEACCH services for preschool children. In S. L. Harris & J. S. Handleman (Eds.), *Preschool education programs for children with autism* (pp. 87–106). Austin, TX: PRO-ED.

Lovaas, O. I. (1981). *Teaching developmentally disabled children: The me book.* Austin, TX: PRO-ED.

Loveland, K., & Tunali, B. (1991). Social scripts for conversational interactions in autism and Down syndrome. *Journal of Autism and Developmental Disorders, 21*(2), 177–186.

Matson, J. L., Sevin, J. A., Box, M. L., Francis, K. L., & Sevin, B. M. (1993). Evaluation and comparison of two methods for increasing spontaneous language in autistic children. *Journal of Applied Behavior Analysis, 26,* 389–398.

McCormick, K. M., Jolivette, K., & Ridgley, R. (2003). Choice making intervention strategy for young children. *Young Exceptional Children, 6*(2), 3–10.

McGee, G. G., Almeida, M. C., Sulzer-Azaroff, B., & Feldman, R. S. (1992). Promoting reciprocal interactions via peer incidental teaching. *Journal of Applied Behavior Analysis, 25,* 117–126.

McGee, G. G., Krantz, P. J., & McClannahan, L. E. (1984). Conversational skills for autistic adolescents: Teaching assertiveness in naturalistic game settings. *Journal of Autism and Developmental Disorders, 14*(3), 319–330.

McGee, G. G., Krantz, P. J., & McClannahan, L. E. (1985). The facilitative effects of incidental teaching on preposition use by autistic children. *Journal of Applied Behavior Analysis, 18,* 17–31.

McLean, J., & Snyder-McLean, L. (1978). *A transactional approach to early language training: Derivation of a model system.* Columbus, OH: Charles Merrill.

Mirenda, P. (2003). Toward functional augmentative and alternative communication for students with autism: Manual signs, graphic symbols, and voice output communication aids. *Language, Speech, and Hearing Services in Schools, 34,* 203–216.

Mirenda, P., & Schuler, A. L. (1988). Augmenting communication for persons with autism: Issues and strategies. *Topics in Language Disorders, 9*(1), 24–43.

National Research Council. (2001). *Educating children with autism.* Committee on Educational Interventions for Children with Autism, Division of Behavioral and Social Sciences and Education. Washington, DC: National Academy Press.

Ogletree, B., & Oren, T. (1998). Structured yet functional: An alternative conceptualization of treatment for communication impairment in autism. *Focus on Autism and Other Developmental Disabilities, 13*(4), 228–233.

Potter, C. A., & Whittaker, C. A. (1997). Teaching the spontaneous use of semantic relations through multipointing to a child with autism and severe learning difficulties. *Child Language, Teaching and Therapy, 13*(2) 177–193.

Potter, C., & Whittaker, C. (2001). *Enabling communication in children with autism.* Philadelphia: Jessica Kingsley.

Prizant, B. M., & Rydell, P. J. (1993). Assessment and intervention considerations for unconventional verbal behavior. In S. F. Warren & J. Reichle (Series Eds.) & J. Reichle & D. Wacker (Vol. Eds.), *Communication and language intervention series: Vol. 3. Communicative alternatives to challenging behavior: Integrating functional assessment and intervention strategies* (pp. 263–297). Baltimore: Brookes.

Prizant, B. M., & Wetherby, A. M. (1998). Understanding the continuum of discrete-trial traditional behavioral to social–pragmatic developmental approaches in communication enhancement for young children with autism/PDD. *Seminars in Speech and Language, 19,* 329–352.

Prizant, B. M., Wetherby, A. M., & Rydell, P. J. (2000). Communication intervention issues for young children with autism spectrum disorders. In A. M. Wetherby & B. M.

Prizant (Eds.), *Autism spectrum disorders: A transactional developmental perspective* (pp. 193–224). Baltimore: Brookes.

Quill, K. A. (1997). Instructional considerations for young children with autism: The rationale for visually cued instruction. *Journal of Autism and Developmental Disorders, 27*(6), 697–714.

Risley, T., & Wolf, M. (1967). Establishing functional speech in children with echolalia. *Behavioral Research and Therapy, 5,* 73–88.

Roper, N., & Dunst, C. J. (2003). Communication intervention in natural learning environments: Guidelines for practice. *Infants and Young Children, 16*(3), 215–226.

Sarokoff, R., Taylor, B., & Poulson, C. (2001). Teaching children with autism to engage in conversational exchanges: Script fading with embedded textual stimuli. *Journal of Applied Behavior Analysis, 34*(1), 81–84.

Schlosser, R. W., & Braun, U. (1994). Efficacy of AAC interventions: Methodologic issues in evaluating behavior change, generalization, and effects. *AAC Augmentative and Alternative Communication, 10,* 207–223.

Schlosser, R. W., & Lee, D. L. (2000). Promoting generalization and maintenance in augmentative and alternative communication: A meta-analysis of 20 years of effectiveness research. *AAC Augmentative and Alternative Communication, 16*(4), 208–226.

Schwartz, I. S., Garfinkle, A. N., & Bauer, J. (1998). The Picture Exchange Communication System. Communicative outcomes for young children with disabilities. *Topics in Early Childhood Special Education, 18*(3), 144–159.

Sherer, M., Pierce, K. L., Paredes, S., Kisacky, K. L., Ingersoll, B., & Schreibman, L. (2001). Enhancing conversation skills in children with autism via video technology: Which is better, "self" or "other," as a model? *Behavior Modification, 25*(1), 140–158.

Shipley-Benamou, R., Lutzker, J. R., & Taubman, M. (2002). Teaching daily living skills to children with autism through instructional video modeling. *Journal of Positive Behavior Interventions, 4*(3), 166–177.

Simon, E. W., Whitchair, P. M., & Toll, D. M. (1996). A case study: Follow-up assessment of facilitated communication. *Journal of Autism and Developmental Disorders, 26*(1), 9–18.

Snyder-McLean, L., Solomonson, B., McLean, J., & Sack, S. (1984). Structuring joint action routines: A strategy for facilitating communication and language development in the classroom. *Seminars in Speech and Language, 5,* 213–228.

Sonnenmeier, R. M. (1994). Script-based language intervention: Learning to participate in life events. In J. Duchan, L. Hewitt, & R. M. Sonnenmeier (Eds.), *Pragmatics: From theory to practice* (pp. 134–148). Englewood Cliffs, NJ: Prentice Hall.

Sundberg, M. L., & Partington, J. W. (1998). *Teaching language to children with autism or other developmental disabilities.* Pleasant Hill, CA: Behavior Analysts.

Sussman, F. (1999). *More than words: Helping parents promote communication and social skills in children with autism spectrum disorders.* Toronto, Ontario: Hanen Centre.

Taylor, B. A., & Harris, S. L. (1995). Teaching children with autism to seek information: Acquisition of novel information and generalization of responding. *Journal of Applied Behavior Analysis, 28*(1), 3–14.

Trillingsgaard, A. (1999). The script model in relation to autism. *European Child and Adolescent Psychiatry, 8*(1), 45–49.

Venter, A., Lord, C., & Schopler, E. (1992). A follow-up study of high functioning autistic children. *Journal of Child Psychology and Psychiatry, 33,* 489–507.

Volden, J., & Johnston, J. (1999). Cognitive scripts in autistic children and adolescents. *Journal of Autism and Developmental Disorders, 29*(3), 203–211.

Watson, L. R. (1985). The TEACCH communication curriculum. In E. Schopler & G. B. Mesibov (Eds.), *Communication problems in autism* (pp. 187–206). New York: Plenum Press.

Watson, L. R., Lord, C., Schaffer, B., & Schopler, E. (1989). *Teaching spontaneous communication to autistic and developmentally handicapped children.* New York: Irvington.

Webb, T. (2000). Can children with autism be taught to communicate using PECS? *Good Autism Practice, 1,* 29–43.

Wetherby, A. M. (1992). *Communication and language intervention for preschool children.* Chicago: Riverside.

Wetherby, A. M., & Prizant, B. M. (1989). The expression of communicative intent: Assessment guidelines. *Seminars in Speech and Language, 10*(1), 77–91.

Whittaker, C. A., & Reynolds, J. (2000). Hand signaling in dyadic proximal communication: Social strengths of children with autism who do not speak. *Child Language Teaching and Therapy, 16*(1), 43–57.

Woods, J., Kashinath, S., & Goldstein, H. (2004). Effects of embedding caregiver-implemented teaching strategies in daily routines on children's communication outcomes. *Journal of Early Intervention, 26*(3), 175–193.

Yoder, P. J., Kaiser, A. P., Alpert, C., & Fischer, R. (1993). Following the child's lead when teaching nouns to preschoolers with mental retardation. *Journal of Speech and Hearing Research, 36,* 158–167.

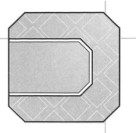

CHAPTER 10

Interventions
To Support the Play
of Children with ASD

Patricia A. Prelock

QUESTIONS TO CONSIDER

In this chapter, you will learn about the role of teaching play to children with autism spectrum disorders (ASD). Several strategies will be described for teaching imitative and independent play, pretend or sociodramatic play, and peer-supported play. You will also learn about the interrelationships among various aspects of play, language, social interaction, and cognition that affect intervention. As you read this chapter, consider the following questions:

1. What strategies could be effective in supporting the imitative and independent play of children with ASD?

2. How can pretend or sociodramatic play be developed for children with ASD?

3. What is the role of peer-supported play in facilitating the social play of children with ASD?

Introduction

Play is an important instrument in the intellectual, linguistic, emotional, and social development of children (Wolfberg, 1995a, 1999). It usually follows a developmental sequence that parallels and reflects the development of language and cognition (Bates, O'Connell, & Shore, 1987). From a language perspective, first words typically develop in concert with the child's use of real objects in symbolic play and combinations of objects in constructive play. When word combinations occur, children are usually performing single-action schemes in their symbolic play and combining four or more structures in their constructive play (Bates et al., 1987). Cognitively, children realize that items of play can serve functions beyond their intended purpose. This facilitates their problem solving, imagination, and creativity (Libby, Powell, Messer, & Jordan, 1998). Chapter 5 described stages of play development, the challenges for children with ASD, and the importance of careful assessment. Because children with ASD show some functional play, teaching play skills that expand their ability to attend to another and to pretend can be an important intervention goal (Charman et al., 1998).

This chapter emphasizes strategies that might be considered in supporting the play development of children with ASD. It will become obvious, however, that supporting a child's play is likely to lead to developments in language, social–emotional, and cognitive skills because of the interrelationships that exist among these developmental domains. In fact, research investigating the effects of developmentally based play instruction has indicated progress in the cognitive and linguistic abilities of children with ASD as well (Rogers & DiLalla, 1991; Rogers, Herblson, Lewis, Pantone, & Reis, 1986).

Following the assessment process, the intervention team has to decide what should be taught and how it should be taught. The literature suggests that children with autism demonstrate little fantasy and symbolism in their play and instead often engage in nonfunctional ritualistic activities using a limited number of objects (Wulff, 1985). It may be that the most effective approaches to supporting play in children with ASD focus less on a typical developmental course and more on the interests of and motivators for the children in which communication and social interaction can be facilitated.

Teaching Play

The approach to and specific strategies for facilitating play skills in children with ASD must consider the challenge this core deficit area presents to children affected by autism, as well as the interrelationships between play, communication, and social interaction. First, engagement must be established if a child is to attend to and maintain attention and interest in play with another. Interventions such as floor time (Greenspan & Wieder,

1998) and relationship development intervention (Gutstein & Sheely, 2002) have been developed to facilitate engagement in children with challenges in joint attention, interaction, and play (see Chapter 11 for further explanation of floor time and relationship development intervention). Once engagement has been established, enticing the child to join activities initiated by his or her play partner is the important next step. Following enticement, children need to be able to establish reciprocal exchanges with their play partners, initiating and responding to one another in turn. This reciprocal exchange is similar to what occurs in discourse and is a fundamental social skill. As soon as this back-and-forth exchange is achieved, the length and complexity of the turns need to increase. This ensures sustained play activities with opportunities for extending the content and complexity of the play. In addition, the play routines need to incorporate planned variations to promote flexibility in play, as children with ASD often become rigid play partners, have established rules, and become anxious and even aggressive when their "rules" are not followed.

When modeling cooperative play activities, the play partner must become an integral part of the child's play. For example, the play partner might have a critical prop that the child with ASD needs to continue the activity. The play might involve a familiar theme such as that of one of the child's favorite stories (e.g., *Caps for Sale*), which is then expanded to include characters or props not in the original story (e.g., boots instead of caps, or squirrels instead of monkeys). The goal is to provide opportunities to increase flexibility in the child's play and eventually move to more abstract play scripts (e.g., *Harry Potter*).

Other strategies can be incorporated into the intervention to support the child's development of play schemes. For example, the use of social stories (Gray, 1995, 1998), as described in Chapter 11, can prepare or prime the child for a future play event with a peer. Defining and then reviewing a play script for a child serves many purposes. It helps to outline and define the "rules" for a particular play event, and it models the language and vocabulary that will be emphasized in the play routine. When the child knows what to expect of a particular play interaction, that familiarity can increase responsiveness and participation in the play event. Practitioners might also establish these skills in their play with a child with ASD before integrating peers into the cooperative play activities.

Structuring an appropriate teaching environment is essential to facilitating the play of children with ASD (Janzen, 1996). This might include planned play sessions, a specific location with limited distractions, and selected play materials of interest to the child and relevant to achieving the intended play intervention goals. Play sessions should have clear beginnings and endings, with active involvement of the child and the use of visual cues to support the child's play choices and prediction of story events.

Several intervention strategies have been used to support the imitative and independent play, pretend or sociodramatic play, and peer-supported play of children with ASD. These strategies are described in the following sections, and the intervention goals, value, and efficacy for children with

ASD are highlighted. Some sample goals for play and the interventions that might be used to support those goals can be found in Table 10.1.

Imitative and Independent Play Strategies

Dawson and Lewy (1989) describe the use of imitation to increase the attentiveness and social responsiveness of children with autism in play. Recognizing Piaget's (1962) early work on the imitation skills of infants and their resulting attentiveness and motor responses to the imitations of others, Dawson and Lewy explored the effects of imitating the behaviors of children with ASD (Dawson & Adams, 1984; Dawson & Lewy, 1989). They found that imitating the behavior of children with ASD increased the children's attentiveness or duration of gaze toward the adult and their social responsiveness, or touching, gesturing, and vocalizing with the adult. Using an imitation strategy in play gives the child with ASD the role of initiator and allows the child to engage in a shared experience that may increase self-awareness.

Modeling and prompting strategies can be effectively used to teach imitative play to children with ASD beyond imitating the behaviors they typically exhibit with toys or objects of play. Using activities that they prefer also increases the likelihood of their engagement and decreases their tendency to

TABLE 10.1
Sample Play Goals and Possible Strategies To Support Those Goals for Children with ASD

Sample Goal	Possible Strategies
To increase both the complexity and the duration of the child's pretend play, moving from adults to peers in structured and unstructured settings.	*Video modeling* (Charlop-Christy & Kelso, 1997) EXAMPLE: Interventionist uses play props to demonstrate on videotape how a child would engage in pretend play with those objects; the interventionist then videotapes two individuals taking turns in a game; the child with ASD watches a 3- to 5-minute video sample that models the appropriate toy play and the game playing between two adults. *Narrative play therapy* (Densmore, 2000) EXAMPLE: Interventionist develops a "play script" in collaboration with a typical peer and a child with ASD. The interventionist narrates the play of both children and then guides them to expand their language understanding and use during play.
To increase the child's expression and use of feelings and ideas through drama and make-believe with adults and peers.	*Floor time* (Greenspan & Wieder, 1997; Wieder, 1997) EXAMPLE: Child with ASD and parent build on the intimate connections already established during rough-and-tumble play to expand to more complex and elaborated play through multiple circles of communication, using highly motivating toys or activities.

avoid play encounters (Koegel, Dyer, & Bell, 1987). Further, children with ASD can be taught to self-monitor their play activities and differentiate between appropriate and inappropriate play (Charlop-Christy & Kelso, 1997).

A first step in teaching imitative play to a child with ASD is to model the desired play action (e.g., pushing a car along the floor) and then immediately give the child an opportunity to imitate that action (e.g., give the child the car to push). If the child does not imitate the action after approximately 5 seconds, the interventionist can repeat the action and say, "Do this" (Charlop-Christy & Kelso, 1997). If the action is not imitated, the child can be physically prompted to perform the action (e.g., by placing the child's hand on the car and pushing it along the table) and then praised and reinforced for doing so. The child is then given another opportunity to imitate the play. If the attempt is unsuccessful, prompting can be reinstated with less directive prompts provided over time. Nondirected play might also be used to support the imitative play skills of children with ASD. The purpose of nondirected play is to provide the child with effective social communication strategies in the context of the natural environment, while the adult plays and communicates alongside the child (Cogher, 1999).

Teaching imitative play supports the child with ASD in learning independent play activities such as putting puzzles together, stacking blocks, and racing cars. When teaching independent play, it is important that interventionists limit their participation over time, so they eventually can remove themselves from the child's play. Providing praise and reinforcement is a powerful motivator until children experience their own satisfaction with successfully completing a task, particularly a preferred task. It is also useful to provide opportunities to play with a variety of toys, interspersing preferred and nonpreferred toys and activities (Charlop-Christy & Kelso, 1997). Correspondence training (teaching children that what they say they will do should relate to what they actually do) and play activity schedules (using photographs to represent play areas) have also been used to teach independent play (Morrison, Sainato, Benchaaban, & Endo, 2002). When using correspondence training to teach independent play, the interventionist teaches the children to select from photographs of play areas those areas in which they wish to play, observes their actual play choices, and then debriefs with them about the play areas they went to compared to the areas they originally selected. The child is prompted with questions or comments such as "Where do you want to play?" "Where do you want to play next?" "Follow your play schedule," and "Look at your play schedule" (Morrison et al., 2002, p. 64). When debriefing with the child following independent playtime, the interventionist might say, "You chose the sand table. Did you play at the sand table?" If the child does not respond, the interventionist might say, "You picked the sand table, and you played at the sand table" or "You didn't play at the sand table today" or "You forgot to play in the sand area today after you were done at the block area."

When teaching imitative play, interventionists might also consider using modeling and reinforcement to facilitate the child's preference for toys and books over engaging in stereotypy or passivity during free time or free play. Research suggests that books and toys can be conditioned as reinforcers and that behaviors associated with looking at books and playing with selected toys can be learned through imitation for children with ASD (Nuzzolo-Gomez, Leonard, Ortiz, Rivera, & Greer, 2002).

Because imitation has been defined as a critical component in play, as well as in language and cognition, and an area of challenge for children with ASD (Lovaas, 1981; Murray-Slutsky & Paris, 2000; Peeters, 1997; Quill, 2000), games such as Follow the Leader and Simon Says might be used. To reflect the "special interests" of the child with autism, the games might be renamed, such as Follow Aladdin or The Hulk Says. Using typical peers to help model and participate in the imitative games provides rich opportunities for children with autism to interact, play, and communicate with their peers.

Self-management strategies, as described in Chapter 13, have also been used to support the appropriate independent play of children with ASD. Children are taught to distinguish appropriate from inappropriate behavior and then learn to manage their own behavior. For example, Stahmer and Schreibman (1992) report on a self-management intervention package to teach three children with autism to increase their independent play skills. Treatment involves discrimination training during which demonstrations of appropriate play (e.g., placing a puzzle piece in a puzzle) and inappropriate play (e.g., spinning or mouthing the puzzle piece) with toys are provided and the children are asked to determine the appropriateness of each demonstration. The children are then asked to provide their own examples of appropriate and inappropriate play with toys. Following that, the children are taught to use a wristwatch that cues time intervals in which to evaluate their play. Reinforcement is given when the entire interval is filled with appropriate play. Children learn to chart their appropriate play behavior, which allows them to obtain a desired reinforcer. The goal in the intervention is to fade the presence of the interventionist over time and to remove the self-management materials (e.g., the wristwatch, monitoring chart) to establish independent and generalized play. Stahmer and Schreibman describe their success in increasing the independent play skills of children with ASD using such self-management strategies.

Intervention Goals. Goals for imitative and independent play should include establishing joint attention around desired objects and actions, prompting and modeling play behaviors, and creating variations of those behaviors. Practitioners might also develop goals around identifying preferred toys and books for the child with ASD and reinforcing opportunities to play with those, as research suggests that the unusual repetitive movements and passive nature of many children with ASD decrease when toy and book play is reinforced (Nuzzolo-Gomez et al., 2002). Imitative play is an appropriate intervention goal for children with ASD who are functioning at an early developmental level and should be used to establish initial social interest in play. Upon that foundation, other play behaviors can be built that establish social interaction and understanding games with rules.

Value for Children with ASD. The use of imitation in play with children with ASD, including imitating facial expressions and vocalizations, creates a context for intervention that is similar to what very young typically developing children experience in their early interactions with adults. Thus, the interventionist "may be providing a social environment that is developmentally appropriate and meaningful" to children with ASD (Dawson & Lewy, 1989, p. 63). Imitation also provides a visual cue and a predictable response for the child with ASD, thereby minimizing the child's information processing load. Imitation, as an intervention strategy, "simplifies, exaggerates and distills many important features of early social interaction" (Dawson & Lewy, 1989, p. 63). It provides a salient model and a response that is predictable and contingent (e.g., the interventionist imitating the child lining up cars, using the same color and car type in the same order).

Using nondirective play to teach imitative and independent play skills is likely to increase children's communication behaviors and their opportunities to engage in pretend play. Further, nondirective play can be used in the home or school setting and across play partners and benefits children with ASD who exhibit limited verbal communication and social interaction skills (Cogher, 1999).

Correspondence training and activity schedules are effective and non-intrusive means of including children with ASD in the play activities of the general education classroom (Morrison et al., 2002). These strategies can be used across settings and for children with ASD who exhibit a range of ability levels. They can also support the organizational skills and engagement of children with ASD during play activities.

Teaching appropriate ways to use books and toys in play and helping to create a preference for such activities over less engaging and socially appropriate behaviors increase opportunities to expand the preferences of children with ASD for all types of activities. Self-management training supports the development of self-awareness in children with ASD, even those with more significant impairments. Both of these approaches to play intervention may facilitate the integration and involvement of children with ASD in inclusive settings. They also are unobtrusive strategies that can decrease the need for the constant presence of an interventionist.

Efficacy. The use of imitation as an intervention strategy for children with ASD has shown positive effects. Dawson and Adams (1984) found that imitating the behaviors of children with ASD led to increased attentiveness, social responsiveness, and less perseverative play with toys. Dawson and Lewy (1989) found that mothers of children with autism could be coached to imitate their children's behaviors, including their vocalizations, body movements, and toy play, which increased the children's social attentiveness. Mothers of 15 children with autism (2 to 6 years of age) were given two sets of identical toys and asked to carry out the imitation strategy for 2 weeks, 20 minutes each day. Dawson and Lewy found that the children focused more on the faces of their moms, indicating a social interest beyond just the contingent actions with the toys. The children also demonstrated greater exploration with a variety of toys and play schemes. The researchers provided empirical support for their contention that children with autism can increase their attention to others "by sensitive interactive strategies that provide simplified, predictable, and highly contingent responses and allow the children to control and regulate the amount of stimulation" (Dawson & Lewy, 1989, p. 69). Lewy and Dawson (1992) investigated the effects of imitative play on the toy play, verbalizations, and actions of 20 preschool children with ASD. They found that child-centered intervention, in which an adult interventionist imitates the behaviors of the child, can effect positive change in the joint attention of children with ASD and may support an increase in the complexity of toy play.

Modeling has been successfully used to support the independent play of children with ASD (Tryon & Keane, 1986). Combining correspondence training and activity schedules has also been used to teach children with ASD independent play skills. Activity schedules serve as verbal mediators, particularly for children with ASD who have no or limited verbal skills, to facilitate independent selection and performance of play activities (Morrison et al., 2002). When children with ASD were taught to look at books and play with toys during free play, they demonstrated a significant decrease in their passivity and stereotypic behaviors (Nuzzolo-Gomez et al., 2002). They also sought out toys and books during their free playtime, thus replacing their less socially appropriate behaviors. Stahmer and Schreibman (1992) found that self-management strategies are successful in increasing appropriate play with toys while decreasing self-stimulatory behavior. They also found that appropriate play skills generalized to novel settings and that learning could be maintained. Parents also reported improved play behaviors when their children were unsupervised at home.

Pretend or Sociodramatic Play Strategies

Play is a natural way for children to manifest their social behaviors (Kim et al., 2003). Therefore, objects of play should be items that promote social behaviors, such as balls, board games, and action figures that require a back-and-forth or reciprocal exchange with another child, or dress-up clothes, housekeeping toys, blocks, puppets, and toy cars or trucks that facilitate pretend scripts and imagination. A review of 13 intervention studies examining how toys were used in groups composed of young children with disabilities revealed that children exhibit more social behavior when playing with social toys like balls than when playing with toys like books (Kim et al., 2003). Further, children in mixed groups, with and without disabilities, demonstrate a reduction in inappropriate play and a higher level of cognitive play, as might be seen in constructive play (Guralnick & Groom, 1988). It appears that the greatest social behavior among preschoolers occurs when social toys are available and children with and without disabilities are part of the play group. Therefore, parents, teachers and other providers might consider increasing the access children with disabilities, including ASD, have to social toys and to children without disabilities.

It may be that a child with ASD has demonstrated some appropriate functional and imitative play but appears stuck in his or her ability to move to imaginative play typical of same-age peers. For example, the child may be highly motivated by a movie such as *Toy Story* or a fairytale like "Goldilocks and the Three Bears." The team can take advantage of that interest and familiarity with the script to set up play opportunities in the classroom with relevant props in clear view. Over time, the teacher may add props or characters not in the original story or script to facilitate the child's thinking and movement toward more imaginative nonscripted play in the context of a setting or theme that is familiar and comfortable to the child. Jarrold, Boucher, and Smith (1996) suggest that another way to develop symbolic or pretend play in children with ASD is to build on what the child does functionally or in a meaningful way with familiar objects by introducing perceptually similar but less meaningful or nonfunctional objects into the play routine.

A number of strategies are available to the interventionist to support the skills the child with ASD requires to have successful play experiences. Using open-ended questions, introducing new characters or plots, providing choices, offering logical sequences, and modeling play expansion are appropriate strategies to facilitate the complexity and duration of a child's play schemes. These techniques provide play experiences and relevant language that the child with ASD can "borrow" to elaborate his play themes at later times. This supports the tendency of children with ASD to recall and rehearse motivating topics.

Because reading books is often a favorite activity for children with ASD, the interventionist can respond directly to this interest. A "book bucket" (a book placed in a container with relevant story props included) can be provided to encourage expanding the play of a child with ASD using tangible objects from a familiar story. The use of the miniature props to act out the story can be modeled as needed. These props provide a visual support, and the script of a familiar story provides a comfortable context in which a child with ASD can explore pretend play. Miniatures also can be used to recreate a specific sequence of activities or events the child has experienced or is familiar with. The interventionist provides a model of the language and social behavior associated with the play that is represented using the miniatures.

Just as prompting and modeling are effective strategies to support communication, as described in Chapter 9, and in supporting imitative play as discussed here, those techniques have value in teaching pretend play. Charlop-Christy and Kelso (1997) recommend the strategic use of prompting, modeling, and reinforcement during pretend-play activities (e.g., playing grocery shopping, playing school, playing doctor) that focus on the child's interests and preferred toys. The interventionist can take turns with the child, playing different roles to expose the child to the actions and language associated with those roles in pretend-play activities.

As discussed in Chapter 9, video modeling has been established as an effective intervention strategy to support the language and communication of children with ASD. It also has application for teaching pretend play to children with ASD as young as preschool (D'Ateno, Mangiapanello, & Taylor, 2003). Defining or explaining pretend or imaginative play to children with ASD is a difficult task. The concept knowledge, language, and perspective needed to be successful in imaginative play are specific areas of deficit for the child with ASD. Watching a video, however, where actual play with toys is modeled or two peers engaged in a game or play activity are viewed, supports the child's observational learning in a controlled context. Video modeling is used to facilitate new behaviors or increase desired behaviors through repeated viewings of the target behaviors in short video clips that emphasize those behaviors (Dowrick, 1999). The interventionist might videotape two adults playing a board game, including the language used to initiate turns and comments, as well as the nonverbal behaviors important to playing a game, such as picking a game piece and moving it along a board. A pretend-play event based on a theme (e.g., grocery shopping, playing school) might also be videotaped to be viewed later and then role-played by the child with ASD.

Floor time, discussed in detail in Chapter 11, is a systematic way for parents and educators to interact with children for 20- to 30-minute interaction periods in order to provide a safe environment for the expression and use of feelings through pretend play. The interventionist provides simplified, relevant language describing the positive and negative feelings associated with the consequences of actions during pretend play (e.g., sharing, turn taking). The development of these social–emotional skills can promote successful play interactions with peers.

Pivotal response training (PRT), also described in Chapter 11, has been adapted to support the sociodramatic play of children with ASD (Thorp, Stahmer, & Schreibman, 1995). In a PRT framework, preferred toys that vary with the child's interests are used, play turns and actions with preferred toys are modeled, and appropriate responses are reinforced. Mastered play themes are interspersed with more novel themes to ensure success. The interventionist actively participates in the play, providing models of what to say and do. For example, if a child has an interest in trains, a theme can be developed related to trains (e.g., going on a trip), and different roles can be modeled (e.g., conductor, passenger) and exchanged between child and interventionist. Imaginary characters can be introduced and dolls or stuffed animals can be involved as characters (e.g., passengers) in the play theme.

Teaching sociodramatic play scripts is a strategy that has been used to support the social and communicative play behavior of children with significant language impairments and related handicaps. Although not specifically identified as an intervention strategy for children with ASD, it has usefulness for supporting the development of their pretend play. This training involves creating a script around a sociodramatic play activity (e.g., going to a restaurant) that incorporates both targeted motor or gestural responses and verbal responses for different roles in the script. Both group and individual training on the script can occur, and an adult interventionist can be used to prompt children to stay with their roles or switch their roles. The adult interventionist can also prompt the children on what to say or do in their roles as needed.

Intervention Goals. Language and cognitive development can be enhanced when the gestures and actions associated with pretend play are modeled in association with developmentally appropriate language (Paul, 1995). It is important to increase both the complexity and duration of play for a child with ASD. For example, an intervention goal might be established to develop contexts and play opportunities in which the child can be challenged to think creatively, moving from a predictable to a more spontaneous play event. Child-directed play and interaction, which is supported by adult caregivers during floor time, promotes trust, intimate connections, more pleasurable affect, and a heightened capacity for abstract thinking (e.g., of how another may feel by observing facial and gestural expression) (Greenspan & Wieder, 1997). Intervention goals should consider ways to increase the child's expression and use of feelings and ideas through drama and make-believe with adults and peers. Language models can be provided to describe how the child with ASD feels at different times during play (e.g., "You are mad because you can't find the toy you wanted") and how his or her adult play partners feel during the interactions (e.g., "This game is fun. It makes me happy! See my smiling face?"). This approach can help the child understand and describe the wide variety of emotions he or she feels and how to interpret the emotions of others (e.g., frustrated, scared, surprised, tired, excited). This skill is particularly important for establishing successful peer relationships. As an example, consider the challenges that Ethan, a 4-year-old with ASD, experiences in his pretend play with an adult. Ethan runs into the interventionist with an angry face, saying, "Hurt you." He does not have the language to describe or expand his play or to compensate for the frustration this is causing. The interventionist takes this opportunity to explore what Ethan is feeling and says, "I'm confused, Ethan. I thought we were having a good time playing this game. But you look mad when your face is like this [mimics his facial expression]. Is something wrong?"

An important intervention goal for script training is to teach children with ASD a sociodramatic play theme that can be incorporated into their peer play. Script training can also be used to facilitate appropriate verbal and gestural productions in play. Overall, intervention goals for pretend play should target developmentally appropriate skills, as these are more likely to generalize to other toys and activities (Lifter, Sulzer-Azaroff, Anderson, & Cowdery, 1993).

Value for Children with ASD. Three-dimensional objects can provide a valuable visual support for children with ASD in the re-creation of stories or to facilitate pretend-play events. Acting out stories allows the pace of events to be slowed, the language to be simplified, and repetition to occur. Script training provides a structure for learning roles in sociodramatic play routines and the language and gestures associated with those roles. It also facilitates story understanding and narrative language production. Pretend-play activities provide an interactive context in which to learn actively and an opportunity for modeling language structure and vocabulary in a novel way. Intervening in this area of play will also lead to increased opportunities to develop and support the language and social interaction skills of children with ASD. It can be implemented in the home setting and taught to family members or caregivers.

Efficacy. Video modeling has been successfully used to support the play of children with ASD across a range of play skills, including independent play, cooperative play, and pretend or make-believe play (Charlop-Christy & Kelso, 1997). Further, video modeling of imaginative play has been used successfully to increase both verbal and motor responses for children with autism (D'Ateno et al., 2003). Both rapid acquisition of play skills and generalized learning of new play behaviors when implementing video modeling for children with ASD have been reported in the literature.

Pivotal response training procedures have also been used to support the sociodramatic play of children with ASD. Thorp and her colleagues (1995) found positive results for several behaviors important to sociodramatic play. Three children with ASD (ages 5, 8, and 9 years) increased the amount of time they exhibited elements of sociodramatic play and improved their language and social skills, all of which were maintained at a 3-month follow-up. This play intervention approach resulted in an increase in initiations and appropriate responses and a decrease in negative behaviors that generalized to novel situations (Thorp et al., 1995). In a study training preschool children with and without disabilities to act out play themes following a sociodramatic play script, children learned critical behaviors for playing "hamburger stand" using a script with three roles (Goldstein, Wickstrom, Hoyson, Jamieson, & Odom, 1988). Adult prompting during the script training led to significant improvements in the children's social and communicative interactions. Goldstein and his colleagues also found that the children's sociodramatic play following script training was more complex and generalized to free play.

Peer-Supported Play Strategies

Typically developing children learn to tell a story in play using objects or props with meaning and negotiating the story line with their peers. If children with ASD fail to use objects to represent meaning, they will be at a disadvantage in interactive play with their peers. Introducing the concept of a "story" and creating a "theme" for play can establish a context for joint attention among peers. Play then becomes a "story in action." Narrative play therapy is one intervention strategy used to teach children with ASD to engage in joint attention and follow the sequence of symbolic play while interacting with their peers in natural settings and learning language in social contexts (Densmore, 2000).

The interventionist using narrative play introduces a story in small, sequential steps through symbolic play using circles of communication. The child learns the language needed to tell the story, how to share objects in play, and how to experience play events with peers to establish joint attention. Densmore (2000) identifies two major goals for teaching the use of narratives during play interactions: to develop joint attention, and to develop a sense of story between partners with an object and agent following an action sequence for approximately 5 to 10 minutes using a narrative with a beginning, middle, and end.

The first goal of establishing joint attention in play includes six levels. In Level 1, a peer partner learns to comment either verbally or nonverbally (e.g., saying, "Look!" or pointing to a rising balloon) to a child with ASD. Level 2 involves teaching the child with ASD to look at the peer partner who commented and continually prompting the children to make comments as they look at, for example, a balloon rising to the ceiling. Visual scripts can be used to prompt comments such as "Cool" and "Awesome" (Densmore, 2000). In Level 3, one of the peer partners might be asked by the interventionist to hold an object, such as the balloon, and then ask the other child if he or she wants to hold it. The children are prompted both to ask questions of one another and to answer those questions. In Level 4, the play partners are encouraged to initiate a back-and-forth exchange with one another, commenting about what they are doing. For example, the children might toss the balloon back and forth and make comments like "Catch it," "Here it comes," or "Look out, it's going to fly away." The interventionist can model such comments as well to prompt the children's play. Densmore (2000) encourages the use of varied tone and pitch patterns to encourage strong emotional connections between the play partners. In Level 5, the play partners are left to play independently so the interventionist can observe any attempts at joint attention. The children are praised for their peer play actions, and data are kept on their commenting and looking at their play partner. By Level 6, the peer partner is prompted to move play objects toward the child with ASD, verbally prompting or gesturing to get the child with ASD to respond. The interventionist uses prompts such as questions to increase the peers' time engaged in commenting during their play.

For the second goal, Densmore (2000) describes another six levels designed to help the play partners create a sense of story with one another about objects and agents in play. Level 7 begins by prompting the child with ASD and the peer play partner to create a story about an object of play (e.g., posing questions about the balloon, where it is going to go, how it is moving). The interventionist encourages the children to follow one another and comment on the object and action of their play. Simple language is introduced in Level 8, and the children's comments are rephrased to support the development of a story. For example, a character might be introduced as riding in a hot air balloon to travel around the world. The interventionist allows the children to name the character or say where the character might be going and then offers simple language to highlight the beginnings of a story (e.g., "David is riding the hot air balloon and lands in Alaska. He is so cold, he decides to come home."). In Level 9, the children's narrative is placed on the computer, and the play partners add photos or pictures to their story, which is placed in a small book. The interventionist might take pictures of the children acting out their story to be added to the book. Both children are given a copy of the narrative with a clear beginning, middle, and end. In Level 10, a videotape is made of the play partners as they create a story about what they are doing together (Densmore, 2000). The children are given an opportunity to watch the video, which is also shared with their parents so that they might learn some strategies from the interventionist to facilitate their child's play with a peer partner at home. Levels 11 and 12 require the interventionist to identify other locations in which he or she might join a child with ASD in play with a peer, narrating their actions, modeling comments, rephrasing verbalizations, and cueing both children to look at one another and their objects of play and make comments so that joint attention is maintained and a sense of story is established.

Other intervention strategies using peers, as described in Chapter 11, and siblings to facilitate the play of children with ASD have been reported in the literature. For example, manual and verbal prompts and modeling are effective strategies to support peer or group play, just as they are useful for developing imitative and pretend play (Charlop-Christy & Kelso, 1997). In addition, incorporating themes into peer or sibling play based on the ritualistic interests of children with ASD leads to increased social skills in play (Baker, 2000). Games such as Memory, Concentration, and Bingo can be modified to incorporate the ritualistic themes of children with ASD as they play with their siblings or peer partners. Pictures of characters and events from a favorite video (e.g., *Aladdin*) might replace the usual pictures in a memory game, for example.

An integrated playgroup intervention model has been used with success to support the play of children with ASD and their typical peers in inclusive settings (Zercher, Hunt, Schuler, & Webster, 2001). There are several features to this model, including well-designed play spaces, play materials with interactive potential, a consistent schedule and routine, a focus on competence, guided participation, developmentally appropriate peer partners, and immersion in play in natural settings (Wolfberg & Schuler, 1993). Typically, the playgroups consist of at least five children, two with ASD (novices) and three to five who are typically developing (experts). The children in the playgroups meet on a regular basis, usually two or more times a week, in a designated play space to socialize for 30 to 60 minutes at a time. An adult interventionist serves as a play facilitator, providing varying levels of support to the players and incorporating the specific interests of the children with ASD into play themes. Essentially, the interventionist serves as an interpreter between the novices and the experts. The interventionist monitors the children's play initiations and scaffolds interactions by adjusting the need for support based on the children's play needs. This integrated playgroup model has been designed to support the quality of play, focus, and language complexity of older elementary children with ASD (Schuler & Wolfberg, 2000; Wolfberg, 1995b).

Intervention Goals. There are some critical goals that can be established using peer-supported play techniques or strategies. These goals include establishing joint attention with peers, developing a sense of story with peer partners in play, and learning to use narrative language to support play activities. Peer-supported or group play can also be used to increase the ability of children with ASD to learn game playing rules (e.g., what to do and how to score in board games, baseball, or soccer) and the possible roles within those games or group activities.

Value for Children with ASD. Narrative play intervention can be compared to floor time, as described in Chapter 11. Like floor time (Greenspan & Wieder, 1998), narrative play supports relationship building for children with ASD, respecting their individual needs and developmental level. It requires making emotional connections with peers in play. Floor time works to build circles of communication between children with ASD and their communication and play partners. Narrative play builds on established circles of communication and moves on to introduce a play theme to teach specific language or social communication using peer support. Creating games based on favorite themes of children with ASD is likely to motivate them and reinforce their participation.

Efficacy. Although no empirical data is currently available on the use of narrative play therapy with peers and children with ASD, Densmore (2000) provides positive case study reports of its effectiveness. There is support for incorporating the favorite themes of children with ASD into their social play with siblings and their school peers (Baker, 2000; Baker, Koegel, & Koegel, 1998). For example, Baker (2000) used the ritualistic themes of three children with ASD (5–6 years of age) to modify a Bingo game that addressed their special interests (e.g., math number lines, car crashing, movies). The children with ASD and their siblings were prompted to play the modified game. The concept of winning was explained and reinforced to ensure understanding on the part of the children with ASD. Results demonstrated that the ritualistic behaviors of children with ASD can be incorporated into games and facilitate their play with their siblings. Baker's findings show that "frequently occurring thematic, ritualistic behaviors, typically viewed as problematic in young children with autism, may be considered intrinsically reinforcing agents for positive change and development" (p. 79). Thus, children with ASD can learn to interact and play with peers through the use of games. Zercher and colleagues (2001) investigated the effects of an integrated playgroup on the joint attention, symbolic play, and language behavior of twin boys with ASD (6 years of age) as they played with three girls (ages 5, 9, and 11 years) who were typically developing. They found that peer-supported play using the integrated playgroup model led to notable increases in shared attention, symbolic play behaviors, and verbal productions for the children with ASD.

Summary

In this chapter, you have learned about several interventions to support the play of children with ASD. The value of teaching imitative, pretend, and peer-supported play in children with ASD has been emphasized. The summary below refers to the questions at the beginning of the chapter and highlights key points you should be familiar with when creating environments and opportunities for supporting the play of children with ASD.

What strategies could be effective in supporting the imitative and independent play of children with ASD?
Adult imitation of children's verbalizations, gestures, and motor movements positively affects the ability of the child with ASD to share attention with others and increase the appropriateness of toy play. Using preferred toys and objects of interest while modeling and prompting play is also an effective strategy to support not only imitative but also independent play. Imitative play may be an important initial goal for children with ASD, particularly those who demonstrate skills at an early developmental level.

How can pretend or sociodramatic play be developed for children with ASD?
Several strategies are defined in the literature as supporting the pretend or sociodramatic play of children with ASD. Techniques include script training, pivotal response training, floor time, video modeling, in vivo modeling, and promoting. Although the level of evidence differs among the reported strategies, each strategy has specific skill development and training techniques that enhance the success of a child with ASD to connect with a typical peer.

What is the role of peer-supported play in facilitating the social play of children with ASD?
Three specific strategies to support the peer and sibling play of children with ASD were discussed in this chapter. These include initiating narrative play therapy, incorporating ritualistic or favorite routines in play, and using an integrated playgroup model. Each of these strategies or instructional models requires children with ASD to establish joint attention with others and to expand their linguistic and social communication skills through narratives and pretend play with peers.

Practice Opportunities

1. Create a sociodramatic play script that is developmentally appropriate for a child with ASD and teach that script to the child and his or her typical peers.

2. Identify the toy preferences of a child with ASD and describe how you will use those toys to provide an enriched play environment for the child and his or her peers.

3. Using video modeling, develop a script for symbolic play with toys that can be used to teach the child with ASD to attend to the critical elements of play with the selected toys.

4. Create an integrated playgroup of at least five children, with no more than two children with ASD. Outline the prompting and scaffolding strategies the interventionist will use to support peer play within the playgroup.

Suggested Readings

Charlop-Christy, M., & Kelso, S. E. (1997). *How to treat the child with autism.* Clarement, CA: Authors.

Although this book is filled with valuable research-based intervention methods beyond teaching play skills, the chapter on play is comprehensive, explaining the categories of play that it is important to develop in children with autism and identifying both procedures and tasks used to teach play skills. The authors highlight the effectiveness of prompting, modeling, self-monitoring, and video modeling to support independent, cooperative, and imaginary play.

Densmore, A. (2000). Speech on location: A narrative play technique to teach expressive language and communication to children with PDD/autism/language delay. *Journal of Developmental and Learning Disorders, 4*(2), 209–239.

This article provides an excellent description of narrative play therapy and provides several examples and scripts for supporting children with ASD and their typical peers in pretend play. Densmore makes connections to the principles of floor time and focuses on the value of establishing joint attention between children with ASD and their typical peers.

Odom, S. L., & McConnell, S. R. (1993). *Play time/social time: Organizing your classroom to build interaction skills.* Tucson, AZ: Communication Skill Builders.

This resource contains three primary components that are useful in supporting the social play of children with ASD: social skills lessons, structured play activities, and strategies for prompting and prompt fading. Each of these components is described in detail, and ways to incorporate them in the classroom are discussed.

Resources

Baldi, H., & Detmers, D. (2000). *Embracing play: Teaching your child with autism* [Video]. Bethesda, MD: Woodbine House.

Beyer, J., & Gammeltoft, L. (1999). *Autism and play.* New York: Jessica Kingsley.

Moor, J. (2002). *Playing, laughing and learning with children on the autism spectrum.* New York: Jessica Kingsley.

Wolfberg, P. J. (1999). *Play and imagination in children with autism.* New York: Teachers College Press.

Glossary

Cooperative play. Two or more children engaged in the same activity and interacting in a cooperative manner.

Group play. Play activities with multiple participants, like group sports, games of tag, and board games.

Imaginative play. Play involving pretend games (e.g., house, restaurant, doctor); also known as creative or sociodramatic play.

Independent play. Solitary play consisting of such activities as block building, coloring, puzzle building, and playing with cars or dolls.

Passivity. Not looking at, searching for, touching, or responding to objects of play.

Stereotypy. Repetitive movements (e.g., hand flapping, finger flicking, rocking) without apparent consequences for the person displaying the behaviors.

References

Baker, M. J. (2000). Incorporating the thematic ritualistic behaviors of children with autism into games: Increasing social play interactions with siblings. *Journal of Positive Behavior Interventions, 3*(2), 66–84.

Baker, M. J., Koegel, R. L., & Koegel, L. K. (1998). Increasing the social behavior of young children with autism using their obsessions. *Journal of the Association for Persons of Severe Handicaps, 23,* 300–309.

Bates, E., O'Connell, B., & Shore, C. (1987). Language and communication in infancy. In J. Osofsky (Ed.), *Handbook of infant development* (pp. 149–203). New York: Wiley.

Charlop-Christy, M., & Kelso, S. E. (1997). *How to treat the child with autism.* Clarement, CA: Authors.

Charman, T., Swettenham, J., Baron-Cohen, S., Cox, A., Baird, G., & Drew, A. (1998). An experimental investigation of social-cognitive abilities in infants with autism: Clinical implications. *Infant Mental Health Journal, 19*(2), 260–275.

Cogher, L. (1999). The use of non-directive play in speech and language therapy. *Child Language Teaching & Therapy, 9,* 7–15.

D'Ateno, P., Mangiapanello, K., & Taylor, B. A. (2003). Using video modeling to teach complex play sequences to a preschooler with autism. *Journal of Positive Behavior Interventions, 5*(1), 5.

Dawson, G., & Adams, A. (1984). Imitation and social responsiveness in autistic children. *Journal of Abnormal Child Psychology, 12,* 209–225.

Dawson, G., & Lewy, A. (1989). Arousal, attention, and the social-emotional impairments of individuals with autism. In G. Dawson (Ed.), *Autism: Nature, diagnosis, and treatment* (pp. 49–74). New York: Guilford Press.

Densmore, A. (2000). Speech on location: A narrative play technique to teach expressive language and communication to children with PDD/autism/language delay. *Journal of Developmental and Learning Disorders, 4*(2), 209–239.

Dowrick, P. W. (1999). A review of self modeling and related interventions. *Applied & Preventive Psychology, 8,* 23–39.

Goldstein, H., Wickstrom, S., Hoyson, M., Jamieson, B., & Odom, S. L. (1988). Effects of sociodramatic script training on social and communicative interaction. *Education and Treatment of Children, 11*(2), 97–117.

Gray, C. A. (1995). Teaching children with autism to "read" social situations. In K. A. Quill (Ed.), *Teaching children with autism: Strategies to enhance communication and socialization* (pp. 219–242). New York: Delmar.

Gray, C. A. (1998). Social stories and comic strip conversations with students with Asperger syndrome and high-functioning autism. In E. Schopler, G. B. Mesibov, & L. J. Kunce (Eds.), *Asperger syndrome or high functioning autism* (pp. 167–194). New York: Plenum Press.

Greenspan, S., & Wieder, S. (1997). An integrated developmental approach to interventions for young children with severe difficulties in relating and communicating. *Zero to Three, 17,* 5–17.

Greenspan, S., & Wieder, S. (1998). *The child with special needs: Encouraging intellectual and emotional growth.* Reading, MA: Addison-Wesley.

Guralnick, M. J., & Groom, J. M. (1988). Peer interactions in mainstreamed and specialized classrooms: A comparative analysis. *Exceptional Children, 54,* 415–425.

Gutstein, S. E., & Sheely, R. K. (2002). *Relationship development intervention with young children: Social and emotional development activities for Asperger syndrome, autism, PDD & NLD.* Philadelphia: Jessica Kingsley.

Janzen, J. (1996). *Understanding the nature of autism.* San Antonio, TX: Therapy Skill Builders.

Jarrold, C., Boucher, J., & Smith, P. (1996). Generativity deficits in pretend play in autism. *British Journal of Developmental Psychology, 14,* 275–300.

Kim, A., Vaughn, S., Elbaum, B., Hughes, M. T., Sloan, C. V. M., & Sridhar, D. (2003). Effects of toys or group composition for children with disabilities: A synthesis. *Journal of Early Intervention, 25*(3), 189–205.

Koegel, R. L., Dyer, K., & Bell, L. K. (1987). The influence of child preferred activities on autistic children's social behavior. *Journal of Applied Behavior Analysis, 20,* 243–252.

Lewy, A. L., & Dawson, G. (1992). Social stimulation and joint attention in young autistic children. *Journal of Abnormal Child Psychology, 20*(6), 555–566.

Libby, S., Powell, S., Messer, D., & Jordan, R. (1998). Spontaneous play in children with autism: A reappraisal. *Journal of Autism and Developmental Disorders, 28,* 487–497.

Lifter, K., Sulzer-Azaroff, B., Anderson, S. R., & Cowdery, G. E. (1993). Teaching play activities to preschool children with disabilities: The importance of developmental considerations. *Journal of Early Intervention, 17*(2), 139–159.

Lovaas, O. (1981). *Teaching developmentally disabled children: The me book.* Austin, TX: PRO-ED.

Morrison, R. S., Sainato, D. M., Benchaaban, D., & Endo, S. (2002). Increasing play skills of children with autism using activity schedules and correspondence training. *Journal of Early Intervention, 25*(1), 58–72.

Murray-Slutsky, C., & Paris, B. (2000). *Exploring the spectrum of autism and pervasive developmental disorders.* San Antonio, TX: Therapy Skill Builders.

Nuzzolo-Gomez, R., Leonard, M. A., Ortiz, E., Rivera, C. M., & Greer, R. D. (2002). Teaching children with autism to prefer books or toys over stereotypy or passivity. *Journal of Positive Behavior Interventions, 4*(2), 80–87.

Paul, R. (1995). *Language disorders from infancy through adolescence: Assessment and intervention.* St. Louis, MO: Mosby.

Peeters, T. (1997). *Autism: From theoretical understanding to educational intervention.* San Diego: Singular.

Piaget, J. (1962). *Play, dreams, and imitation.* New York: Norton.

Quill, K. (2000). *Do–watch–listen–say: Social and communication intervention for children with autism*. Baltimore: Brookes.

Rogers, S. J., & DiLalla, D. L. (1991). A comparative study of the effects of a developmentally based instructional model on young children with autism and young children with other disorders of behavior and development. *Topics in Early Childhood & Special Education, 11*(2), 29–47.

Rogers, S. J., Herblson, J. M., Lewis, H. C., Pantone, J., & Reis, K. (1986). An approach for enhancing the symbolic, communicative, and interpersonal functioning of young children with autism or severe emotional handicaps. *Journal of the Division of Early Childhood, 10*(2), 135–145.

Schuler, A. L., & Wolfberg, P. J. (2000). Promoting peer play and socialization: The art of scaffolding. In A. M. Wetherby & B. M. Prizant (Eds.), *Autism spectrum disorders: A transactional developmental perspective* (pp. 251–277). Baltimore: Brookes.

Stahmer, A. C., & Schreibman, L. (1992). Teaching children with autism appropriate play in unsupervised environments using a self-management treatment package. *Journal of Applied Behavior Analysis, 25*(2), 447–459.

Thorp, D. M., Stahmer, A. C., & Schreibman, L. (1995). Effects of socio dramatic play training on children with autism. *Journal of Autism and Developmental Disorders, 25*(3), 265–282.

Tryon, A. S., & Keane, S. P. (1986). Promoting imitative play through generalized observational learning in autistic-like children. *Journal of Abnormal Child Psychology, 14*, 537–549.

Wieder, S. (1997). Creating connections: Intervention guidelines for increasing interaction with children with multisystem development disorder (MSDD). *Zero to Three, 17*, 19–27.

Wolfberg, P. J. (1995a). Enhancing children's play. In K. Quill (Ed.), *Teaching children with autism* (pp. 193–218). New York: Delmar.

Wolfberg, P. J. (1995b). Supporting children with autism in play groups with typical peers: Description of a model and related research. *International Play Journal, 3*, 38–51.

Wolfberg, P. J. (1999). *Play and imagination in children with autism*. New York: Teachers College Press.

Wolfberg, P. J., & Schuler, A. L. (1993). Integrated playgroups: A model for promoting the social and cognitive dimensions of play in children with autism. *Journal of Autism and Developmental Disorders, 23*, 467–489.

Wulff, S. (1985). The symbolic and object play of children with autism: A review. *Journal of Autism and Developmental Disorders, 15*, 139–148.

Zercher, C., Hunt, P., Schuler, A. L., & Webster, J. (2001). Increasing joint attention, play and language through peer supported play. *Autism: The International Journal of Research & Practice, 5*(4), 374–398.

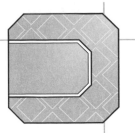

CHAPTER 11

Interventions To Support the Social–Emotional Needs of Children with ASD

Patricia A. Prelock

QUESTIONS TO CONSIDER

In this chapter, you will learn about four intervention models that foster the social–emotional development of children with autism spectrum disorders (ASD) through building relationships, establishing environmental supports, and defining the expectations for interaction. You will also learn specific strategies for facilitating the peer interactions and increasing the social awareness of children with ASD. As you read this chapter, consider the following questions:

1. What models of intervention guide programming for meeting the social–emotional needs of children with ASD?

2. How effectively can peers be used to support the social interaction skills of children with ASD?

3. How can pivotal behaviors be used to support the social interaction of children with ASD in natural settings?

4. What are some strategies for supporting the social understanding and social communication of children with ASD?

Introduction

Developing social competence is an essential skill for all children and a particularly important goal for children with ASD who experience significant deficits in their social–emotional development. Considering another's actions, feelings, and thoughts and integrating relevant social cues into an interaction are notable difficulties for children with ASD. Difficulties attending to and processing social information impede the ability to engage in appropriate social behavior and certainly affect learning (R. L. Koegel, Koegel, Frea, & Smith, 1995; Webb, Miller, Pierce, Strawser, & Jones, 2004). Because of their challenges in interpersonal interaction and relationships, individuals with ASD often avoid social encounters and experience social isolation. Therefore, it is critical to consider interventions for supporting the social–emotional development of children with ASD.

The speech–language pathologist (SLP) has a significant role to play in supporting the social–emotional development of children with ASD, in collaboration with the family and the educational team. Several strategies discussed in Chapters 9 and 10 can be considered here, as children require communication and play skills to participate fully in social exchanges and activities with peers and adults across a variety of environments. Models of intervention are described to support program planning, and specific strategies are highlighted that have been described as successful in facilitating the social skills of children with ASD. Each of the intervention models discussed should be interpreted with caution, however, as there is limited to no empirical research to support the use of these models in facilitating the social skills of children and adolescents with ASD.

Models of Intervention

Several interventions are described in the literature as supporting the social–emotional development of children with ASD. Specifically, interventions are designed to support a child's connection with another, build strategies for social interaction and social communication, and facilitate social skills across settings and communication partners. Four models or frameworks for intervention that I have found particularly useful in establishing meaningful connections between children with ASD and their communication partners are described in the sections that follow. The developmental individual-difference relationship-based (DIR) or floor time model (Greenspan & Wieder, 1998); the relationship development intervention (RDI) model (Gutstein & Sheely, 2002a, 2002b); the social communication, emotional regulation, and transactional supports (SCERTS) model (Prizant, Wetherby, Rubin, & Laurent, 2003; Prizant, Wetherby, Rubin, Laurent, & Rydell, 2004); and the do–watch–listen–say framework (Quill, 2000) were selected because of the value they have for children with ASD across a range of ages and ability levels, the strong theoretical foundation on which the models were developed, the clear connections made to functional and meaningful program goals, and the comprehensive way in which the intervention models have been described, ensuring easy access for the practitioner.

Developmental Individual-Difference Relationship-Based Model

The DIR, or floor time, intervention model is designed to facilitate affect, attachment, and a sense of relatedness between a child with special needs and a caregiver or interaction partner (Greenspan & Wieder, 1997a, 1997b, 1998, 2000, 2001). Emphasizing a global view of the child, Greenspan and Wieder (2001) focus their intervention model on "an integrated understanding of human development" (p. 18). The facilitation of social–emotional development through mastery of six developmental benchmarks or milestones provides a comprehensive picture of the child's development. The six milestones are the abilities (a) to regulate and share attention; (b) to engage with warmth, trust, and intimacy; (c) to establish two-way communication; (d) to problem solve; (e) to use ideas in a functional way; and (f) to build bridges between ideas (Greenspan & Wieder, 1998, 2001).

To address mastery of these milestones, Greenspan and Wieder (1998, 2001) established four major goals for floor time: to encourage attention and intimacy, to establish two-way communication, to cultivate the expression of ideas and feelings, and to connect logical thought. The intervention involves 20- to 30-minute interaction periods 6 to 10 times throughout the day in which the parent or interaction partner "gets down on the floor" with the child and engages in activities ranging from rough-and-tumble play to acting out adventures with toys (Greenspan & Wieder, 1998). Floor time is a child-centered intervention approach in which the interaction partner facilitates the initiation of interactions, at first nonverbally, in response to the subtle movements or gestures of a child. It involves creating a meaningful link between emotions and behaviors, as well as encouraging problem solving and abstract thought. It is the adult's role to follow the child's lead, expand on the child's actions, and attempt to turn every behavior into a circle of communication.

Circles of communication are critical components of this approach. A *circle of communication* opens when a child or adult initiates an interaction or tries to engage another (verbally or nonverbally) and closes when there is a response to the initiation or when the interaction ends (Greenspan & Wieder, 1998). During floor time, interventionists learn to capitalize on a child's motivation and interests, such as a perseveration a child with ASD might have with an object or action that creates an opportunity for interaction. For example, if a child is opening and closing doors repeatedly, the interventionist might open a circle of communication by placing her hand or body in the way of the child so that the child must react in order to continue the action. The child may close the circle by moving the interventionist's hand or body out of the way and continuing the action. The interventionist learns not to be rejected by the child's closing of the circle and waits for another opportunity to open a circle. In the previous example, it might be that the clinician is working to establish more functional or meaningful opportunities to use the child's interests by using pet cages with doors that open and close and are part of the props for a pet store in a sociodramatic play area in a preschool setting. After several attempts to open a circle by placing her hand in the way of the child closing a pet cage door and the child closing the circle by pushing her hand away, the interventionist might delay her next attempt. The child then opens a circle by looking at the interventionist, who then closes the circle by placing a stuffed animal in the cage before the child closes the door. Initially, circles are simple and contain reactions, not interactions. They also communicate emotions and take advantage of a child's natural motivation, increasing the likelihood that a response will occur through enticement (e.g., the interventionist building a tower of the child's favorite blocks) and playful obstructions (e.g., desired blocks are out of reach and require an adult to gain access). Greenspan and Wieder (1998) believe that as circles of communication increase in length and complexity, the child's proficiency in relating increases, which leads to higher levels of emotional development. This exploration of emotions is a critical component of floor time and appears to facilitate a child's understanding of abstraction (Stacey, 2003). Through a series of circles of communication, interaction partners help the child to master each emotional milestone, ensuring that the child is able to demonstrate target behaviors even when experiencing emotional extremes.

Intervention Goals. The first intervention goal is to encourage attention and intimacy. To do this, the interactive partner must support the child's ability to maintain mutual attention and engagement by teaching the child to tap into the interactive partner's presence and enjoy involvement with the partner. For example, as a child with ASD bolts across a room, seemingly to run away, the interaction partner could initiate a "race," running across the room in response to "Ready, set, go."

The second goal is to establish two-way communication. This is done by using and responding to subtle facial expressions and engaging in dialogue without words. The interactive partner facilitates the use of dialogue that capitalizes on the child's emotions and the use of hands, face, and body to communicate intention. For example, when a father is playing an "I'm gonna get you" game with his son who has ASD, he might wait until his son lifts his arms to be tickled or peaks his head up from behind a couch before initiating the routine.

The third goal is designed to encourage the expression and use of feelings and ideas. This is done through drama and make-believe, during which a child learns to express his needs, wishes, feelings, and expression. For example, as a clinician and a child with ASD play with some characters from the child's favorite video, the clinician might change the typical script by adding a character, by asking why a character is doing something, or by describing the feelings a character has when the child says or does something.

The final goal requires the interventionist to help the child to link ideas to feelings, to connect thoughts in logical ways, so that he or she develops a logical understanding of the world. For example, a child might then be able to explain to the clinician in play why an animal is thirsty, how thirsty the animal is, what the animal likes to drink, how the animal might feel when he does not get enough to drink, and what could be done if the animal cannot get what he likes to drink. Thus, the child would be opening and closing multiple, complex circles of communication and elaborating on the content, themes, and emotions that are offered by the interactive partner.

Value for Children with ASD. A notable advantage of floor time is its focus on what motivates a child, although families and practitioners must be careful not to limit play and interaction to activities of a specific and restricted interest. The child's interests can shape the intervention, increasing the likelihood of successful engagement, at least initially, through that interest. Because the interventionist is not structuring the intervention on activities that are of little interest to the child, gaining trust and forming emotional bonds are facilitated. Floor time allows the child to direct the intervention, and there are no preconceived notions of what constitutes a correct response. Further, the literature indicates that "conditional and unqualified acceptance have been found to be more facilitative of communicative success and growth in children" (Prizant & Wetherby, 1998, p. 337).

The focus on developmentally appropriate interactions with a child also is a strength of this intervention approach. Floor time does not require a separate curriculum; instead, it builds on the child's play, following the child's lead and encouraging a greater number of circles of communication with a variety of communicative partners. All behavior is treated as purposeful, and the environmental arrangement at home, at school, or in the community can be adjusted to accommodate the child's developmental strengths and interests.

The involvement of families in intervention planning and implementation for children with ASD is critical (Dawson & Osterling, 1997; see Chapters 2, 3, and 8 for further discussion). Greenspan and Wieder (2000) believe family involvement is a central component of floor time. They explain that the "interaction patterns between the child and caregivers and family members bring the child's sensory and motor needs and sensitivities into the larger developmental picture and can contribute to the negotiation of the child's functional developmental capacities" (p. 283). An additional benefit of involving the family and working within the home, as espoused in the floor time approach, is the increased likelihood of generalization. Children with disabilities generalize their communication skills to a greater extent in environments similar to those in which they are taught (Roberts, Prizant, & McWilliam, 1995).

Children with ASD have marked difficulty with pragmatics, or the use of language. Joint attention and turn taking, pragmatic skills critical to successful interaction, may be especially problematic. The early stages of linguistic development, prior to the actual use of words, serve as a useful framework for the initial stages of intervention, in that children must attain skills in engagement, affect, and intentionality if they are to develop language (Gerber, 2003). Interventionists employing the floor time approach do not assume that if a child speaks, essential pragmatic skills are present. Because this approach does not initially require verbal interactions and instead emphasizes balanced reciprocal partnerships in achieving communication, it is well suited for children with ASD who display limited verbal communication. It is also useful as a strategy for children with ASD who have a foundation in verbal communication but struggle to capitalize on expressing their knowledge in meaningful social contexts such as play with peers. In the example of Halsey that follows, the team understands the importance of capitalizing on Halsey's interests, knowing his level of social and emotional development, and creating opportunities for play with his peers in their application of the floor time approach in the preschool environment.

Halsey is a 5-year-old boy with ASD who is verbal with some immediate and delayed echolalia, as well as challenges in his understanding of abstract terms and complex language structure. He engages in some repetitive behaviors and exhibits limited peer interactions. To facilitate his social and emotional development, the team decided that floor time could be an effective intervention, because, although other strategies had fostered his academic performance and ability to attend, peer relationships and play continued to be a struggle. Halsey can maintain his attention in contexts that focus on his interests, and he can engage with family members and selected adults in two-way communication exchanges. Although he has the requisite skills for achieving the first two goals in the floor time approach, he is unable to express his emotions, engage in dramatic play, or make logical connections. Based on this profile, his educational team, in collaboration with his family, determined that his floor time intervention should begin with Goal 3, fostering the expression and use of feelings and ideas through an emphasis on dramatic play and make-believe. At preschool, Halsey likes the costumes in the dress-up area but has yet to engage in pretend play with his peers during free time. The team decided to capitalize on his interests by introducing a play theme based on *Harry Potter,* a favorite topic for Halsey. Through the use of props and scripts adapted from the *Harry Potter* stories, the team facilitated Halsey's ability to increase the number of verbal circles of communication he was able to open and close with his peers and promote his expression of emotions.

By setting up opportunities for imaginative play based on familiar and motivating content, the team successfully scaffolded Halsey's ability to connect with his peers. As an intervention approach to support social interaction, emotional thinking, and two-way communication, floor time provides a unique opportunity for children with ASD to advance their social–emotional development while nurturing their language development.

Efficacy. The floor time approach is supported primarily through chart reviews and testimonials; a review of the literature reveals anecdotal but little empirical support for it (Armour & Kuster, 2002). In a retrospective chart review, outcome patterns based on clinical observations and detailed notes taken as part of the *Functional Emotional Assessment Scale* (Greenspan, 1992) were described for 200 children. Outcomes were examined at two levels: overall pattern of social–emotional behavior and severity of autistic symptoms (Greenspan & Wieder, 1997a). Three different patterns emerged from the chart review: good to outstanding outcomes (58%, or 116 children), medium outcomes (25%, or 50 children), and ongoing difficulties (17%, or 34 children). A range of severity of symptoms was reported for the three groups, indicating that the group with continuing difficulties included a greater percentage of children (70%) with a significant degree of impairment (score of 40 or more on the *Childhood Autism Rating Scale*) compared to the good to outstanding group (20%) and the medium group (45%). Thus, the children with greater autistic symptomatology at the initiation of intervention were more likely to be in the continuing difficulties group, although progress was noted for children with a range of autistic symptoms, as children with mild, moderate, and severe deficits were found in both the good to outstanding and medium outcome groups.

In addition, Greenspan and Wieder (1997a) analyzed videotaped interactions with caregivers of a subset of 20 children from the good to outstanding outcomes group who made the most progress. They noted that these children continued to improve their functioning, especially their socialization, the longer they were in intervention. They also found this group to be indistinguishable from a group of 14 children with no history of challenges. Greenspan and Wieder reported that those children in the good to outstanding group "were able to use their emerging symbolic skills both creatively and logically" (p. 118). These children were described as more purposeful and organized in their approach to problem solving and interacting with others. They also increased their trust and intimate connections with their parents, managed two-way symbolic communication, displayed a more pleasurable affect, and exhibited a heightened capacity for abstract thinking.

In another study, a variation of floor time was compared with an adult-directed, structured approach that yielded statistically significant outcomes, favoring floor time (DeGangi & Greenspan, 1997). Further, anecdotal reports exist regarding the value of floor time in supporting the emotional development of young children with autism (Stacey, 2003).

Greenspan and Wieder (1997a) identified some notable limitations in their chart review. Assessment procedures used for identifying children with ASD differed for the 200 children in their retrospective study. The sample was selective, and the results cannot necessarily be applied to other populations with ASD. Information in the charts was drawn from clinician notes and observations and not through clinical ratings by objective and reliable raters. There was also variability in the degree to which the families of each child were able to administer the floor time intervention. Therefore, not all of the children received identical treatment. In summary, although some evidence suggests that floor time is effective in increasing the number of communication circles used by children with ASD and facilitating engagement and an ability to relate to others, additional research is needed (Greenspan & Wieder, 1997a).

Relationship Development Intervention Model

The RDI model (Gutstein & Sheely, 2002a, 2002b) is similar to the floor time model in that it builds on the sharing and joint attention that naturally occur between parents and their children. It is designed, however, to support relationship development for children, adolescents, and adults with ASD through the implementation of three cardinal principles of intervention: functions precede means or skills, social referencing, and coregulation (Gutstein, 2000). Gutstein specifies both the particular behaviors to be developed and the sequence in which those behaviors might be developed within his relationship model.

The first principle is to teach function before skills because function is the reason for a particular behavior or skill. Gutstein believes that emotion sharing or excitement sharing is one of the first and most basic functions that should be developed in a child. Competence, including proficiency, perseverance, responsibility, and resilience, is another important function Gutstein emphasizes in preparing children for their relationship development. Children must be proficient in sharing their emotions, stick with the event or experience that excites them, take responsibility for their role in an interaction, and bounce back when the experience does not go quite the way that is expected. The interventionist must determine a child's developmental readiness prior to teaching skills. The goal is to ensure that the individual has a strong foundation on which to build those skills necessary for meaningful relationships. A balance between two strategies, guiding and pacing, is necessary. *Guiding* requires choosing relevant objectives for establishing sharing experiences, maintaining control of the critical elements of an event, limiting variations within that event, and setting clear limits for expected behavior. *Pacing* involves modifying one's communication style and pace for practicing particular skills to ensure mastery, and breaking down complex events or tasks into simpler ones while requiring a child to take greater responsibility for regulating his or her behavior. For example, while a dad and his son are playing the drums together, the dad would not be using his voice but instead would be guiding his son by smiling and nodding his head and maybe showing the child how to hold the drumsticks. The child then imitates his dad's movement patterns, using only one drumstick at a time.

The second intervention principle in the RDI model is social referencing, or the ability to perceive and process information important in social relationships (Gutstein, 2000). The ability to reference socially is the foundation for experience sharing, which depends on interactive partners being able to evaluate a match or mismatch in what they are experiencing with one another. Indirect prompts are used to facilitate experience sharing. Although such prompts do not tell the child exactly what to do, they do provide important information on the next steps. For example, while a child is picking out objects from a grab bag, instead of stating, "Pick an object from the bag," the interventionist might say to the child, "What surprise do you have for me?" *Spotlighting* is a strategy the interventionist uses to find a way to make the learning opportunity stand out. The interventionist learns to create a contrast for the child, such as using a quiet versus a loud voice or pretending that plastic bugs taken out of a box are real and acting afraid. Once spotlighting is modeled for the child, roles are switched so that the child can react to the event or experience that was just shared with the interventionist. Thus, the interventionist models a script for the child and then gives the child an opportunity to carry out the script with increased competence. Motivation for experience sharing is emphasized and requires the retention of positive episodic memories, such as remembering celebrations following an activity with a parent (e.g., a father and son giving each other a "high five" after drumming together or during an activity; mother and son hugging when engaged at the piano). It might also involve stopping an action and mentioning to a child a memory of a favorite event such as going to the beach and then describing that experience. To reinforce episodic memories for children with ASD, Gutstein (2003) suggests using a memory book that includes photos of a special family event so that each family member can share what he or she remembers about this special event at mealtime or during a quiet family time.

Developing frameworks for sharing experiences is a key element of the RDI model. When creating a framework, the interventionist identifies the central elements of an activity and keeps those the same, while peripheral elements begin to change. For example, in the common and simple activity of peekaboo, there is a basic hiding-and-revealing relationship. This framework evolves over time from hiding behind a blanket or pillow and revealing one's face while playing peekaboo with an infant, to hiding and revealing objects with toddlers to create an element of surprise, to playing hide-and-seek with a preschooler. The interventionist might also consider the following examples in developing an understanding of frameworks (Gutstein, 2003).

Activity:

Interventionist sends a car down an incline to a child at the other end.

Central element: Sender–receiver roles (interventionist–child)
Peripheral element: Car

⬦ **Activity:**

Interventionist gives the child fruit to send down the incline to a parent.

Central element: Sender–receiver roles (child–parent)
Peripheral element: Fruit (replaces the car)

⬦ **Activity:**

Child places fruit in a truck and pushes the truck to the parent.

Central element: Sender–receiver (child–parent)
Peripheral element: Truck (replaces the incline)

This sender–receiver framework is replaced with a more complex version in the following example.

The parent is a storekeeper who "calls" the child (playing a farmer) on a play telephone and asks for different kinds of apples, berries, or pears to be delivered to the store. The child loads up the truck and sends the requested fruit to the store. If the child gets stuck loading the truck or selecting the requested fruit, the "storekeeper" might say, "I wonder when that truck will arrive" or "I sure hope that delivery comes soon."

This concept of frameworks can be expanded by changing the farmer–storekeeper role to a car factory–car dealer role (Gutstein, 2003).

The third cardinal principle is learning coregulation or the ongoing fine-tuning of actions to seek feedback from interactive partners (Gutstein, 2000, 2003). Coregulation appears to be critical to establishing competence in experience sharing because it is a process for altering individual actions based on the expected and ongoing actions of others. For example, if an interventionist places a ball between herself and a child and requires that they walk with the ball between them, picking up the pace as they go, the movement of one depends on the other. Another example might include an interventionist and a child hitting drums in synchrony while chanting, "Get away, spider" or "Where is my train?" periodically stopping what is said or done. What is said and done can be varied to create several frameworks in which the child must coregulate with an interactive partner by changing the drumbeat, the chant, or the pace. Competence in coregulating experience sharing requires practice, so activities are built on that require the child and adult to work together in the interaction. For example, if a child is standing on a treadmill and at first wants a parent to catch him when he jumps off, the next time the child might be sitting on the treadmill and asking to be caught when he jumps off. Or a child might be engaged in a reciprocal activity with an adult but will learn not to take a turn until signaled by a head shake or nod from an interactive partner. Competence in experience sharing develops in simple settings with simple partners. Intervention begins in comfortable environments with familiar partners and gradually moves to more complex settings and less familiar patterns. This evolution of experience sharing depends on the child's mastery level for each level of intervention. Objects that might compete for attention (e.g., video games, TV, action figures, objects of obsessive interest) are avoided until the child has mastered some frameworks for experience sharing. Adults, and particularly parents, are the initial partners, as most young children without ASD prefer adults the first 2 years of life. Adults are usually effective at balancing safety with challenge to facilitate experience sharing. When moving to peer dyads, Gutstein (2003) recommends using a single typical peer who has skills in referencing and regulation similar to those of the child with ASD, so that there will be plenty of opportunities to practice and negotiate referencing and regulation within a peer interaction.

Gutstein (2003) also offers some principles to consider when implementing RDI with teenagers with ASD. He recommends that interventionists work to form an alliance with the teens—sit side by side, withhold asking questions, and place the teen in the more competent role during activities of experience sharing. Further, he suggests that the interventionist may need to be prepared to work without the parents, at least initially.

Intervention Goals. Overall, there are six levels to the RDI model and 28 stages. Within each stage, goals are established, as well as a process for evaluating mastery of stage acquisition. For example, Level 1, Laying the Foundation for Relational Development, has four stages: emotional attunement and attending; social referencing; excitement sharing or regulating; and coordinating actions, as in simple games. During *emotional attunement or attention,* the interventionist's goal is to seek the child's face-to-face gazing through sharing joy and laughter or soothing distress. Mastery is achieved when the child meets the adult's gaze with the specific intent of sharing emotions of pleasure or distress, receives comfort without having to make physical contact, initiates excited emotion sharing during a brief pause in a mutually pleasurable activity, and shares reinforcing laughter. The goal for *social referencing* is to have the child seek the adult's facial expressions as a reference point for subsequent actions, particularly in uncertain situations. The goal is to teach referencing, not eye contact. Mastery in this case is the child's ability to shift gaze when uncertain or confused and to look to the adult's face as a reference point for determining what to do next. The goal for *excitement sharing or regulating* is to facilitate a preference for increased challenge and excitement by providing novel elements and versions of experience sharing frameworks. Mastery of this goal is evaluated in several ways: The child responds to adult-introduced changes in familiar frameworks, recalls activities with novelty and variation as more enjoyable than familiar repeated activities, and chooses to have the adult add novelty during joke telling. During *coordinated actions,* the goal is to have the child enjoy coordinating his or her actions with the adult while engaged in simple shared-activity frameworks. Mastery of this goal occurs when the child chooses to engage in enjoyable shared activities, even when offered options of performing versions of the activities alone.

Goals and evaluation of mastery are provided for each of the stages within the five remaining levels (i.e., Becoming an Apprentice; You and Me Working Together as Partners; Sharing Our Worlds, Sharing Our Minds; The Inner Game; and True Friends) of the RDI model (Gutstein, 2000). Gutstein and Sheely (2002a, 2002b) have simplified the names of the six levels to Novice, Apprentice, Challenger, Voyager, Explorer, and Partner to represent the roles the children are taking on in their relationship development. The stages within these levels include goals around perspective taking, imagination sharing, integrating ideas, reciprocal conversations, building friendships, self-regulation, emotional awareness, group participation, and identity development.

Gutstein (2003) recommends that Individualized Education Program (IEP) objectives for children involved in the RDI model should start with appropriate functions and then skills in social, self-regulation, emotional awareness, relative thinking, and executive functions. He encourages teams to develop objectives that consider intervention opportunities both at home and at school with clear reevaluation dates and criteria established for mastery. He recommends that formal reevaluation of the RDI process should occur at least every 16 weeks and that objectives should not be considered mastered unless they have been generalized across settings and communication partners.

Value for Children with ASD. The systematic approach to relationship building that is the foundation for the RDI model is responsive to the needs of both children and youth with ASD. RDI is responsive to addressing the core deficits in autism, particularly in the area of social impairment. Intervention is built around function before skills and establishes natural opportunities for sharing emotions; referencing actions, objects, and people; and coordinating and regulating actions with another. Flexibility is built in through numerous variations of frameworks for interacting, settings in which the interactions might occur, and individuals who serve as interactive partners. It is a partnership model of intervention that engages both the parents and the school team. An assessment framework is used with goals and objectives established for skill mastery within intervention contexts. Parent training, support, and coaching are provided as part of the intervention, as is direct service from a trained interventionist. Notably, the commitments for training time and cost may be prohibitive and could affect the ease with which RDI is implemented for a particular child with ASD. For example, interventionists must have an initial 2-day training, followed by a 4-day training and weekly supervision by a certified RDI interventionist. Parents are expected to be involved in an initial 12-hour training, followed by monthly support groups with a certified RDI interventionist. Accessibility of training and supervision is likely to be limited for many children with ASD and their families.

Efficacy. Because RDI is a fairly new systematic program, published research on its effectiveness is not currently available. Gutstein (2003) is engaged in preliminary research, however, and reports positive results for RDI intervention with 10 children, ages 5 to 11 years, who improved in their communication, reciprocal social interaction, and overall social and communication performance from pre- to postassessment on the *Autism Diagnostic Observation Schedule* (ADOS; Lord, Rutter, DiLavore, & Risi, 1999). There were notable changes in the ADOS classification for the 10 children. Prior to initiating RDI, 9 of the children were considered autistic, and 1 child was identified as on the autistic spectrum. After participating in RDI, 4 of the children remain classified as autistic, 3 were reclassified as on the autistic spectrum, and the remaining 3 children were classified as not on the spectrum. Gutstein also reports favorable perceptions by parents ($N = 20$), who rated their children's performance in several target areas as *significantly improved, somewhat better,* or *about the same.* Areas where parents rated some improvement at least 80% of the time included excitement/enthusiasm, teacher reports, communication/nonverbal language, initiation, eye contact, and family interaction. There were also notable improvements in desire to be with others, sharing emotions, paying attention, and behavior. Because these are preliminary results with a small number of participants, the results must be interpreted cautiously. The use of the ADOS as an outcome measure is less likely than other measures of day-to-day social performance to provide a valuable account of generalized social skills in meaningful contexts as a result of participating in RDI intervention. Systematic and ongoing research of the RDI model will be critical to understanding its potential value for children with ASD.

The Social Communication, Emotional Regulation, and Transactional Supports Model

The SCERTS model, developed by Prizant and his colleagues (Prizant et al., 2003; Prizant et al., 2004), is a comprehensive approach to facilitating the social–emotional and communication abilities of children with ASD in their home and school settings. The authors believe that improved social communication and emotional regulation are primary developmental goals that intervention programs must recognize and prioritize as targets for young children with ASD, and that transactional supports allow meaningful learning experiences to occur in a child's everyday activities at home and in school. Therefore, they emphasize using a variety of caring partners in typical social routines.

The first component of the model, *social communication,* emphasizes goals that increase children's competence and confidence in actively participating in social events in which they can derive pleasure and joy from their interactions with other children and adults. Two major objectives are emphasized in children's social communication: an increased capacity for joint attention so that children share their emotion and express their intentions with their social communication partners, and an increased capacity for symbol use or communicative means (preverbal and verbal), so that children develop sophisticated and abstract ways of communicating (Prizant et al., 2004). By supporting children's ability to attend and respond to social overtures that are typical of reciprocal interactions and to communicate for a variety of purposes, the practitioner helps the child to learn to participate in emotionally satisfying social interactions (Prizant et al., 2004).

Emotional regulation, the second component of the model, emphasizes goals that support children's ability to manage their emotional arousal and availability to learn. Prizant and his colleagues propose that children are "available learners" when they can attend to and focus on relevant information within an activity, process information verbally and nonverbally, stay socially engaged, initiate interactions using more complex language, respond within reciprocal exchanges, and participate actively in daily events (Prizant et al., 2004). To accomplish this, children must have the emotional regulatory capacity to remain organized in stressful events (self-regulation), seek or respond to the support of others in stressful circumstances (mutual regulation), and recover from stressful events through self or mutual regulation (recovery from dysregulation) (Prizant et al., 2004). Ultimately, by supporting a child's ability to adapt to and cope with his or her daily emotional challenges, practitioners can facilitate optimal arousal conducive to learning.

The final component of the SCERTS model, *transactional supports,* considers interpersonal, learning and educational, family, and service provider supports. These supports are considered because the authors emphasize the importance of developing trusting relationships with social partners in everyday activities. Interpersonal supports involve adjustments in language, emotional expression, and interaction style that communicative partners make to facilitate the ability of a child with ASD to understand language, engage in interaction, maintain regulated states, and experience emotionally satisfying social events (Prizant et al., 2004). Communicative partners include both adults and peers who become responsive partners and provide appropriate models for social interaction, language, and play. Learning and educational supports consider the arrangement of the settings in which a child with ASD learns and interacts, so that social communication and emotional regulation are fostered (Prizant et al., 2004). These supports might include visual symbols, pictures, or schedules and curriculum adaptations to enhance the child's opportunities for learning success. Family supports involve sharing educational resources or instructing family members to support their child's social communication and emotional regulation in daily routines. It might also include providing emotional support for the family to facilitate coping with and adapting to their child's challenges (Prizant et al., 2004). The final level of support, which comes from professionals and other service providers, involves creating opportunities that facilitate the intervention skills of practitioners, as well as emotional support for dealing with the challenges often presented by children with ASD.

Although Prizant and his colleagues (Prizant et al., 2003; Prizant et al., 2004) discuss the three components of the SCERTS model individually, they assert that they recognize the interdependence among these aspects of a child's development. They have also found in their recent work that although the SCERTS model was originally designed for use with young children with ASD, social communication, emotional regulation, and transactional supports are valued life-span abilities and are appropriate for conceptualizing intervention through adulthood. Further, they assert that an ideal intervention style when implementing the SCERTS model is one that would include sufficient "structure to support a child's attentional focus, situational understanding, emotional regulation, and positive emotional experiences, but that also fosters initiation, spontaneity, flexibility, problem-solving, and self-determination" (Prizant et al., 2003, p. 310).

Intervention Goals. Prizant and his colleagues (Prizant et al., 2003; Prizant et al., 2004) provide several examples of goals that might be appropriate in each of the three components of SCERTS. Social communication goals are provided for both joint attention and symbol use and consider the communication level of the child (intentional communication, emerging and early multiword, or sentence and discourse). For example, at the intentional communication level, a goal for joint attention might be to establish shared affect (by smiling), while a goal for symbol use might be to use contact gestures to establish intent (showing an object) (Prizant et al., 2004). At the emerging and early multiword level, a joint attention goal might be to attract attention to oneself (by calling a play partner's name), and a goal for symbol use might be establishing conventional use of objects in play (by pretending to drink from a cup). At the sentence and discourse level, a joint attention goal might be to facilitate perspective taking (by using theory of mind tasks), whereas a goal for symbol use might be to develop vocabulary to express a variety of emotions (by identifying confusion or frustration).

Emotional regulation goals also involve goals for joint attention and symbol use at both sensory–motor/prelinguistic and cognitive/linguistic levels (Prizant et al., 2004). For example, at the sensory–motor/prelinguistic level, a joint attention goal might expand the use of a sensory–motor strategy to facilitate ease of transition within a routine (by using a transition object), whereas a goal for symbol use might increase the use of socially appropriate gestures for social control (by pushing away to protest) (Prizant et al., 2004). At the cognitive/linguistic level, a joint attention goal might be to increase attention to tasks (by using verbal mediation), whereas a goal for symbol use might be to increase understanding of social conventions (by using social stories).

A variety of transactional support goals are offered in the SCERTS model. Interpersonal support goals might include identifying interaction styles that support interactions with children with ASD; learning and education support goals might modify the curriculum to make the language accessible for children with ASD; and family support goals might provide families with emotional support through parent groups, whereas a support goal for professionals and other service providers might include training in targeted intervention skills.

Value for Children with ASD. Prizant and his colleagues describe the SCERTS model as value based, in that it is grounded in explicitly stated principles that guide their intervention efforts (Prizant et al., 2004). They emphasize respect for the child and family and focus on meaningful goals that facilitate a child's function in his or her daily environment. The priorities of the SCERTS model are consistent with those identified by the National Research Council (2001). These include the development of spontaneous communication, social connections and play with peers, and functional skills in daily activities. Parents of children with ASD have also reported such priorities, indicating that they worry most about their children's lack of functional communication, responsiveness to and relationships with family members and peers, and behavior (Bristol & Schopler, 1984). These difficulties, Prizant and colleagues suggest, are a result of the children's deficits in social communication and emotional regulation.

The SCERTS model is not a curriculum that specifies skills to be taught. Instead, it emphasizes developmental capacities and supports important to developing a child's functional skills. It is systematic but flexible, not prescribing what should be done but guiding the practitioner to facilitate learning by following the child's lead and building on respectful social connections.

Efficacy. A key challenge for practitioners is to determine what intervention approaches or strategies are effective for individual children and their families (Prizant & Wetherby, 1998). Most often, outcome measures reported for children with ASD focus on improvements in scores on intelligence tests and where a child is placed following intervention. This approach to examining intervention effectiveness risks ecological validity because it does not consider performance changes in the context of natural environments and because it fails to consider treatment across the core deficits identified for ASD (Prizant et al., 2003). There is a need for more dynamic approaches to assessing intervention effectiveness that consider success or competence in communication and social exchanges, peer relationships, and emotional regulation across a child's natural environments and interactive partners. Although efficacy data are not available for use of the SCERTS model, it does provide a framework within which to address the core deficits of autism. Further, it emphasizes the recommended priorities for outcome measures suggested by the National Research Council (2001), including gains in spontaneous initiation to communicate in functional ways and generalizing abilities across tasks, interactive partners, and settings. It also facilitates individualized intervention planning, considering a child's strengths and challenges and incorporating intervention strategies that are evidence based along a continuum of contemporary behavioral and developmental social–pragmatic approaches (Prizant et al., 2003).

Do–Watch–Listen–Say Framework

Quill (2000) describes social experiences as complex, ever changing, and requiring social skills that allow a child to understand social and emotional events across a variety of contexts. Quill proposes a do–watch–listen–say framework that engages the child with ASD at cognitive, social, linguistic, and communicative levels. For example, the ability to know what to *do* in a social context requires a level of cognitive understanding that allows a child to know how things are related. The ability to *watch* others is a highly desirable socialization skill, as it contributes to a child's understanding of how to imitate, share, take turns, use gestures, and express feelings. The ability to *listen* is a language skill that ensures that a child has assigned meaning to objects and actions, as well as the nonverbal and verbal behaviors of others. Finally, communication skills guide the ability to know what to *say*, how to initiate and maintain interactions and communicate socially relevant messages. For example, in the social play of a preschool, a child might explore using blocks (*do*), look at the behaviors of his peers as they share their books or take turns on completing a construction project (*watch*), and attend to what is being said (*listen*) so that a response can be provided to requests and comments. Finally, the child learns to imitate and sustain his communicative interactions (*say*). Quill defines social mastery, then, as the child's ability to do–watch–listen–say within a social context.

Intervention Goals. When planning social skills intervention, Quill (2000) suggests there is a hierarchy of skills to consider within each of the four do–watch–listen–say domains that can guide intervention goals for children with ASD. For example, in the domain of *do*, the goal is to provide social play opportunities that involve functional, close-ended activities (e.g., cause–effect toys) gradually moving to open-ended activities (e.g., sand table) and then working toward creative activities (e.g., imaginative play). In the *watch* domain, the goal is first to help the child learn to share physical space, then to share toys and materials, and finally to take turns. For the *listen* domain, the goals involve teaching the child to respond to gestural messages first and then moving to nonverbal prosocial behaviors and eventually to verbal messages. For the final domain, *say*, the goals focus on initiating nonverbal prosocial messages, then nonverbal requests and comments, verbal prosocial messages, and then verbal requests and comments. A final goal in this domain is maintaining a conversational exchange with a social partner.

Quill (2000) also defines nine areas of social and communication development that can be used by teams to guide target goals and objectives for intervention planning. There are core skills (nonverbal interaction, imitation, and organization), social skills (play, group, and community), and communication skills (basic communicative, socioemotional, and basic conversational) that should be considered to maximize a child's social and communicative competence, mirror that of same-age peers, increase spontaneity, and build generalization (Quill, 2000). The individual needs of children with

ASD should be a primary consideration in goal setting. In addition, the team needs to consider some core abilities children exhibit in their social environments, including social observation, imitation, and organizational skills. An assessment of these abilities guides the selection of intervention strategies. For example, if a child likes to observe or imitate his peers, modeling is an effective teaching strategy for the team to consider (Quill, 2000).

Value for Children with ASD. The do–watch–listen–say framework is responsive to the challenges children with ASD often face in social contexts. It supports a strengths perspective, in that the focus is on building social skills rather than managing difficult behaviors. The assumption is that developing social communication skills in children with ASD will decrease problem behaviors (Quill, 2000). The framework considers the individual needs of the child with ASD and focuses on core social and communication skills. A process for assessment that guides intervention planning and a core social skills curriculum is provided. The curriculum specifies potential goals and objectives, activities in which the goals and objectives can be met, and strategies to facilitate goal achievement.

Efficacy. The do–watch–listen–say framework is grounded in what is known about good practice for supporting the socioemotional development and social communication skills of children with ASD. The framework encourages ongoing assessment, individualization of curriculum goals, and data collection to determine progress and gains in social skills across contexts. There is no specific data available at this time, however, to document the efficacy of this framework for children with ASD.

Strategies To Support Social Interaction and Social Communication

The literature offers several strategies that have been used effectively to facilitate the social interaction of children and adolescents with ASD. These strategies can be used in addition to those described in Chapters 9 and 10 that describe ways to foster communication and play with a variety of social partners across environmental contexts. Peer intervention strategies, cognitive behavioral interventions, pivotal response training, comic strip conversations, and social stories were selected for description and review because of their frequent application to and reported value for children and adolescents with ASD.

Peer Intervention Strategies

Considering the significant deficit in social interaction skills that characterizes autism, practitioners, families, and researchers should recognize the importance of providing opportunities for children with ASD to establish and successfully engage in positive peer relationships. Adult-mediated interventions in which teachers reinforce attention to peers or prompt interactions with typical peers have been used to facilitate the social interactions of children and adolescents with ASD and their typical peers (for a review, see Paul, 2003). Such adult support, however, has sometimes led to adult dependency and potential disruption of child-to-child interactions (Paul, 2003). More recently, peers have been used as the primary intervention agents to support the social skill development of children with ASD.

Early research focused on the immersion of children with social interaction challenges in socially active peer groups (Bricker, 1978), as well as on increasing access to socially competent peers (Apolloni, Cooke, & Cooke, 1977). Research then moved to training peers as interventionists (Goldstein, Kaczmarek, Pennington, & Shafer, 1992; Hoyson, Jamieson, & Strain, 1984; Kohler, Strain, Maretsky, & DeCesare, 1990; Lee & Odom, 1996; Odom & Strain, 1986; Roeyers, 1996; Strain & Cordisco, 1994; Strain, Kohler, & Goldstein, 1996) and finally to training both children with ASD and their socially competent peers (Kamps et al., 1992; Simpson, Myles, Sasso, & Kamps, 1997). Group friendship activities (Cooper & McEvoy, 1996) and "buddy skills" (English, Goldstein, Kaczmarck, & Shafer, 1996) have also been used to support friendship building between young children with disabilities and their typical peers. The establishment of social interaction is a critical dimension of the long-term success for many children with ASD. Research suggests that children with ASD who have opportunities to experience peers without disabilities will increase the time they spend in interaction, their responsiveness to partner initiations, and their attempts to initiate (Goldstein et al., 1992; Roeyers, 1996).

Several strategies have been used to facilitate interactions among children with ASD and their typical peers. *Proximity,* or placing typical peers who are socially competent with children with disabilities and directing them to play together without specific training is one strategy that has been used. *Prompting and reinforcing* is a combination strategy in which socially competent peers are trained first to prompt a child with disabilities to play and then to reinforce the child's responses. Teachers have also been used to prompt engagement among children with and without ASD. For example, in *antecedent prompting* (Simpson et al., 1997), a child with ASD is paired with a socially competent peer who is instructed to remain in proximity to the child with ASD. The teacher provides periodic prompts to the child with ASD to engage in social interaction. The teacher initially waits for a response, and if there is none, provides a physical prompt. The advantage of this strategy is that it can be used in natural contexts, although it may disrupt ongoing social encounters among children. *Peer initiation* is a strategy in which typical peers are trained to make social initiations to children with disabilities. For example, typical peers would be taught to initiate with children with ASD by sharing, suggesting play ideas, showing affection, and providing assistance (Lee & Odom, 1996). Teachers are also taught to remind typical peers to use their initiation strategies with the child with ASD while in the classroom.

In addition, *peer tutoring* (Simpson et al., 1997), in which children with ASD work in dyads with socially competent peers, has been effectively used in inclusive classroom settings. Peer tutors are informed of the basic characteristics of students with autism. The teacher helps to define and structure the actual tutoring task, such as what materials are to be used, how directions and reinforcement should be given, and how to manage inappropriate behaviors. Informal interaction periods are also scheduled between tutoring tasks so that the peer dyads can establish some social connections besides learning academic tasks. Peer tutoring can be used in elementary, middle, and high schools, and often peer tutors are taken from an upper grade to work with a student with ASD from a lower grade, although they can be from the same grade. For example, the SLP might work with the fifth-grade teacher to identify potential peer tutors to work with a third-grade student with ASD around facilitating reading comprehension and language skills when reading short stories and responding to questions about those stories. The peer tutor and the student with ASD would be given a choice of stories that meet the reading standards to read from, including some that have preferred themes or topics for the student with autism. The peer tutor would have a format to assess the understanding of the student with ASD of the main idea and identification of the main characters. Together, the students make story character puppets and other simple props to reenact the story in a play or drama format. The students take turns role-playing the different characters. They complete an assessment rubric together (see Figure 11.1 for a sample) that visually evaluates the ability of the student with ASD to describe a three-part story sequence in which the events clearly match the story and are presented in order, as well as to work cooperatively with the peer tutor.

A specific approach to peer-mediated intervention for children with ASD has been described by Strain and his colleagues as part of a comprehensive early intervention program known as Learning Experiences ... An Alternative Program (LEAP), designed for preschoolers with social communication disorders and their families (Strain & Cordisco, 1994; Strain et al., 1996). This approach involves teaching typical peers to initiate play with children with ASD through role-play, adult cueing around play materials and activities, and reinforcement. Parents are also engaged in the peer-mediation training as they support their other children in interactions with the sibling with ASD. As part of the curriculum for peer-mediated intervention within LEAP, Strain (2001) emphasizes six key friendship behaviors: sharing, suggesting play ideas, showing affection, assisting others, establishing lengthy social encounters, and demonstrating reciprocity. His curriculum for supporting the peer interactions of children with ASD and their typical peers teaches five key social skills: getting a friend's attention, sharing a toy, requesting a toy, suggesting play ideas, and complimenting what the friend is doing. Intervention around each skill involves four basic steps (Strain, 2001):

1. The interventionist introduces the skill to a typical peer, describing it and providing a rationale. For example, an important skill for learning to share is being

Sample Assessment Rubric for Peer Tutoring

Skill	Wow, I Did It!	Pretty Good	Need Some Help
Identifying a 3-part story sequence	___ There is a three-part sequence to my play. ___ The sequence matches the story. ___ The sequence is easy to follow.	___ There is a 3-part sequence to my play. ___ Some parts match the story. ___ Some parts can be followed.	___ Parts of the sequence are missing. ___ Difficult to tell what matches the story. ___ The sequence is hard to follow.
Knowing the characters	___ I have my main character. ___ My main character looks like the main character in the story. ___ I have at least two more characters from the story. ___ My other characters look like those from the story.	___ I have my main character. ___ My main character looks somewhat like the main character in the story. ___ I have at least one more character from the story. ___ My other character may or may not look like those from the story.	___ My main character is missing. ___ My main character does not look like the main character in the story. ___ I have no other characters from the story. OR ___ My other characters do not look like those from the story.
Cooperating as a peer partner	___ I cooperated with my peer partner. ___ I listened to what my peer partner said. ___ I talked to my peer partner. ___ I did my best work on the play. ___ I am proud of my work.	___ I cooperated some of the time with my peer partner. ___ I listened some of the time to what my peer partner said. ___ I talked to my peer partner some of the time. ___ I worked on the play. ___ I did okay but could do better.	___ I need to cooperate with my peer partner. ___ I need to listen to what my peer partner says. ___ I need to talk to my peer partner. ___ I need to complete my play. ___ I let my peer partner do most of the work. I need to do the work next time.

FIGURE 11.1. Sample assessment rubric for peer tutoring.

able to get a child's attention. This skill might be introduced in the following way: "Today we are going to learn how to get our friends to do fun things with us. It is important that friends learn to have fun with one another. One way to get a friend to have fun, like talking or playing a game, with you is by getting his attention." Then the specific skill of getting attention might be described in this way: "One way to get our friends to have fun together is by getting their attention. To get a friend's attention, you look at your friend, you say your friend's name, you gently tap your friend's shoulder or arm if he is not looking at you. You keep trying until you get your friend's attention."

2. The interventionist demonstrates the skill for the typical peer. The interventionist might say the following: "Let's practice getting your friend Mark's attention so that he looks at you. Watch me. I'm going to get Mark's attention. Tell me if I am doing it right." and then "Did I get Mark's attention? You're right, I did get Mark's attention. I looked at Mark, said his name, and gently touched him on the arm."

3. The typical peer rehearses the skill with the interventionist. For example, the interventionist might say: "Now let's have you practice getting a friend's attention. Let's pretend I am your friend and you are trying to get my attention. Remember to look at me, say my name, gently touch me on my arm if I'm not looking at you, and keep trying until you get my attention." The interventionist can then trade places with the child and try to get the child's attention. The child is then asked to tell the interventionist if she did it right.

4. The typical peer practices or rehearses the skill with another child. It could be another typical peer and ultimately the target child with ASD. In this step, the interventionist explains that it is time to practice with a peer or friend and says something like: "I am going to have David come over and practice with us. Christopher, you practice getting David's attention. Remember, you are going to look at him, say his name, gently touch him on the arm or shoulder if he is not looking at you, and keep trying until you get his attention." The interventionist provides feedback as needed and praises the child for looking at his friend and getting the friend's attention.

These four basic steps are repeated for each of the social skills to be taught (i.e., sharing a toy, asking for a toy, suggesting to a friend what to do with a toy, and saying nice things about the friend or what the friend is doing). Some skills have additional steps like demonstrating the skill the right way and then the wrong way. Tracking forms are used to collect data on the trained behaviors the typical peers demonstrate and the responses of the children with ASD. Time engaged is also documented.

Intervention Goals. Research has established some benchmarks for social behavior (e.g., proximity to other children, social bids, engagement) that should be considered in the development of social intervention goals for children with ASD (McGee, Feldman, & Morrier, 1997). This research examines social behavior in children without disabilities so that expectations for social bids and social play in children with ASD are not "out of sync" with what might be expected of same-age peers who are developing in a typical manner. McGee and colleagues suggest that "key peer behaviors must be assessed across time and a variety of activities, if sweeping, fundamental change in social learning is the goal" (p. 363). Without consistent observation across contexts and over time, practitioners may misinterpret generalized social gains based on intervention goals achieved in a specific setting with identified supports.

With these benchmarks in mind, several intervention goals for facilitating peer interactions can be identified for children with ASD, although all goals should be individualized. For example, if a team wishes to teach interaction concepts important to establishing friendships, they might incorporate some of the following into an IEP:

- The child will accept an object from another child by taking that object and using it in play.
- The child will offer an object to another child.
- The child will respond to an idea for play from a peer.
- The child will suggest an idea for play with a peer.
- The child will allow a peer to help him complete a task.
- The child will help a peer to complete a task.
- The child will accept affection (e.g., patting, hugging, holding hands) from a peer.
- The child will show affection toward a peer.
- The child will respond with appropriate affect to statements of praise from a peer.
- The child will make appropriate statements of praise to a peer.

In peer tutoring, goals might relate to working cooperatively or collaboratively with a peer tutor on an academic task, taking turns in conversation around a shared topic of interest, responding to questions, asking questions, and commenting on what a communication partner says. For older students and adolescents, goals might center around getting or giving assistance, such as initiating a conversation when a peer comes into school, offering to help a peer who cannot open a door because his arms are full, volunteering to take on a role in a cooperative learning group with a small group of peers, and asking questions about a topic of interest shared by a peer. Social goals and potential strategies that can be used with peers and children with ASD are highlighted in Table 11.1.

Parents of children with disabilities have also identified specific goals for friendship building with typical peers (Overton & Rausch, 2002). Eleven mothers were interviewed via focus groups in which general questions were posed to the group to initiate a discussion about friendship issues for their children. The results indicated that the mothers believed that friendships influence a number of goals related to quality-of-life issues, including their desire for their children to be happy; to evidence strong self-esteem, self-confidence, and self-acceptance; and to develop social competence (Overton

TABLE 11.1

Sample Social Interaction Goals and Possible Strategies
To Support Those Goals for Children with ASD

Sample Goal	Possible Strategies
To increase two-way communication and dialogue between a child with ASD and his communication partners, moving from interactions with adults to peers in both structured and unstructured situations.	*Floor time* (Greenspan & Wieder, 1997b, 1998) EXAMPLE: Interventionist works in the home setting with the parents of a child with autism to facilitate opening and closing circles of communication; play dates are scheduled with typical peers; interventionist models appropriate floor time strategies for the peers.
To increase initiations with a communicative partner, moving from interactions with adults to play with peers.	*Peer-mediated intervention* (McGee, Feldman, & Morrier, 1997; Roeyers, 1996; Strain, Kohler, & Goldstein, 1996) EXAMPLE: Peers are taught to initiate play with a child with ASD at a preschool setting after role playing and learning specific strategies to gain the child's attention and interest from adult models. *Antecedent prompting* (Simpson, Myles, Sasso, & Kamps, 1997) EXAMPLE: Child with ASD is paired with a socially competent peer; the peer is instructed to remain in proximity with the child, and the teacher provides periodic prompts (using time delay) to encourage the child with ASD to engage in social interaction.
To increase the child's participation in group activities in the classroom.	*Pivotal response training* (L. K. Koegel, Koegel, & Carter, 1998; L. K. Koegel, Koegel, Harrower, & Carter, 1999) EXAMPLE: Child with ASD is placed in a classroom that has incorporated the child's preferred toys and topics of interest; SLP and parent "prime" the student by reading the story to be presented in opening group the day before; teacher models how the child is to respond to questions asked during the morning greeting.

& Rausch, 2002). Mothers reported that having friends positively affects these goals, while not having friends negatively affects them. Several peer-specific goals were also identified, including (a) being accepted and included by peers; (b) having peers to play with on a consistent basis; (c) having peers of the same age; (d) having one or more "best" friends; (e) having loyal friends who will defend them; (f) taking responsibility for developing their own friendships; (g) maintaining friendships over time; (h) distinguishing someone who is a real friend from someone who is not; and (i) having friends who are not in trouble. Parents' goals for establishing friendships and achieving broader quality-of-life goals have important implications for SLPs and other members of the educational team in developing an IEP that is responsive to the family's goals and creating a program that addresses these goals and provides broad opportunities to connect with peers in meaningful ways.

Value for Children with ASD. Incorporating peer intervention strategies into the educational programs of children with ASD is critical. Parents consider the development of peer relationships and friendships as primary goals for their children (Overton & Rausch, 2002). When children with ASD are involved with their typical peers, they increase their time engaged, functional language use, and play skills. They also decrease their self-stimulatory behavior. Peer interventions provide meaningful opportunities for children with ASD to learn, generalize, and maintain their social skills (Roeyers, 1996).

Efficacy. There is consistent support for the use of peer training in facilitating interactions among peers with and without disabilities. Kamps and colleagues (1992) used social skills groups to facilitate interactions between three students with autism and their typical peers in a first-grade classroom. They found that training students with autism and their peers to initiate, respond to initiations, greet, accept compliments, take turns, share, ask for help, and include others led to an increase in time engaged and more frequent and lasting social interactions among the children. Lee and Odom (1996) found increased interactions among typical peers and children with disabilities. A reduction of stereotypic or unusual behaviors by the children with disabilities was also noted, suggesting that increased social engagement led to a more motivating and socially satisfying environment and reduced the need for other types of sensory stimulation. Roeyers (1996) reported on an intervention with 85 children with ASD and 48 typically developing peers (5 to 13 years of age). The children with ASD were selected from 13 elementary schools with categorical classrooms for this population and institutions for children with mental retardation in Belgium. The typical peers were drawn from local schools in the neighborhoods where the children with ASD lived. Intervention included initial training of the typical peers via videotape viewing of children with autism, instruction about the disorder at their comprehension level, and some role playing. Areas of training included how to react to aggressive behavior, being at the same eye level, and ways to get the attention of a child with ASD (Roeyers, 1996). Staff were trained not to intervene in the peer play sessions and to limit their responses to the children with ASD. They also debriefed with the typical peers, evaluating each play session with them and answering their questions about autism. Typical peers were prompted before the beginning of each play session with a child with ASD to try to get the child to play with them. Several positive results were found. The children with ASD increased their time spent in interaction and the length of sustained interaction, as well as their responsiveness to their peer partner's initiations. There was also an increase in the number of initiations made by the children with ASD and in their presocial behaviors (e.g., solitary play), while a decrease in self-stimulatory behaviors, which usually interfere with interaction, occurred (Roeyers, 1996).

Strain and colleagues (1996) describe several positive program outcomes for the peer-mediated intervention and parent training that is implemented within LEAP. Children with ASD show a reduction of symptoms and an increase in developmental progress as measured by cognitive and language assessments after 2 years of intervention. Observations in natural settings (e.g., home, school) suggest more appropriate social behavior and engagement, as well as skill maintenance following 2 years of intervention. Nearly half of the students participating in LEAP were enrolled in general education classrooms. Several experiments yielded positive outcomes for facilitating communication and social interaction using peer mediation. For example, peers' use of facilitative strategies resulted in increased communicative interaction in preschool children with ASD, including turn taking and on-topic responsiveness to peer initiations when both children were reinforced, and a decrease in nonsocial, less desirable behavior (Goldstein & Wickstrom, 1986). Increases in initiation by children with ASD were inconsistent, however, as were maintenance and generalization effects. Research has resulted in the following important findings: typical peers as young as 3 years old can be taught to engage with socially withdrawn peers (Strain, 1977; Strain, Shores, & Timm, 1977); peer mediation leads to immediate effects, indicating that some of the poor social abilities of children with ASD could be a result of unresponsive educational contexts (Strain, 1977; Strain & Odom, 1986); and no negative outcomes have been reported for typical peers participating in peer-mediated intervention—instead, improvements in their social relationships with other children are likely to occur (Strain, 1987).

Social skills interventions are also being carried out to support the social interactions of school-age and adolescent children with ASD. T. D. Barry and her colleagues (2003) examined the effectiveness of a clinic-based social skills group for four elementary children with autism who had high cognitive abilities. Over eight sessions, the students were taught specific social skills, including greeting, conversation, and play. Following intervention, they were observed interacting with their peers, who received some education about how to play with children with ASD. Results indicated improvement in greetings and play and less success in conversational skills. The children themselves reported feeling support from their peers. Parent reports indicated improvements in greeting only. The researchers recognize the challenges of delivering social skills interventions in a clinical setting and the impact on generalized learning in more natural settings. Morrison, Kamps, Garcia, and Parker (2001) provide additional support for peer-mediated intervention to support the social skills of school-age students with ASD. They used peer training to teach requesting, commenting, and sharing during game play and compared self- versus peer monitoring. Using direct instruction, the interventionist introduced and defined the target social skill and then had the typical peers and students with ASD give examples. Following this, monitoring sheets and pens were distributed, and the students were trained in how to monitor the occurrence of each social behavior. For example, during self-monitoring for requesting, students placed a check in one of the boxes each time they made a request. Tangible rewards were given when students made a request and marked it on the monitoring sheet. During peer monitoring, a peer monitored the use of requests by the student with ASD and then rewarded the student when a request was made. Results indicated that both peer and self-monitoring resulted in increased initiations by students with ASD and increased time spent in social interactions (Morrison et al., 2001).

Kamps and her colleagues (2002) investigated the effectiveness of peer training on social skills and cooperative learning groups across two studies, including a total of 39 students with ASD ranging in age from 7 to 14 years. Intervention for cooperative learning groups included training typical peers to tutor their partners with ASD in social studies vocabulary and facts and to complete a team activity. Intervention for social skills groups emphasized training in initiation and responding, cooperating, and engaging in positive play interactions (Kamps et al., 2002). Results indicated increased social interaction among peers, with generalization effects favoring cooperative learning groups. Kamps and colleagues state that the tutoring aspect and multiple components (academic and social) of the cooperative groups may explain the more robust results. In their follow-up study, they used trained and untrained peers in a variety of peer-mediated programs, including social skills–play groups, lunch buddy groups, recess buddy groups, and tutoring activities. Trained peers participated in at least one of the peer-mediated programs and received training in prompting and reinforcing social interaction, while untrained peers did not. Results indicated notable increases in time engaged and reciprocal interactions and some change in on-topic language for students with ASD when they were matched with trained versus untrained peers. The researchers discuss the value of peer training and structured group activities to support relationship building and skill generalization for students with ASD.

Although the research suggests that older children with ASD, and in particular Asperger syndrome, continue to prefer family or adult company over peers, they can and often do develop at least one peer friendship by middle or high school (Church, Alisanski, & Amanullah, 2000). These social outcomes appear to be better for children with autism who have higher cognitive ability. Orsmond, Krauss, and Seltzer (2004) also found that peer relationships and friendships are poorer for adolescents and adults with autism, and that individual characteristics such as a lesser degree of social impairment predict those individuals who will have greater participation in social and recreational activities. They further reported that characteristics of the environment, such as participation of the maternal parent in the activities, increased services received, and opportunities for inclusion predicted participation in social and recreational events. Orsmond and colleagues suggest that intervention programs should facilitate actual participation in recreational and social events to support friendship building.

Staff training also appears to have a role in successful social connections between typical peers and students with disabilities. Schepis, Reid, Ownbey, and Clary (2003) provided training videos to staff with examples of ways to prompt and praise cooperative interactions during free play, in addition to giving specific instructions and direct feedback on the job. Results indicated increases in cooperative interactions between the child with disabilities and typical peers for trained versus untrained staff.

Cognitive Behavioral Interventions

Cognitive behavioral interventions are often employed for children with ASD who have higher cognitive skills. Although children with autism who are considered higher functioning usually have an interest in social interaction, they often remain socially isolated because of their difficulties in social cognition and emotion recognition (Bacon, Fein, Morris, Waterhouse, & Allen, 1998; Bauminger, 2002). Social cognition involves recognition and interpretation of both verbal and nonverbal social and emotional cues, understanding of social behaviors and the consequences of those behaviors in a variety of social events, and identification of the mental state of another person (Crick & Dodge, 1994). Emotion recognition involves the capacity to differentiate between affective states through an understanding of facial, gestural, and verbal expressions and the meaning of those expressions (Buitelaar, Van der Wees, Swaab-Barneveld, & Van der Gaag, 1999).

Interpersonal problem solving is one strategy in cognitive behavioral intervention that is used to facilitate a child's ability to attend to both internal (e.g., feelings) and external (e.g., facial expressions) social cues, as well as to gain knowledge about different ways to respond in social situations and the consequences of the particular behavior selected (Kendall & Braswell, 1993). Several curriculums are available, such as Spivak and Shure's (1974) problem-solving model, as well as a number of commercially available programs (see the "Resources" section at the end of this chapter for social skills programs that emphasize problem solving). Basically, instruction is provided in key concepts that children must understand to be successful in a social interaction with a peer (e.g., what a friend is, how and why one listens to a friend, what a social conversation is).

Training in *affective education* is another strategy that might be employed. The focus of this strategy is to enhance children's recognition of their own as well as others' emotions, linking particular social situations to the emotions elicited (Kendall & Braswell, 1993). Training can begin with simple emotions (e.g., happiness, anger), teaching rules about the emotion and how to identify it, particularly in social contexts. Commercial programs for teaching emotion recognition are also available (see the "Resources" section).

Intervention Goals. Bauminger (2002) and Howlin (1998) propose two major goals for the use of cognitive behavioral interventions with children with ASD who are higher functioning. The first is to expand children's understanding of the mental states of others. The second is to scaffold children's ability to apply what they know so that they can establish reciprocal social interactions. Practitioners should consider these as primary goals for supporting the social cognition and emotion recognition of children with ASD, but they may wish to establish additional goals that are individualized and responsive to the particular social–emotional needs of a specific child.

Value for Children with ASD. Cognitive behavioral interventions have particular value for children with ASD who have higher cognitive and linguistic abilities, as these interventions require the ability to recognize and talk about problems, to think about solutions, and to recognize different emotions in a variety of social contexts. The strategies involved in cognitive behavioral therapy facilitate a child's problem solving, as well as recognition and interpretation of various social cues. Learning these skills is particularly important for children with ASD, because they often wish to have social connections but are challenged by their lack of emotion recognition and their poor problem solving.

Efficacy. Bauminger (2002) studied the effectiveness of a cognitive behavioral intervention program designed to facilitate the social cognition, emotional understanding, and social interaction skills of children with autism who were high functioning. Using social interpersonal problem-solving and affective education strategies, Bauminger found that the children increased their ability to initiate, establish eye contact, and share experiences with their peers, as well as show interest in them following intervention. Problem-solving intervention led to more relevant and less asocial solutions to social events, whereas emotion education led to greater recognition and understanding of complex emotions.

Pivotal Response Training

The concept of teaching pivotal behaviors recognizes that most children with significant disabilities, including children with ASD, require treatment for several behaviors, and that a more efficient and effective intervention approach might be to target specific behaviors that are likely to lead to changes in several other behaviors not directly targeted. Although it is a useful strategy to facilitate both communication and play, pivotal response training (PRT) is discussed in this chapter because of its potential significant impact on the social interaction of children with ASD. R. L. Koegel and his colleagues (1989) have designed training procedures to teach children with ASD "pivotal" behaviors, those behaviors that are central to a child's day-to-day functioning, with the ultimate goal of facilitating generalized improvements across contexts. Two pivotal behaviors described in their training procedures are *motivation* and *responsivity to multiple cues*. Challenges in these behaviors are frequently associated with poorer performance for children with ASD, whereas improvements in these areas effect positive change. Motivation, particularly to learn new tasks or engage socially, is frequently reported as lacking in children with ASD (L. K. Koegel & Koegel, 1986; R. L. Koegel,

Dyer, & Bell, 1987). Stimulus overselectivity has also characterized the challenges of children with ASD, in that they fail to use all the information in their environment to learn and respond in social contexts (Schreibman, 1988). This failure to respond to a variety of environmental cues interferes with learning; therefore, it is important that children with ASD be supported to be responsive to multiple cues.

Various components are involved in teaching pivotal behaviors. The first is providing a question, instruction, or opportunity for a child to respond. Opportunities to respond that are not dictated by questions or instructions are important because they facilitate spontaneous behavior. When instructions and questions are given, they should be appropriate to the task, clear, and uninterrupted while the child's attention is maintained. For example, if it is time to get ready to go home on the bus, a teacher might go to a child, get his attention by tapping him on the shoulder and saying his name, and then simply stating, "Tommy, get your coat."

Another component or strategy for teaching pivotal behaviors is interspersing maintenance tasks (those the child can already perform) with novel tasks (those the child will be learning). Interspersing maintenance trials in a novel task or event can increase a child's motivation and confidence because, while the child is challenged by the novel tasks, he or she can experience success with the tasks that are known. For example, if a child with ASD knows all her colors and loves matchbox cars, you might rotate asking what color a car is (what she knows) with what kind of car it is (new information she is learning). You could permit the child to play with the car for which she identified the color correctly. If the child does not know the type of car, you could model the correct answer, prompt her to respond, and reward her with being able to play with the car once she repeats the name.

A third strategy likely to enhance a child's motivation to participate in a particular task is known as *shared control,* or giving the child some choice in selecting a learning task. Although choices must be managed so that children do not engage in dangerous or inappropriate behavior, giving them some level of control over selecting the toys they want or the topics they wish to talk about can be highly motivating and can facilitate meaningful social exchanges. Shared control also leads to turn taking, such that there is a natural give-and-take between the interventionist and the child. For example, a parent might give a child a choice about which book he wants to have read at bedtime and then engage in turn taking as they look at the book together, identify the pictures, and talk about what is happening.

Strategies that facilitate opportunities to respond spontaneously, intersperse maintenance tasks, and allow for shared control of the teaching events increase motivation in the child with ASD (R. L. Koegel et al., 1989). It is also critical to structure learning environments so that the children can respond to multiple cues. Children need to be given opportunities to respond to multiple cues or multiple components, such as recognizing that the yellow balloon is different from the red balloon or that the red box is different from the red ball, as they engage with those objects in the play environment.

R. L. Koegel and his colleagues (1989) suggest that children who are exposed to multiple cues versus single cues like "ball" or "balloon" are likely to be more responsive in their learning.

Pivotal response training also requires the interventionist to consider the consequences of a child's behaviors. R. L. Koegel et al. (1989) suggest that three considerations are important in reinforcing a child's behavior: First, reinforcement should be contingent on a child's actual behavior. For example, a child might request a glass of juice. A parent could take that opportunity to engage the child in an interaction and ask, "Who has the juice?" When the child responds, "You do," the parent would immediately give the child the juice. The parent's response or reinforcement is immediate, appropriate, and dependent on the child's response. Second, all goal-directed attempts at responding to questions, instructions, or opportunities to respond should be reinforced, as research suggests that motivation for children with ASD can be enhanced if they are reinforced for their attempts to respond (R. L. Koegel et al., 1989). This means that interventionists should reinforce children for their attempts to respond even if the responses are not completely correct. The attempt should be reasonable, however; the child should be directing attention to the task at hand and putting forth some effort in the attempt to respond. For example, if an interventionist is looking at a book and comes to a picture with a frog jumping from one lily pad to another, he might say to the child with ASD, "What is the frog doing?" If the child points to the frog and says, "Green frog," the interventionist might say, "Yes, it is a green frog. What's the frog doing? Is he jumping?" The child might say, "Jumping," and the interventionist follows with, "Yes, he is jumping. What is *he* doing?" (pointing to another jumping frog).

A third consideration of the consequence of a child's response is that the reinforcement should be related to the targeted behavior; that is, the reinforcement should be a natural consequence of the behavior (R. L. Koegel et al., 1989). For example, if a child says, "Ball" when he sees the interventionist take a ball out of a bag, a natural reinforcing consequence would be to roll the ball to the child. Natural reinforcement such as this is similar to what a child would receive in his day-to-day interaction, thus increasing the likelihood of generalized learning.

Other pivotal behaviors described by L. K. Koegel and Koegel (2001) include self-initiation, empathy, self-regulation, and social interaction. Teaching pivotal behaviors involves some level of play, modeling, shaping, and priming to increase a child's engagement and social communication. The interventionist uses multiple cues, capitalizes on a child's motivators or interests, offers the child choices, provides reinforcers in the form of natural consequences, reinforces communication attempts, and incorporates self-management (L. K. Koegel, Koegel, Harrower, & Carter, 1999). To monitor implementation of the intervention, consider the following questions:

- Did I have the student's attention?
- Did I use clear and simple directions?

- Did I follow the student's lead or choices?
- Am I providing a mixture of learned skills with new skills?
- Did I reinforce good attempts?
- Am I rewarding the student with what he is asking for?
- Am I reinforcing immediately?

Intervention Goals. Pivotal response training focuses on identifying and teaching pivotal behaviors (L. K. Koegel, Koegel, & Carter, 1998; L. K. Koegel, Koegel, Harrower, & Carter, 1999). Pivotal behaviors are those central to wide areas of functioning. Change in a pivotal behavior is believed to have widespread positive effects across other behaviors (L. K. Koegel et al., 1998). An overwhelming number of individual skills need to be taught to children with autism. Intervention goals should target specific pivotal behaviors (e.g., empathy, self-initiation, social interaction, motivation, self-regulation) that effect change across several behaviors, which increases the effectiveness of intervention.

Value for Children with ASD. Pivotal response training is a valuable intervention for children with ASD because it recognizes the importance of capitalizing on a child's interests and finding objects, actions, people, and events that motivate the child. It is used to support initiation, self-regulation, and empathy in the context of social situations, all areas of need for this population. Because children with ASD often experience stimulus over-selectivity, they fail to use the available information in their environment to respond socially. Pivotal response training facilitates the responsiveness of children with ASD to multiple cues in their natural environments.

Efficacy. Pivotal response training (PRT) has been used successfully to increase social interaction in toy play between typical peers and children with ASD (L. K. Koegel & Koegel, 2001). Improvement in sound production has also been reported for five children with autism in response to a systematic approach to intervention using motivators within a natural language teaching framework (R. L. Koegel, Camarata, Koegel, Ben-Tall, & Smith, 1998). Although speech and language intervention was successful in this context, generalized learning did not occur. Koegel and his colleagues indicated that it did not occur because the stimuli lacked salience. Thus, the natural environment was not sufficient to support learning. Some systematic teaching is needed, combined with motivating and meaningful contexts. Pierce and Schreibman (1995) found that two children with autism were successful in their ability to engage in a variety of complex social and attentional behaviors (e.g., initiation, joint attention) using peer-mediated PRT, and they replicated those findings in a later study (Pierce & Schreibman, 1997). Stahmer (1995) demonstrated that the use of PRT improved symbolic play skills in seven children with autism. Children with ASD were also successfully taught self-initiations using PRT, suggesting the importance of initiations for increasing the functions of language beyond requesting (L. K. Koegel, Koegel, Shoshan, & McNerney, 1999).

Comic Strip Conversations

Comic strip conversations use simple drawings to illustrate an ongoing conversation while providing visual support for students with ASD who have difficulty understanding the rapid exchange of information that occurs in a back-and-forth communication (Gray, 1994, 1998). The comic strip is used to work through a problem that the student with ASD has experienced, and together the interventionist and the student identify solutions using simple drawings and written words, representing both the thoughts and the words of the participants.

When creating a comic strip conversation with a student with ASD, the interventionist identifies in a systematic way who is part of the challenging event and what the participants say or do. The thoughts, feelings, and words of the individuals are represented in the comic strips. Gray (1994, 1998) suggests that comic strip conversations serve as a prerequisite strategy to social story development, which is discussed under "Social Stories" later in this chapter.

Gray (1994, 1998) offers suggestions for what materials to use in creating a comic strip conversation. The interventionist could use a laminate marker board, paper, or chalkboard. There are advantages and disadvantages to each. For example, a laminate board is flexible—changes can be made easily—but the drawings cannot be saved to refer to at a later time. Paper has the advantage of being easy to save for later reference, but it does not allow easy changes. An advantage of a chalkboard is the large amount of space available for drawing and making changes as needed, but like the laminate board, it is not permanent.

To begin the comic strip conversation drawing, the interventionist helps the student with ASD understand that it is okay to draw while talking. The student is given the opportunity to lead the conversation, and the drawing materials are readily accessible to both the interventionist and the student. The goal is to have the student with ASD do most of the drawing, writing, and talking. The conversation with the student begins as an interview, during which the interventionist, as a conversational partner, asks or writes questions with the student, gradually moving to a conversation-like format. Simple symbols are introduced that represent such things as talking, a person, listening, more than one person talking at the same time, and loud versus quiet words. Symbols are added over time as the student with ASD becomes familiar with the drawing process. Gray (1994) provides basic symbols that are easy and quick to draw with clear meanings. Personal symbols can be added by the student and can include specific people, places, and concepts. To begin, the student with ASD is encouraged to select a topic of interest to talk about, so that the drawing symbols can be introduced and understood. These symbols are eventually applied to more challenging situations that require some problem solving.

The actual drawing process starts with the placement of a location symbol, which is drawn in the upper left-hand corner of the drawing area. For example, if there was an episode in gym while playing basketball, the symbol might be a gym floor with a basketball hoop. The focus of the comic strip then becomes the events of the specific situation. The sequence of the events is organized in boxes or frames that can be drawn ahead of time and can be numbered or not.

The interventionist gathers information about the challenging event by asking several questions and collaborating with the student in the drawing. As an example, the interventionist might ask, "Where are you?" and then the student draws a person symbol, and his name is written beneath the symbol. The next question might be, "Who else is here?" Person symbols are added, and their names are placed beneath each one. In the basketball incident, three students were involved, so person symbols for all three are drawn, and they are given names: Taylor (the child with ASD), George, and Billy. The student is then asked, "What are you doing? What did others do?" and related actions or items are drawn to represent the activity. In the basketball incident, Taylor said that Billy threw the ball to George, and then Taylor ran to George and took the ball from him. These actions were represented in simple drawings of person symbols either holding or throwing the basketball. Using a "talk" symbol, the student is then asked to indicate what was said when the actions occurred. Returning to the example, the talk symbol was filled in as follows: Billy was not reported to say anything. George said, "Throw the ball—I'm open." Taylor said, "I want that ball." In the next frame, a person symbol is drawn to represent the teacher, Mr. Marcus. The talk symbol for the teacher is filled in with: "Taylor, that is not the way we play basketball. You need to sit out of the game for a while." In the next step of the drawing, the student is asked what he was thinking when he said what he did. The same is asked for the other participants in the event and thoughts are written in the "thought" symbols. For example, Taylor stated what he was thinking as, "I never get the ball. My classmates don't like me. They don't want me to have the ball." Taylor assumed that Billy was thinking, "I don't like Taylor, so I am going to throw the ball to George." Taylor assumed that George was thinking, "I'll make sure Taylor doesn't get the ball." In the next frame of conversation, the adult communication partner has an opportunity to share with the student other possible perspectives on the thoughts of the participants. Initially, the interventionist asks the student what else the individuals in the event might have been thinking. If the student is unable to think of anything, the interventionist offers some possibilities, working toward a balance between retaining the student's perspective and sharing accurate social information. All answers are accepted as valid while the interventionist works with the student to clarify how others communicate and what perspectives they might have. For example, the interventionist might help the student to realize that Billy might have been thinking, "George is open so he can get the ball to score the points for our team," and that George might have been thinking, "I hope Billy can get the ball to me so I can help our team score two points."

To complete the comic strip conversation, the student summarizes the key points of the event, pointing to the pictures that represent each aspect of the event. New solutions (e.g., call to your classmate to throw you the ball when you are close to the hoop, ask for a turn to throw the ball, learn more about the game so you know what to do) are identified as alternatives to the original behavior, and those solutions are put in writing. Together, the interventionist and the student create a potential plan for each solution, emphasizing the advantages and disadvantages of each, eliminating solutions that are not feasible and prioritizing the preferred solutions.

Gray (1994, 1998) also describes the use of color to identify emotional content or the motivation behind what is said in a comic strip conversation and recommends that colors be introduced gradually, starting with basic emotions (e.g., anger, happiness, sadness) and moving to more complex emotions (e.g., pride, confusion). It is important to help the student recognize that more than one emotion can occur in a single statement, indicating conflicting feelings. Although Gray offers colors to represent different emotions and feelings, I have found that it is best to allow the student with ASD to determine what colors represent which emotions and feelings. In working with students with more advanced cognitive and linguistic ability, the interventionist could use sharp edges on the talking symbols to indicate anger or frustration and wavy lines to indicate uneasiness or a lack of self-confidence.

Intervention Goals. Comic strip conversations are used to clarify information that may be confusing to a child with ASD. Intervention goals established around the use of comic strip conversations might include learning to explain the response of others in difficult social encounters, to increase understanding of the perspective of another, to prepare for a new or unfamiliar social situation or event, or to identify the motivation behind a particular behavior (Gray, 1998).

Value for Children with ASD. The reported effectiveness of visual supports to structure the learning of students with autism may also support comprehension of a conversation. Because children with autism have difficulty recognizing the beliefs and motivations of others, a strategy that can visually represent those beliefs and intents provides a needed support. Thus, comic strip conversations offer a strategy that allows children with ASD to capitalize on their visual strengths, organize the events of an activity, and solidify abstract thoughts and ideas. It is a strategy most often used with children who have Asperger syndrome or those children with autism who have higher cognitive abilities (Gray, 1998).

Efficacy. To date, no empirical research examines the efficacy of comic strip conversations. Gray (1998), however, provides anecdotal support for clinicians using comic strip conversations for individual students with Asperger syndrome or students with ASD who display higher cognitive abilities. These students have demonstrated "the ability to accurately identify what another person is thinking, feeling and/or what is motivating a given response" (p. 194). Glaeser, Pierson, and Fritschmann (2003) also describe the successful use of comic strip conversations for two students, one of whom had ASD. A reduction in playground and classroom incidents occurred for both students after employing comic strip conversations to facilitate their problem solving. Teachers also reported less frustration and anger for these students.

Social Stories

Children with ASD experience social deficits at several levels, including social recognition (e.g., lack of interest in others), social communication (e.g., limited facial, gestural, and oral communication), and social imagination (e.g., decreased pretend play and perspective taking) (Wing, 1988). Gray (1995b) describes children with ASD as exhibiting "unique perceptions of people and events … [and as] impaired in their ability to understand and interpret social cues accurately" (p. 219). Challenges in processing environmental information explain some of their poorly developed social skills (Quill, 1995) and indicate a need for alternative strategies (Gray & Garand, 1993). Some children with ASD require more than visual supports to manage their behavior, such as explicit directions or guidelines (Kuttler, Myles, & Carlson, 1998). Gray (1995b) explains that social stories are like "social reading," in which a child's understanding of a social situation improves through the use of visual instruction. Social stories incorporate directions and explicitly stated guidelines to support the social behavior of children with ASD.

The goal of social stories is "to minimize potentially confusing instructional interactions … [by providing] students direct access to social information" (Gray & Garand, 1993, p. 2). Gray (1998) challenges the practitioner to consider that the perspective of an individual with ASD is not necessarily wrong; it is just different. She states, "There are no 'bizarre' behaviors, only human responses that originate from experiences not fully understood" (p. 168).

Social stories are usually composed of two to five short sentences and may include printed words alone or words paired with pictures (Gray & Garand, 1993). Each sentence takes one of four forms: A *descriptive* sentence provides information about the setting, people, or activities (e.g., "Usually, I go to gym class on Tuesdays and Thursdays with my third-grade class"). A *directive* sentence informs children of what they need to do in a given setting (e.g., "When I go to gym class, I listen to what my teacher tells the class to do"). A *perspective* sentence describes the feelings, beliefs, or reactions of others (e.g., "My teacher likes it when I listen to what he says"). A *control* sentence is written by the child with ASD in order to identify strategies he or she might use to recall the information in a social story (e.g., "When I listen to my teacher's instructions, I will draw a picture in my head of what the teacher is telling us to do") (Gray, 1995a). One directive sentence for every two to five descriptive, perspective, or control sentences is recommended, although the precise number of each sentence type is dependent on the needs of the student (Gray, 1995b; Gray & Garand, 1993). Social stories use situations from a child's actual experience to visually present social information while incorporating reading and writing (Gray, 1995b). To construct an effective social story, "it is critical … to consider the perspective of the student for whom the story is written. Through careful observation, the author focuses on what a student may see, hear, and feel in the targeted situation" (Gray & Garand, 1993, p. 3).

Gray (1995b) offers several guidelines for creating social stories for children with ASD. It is important to begin with some background information about the child and the social situations that present challenges. The practitioner must determine where the social situation occurs, who is involved, how long the event is, how it begins and ends, what happens, and why it happens. This information is usually collected through interviews with those working with the student and familiar with the situation. Gray also recommends that the situation be observed to identify potential changes and determine possible motivators that might predict the student's response. It is critical to observe and record the information observed as objectively as possible (Gray, 1995b). Further, the practitioner must attempt to assume the perspective of the student with ASD. This will lead to more accurate understanding of the child's feelings. In addition, to facilitate perspective taking on the part of the student, the practitioner can ask questions about the relevant cues and responses to the cues in the social situation for which a social story is being developed (e.g., "What would your classmates do?" "What do your classmates do when the gym teacher says … ?" "What would your teacher say?" "What would your classmates say?"). It is common to place too many directive statements in the social story, which limits children's ability to come up with their own ideas or responses to a situation. Although some children require the use of clear directive statements, others respond well to an abundance of descriptive and prescriptive sentences. Practitioners are encouraged to avoid terms such as "always" in their story, as it is unlikely that something will always occur. Words like "sometimes" and "usually" can be substituted to teach and model some flexibility in events. Typically, the stories are written in the present tense and the first person is used. The social stories are given a title in question form. In addition, illustrations or drawings are sometimes useful to students to supplement the written story. Figure 11.2 presents three social stories developed for a third-grade child with ASD about his challenges playing ball with his friends, taking a test, and handling an unexpected visitor in class.

Using social stories for children with lower cognitive abilities may require some modifications, including the use of simple sentences with associated pictures or visual symbols. Swaggart et al. (1995) outline strategies practitioners might consider in their development of social stories for children with ASD. First, the social behavior requiring change should be identified. It should be responsive to the child's educational goals and address a social deficit that interferes with the child's ability to participate in his home, school, or community. Second, practitioners need to operationalize or clearly define the behaviors for which they are collecting data. For example, the team needs to decide how to define an appropriate greeting or an aggressive act. Third, baseline data should be collected so comparisons can be made

Social Story 1

How do you play ball with friends? (title)

Sometimes kids play ball with their friends. (descriptive)

At my school, Main Street Elementary, some friends play ball at recess. (descriptive)

Usually, one friend throws the ball, and the other friend catches the ball and then throws the ball back again. (descriptive)

Sometimes a third friend plays ball. (descriptive)

They have fun throwing the ball back and forth. (perspective)

Friends take turns throwing the ball back and forth. (descriptive)

Sometimes I don't want to throw the ball back when I play catch with my friends. (descriptive)

That makes my friends angry. (perspective)

When my friends throw me a ball, I will try to throw the ball back to them. (directive)

That's called playing with friends. (descriptive)

Before I go out to recess, I will read my social story about playing with friends. (control)

Social Story 2

How do you take a test? (title)

I am in Mrs. Reed's third-grade class. (descriptive)

There are 21 other children in my class. (descriptive)

Sometimes we have a test. (descriptive)

We cover our work with a study folder. (descriptive)

Sometimes I try to look at other kids' work or ask them for the answer. (descriptive)

When I do this, they get mad. (perspective)

They think I am cheating. (perspective)

Cheating on a test means using someone else's answers as my own. (descriptive)

When I take a test, I will try to keep my eyes on my paper and not talk to my classmates. (directive)

Before each test, I will read my story about cheating! (control)

(continues)

FIGURE 11.2. Sample social stories for a third-grade student with ASD.

Social Story 3

What to do when an unexpected visitor comes to class. (title)

I am in Ms. Johnson's class. (descriptive)

Usually, Martha helps me in Ms. Johnson's class. (descriptive)

Sometimes people that I don't expect in my classroom want to visit. (descriptive)

That is okay. (control)

Sometimes people who visit my classroom like to be included in our activities. (perspective)

When visitors want to join in the activity I am doing, I will try to look at them, smile, and say, "Hi." (directive)

It is okay to smile at our classroom visitors. (control)

FIGURE 11.2. *Continued.*

about the impact of intervention. For instance, the number of appropriate greetings or aggressive acts would be counted over a period of time to determine the trend and stability of those behaviors prior to intervention. As previously mentioned, descriptive, perspective, and control sentences are used more often than directive sentences. Depending on the ability level of the child with ASD, team members need to determine how many sentences per page are manageable for the child to process. During intervention, the social story is read to the student each day, prior to an activity or event targeted in the story. Data collection occurs throughout intervention, and the results are reviewed to determine effectiveness. If intervention must be changed, one component (e.g., the content of the story, who reads the story, how often it is read) is changed at a time to determine what factor contributes to the desired behavior change. To ensure maintenance and generalized use of the target behavior, time between social story readings can be increased, the children can read their own stories, and over time children can develop their own social stories (Swaggart et al., 1995).

Gray (1995b) offers several variations on the use of social stories to support the perspective of the student with ASD in social contexts. She describes a process of "social review," in which videotaping is used to assess a student's understanding of a social situation and assist the student in developing appropriate social skills relevant to the situation. Critical phrases from the video can be listed, and the student can compare his response to that of his peers. This social review can also be applied to selected television programs or videos that offer an opportunity to gain experience in reading a social situation. For example, the student with ASD and a practitioner might watch a sitcom or cartoon with the volume off to identify gestures and facial expressions, predict emotions, and speculate on what is being said. Following this, the program would be viewed with the volume on to evaluate the accuracy of the predictions. Other social story variations might include checklist stories (to teach new routines), skills stories (to teach specific social skills), and judgment stories (to teach ways to make appropriate judgments), among others (Gray, 1995b).

Intervention Goals. Several goals can be developed using social stories to facilitate the social interaction, play, and pragmatic communication of children with ASD. For example, the team might use social stories to facilitate a student's understanding of the social script for working in cooperative work groups in the general education classroom. Social stories might be used to decrease interruptions during story time in the classroom. They might also be used to increase the perspective of the student with ASD about the feelings of a peer in an interactive computer game activity when the student with ASD is not willing to take turns during the game. Social stories are often used to explain an event or a story, teach a routine and variations to that routine, and address undesirable behaviors. Further, they can be used as part of most social skills curriculums to facilitate students' understanding of appropriate versus inappropriate behavior in social contexts. Simpson (1993) offers suggestions for implementing goals related to the use of social stories across settings throughout the day, so that the targeted behavior is reinforced and effectiveness is monitored. For example, a chart could be developed with a list of the behaviors targeted in the social story on one side and space on the other side to draw a smiley face and provide a sticker next to the behavior that is observed.

Value for Children with ASD. Social stories intervention is reported to be effective for children with ASD because it draws on what is personally relevant and motivating for the child. As children with autism have more relative strength with visual information than verbal information, social stories are an appropriate means of explaining and describing confusing social situations. In addition, the activities are commonly identified as good practice for persons with ASD (Gray, 1995b; Smith, 2001). Social stories are designed to reduce the factors identified as potentially confusing during a social interaction or event in order to provide students with ASD "direct access to social information" (Gray & Garand, 1993, p. 2). Social stories are written to describe a social situation and to provide information about relevant social cues in that situation, highlighting what the cues mean and why they occur. They are responsive, therefore, to the social challenges often reported for children and adolescents with ASD. Social stories have been effectively used with preschoolers, school-age children, adolescents, and adults, particularly those interested in written or literacy-based material (Swaggart et al., 1995).

Efficacy. Social stories have been successfully used to teach specific social skills (e.g., greeting) and behavioral skills (e.g., decreased aggressive acts) in children with autism who exhibit a range of ability levels. Research results report fewer inappropriate social behaviors for children with ASD in the home and school setting following the use of social stories (Cullain, 2000; Kuoch & Mirenda, 2003; Kuttler et al., 1998; Norris & Dattilo, 1999; Romano, 2002; Smith, 2001; Swaggart et al., 1995).

Specifically, Gray and Garand (1993) provide anecdotal support for the use of social stories for three children with ASD. They also report on evidence shared by practitioners using this intervention strategy. Norris and Dattilo (1999) examined the effects of social story use for a girl with ASD in a general education classroom. The child was 8 years of age, with verbal communication skills and below-average cognitive ability. Using an AB research design, Norris and Dattilo saw reductions in inappropriate behaviors and little change in appropriate behaviors, based on the social story they developed to target lunch skills.

Swaggart and her colleagues (1995) used social stories to teach appropriate social behaviors to three children with autism, one 11-year-old female and two 7-year-old males. The targets for the 11-year-old were to increase appropriate greetings and to decrease aggressive acts. For the 7-year-olds, the target behavior was sharing. Swaggart et al. did not conform to the sentence-type ratio that Gray (1994, 1995b) employed and instead used many more directive than descriptive, perspective, or control sentence types, as well as employing some traditional behavioral strategies (e.g., response-cost, social and tangible reinforcement) to train the targeted social skills. Results indicated increased appropriate behavior and decreased inappropriate behavior for all three children. Swaggart et al. caution the reader, however, that their intervention was designed to be accessible to teachers and lead to functional outcomes in natural settings and would not stand up to more rigorous experimental research designs.

Kuttler and colleagues (1998) describe the use of social stories for a 12-year-old boy with ASD to reduce tantrum behavior during morning work time and lunch. Social stories were developed to reduce those behaviors (e.g., dropping to the floor, screaming, swearing) that preceded a tantrum and to address the student's challenges with waiting, unexpected transitions, and free time. A social story for lunchtime and one for work time were created and read immediately prior to those events. Results revealed a reduction in the behaviors preceding a tantrum and an increase in desired behavior. The researchers noted that the visual schedules used prior to this intervention were insufficient, and that some students with ASD might require more explicit "directions, choices, or a rationale to transition or manage their own behavior" than provided in a social story (p. 181).

Smith (2001) describes a unique approach to examining the effectiveness of social story use. She trained practitioners on how to develop and use social stories for students with ASD in their settings and then followed up with a second training in which the participants rated the effectiveness of the social stories they had developed and used. The rating scale ranged from zero (*not at all successful*) to 10 (*completely successful*). Results indicated that 19 stories were developed, 13 of which had ratings between 7 and 10, with

5 of those rated at 10. Parents and teachers reported greatest success when the social stories were read frequently.

Thiemann and Goldstein (2001) paired video feedback with social stories to improve the use of social skills (i.e., securing attention, initiating comments and requests, making contingent responses) in five children with ASD (6 to 12 years of age). They also paired the children with typical peers to take part in social activities that would allow them to practice the social skills emphasized in the social stories. The typical peers participated in an orientation regarding expectations for talking with friends prior to the intervention. Social stories were written for each of the four social skills previously identified. The children with ASD read the social stories and engaged in role playing around the story using written cue cards provided by the examiner. A 10-minute social interaction period was then provided to create opportunities for the children with ASD to use their social skills with typical peers. The examiner provided prompting (e.g., pointing to a written cue from the story) as needed. Following this interaction period, the children with ASD and their typical peers reviewed a video of their interaction period, evaluating the effectiveness of their social responses. Targeted social behaviors increased following intervention for all five children, and for at least one of the children some generalization was seen in the classroom. The findings support the use of visual cues to facilitate social development among children with ASD and their typical peers. Thiemann and Goldstein note, however, that it is difficult to determine which of the visual supports used were most beneficial, because written cues, video replay, and social stories were incorporated into the intervention.

Using social stories for three boys with ASD (3 to 6 years old), Kuoch and Mirenda (2003) found a reduction in the rate of problem behaviors that was maintained once social story intervention was completed. Their research design included a condition of the effect of adult attention alone, as compared to the adult presenting the social story. Their data support the notion that it is the social story, not the adult attention that goes along with reading the social story, that is responsible for the changes in behavior.

L. M. Barry and Burlew (2004) used social stories to teach two children with ASD with significant behavioral impairment to make choices and play appropriately with the materials selected within a play or activity center. They also used a social story to facilitate play with other students in the classroom, including sharing, taking turns, and talking to a peer. The children were 7 and 8 years of age, and intervention took place in a first-grade special education classroom. Both children exhibited gains in their ability to make choices independently and to play appropriately with the material in an activity center. One of the children also gained appropriate peer interaction skills that facilitated her placement in a general education classroom.

Adams, Gouvousis, VanLue, and Waldron (2004) used a social story in the home environment for a 7-year-old boy with Asperger syndrome who was experiencing frustration during homework time. Four behaviors were targeted in the social story, including crying, hitting, screaming, and falling. These frustration behaviors were reduced, although not eliminated, following the introduction of the social story. The child also increased his oral communication to express his needs or worries during homework time.

Gray and Garand (1993) reported positive results for children with autism who exhibited higher cognitive skills, and others (Kuttler et al., 1998; Swaggart et al., 1995) found positive outcomes for children who fell in the moderate to severe range of autism. Gray (1998) states the need for explicit research and makes mention of negative outcomes that she attributes to "stories that did not adhere to the guidelines" (p. 193). There are limitations to the current research, however, in that a narrow range of outcomes has been targeted, and methodological designs have been generally weak. Additional research is needed to provide strong evidence for this frequently employed intervention strategy.

Other Intervention Suggestions To Support the Social Behavior of Children with ASD

Often the social behavior of children with ASD is affected by communication challenges that impinge on the social reciprocity needed for engaging in conversation and play. Chapters 9 and 10 highlighted several strategies that support not only the communication and play of children with ASD but also the development of their social behavior across communication partners. Children with ASD may require specific instruction to explain what a conversation is (e.g., staying on same topic, taking turns), how to develop skills in question asking, and ways to end a conversation. They may also require support for maintaining a conversational topic in a social exchange. For example, an SLP might visually represent on-topic comments by placing a block for each statement on top of another, representing the building of a sustained conversation. The block would be placed elsewhere if an off-topic comment occurred. If the child was monopolizing the conversation, a larger block might be placed on the stack, knocking over the smaller blocks and indicating too much talk.

Because many children with ASD do not recognize or understand the value of eye gaze during social encounters, the SLP may wish to "cue in" the child about why the SLP is doing what she is doing. For example, she might say, "I am moving my eyes and face toward Diane's so she knows I am paying attention to what she is saying." Using natural consequences might also be effective. For example, when a child is talking to the SLP but not looking in the SLP's general direction, the SLP might walk away. The SLP might explain that she moved away because she did not know the child was talking specifically to her. Developing gesture dictionaries can be useful in highlighting the intent of nonverbal gestures. For example, the practitioner can pair a body part (e.g., moving the head up and down) with its communicative intent (e.g., means yes). Students can also be asked to look at cartoons or watch selected TV programs without sound and determine the emotions of the characters by matching them to graphic representations of emotions.

If an ultimate goal of the team is to reinforce social skills, it is important to point out to students with ASD what they are doing right, using consistent, immediate, and specific feedback about a social attempt. Allowing students, particularly those with cognitive and verbal strengths, to generate alternative ways to react in a social situation is a powerful way for them to self-manage their difficult social encounters. It is not enough to teach a social skill or behavior; it is critical to explain why that social behavior is important for establishing relationships and building friendships. Students with ASD must understand the social feedback loop—that is, knowing that what one says and does affects another and affects one's ability to continue an interaction.

A "power card" strategy might also be incorporated into a child's intervention program as a reminder for particular social behaviors. A power card (Gagnon, 2001) is a visually based strategy designed to promote desired skills by relating them to the special interest of a child with ASD. Keeling, Myles, Gagnon, and Simpson (2003, p. 107) used the power card strategy to teach sportsmanship skills to a 9-year-old girl with autism. They developed a power card script with a brief description of the child's special interest or hero (the PowerPuff Girls), a troubling situation (losing a game), and the "hero's" solution to the problem ("Take a deep breath; say 'Good job' to your friend; or say 'Maybe next time'"). Simple steps to solving the targeted problem are outlined, and a comment is written that encourages the child to try the "hero's" solution to the problem. Keeling and her colleagues found the power card strategy to be effective in reducing the child's screaming and whining when she lost a game. A power card script can also be adapted from a social story. For example, in the first social story in Figure 11.2, a power card based on the child's hero, the Hulk, might be created as follows:

◆ The Hulk says:
1. Remember to throw the ball back when you play catch with your friends.
2. Don't forget to ask, "Can you throw me the ball?" Or you can say, "Throw me the ball. I'll catch it."

The power card strategy has particular value for children with ASD because it builds on their visual strengths, capitalizes on their special interests, and prepares them for challenging situations.

Another central aspect of supporting social competence in children with ASD is theory of mind (Howlin, Baron-Cohen, & Hadwin, 1999; Ozonoff & Miller, 1995). It is often difficult for children with ASD to understand that a person or social partner they encounter might have a perspective different from their own. Further, it is hard for them to recognize that people can have more than one emotion about a particular experience. In a "theory of mind" approach to intervention, students learn to define emotions based on photographs presented to them, draw faces and facial expressions representing a variety of emotions, and begin to understand desire-based and belief-based emotions. Teaching is broken down into small steps using typical developmental sequences as a guide and occurs in the child's natural environment, incorporating systematic intrinsic rewards derived from the task or activity (Howlin et al., 1999). Howlin and colleagues taught children with ASD five levels of mental state concepts focused on understanding informational states (e.g., from simple perspective taking to false-belief understanding), emotion (e.g., from recognition of pictures to belief-based emotions), and pretense (e.g., from sensorimotor to pretend play). Basic principles underlying these mental state concepts include (a) perception leads to knowledge (i.e., individuals will know something if they saw it or heard about it); (b) actions or objects satisfy desires (i.e., if individuals want something, they will be delighted to receive it, and if they do not receive it, they will be unhappy); and (c) pretense involves the substitution of objects or the suspension of an outcome (i.e., when pretending, an individual does so for fun and with no expectation of using an object in a typical way). Howlin and her colleagues report positive outcomes for the mental state concepts taught and maintenance of improved understanding following completion of the intervention.

The notion that "perception leads to knowledge" is taught by demonstrating that an object's location can be known only if its placement is directly observed or verbally related. The teaching of this principle often makes use of a false-belief task (Perner & Wimmer, 1983). This involves telling a story in which an object is moved from an original location to a new location without the knowledge of the individual who originally placed the object. The child with ASD is asked to predict where that individual will search for the object. Another strategy used to teach perspective taking is blindfolding an interventionist and asking the child with ASD to lead the interventionist through a maze while describing the location of physical obstacles. Other approaches include role playing and conversations centering on hypothetical people and events in order to demonstrate that what one individual sees or knows may not be what another individual sees or knows.

Ozonoff and Miller (1995) examined the effectiveness of a social skills training program that provided theory of mind instruction in the underlying social–cognitive principles necessary to infer the mental states of others. Their pre- to postintervention assessments indicated meaningful change for the intervention group, but no difference in teacher and parent ratings of the children's social competence. They suggested the need to consider the value of the intervention provided. Intervention certainly needs to serve a function that will be meaningful to the individual with ASD.

Although individuals with ASD can be trained to pass theory of mind tasks that assess the understanding of emotions, desires, beliefs, or pretense, outcomes are not associated with ratings of enhanced social competence (Ozonoff & Miller, 1995) or more meaningful and spontaneous communicative behaviors (Hadwin, Baron-Cohen, Howlin, & Hill, 1996, 1997; Swettenham, 1996). Yet because theory of mind remains important for the development of social competence in children with ASD, intervention strategies need to continue to examine ways of enhancing theory of mind development.

Other types of social skill groups also have been used to support the social competence of children, adolescents, and young adults with ASD (Mesibov, 1984; Webb et al., 2004; Williams, 1989). For example, Webb and her colleagues used the SCORE Skills program (Vernon, Schumaker, & Deshler, 1996) to teach social skills to adolescents with ASD who exhibited high cognitive abilities. The SCORE program is designed to support students in systematically acquiring, mastering, and using five key social skills: sharing ideas, complimenting others, offering help or encouragement, recommending changes nicely, and exercising self-control. Ten students (ages 12 to 17 years) participated in a 10-week training program that incorporated the strategy steps (e.g., tell your ideas, say something nice) and body language expectations (e.g., sound—pleasant; expression—pleasant; eye contact) used in the SCORE Skills program. The following instructional sequence from the SCORE program was used to support the development of each of the five social skills (adapted from Webb et al., 2004):

- *Provide an advanced organizer:* Review previously learned skills and explain current objectives.
- *Introduce the skill:* Name it, identify words associated with it, and explain its importance.
- *Discuss each step:* Define and explain each skill step.
- *Model the skill:* Demonstrate what the skill looks like.
- *Practice verbally:* Rehearse the name of each skill step.
- *Practice through role playing:* Practice the skill with a partner.
- *Review and prepare for next time:* Review what was learned and identify what is next.
- *Apply learning:* Apply skills in real situations.

Results indicated that adolescents with ASD who have high cognitive abilities can learn the five social skills taught in the SCORE program and can do so by working in a cooperative group setting. Parents were also satisfied that the training program benefited their children.

There are essential components to implementing an effective social skills curriculum for children with ASD. Krasny, Williams, Provencal, and Ozonoff (2003) emphasize the following components as part of their PROGRESS curriculum for supporting the social skills of children with ASD:

- Make abstract concepts concrete by defining the targeted skills and providing visual cues and prompts as needed.
- Ensure structure and predictability so that the routine is evident and has a clear beginning and ending.
- Scaffold language through modeling, scripting, and providing visual supports.
- Offer multiple learning opportunities that include varying materials and activities and involve different sensory systems.

- Include focused activities that involve group work, teach perspective taking, highlight student interests, and promote cooperation.
- Encourage self-esteem and self-awareness by creating a welcoming environment that builds on a child's strengths and provides constructive feedback.
- Select and prioritize functional goals that are relevant to the social skill development of the individual student.
- Provide a systematic program in which skills are taught sequentially and complex behaviors are simplified.
- Employ practice and opportunities for generalization by involving varied social partners in the home, school, and community.

Practitioners who are able to incorporate these central principles in their social skills intervention program for children with ASD are most likely to achieve success.

Summary

This chapter has discussed ways to facilitate the social and emotional needs of children with ASD. It is clear that students with ASD require some direct instruction in social skills, and several models of intervention were reviewed. Specific strategies that have had some success were highlighted, including the use of typical peers, pivotal response training, and social stories. It is important that teams analyze important social skills for particular events, use modeling to teach those skills, and offer multiple exemplars and opportunities to support the learning of those social skills in natural settings. The summary that follows refers to the questions at the beginning of the chapter and highlights key points you should be familiar with to prepare interventions that are responsive to the social and emotional needs of children with ASD.

What models of intervention guide programming for meeting the social–emotional needs of children with ASD?

Four models were described that can be used to support intervention programming for children with ASD across age and ability levels. The DIR or floor time model is designed to facilitate affect, attachment, and a sense of relatedness between a child with ASD and his or her interaction partner. The RDI model supports relationship development for children, adolescents, and adults with ASD through central intervention principles that focus on learning functions before skills, social referencing, and coregulation. The SCERTS model suggests that social communication, emotional regulation, and transactional supports are primary milestones that intervention programs should prioritize as goals for young children with ASD, and that meaningful learning experiences occur in a child's natural environment. Quill's (2000) do–watch–listen–say framework teaches the child with ASD how to know what to do in a social context; how to watch others to learn to imitate, share, take turns, use gestures, and express feelings; how to listen to others and to instructions to ensure that the child has assigned appropriate meaning to objects and actions, as well as the nonverbal and verbal behaviors of others; and how to know what to say.

How effectively can peers be used to support the social interaction skills of children with ASD?

Several empirically tested peer-mediation strategies have been used to support the social competence of children with ASD. Typically, these strategies involve peer models and reinforcement of targeted social behaviors. Promoting peer effort and altering peer expectations of children with ASD is important to the success of peer-mediated intervention; research should continue to explore the role of peers and their expectations for social engagement with special populations (DiSalvo & Oswald, 2002).

How can pivotal behaviors be used to support the social interaction of children with ASD in natural settings?

Children with ASD require treatment for several behaviors. Pivotal response training is an efficient and effective intervention approach that teaches or promotes specific behaviors that are central to the day-to-day functioning of a child with ASD and are likely to lead to changes in other behaviors. R. L. Koegel and his colleagues (1989) have designed intervention procedures that can be implemented in the natural environment with the ultimate goal of teaching these "pivotal" behaviors (e.g., self-initiation, motivation, responsivity to multiple cues, empathy, self-regulation, and social interaction) to facilitate generalized learning across contexts.

What are some strategies for supporting the social understanding and social communication of children with ASD?

Children with social cognition challenges have difficulty interpreting social situations and, as a result, behave inappropriately in those situations. Social stories benefit children with ASD by directly targeting those areas of relative weakness (Gray & Garand, 1993). Because children with autism have difficulty taking the perspective of other individuals and are unable to "read" people, social stories can explain and describe everyday occurrences in a way that allows children with autism to act in a more expected way. Comic strip conversations pair visual illustrations with written words to make explicit the intentions of others. They are used to review past experiences or incidents that may have been overwhelming to the individual with autism (Gray, 1998). Training programs have also been used to support social skill development with success for children and adolescents with ASD and higher cognitive abilities. Recently, theory of mind interventions have been used to promote perspective taking in individuals with ASD.

Practice Opportunities

1. Identify a difficult social situation or challenging social behavior for a child or adolescent with ASD and create a social story that will support the child's understanding of the situation and facilitate more desirable social behaviors.

2. Identify peers who are appropriate candidates for peer-mediated intervention and develop a peer intervention program that will support the social interaction skills of a young child with ASD.

3. Select a model of intervention for supporting the needs of a child with ASD, develop intervention goals, and create a plan for implementing the intervention in the home and school environments with a variety of interactive partners.

4. Identify two pivotal behaviors important to the social–emotional development of a child with ASD and establish an intervention plan around those behaviors in an inclusive classroom setting.

Suggested Readings

Bolick, T. (2001). *Asperger syndrome and adolescence: Helping preteens and teens get ready for the real world.* Gloucester, MA: Fair Winds Press.

> The author presents several helpful strategies for supporting the social skills of older school-age and adolescent students with ASD in the general education classroom and at home. She offers practical examples of the challenges often faced by students with ASD and then provides solutions based on her collaboration with the students. She also provides clear and meaningful suggestions for teachers and families.

McConnell, K., & Ryser, G. (2000). *Practical ideas that really work for students with autism spectrum disorders.* Austin, TX: PRO-ED.

> As a workbook for educators who are supporting the social learning of children with ASD, this resource is appropriate for children in preschool through Grade 12. It includes two components, a "Book of Practical Ideas" and an evaluation form. Thirty-seven instructional strategies emphasizing improvement in social interaction and communication skills are included in the book. A rating scale and ideas matrix are included as part of the evaluation form. The rating scale can be used to evaluate behaviors that interfere with student learning and social interaction. The ideas matrix links the rating scale results to intervention ideas.

Quill, K. A. (2000). *Do–watch–listen–say: Social and communication intervention for children with autism.* Baltimore: Brookes.

> This book includes an assessment tool and numerous ideas that promote social communication skills in children with ASD. Questionnaires and checklists are included for teachers and related service providers to profile a child's

abilities in 100 subskill areas. Each subskill area is linked to activities that teach solitary and social play, social communication, social reciprocity, and imitation.

Resources

Social Skills Books and Articles

Cartledge, G., & Kiarie, M. W. (2001). Learning social skills through literature for children and adolescents. *Teaching Exceptional Children, 34*(2), 40–47.

Gray, C. (2000). *The new social storybook: Illustrated edition*. Arlington, TX: Future Horizons.

Gray, C., & White A. L. (2002). *My social stories book*. Philadelphia: Jessica Kingsley.

Johnson, A. M., & Susnick, J. L. (2000). *Social skills stories: Functional picture stories for readers and nonreaders K–12*. Solana Beach, CA: Mayer-Johnson.

MacDonald, J. D. (2004). *Communicating partners: 30 years of building responsive relationships with late talking children*. New York: Jessica Kingsley.

McAfee, J. (2002). *Navigating the social world: A curriculum for individuals with Asperger's syndrome, high functioning autism and related disorders*. Arlington, TX: Future Horizons.

McClannahan, L. E., & Krantz, P. J. (1999). *Activity schedules for children with autism: Teaching independent behavior*. Bethesda, MD: Woodbine House.

Moyes, R. A. (2001). *Incorporating social goals in the classroom: A guide for teachers and parents of children with high-functioning autism and Asperger syndrome*. Philadelphia: Jessica Kingsley.

Siperstein, G. N., & Rickards, E. P. (2004). *Promoting social success: A curriculum for children with special needs*. Baltimore: Brookes.

Snell, M. E., & Janney, R. (2000). *Social relationships and peer support*. Baltimore: Brookes.

Sonders, S. A. (2002). *Giggle time—Establishing the social connection: A program to develop the communication skills of children with autism, Asperger syndrome and PDD*. New York: Jessica Kingsley.

Weiss, M. J., & Harris, S. J. (2001). *Reaching out, joining in: Teaching social skills to young children with autism*. Bethesda, MD: Woodbine House.

Winner, M. G. (2000). *Inside out: What makes a person with social cognitive deficits tick?* San Jose, CA: Michelle Garcia Winner.

Winner, M. G. (2002). *Thinking about you thinking about me: Philosophy and strategies to further develop perspective taking and communicative abilities for persons with social cognitive deficits*. San Jose, CA: Michelle G. Winner.

Social Skills Activities and Programs

Begun, R. W. (Ed.). *Ready-to-use social skills*. Eau Claire, WI: Thinking Publications.

Appropriate for preschool and kindergarten, 50 lessons are provided to develop children's social communication, self-control, self-esteem, and respect for others' rights. The teacher can model the social skills emphasized using puppets and flannel board cutouts.

Gajewski, N., Hirn, P., & Mayo, P. *Social skills strategies: A social–emotional curriculum for adolescents* (2nd ed.). Eau Claire, WI: Thinking Publications.

An inclusive curriculum used in numerous schools across the United States, this resource targets students in Grades 6 through 12. Fifty-seven different social skills are highlighted, with consideration given to special populations like those with language disorders and at risk for social challenges. Two skill books are included. One addresses general introductory interaction skills such as listening, accepting "no," asking for help, interrupting, using body language, and choosing the right time and place. The second book emphasizes more advanced skills in the areas of personal management, emotional expression, and peer interaction, such as dealing with anger, dealing with disappointment, accepting consequences, joining in, being assertive, and maintaining a friendship.

Gajewski, N., Hirn, P., & Mayo, P. *Social star program.* Eau Claire, WI: Thinking Publications.

This curriculum is designed for students in second through fifth grades and emphasizes three skill levels: general interaction, peer interaction, and conflict resolution and community interaction skills. Hands-on activities are used to support students in both general and special education classrooms. Students learn a cognitive planning strategy they can apply to all three social skill levels, with individual social skills emphasized at each.

Gray, C. *The new social story book.* Los Angeles: Western Psychological Services.

This book provides over 200 stories that focus on supporting the understanding of children with ASD in such content areas as people and pets, personal care, helping around the house, cooking, and parties. The sample stories are simple and clear with five or six sentences each. Strategies for creating stories are also included.

Gray, C., & White, A. L. *My social stories book.* Philadelphia: Jessica Kingsley.

The stories in this book are short narratives that take children (ages 2–6 years old) through basic activities such as bathing, brushing teeth, wearing new clothes, shopping, visiting the doctor, and going to school. Over 150 stories are included, with line drawings.

Hanken, D., & Kennedy, J. *Getting to know you! A social skills curriculum.* Austin, TX: PRO-ED.

This curriculum is designed for children in first through ninth grades and emphasizes developing interpersonal relationships and friendships, identifying and expressing feelings, making decisions, and self-acceptance.

Koenig, T., & Meyer, B. *Caring kids.* Eau Claire, WI: Thinking Publications.

Six different lessons are included, which are appropriate for children in first through third grades. Several social–emotional skills are emphasized, including listening, dealing with feelings, working and playing together, and being a part of a community. In addition, character traits such as kindness, respect, responsibility, and self-discipline are integrated in the social lessons.

LoGiudice, C., & McConnell, N. *Room 28: A social language program.* East Moline, IL: LinguiSystems.

This program is designed to support students in Grades 6 through 12 as they learn to understand, manage, and deal with social situations. Through role playing, small group discussions, and some independent work, students learn verbal and nonverbal communication skills important in social interactions; they also learn to recognize and control their emotions and to understand ways to solve problems and resolve conflict.

Mannix, D. *Social skills activities for secondary students with special needs.* Austin, TX: PRO-ED.

Divided into two parts, this activity book emphasizes basic social skills in Part 1 and social skills in action in Part 2. Basic social skills highlighted include listening, understanding others' viewpoints, managing emotions, making and keeping friends, reacting to peer pressure, and being flexible. Part 2 features ways to apply social skills in real situations such as home, school, and community.

Marquis, M. A., & Addy-Trout, E. *Social communication: Activities for improving peer interactions and self-esteem.* Eau Claire, WI: Thinking Publications.

Focusing on 12- to 16-year-olds, this tool supports students' effective communication as self-advocates. The social communication skills addressed include communicating with others, decision making and problem solving, enhancing self-esteem, and exploring self-concepts.

Mayo, P., Hirn, P., Gajewski, N., & Kafka, J. *Communicate Junior: An educational activity to reinforce social skills in elementary-age children.* Austin, TX: PRO-ED.

This game board activity combines social communication skills and cooperative learning. It emphasizes the following skill areas: facial expressions, eye contact, voice and body language; conversation; manners; time and place; listening and following rules; sharing, taking turns, and ignoring; and hygiene.

Mayo, P., Hirn, P., Gajewski, N., & Kafka, J. *Social skills communicate junior.* Eau Claire, WI: Thinking Publications.

Appropriate for Grades 1 through 4, this resource combines skills needed for effective cooperative learning and social communication. Twelve basic skills are emphasized: eye contact, facial expressions, manners, body language, listening, voice (including tone and volume), conversations, time and place, following rules, sharing and taking turns, ignoring, and hygiene.

Mayo, P., & Waldo, P. *Communicate: An educational activity to reinforce social–communication skills during adolescence.* Eau Claire, WI: Thinking Publications.

Appropriate for children in 5th through 12th grades. Strategies are provided for developing several social–emotional skills, including giving advice, interrupting, dealing with anger, offering help, listening, and making introductions.

Mayo, P., & Waldo, P. *Social skills communicate: An educational activity to reinforce social skills during adolescence.* Eau Claire, WI: Thinking Publications.

This activity highlights 57 different social skills and addresses the social–emotional challenges of students in Grades 5 through 12. Strategies include asking for permission, introducing self, using manners, giving advice, giving a compliment, offering help, being honest, and dealing with peer pressure.

McConnell, N., & LoGiudice, C. *That's life! Social language.* East Moline, IL: LinguiSystems.

This manual was developed to support the social language skills of students, 12 to 18 years of age, with language and learning disorders that affect their ability to fit in with their peers. Through role playing, discussion, interactive tasks, and direct instruction, several social skills are practiced. These include recognizing nonverbal cues, using nonverbal cues, initiating conversation, maintaining conversation, terminating or closing a conversation, making friends, maintaining friendships, learning self-control, resisting peer pressure, managing conflict, and solving problems.

McGann, W., & Werven, G. *Social communication skills for children: A workbook for principle-centered communication.* Austin, TX: PRO-ED.

This workbook features practice scenarios for problem solving using communication skills. It is most appropriate for use with children ages 8 to 11 years of age. Some of the content focus includes learning to participate socially with peers; understanding the principles that guide social communication; applying the principles of social communication in real contexts; and practicing social skills in a variety of settings and situations.

Moyes, R. A. *Incorporating social goals in the classroom: A guide for teachers & parents of children with high-functioning autism & Asperger syndrome.* Los Angeles: Western Psychological Services.

This guidebook provides hands-on social skills activities for children with autism who have high cognitive skills or have been identified with Asperger syndrome. Content areas include taking turns, understanding idiomatic expressions, and perceiving vocal tone and body language.

Reese, P. B., & Challenner, N. C. *Autism & PDD adolescent social skills lessons.* East Moline, IL: LinguiSystems.

This resource includes rebus lessons to support the social skills of older students and adolescents (12–18 years of age). The five areas of focus include health and hygiene, interacting, managing behavior, vocational schools, and secondary schools.

Reese, P. B., & Challenner, N. C. *Autism & PDD: Intermediate social skills lessons.* East Moline, IL: LinguiSystems.

Using rebus stories, social skills are supported for students 8 to 12 years of age. Topics emphasize learning about unfair situations, when to hug, obsessing on a topic, leaving elementary school, and expressing anger.

Reese, P. B., & Challenner, N. C. *Autism & PDD primary social skills lessons.* East Moline, IL: LinguiSystems.

This resource includes structured rebus lessons to support social skills learning for children, ages 3 to 8 years. Pictures are provided to facilitate children's ability to "read" the social lessons. The lessons cross five areas: community, school, home, behavior, and getting along. They include social skills such as using a quiet voice, going on a field trip, and getting a checkup.

Rider, T. *Let's share our feelings.* Oceanside, CA: Academic Communication Associates.

Pragmatic activities are used to support children, ages 4 through 10, in understanding their feelings and the feelings of others so they can be effective communicators in social situations. Children listen to stories and then respond to the actions and feelings of the characters in the stories.

Schilling, D., & Palomares, S. *Social skills activities for the elementary grades.* Austin, TX: PRO-ED.

Included in this book are several activities designed to help children, kindergarten through sixth grade, effectively relate to others and interact in a deliberate and fun way. Topics include managing anger and fear, making positive choices, communicating effectively, understanding body language, making and keeping friends, cooperating with others, and managing conflicts.

Skillstreaming series: Skillstreaming the elementary school child (Rev. ed.) and *Skillstreaming the adolescent* (Rev. ed.). Eau Claire, WI: Thinking Publications.

> Modeling, role playing, feedback, and transfer training are used to teach students social skills for successful communication with their families, teachers, and peers. There are 60 social communication behaviors in the elementary school edition and 50 in the adolescent edition. This series supports students dealing with interpersonal conflicts, challenges in self-control, and negative attitudes. The activities are particularly effective for group work.

Snell, M., & Janney, R. *Social relationships and peer support.* Baltimore: Brookes.

> This book provides a number of strategies that can be used to foster social relationships in school settings. Included are ways to assess, develop, and implement friendship building among students within and outside of school settings.

Walker, H. M., McConnell, S., Holmes, D., Todis, B., Walker, J., & Golden, N. *The Walker social skills curriculum: The ACCEPTS program.* Austin, TX: PRO-ED.

> This social skills curriculum emphasizes social–behavioral competencies to support the successful adjustment of students to the demands and expectations of inclusionary environments. ACCEPTS (A Curriculum for Children's Effective Peer & Teacher Skills) includes a placement test, instructional procedures, scripts, videos, role plays, and guidelines for teaching the curriculum. Activities are included for use in one-on-one, small group, and whole-class instruction.

Weiss, M. J., & Harris, S. L. *Reaching out, joining in: Teaching social skills to young children with autism.* Bethesda, MD: Woodbine House.

> Appropriate for parents of children with ASD, preschool through the early primary grades, this resource introduces social skills that parents can help their children learn, including play skills, the language of social skills, understanding another person's perspective, and functioning in an inclusive classroom. The resource includes tips for games, modeling, and role playing.

Wilson, C. C. *Room 14: A social language program.* East Moline, IL: LinguiSystems.

> The activities within this program are used for students in Grades 1 through 5 who have difficulty making and keeping friends, demonstrating self-control, exhibiting and managing feelings, and fitting in at school. The program includes stories, comprehension activities, and lesson plans.

Peer Tutoring Articles

Fulk, B. M., & King, K. (2001). Classwide peer tutoring at work. *Teaching Exceptional Children, 34*(2), 49–53.

Greenwood, C. R., Arreaga-Mayer, C., Utley, C. A., Gavin, K. M., & Terry, B. (2001). Classwide peer tutoring learning management system: Applications with elementary level English language learners. *Remedial and Special Education, 22,* 34–47.

Harper, G. F., Maheady, L., Mallette, B., & Karnes, M. (1999). Peer tutoring and the minority child with disabilities. *Preventing School Failure, 43,* 45–51.

Mortweet, S. L., Utley, C. A., Walker, D., Dawson, H. L., Delquadri, J. C., Reddy, S. S., et al. (1989). Classwide peer tutoring: Teaching students with mild retardation in inclusive classrooms. *Exceptional Children, 65,* 524–536.

Glossary

Checklist stories. Social story variations used to teach new routines.

Circle of communication. A critical component of floor time intervention involving initiation of an interaction either verbally or nonverbally and a response to the initiation.

Control sentences. Sentences used in a social story that identify strategies to recall information in the story.

Descriptive sentences. Sentences used in a social story to provide information about a particular social situation.

Directive sentences. Sentences used in a social story to provide information about what to do in a particular social situation.

False-belief task. Telling a story in which an object is moved from an original location to a new location without the knowledge of the main protagonist and asking the observer to predict where the protagonist will search for the object.

Floor time. A child-centered intervention approach involving 20- to 30-minute interaction periods that occur throughout the day, in which an interaction partner gets down on the floor with a child and engages in activities that range from rough-and-tumble play to acting out adventures with toys.

Judgment stories. Social story variations used to teach ways to make appropriate judgments.

Perspective sentences. Sentences used in a social story to provide information about the thoughts, feelings, moods, and beliefs of others.

Skills stories. Social story variations used to teach specific social skills.

Social review. Using videotaping to assess student perception of a social event and assist in developing social skills appropriate to that event.

References

Adams, L., Gouvousis, A., VanLue, M., & Waldron, C. (2004). Social story intervention: Improving communication skills in a child with autism spectrum disorders. *Focus on Autism and Other Developmental Disabilities, 19*(2), 87–94.

Apolloni, T., Cooke, S. A., & Cooke, T. P. (1977). Establishing a normal peer as a behavioral model for developmentally delayed toddlers. *Perceptual and Motor Skills, 44,* 241–251.

Armour, J., & Kuster, J. M. (2002). Floor time and evidence-based practice. *Perspectives in Language Learning and Education, 9*(2), 16–20.

Bacon, A. L., Fein, D., Morris, R., Waterhouse, L., & Allen, D. (1998). The responses of autistic children to the distress of others. *Journal of Autism and Developmental Disorders, 28,* 129–142.

Barry, L. M., & Burlew, S. B. (2004). Using social stories to teach choice and play skills to children with autism. *Focus on Autism and Other Developmental Disabilities, 19*(1), 45–51.

Barry, T. D., Klinger, L. G., Lee, J. M., Palardy, N., Gilmore, T., & Bodin, S. D. (2003). Examining the effectiveness of an outpatient clinic social skills group for high-functioning children with autism. *Journal of Autism and Developmental Disorders, 33*(6), 685–701.

Bauminger, N. (2002). The facilitation of social–emotional understanding and social interaction in high functioning children with autism: Intervention outcomes. *Journal of Autism and Developmental Disorders, 32*(4), 283–298.

Bricker, D. D. (1978). A rationale for the integration of handicapped and nonhandicapped preschool children. In M. J. Guralnick (Ed.), *Early intervention and the integration of handicapped and nonhandicapped children* (pp. 3–26). Baltimore: University Park Press.

Bristol, M. N., & Schopler, E. (1984). A developmental perspective on stress and coping in families of autistic children. In J. Blacher (Ed.), *Severely handicapped young children and their families: Research and review* (pp. 91–141). New York: Academic Press.

Buitelaar, J. K., Van der Wees, M., Swaab-Barneveld, H., & Van der Gaag, R. J. (1999). Verbal memory and performance IQ predict theory of mind and emotion recognition ability in children with autism spectrum disorders and in psychiatric control children. *Journal of Child Psychology and Psychiatry, 40,* 869–881.

Church, C., Alisanski, S., & Amanullah, S. (2000). The social, behavioral, and academic experiences of children with Asperger syndrome. *Focus on Autism and Other Developmental Disabilities, 15*(1), 12–20.

Cooper, C. S., & McEvoy, M. A. (1996). Group friendship activities: An easy way to develop the social skills of young children. *Teaching Exceptional Children, 29,* 67–69.

Crick, N. R., & Dodge, K. A. (1994). A review and reformulation of social-information processing mechanisms in children's social adjustment. *Psychological Bulletin, 115,* 74–101.

Cullain, R. E. (2000). The effect of social stories on anxiety levels and excessive behavioral expressions of elementary school aged children with autism (Doctoral dissertation, Union Institute Graduate College, 2000). *Dissertation Abstracts International, 62,* 2383.

Dawson, G., & Osterling, J. (1997). Early intervention in autism. In M. J. Guralnick (Ed.), *The effectiveness of early intervention* (pp. 307–326). Baltimore: Brookes.

DeGangi, G. A., & Greenspan, S. I. (1997). The effectiveness of short-term interventions in treatment of inattention and irritability in toddlers. *The Journal of Developmental and Learning Disorders, 1,* 277–298.

DiSalvo, C. A., & Oswald, D. P. (2002). Peer-mediated interventions to increase the social interaction of children with autism: Consideration of peer expectancies. *Focus on Autism and Other Developmental Disabilities, 17*(4), 198–207.

English, K., Goldstein, H., Kaczmarek, L., & Shafer, K. (1996). "Buddy skills" for preschoolers. *Teaching Exceptional Children, 29,* 62–66.

Gagnon, E. (2001). *Power cards: Using special interests to motivate children and youth with Asperger syndrome and autism.* Shawnee Mission, KS: Autism Asperger Publishing.

Gerber, S. (2003). A developmental perspective on language assessment and intervention for children on the autistic spectrum. *Topics in Language Disorders, 23*(2), 74–94.

Glaeser, B. C., Pierson, M. R., & Fritschmann, N. (2003). Comic strip conversation: A positive behavioral support strategy. *Teaching Exceptional Children, 36,* 14–19.

Goldstein, H., Kaczmarek, L., Pennington, R., & Shafer, K. (1992). Peer-mediated intervention: Attending to, commenting on, and acknowledging the behavior of preschoolers with autism. *Journal of Applied Behavior Analysis, 25,* 289–305.

Goldstein, H., & Wickstrom, S. (1986). Peer intervention effects on communicative interaction among handicapped and nonhandicapped preschoolers. *Journal of Applied Behavior Analysis, 19,* 209–214.

Gray, C. A. (1994). *Comic strip conversations.* Arlington, TX: Future Education.

Gray, C. A. (1995a). *Social stories and comic strip conversations: Unique methods to improve social understanding.* Jenison, MI: Carol Gray.

Gray, C. A. (1995b). Teaching children with autism to read social situations. In K. A. Quill (Ed.), *Teaching children with autism: Strategies to enhance communication and social ization* (pp. 219–242). New York: Delmar.

Gray, C. A. (1998). Social stories and comic strip conversations with students with Asperger syndrome and high functioning autism. In E. Schopler, G. B. Mesibov, & L. J. Kunce (Eds.), *Asperger syndrome or high functioning autism?* (pp. 167–194). New York: Plenum Press.

Gray, C. A., & Garand, J. D. (1993). Social stories: Improving responses of students with autism with accurate social information. *Focus on Autistic Behavior, 8*(1), 1–10.

Greenspan, S. I. (1992). The basic model: The influence of regulatory and experiential factors on the six organizational levels of experience. In S. I. Greenspan, *Infancy and early childhood: The practice of clinical assessment and intervention with emotional and developmental challenges* (pp. 3–28). New York: Teachers College Press.

Greenspan, S. I., & Wieder, S. (1997a). Developmental patterns and outcomes in infants and children with disorders in relating and communicating: A chart review of 200 cases of children with autistic spectrum diagnoses. *Journal of Developmental and Learning Disorders, 1,* 87–141.

Greenspan, S. I., & Wieder, S. (1997b). An integrated developmental approach to interventions for young children with severe difficulties in relating and communicating. *Zero to Three, 17,* 5–17.

Greenspan, S. I., & Wieder, S. (1998). *The child with special needs: Encouraging intellectual and emotional growth.* Reading, MA: Addison-Wesley.

Greenspan, S. I., & Wieder, S. (2000). A developmental approach to difficulties in relating and communicating in autism spectrum disorders and related syndromes. In A. M. Wetherby & B. M. Prizant (Eds.), *Autism spectrum disorders: A transactional developmental perspective* (pp. 279–306). Baltimore: Brookes.

Greenspan, S., & Wieder, S. (2001). *Floor time techniques and the DIR model: For children and families with special needs.* Bethesda, MD: ICDL Publications.

Gutstein, S. E. (2000). *Autism/Aspergers: Solving the relationship puzzle.* Arlington, TX: Future Horizons.

Gutstein, S. E. (2003, June). *Solving the relationship puzzle: Opening doors to friendship.* Presentation at the annual Vermont Summer Autism Institute, Burlington.

Gutstein, S. E., & Sheely, R. K. (2002a). *Relationship development intervention with children, adolescents & adults: Social and emotional development activities for Asperger syndrome, autism, PDD & NLD.* Philadelphia: Jessica Kingsley.

Gutstein, S. E., & Sheely, R. K. (2002b). *Relationship development intervention with young children: Social and emotional development activities for Asperger syndrome, autism, PDD & NLD.* Philadelphia: Jessica Kingsley.

Hadwin, J., Baron-Cohen, S., Howlin, P., & Hill, K. (1996). Can we teach children with autism to understand emotions, belief, or pretense? *Development and Psychopathology, 8,* 345–365.

Hadwin, J., Baron-Cohen, S., Howlin, P., & Hill, K. (1997). Does teaching theory of mind have an effect on the ability to develop conversation in children with autism? *Journal of Autism and Developmental Disorders, 27*(5), 519–537.

Howlin, P. (1998). Practitioner review: Psychological and educational treatments for autism. *Journal of Child Psychology and Psychiatry, 39,* 307–322.

Howlin, P., Baron-Cohen, S., & Hadwin, J. (1999). *Teaching children with autism to mindread: A practical guide.* New York: Wiley.

Hoyson, M., Jamieson, B., & Strain, P. S. (1984). Individualized group instruction of normally developing and autistic-like children: The LEAP curriculum model. *Journal of the Division for Early Childhood, 8,* 157–172.

Kamps, D. M., Leonard, B. R., Vernon, S., Dugan, E. P., Delquadri, J. C., Gershon, B., et al. (1992). Teaching social skills to students with autism to increase peer interactions in an integrated first-grade classroom. *Journal of Applied Behavior Analysis, 25*(2), 281–288.

Kamps, D. M., Royer, J., Dugan, E. P., Kravits, T., Gonzalez-Lopez, A., Garcia, J., et al. (2002). Peer training to facilitate social interaction for elementary students with autism and their peers. *Exceptional Children, 68*(2), 173–187.

Keeling, K., Myles, B. S., Gagnon, E., & Simpson, R. L. (2003). Using the power card strategy to teach sportsmanship skills to a child with autism. *Focus on Autism and Other Developmental Disabilities, 18*(2), 105–111.

Kendall, P. C., & Braswell, L. (1993). *Cognitive–behavioral therapy for impulsive children* (2nd ed.). New York: Guilford Press.

Koegel, L. K., & Koegel, R. L. (1986). The effects of interspersed maintenance tasks on academic performance in a severe childhood stroke victim. *Journal of Applied Behavior Analysis, 19,* 425–430.

Koegel, L. K., & Koegel, R. L. (2001, June). *Improving socialization, behavior and communication in children with autism and Asperger's syndrome.* Presentation at the annual Vermont Summer Autism Institute, Burlington.

Koegel, L. K., Koegel, R. L., & Carter, C. M. (1998). Pivotal responses and the natural language paradigm. *Seminars in Speech & Language, 19,* 355–372.

Koegel, L. K., Koegel, R. L., Harrower, J. K., & Carter, C. M. (1999). Pivotal response intervention I: Overview of approach. *Journal of the Association of Persons with Severe Handicaps, 24,* 174–185.

Koegel, L. K., Koegel, R. L., Shoshan, Y., & McNerney, E. (1999). Pivotal response intervention II: Preliminary long-term outcome data. *Journal of the Association of Children with Severe Handicaps, 24,* 186–198.

Koegel, R. L., Camarata, S., Koegel, L. K., Ben-Tall, A., & Smith, A. E. (1998). Increasing speech intelligibility in children with autism. *Journal of Autism & Developmental Disorders, 28*(3), 241–251.

Koegel, R. L., Dyer, K., & Bell, L. K. (1987). The influence of child preferred activities on autistic children's social behavior. *Journal of Applied Behavioral Analysis, 20,* 243–252.

Koegel, R. L., Koegel, L. K., Frea, W. D., & Smith, A. E. (1995). Emerging interventions for children with autism. In R. L. Koegel & L. K. Koegel (Eds.), *Teaching children with autism: Strategies for initiating positive interactions and improving learning opportunities* (pp. 1–15). Baltimore: Brookes.

Koegel, R. L., Schreibman, L., Good, A., Cerniglia, L., Murphy, C., & Koegel, L. K. (1989). *How to teach pivotal behaviors to children with autism: A training manual.* Santa Barbara: University of California.

Kohler, F. W., Strain, P. S., Maretsky, S., & DeCesare, L. (1990). Promoting positive and supportive interactions between preschoolers: An analysis of group-oriented contingencies. *Journal of Early Intervention, 14*(4), 327–341.

Krasny, L., Williams, B. J., Provencal, S., & Ozonoff, S. (2003). Social skills interventions for the autism spectrum: Essential ingredients and a model curriculum. *Child and Adolescent Psychiatric Clinics in North America, 12,* 107–122.

Kuoch, H., & Mirenda, P. (2003). Social story interventions for young children with autism spectrum disorders. *Focus on Autism and Other Developmental Disabilities, 18*(4), 219–227.

Kuttler, S., Myles, B. S., & Carlson, J. K. (1998). The use of social stories to reduce precursors to tantrum behavior in a student with autism. *Focus on Autism and Other Developmental Disabilities, 13*(3), 176–182.

Lee, S., & Odom, S. L. (1996). The relationship between stereotypic behavior and peer social interaction for children with severe disabilities. *Journal of the Association for Persons with Severe Handicaps, 21*(2), 88–95.

Lord, C., Rutter, M., DiLavore, P. C., & Risi, S. (1999). *Autism Diagnostic Observation Schedule–Generic.* Los Angeles: Western Psychological Services.

McGee, G. G., Feldman, R. S., & Morrier, M. J. (1997). Benchmarks of social treatment for children with autism. *Journal of Autism and Developmental Disorders, 27,* 353–364.

Mesibov, G. B. (1984). Social skills training with verbal autistic adolescents and adults: A program model. *Journal of Autism and Developmental Disorders, 14,* 395–404.

Morrison, L., Kamps, D., Garcia, J., & Parker, D. (2001). Peer mediation and monitoring strategies to improve initiations and social skills for students with autism. *Journal of Positive Behavior Interventions, 3*(4), 237–250.

National Research Council. (2001). *Educating children with autism.* Washington, DC: National Academy Press.

Norris, C., & Dattilo, J. (1999). Evaluating effects of a social story on a young girl with autism. *Focus on Autism and Other Developmental Disabilities, 14,* 180–186.

Odom, S., & Strain, P. S. (1986). Peer mediated approaches to promoting children's social interaction: A review. *American Journal of Orthopsychiatry, 54,* 544–557.

Orsmond, G. I., Krauss, M. W., & Seltzer, M. M. (2004). Peer relationships and social and recreational activities among adolescents and adults with autism. *Journal of Autism and Developmental Disorders, 34*(3), 245–256.

Overton, S., & Rausch, J. L. (2002). Peer relationships as support for children with disabilities: An analysis of mothers' goals and indicators for friendship. *Focus on Autism and Other Developmental Disabilities, 17*(1), 11–29.

Ozonoff, S., & Miller, J. N. (1995). Teaching theory of mind: A new approach to social skills training for individuals with autism. *Journal of Autism and Developmental Disorders, 25*(4), 415–433.

Paul, R. (2003). Promoting social communication in high functioning individuals with autistic spectrum disorders. *Child & Adolescent Psychiatric Clinics in North America, 12,* 87–106.

Perner, J., & Wimmer, H. (1983). Beliefs about beliefs: Representation and the constraining function of wrong beliefs in young children's understanding of deception. *Cognition, 13,* 103–128.

Pierce, K., & Schreibman, L. (1995). Increasing complex play in children with autism via peer-implemented pivotal response training. *Journal of Applied Behavior Analysis, 28,* 285–295.

Pierce, K., & Schreibman, L. (1997). Multiple peer use of pivotal response training to increase social behaviors of classmates with autism: Results from trained and untrained peers. *Journal of Applied Behavior Analysis, 30*(1), 157–160.

Prizant, B. M., & Wetherby, A. M. (1998). Understanding the continuum of discrete-trial traditional behavioral to social–pragmatic, developmental approaches in communication enhancement for young children with ASD. *Seminars in Speech and Language, 19,* 329–353.

Prizant, B. M., Wetherby, A. M., Rubin, E., & Laurent, A. C. (2003). The SCERTS model: A transactional, family-centered approach to enhancing communication and socio-emotional abilities of children with autism spectrum disorders. *Infants and Young Children, 16*(4), 296–316.

Prizant, B. M., Wetherby, A. M., Rubin, E., Laurent, A. C., & Rydell, P. (2004). *The SCERTS model: Enhancing communication and socioemotional abilities of children with autism spectrum disorders.* Port Chester, NY: National Professional Resources.

Quill, K. A. (1995). Visually cued instruction for children with autism and pervasive developmental disorders. *Focus on Autistic Behavior, 10,* 10–20.

Quill, K. A. (2000). *Do–watch–listen–say: Social and communication intervention for children with autism.* Baltimore: Brookes.

Roberts, J. E., Prizant, B., & McWilliam, R. A. (1995). Out-of-class versus in-class service delivery in language intervention: Effects on communication interactions with young children. *American Journal of Speech–Language Pathology, 6*(2), 40–49.

Roeyers, H. (1996). The influence of nonhandicapped peers on the social interactions of children with a pervasive developmental disorder. *Journal of Autism and Developmental Disorders, 26,* 303–320.

Romano, J. (2002). Are social stories effective in modifying behavior in children with autism? (Doctoral dissertation, Fairleigh Dickenson University, 2002). *Dissertation Abstracts International, 62,* 2383.

Schepis, M. M., Reid, D. H., Ownbey, J., & Clary, J. (2003). Training preschool staff to promote cooperative participation among young children with severe disabilities and their classmates. *Research & Practice for Persons with Severe Disabilities, 28*(1), 37–42.

Schreibman, L. (1988). *Autism.* Newbury Park, CA: Sage.

Simpson, R. L. (1993). Tips for practitioners: Reinforcement of social story compliance. *Focus on Autistic Behavior, 8,* 15–16.

Simpson, R. L., Myles, B. S., Sasso, G. M., & Kamps, D. M. (1997). *Social skills for students with autism* (2nd ed.). Reston, VA: Council for Exceptional Children.

Smith, C. (2001). Using social stories to enhance behaviour in children with autistic spectrum difficulties. *Educational Psychology in Practice, 17*(4), 337–345.

Spivak, G., & Shure, M. B. (1974). *Social adjustment of young children: A cognitive approach to solving real life problems.* San Francisco: Jossey-Bass.

Stacey, P. (2003, January/February). Floor time. *The Atlantic Monthly,* pp. 127–134.

Stahmer, A. (1995). Teaching symbolic play skills to children with autism using pivotal response training. *Journal of Autism and Developmental Disorders, 25,* 123–141.

Strain, P. S. (1977). Training and generalization effects of peer social initiations on withdrawn preschool children. *Journal of Abnormal Child Psychology, 5,* 445–455.

Strain, P. S. (1987). Parent training with young autistic children: A report on the LEAP model. *Zero to Three, 7,* 7–12.

Strain, P. S. (2001, June). *Teaching and evaluating peer mediated intervention.* Presentation at the annual Vermont Summer Autism Institute, Burlington.

Strain, P. S., & Cordisco, L. K. (1994). LEAP preschool. In S. L. Harris & J. S. Handleman (Eds.), *Preschool education programs for children with autism* (pp. 225–244). Austin, TX: PRO-ED.

Strain, P. S., Kohler, F. W., & Goldstein, H. (1996). Learning experiences, an alternative program: Peer mediated interventions for young children with autism. In E. Hibbs & P. Jensen (Eds.), *Psychosocial treatments for child and adolescent disorders: Empirically based strategies for clinical practice* (pp. 573–586). Washington, DC: American Psychological Association.

Strain, P. S., & Odom, S. L. (1986). Peer social initiations: An effective intervention for social skills deficits of exceptional children. *Exceptional Children, 52,* 543–551.

Strain, P. S., Shores, R. E., & Timm, M. A. (1977). Effects of peer initiations on the social behavior of withdrawn preschoolers. *Journal of Applied Behavior Analysis, 10,* 289–298.

Swaggart, B. L., Gagnon, E., Bock, S. J., Earles, T. L., Quinn, C., Myles, B. S., et al. (1995). Using social stories to teach social and behavioral skills to children with autism. *Focus on Autistic Behavior, 10*(1), 1–16.

Swettenham, J. (1996). Can children be taught to understand false belief using computers? *Journal of Child Psychology & Psychiatry & Allied Disciplines, 37*(2), 157–165.

Thiemann, K. S., & Goldstein, H. (2001). Social stories, written text cues, and video feedback effects on social communication of children with autism. *Journal of Applied Behavior Analysis, 34,* 425–446.

Vernon, D. S., Schumaker, J. B., & Deshler, D. D. (1996). *The SCORE skills: Social skills for cooperative groups.* Lawrence, KS. Edge Enterprises.

Webb, B. J., Miller, S. P., Pierce, T. B., Strawser, S., & Jones, W. P. (2004). Effects of social skill instruction for high-functioning adolescents with autism spectrum disorders. *Focus on Autism and Other Developmental Disabilities, 19*(1), 53–62.

Williams, T. A. (1989). Social skills groups for autistic children. *Journal of Autism and Developmental Disorders, 19,* 143–155.

Wing, L. (1988). The continuum of autistic characteristics. In E. Schopler & G. B. Mesibov (Eds.), *Diagnosis and assessment in autism* (pp. 91–110). New York: Plenum Press.

CHAPTER 12

Health-Care Considerations for Children with ASD

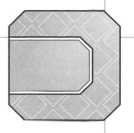

Stephen H. Contompasis and Patricia A. Prelock

QUESTIONS TO CONSIDER

Children with autism spectrum disorders (ASD) share the health concerns typical for all children, but they have additional considerations that are likely to affect or exacerbate their core deficits in social interaction, communication, and behavior. The health intervention supports presented in this chapter will address the following three questions:

1. What is the role of a "medical home" in the health care that children with ASD require?

2. What is the importance of a coordinated and comprehensive plan for addressing the health issues of children with ASD?

3. What health-related strategies can be considered to support the ability of children with ASD to interact socially, communicate, play, and sustain their behavior so that they can learn and actively participate in their environments?

---

*The authors contributed equally to this chapter.

541

Introduction

In addition to routine health care, children with ASD require a coordinated and comprehensive approach to those health issues unique to their developmental condition. New concepts for health care such as the "medical home" are being developed and implemented across the country in pediatric practices. In this chapter, we discuss the potential role of the medical home in the care of children with ASD and ways to identify problems characteristic of children with ASD that require specific and ongoing medical attention. We also describe strategies to support the health of children with ASD that can have both a direct and an indirect impact on the quality of the children's social interactions, communication, play, and behavior. Although the primary responsibility for health care may lie with a child's physician, we will discuss the importance of an interdisciplinary, collaborative approach to supporting the health and quality of life of children with ASD.

Role of a "Medical Home" for Children with ASD

In recent years, the American Academy of Pediatrics (AAP) has suggested that all children with disabilities have a "medical home" that provides for their ongoing care (AAP, 1992). Unfortunately, the interpretation of the medical home concept has been fraught with challenges, including lack of reimbursement for services physicians provide while caring for children in a medical home. This has precipitated a new policy statement with a more comprehensive interpretation and expanded view (AAP, 2002). The new policy states that "the medical care of infants, children, and adolescents ideally should be accessible, continuous, comprehensive, family centered, coordinated, compassionate and culturally effective" (p. 184) and that well-trained primary care physicians should deliver, maintain, and facilitate all aspects of the care.

The medical home is typically an office-based practice that is committed to the development of partnerships with families who have children with special health needs. Some pediatric practices that have adopted the concept of a medical home use a care coordinator within their office, who can facilitate timely and effective interactions among families, their educationally based teams, and other health specialists. As part of the medical home concept, a medical care plan and medical information exchange form with schools could be developed. These structural changes in pediatric practices seem to make a positive difference in the care of children with special health needs and their families. It is just these kinds of changes that would enhance the health care of children with ASD, who frequently are plagued by seizures and often have difficulties with sleep, toileting, transitions, and related behaviors.

Coordination among interdisciplinary personnel (e.g., psychologists, speech–language pathologists, audiologists, occupational therapists), agencies (e.g., schools, developmental and mental health agencies), and specialty health providers (e.g., psychiatrists, neurologists, and developmental pediatricians) is an implied theme in the AAP's (2002) policy statement regarding the establishment of a medical home. Principles of care that are strongly emphasized in the policy statement include continuity of services, information interpretation, accurate record keeping, and communication among all parties involved in the care of the child with special health care needs. Table 12.1 summarizes the specific tenets for a medical home. Considering the number of potential health challenges experienced by children with ASD (as described in subsequent sections of this chapter) and the pervasive nature of their deficit, establishing the principles of care described for a medical home would be an effective and efficient response to meeting their needs. Primary care physicians who take the time to coordinate a medical home for children with disabilities actively attain knowledge regarding

TABLE 12.1

Tenets for Establishing a Medical Home

1. Provide family-centered care by partnering with families, respecting their diversity, and recognizing their ongoing presence in their child's life.

2. Share clear and unbiased information with families about their children's medical care, available organizations, and specialty and community services.

3. Provide primary care, including acute, chronic, and preventive services (e.g., immunizations, growth and developmental assessments, screenings, counseling).

4. Ensure that ambulatory and inpatient care for acute illnesses will be continuously available.

5. Provide care over an extended period to ensure continuity and plan and organize transitions in health care with child and family.

6. Identify the need for subspecialty consultation and referrals, collaborate with other care providers, articulate each provider's role, and establish shared management plans in partnership with the child and family.

7. Interact with school and community agencies to ensure that the special health needs of the individual child and family are addressed.

8. Provide care coordination services and implement a specific care plan as part of an organized team that includes the family, the family's physician, and other service providers.

9. Maintain an accessible, confidential central record and database that contains all pertinent medical information about the child, including information about hospitalizations.

10. Provide developmentally appropriate and culturally competent assessments and counseling to ensure a coordinated and successful transition to adult health care.

Note. Adapted from "The Medical Home," by the American Academy of Pediatrics, 2002, *Pediatrics, 110*(1), pp. 184–186. Copyright 2002 by American Academy of Pediatrics. Adapted with permission.

specific developmental disorders and their health implications. Families of children with ASD might seek out primary care practices that are committed to the medical home concept because of the likely benefit to their children's health.

A Plan for Coordinated and Comprehensive Health Care for Children with ASD

Several models of case management have been described in the social work, health care, and early intervention literature (Appleton et al., 1997; Case-Smith, 1991; Freedman, Pierce, & Reiss, 1987; Gonzalez-Calvo, Jackson, Hansford, Woodman, & Remington, 1997; Jackson, Finkler, & Robinson, 1992; S. Steele, 1993). Case management is generally conceived of as a process for coordinating the services for individuals with special needs. Diverse theoretical origins of the case management concept, however, have led to various interpretations and applications (Etheridge, 1989). Further, there has been a shift in terminology from *case management* to *care coordination*. The term *care coordination* will be used throughout this chapter because it more accurately describes the service provision required for children with complex health and developmental needs, particularly children with ASD.

Traditionally, nurses and social workers have been primarily responsible for care coordination (Weil & Karls, 1985). It has been described in the nursing literature as a service delivery system focused on achieving effective outcomes in a time- and resource-efficient manner (Etheridge, 1989). The social work literature defines care coordination as providing individualized services and connecting individuals to other community services and informal support networks (Fiene & Taylor, 1991; Rothman, 1991). Although not explicitly stated as a responsibility in the past, more recent policy statements indicate a significant role for pediatrics in care coordination. The AAP Committee on Children with Disabilities (1999) describes care coordination as a process of linking services and resources to children with special health needs and their families to achieve optimal health outcomes. Whatever discipline is involved in care coordination, there is agreement that it is a process for supporting families in identifying the services they need and facilitating the coordination of those services.

Several models exist for implementing the principles of care coordination proposed for medical homes. Some practices have instituted periodic care conferences in the primary care office or alternative community site (e.g., school or agency). A care conference involves the participation of all key members of a child's community team or teams. Key members might include families, the child as appropriate, health personnel from the child's medical home (pediatrician or family physician, office-based nurse), health personnel from school or home health (school nurse, home health nurse), developmental services providers and case managers, educational case managers representing the child's special education process, and related service providers (occupational therapist [OT], physical therapist [PT], speech–language pathologist [SLP], psychologist from school or community health services). The agenda of the care conference should reflect current issues affecting the child's health and service needs that require interdisciplinary and interagency input. There should be sufficient time scheduled to allow for discussion, information sharing, brainstorming and problem solving, action planning, and tracking the progress of previously assigned tasks. Minutes of the meeting, with action plans and assigned responsibility for follow-through, are an effective means of ensuring positive outcomes. Care conferences require a commitment of all team members to attend. Practitioners are learning, however, that the time spent in a care conference may be more efficient than multiple phone calls. Ideally, care conferences should be part of an agency's work plan or should be reimbursed adequately through health care plans so that practitioners attend without concern about the need for additional resources.

Physicians have also found value in using a plan to provide care for children with chronic or disabling conditions. Two effective formats are proposed in the sections that follow (preventive medical checklists and problem-oriented medical records) that can improve health outcomes for individuals with autism by anticipating (and thereby possibly preventing) secondary complications and by more effectively managing problems as they arise.

Strategies To Support the Health Care of Children with ASD

Primary health care providers, families, and other practitioners can participate in the implementation of several strategies designed to improve the health and quality of life of children with ASD. Some of these strategies include routine health care maintenance, use of a preventive medical checklist specific to the child's condition (ASD), and maintenance of a problem-oriented medical record to address identified concerns (e.g., monitoring of seizures or epilepsy, genetic testing and counseling, diet and nutritional support). Considering the health domains proposed by the World Health Organization (2001), identifying health challenges and strategies to address those challenges should occur at two basic levels: body functions and structures, and activity and participation. Recognition of functioning and disability at both of those levels, as well as the potential contextual factors (e.g., environmental and personal) involved is likely to broaden the preventive and treatment efforts of those participating in providing health services to individuals with autism. Both preventive activities and those directed at identified problems can be brought to the care conference agenda, as they may require interdisciplinary and interagency collaboration. As will be discussed in the following paragraphs, all practitioners must collaborate in their efforts both to inform one another and to prepare children with autism and their families for the health experiences they are likely to encounter. A problem list such as the one found in Table 12.2 can be used as a guide for the collaborative discussions and action planning needed to address the health care of a child with ASD.

Routine Health Care Maintenance and Preventive Medical Checklists

Pediatric health care practitioners are familiar with the concept of using preventive medical guidelines and checklists to enhance the routine health care maintenance of children in their practices. Guidelines currently in use include the Medicaid/EPSDT (Early and Periodic Screening, Diagnostic, and Treatment Program) Schedule, and the Bright Futures Guidelines for Health Supervision of Infants, Children, and Adolescents (Green, 1994). At a minimum, children with ASD should be seen for routine health maintenance visits at the prescribed intervals for children without disabilities. The American Academy of Pediatrics supports the use of these guidelines in their policy statement "Recommendations for Preventative Pediatric Health Care." The AAP Committee on Practice and Ambulatory Medicine (2000) further notes that these guidelines for routine health visits are designed for the care of children who are receiving competent parenting, have no manifestations of any important health problems, and are growing and developing in a satisfactory fashion. Additional visits may become necessary if circumstances suggest variations from normal. A periodicity schedule can be found at http://www.aap.org/policy/re9939.html (American Academy of Pediatrics, 2000) that outlines the ages for routine health maintenance visits and the suggested activities for monitoring, including growth, interval health problems, vision and hearing screening, developmental screening, and anticipatory guidance around a number of health, developmental, and safety concerns. Currently, the periodicity guidelines suggest visits in infancy at 1, 2, 4, 6, 9, and 12 months; in early childhood at 15, 18, and 24 months and 3 and 4 years; in middle childhood at 5, 6, 8, and 10 years; and yearly through adolescence. Children with ASD who have more complicated presentations (e.g., seizure disorder, severe behavioral manifestation requiring medication and other supports, nutritional or growth deficiency secondary to a limited diet) should be seen more frequently to address their current problem list.

Practice guidelines and preventive medical checklists have been developed for a number of chronic childhood conditions. In general, they should be based on best available medical literature. Often, a panel of experts in the field creates these guidelines. The American Academy of Pediatrics Web site houses a number of clinical practice guidelines at http://www.aap.org/policy/paramtoc.html, including the American Academy of Neurology practice parameters for the screening and diagnosis of autism. These do not provide a comprehensive approach to ongoing preventive care, however. A number of useful preventive medical checklists have been developed for disorders such as Fragile X syndrome (Wilson & Cooley, 2000), but no specific checklist has been developed for ASD. To assist health practitioners

TABLE 12.2

Problem List for Jason, a Child with ASD

Problem	WHO Classification Level	Plans (typically diagnostic, therapeutic, or patient and family education)
1. Jason is now 5, and his parents want him to be toilet trained.	Activity and participation, limitations or restrictions, and context (i.e., personal and environmental factors)	a. Parents and school to collect charted data on current bowel movements and diaper checks for frequency of urination. b. History and physical exam to rule out chronic constipation and stool withholding and soiling pattern (encopresis). c. Physician to contact behavioral psychologist for possible protocols effective in toilet training children with autism. d. Team to meet to coordinate a behavioral plan to address toileting across home and school. e. Add this concern to ongoing agenda at care coordination meetings held monthly between pediatric office, home, school, and mental health agency.
2. Jason is having increased periods of inattentiveness, and school personnel have wondered about seizure activity.	Body functions and structures and impairments, activity and participation, and context (i.e., personal and environmental factors)	a. Review current concern with parents and school nurse. b. Ask for and review videotape of suspicious behaviors at school. c. Arrange for EEG and consultation with pediatric neurologist if videotape confirms likely seizure-related behaviors. d. Add this concern to ongoing agenda at care coordination meeting.
3. Jason is eating only white and yellow foods (diet limited to plain toast, milk, macaroni with cheese, and popcorn).	Body functions and structures and impairments	a. Provide parents with a 3-day dietary recall. b. History and physical exam to include features of nutritional deficiency. c. Office visits to update growth measurements. d. Provide 3-day recall to referring nutritionist for evaluation. e. Add multivitamin if indicated. Arrange for behavioral psychology consultation to develop plan to expand Jason's willingness for new foods if analysis reveals any dietary deficiency. f. Attempt to increase dietary fiber intake (related to problem #1). g. Add this concern to ongoing agenda at care coordination meetings held monthly between pediatric office, home, school, and mental health agency.

in providing a more comprehensive plan for health care maintenance for children with autism, Figure 12.1 presents a possible format for a preventive medical checklist.

Physicians, nurses, and office staff must acquaint themselves with techniques for interviewing, information gathering, and information sharing, as demanded by the unique communication and behavioral challenges often presented by a child with ASD. Working closely with parents and related service providers (e.g., speech–language pathologists, audiologists, occupational therapists, and behavioral interventionists) is a must when working with children who might be nonverbal, have variable receptive language and cognition, and have atypical sensory experiences or behavioral responses. Office-based practices for screening (i.e., for vision and hearing) may need to be adapted for the individual with ASD, or a referral for a specialty evaluation (i.e., with an ophthalmologist or audiologist) may be necessary.

Equally important is the opportunity and responsibility of other practitioners to communicate with primary care physicians so that they might be better prepared to address the health care needs of the child with ASD. For example, through the communication systems established for children with ASD, SLPs can help develop methods for answering simple yes–no questions or communicating pain and discomfort to the physician. If the child uses an augmentative communication system (e.g., sign language, communication board, Picture Exchange Communication System, electronic device), the SLP can do some pretraining of relevant vocabulary and preprogram the communication system used by the child. The SLP might also prepare a script or social story to prime the child for a primary care visit. An OT might share with the physician sensory strategies that can be used to effectively check the blood pressure, take the temperature, or examine the oral cavity of a child with ASD who has tactile defensiveness or oral sensitivity. The OT might also prepare the child with sensory issues for some of the sensory tasks he or she will experience at the primary care visit.

Specific Considerations for a Preventive Medical Approach for Children with Autism

Several areas should be given special consideration in the care of children and adolescents with ASD. These include speculated etiologies and complementary alternative medicine; diet and nutrition; growth; seizure activity; mental health; psychopharmacology; dental care; orthopedic care and physical therapy; self-care, activities of daily living, and occupational therapy; pain or acute illness; safety and sexuality; and sleep. Each of these areas of health is briefly described in the following paragraphs.

Speculated Etiologies and Complementary Alternative Medicine. Families often search for the cause of their child's autism, which may lead to speculation regarding etiologies and the subsequent use of complementary alternative medicine approaches to treatment. The desire to cure

Health Care Checklist for Children with ASD

Child's name:_____   Health care provider:_____

List identified clinical concerns:

General _____   Surface _____

Facial _____   Internal _____

Skeletal _____   Neural _____

Health Care Activity	Target Dates	Accommodations Needed	Outcomes	Follow-up Needed
Monitor growth				
Review nutritional status and eating patterns				
Assess seizure activity				
Review medications				
Review sleep patterns				
Review toileting needs				
Assess vision				
Assess hearing				
Assess communication development				
Review opportunities for social experiences				
Assess behavior				

FIGURE 12.1. Health care checklist for children with ASD.

the child's autism by finding the cause is certainly a strong motivator for parents of diagnosed children. The use of complementary and alternative medicine (CAM) in general to treat chronic illness or disability is increasing in the United States (Eisenberg et al., 1998). This is especially evident among parents of children with autism and related disorders, where use of CAM may be as high as 60% or more (Nickel, 1996).

It may be challenging to pediatricians to remain current and to distinguish among accepted biomedical treatments, unproven therapies, and alternative therapies. To best serve the interests of children, and to maintain trusting relationships with families, it is important to maintain a scientific perspective, to provide balanced advice about therapeutic options, and to guard against bias. Pediatricians might consider using specific strategies from the American Academy of Pediatrics, such as those found in the statement of the AAP Committee on Children with Disabilities (2001). Those strategies can be used to support the intervention decision making of teams working with children with ASD and their families, as discussed in Chapter 8. Pediatricians may also be able to summarize critical information about current thinking on the etiology of autism (see Chapter 1), which implicates genetics and neurobiology over other causal theories, to direct the family's energies toward more evidence-based educational and therapeutic practices that can improve outcomes in children with autism.

Diet and Nutrition. Often the behavior patterns of children with autism include rigid and inflexible food preferences (Quinn & Levine, 1995; Raiten & Massaro, 1986; Volkmar & Wiesner, 2004). Such preferences can relate to color (e.g., white or yellow foods), taste (e.g., salty or sweet foods), or texture (e.g., crunchy or soft foods). Further, children with ASD can become more selective over time regarding their food preferences (e.g., refusing foods that they had previously eaten) (Quinn & Levine, 1995). Families and practitioners who observe the daily food intake of children with ASD report their concerns and challenges in helping them achieve a balanced, healthy diet. These concerns are warranted because children with ASD who exhibit highly rigid food preferences may have a diet deficient in major nutrient groups, such as proteins, carbohydrates, fats, or fibers, or in vitamins and micronutrients (i.e., calcium, iron, zinc, or selenium). Referral to a registered dietician who can perform a dietary recall and analysis can be helpful. This analysis may lead to a need for nutritional adjustments, such as the addition of vitamins and minerals.

Changing the diet and nutritional intake of children with ASD requires a coordinated effort among families and interdisciplinary professionals who provide services. For example, in consultation with a nutritionist, an OT can gradually begin to introduce different food types into a child's daily snacks with textures the child can tolerate and nutrients the child needs. The same can occur in the home. Also, the SLP can develop a social story focusing on snacks that children and adolescents enjoy that have the nutrients the child or adolescent with ASD requires. In severe cases of rigid food and nutritional intake, a behavioral psychologist with experience shaping the behavior of children with ASD may be needed to support the introduction of a varied diet.

Helpful mealtime strategies such as the following have been described for children with ASD (Quinn & Levine, 1995):

- scheduling routine mealtimes and environments;
- providing supportive seating at the table;
- creating a comfortable, calm environment for eating;
- determining whether a child would be more or less calm with the presence of music or a video; and
- determining whether a child's ability to sit at mealtime is influenced by the presence or absence of others.

It should also be noted that the use of vitamins has been implicated as one complementary or alternative treatment strategy for autism. Based on orthomolecular theory that suggests treating a condition by providing normally present substances in optimal concentrations, substances such as vitamin B_6 and magnesium have been used to reduce the symptoms of autism (Pfeiffer, Norton, Nelson, & Shott, 1995). Pfeiffer and colleagues have critically examined several studies investigating vitamin therapy in individuals with autism. Although most of the studies provided favorable reports of the efficacy of vitamin treatment, Pfeiffer et al. point out several methodological flaws that indicate a cautious interpretation of the results is needed. Primary care providers and their collaborators must be open to hear and understand families' requests for biochemical interventions such as vitamin therapy. They must also be informed, however, about the outcome measures used, as well as the characteristics of the individuals used as participants in the published research; and they must be cautious about interpretation without verification of replicability and long-term effects.

Elimination diets, such as a gluten- and casein-free diet, have also been used as complementary and alternative treatment strategies to reduce the symptoms of ASD. Proponents of the gluten- and casein-free diet suggest that particular peptides break down products from the gluten and casein proteins that are absorbed by the gut, and that they have opioid properties that can affect the brain either directly or indirectly through the immune system. Children with ASD are selected to participate in this treatment based on urine testing for these opioid peptides. Few double-blind placebo studies have been done to assess the efficacy of this diet-related treatment, although Knivsberg, Reichelt, Nodland, and Hoien (1995) studied 15 children with ASD using this dietary treatment and found positive results. One year and 4 years following initiation of the diet in the Knivsberg et al. study, the children continued to demonstrate positive effects in the areas of social interaction, communication, and learning. A reduction in "odd" behavior was also reported. Again, however, practitioners are reminded to hear what families have to say, carefully define a process for examining the effects of a nutritional intervention, and cautiously interpret results that have not been replicated or sustained over time (Adams & Conn, 1997). The American Academy of Neurology Practice Guidelines (Filipek et al., 2000) reports,

> There is inadequate supporting evidence for hair analysis, celiac antibodies, allergy testing (particularly food allergies for gluten, casein, candida, and other molds), immunologic or neurochemical abnormalities, micronutrients such as vitamin levels, intestinal permeability studies, stool analysis, urinary peptides, mitochondrial disorders (including lactate and pyruvate), thyroid function tests, or erythrocyte glutathione peroxidase studies. (p. 474)

Growth Monitoring. Because of the potential for a selective diet in this population, it is particularly important that primary care providers track and monitor the growth of children with ASD. Tracking of anthropometric data (i.e., specific growth measurements typically included in routine health maintenance visits), including height, weight, head circumference, and weight-to-height ratio or body mass index, should be part of the routine care for all children with ASD. Despite their selective appetites, however, most children with ASD are average or above average in size (Quinn & Levine, 1995).

Monitoring of Seizures. Children with ASD are at a significantly increased risk for the development of seizures. Seizures are caused by abnormal electrical discharges in the brain, whereas epilepsy, or seizure disorder, is a condition in which an individual experiences recurrent seizures. Seizures are usually generalized (tonic-clonic, absence, atonic, akinetic) or partial (simple and complex), depending on the involvement of the brain (Volkmar & Wiesner, 2004). They are associated with unusual sensations, uncontrollable muscle spasms, and often a loss of consciousness. The onset of seizures in children with ASD peaks in early childhood and again in adolescence (Filipek et al., 2000). Approximately 7% to 14% of children with ASD will develop a seizure disorder. By adolescence and adulthood, the prevalence rises to nearly 30% (Rossi, Posar, & Parmegiani, 2000).

Depending on their level of expertise, physicians may wish to develop their own plans for evaluating seizures or suspected seizures, or they may wish to consult with a neurologist. The child with ASD who demonstrates some regressive symptoms (e.g., loss of previous language skill) may require further evaluation, even though the link between regression in autism and epileptiform syndromes (i.e., Landau–Kleffner syndrome) remains poorly defined (Rapin, 1997; Rapin & Tuchman, 1997).

Physicians must also communicate with families and other practitioners involved in the service delivery of children with ASD who have extended opportunities to observe the child's daily behavior and can offer both qualitative and quantitative data on suspected seizure activity. For example, a physician might ask a teacher or instructional assistant to describe and count the number of suspected seizure-like behaviors observed during the course of a week. A format for documenting the observed behaviors might be agreed upon so that the data collected have a consistent context and structure and can be used over time. An example of a format that might be used can be found in Figure 12.2.

Teachers, related service providers, and families can also report any regression in language and learning performance that is new and for which other explanations have been ruled out. Periodic videotaping of the daily routines and activities of a child with ASD can be a useful tool for retrospectively reviewing a child's behavior, movement, language, and speech when later regression is observed. Further, there are some subtle symptoms potentially indicative of a seizure disorder that all service providers can observe. Thiele (2001) describes some of these observable symptoms as

- brief staring spells,
- periods of confusion,

Suspected Seizure Activity

Child's name: _____   Observer: _____

Location: _____   Primary health care provider: _____

Date	Time of Day	Activity in Which Child Is Engaged	Antecedent Event[a]	Behavior Observed[b]	Consequent Event[c]

FIGURE 12.2. Format for observing suspected seizure activity. [a]Describe what the child is doing prior to the observed behavior. [b]Describe actual behavior and note the approximate duration. [c]Describe what the child does after the observed behavior, noting anything you do to regain the child's attention.

- head dropping,
- sudden loss of muscle tone,
- episodic rapid blinking of eyes rolling upward,
- blank facial expression with odd mouth and face movements,
- aimless or dazed walking or repetitive movements not appropriate to a situation or environment, and
- involuntary arm or leg jerking.

It is important that families and practitioners be aware of ways to help a child who is having a seizure. Typically, the child should be placed on the floor with no objects nearby and clothing loosened around the child's head and neck. Objects should not be placed in the child's mouth, and movements should not be restrained. Following the seizure, the child should be placed on his side, and medical services should be contacted immediately if the child is having trouble breathing, has hurt his head, or seems ill in any way. Further, if this is the first seizure the child has experienced, or if the child has recurrent seizures but a seizure occurs that is longer lasting or different from usual, medical care should be pursued. Educational teams should develop safety protocols, in collaboration with families and their children's primary health care providers, for any child or adolescent with ASD who has experienced a seizure. All members of the team should be aware of the protocol and should be trained in how to support the child with ASD should a seizure occur. Team members should also be knowledgeable of the types of antiepileptic drugs that can be used to suppress seizures in children with ASD, as some medications may impact language, learning, and attention.

Mental Health Monitoring. Individuals with mental retardation and developmental disabilities are estimated to be three to four times more likely than those in the general population to experience an emotional, behavioral, or psychiatric disorder (National Institutes of Health, 2001). Difficulty recognizing the behavioral manifestations of depression, anxiety, or psychoses against the backdrop of atypical behavior or the symptoms of ASD may cause underdiagnosis and undertreatment. To ensure more careful discrimination of mental health in the population of children and adolescents with ASD, health practitioners should include in their history taking an assessment of any changes in behavior that may be symptomatic of an underlying mental health condition. The reported and observed presence of such changes warrants further evaluation and referral. Other practitioners involved in the daily care of children and adolescents with ASD, as well as families, should be informed of the signs of any mental health problems, so that they can report and describe the symptoms observed during care conferences with the children's primary health care provider.

Psychopharmacology. Because the exact pathogenesis of ASD is unknown, specific treatments aimed at the underlying abnormalities is difficult (Vitiello, 2000). There is evidence, however, that supports the use of psychopharmacologic agents to treat certain patterns of emotion, aggressive mood and self-injury, compulsive or stereotyped behavior, attention, and sensory dysfunction in individuals with autism (Campbell, Perry, Small, & Green, 1987; Holm & Varley, 1989; King et al., 2001; Vitiello, 2000).

Medications most often used for children with ASD include anticonvulsant drugs, tranquilizers, stimulant medications, antidepressants, anxiolytic (antianxiety) medications, and beta-blockers (des Portes, Hagerman, & Hendren, 2003; Fisman, 1997; Heflin & Simpson, 1998; Tsai, 1992; Wilens, 1999). Antiseizure drugs (e.g., phenobarbital, Tegretol, Dilantin, valproic acid [trade names Depakene, Depakote], Clonopin, Mysoline) are among the most common medications prescribed because of the increased evidence of seizures in children with ASD (Tsai, 1998). The ability of these drugs to decrease seizure activity is variable across children, and side effects such as drowsiness and motor tics have been reported. Generally, though, seizure medications have been considered effective (Tsai, 1998).

The major tranquilizer medications (or neuroleptics) have been prescribed more in the past to reduce responses such as severe anxiety, aggression, agitation, hyperactivity, and self-stimulatory behavior (Gordon, 2000; Volkmar, 2001). Frequently used tranquilizers include Thorazine, Mellaril, Trilafon, Stelazine, Prolixin, and Haldol. Because of the many associated side effects of the major tranquilizers, such as drowsiness, blurred vision, impaired motor performance, tremors, and tardive dyskinesia (a lifelong and disfiguring motor disorder), physicians often use other safer medications with similar benefits. Physicians may still prescribe tranquilizers as necessary, however, to help reduce disorganized thinking and to assist with other behavioral concerns (Heflin & Simpson, 1998).

Stimulant medications (e.g., Ritalin, Adderall, Dexedrine) are used to stimulate concentration and attention and reduce overactivity and behavioral problems (Gordon, 2000). Although side effects appear to be minimal, debate continues over perceived effectiveness in children with ASD. Antidepressant medications are also used broadly to manage attention deficits and hyperactivity as well as enuresis, school phobia, sleep disturbance, aggression, and obsessions. The most commonly used and reportedly most effective class of antidepressant medications for children with ASD are the tricyclic antidepressants (e.g., Elavil, Norpramine, Pamelor, Tofranil). Side effects of these medications include nausea, loss of appetite, dry mouth, irritability, insomnia, and fatigue (Heflin & Simpson, 1998). Possible cardiovascular side effects and seizure threshold reduction suggest caution in using antidepressants for children with ASD (Aman & Langworthy, 2000).

Use of newer antidepressant medications that block serotonin reuptake in the brain (SSRIs, or selective serotonin reuptake inhibitors) has shown mixed responses, with recent reports indicating no improvement in behavior. Prozac and Risperodal have been described as useful, yet effectiveness for children with ASD is poorly understood (M. M. Steele, 1997).

Antianxiety medications tend to have fewer side effects than many other medications and are generally considered to be effective for children with ASD. Most common among the antianxiety medications are Librium, Valium, Xanax, Atavin, Atarax, and Equanil (Heflin & Simpson, 1998).

Beta-blockers have been reported to be effective in reducing aggression, although empirical support is lacking (Heflin & Simpson, 1998). No single psychopharmacological intervention has been identified as the medication of choice to address aggression in individuals with ASD (King, 2000). Lithium is used to treat aggressiveness and hyperactivity, but its effectiveness for children with ASD is unknown.

A summary of the current research suggests that certain behaviors such as aggression, stereotypies, and self-injury may improve with pharmacological treatment, whereas improvement in the core deficits of autism (e.g., social interaction, communication) remains unclear. Both practical and conceptual problems have complicated the research findings to date (Volkmar, 2001). From a practical standpoint, variation in symptom expression for autism, problems in research design, and the lack of longitudinal studies have plagued past research. Often the procedures used to reflect change in behavior following pharmacological treatment have not considered the expertise in behavioral psychology (Volkmar, 2001). On the theoretical side, the tendency has been to apply treatment and consider the "why" afterwards. Interesting conceptual views about the diversity in the neurochemical systems of individuals with autism have been developed (Volkmar, 2001). These theoretical views, however, have not been able to account for the basic deficits in autism.

Consultation with or referral to a psychiatrist with experience treating children and adolescents with autism or other developmental disabilities is an important aspect of comprehensive, coordinated care. The primary care physician, however, can and should take an active role in prescribing, and monitoring the possible effects of, any medication used for a child with ASD. The primary care physician also has a responsibility to inform and communicate with families and service providers about the medications prescribed and possible effects to be monitored. Collaboration with other practitioners and families who have a consistent view of the child's behavior is critical in the use of psychopharmacology. Through care conferences and medical information exchanges with school personnel, the primary care provider can obtain accurate and reliable data on both positive changes in behavior and undesirable side effects.

Ultimately, the goal of medication for children with ASD is to help them take advantage of their learning opportunities across the core deficit areas (Gordon, 2000). As an intervention, pharmacology is also only one aspect of what should be a comprehensive treatment approach for children with ASD. (For a more comprehensive overview of psychopharmacological treatment in autism, see Campbell et al., 1987; Holm & Varley, 1989; or Volkmar, 2001.)

Dental Care. Because of the specific challenges related to the core deficits in autism, dental health may be compromised in several ways (Volkmar & Wiesner, 2004). Some children with ASD exhibit oral sensitivity and are highly resistant to routine hygiene measures. For example, many families report limits in their ability to accomplish tooth brushing with their children. Other children with ASD may have abnormal dietary practices (e.g., prolonged bottle dependence and bottle carrying) or an inability to clear food particles from their mouths. Further, sensory behaviors (e.g., tooth grinding) or self-injurious behaviors (e.g., hits to the face) and complications of seizures or medication (e.g., trauma, gum hyperplasia) may be observed in this population. All of these dental care challenges may require more aggressive management. On occasion, examinations and treatments may require appropriate and safe anesthesia techniques.

Coping with a visit to the dentist's office is often an additional stressor for families of children with ASD. The SLP can support families in planning ahead for a dental visit by putting together a social story or social script that outlines the steps of the visit. Opportunities to act out a play script or view a video model for "going to the dentist" with the accompanying social communication can be included as part of the plan for speech–language intervention.

Orthopedic Care and Physical Therapy. Although motor disability is not a typical hallmark of autism, differences in motor ability, tone, and posture can be seen in that population (see Chapter 7). Primary care providers may play a role in referring children with ASD for appropriate physical therapy support. This might be done for the child with hypotonia and motor delays or for the child with asymmetric muscle tone or posture who is at risk for contracture or scoliosis. It is important that primary care providers collaborate with physical therapists to determine the best course of action for individual children. SLPs are likely to be a part of the interdisciplinary team that supports the motor needs of children with ASD. It is important that strategies for physical therapy support are reinforced as SLPs implement their intervention plans.

Self-Care, Activities of Daily Living, and Occupational Therapy. Similar to all children with developmental disabilities, children with ASD may experience delays in the development of their self-care skills, such as dressing, bathing, grooming, and toileting. It is possible that children with ASD have a less inherent drive to comply with the social pressures related to self-care than is typical for children without ASD. Toilet training is often delayed while dealing with other priority goals such as language and communication. An interdisciplinary approach to toilet training using communication, behavioral, sensory, and nutritional support is critical. Appropriate dietary and medical management of constipation is a must for successful toilet training. Knowledgeable pediatricians who collaborate with families and other practitioners can effectively address issues of constipation in children with ASD. For example, the nutritionist can support a diet that is responsive to the child's needs; an occupational therapist can evaluate the child's fine motor and adaptive abilities, clothing requirements, and the bathroom environment; and an SLP can design a communication system that gives the child a vehicle for communicating toileting needs. The SLP can also collaborate with the family and the instructional assistant to create a social story or script for implementing the toileting process. A psychologist can be asked to initiate a protocol to shape the child's behavior toward successful and independent toileting skills.

Pain or Acute Illness. Children with autism are at risk for underreporting pain symptoms from injury or illness, which places them at risk for later diagnosis and complications. It has been suggested that children with ASD send less clear affective messages using facial expressions than do children without ASD (Mundy & Sigman, 1989). It may be difficult to interpret what children with ASD are feeling just by looking at their facial expressions. This is an important distinction from other children, since families often use children's facial expressions, particularly when their communication skills are limited, to detect pain, discomfort, and illness. Further, the ability to coordinate multiple nonverbal cues increases the salience of a communicative act, as well as the likelihood of a response (Stone, Ousley, Yoder, Hogan, & Hepburn, 1997), yet children with ASD are limited in their ability to coordinate gestures with vocalizations (Wetherby, Prizant, & Hutchinson, 1998).

Recent research examining the expression of pain in children with autism during needle sticks for blood drawing or injections indicates that children with autism exhibit notable facial pain reactions, and that parental reports of pain are fewer than actual observed pain responses (Nader, Oberlander, Chambers, & Craig, 2004). The children's pain responses were similar to those of a comparison group without autism, although the facial responses to pain of the children with autism exceeded those of children without autism. Further, although parental reports of pain did not differ between the two groups, there was closer alignment between parental report and observed pain response for the children without autism than for the children with autism (Nader et al., 2004). These findings are in contrast with previous research suggesting that children with autism display pain insensitivity (American Psychiatric Association, 2000; Baranek & Berkson, 1994; Gillberg, 1995). Given their challenges in language and social responsiveness, children with ASD have a distinct disadvantage in pain expression and interpretation. They are also at risk for undermanagement of pain because of varying beliefs about pain sensitivity in this population (Nader et al., 2004). It is important, therefore, that families, primary health care providers, and other practitioners involved in the care of this population be alert to these challenges.

Health practitioners should listen carefully to parents and caregivers who notice changes in a child's behavior or sense that a child "just isn't himself." A more comprehensive examination may be required if the individual cannot isolate the location of pain or discomfort. It is important for all providers to include in a child's educational plan a method for the child to report pain, injury, or illness symptoms. Use of picture symbols representing pain may be a useful strategy. The SLP can work with the family and other practitioners to develop a communication system that provides opportunities for children with ASD to communicate their pain or discomfort in a manner that is meaningful to them and can be interpreted by others. In addition, practitioners and families can engage in some preassessment of behaviors that may be related to pain and watch for changes in these behaviors as they relate to health conditions such as ear infections, fevers, flu, and colds. This observation can provide a baseline for understanding and interpreting the subtle symptoms children with ASD may be exhibiting. Figure 12.3 provides one example of a preassessment of pain and illness that may be useful.

Safety and Sexuality. Personal safety is a real concern for any child with social, communication, and cognitive challenges. Children with ASD often take longer to understand safety concepts and exhibit unusual sensory interests that put them at risk for accidents that could potentially lead to death (Volkmar & Wiesner, 2004). Issues to consider include but are not limited to pica and lead intoxication, other accidental poisoning, street safety (e.g., because of wandering and bolting), and water safety (e.g., because of approaching water without fear). Childproofing the house or other environments of the child with autism may need to be extended beyond what parents would typically do for other children. Evaluation of blood lead level is indicated in cases of pica. Appropriate medical treatments and environmental treatments (painting old surfaces, providing ground cover outside houses where lead paint has been scraped, and other measures) are also indicated. The removal of lead from a house should be managed by a professional service and in consultation with the local health department to avoid actually increasing the amount of lead in the environment while repairs are attempted. A child with iron deficiency anemia and pica should receive treatment for the iron deficiency. For general safety, medical alert bracelets or other forms of identification should be considered, particularly for children with ASD who have insufficient verbal communication skills and who may wander off and become lost. Social stories, scripting, and video review (as discussed in Chapter 9) are strategies that can be used by teachers and families who are concerned about specific aspects of street and water safety to enhance the safety awareness of children with ASD.

Further, children with ASD may not develop the same understanding of the dangers in society as other children. Therefore, they are at greater potential risk for abuse (physical and sexual) and are less likely to be able to report or describe instances of abuse. In particular, children with mental retardation tend to be more vulnerable to sexual exploitation. A lack of knowledge of what is acceptable behavior, the desire and need to be accepted by peers, and an unconditional trust in others all contribute to an increased risk (Sobses, 1991). Some families and providers have used visuals to enhance children's awareness of those individuals with whom they can be safe. Concentric circles are drawn with names of those closest to the child placed in the center of the circle. Gradually, those less familiar or unknown to the child are placed in the outer circles. The child with ASD is then taught acceptable ways to touch or be touched by those closest to him compared to those who are less familiar or strangers.

Assessment of Pain or Illness for Children with ASD

Child's name: _____

Observer: _____ Date: _____

What gestures does the child use when he or she appears to be in pain or not feeling well? (Check all that apply.)

☐ Pulls at area of the body that hurts.

☐ Points to area of the body that hurts.

☐ Rubs area of the body that hurts.

☐ Takes another's hand and touches the area that hurts.

☐ Protects area of the body that hurts.

☐ Flails arms or hands more than usual.

☐ Reaches for comfort when not expected.

☐ Other:_____

What changes in behavior are observed when the child appears to be in pain or not feeling well? (Check all that apply.)

☐ Withdraws more than usual.

☐ Talks or makes sounds less than usual.

☐ Screams more than usual.

☐ Increases crying.

☐ Changes sleeping pattern. (Describe: _____)

☐ Changes eating pattern. (Describe: _____)

☐ Becomes more agitated than usual.

☐ Changes activity level. (Describe: _____)

☐ Other:_____

What facial expressions are observed when the child appears to be in pain or not feeling well? (Check all that apply.)

☐ Grimaces

☐ Closes eyes

☐ Pouts

(continues)

FIGURE 12.3. Assessment of pain or illness for children with ASD.

☐ Quivers lips

☐ Grinds teeth more than usual

☐ Covers ears more than usual

☐ Other:_____

What vocal behaviors are observed when the child appears to be in pain or not feeling well? (Check all that apply.)

☐ Moans

☐ Whines

☐ Whimpers

☐ Screams or cries out

☐ Uses a specific sound or word. (Describe: _____)

☐ Other:_____

What physiological behaviors are observed when the child appears to be in pain or not feeling well? (Check all that apply.)

☐ Shivering or shaking

☐ Changes in skin color

☐ Perspiration

☐ Breathing changes. (Describe: _____)

☐ Other:_____

FIGURE 12.3. *Continued.*

Changes in behavior without an apparent source of pain or illness should heighten the practitioner's suspicion of potential abuse. Increased anxiety, depression, agitation or aggression, avoidance of particular situations or people, and withdrawal are additional signs of abuse (Volkmar & Wiesner, 2004). Teaching children with ASD social and safety boundaries and the communication skills to respond to unsafe situations is worth advocating for in educational or developmental service plans.

Sleep Problems. Research suggests that children with ASD may be more likely to experience difficulties with sleep than other groups of children (des Portes et al., 2003; Richdale, 1999; Richdale & Prior, 1995). Problems have been identified in the onset of sleep, sleep maintenance, early waking, irregular sleep–wake patterns, and sleep routines and occur with high frequency regardless of intellectual level (Richdale, 1999). Although the causes of sleep problems in autism are currently unknown, there are important associations between difficulties with sleep in children with ASD and communication challenges and difficult behavior during the day. Richdale (1999) suggests that "routines and social cues are thought to help young infants develop stable sleep–wake patterns with the longest sleep occurring during the night hours" (p. 62). Children with ASD who exhibit social communication impairments are likely to have difficulty using those cues to control their rhythms, leading to sleep–wake problems (Johnson, 1996; Richdale, 1999).

Sleep disturbances in autism create additional stress for families and require intervention strategies that are responsive to the needs of the child and the family. Intervention requires an interdisciplinary perspective in which a thorough history is taken regarding past and current sleep–wake behaviors and patterns. Both behavioral strategies and pharmacological treatments related to regulating the sleep–wake cycle (e.g., the use of melatonin) have been used to manage reported sleep difficulties. Other pharmacological treatments to address sleep problems have included clonidine and trazodone (des Portes et al., 2003). Families who have received some help managing their children's sleep problems most often report satisfaction with behavioral approaches (Wiggs & Stores, 1996). Establishing appropriate bedtime routines is one behavioral strategy for which effectiveness has been reported (Piazza, Fisher, & Sherer, 1997; Richdale, 1999). The speech–language pathologist may provide support to families of children with ASD who display sleep problems by working with the team to design a bedtime script that can be pictured or to develop a social story around a bedtime routine that can be read each night to the child, identifying the relevant social behaviors associated with going to sleep.

Summary

This chapter has discussed the quality of health care a child with ASD should have access to and the level of collaboration required among all parties involved to ensure the child's quality of life. Specific medical needs related to autism itself can arise and are affected by the communication, social, and behavioral challenges inherent in the disorder. A medical home can and should be established to address the medical needs of children with ASD, and specific strategies can be employed among all practitioners involved to ensure consistent, efficient, and effective health care. The key questions posed at the beginning of this chapter are addressed in the following paragraphs.

What is the role of a "medical home" in the health care that children with ASD require?

The medical home must accommodate the specific and individual differences of children with ASD. Maintenance of a problem list and collaboration with families and other practitioners involved in the care of children with

ASD are important strategies for ensuring coordinated care. The medical home concept is particularly well suited to the care of children with ASD, because of their often subtle but intense and variable health needs.

What is the importance of a coordinated and comprehensive plan for addressing the health issues of children with ASD?

The role of case management, or care coordination, has evolved over the years to support more effectively the needs of children with special health and developmental concerns. With the potential for a variety of health-related conditions, the child with ASD is a particularly good candidate for development of a comprehensive and well-coordinated plan. Although the core deficit areas for ASD make it difficult for physicians to complete their assessments in a traditional way, their collaboration with families and other practitioners is more likely to lead to an integrated plan for the child's health.

What health-related strategies can be considered to support the ability of children with ASD to interact socially, communicate, play, and sustain their behavior so that they can learn and actively participate in their environments?

All practitioners interested in responsive care for children with ASD can participate in the implementation of several strategies designed to improve the children's health and quality of life. Primary health care providers can and should collaborate with families and other practitioners to ensure efficient and effective health care maintenance, seizure monitoring, genetic follow-up, adequate nutrition and growth, mental health support, dental follow-up, therapeutic support for motor difficulties, development of self-care skills, and responses to safety and sexuality concerns. Although health concerns are often seen as the primary responsibility of the physician, it has become clear that because the communication, social interaction, and behavioral deficits so often characteristic of children with ASD affect the accessibility and consistency of adequate health care, it is important to engage families and related service providers (e.g., SLPs, psychologists, nurses) in the implementation of coordinated care. For example, SLPs can identify children's challenges in communication and determine how those challenges may affect the ability of children and adolescents with ASD to express their pain or discomfort. Collaboration among health care and related service providers increases the likelihood that children with ASD will participate fully in their home, school, and community activities.

Practice Opportunities

1. As a team, complete Figure 12.3 for a child with ASD whom you suspect may be having pain or not feeling well although neither the family nor the practitioners who work with the child can detect a consistent pattern of behavior indicating pain or ill health.

2. Create a social story for a child with ASD who is preparing to go on a field trip with his class but has a tendency to bolt and for whom safety concerns are affecting his ability to participate with his class.

3. If you know a child with ASD who exhibits seizure-like activity, complete the observation form in Figure 12.2 and share that information with the child's primary health care provider.

4. Set up a care conference for a child with ASD who has several health concerns, including constipation, a limited diet, and seizure-like activity. As a team, establish an agenda for the conference and determine a format for medical information to be shared among the team players across settings.

Suggested Readings

American Academy of Pediatrics, Committee on Children with Disabilities. (2001). Counseling families who choose complementary and alternative medicine for their child with chronic illness or disability. *Pediatrics, 107*(3), 598–601.

To best serve the interest of children, it is important to maintain a scientific perspective, to provide balanced advice about therapeutic options, to guard against bias, and to establish and maintain a trusting relationship with families. This statement provides information and guidance when counseling families about complementary and alternative medicine.

American Academy of Pediatrics, Committee on Children with Disabilities. (2001). Technical report: The pediatrician's role in the diagnosis and management of autistic spectrum disorder in children. *Pediatrics, 107,* 1221–1226.

Because pediatricians share the challenge of making an accurate and early diagnosis and implementing a timely intervention program, collaboration between pediatricians and the families they serve is essential. This technical report provides 12 key recommendations that have important implications for consultation among all health practitioners interested in the care of children with ASD.

Filipek, P. A., Accardo, P. J., Ashwal, S., Baranek, G. T., Cook, E. H., & Dawson, G. (2000). Practice parameters: Screening and diagnosis of autism: Report of the Quality Standards Committee of the American Academy of Neurology and the Child Neurology Society. *Neurology, 55,* 468–479.

This article summarizes the practice guidelines for both surveillance and diagnostic assessment of children suspected of ASD. The practice parameters were developed in collaboration with practitioners from a variety of disciplines interested in the quality health care of children with ASD.

Volkmar, F. R., & Wiesner, L. A. (2004). *Healthcare for children on the autism spectrum: A guide to medical, nutritional, and behavioral issues.* Bethesda, MD: Woodbine House.

This book provides families and professionals with a comprehensive look at the health care issues that affect individuals with ASD. The authors provide critical information related to handling such concerns as emergency room visits, safety, sleep problems, seizure disorders, dental care, medications for challenging behaviors, nutrition, growth, and sexuality.

Resources

Information on Dental Care

American Dental Association. (1991). *Dental care for special people.* Chicago: Author.

Chicago Dental Society, http://www.chicagodentalsociety.org

Kunz, J. R. M., & Finkel, A. J. (1987). *The American Medical Association family medical guide.* New York: Random House.

National Foundation of Dentistry for the Handicapped 1997–1998 NFDH Report; 1800 15th Street, Unit 100, Denver, CO 80202, 303/534-5360, 303/534-5290 (fax).

National Institute of Dental Research Public Information Office, 31 Center Drive, MSC 2290, Bethesda, MD 20892-2290.

Information on Medications

Research Units in Pediatric Psychopharmacology. (2002). Risperidone in children with autism and serious behavioral problems. *New England Journal of Medicine, 347,* 314–321.

Tsai, L. (2001). *Taking the mystery out of medications in autism and Asperger syndrome: A guide for parents and non-medical professionals.* Arlington, TX: Future Horizons.

Wilens, T. E. (1999). *Straight talk about psychiatric medications for kids.* New York: Guilford Press.

Information on the Medical Home

American Academy of Pediatrics, *AAP Clinical Practice Guidelines,* http://www.aap.org/policy/paramtoc.html

American Academy of Pediatrics, *Recommendations for Preventative Pediatric Health Care,* http://www.aap.org/policy/re9939.html

Information on Nutrition

American Dietetic Association, http://www.eatright.org

Jackson, L. (2002). *A user guide to the GF/CF diet for autism, Asperger syndrome and AD/HD.* Philadelphia: Jessica Kingsley.

Legge, B. (2002). *Can't eat, won't eat: Dietary difficulties and autistic spectrum disorders.* Philadelphia: Jessica Kingsley.

Tamborlane, W. V. (1997). *The Yale guide to children's nutrition.* New Haven, CT: Yale University Press.

Information on Safety

Davis, B., & Schunick, W. G. (2002). *Dangerous encounters—Avoiding perilous situations with autism: A streetwise guide for all emergency responders, retailers and parents.* Philadelphia: Jessica Kingsley.

Debbaudt, D. (2001). *Autism, advocates, and law enforcement professionals: Recognizing and reducing risk situations for people with autism spectrum disorders.* Philadelphia: Jessica Kingsley.

Kahn, R. (2001). *Too safe for strangers.* Arlington, TX: Future Horizons.

Kahn, R., & Chandler, S. (2001). *Too smart for bullies.* Arlington, TX: Future Horizons.

Information on Seizures and Epilepsy

Epilepsy Foundation, http://www.epilepsyfoundation.org

Moshe, S. L., Pellock, J. M., & Salon, M. C. (1992). *The Parke-Davis manual on epilepsy.* New York: KSF Group.

Information on Sexuality

Amory, I. B. (1980). *Sexual behavior and awareness: Social awareness, hygiene, and sex education for the mentally retarded and developmentally disabled.* Springfield, IL: Charles C Thomas.

Johnson, W. R., & Kempton, W. (1981). *Sex education and counseling of special groups: The mentally and physically disabled, and elderly.* Springfield, IL: Charles C Thomas.

Kempton, W. (1991). *Sex education for persons with disabilities that hinder learning: A teacher's guide* (2nd ed.). Hartford, PA: James Stanfield.

Kempton, W., Gordon, S., & Bass, M. (1986). *Love, sex, and birth control for the mentally retarded: A guide for parents.* Philadelphia: Planned Parenthood Association of Southwestern Pennsylvania.

Kroll, K., & Klein, E. (1992). *Enabling romance: A guide to love, sex, and relationships for disabled people (and the people who can help them).* New York: Crown.

McCarthy, W., & Feger, L. (1984). *Sex education and the intellectually handicapped.* Sydney, Australia: ADIS Health Science Press.

McKee, L., & Blacklidge, V. (1981). *An easy guide for caring parents: A book for parents of people with mental handicaps—Sexuality and socialization.* Walnut Creek, CA: Planned Parenthood of Contra Costa.

National Information Center for Children & Youth with Disabilities. (1992). Sexuality education for children and youth with disabilities. *NICHCY News Digest.* Retrieved May 5, 2005, from http://www.nichcy.org

Newport, J., & Newport, M. (2002). *Autism–Asperger's & sexuality: Puberty and beyond.* Arlington, TX: Future Horizons.

Realmuto, G. M., & Ruble, L. A. (1999). Sexual behaviors in autism: Problems in definition and management. *Journal of Autism and Developmental Disorders, 29*(2), 121–127.

Rowe, W. (1987). *Sexuality and the developmentally handicapped.* Queenston, Ontario: Edwin Mellen Press.

Schwier, K. M., & Hingsburger, D. (2000). *Sexuality: Your sons and daughters with intellectual disabilities.* Baltimore: Brookes.

Sobses, D., Gray, S., Wells, D., Pyper, D., & Reimer-Heck, B. (Eds.). (1991). *Disability, sexuality and abuse: An annotated bibliography* (pp. ix–xii). Baltimore: Brookes.

Valenti-Hein, D. C., & Mueser, K. T. (1991). *The dating skills program: Teaching social–sexual skills to adults with mental retardation.* Orland Park, IL: International Diagnostic Systems.

Way, P. (1982). *The need to know: Sexuality and the disabled child for parents of children with physical, sensory, or developmental disabilities.* Eureka, CA: Planned Parenthood Association of Humboldt County.

Information on Sleep

Durand, V. M. (1998). *Sleep better! A guide to improving sleep for children with special needs.* Baltimore: Brookes.

Glossary

Absence seizure. A generalized nonfocal seizure that involves a temporary loss of consciousness characterized by staring, eye fluttering, or possibly facial twitching.

Akinetic. A generalized nonfocal seizure that involves brief muscle jerks in the arms or head.

Anthropometric. Relating to the measurement of the body.

Atonic. A generalized nonfocal seizure that can involve loss of muscle tone and possible loss of consciousness.

Body mass index. Generated by a mathematical formula using weight and height measurements, indicates levels of body fat to other body mass.

Care conference. A conference of families and service providers to discuss care plans for a child.

Care coordination. Service provision required for children with complex health and developmental needs.

Casein. Protein found in milk and milk products.

Case management. A process for coordinating the services for individuals with special needs.

Complex partial seizure. An abnormal variable response to the environment that can involve a person losing consciousness; usually starts in one part of the brain and generalizes to other parts.

Contracture. Abnormal angle of a joint usually caused by severely increased muscle tone or spasticity and limiting the normal movement of that joint.

Fragile X syndrome. A genetic condition previously known to cause a fragile site on the X chromosome and now recognized by excess copies of a "nonsense" sequence of DNA. Can expand itself in each generation, leading to a "carrier state," or full expression with mental retardation, abnormal physical features, and odd or autistic behavior.

Gluten. A protein in wheat and rye and to a lesser extent in oats and barley.

Landau-Kleffner syndrome. Also known as epileptiform aphasia, or electrical status epilepticus during slow-wave sleep (ESES); a syndrome defined by onset of abnormal electrical brain wave discharges, with resultant loss of language skills. Unclear association with language regression in autism.

Medical home. An office-based practice committed to the development of partnerships with families who have children with special health needs.

Neurotransmitter. A chemical substance secreted across the nerve synapse (junction) to stimulate successive transmission of nerve impulses.

Opioid properties. Chemical effects similar to those of opium or other narcotic medication.

Orthomolecular theory. Theory that a condition can be treated by providing normally present substances in optimal concentrations.

Peptides. Chains of amino acids that combine to form proteins.

Pica. Eating of nonfood substances.

Problem list. List of an individual's medical problems (active or inactive) within the problem-oriented medical record.

Problem-oriented medical record. A medical records system that contains a database of historical information, laboratory results, and physical exam findings; a problem list of active and resolved problems; initial plans that address the problems; and progress notes that document ongoing efforts to resolve a problem.

Psychopharmacology. Study of the effects of medications on mind and behavior.

Scoliosis. Curvature of the spine often caused by imbalances of muscle tone or weakness.

Serotonin. One of the chemical neurotransmitter substances implicated in the etiology or treatment of central nervous system disorders.

Simple partial seizure. Seizure that is manifested in only one part of the body—for example, by the eyes rolling back or the head dropping.

Tonic-clonic seizure. A generalized nonfocal seizure with a variety of symptoms, including loss of consciousness and an alteration of contracting and relaxing muscle groups.

Tricyclic. Containing three closed chains in the molecular structure.

References

Adams, L., & Conn, S. (1997). Nutrition and its relationships to autism. *Focus on Autism and Other Developmental Disabilities, 12*(1), 53–58.

Aman, M. G., & Langworthy, K. S. (2000). Pharmacotherapy for hyperactivity in children with autism and other pervasive developmental disorders. *Journal of Autism and Developmental Disorders, 30*(5), 451–459.

American Academy of Pediatrics. (1992). The medical home. *Pediatrics, 90,* 774.

American Academy of Pediatrics. (2002). The Medical Home, *Pediatrics, 110*(1), 184–186.

American Academy of Pediatrics Committee on Children with Disabilities. (1999). Care coordination: Integrating health and related systems of care for children with special health care needs. *Pediatrics, 104*(4), 978–981.

American Academy of Pediatrics Committee on Children with Disabilities. (2001). Counseling families who choose complementary and alternative medicine for their child with chronic illness or disability. *Pediatrics, 107*(3), 598–601.

American Academy of Pediatrics Committee on Practice and Ambulatory Medicine. (2000). Recommendations for preventive pediatric health care (RE9939). *Pediatrics, 105*(3), 645.

American Psychiatric Association. (2000). *Diagnostic and statistical manual of mental disorders* (4th ed., text rev.). Washington, DC: Author.

Appleton, P. L., Boll, V., Everett, J. M., Kelly, A. M., Meredith, K. H., & Payne, T. G. (1997). Beyond child development centres: Care coordination for children with disabilities. *Child: Care, Health and Development, 23*(1), 29–40.

Baranek, G. T., & Berkson, G. (1994). Tactile defensiveness in children with developmental disabilities: Responsiveness and habituation. *Journal of Autism and Developmental Disorders, 24,* 457–471.

Campbell, M., Perry, R., Small, A. M., & Green, W. H. (1987). Overview of drug treatment in autism. In E. Schopler & G. Mesibov (Eds.), *Neurobiological issues in autism* (pp. 341–356). New York: Plenum Press.

Case-Smith, J. (1991). Occupational and physical therapists as case managers in early intervention. *Physical and Occupational Therapy in Pediatrics, 11*(1), 53–70.

des Portes, V., Hagerman, R. J., & Hendren, R. L. (2003). Pharmacotherapy. In S. Ozonoff, S. J. Rogers, & R. L. Hendren (Eds.), *Autism spectrum disorders: A research review for practitioners* (pp. 161–186). Washington, DC: American Psychiatric Publishing.

Eisenberg, D. M., Davis, R. B., Ettner, S. L., Appel, S., Wilkey, S., Van Rompay, M., et al. (1998). Trends in alternative medicine use in the United States, 1990–1997: Results of a follow-up national survey. *Journal of the American Medical Association, 280,* 1569–1575.

Etheridge, M. L. (Ed.). (1989). *Collaborative care: Nursing case management.* Chicago: American Hospital Publishing.

Fiene, J. I., & Taylor, P. A. (1991). Serving rural families of developmentally disabled children: A case management model. *Social Work, 36*(4), 323–327.

Filipek, P. A., Accardo, P. J., Ashwal, S., Baranek, G. T., Cook, E. H., & Dawson, G. (2000). Practice parameters: Screening and diagnosis of autism: Report of the Quality Standards Committee of the American Academy of Neurology and the Child Neurology Society. *Neurology, 55,* 468–479.

Fisman, S. (1997). Pharmacotherapy of the pervasive developmental disorders: A practical approach. *Child and Adolescent Psychopharmacology News, 2*(4), 1–4.

Freedman, S. A., Pierce, P. M., & Reiss, J. G. (1987). REACH: A family-centered, community-based case management model for children with special health needs. *Children's Health Care, 16*(2), 114–117.

Gillberg, C. (1995). Endogenous opioids and opiate antagonists in autism: Brief review of empirical findings and implications for clinicians. *Developmental Medicine and Child Neurology, 37,* 239–245.

Gonzalez-Calvo, J., Jackson, J., Hansford, C., Woodman, C., & Remington, N. (1997). Nursing case management and its role in perinatal risk reduction: Development, implementation, and evaluation of a culturally competent model for African-American women. *Public Health Nursing, 14*(4), 190–206.

Gordon, C. T. (2000). Psychopharmacological treatments for symptoms and behaviors in autism spectrum disorders. *Advocate, 33*(6), 28–31.

Green, M. (Ed.). (1994). *Bright futures: Guidelines for health supervision of infants, children, and adolescents.* Arlington, VA: National Center for Education in Maternal and Child Health.

Heflin, L. J., & Simpson, R. L. (1998). Interventions for children and youth with autism: Prudent choices in a world of exaggerated claims and empty promises. Part I: Intervention and treatment option review. *Focus on Autism and Other Developmental Disabilities, 13*(4), 194–211.

Holm, V. A., & Varley, C. K. (1989). Pharmacological treatment of autistic children. In G. Dawson (Ed.), *Autism: Nature, diagnosis and treatment* (pp. 386–404). New York: Guilford Press.

Jackson, B., Finkler, D., & Robinson, C. (1992). A case management system for infants with chronic illnesses and developmental disabilities. *Children's Health Care, 21*(4), 224–232.

Johnson, C. R. (1996). Sleep problems in children with mental retardation and autism. *Child and Adolescent Psychiatric Clinics of North America, 5,* 673–683.

King, B. H. (2000). Pharmacological treatment of mood disturbances, aggression, and self-injury in persons with pervasive developmental disorders. *Journal of Autism and Developmental Disorders, 30*(5), 439–445.

King, B. H., Wright, M., Handen, B. L., Sikich, L., Zimmerman, A. W., MacMahon, W., et al. (2001). Double-blind, placebo-controlled study of amantadine hydrochloride in the treatment of children with autistic disorder. *Journal of the American Academy of Child and Adolescent Psychiatry, 40,* 658–665.

Knivsberg, A. M., Reichelt, K. L., Nodland, M., & Hoien, T. (1995). Autistic syndromes and diet: A follow-up study. *Scandinavian Journal of Educational Research, 39*(3), 223–236.

Mundy, P., & Sigman, M. (1989). Specifying the nature of the social impairment in autism. In G. Dawson (Ed.), *Autism, nature, diagnosis and treatment* (pp. 3–21). New York: Guilford Press.

Nader, R., Oberlander, T. F., Chambers, C. T., & Craig, K. D. (2004). Expression of pain in children with autism. *Clinical Journal of Pain, 20*(2), 88–97.

National Institutes of Health. (2001). *Emotional and behavioral health in persons with mental retardation/developmental disabilities: Research challenges and opportunities* [Executive Summary]. Rockville, MD: Author.

Nickel, R. E. (1996). Controversial therapies for young children with developmental disabilities. *Infants and Young Children, 8,* 29–40.

Pfeiffer, S. I., Norton, J., Nelson, L., & Shott, S. (1995). Efficacy of vitamin B_6 and magnesium in the treatment of autism: A methodology review and summary of outcomes. *Journal of Autism and Developmental Disorders, 25*(5), 481–493.

Piazza, C. C., Fisher, W. W., & Sherer, M. (1997). Treatment of multiple sleep problems in children with developmental disabilities: Faded bedtime with response cost versus bedtime scheduling. *Developmental Medicine and Child Neurology, 39,* 414–418.

Quinn, H. P., & Levine, K. (1995). Nutrition concerns for children with pervasive developmental disorder/autism. *Nutrition for Children with Special Health Care Needs Focus, 10*(5), 1–7.

Raiten, D. J., & Massaro, T. (1986). Perspectives on the nutritional ecology of autistic children. *Journal of Autism and Developmental Disorders, 16*(2), 133–143.

Rapin, I. (1997). Autism. *New England Journal of Medicine, 337,* 97–104.

Rapin, I., & Tuchman R. F. (1997). Regression in pervasive developmental disorders: Seizures and epileptiform electroencephalogram correlates. *Pediatrics, 99,* 560–566.

Richdale, A. L. (1999). Sleep problems in autism: Prevalence, cause and intervention. *Developmental Medicine & Child Neurology, 41,* 60–66.

Richdale, A. L., & Prior, M. R. (1995). The sleep–wake rhythm in children with autism. *European Child and Adolescent Psychiatry, 4,* 175–186.

Rossi, P. G., Posar, A., & Parmegiani, A. (2000). Epilepsy in adolescents and young adults with autistic disorder. *Brain Development, 22,* 102–106.

Rothman, J. (1991). A model of case management: Toward empirically based practice. *Social Work, 36*(6), 520–528.

Sobses, D. (1991). Toward a scientific understanding: An introduction. In D. Sobses, S. Gray, D. Wells, D. Pyper, & B. Reimer-Heck (Eds.), *Disability, sexuality and abuse: An annotated bibliography* (pp. ix–xii). Baltimore: Brookes.

Steele, M. M. (1997). The use of risperidone in pervasive developmental disorders. *Child and Adolescent Psychopharmacology News, 2*(4), 5, 8.

Steele, S. (1993). Nurse and parent collaborative case management in a rural setting. *Pediatric Nursing, 19*(6), 612–615.

Stone, W. L., Ousley, O. Y., Yoder, P. J., Hogan, K. L., & Hepburn, S. L. (1997). Nonverbal communication in two- and three-year-old children with autism. *Journal of Autism and Developmental Disorders, 27*(6), 677–696.

Thiele, E. (2001, June). *Seizure disorders and their relationship to patterns of developmental disability.* Presentation at the annual Vermont Rural Autism Project Summer Institute, Burlington.

Tsai, L. Y. (1992). Medical treatment in autism. In D. E. Berkell (Ed.), *Autism: Identification, education and treatment* (pp. 151–184). Hillsdale, NJ: Erlbaum.

Tsai, L. Y. (1998). Medical interventions for students with autism. In R. L. Simpson & B. S. Myles (Eds.), *Educating children and youth with autism: Strategies for effective practice* (pp. 277–314). Austin, TX: PRO-ED.

Vitiello, B. (2000). Current research highlights in child and adolescent psychopharmacology. *Current Psychiatric Reports, 2*, 110–116.

Volkmar, F. R. (2001). Pharmacological interventions in autism: Theoretical and practical issues. *Journal of Clinical Child Psychology, 30*(1), 80–87.

Volkmar, F. R., & Wiesner, L. A. (2004). *Healthcare for children on the autism spectrum: A guide to medical, nutritional, and behavioral issues.* Bethesda, MD: Woodbine House.

Weil, M., & Karls, J. M. (1985). Historical origins and recent developments. In M. Weil & J. M. Karls (Eds.), *Case management in human service practice* (pp. 1–28). San Francisco: Josssey-Bass.

Wetherby, A. M., Prizant, B. M., & Hutchinson, T. A. (1998). Communicative, social/affective, and symbolic profiles of young children with autism and pervasive developmental disorders. *American Journal of Speech–Language Pathology, 7*, 79–91.

Wiggs, L., & Stores, G. (1996). Sleep problems in children with severe intellectual disabilities: What help is being provided? *Journal of Applied Research in Intellectual Disabilities, 9*, 160–165.

Wilens, T. E. (1999). *Straight talk about psychiatric medications for kids.* New York: Guilford Press.

Wilson, G. N., & Cooley, W. C. (2000). *Preventive management of children with congenital anomalies and syndromes.* Cambridge, England: Cambridge University Press.

World Health Organization. (2001). *International classification of functioning, disability and health.* Geneva: Author.

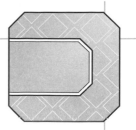

CHAPTER 13

Inclusionary Practice for Children with ASD

Patricia A. Prelock

QUESTIONS TO CONSIDER

In this chapter, you will learn about the benefits and challenges of inclusive education for children with autism spectrum disorders (ASD) and about strategies that effective Individualized Education Program (IEP) teams might use to support the learning experience for this population. You will also learn how educational teams can support the integration and transitions of children with ASD in an educational setting. As you read this chapter on inclusionary practice for children with ASD, consider the following questions:

1. What is the role of inclusive education for children with ASD?

2. What are the strategies that effective IEP teams can use to ensure an inclusive educational community for children with ASD?

3. How can teams support the integration and transitions of children with ASD across grade levels in general education settings?

Introduction

Special education has experienced dramatic reform over the last 30 years. Minimum education requirements for children with disabilities were first established with the Education of the Handicapped Act in 1970 (Public Law [P.L.] 91-230). Its amendment in 1975 to the Education for All Handicapped Children Act, (P.L. 94-142) provided the framework for special education as it is known today (Moore-Brown & Montgomery, 2001). It mandated the provision of a free appropriate public education for children with disabilities, ages 5 to 21 years, in the least restrictive environment possible.

Several revisions and amendments have occurred since then, as well as initiatives to ensure better educational opportunities for special populations. The Regular Education Initiative (REI) in 1985 evolved as a result of research suggesting the benefits of mainstreaming for children with special education needs. In 1986, P.L. 99-457 was added to institute services for preschoolers (3 to 5 years), as well as to initiate transition services and services to children under 3 years old. The 1990 amendments renamed the law (P.L. 101-476) to the Individuals with Disabilities Education Act (IDEA). It was in these amendments that new definitions for eligibility were provided, including a separate category for autism. That same year, the Americans with Disabilities Act (P.L. 101-336) was also signed, to define those practices considered discriminatory and illegal and to ensure reasonable accommodations for individuals with disabilities. Amendments to IDEA occurred again in 1997 to address issues like access to the curriculum and discipline policies. Most recently, the 2004 reauthorization of IDEA requires additional accountability for the delivery of services and greater recognition of the role of the general education teacher and the family in the educational planning for a child with special needs.

With all of this change to special education, struggles remain at several levels. Some of these include improvement in scholastic performance, access to the general education curriculum, support for successful transitions, placement in the least restrictive environment, prevention of school dropouts, behavior management, service coordination, full family participation, and resolution of disputes through mediation. Schools also struggle to effectively hire, train, and maintain special educators in their systems. Therefore, the challenges so often experienced by families with children affected by autism are part of a larger system of service that is struggling to do the job IDEA intended for all children with special education needs.

The focus of this chapter is inclusive education for children and adolescents with ASD. I recognize, however, that an inclusive environment may not be the least restrictive environment for those students with ASD who have intensive behavioral, educational, and vocational needs. They may require a more segregated, centered-based program with highly trained and experienced personnel who can manage the significant challenges that often accompany children with autism. Although the hope remains for all children to be educated within their home community and school, students have a right to an education that addresses their needs in a meaningful way, and parents have a right to request an educational program that is responsive to their child's needs.

Inclusive Education for Children with ASD

The inclusion movement began in 1985 with the REI, mentioned in the introduction, which called for increased integration of children with special needs. Unfortunately, the movement was driven by special education with no input from general education, which had its own educational reform agenda (i.e., commitment to excellence, meaning more time in school and more standards, courses, and homework) that would be seen by many as being in conflict with the REI (Moore-Brown & Montgomery, 2001). More common ground in which general and special education work in partnership to break the barriers between them and transform the educational system is needed (Paul, Yang, Adiegbola, & Morse, 1995). Again, families of children with ASD are caught in the crossfire.

Giangreco, Cloninger, Dennis, and Edelman (2000) contrast traditional versus inclusion-oriented approaches to educating students with a range of diverse needs. Instruction types and teacher and student roles are different across approaches. For example, in a traditional instructional environment, the teacher is the leader and problem solver, while students are passive learners. In contrast, an inclusive instructional approach views the teacher's role as more collaborative, and learning and problem solving are achieved through collaboration between students and teachers. In traditional classrooms, similar ability levels dictate how children are grouped, and curriculum is determined by grade placement, while inclusive classrooms group students heterogeneously, and curriculum is not tied to grade level. Most important, students who do not "fit" well in a general education context are excluded from activities in a traditional model, but an inclusive model includes all students in the general education activities. Further, children being educated in an inclusive model are evaluated using individually developed criteria, as opposed to common standards, and the educational team assumes ownership for learning success for all students (Giangreco et al., 2000). Thus, inclusive educational environments create a place where everyone belongs and is supported to achieve their full potential. Students with ASD have the right to an inclusive education, and teams have a responsibility to define how best an inclusive approach to education might support the needs of students with ASD.

When it is thoughtfully developed and implemented, inclusion provides integration for a student at three levels: social, environmental, and programmatic. It can also be highly successful and richly supported by qualified and committed general and special educators who believe in the strengths of children and in building on those while accommodating the weaknesses without compromising learning potential. Full inclusion is characterized by heterogeneous grouping; that is, children of all abilities share the learning environment and a sense of community in which all children are perceived as belonging to the group. Participation in activities is inclusive, although the expected outcomes are individualized. Efforts for children with ASD should be no different. Practitioners must ensure that these children also have access to an individualized and balanced educational experience that allows them the benefits of sharing the experiences of their peers and fully participating in activities.

Many benefits of inclusive education for children with disabilities, including children with ASD, have been documented in the research (Harrower & Dunlap, 2001). For example, children with disabilities who have been fully included receive more social support, exhibit greater engagement and social interaction, have a larger number of friends, and have IEP goals that are more advanced than children with disabilities in noninclusive settings (Fryxell & Kennedy, 1995; Hunt, Farron-Davis, Beckstead, Curtis, & Goetz, 1994; Hunt & Goetz, 1997). The research also indicates that children without disabilities can be effective peer models for children with disabilities. Specifically, typical peer models, as discussed in Chapter 11, can be used effectively to support the social skill development of children with ASD (Kamps, Barbetta, Leonard, & Delquadri, 1994; Roeyers, 1996). In fact, students with severe disabilities in inclusive educational programs make significantly greater gains in their independence and social competence than their peers in self-contained programs (Fisher & Meyer, 2002).

Effective inclusionary practices have also been examined in early education. For example, Rafferty, Piscitelli, and Boettcher (2003) found that preschoolers with a range of disabilities in inclusive settings made greater progress in their language and social skill development than preschoolers with disabilities in segregated settings. The researchers caution, however, that all placement decisions should be individually determined and periodically reevaluated to determine the effectiveness with which children's goals and needs are being addressed. Much of the research on inclusive practices has also been done in model programs, from which the generalizability of the findings has been questioned (Buysse & Bailey, 1993). Yet research has also demonstrated that children both with and without disabilities can benefit from inclusion in early childhood settings. This is an important valued outcome for including children with ASD with their typical peers (Simpson & Sasso, 1992).

To examine further the components of quality inclusion in early childhood, Buysse, Skinner, and Grant (2001) conducted 92 individual interviews with families and professionals across 19 settings identified as high-quality inclusive preschool programs. Their results were presented across several dimensions: contributors, challenges, and strategies related to quality inclusive childcare; family involvement and support related to quality inclusive childcare; and the benefits of quality inclusive childcare. A global dimension of quality inclusion was the provision of developmentally appropriate practice. For serving children with disabilities, staff-to-child ratios and the integration of interventions and special services into classroom routines and activities were most often mentioned. A consistent challenge to achieving quality inclusion was individually addressing the needs of children with a variety of disabilities. Strategies for achieving success included consultation and collaboration with other professionals and using a variety of child-focused strategies (e.g., peer mediation intervention, environmental arrangement). Further, successful inclusive childcare settings had a family-friendly philosophy and procedures in place to communicate consistently and effectively between home and school. Finally, a powerful benefit of these inclusive settings was the improved development and learning of children with disabilities and the increased acceptance of children with differences. Although not specific to a population of children with ASD, the results of the study by Buysse and her colleagues provide a framework for both developing and evaluating quality inclusive education in early childhood settings for any child with a disability.

Educational placement options have expanded across the nation for children with ASD, moving from more center-based programs to special classes within general education programs and to integration within the general education classroom. Successful inclusionary efforts, however, require careful planning, development, and implementation (Wagner, 1998). In her description of the Emory Autism Resource Center Inclusion Project, Wagner identifies several components critical to successful inclusion. First, schools and the teams that serve children with ASD must believe that an inclusive setting can meet the needs of the students and that the students should have access to the learning that occurs in environments with typical peers. Second, support must exist within the administration to give teachers the type of support they will require to be optimally effective with the student with ASD. Third, teachers and instructional assistants require training in what autism is; how the core deficits affect learning, communication, social interaction, and behavior; and ways to effectively address the needs of children with ASD in the classroom. Fourth, special education support in the form of an inclusion coordinator or integration specialist is needed to ensure that the IEP is implemented and that guidance and support are provided to the primary interventionists. Fifth, collaboration among general education, special education, and families in the form of regular meetings involving all key interventionists and consistent communication are crucial if a student's program is to be appropriately modified and successfully implemented. Sixth, the use of an instructional assistant, teaching aid, or some level of trained individual support is needed for the student to have full access to the available academic and social opportunities in school. Seventh, a general education environment must be able to meet the IEP goals established for students with ASD, achieving progress that is data supported. Finally, with consistent and effective support from an integration specialist or inclusion coordinator, an instructional assistant or aid, and the administration, the general education teacher must take ownership for children with ASD if they are to become a part of the classroom community (Wagner, 1998).

Searching for educational programs that are equipped to manage the impairment children with ASD experience is not an easy task. Families want to consider programs that provide opportunities for their children to engage in a full range of activities that support their ultimate participation in the broader community, as described by the World Health Organization (2001) and mentioned throughout this book. Families should raise several questions as they consider the educational options for their children. Gartner and Lipsky (2000) highlight the role collaboration has in quality inclusive education. Based on the principles of collaborative schools, families might ask the following questions:

- What is happening at this school that tells me quality education is occurring?
- Have norms been collaboratively established for assessing students' ongoing improvement?
- Do teachers see themselves as responsible for the instructional process and the outcomes of their students?
- Is the administration working collaboratively with parents and teachers to achieve a quality educational environment?
- Are general education teachers involved in making decisions and implementing the goals of students with disabilities?
- How do general and special education teachers and related service providers partner to achieve effective education for students with disabilities?

Villa and Thousand (2000) suggest additional elements to establish and implement successful inclusive education. Based on their suggestions, families might also ask,

- Is diversity valued in this school?
- Is the principal an active school leader?
- Is there a sense of belonging, support, and acceptance for students with disabilities, specifically ASD, in this program?
- What is the array of services available and offered to meet the needs of children with disabilities, in particular, children with ASD?
- Is technology available to students, and are modifications made that maintain the integrity of learning while adjusting to the learning style and needs of the individual student?
- Are parents seen as equal partners in the educational journey of their children?

Ruble and Dalrymple (2002) have proposed a consultation framework known as the Collaborative Model for Promoting Competence and Success (COMPASS), which has significant implications for the effective inclusion of children with ASD in general education settings. Their model supports building bridges between home and school through collaboration during program planning. The overall goal of COMPASS is to facilitate competence in children with ASD. Ruble and Dalrymple suggest that programs that evolve from a collaborative consultation model result in more consistent programming that ensures better skill maintenance and generalization. COMPASS requires the collaborative team that supports a child with ASD to identify the risk factors or barriers to learning and the supports needed to achieve success (Ruble & Dalrymple, 2002). They define four key steps in the process of maintaining a balance between challenges and supports likely to affect successful programming for children with ASD:

- identifying environmental challenges (external factors that affect learning, such as noise level, no access to typical peers, lack of instructor training) and personal challenges (core deficits noted during assessment);
- identifying environmental supports and resources (e.g., adaptations, visual strategies, structured teaching) and personal supports and resources (e.g., strengths, interests, motivators);
- identifying and prioritizing goals through team consensus; and
- developing action plans to address the identified goals.

The COMPASS model offers team members a theoretically and conceptually sound approach to consulting around program development for children with ASD.

Simpson and Sasso (1992) suggest that educational teams ask some hard questions and objectively assess the ability of children with ASD who are included in the general education classroom to initiate more positive interactions with peers, use more meaningful expressive language in the classroom, and demonstrate functional skills to a greater extent than children with ASD who are placed in special education settings. They also suggest that practitioners should expect children without disabilities to exhibit more positive interactions with children with ASD, when they have had experiences with them, than typical peers who have not had an inclusive experience with children with ASD.

Whatever families decide for their children with ASD, the quest for inclusive education must lead to children being able to achieve the academic, social, vocational, and personal goals that have been established by them and their families. The development and implementation of these goals must be a collaborative effort with the practitioners who will support the children with ASD throughout their educational experience. Family–professional connections are key to an inclusive education for children with ASD, and teachers play a critical role. Kluth (2003) describes it this way: "Teachers must listen to families and work to understand their experiences, traditions, histories, rituals, and beliefs. Teachers will benefit from learning to understand how families view themselves, the students' school experiences, and the partnership between the school and the home" (p. 61).

Strategies for Effective IEP Teams

The inclusion of autism as a disability category in 1990 should have increased the ease with which IEPs are developed for children with ASD. In fact, the

IEP process is a challenge for most teams. Families are usually under a great deal of stress and require relief through respite or alternative placements. Often, teams are ill equipped to address the immediate crisis needs that affect the ability of the child with ASD to function.

IDEA mandates that the IEP address the individual needs of children. Consideration needs to be given to the child's age, family priorities, medical issues, social interaction, functional skills, and ability to generalize and maintain a particular skill level (Fouse, 1996). Some basic goals are described in the literature as important to the learning success of children with ASD. These include functional abilities in the following areas: maintaining attention to task; imitating across modalities; identifying words, pictures, and objects receptively and expressively; matching, sorting, and sequencing to support academic skills; feeding, dressing, and toileting; and participating with peers in toy and game play (Mulick & Butter, 2002).

Effective IEP teams share several characteristics. Hammar and Malatchi (2001) suggest seven habits teams might follow based on Covey's (1989) habits of highly effective people. The first is "Be proactive." This requires a shift in thinking, from deficits to capacities, in teams, children, and families. The second habit is "Begin with an end in mind." That is, know the student's potential, fears, and hopes for the future. "Put first things first" is the third habit, reminding teams to prioritize goals and objectives. The fourth habit, "Think win-win," requires teams to build consensus around desired goals and develop guidelines for achievement and assessment of progress. "Seek first to understand and then to be understood" serves as habit five, indicating that effective IEP teams are willing and able to listen to and understand what parents, students, and other team members are saying. The sixth habit is "Synergize." This is a critical goal for the IEP team and one that can be accomplished through reviewing the assessment data, answering the questions that need to be asked, and striving to create a meaningful educational program. The final habit is "Sharpen the saw," or evaluate and celebrate the achievements of all involved in the IEP, particularly the student with ASD.

There are basic principles of collaboration that teams must demonstrate if they are to effectively carry out the IEP goals and objectives for students with ASD. Kluth (2003) offers some basic principles to ensure a collaborative approach to goal implementation. First, team members must establish some common goals and values. For example, a team committed to inclusive education might believe that "all students can learn and that those learners have a right to be educated with their peers" (p. 250). Second, there needs to be parity and role sharing among team members. That is, team members should share roles and responsibilities so that knowledge among them is expanded and access to supports for the children increases. Finally, a structure to plan and communicate among team members across settings must be created. Kluth proposes several strategies to support planning, such as regularly scheduled team meetings, mini team meetings with core participants focused on a goal, and activity and lunch meetings. She also suggests the use of e-mail, lesson binders with access to all team members, and a dialogue notebook in which team members communicate with one another about their ideas, thoughts, and concepts. Effective IEP teams create a structure or framework within which they can plan how to implement an individualized program for a child with ASD and communicate about its effectiveness and about what adjustments are needed to make the plan work.

Supporting Integration and Transitions Within General Education Settings

The question of inclusion for children with ASD is a complex one for every child and family. It must consider the core deficits reported for children along the spectrum, particularly social and communication impairments, and the impact those deficits are likely to have in general education settings. As previously discussed, inclusion means that students of varying ability levels learn together and have access to the same activities and social and academic opportunities. It does not mean that children with disabilities are isolated in separate classrooms or placed in general education classrooms without the needed services and supports necessary to meet their individual needs. Nor does it mean that safety is jeopardized or that unreasonable demands are placed on teachers and administrators.

Different models of inclusion will have to be considered for each child. The family and educational team must be diligent in their efforts to achieve successful integration, including having accountability for meeting the child's individual goals. They also need to consider the transitions that will occur from grade to grade. Possible models of inclusion to support the needs of children with ASD are discussed in the following paragraphs, as are approaches to achieving successful transitions across grade levels. It is important that practitioners consider not only where children with ASD are included but also how to evaluate and teach them so they can truly experience social integration (Gena & Kymissis, 2001).

Models of Inclusion

Several models of inclusion have been described in the literature for children with disabilities (Idol, 1997). All of them may have value in addressing the priority goals established for individual children with ASD, although particular challenges occur in implementation because of the core deficits characteristic of ASD. Teams may need to consider even more creative approaches to establish some level of integration in the school or larger community, depending on the particular strengths and challenges of individual children.

First, the team may decide to place a child in a *general education classroom with modifications* to the curriculum and instructions. A child with ASD who has generally strong cognitive skills and adequate communication skills might be provided with this level of support. Modifications could include scripting classroom activities and expectations, providing visual supports to facilitate transitions between activities, and using instructions tailored to the child's comprehension and performance levels. The success of this model of inclusion lies in its ability to address the child's specific social impairment. The social deficit in autism, particularly for children with strong cognitive and communication abilities, is likely to compromise fluent social exchanges with peers in cooperative learning groups, at recess and lunch, on bus rides, and in other situations that are less structured and predictable.

Another model of inclusion is full-day placement in a *general education classroom with the support of a one-to-one aid* or instructional assistant, as well as curricular modifications. In this model, children are provided with consistent adult support to facilitate or scaffold learning and social opportunities. The curriculum is adjusted appropriate to children's individual needs as determined by their IEPs. The challenge of this model for children with ASD is often the lack of training provided to the aid or instructional assistant in understanding the impairments characteristic of autism and how they might manifest themselves in an educational setting. Another challenge is the limited supervision provided to the aids in implementing the programs designed for children with ASD. This model requires ongoing and consistent collaboration among team members, including time to plan, model intervention strategies, collect data, and evaluate progress. This is a typical model of inclusion for children with ASD whose families and educational teams value the social opportunities in an environment of peers without disabilities and know that the children cannot succeed in the classroom independent of the structure and support provided by a consistent adult.

A third model for inclusive education is full-day placement in a *general education classroom with the development and supervision of a plan by an integration or inclusion specialist.* In this circumstance, someone familiar with autism and knowledgeable about the curriculum, the need for positive behavioral supports, and strategies for capitalizing on children's strengths and managing their challenges is assigned the task of developing a program that can be implemented by the general education teacher but requires a level of supervision and support to ensure that it is carried out effectively.

Another model of inclusive practice *combines placement* in a general education class (in areas where the child can access the curriculum with varying levels of support) and a resource room or special classroom (to support the child's individual learning and life skills needs). This might mean placing a student with ASD in a science class where there are opportunities for hands-on learning experiences with some modifications in expectations for assignments but required knowledge of basic content is commensurate with that of typical peers. For math, a particularly challenging area of learning, the same student might participate in a resource room or functional skills class, where basic math concepts critical to daily living, such as purchasing items of varying amounts, making change, and recognizing whether items cost more or less than the amount of money available, are emphasized. A special education teacher might provide some direct instruction in that academic area, along with an opportunity for the student to apply the new knowledge by working at the school store.

A more *individualized approach* to inclusion allows a student with ASD to participate in activities that do not require specific academic skills but provide opportunities to engage with peers. In this situation, students may receive all of their academic and life skills learning in a special education classroom but join their peers for lunch, recess, and specials like art, music, library, and physical education.

Finally, an inclusive strategy often used to create opportunities for students with ASD to have experiences with typical peers is the use of a *peer buddy program*. In this program, peers without disabilities who demonstrate particular skills in learning may be paired with students with ASD to support their understanding of a story they are reading or their completion of a math assignment. The peer buddy concept can employ the student with ASD as the supporting peer, as well. A teacher might identify a particular talent of the student with ASD, such as computer skills, and create opportunities for that student to work in the computer lab as a peer buddy or to work with individual students in the school who are having difficulty navigating the computer.

Whatever decisions are made about the type of inclusive opportunities provided for a child with ASD, the team should consider several points. First, it is important to define the goal for the inclusive activity and determine how the opportunity will facilitate the child's social interaction, communication, and behavior. Second, some direct support or scaffolding may be needed to ensure that the inclusive activity is successful. For example, when the child is fully included, his or her peers and teacher will require some explanation of the child's unique interests, communication style, and behavior. For some students, a paraprofessional or instructional assistant may be needed in the classroom. When using a combination model, some analysis of the curriculum (see Chapter 8) will be necessary if the child with ASD is going to be asked to participate in a particular content area. If a partial model of inclusion is used, the child with ASD will need support in transitioning from activities and communication partners who are known and predictable to less predictable environments and a variety of potential communication partners. The peer buddy system also will work only if both parties are clear about their roles and task expectations. Third, training will be required of those who are going to be supporting children with ASD in inclusive settings. Fourth, regularly scheduled planning meetings, with the general education teacher, the special educator, and related service providers like the speech–language pathologist (SLP) who have ongoing contact with the child, will be needed to ensure a shared mission toward achieving the child's learning goals. Finally, the team—including the family—will need to examine the benefits and challenges of the inclusive model selected, collecting data on a regular basis to determine how the practices being used are leading to positive growth for the child involved. A model of inclusive education for children with disabilities, and particularly children with ASD, must be carefully designed, comprehensive, and devote time to "providing activities that aid in the formation of positive dispositions such as caring, in preparing students to better understand others, and in developing skills that help the successful interaction and communication among students" (Cooper, Griffith, & Filer, 1999, p. 114).

Facilitating Integration

One of the challenges facing teams in making sure children with ASD "fit in" is a lack of understanding of who the child is and what he or she brings to a classroom environment. Children with ASD pose challenges to general education teachers because of their difficult social interactions and the impression they give that interaction with teachers or students in the classroom is not a high priority. Often paraprofessionals assume responsibility for the educational program of a child with ASD in an inclusive classroom, which can limit interactions with the general education teacher (Robertson, Chamberlain, & Kasari, 2003). Because one of the goals of inclusion is to facilitate positive interactions among children with and without disabilities, the relationship between a child with ASD and his or her teacher can affect the child's social status. Further, children with ASD must be able to access the classroom curriculum, as discussed in Chapter 8, and be prepared for the day-to-day instruction. Best practice suggests that the curriculum content needs to consider "(a) student-chosen, high-interest topics and books; (b) opportunities to engage in a variety of activities; and (c) cooperative learning experiences for difficult material" (Simpson, 1994, p. 12). The ultimate goal is to create a classroom environment in which everyone can learn.

Successful inclusion for supporting the communication and learning of children with ASD requires collaborative teaming, related services in the classroom, and instructional lessons designed to support communication and learning (Sonnenmeier & McSheehan, 2002). For example, the SLP needs to build consensus with the team around those communication supports to be used in the classroom, including how to implement them, who will be responsible for carrying them out, and in what context data will be collected to assess effectiveness. Related services, including speech–language intervention, need to be provided in the classroom, where natural opportunities can be created throughout the day to support the student's participation. Lesson design must consider materials of interest, opportunities in which to engage with motivating materials, use of visual supports, type of instruction, models for target behavior, and choices. With strategic supports in the classroom, students with ASD should be able to demonstrate their ability to learn (Sonnenmeier & McSheehan, 2002).

Teachers might also reconsider their lesson preparation, so that they can be responsive to the social, communication, and learning challenges students with ASD bring to the classroom. Marks and her colleagues (2003) offer several tips for teachers, including highlighting important concepts, establishing different ways to complete assignments, preparing for instructional transitions, and maximizing comprehension and content retention through the use of graphic or visual organizers and mnemonic devices. These antecedent management strategies help to create a responsive classroom environment, as opposed to one that is focused on managing consequences for behavior (Marks et al., 2003).

Several intervention strategies might be considered in an attempt to facilitate integration of a child with ASD into an inclusive setting. Some strategies support the child's attention and participation in daily learning tasks (e.g., priming), whereas others foster the child's engagement with typical peers (e.g., peer tutoring). As children with ASD learn to initiate communication in natural settings and respond to the initiations of their peers, positive relationships emerge. Schwartz, Billingsley, and McBride (1998) propose that strategies that occur in the natural environment, with individual teaching opportunities provided throughout the day that are child initiated and offer natural consequences, are most effective. A number of possible strategies that facilitate success in inclusive settings are described in the paragraphs that follow.

Priming. This intervention method previews information or activities that a child with ASD is likely to find difficult in the classroom. Priming is designed "to increase a child's competence in a given area before problems have a chance to develop" (Wilde, Koegel, & Koegel, 1992, p. 5). Typically, an interventionist and often a parent carries out priming the afternoon or evening before the material is to be presented in the classroom. It is important that the priming be as close an approximation as possible to what will occur the following day in the classroom. For example, if a teacher is going to be reading a particular book and asking specific questions of the group about what was read, priming that occurs the previous day will preview the book by reading the section the teacher will be presenting and asking questions of the child to encourage responses that will be probed in the classroom. Generally, short meaningful sessions seem to be most effective in familiarizing the child with what will be presented the following day (Wilde et al., 1992). If particularly challenging information is being presented the following day, it may be that only a portion of the lesson is reviewed with the child. For example, if students are expected to respond to questions in complete sentences and the child with ASD has limitations in sentence structure, the goal might be to familiarize the child with the basic vocabulary that is related to the pictures in the story. Wilde and her colleagues suggest that this allows the child to attend to and participate in the discussion and may facilitate comprehension and a sense of success in being able to follow along during the story reading.

There are four basic steps to implementing priming: collaboration, communication, priming, and feedback (Wilde et al., 1992). In the first step, the team collaborates to determine who will be participating in the priming (e.g., parents, teachers, paraprofessionals). The second step, communication, requires a timely and efficient method for a back-and-forth exchange between the primer and the teacher, so the material to be covered in class is clear and specific assignments are developed in a timely fashion. The team might use a calendar or priming memos to the parties involved. The actual priming procedures characterize the third step, in which a specific time and place are identified for the priming, so that a routine is established for the child and the primer. The goal is to familiarize the child with the material and not necessarily require proficiency with the content (Wilde et al., 1992). The child should be rewarded for trying during the priming sessions, as research suggests that encouraging the child's attempts to respond will improve response accuracy through trial and error (R. L. Koegel, O'Dell, & Dunlap, 1988). The child can be stretched to understand or respond to the material without requiring full comprehension, because motivation is often high when children are challenged in their learning just beyond their current skill level (Csikszentmihalyi & Nakamura, 1989). Choices can also be offered during the priming sessions to provide the child with a sense of control over his or her learning, which often leads to increased motivation to participate (Wilde et al., 1992). An important caution is that the job of the primer is to introduce and not "teach" the material or do the assignment for the child. Priming provides a simple scaffold for transitioning a child to new learning. The final step in the priming process is feedback. The effectiveness of priming can be assessed by first evaluating the child's behavior, attention, and response to the classroom task when material is *not* sent home to be primed. Then the team can assess differences in behavior, attention, and response when material *is* primed. The team should set up a feedback form, so that assignments are clear, a record of those that are primed and not primed is kept, and comments are provided by both the primer and the teacher regarding how the priming session went and what behaviors were observed in the classroom following primed and unprimed tasks.

For children who resist priming sessions, Wilde and colleagues (1992) provide several ideas for trouble-shooting. For example, if a child initially resists attending the sessions, the primer might begin with very short sessions (e.g., less than a minute) or very limited response requirements, and then gradually build up the time together and the child's level of participation. Rewards that the child chooses might be given for participation in a priming session, although Wilde et al. (1992) suggest that strategy as a last resort. Peers or siblings can be involved in the priming if that appeals to the child with ASD and decreases potential disruptions by siblings in the home. Team members must recognize that priming can facilitate the child's classroom performance and comprehension of critical learning materials; therefore, team communication around learning tasks is essential. Finally, in some situations, a child may be primed to respond in a way that is not appropriate to the actual classroom lesson. For example, a child might be primed to name pictures on each page of a story, but the teacher's expectation is that the student will answer questions about the story's events. It is important that the child be prepared to take on the expected role in the classroom activity or task and for the primer to remember that the goal is to facilitate comprehension and participation and not teach exact responses or undesirable classroom behavior.

The available research suggests that priming is an effective strategy for children with ASD. Two preschoolers with autism were provided with a "priming strategy" to increase their spontaneous initiation with their typical peers (Zanolli, Daggett, & Adams, 1996). Independent training of the peers also occurred. They were taught to respond to the initiations of and reinforce attempts at engagement by the children with autism. Priming successfully increased the rate of spontaneous initiations of the preschoolers with autism. Typical peers effectively responded to their initiations over the course of the study with few teacher prompts. Priming has also been used as a strategy to expose children with autism to assignments in general education classrooms before the assignments are made in those classrooms, in an effort to support their learning and decrease problem behaviors (L. K. Koegel, Koegel, Frea, & Green-Hopkins, 2003). L. K. Koegel and her colleagues (2003) found that two students with autism increased their ability to respond to classroom instruction and reduced their problem behaviors in the general education classroom following the implementation of priming sessions.

Priming appears to be beneficial for all students and requires minimal effort (Wilde et al., 1992). It enables parents, paraprofessionals, general and special educators, and related service providers to take an active role in the child's education and is designed to be a positive experience for the child with ASD.

Prompting. Prompting, as discussed in Chapter 9, helps a student learn through a process of guiding his or her responses so that a correct response is achieved and can be reinforced, increasing the likelihood that the correct response will be selected in subsequent presentations of the task (Charlop-Christy & Kelso, 1997). This strategy has been effectively used with children with ASD to facilitate their responses in an inclusive setting. The complexity of the academic curriculum and traditional instruction in a general education setting will often require prompted responses (Harrower & Dunlap, 2001). Sainato, Strain, Lefebvre, and Rapp (1987) reported the successful use of teacher prompting to facilitate transitions in the classroom for three preschoolers with autism. Prompts such as pointing or physical guidance can be used in the classroom setting to facilitate a response. For example, if a teacher asks a student to give her a blue ball, she would wait for a response and then either point to the ball or physically guide the child's hand to the blue ball. Prompts must be faded, however, so that the child responds to task stimulus on his own. The process is gradual and involves moving from the most to least directive prompt (Charlop-Christy & Kelso, 1997). Teachers may also use prompts with typical peers in the classroom, guiding them to model a particular behavior or prompt a behavior for a student with ASD.

Addressing Unconventional Verbal Behavior in the Classroom.
In general, interventions for reducing unconventional verbal behavior such

as echolalia should be positive and supportive. Supporting students with ASD who are using echolalia requires both creative and sensitive responding. First, the student may need some reassurance, as descriptions of echolalic behavior, as discussed in Chapter 4, indicate that increased anxiety or frustration is often associated with such behavior. Making statements like "I can see that you are trying to tell me something; let me see if I can figure it out" might help (Kluth, 2003, p. 113). Often, children with ASD are echoing a video, movie, or cartoon script, and becoming familiar with the scripted phrases the student uses may provide some understanding as to why a student uses a particular phrase in a specific situation. The team could work with the family to create a dictionary of scripted phrases, identifying what they typically mean or describing the function they may serve. This could enable teachers to respond more appropriately and provide verbal models or visual supports for more conventional ways of communicating a need. Writing might also be employed when a student appears to be using echolalia or other unconventional verbal behavior because he is confused or does not understand an instruction, question, task, or activity. Providing choices that can be pointed to or written questions or directions may facilitate understanding (Kluth, 2003).

Understanding Peer Cultures and Fostering Peer Connections.
Wolfberg and her colleagues (1999) studied peer cultures in children with a variety of challenges, including autism. They observed the participation and social connection of children with disabilities with their typical peers in inclusive preschool and related community settings. Their findings indicated that children with disabilities expressed a desire to participate in the culture of their preschool peers (i.e., to share a sense of group identity, which is constantly negotiated and reconstructed and includes norms or rules of behavior that are linked to events, play, and discourse) (Corsaro, 1985, 1992). Children with disabilities watched, followed, touched, and imitated their peers, as well as shared, gestured, and talked with their peers (Wolfberg et al., 1999). Some children even talked or wrote about their peers with other adults, including teachers and family members. Half of the children studied took roles in peer play, and more than half associated most with peers who shared some common ground like a familiar communication system or a play interest. Peers were generally responsive to the social communication attempts by children with disabilities and made adjustments to normalize their unconventional behaviors. Some peers offered help and guidance, demonstrating genuine caring for the children with disabilities.

Exclusion from the peer culture, however, was also observed. Wolfberg and her colleagues (1999) noted that apathy and indifference by typical peers were frequent occurrences, as were misinterpretations of the social cues exhibited by children with disabilities in their attempts to engage socially. Space and property conflicts, tattling and gossiping, and the formation of cliques also explained some of the exclusion observed for children with disabilities. The results of the study indicate a need for practitioners to recognize and understand the social and cultural contexts that exist in inclusive environments if successful connections and friendships are to be formed between children with and without disabilities.

Wolfberg et al. (1999) suggest that teachers might consider their roles as "social–cultural interpreters," in which they help typical peers to recognize and respond to the cues of children with disabilities. In the case of a child with ASD, goals might be established that include the communicative behaviors most typically used in the peer culture in which the child is included. Because shared interests seem to be a viable way to make connections among peers, teachers might work with the children to establish some common ground for play. They might also work to shape the unconventional behavior of a child with ASD to be more in line with the peer culture of the classroom. To decrease exclusion and increase empathy and caring among children, the teacher might employ group friendship activities or story telling that could help typical peers think about what it might be like to be excluded from an activity (Wolfberg et al., 1999).

Before educational teams can support the social skill behaviors of students with ASD, they must have a solid understanding of the unique strengths and challenges the students bring to social situations in the educational setting. They must also be able to assess potential friendships between children with ASD and their typical peers if they wish to build friendship networks. Therefore, the team might incorporate some observation tools or checklists that can identify challenging areas, guide intervention planning, and evaluate progress (Moyes, 2001). A teacher checklist is provided in the *Skillstreaming Curriculum* (McGinnis & Goldstein, 1997), which has teachers evaluate children's observed social behavior for skills such as listening when someone is speaking, knowing when and how to ask for help, and expressing appreciation for help given. The teacher rates the child's use of each skill in the classroom on a scale from *almost never good* to *almost always good*. Students are also given an opportunity to rate their social behavior in a similar manner by answering specific questions related to the ease with which they listen to others, ask for help, and thank people, among others. The parent is provided with a checklist similar to the teacher checklist to provide input on the child's social skills.

The *Observation Profile* (Cumine, Leach, & Stevenson, 1998) might also be used by the team to assess a variety of behaviors important to success in the classroom. The behaviors observed include social interaction (e.g., ability to use gestures, body posture, facial expression, and eye gaze in group interaction); social communication (e.g., ability to initiate conversation); social imagination and flexible thinking (e.g., ability to play imaginatively with others); and motor and organizational skills (e.g., ability to sit among peers in a large group like an assembly) (Cumine et al., 1998). Both teachers and parents can use this observation format to identify areas of concern from a rating of 1 (*no cause for concern*) to a rating of 5 (*great cause for concern*). The *Walker Social Skills Curriculum: The Accepts Program* (Walker & McConnell, 1988) also has a format for teachers to rate skills, on a scale of 1 (*not descriptive or true*) to 5 (*very descriptive or true*) in the areas of social interaction, friendship, coping, and getting along.

Goldman and Buysse (2002) offer an approach to assessing friendships in the classroom by means of the *Playmates and Friends Questionnaire for Teachers–Revised.* In this questionnaire, teachers are asked to identify who the child with ASD plays with, how often, and whether the child has any special friends. Teachers are also asked to document any friendship strategies they use to support the friendship building among children with ASD and their typical peers (e.g., giving free-choice time for the friends to play together, providing suggestions to resolve conflicts between friends, inviting friends to play together).

Following an assessment of the social behavior of students with ASD, a social skills program or curriculum might be selected by the team to implement in the classroom. For example, the *Skillstreaming* curriculum (McGinnis & Goldstein, 1997), which includes a framework for young children, elementary-age children, and adolescents, might be selected. It is a particularly useful tool, because it identifies particular social skills to be emphasized, provides "skill cards" for students that list steps to follow to achieve each skill, provides lesson plans for implementation, and supports social skill development at school and home. The team may decide to create a social skills group with socially competent peers and an individually designed curriculum based on the pragmatic language and social communication difficulties exhibited by students with ASD (Moyes, 2001).

Teachers can play a critical role in friendship building for children with ASD, in that they can serve as social coaches or provide social opportunities within the classroom to capitalize on potential relationships with typical peers (Danko & Buysse, 2003). Teachers can model how to play by offering suggestions on what to do with objects in play or by taking on a particular role in play and modeling the language that goes with it. They can also provide social opportunities within the classroom or the school day to help children with ASD make connections with friends. Danko and Buysse offer the following consideration for teachers who wish to facilitate friendships among children with ASD and their typical peers:

- Create opportunities for children with ASD to display their specific talents (e.g., knowledge of trains), desired activities (e.g., jumping on a trampoline), or favorite characters (e.g., Sponge Bob Square Pants).
- Identify common interests among talents, activities, and characters for children with ASD and their typical peers.
- Adjust the curriculum and include activities and materials that fit with the talents and the favorite activities and characters of the children with ASD.

The SLP will have a significant role in supporting the social skills and friendship building of children with ASD. The SLP can help to develop appropriate IEP goals that will support the development of social interactions in inclusive settings. These might include

- increasing opportunities for social interactions with peers across settings (e.g., classroom, cafeteria, specials, lunchroom, recess);
- increasing turn taking during social contexts (e.g., greetings, conversational exchanges, game playing); and
- improving the quality of interactions with peers and adults (e.g., making appropriate initiations, attending to a communication partner, responding to questions asked).

The SLP might also establish some training needs for the school staff and peers to support the success of social interaction for the child with ASD. For example, the SLP might begin with increasing staff awareness of the importance of social opportunities for children with ASD. Collaborating with teachers and parents to recruit potential typical peers that could serve as effective models, lunch buddies, and tutors could follow. Training typically developing peers to be models or tutors comes next, followed by implementation of peer-mediated social skills strategies (see Chapter 11 for an explanation). Further, any specific strategies the SLP is using to develop the social skills of students with ASD in one-on-one intervention (e.g., social stories, comic strip conversations, video modeling) need to be incorporated in the classroom.

Facilitating Literacy Learning. Current research suggests that literacy learning for children with disabilities is similar to literacy learning for those without disabilities and that home environments that provide rich opportunities for communicating and consistent access to print materials facilitate literacy in all children. Further, it is becoming more apparent that children with ASD "benefit from literacy instruction that incorporates the use of multiple instructional strategies that are carefully matched to the stages or phases of development through which all readers pass on their way from emergent reading to skilled reading" (Mirenda, 2003, p. 275). Practitioners should capitalize on the interest children with ASD often show in books, even if the selection of topics is narrow and determined by a specified interest. For example, if a child with ASD has an interest in books about trains, the educational team needs to consider ways to guide that interest and show the child that he or she can not only read about trains but also draw them, spell words related to them, write about them, and talk about them. When the child is ready to move on to another topic of interest, similar literacy opportunities can be provided and reinforced. Koppenhaver and Erickson (2003) found that when they introduced a variety of reading and writing tools and opportunities to three preschool children with ASD, the children's interest in and exploration and use of those materials increased in sophistication over a 5-month period. Speech-generating devices and computers with print and speech feedback appear to be responsive to the unique learning and processing styles of children with ASD and can be used to facilitate spelling (Blischak & Schlosser, 2003). Written narratives have also been explored for this population. Bedrosian, Lasker, Speidel, and Politsch (2003) describe a study with an adolescent boy with ASD who was successfully taught story planning and writing using story grammar maps, AlphaTalker messages, and peer support. Recognizing the value of visual input for children with ASD and using Oelwein's (1995) methodology for supporting the reading development of children with Down syndrome, Broun (2004) facilitated sight word recognition, vocabulary development, readiness skills, and comprehension in her students with ASD. Literacy is important to communicating, interpreting information, and learning in the classroom. Through print, practitioners can capitalize on the visual strengths of children with ASD, helping them to organize their internal language so they can respond in meaningful ways in the classroom.

Supporting Inclusive Leisure Activities. Inclusive community-based recreational activities are often ignored for children with ASD. Frequently, children with ASD participate in leisure activities separate from their peers. It is important, however, to consider the value of such recreational activities with peers without disabilities. Fennick and Royle (2003) describe a pilot project that explored training students in teacher education and health professional programs in a university setting. Students serving as "activity coaches" were trained in ways to support children with disabilities, including children with ASD, for participation in specific activities using accommodations appropriate to the children's disabilities. The activity coaches worked with instructors in swimming and gymnastic classes to support the inclusion of children with disabilities (7 to 11 years of age), five of whom had autism, with their typical peers. The children expressed enjoyment and improvement in their individual recreational activities, although their levels of being included with their peers during the activities varied. The authors reported some challenges in implementing the program, including scheduling difficulties, time constraints, and cultural differences related to how time is spent after school and with family. These first steps toward making needed community connections and modeling inclusive practice, however, are important as practitioners consider the ongoing intervention and recreational supports accessible to children with ASD.

Self-Management. Strategies for self-management are used to facilitate independence in the classroom and shift some responsibility for behavior from the teacher to the student. Students learn to differentiate between what is and is not appropriate behavior. They also evaluate their own behavior (e.g., by circling a happy or sad face or marking a checklist), monitor that behavior over time (e.g., checking in several times throughout the day, comparing their results with those of an adult), and self-reinforce when they have met the expected behavior requirement (e.g., earning reinforcement points to be traded in for a desired item) (Callahan & Rademacher, 1999;

Harrower & Dunlap, 2001). For example, four children with ASD were taught to improve their responses to verbal initiations by recording their correct responses to questions on a wrist counter (L. K. Koegel, Koegel, Hurley, & Frea, 1992). A second-grade student with ASD increased his on-task behavior in the classroom following the implementation of self-management and reinforcement procedures (Callahan & Rademacher, 1999). Pictorial self-management has also been reported as successful with three students with ASD who managed and maintained their behavior without the aid of an adult across settings using pictures to manage their behavior (Pierce & Schreibman, 1994). Reduction of inappropriate vocalizations (e.g., echolalic words or phrases, humming) in the classroom has also been achieved by applying self-management techniques (Mancina, Tankersley, Kamps, Kravits, & Parrett, 2000). Teaching self-management strategies has led to the independent functioning of students with disabilities, including those with ASD, in the classroom setting with decreased adult dependence and increased opportunities for successful peer interaction, improved social skills and classroom performance, and reduced disruptive behaviors (L. K. Koegel, Harrower, & Koegel, 1999; L. K. Koegel et al., 1992; Reid, 1996; Strain, Kohler, Storey, & Danko, 1994).

Supporting Transitions

There are a number of assistance activities that can support the success of children with ASD in the classroom, particularly as they are trying to fit in with their typical peers. Many of these activities support the transitions children with ASD must manage on a daily basis within the general education classroom (Gray, 1995). They might include a visually presented class or activity schedule (pictured or written) to support a smooth transition from one task to another, or a desk map that visually represents where things are or should be so they can be easily and independently retrieved and replaced (Gray, 1995; Hodgdon, 1998; McClannahan & Krantz, 1999; Moyes, 2001). As an alternative to verbal instruction, picture or visual schedules foster understanding of the classroom structure and help to prepare for a transition or change. Picture schedules have been successfully used to alert students with disabilities of daily classroom activities and changes in those activities (Hall, McClannahan, & Krantz, 1995). The use of activity schedules in the classroom has also resulted in decreased aggression and increased cooperation (Dooley, Wilczenski, & Torem, 2001). They are easy to construct and can be used by the teacher, instructional assistant, or paraprofessional, as well as related service providers, to support and predict the daily classroom routine for the student with ASD. The visual schedule serves, in a way, as a "prime" to prepare the student for what is to come or for the order of events for the day. To inform the student of any changes, a calendar or note with an agreed-upon symbol to indicate change (e.g., a red flag, a stop sign) could be used. A desk map could be created to help a student with ASD stay organized so access to materials does not delay his or her active participation or movement between activities. A direction card or a mini schedule can also be used to list simple task directions or the steps to be followed in a single time slot (Moyes, 2001). These can be placed right on the student's desk or inside individual assignment folders. Gray (1995) suggests that having a list of school rules and the reasons for those rules might facilitate the student's response to those rules and, again, support daily transitions. Walking through a change or practicing what is going to happen when a particular transition is going to occur (e.g., a fire drill, reviewing a new story, going to the bathroom, changing classes) might also be incorporated into the intervention plan for a student with ASD (Moyes, 2001). Again, this practice serves as a prime to prepare the child for a novel event, a variation in a familiar activity, or a new learning opportunity. Classroom transitions, challenging events for children with ASD, can be supported through a variety of class or activity schedules that help with organization, predictability, and preparedness.

Summary

In this chapter, you have learned a great deal about inclusionary practices to support the education of children with ASD. You have also read about those considerations that need to be made when employing an inclusionary model for children with ASD. The strengths of such a model include the following opportunities: to interact with typical peers, creating a more typical social framework and access to strong communication models; to increase awareness and acceptance by typical peers and adults; to raise awareness of and expectations for competence in the child with ASD; and to experience a rich curriculum that supports valued life outcomes. The challenges of an inclusive model include a failure to individualize the curriculum; a lack of training and support for the educational team; an absence of curricular modifications; and a poor understanding of the strengths and challenges of the child with ASD. Inclusion for children with ASD is complex and should be a choice for children with ASD and their families. The summary that follows refers to the questions at the beginning of the chapter and highlights key points you should be familiar with as you work toward creating inclusionary environments and opportunities for children with ASD.

What is the role of inclusive education for children with ASD?

Children with ASD can and do benefit from participating in inclusive classroom settings, although they require specialized supports to ensure their success (Harrower & Dunlap, 2001). The literature documents the value of typical peers in supporting social skill development and friendship building for children with ASD. Research also reports the value of inclusive practice for children without disabilities. The challenge for families and educational teams, however, is arranging the time, supports, and effective planning to make inclusion work. Several questions need to be asked about a school's philosophy and implementation of inclusive practices for children with ASD and about the school's approach to collaborating around the challenges of different skill levels and the unique needs characteristic of a child with ASD.

What are the strategies that effective IEP teams can use to ensure an inclusive educational community for children with ASD?

The literature suggests that team members must share some common goals and values if they are to implement an inclusive program successfully for children with ASD. This requires taking and sharing responsibility for goal achievement and establishing some "healthy habits" for working together to create a plan, identify valued outcomes, and ensure communication across all the participants. Team members, including families and the student with ASD, should be clear on their hopes, dreams, and fears of an inclusive program and address them with effective supports and collaborative planning.

How can teams support the integration and transitions of children with ASD across grade levels in general education settings?

Several strategies have been reported as effective in facilitating the integration of children with ASD in general education classrooms. These include antecedent methods (e.g., priming, prompting, visual scheduling), which help to prevent or at least decrease problem behaviors; self-management strategies, which foster independence and shift responsibility for behavior and performance from the teacher to the child; and peer-mediated interventions (e.g., peer tutoring, peer supports, cooperative learning), which facilitate the participation of children with ASD in the educational setting (Harrower & Dunlap, 2001).

Practice Opportunities

1. Using the questions derived from the principles of collaborative schools or the elements of successful inclusive programs as a guide, review as a team your school's philosophy and implementation of inclusive practices for children with ASD.

2. A student with ASD is having difficulty handling the instructional time devoted to reading short stories to the entire class, often displaying inappropriate behavior. Determine how you might use priming to support this student's learning and behavior in the general education classroom.

3. Create a visual schedule to support the daily transitions of a child with ASD.

4. Design a peer-tutoring plan for a student with ASD and prepare a peer tutor to facilitate the student's academic performance and social connection with the peer tutor.

Suggested Readings

Fouse, B. (1996). *Creating a "win–win IEP" for students with autism: A how-to manual for parents and educators.* Arlington, TX: Future Horizons.

This book is designed to facilitate collaboration among parents and educators to address the challenges of children with ASD from the point of referral through the development of an IEP. The IEP process is seen as one enhanced by the ability of practitioners and families to take joint ownership of all roles and responsibilities in implementing and evaluating a student's performance.

Kluth, P. (2003). *"You're going to love this kid!" Teaching students with autism in the classroom.* Baltimore: Brookes.

The author of this book addresses inclusion from both ideological and pedagogical perspectives and proposes new ways to think about students with ASD. She emphasizes ways students with ASD can participate in the curriculum with appropriate and creative supports. She defines the characteristics of inclusive classrooms, identifies ways to connect with families, provides guidelines for lesson planning, and offers several teaching strategies to support the engagement of students with ASD in their classroom learning.

Moyes, R. A. (2001). *Incorporating social goals in the classroom: A guide for teachers and parents of children with high-functioning autism and Asperger syndrome.* Philadelphia: Jessica Kingsley.

Moyes offers the reader a clear perspective on the social challenges students with ASD face and how those challenges affect classroom performance. She provides practical and numerous examples of social goals that are appropriate for inclusion in an IEP and supports those goals with clear, concrete, and creative lesson plans that can be matched to the individual needs of students with ASD.

Wagner, S. (1998). *Inclusive programming for elementary students with autism.* Arlington, TX: Future Horizons.

This book provides both a model and a context for implementing inclusive practice with students affected by autism. Emphasizing the critical impact of social skills in general education settings, Wagner offers several strategies for positively affecting social behavior. She also identifies teaching strategies that can be effective in capitalizing on the support provided by paraprofessionals. Suggestions for data collection in inclusive settings are offered, as well as approaches to successful transitions from elementary to middle school.

Resources

Anderson, W., Chitwood, S., & Hayden, D. (1997). *Negotiating the special education maze: A guide for parents and teachers.* Bethesda, MD: Woodbine House.

Bauer, A., & Shea, T. M. (1999). *Inclusion 101: How to teach all learners.* Baltimore: Brookes.

Delmolino, L., & Harris, S. L. (2004). *Incentives for change: Motivating people with autism spectrum disorders to learn and gain independence.* Bethesda, MD: Woodbine House.

Dowty, T., & Cowlishaw, K. (2001). *Home educating our autism spectrum children.* Philadelphia: Jessica Kingsley.

Doyle, M. B. (2002). *The paraprofessional's guide to the inclusive classroom: Working as a team* (2nd ed.). Baltimore: Brookes.

Fouse, B. (1996). *Creating a "win-win IEP" for students with autism: A how-to manual for parents and educators.* Arlington, TX: Future Horizons.

Giangreco, M. F. (1997). *Quick-guides to inclusion: Ideas for educating students with disabilities.* Baltimore: Brookes.

Giangreco, M. F. (1998). *Quick-guides to inclusion 2: Ideas for educating students with disabilities.* Baltimore: Brookes.

Hesmondhalgh, M., & Breakey, C. (2001). *Access and inclusion for children with autistic spectrum disorders.* Philadelphia: Jessica Kingsley.

Kluth, P. (2003). *"You're going to love this kid!" Teaching students with autism in the classroom.* Baltimore: Brookes.

Lipsky, D. K., & Gartner, A. (1997). *Inclusion and school reform: Transforming America's classrooms.* Baltimore: Brookes.

McGregor, G., & Vogelsberg, T. (1999). *Inclusive schooling practices: Pedagogical and research foundations: A synthesis of the literature that informs best practices about inclusive schooling.* Baltimore: Brookes.

Moyes, R. A. (2001). *Incorporating social goals in the classroom: A guide for teachers and parents of children with high-functioning autism and Asperger syndrome.* Philadelphia: Jessica Kingsley.

Moyes, R. A. (2003). *I need help with school! A guide for parents of children with autism and Asperger's syndrome.* Arlington, TX: Future Horizons.

Myles, B. S., & Adreon, D. (2001). *Asperger syndrome and adolescence: Practical solutions for school success.* Shawnee Mission, KS: Autism Asperger Publishing.

Putman, J. W. (1998). *Cooperative learning and strategies for inclusion: Celebrating diversity in the classroom* (2nd ed.). Baltimore: Brookes.

Stainback, S., & Stainback, W. (1996). *Inclusion: A guide for educators.* Baltimore: Brookes.

Twachtman-Cullen, D., & Twachtman-Reilly, J. (2002). *How well does your IEP measure up? Quality indicators for effective service delivery.* Higganum, CT: Starfish Specialty Press.

Watthen-Lovaas, N., & Lovaas, E. E. (1999). *The reading and writing program: An alternative form of communication.* Los Angeles: Lovaas Institute for Early Intervention.

Glossary

Eligibility. Determination of a disability based on assessment results and the need for special education services.

Free appropriate public education. The provision without charge of special education and related services that meet educational standards and include an appropriate educational environment that conforms to a student's IEP.

Inclusion. Philosophy that promotes access to activities, situations, and environments for students with disabilities by providing the necessary accommodations and supports.

Individualized Education Program (IEP). A written description of the special education placement and program designed for students with disabilities.

Least restrictive environment. An educational setting for students with disabilities that gives them as close to a general education as possible, including opportunities to interact with peers without disabilities.

Regular Education Initiative. An educational movement that outlined reforms in special education, including increased opportunities for children with disabilities in general education.

References

Bedrosian, J., Lasker, J., Speidel, K., & Politsch, A. (2003). Enhancing the written narrative skills of an AAC student with autism: Evidence-based research issues. *Topics in Language Disorders, 23*(4), 305–324.

Blischak, D. M., & Schlosser, R. W. (2003). Use of technology to support independent spelling by students with autism. *Topics in Language Disorders, 23*(4), 293–304.

Broun, L. T. (2004). Teaching students with autistic spectrum disorders to read: A visual approach. *Teaching Exceptional Children, 36*(4), 36–40.

Buysse, V., & Bailey, D. B. (1993). Behavioral and developmental outcomes in children with disabilities in integrated and segregated settings: A review of comparative studies. *The Journal of Special Education, 26*, 434–461.

Buysse, V., Skinner, D., & Grant, S. (2001). Toward a definition of quality inclusion: Perspectives of parents and practitioners. *Journal of Early Intervention, 24*(2), 146–161.

Callahan, K., & Rademacher, J. A. (1999). Using self-management strategies to increase the on-task behavior of a student with autism. *Journal of Positive Behavior Interventions, 1*(2), 117–122.

Charlop-Christy, M. H., & Kelso, S. E. (1997). *How to treat the child with autism.* Claremont, CA: Authors.

Cooper, M. J., Griffith, K. G., & Filer, J. (1999). School intervention for inclusion of students with and without disabilities. *Focus on Autism and Other Developmental Disabilities, 14*(2), 110–115.

Corsaro, W. A. (1985). *Friendship and peer culture in the early years.* Norwood, NJ: Ablex.

Corsaro, W. A. (1992). Interpretive reproduction in children's peer cultures. *Social Psychology Quarterly, 55*, 160–177.

Covey, S. (1989). *The seven habits of highly effective people.* New York: Fireside Press.

Csikszentmihalyi, M., & Nakamura, J. (1989). The dynamics of intrinsic motivation: A study of adolescents. *Research on motivation in education* (Vol. 3). New York: Academic Press.

Cumine, V., Leach, J., & Stevenson, G. (1998). *Asperger syndrome: A practical guide for teachers.* London: David Fulton.

Danko, C. D., & Buysse, V. (2003). Thank you for being a friend: Fostering friendships for children with autism spectrum disorder in inclusive environments. *Young Exceptional Children, 6*(1), 2–9.

Dooley, P., Wilczenski, F. L., & Torem, C. (2001). Using an activity schedule to smooth school transitions. *Journal of Positive Behavior Interventions, 3*(1), 57–61.

Fennick, E., & Royle, J. (2003). Community inclusion for children and youth with developmental disabilities. *Focus on Autism and Other Developmental Disabilities, 18*(1), 20–27.

Fisher, M., & Meyer, L. H. (2002). Development and social competence after two years for students enrolled in inclusive and self-contained educational programs. *Research & Practice for Persons with Severe Disabilities, 27*(3), 165–174.

Fouse, B. (1996). *Creating a "win–win IEP" for students with autism: A how-to manual for parents and educators.* Arlington, TX: Future Horizons.

Fryxell, D., & Kennedy, C. H. (1995). Placement along the continuum of services and its impact on students' social relationships. *Journal of the Association for Persons with Severe Handicaps, 20*, 259–269.

Gartner, A., & Lipsky, D. K. (2000). Inclusion and restructuring: A new synergy. In R. A. Villa & J. S. Thousand (Eds.), *Restructuring for caring and effective education: Piecing the puzzle together* (pp. 38–55). Baltimore: Brookes.

Gena, A., & Kymissis, E. (2001). Assessing and setting goals for the attending and communicative behavior of three preschoolers with autism in inclusive kindergarten settings. *Journal of Developmental and Physical Disabilities, 13*(1), 11–26.

Giangreco, M. F., Cloninger, C. J., Dennis, R. E., & Edelman, S. W. (2000). Problem solving methods to facilitate inclusive education. In R. A. Villa & J. S. Thousand (Eds.), *Restructuring for caring and effective education: Piecing the puzzle together* (pp. 293–327). Baltimore: Brookes.

Goldman, B. D., & Buysse, V. (2002). *Playmates and Friends Questionnaire for Teachers–Revised.* Chapel Hill: University of North Carolina at Chapel Hill, Frank Porter Graham Child Development Institute.

Gray, C. A. (1995). Teaching children with autism to "read" social situations. In K. A. Quill (Ed.), *Teaching children with autism: Strategies to enhance communication and socialization* (pp. 219–242). New York: Delmar.

Hall, L. J., McClannahan, L. E., & Krantz, P. J. (1995). Promoting independence in integrated classrooms by teaching aides to use activity schedules and decreased prompts. *Education and Training in Mental Retardation, 30,* 208–217.

Hammar, E., & Malatchi, A. (2001, Fall). Seven habits of highly effective IEP teams. *Center Connections,* pp. 4–5.

Harrower, J. K., & Dunlap, G. (2001). Including children with autism in general education classrooms: A review of effective strategies. *Behavior Modification, 25*(5), 762–784.

Hodgdon, L. A. (1998). *Visual strategies for improving communication.* Troy, MI: Quirk Roberts.

Hunt, P., Farron-Davis, F., Beckstead, S., Curtis, D., & Goetz, L. (1994). Evaluating the effects of placement of students with severe disabilities in general education versus special classes. *Journal of the Association for Person with Severe Handicaps, 19,* 200–214.

Hunt, P., & Goetz, L. (1997). Research on inclusive educational programs, practices, and outcomes for students with severe disabilities. *Journal of Special Education, 31,* 3–29.

Idol, L. (1997). Key questions related to building collaborative and inclusive schools. *Journal of Learning Disabilities, 30*(4), 384–394.

Kamps, D., Barbetta, P. M., Leonard, B. R., & Delquadri, J. (1994). Classwide peer tutoring: An integration strategy to improve reading skills and promote peer interactions among students with autism and general education peers. *Journal of Applied Behavioral Analysis, 27,* 49–61.

Kluth, P. (2003). *"You're going to love this kid!" Teaching students with autism in the classroom.* Baltimore: Brookes.

Koegel, L. K., Harrower, J. K., & Koegel, R. L. (1999). Support for children with developmental disabilities in full inclusion classrooms through self-management. *Journal of Positive Behavior Interventions, 1,* 26–34.

Koegel, L. K., Koegel, R. L., Frea, W., & Green-Hopkins, I. (2003). Priming as a method of coordinating educational services for students with autism. *Language, Speech, and Hearing Services in Schools, 34*(3), 228–235.

Koegel, L. K., Koegel, R. L., Hurley, C., & Frea, W. D. (1992). Improving social skills and disruptive behavior in children with autism through self-management *Journal of Applied Behavior Analysis, 25,* 341–353.

Koegel, R. L., O'Dell, M., & Dunlap, G. (1988). Producing speech use in nonverbal autistic children by reinforcing attempts. *Journal of Autism and Developmental Disorders, 18,* 525–538.

Koppenhaver, D. A., & Erickson, K. A. (2003). Natural emergent literacy supports for preschoolers with autism and severe communication impairments. *Topics in Language Disorders, 23*(4), 283–292.

Mancina, C., Tankersley, M., Kamps, D., Kravits, T., & Parrett, J. (2000). Brief report: Reduction of inappropriate vocalizations for a child with autism using a self-management treatment program. *Journal of Autism and Developmental Disorders, 30*(6), 599–606.

Marks, S. U., Shaw-Hegwer, J., Schrader, C., Longaker, T., Peters, I., Powers, F., et al. (2003). Instructional management tips for teachers of students with autism spectrum disorders (ASD). *Teaching Exceptional Children, 35*(4), 50–54.

McClannahan, L. E., & Krantz, P. J. (1999). *Activity schedules for children with autism: Teaching independent behavior.* Bethesda, MD: Woodbine House.

McGinnis, E., & Goldstein, A. (1997). *Skillstreaming the elementary child.* Chicago: Research Press.

Mirenda, P. (2003). "He's not really a reader …": Perspectives on supporting literacy development in individuals with autism. *Topics in Language Disorders, 23*(4), 271–282.

Moore-Brown, B. J., & Montgomery, J. K. (2001). *Making a difference for America's children: Speech–language pathologists in public schools.* Eau Claire, WI: Thinking Publications.

Moyes, R. A. (2001). *Incorporating social goals in the classroom: A guide for teachers and parents of children with high-functioning autism and Asperger syndrome.* Philadelphia: Jessica Kingsley.

Mulick, J. A., & Butter, E. M. (2002). Educational advocacy for children with autism. *Behavioral Interventions, 17,* 57–74.

Oelwein, P. (1995). *Teaching reading to children with Down syndrome: A guide for parents and teachers.* Bethesda, MD: Woodbine House.

Paul, J. L., Yang, A., Adiegbola, M., & Morse, W. (1995). Rethinking the mission and methods: Philosophies for educating children and the teachers who teach them. In J. L. Paul, H. Rossellini, & D. Evans (Eds.), *Integrating school restructuring and special education reform* (pp. 9–29). Fort Worth, TX: Harcourt Brace.

Pierce, K. L., & Schreibman, L. (1994). Teaching daily living skills to children with autism in unsupervised settings through pictorial self-management. *Journal of Applied Behavior Analysis, 27,* 471–481.

Rafferty, Y., Piscitelli, V., & Boettcher, C. (2003). The impact of inclusion on language development and social competence among preschoolers with disabilities. *Exceptional Children, 69*(4), 467–479.

Reid, R. (1996). Research in self-monitoring with students with learning disabilities. The present, the prospects, the pitfalls. *Journal of Learning Disabilities, 29,* 317–331.

Robertson, K., Chamberlain, B., & Kasari, C. (2003). General education teachers' relationships with included students with autism. *Journal of Autism and Developmental Disorders, 33,* 123–130.

Roeyers, H. (1996). The influence of nonhandicapped peers on the social interactions of children with a pervasive developmental disorder. *Journal of Autism and Developmental Disorders, 26,* 303–320.

Ruble, L. A., & Dalrymple, N. J. (2002). COMPASS: A parent–teacher collaborative model for students with autism. *Focus on Autism and Other Developmental Disabilities, 17*(2), 76–83.

Sainato, D. M., Strain, P. S., Lefebvre, D., & Rapp, N. (1987). Facilitating transition times with handicapped preschool children: A comparison between peer-mediated and antecedent prompt procedures. *Journal of Applied Behavior Analysis, 20,* 285–291.

Schwartz, I. S., Billingsley, F. F., & McBride, B. M. (1998, Winter). Including children with autism in inclusive preschools: Strategies that work. *Young Exceptional Children,* pp. 19–26.

Simpson, R. L. (1994). School reform and children and youth with autism. *Focus on Autistic Behavior, 9*(2), 9–14.

Simpson, R. L., & Sasso, G. M. (1992). Full inclusion of students with autism in general education settings: Values versus science. *Focus on Autistic Behavior, 7*(3), 1–13.

Sonnenmeier, R., & McSheehan, M. (2002, Spring). Communication and learning: Creating systems of support for students with autism. *The Communicator,* pp. 23–25.

Strain, P. S., Kohler, F. W., Storey, K., & Danko, C. D. (1994). Teaching preschoolers with autism to self-monitor their social interactions: An analysis of results in home and school settings. *Journal of Emotional and Behavioral Disorders, 2,* 78–88.

Villa, R. A., & Thousand, J. S. (2000). Setting the context: History of and rationales for inclusive schooling. In R. A. Villa & J. S. Thousand (Eds.), *Restructuring for caring and effective education: Piecing the puzzle together* (pp. 7–37). Baltimore: Brookes.

Wagner, S. (1998). *Inclusive programming for elementary students with autism.* Arlington, TX: Future Horizons.

Walker, H. M., & McConnell, S. (1988). *Walker Social Skills Curriculum: The Accepts Program.* Austin, TX: PRO-ED.

Wilde, L., Koegel, L. K., & Koegel, R. L. (1992). *Increasing success in school through priming: A training manual.* Santa Barbara: University of California.

Wolfberg, P. J., Zercher, C., Lieber, J., Capell, K., Matias, S., Hanson, M., et al. (1999). "Can I play with you?" Peer culture in inclusive preschool programs. *Journal of the Association of Persons with Severe Handicaps, 24*(2), 69–84.

World Health Organization. (2001). *International classification of functioning, disability, and health.* Geneva, Switzerland: Author.

Zanolli, K., Daggett, J., & Adams, T. (1996). Teaching preschool age autistic children to make spontaneous initiation to peers using priming. *Journal of Autism and Developmental Disorders, 26*(4), 407–422.

Epilogue

As you reflect on the chapters in this text, hopefully you have gained greater insight into the nature of autism and the range of symptoms that characterize autism spectrum disorders. There are three notable points to consider in your reflection. First, it is becoming increasingly clear that a neurobiological and genetic basis of autism exists. Second, infant diagnosis is a new and growing area of research critical to the understanding and management of the disorder. And third, social impairment has remained a hallmark of the disorder since Leo Kanner's description in 1943.

Families are crucial partners in assessment and intervention planning for their children with ASD. They are often the only constant in their child's life and are challenged day to day by the pervasive nature of the disorder. Practitioners must consider and respect, however, variations in the ability of families to cope with and manage the needs of their children with ASD. As partners in the assessment and intervention process, families contribute much to practitioners' understanding of the communication, play, and social interaction challenges and strengths of children with ASD.

Before intervention and program planning can be determined for any child or adolescent with ASD, creating a profile of strengths and weaknesses across the core deficit areas should be a priority. This is the primary way to determine what specific needs should be addressed. A comprehensive and interdisciplinary assessment of communication, play, and social–emotional development should be considered for all children with ASD to guide the process for educational or program planning.

Decision making around intervention selection is a complex issue. Families want any and all supports that have the potential for making a difference in their children's behaviors across all areas of development. Unfortunately, evidence to support many interventions of choice are lacking. Practitioners have a responsibility to be informed about interventions and the level of evidence to support their use. Further, practitioners who are not technically proficient in the implementation of particular evidenced-based interventions must pursue training or obtain the support of professionals who do have the knowledge and skill required.

Although intervention that targets all the core areas of deficit in autism is a priority, a primary focus for intervention must be the social skill development of children and adolescents with ASD, as that area of impairment affects them throughout life. Children with ASD require direct instruction that focuses on behaviors that have been targeted to support social interaction and that are developmentally appropriate across contexts (Paul, 2003).

Children with ASD also require numerous opportunities to practice their new skills in several contexts, so that generalization can occur. Further, peers can be effective in supporting the social interactions of children with ASD when they are taught specific strategies to facilitate the inclusion of a child with ASD in their play or social event. Social skills training should incorporate the use of visual supports, foster children's ability to "read" social cues, increase awareness of pragmatic and conversational rules, improve prosody, and engage children in self-monitoring to take responsibility for their own behavior (Klin & Volkmar, 2000).

At present, children and adolescents with ASD are placed in inclusive or integrated settings, where they have opportunities to engage with typical peers in their own educational community, as well as in segregated settings with children who share a similar diagnosis or learning profile and professionals specifically trained in autism. Whatever educational setting or intervention option is selected, all intervention programs need to be individualized. This requires time, collaboration, and an effective decision-making process.

Current research continues to guide practitioners' thinking about autism and its related disorders. Although patterns of behavior are characteristic of ASD, each child with this diagnosis is unique. This book has exposed you to various models and approaches to assessment and intervention. The task is now yours to pull from the chapters what you need to guide your program planning for individual children with ASD.

Over the last 20 years of working with children with autism and related disorders, my beliefs about how they think, communicate, and behave has evolved from recognizing only what is different or disordered to understanding what is unique but meaningful in their approaches to managing the complexities of a world they struggle to understand. Children and adolescents with autism have taught me to think about their competence, to recognize the strengths of their families, and to trust in a collaborative, interdisciplinary approach to address their challenges.

References

Kanner, L. (1943). Autistic disturbances of affective contact. *Nervous Child, 2,* 217–250.

Klin, A., & Volkmar, F. V. (2000). Treatment and intervention guidelines for individuals with Asperger syndrome. In A. Klin, F. V. Volkmar, & S. S. Sparrow (Eds.), *Asperger syndrome* (pp. 340–366). New York: Guilford Press.

Paul, R. (2003). Promotion social communication in high functioning individuals with autistic spectrum disorders. *Child and Adolescent Psychiatric Clinics in North America, 12,* 87–106.

Author Index

Abell, F., 32, 33
Academy of Neurology, 37
Achenbach, T. M., 287
Adams, A., 462, 465
Adams, L., 520, 552
Adams, T., 587
Adiegbola, M., 575
Adrien, J., 14, 23, 24, 255
Aicardi, J., 8
Aitken, K., 5, 306
Alisanski, S., 174, 253, 505
Allen, D., 506
Allen, G., 30, 34
Allen, J., 12, 13, 46, 235, 284, 305
Almeida, M. C., 417
Almond, P., 44, 114, 287
Almy, M., 223
Alpert, C., 416
Alpert, C.L., 412, 442
Altemeier, W. A., 230, 260
Alward, K., 229
Aman, M. G., 555
Amanullah, S., 174, 253, 505
American Academy of Child and
    Adolescent Psychiatry, 22,
    25, 31, 348, 353
American Academy of Pediatrics
    (AAP), 22, 26, 37, 373, 542,
    543, 544, 546, 550
American Psychiatric Association
    (APA), 4, 5, 6, 7, 8, 9, 10, 11,
    30, 168, 247, 252, 256, 305,
    558
Amorosa, H., 29
Anderson, S. R., 354, 469
Andrellos, P. J., 331–332
Andrews, A. B., 98
Anzalone, M. E., 304, 306, 307,
    312, 316, 317
Apolloni, T., 497
Appleton, P. L., 544
Arcidiacono, L., 258
Arick, J. R., 44, 48, 114, 287
Arin, D. M., 8
Armour, J., 485
Arnold, C. L., 405
Asperger, H., 5, 9
Attwood, A., 184
Attwood, A. J., 12, 15, 43, 305
Autism Task Force of Vermont, 78

Autism Society of America, 305
Avery, D. L., 354
Aylward, E. H., 32, 33

Bacon, A. L., 506
Bailey, A., 32, 35
Bailey, A. J., 35
Bailey, D., 223
Bailey, D. B., 367, 576
Bailey, J. N., 32
Baird, G., 19
Baker, M. J., 473
Balla, D., 21, 287
Baltaxe, C. A., 269
Baltaxe, C. A. M., 31
Baltaxe, C. M., 174, 194
Balzer-Martin, L. A., 330–331, 337
Baranek, G., 14, 22, 23, 24, 306, 558
Barbetta, P. M., 576
Baron-Cohen, S., 12, 19, 20, 23, 24,
    25, 33, 171, 230, 231, 232,
    234, 235, 239, 260, 261,
    262, 263, 264, 269, 284,
    290, 305, 319, 327, 522, 523
Barrett, M., 196, 197
Barron, J., 307
Barron, S., 173, 175, 181, 184, 185,
    230, 307
Barry, L. M., 520
Barry, T. D., 504
Bartolucci, G., 194
Barton, M. L., 18, 48, 305
Bates, E., 170, 174, 191, 225, 227,
    460
Bates, M. S., 70
Battacchi, M. W., 258
Bauer, A. M., 101
Bauer, J., 402
Bauman, M. L., 8, 32, 312, 319
Bauminger, N., 263, 506, 507
Bax, M., 28
Beatson, J. E., 65–92, 98, 101
Beckstead, S., 576
Bedroisian, J., 592
Beebe-Frankenberger, M. E., 349
Bell, L. K., 463, 508
Belsky, J., 224, 225
Ben-Tall, A., 416, 510
Benaroya, S., 230
Benchaaban, D., 463

Bennetto, L., 260
Bergen, D., 225
Berkson, G., 306, 558
Bernabei, P., 255
Berument, S. K., 45
Beukelman, D., 401
Bieberich, A. A., 175
Biklen, D., 307
Billingsley, F. F., 585
Billstedt, E., 31
Bishop, D. V. M., 204–205
Bishop, K. K., 98
Bitner, B., 69
Blagden, C., 196
Bleiberg, E., 31
Blischak, D. M., 592
Bock, S. J., 43
Boddaert, N., 33, 34
Boettcher, C., 576
Bolick, T., 256, 268
Bondy, A., 348, 399, 402, 403–405,
    407
Bothuyne, S., 257
Boucher, J., 231, 232, 234, 258,
    269, 467
Boulware, G. L., 94
Bower, C., 8
Bowers, L., 191, 197
Bowlby, J., 254
Bowler, D. M., 232, 263
Box, M. L., 419
Boyle, T. D., 437
Bracken, K. N., 273
Brady, M., 306
Braswell, L., 506
Braun, U., 401
Braverman, M., 232
Brewer, E. J., 98
Bricker, D., 204, 497
Brierly, L. M., 230
Briggs, M. H., 76, 77
Bristol, M. N., 494
Broder, C., 69
Brook, S. L., 232
Brookins, G. K., 70
Broun, L. T., 592
Brown, C., 336
Brown, E., 169, 254, 255, 257
Brown, J., 398
Brown, J. R., 81, 83

Brown, W. H., 269, 273
Brownell, C. A., 254, 255
Bruner, J. S., 186
Bryson, S. E., 22, 260
Buffington, D. M., 171
Buhrmester, D., 273
Buitelaar, J. K., 10, 506
Burghardt, G., 223
Burlew, 520
Butter, E. M., 580
Buxton, R. B., 34
Buysse, V., 576, 577, 590

Calculator, S., 373
Callahan, K., 592, 593
Camaioni, L., 169, 170, 171, 255
Camarata, S., 416, 510
Campbell, D., 331
Campbell, M., 555, 556
Campbell, S., 319
Capps, L., 178, 435
Cardillo, J., 356
Carlson, J. K., 514
Caro-Martinez, L., 171, 260
Carpenter, M., 402
Carpenter, M. H., 426
Carper, R. A., 34, 176
Carriger, M. S., 254
Carter, A., 253, 257
Carter, A. S., 287
Carter, C. M., 268, 271, 412, 416,
    502, 509–510
Carter, M., 402
Case-Smith, J., 544
Cavallaro, C. C., 96, 120
Celani, G., 258, 259
Chamberlain, B., 584
Chambers, C. T., 558
Charlop-Christy, M. H., 218,
    402, 407, 418, 420, 421,
    422–426, 427, 462, 463,
    467, 470, 472, 587
Charlop, M., 419, 421, 422, 424,
    425, 442
Charman, T., 20, 48, 230, 231, 234,
    255, 256, 460
Chawarska, K., 22
Chen, Y., 70
Child Neurology Society, 37
Chorpita, B. F., 349–353
Christian, W.P., 354
Church, C., 174, 253, 505
Cicchetti, D., 12, 21, 253, 287
Cisar, C., 430
Clark, C., 306
Clary, J., 505–506
Cloninger, C. J., 98, 358, 361–362,
    367, 370, 575
Cogher, L., 463, 465
Cohen, D., 4, 253, 254, 256, 262
Cohen, W. I., 72

Colarusso, R. R., 331, 336
Coleman, S. L., 421
Conn, S., 552
Constantino, J. N., 266, 267
Contompasis, S., 3–63, 98,
    541–571
Cook, E. H., 319
Cook, E. H., Jr., 31
Cooke, S. A., 497
Cooke, T. P., 497
Cooley, W. C., 546
Coonrod, E. E., 49, 112
Cooper, C. S., 497
Cooper, M. J., 584
Cordisco, L. K., 497, 498
Corsaro, W. A., 588
Costall, A., 230
Coster, W. J., 331–332, 337
Courchesne, E., 30, 32, 33, 34, 176
Covey, S., 580
Cowdery, G. E., 469
Craig, J., 231, 232
Craig, K. D., 558
Crawford, S., 331
Creaghead, N. A., 429
Crick, N. R., 506
Critchley, H. D., 312, 319
Cronin, P., 9, 14, 20
Csikszentmihalyi, M., 586
Cullain, R. E., 519
Cumine, V., 589
Cumley, C. D., 373
Curcio, F., 171, 260
Curtis, D., 576

Daggett, J., 587
Dake, L., 435–436
Dalrymple, N., 578–579
Daly, K., 47
Daneshvar, S., 424, 425, 426
D'Angiola, N., 31
Daniel, S., 223
Danko, C. D., 590, 593
Darrah, J., 321, 331, 336
D'Ateno, P., 468
Dattilo, J., 591
Dawson, G., 14, 23, 24, 29, 30, 31,
    34, 169, 176, 255, 257, 263,
    264, 265, 284, 305–307,
    349, 355, 372, 462, 465, 483
Deal, A., 98
Dean, A., 32
DeBacker, I., 319
DeCasper, A., 254
DeCesare, L., 497
Deeney, T., 332
DeGangi, G., 276, 282, 330–331,
    337, 485
Delmolino, L., 412
Delprato, D. J., 412, 416, 417
Delquadri, J., 576

Dennis, B., 426
Dennis, R. E., 70, 71, 98, 303–343,
    361, 366, 367, 370, 575
Densmore, A., 462, 471
Department of Health and Human
    Services, 81
Deruelle, C., 259
Des Portes, V., 555, 561, 562
Deshler, D. D., 524
Dettmer, S., 402
DeVellis, R., 47
Dewey, D., 331
Dharmanu, C., 22
Dias, K., 8
Diehl, S., 373
Diehl, S. F., 98
Dietz, J., 316
DiLalla, D. L., 460
DiLavore, P. C., 21, 22, 45, 114,
    241, 286, 491
DiMarco, R., 441
Dinno, N., 14
DiPietro, E. K., 354
DiSalvo, C. A., 526
Djukic, A., 22
Dodge, K. A., 506
Donnellan, A., 307, 317, 318
Dooley, P., 593
Dore, J., 170, 174, 193
Dove, C., 425
Dowrick, P. W., 14, 425, 468
Dragich, J., 8
Duchan, J. F., 182, 183, 373, 408,
    427, 428
Ducker, A., 69, 251–301
Dunlap, G., 355, 416, 576, 586,
    587, 593, 595
Dunn, W., 316, 317, 328, 331, 336,
    337
Dunst, C. J., 68, 69, 98, 441
Dyer, K., 417, 463, 508

Edelman, S. W., 67, 98, 303–343,
    361, 366, 367, 370, 575
Edwards, G. L., 354
Effgen, S. K., 367
Egaas, B., 33
Egel, A. L., 421
Ehlers, S., 46
Eichinger, J., 367
Eisenberg, D. M., 550
Eisenberg, L., 70
Eisenmajer, R., 10
Elliot, S. N., 273, 288
Elliott, G. R., 253
Endo, S., 463
English, K., 497
Erickson, K. A., 591
Etheridge, M. L., 544
Evans, J., 399

Fadiman, A., 67, 68, 70, 71, 72, 73
Fair, M.E., 273
Fallin, D., 35
Farley, S., 367
Farron-Davis, F., 576
Fay, W., 172, 174, 175
Fein, D., 18, 48, 232, 267, 305, 506
Fein, G., 228
Feinstein, C., 267
Feldman, H. M., 72
Feldman, R. S., 175, 417, 500, 502
Fennick, E., 592
Fenske, E. C., 353
Fenson, L., 21, 203
Fernandez, M. C., 230, 260
Feuerstein, R., 96
Fewell, R., 225, 226–227, 244, 331, 336
Fidler, D. J., 32
Fiene, J. I., 544
Fifer, W., 254
Filer, J., 584
Filer, J. D., 108
Filipek, P. A., 4, 22, 24, 26, 36, 327, 552
Fine, J., 194
Finkler, D., 544
Finnerty, J., 202
Fischer, R., 416
Fishel, P. T., 230, 260
Fisher, M., 576
Fisher, W. W., 562
Fisman, S., 555
Fogel, A., 319
Folio, M. R., 331, 336
Fombonne, E., 4, 22, 36
Ford, V., 73, 77
Forest, M., 98, 357
Foster, L. G., 306
Fouse, B., 580
Francis, K. L., 419
Frea, W., 405, 480, 587
Frea, W. E., 593
Freeman, B. J., 9, 14, 20, 353, 360
Freeman, K. A., 421
Freeman, S., 435–436, 544
Friesen, B. J., 67
Friesen, D., 266
Frith, U., 5, 9, 261
Fritschmann, N., 513
Frost, L., 348, 399, 402, 403–405, 407
Fryman, J., 19, 307
Fryxell, D., 576
Furman, W., 273
Furney, K. S., 357

Gagnon, E., 522
Ganz, J. B., 402
Garand, J. D., 514–515, 518, 519, 521, 526

Garcia, J., 504
Garfin, D., 168
Garfinkle, A. N., 352, 402
Garnett, M. S., 12, 15, 43, 305
Gartner, A., 578
Garvey, C., 223
Gazdag, G., 171
Geller, E., 274
Gena, A., 581
Gepner, B., 259
Gerber, S., 484
Gerlach, E. K., 371
Gerson, R., 96, 103
Ghaziuddin, N., 31, 32
Giangreco, M. F., 67, 70, 71, 98, 358–359, 361–362, 365–370, 382, 383, 575
Gillberg, C., 8, 9, 12, 13, 46, 235, 255, 284, 305, 558
Gilliam, J. E., 47–48
Ginsberg, G., 194
Glaeser, B. C., 513
Gleitman, L., 182
Goetz, L., 576
Golden, G. S., 372
Goldman, B. D., 590
Goldstein, A., 589, 590
Goldstein, G., 185
Goldstein, H., 271, 349, 402, 430, 440, 470, 497, 502, 504, 520
Goldstein, S., 31
Gonzalez-Calvo, J., 544
Good, B., 70
Goodman, G., 427
Gordon, C. T., 555, 556
Gould, J., 230
Gouvousis, A., 520
Grandin, T., 317
Grant, S., 576
Gray, C. A., 461, 511, 513–515, 517–519, 521, 526, 593, 594
Green, J. A., 18, 48, 305
Green, M., 546
Green, W. H., 555
Green-Hopkins, I., 587
Greenspan, S. I., 277–282, 294, 306, 329, 348, 349, 438–439, 460–462, 469, 473, 480–483, 485–486, 502
Greer, R. D., 464
Greiner, N., 441
Gresham, F. M., 273, 288, 349
Grice, P., 178
Griffith, E. G., 264
Griffith, K. G., 584
Groce, N. E., 72
Groen, A. D., 372
Groom, J. M., 466
Grossman, J., 257
Grynfeltt, S., 259

Gupta, N., 9
Guralnick, M. J., 269, 466
Gutstein, S. E., 461, 480, 486–491

Hadwin, J., 239, 522, 523
Hagberg, B., 8
Hagerman, R. J., 555
Haley, S., 331–332, 337
Hall, L., 367, 593
Hall, S., 329
Halliday, M., 170
Haltiwanger, J. T., 331–332
Hamby, D. W., 68
Hammar, E., 580
Hammill, D. D., 331, 336
Handen, B. L., 31
Haney, M., 96, 120
Hanft, B. E., 306
Hanner, M. A., 190
Hansford, C., 544
Happe, F., 168
Hardan, A. Y., 319
Harding, B., 32
Harris, N. S., 34, 176
Harris, P., 231
Harris, S. L., 412, 419, 437
Harrower, J. K., 268, 271, 502, 509–510, 576, 587, 593, 595
Harry, B., 70, 71, 72, 74, 77, 78, 79, 81, 82
Hart, B., 412, 442
Hartman, A., 103
Hartup, W. W., 226
Hasbury, D., 98, 357
Hauck, M., 267
Heflin, L. J., 348, 349, 371, 555, 556
Hendren, R. L., 319, 555
Hendrickson, J. M., 271
Hepburn, S. L., 171, 558
Herbert, M. R., 34
Herblson, J. M., 460
Heriza, C. B., 321
Hertzig, M. E., 178
Hesselink, J. R., 34
Hetzroni, O. E., 434
Hill, D., 306, 308
Hill, K., 523
Hobson, R. P., 201, 266
Hodgdon, L. A., 400, 442, 593
Hogan, K. L., 49, 171, 558
Hoien, T., 551
Holcombe, A., 269
Holdgrafer, G., 178
Holm, V. A., 555, 556
Hood, B., 264
Hood, M., 425
Horst, L., 70
Houwink-Manville, I., 8
Howard, P., 367
Howlin, P., 9, 239, 506, 522, 523
Hoyson, M., 271, 430, 470, 497

Huber, H., 355
Huisingh, R., 191, 196, 197
Humphry, R., 78
Hunt, P., 472, 576
Hurley, C., 593
Hurth, J., 355
Hutchins, V. L., 98
Hutchinson, T. A., 170, 256, 558
Hutt, C., 223
Hyman, S. L., 371–372
Hynd, G., 29

Idol, L., 581
Ingenmey, R., 419
Ingram, J., 312
Iovannone, R., 355
Iverson, V. S., 98, 358
Izeman, S., 353, 355

Jackson, A. E., 259–260
Jackson, B., 544
Jackson, J., 544
Jamieson, B., 430, 470, 497
Janota, I., 32
Janzen, J., 461
Jarrold, C., 231, 232, 233, 234, 236,
    264, 269, 467
Jensen, M. R., 96
Jeppson, E. S., 98
Jernigan, T. L., 34
Jette, A. M., 324
Jick, H., 36
Joe, J. R., 68, 72
Johnson, A., 98
Johnson, B.H., 98
Johnson, C. R., 31, 562
Johnson, M. H., 254
Johnston, J., 430
Johnston, S., 399, 401
Jolivette, K., 415
Jones, W. P., 480
Jordan, R., 228, 460

Kaczmarek, L., 284, 497
Kagawa-Singer, M., 70
Kaiser, A. P., 412–416, 442
Kalyanpur, M., 70, 71, 72, 74, 77,
    78, 79, 81, 82
Kaminer, R., 98, 101
Kaminski, R., 225, 226–227, 244
Kamps, D., 406, 497, 502, 503,
    504, 505, 576, 593
Kaniel, S., 96
Kanner, L., 4, 5, 37, 173, 181–182,
    304, 305
Kaplan, B., 331
Karls, J. M., 544
Kasari, C., 159, 256, 263, 350, 352,
    584
Kashinath, S., 440
Kaston, A. J., 70

Kavanagh, K. H., 67, 68–69
Kaye, J. A., 36
Keane, S.P., 466
Keeling, K., 522
Keen, D., 402
Kehres, J., 178, 435
Kellett, K., 402
Kelly-Byrne, D., 223
Kelso, J. A. S., 319
Kelso, S. E., 418, 420, 422, 424,
    462, 463, 467, 470, 472, 587
Kemmerer, K., 406
Kemper, T., 8, 32
Kemper, T. L., 312, 319
Kendall, P. C., 506
Kennedy, C. H., 576
Keshaven, M. S., 319
Kiefer-O'Donnell, R., 67
Kientz, M. A., 316, 329
Kim, A., 466
Kim, K., 171
Kincaid, D., 355
King, B. H., 555
King, N., 223
Kirchner, D. M., 174, 191
Kiresuk, T., 356
Klein, L. S., 230
Klein, M., 329
Kleinman, A., 70, 73
Klin, A., 4, 10, 12, 21–22, 29, 252,
    253, 254, 257, 258, 259, 288
Kluth, P., 579, 580, 588
Knivsberg, A. M., 551
Koegel, L. K., 268, 271, 304, 316,
    319, 412, 416, 473, 480,
    508–510, 585, 587, 593
Koegel, R., 174, 232, 268, 271, 304,
    316, 319, 412, 416, 417, 421,
    463, 473, 480, 507–510,
    585, 586, 587, 593
Kohler, F. W., 349, 497, 502, 593
Koppenhaver, D. A., 591
Kramer, H. C., 253
Krantz, P., 171, 353, 402, 417, 429,
    431, 435, 593
Krashen, S., 182
Krasnegor, N. A., 311
Krasny, L., 524
Krauss, M. W., 505
Kravits, T., 593
Kravitz, T. R., 406
Krug, D. A., 44, 48, 114, 287
Kuoch, H., 519, 520
Kuster, J. M., 485
Kuttler, S., 514, 519, 521
Kymissis, E., 581

Lahar, S., 364
Lainhart, J. E., 32
Laird, J., 72, 78, 79, 103
Lamb, J. A., 35

Landa, R., 32, 180, 181, 184, 188,
    191, 193, 194, 195
Landau, B., 182
Lang, J., 12
Langdell, T., 258
Langworthy, K. S., 555
Lasker, J., 592
Laurent, A. C., 480
Law, M., 330
Le, L., 402, 421
Leach, J., 589
Leary, M., 306, 307, 308, 317, 318
LeBlanc, L. A., 402, 425, 426
LeCouteur, A., 21, 44, 284
Lee, A., 201, 266
Lee, D. L., 401
Lee, N. L., 35
Lee, S., 497, 503
Lefebvre, D., 587
Lemanek, K. L., 230, 260
Leonard, B. R., 576
Leonard, H., 8
Leonard, M. A., 464
Leslie, A., 225, 261
Levi, G., 255
Levine, K., 550, 551, 552
Levy, S. E., 371–372
Lewis, D., 438–439
Lewis, H. C., 460
Lewis, V., 231, 232, 234, 258, 269
Lewy, A., 263, 264, 265, 462, 465
Libby, S., 228, 230, 244, 460
Liddle, K., 406, 407
Lidz, C. S., 97
Lifter, K., 469
Light, J. C., 441
Like, R. C., 82
Linder, T. W., 240, 241
Lindschau, A., 98
Lipsky, D. K., 578
LoGiudice, C., 191, 197
Lord, C., 4, 12, 19, 20, 21, 23, 24,
    30, 34, 44, 45, 95, 114,
    168, 169, 175, 176, 178,
    181, 199, 200, 201, 232,
    241, 252, 253, 255, 256,
    265, 269, 271, 284, 286,
    288, 305, 306, 307, 317,
    323, 348, 431, 432, 491
Losardo, A., 96
Lotter, V., 169
Lovaas, O. I., 168, 349, 353, 412
Loveland, K., 429–430
Lubetsky, M., 31
Luce, S. C., 417
Ludemann, P. M., 254
Ludlow, L. H., 331–332
Luthert, P., 32
Lutzker, J. R., 422
Lyon, G. R., 311

MacMillan, D. L., 349
Madsen, K. M., 36
Magill, J., 265, 269, 271
Magrab, P. R., 98
Mahoney, G. J., 108
Mailloux, Z., 316
Malach, R. S., 68, 72
Malatchi, A., 580
Malhotra, S., 9
Mancina, C., 593
Mangiapanello, K., 468
Mann, L., 175
Manoach, D., 29
Maretsky, S., 497
Maria Del Mar, M. M., 36
Markowitz, P., 232
Marks, S. U., 584–585
Mars, A. E., 14, 17
Masland, R. L., 372
Massaro, T., 550
Matson, J. L., 419
Mauk, J. E., 14
Maurer, R. G., 19
Maurere, R. G., 307
Mauthner, N., 232
Maxwell, K., 402
Mayes, L., 254
McBride, B. J., 94
McBride, B. M., 585
McClannahan, L., 171, 353, 402,
    417, 429, 431, 435, 593
McCollum, J. A., 70
McConnell, S., 589
McCormick, K. M., 415, 416
McCubbin, H. I., 70
McCune, L., 223, 225
McDonough, L., 230, 231, 233,
    234, 244
McEachin, J. J., 168
McEvoy, M. A., 497
McEvoy, R., 260
McGee, G. G., 175, 305, 417, 435,
    500–502
McGee, J., 307, 317, 323
McGinnis, E., 589, 590
McGoldrick, M., 96, 103
McKenzie, B. E., 307
McKissick, F., 257
McLean, J., 186, 408, 442
McNerney, E., 268
McPherson, M., 98
McSheehan, M., 584
McWilliam, R. A., 367, 483
Meloni, I., 8
Meltzoff, A. N., 34, 169, 257
Mentis, M., 232
Mesibov, G. B., 524
Messer, D., 228, 460
Meyer, E. C., 266, 268–269
Meyer, L. H., 576
Mildenberger, K., 29

Miller, B. L., 374, 388
Miller, H., 329
Miller, J., 181, 185
Miller, J. N., 522, 523
Miller, S. P., 480
Milone, A., 169
Milstein, J. P., 422, 425
Minderaa, R. B., 260
Minshew, N. J., 185, 319
Mirenda, P., 187, 399, 400, 401,
    402, 519, 520, 591
Monaco, A. P., 35
Montgomery, J. K., 574–575
Moore-Brown, B. J., 574–575
Morgan, L., 271
Morgan, S. B., 175
Morrier, M. J., 500, 502
Morris, R., 506
Morris, S., 329
Morrison, L., 504, 505
Morrison, R. S., 463, 465, 466
Morse, W., 575
Morton, J., 254
Most, R., 224, 225
Mount, B., 357
Moyes, R. A., 589, 590, 594
Muhle, R., 35
Mulcahy, R. F., 178
Mulick, J. A., 580
Mullen, E. M., 21
Mundy, P., 159, 170, 171, 175, 255,
    256, 257, 258, 263, 265, 267,
    269, 558
Muratori, F., 169
Muris, P., 274
Murphy, E. S., 101
Murray, D., 398
Murray-Slutsky, C., 464
Myles, B. S., 43, 402, 497, 502, 514,
    522

Nader, R., 558
Naidu, S., 8
Nakamura, J., 586
National Institutes of Health, 554
National Research Council, 348,
    349, 353, 373, 494
NcNerney, E., 520
Nelson, C., 67, 399
Nelson, K., 182
Nelson, L., 551
Newschaffer, C. J., 35
Newton, M. S., 72
Nickel, R. E., 360, 371, 550
Nicolson, R., 33
Nodland, M., 551
Norman, K., 253
Norris, C., 519
Norton, J., 551
Notari-Syverson, A., 96
Noterdaeme, M., 29

Nourot, P. M., 223, 229
Nuzzolo-Gomez, R., 464, 466
Nye, J., 19, 307

Oberlander, T. F., 558
O'Brien, J., 98, 357
Ochs, E., 174
O'Connell, B., 225, 460
O'Dell, M. C., 416, 586
Odom, S. L., 269, 430, 470, 497,
    503, 504
Oelwein, P., 592
Ogletree, B. T., 356, 441
Olson, G., 254
Oren, T., 356, 441
Orman, J., 191, 196, 197
Orsmond, G. I., 505
Ortiz, E., 464
Osborn, A., 98, 361
Osofsky, J. D., 307
Osterling, J., 14, 23, 24, 34, 169,
    255, 257, 284, 306, 349, 355,
    372, 483
Oswald, D. P., 526
Ousley, O. Y., 49, 171, 558
Overton, S., 501–503
Ownbey, J., 505–506
Ozonoff, S., 34, 181, 185, 263, 522,
    523, 524

Palazolo, K., 399
Palmer, B. C., 190
Pandina, G. J., 319
Pantone, J., 460
Papoudi, D., 5, 306
Parham, L. D., 316
Paris, B., 464
Parker, D., 504
Parmegiani, A., 552
Parnes, S. J., 98, 361
Parr, J. R., 35
Parrett, J., 593
Partingon, J. W., 412, 416
Parton, M. B., 223–224
Patterson, J., 67, 69, 228
Paul, R., 169, 175, 178, 181, 469,
    497, 575
Pearpoint, J., 357
Peck, C. A., 169, 201, 202
Peeters, T., 464
Peña, E. D., 96, 97
Pennington, B., 232, 260, 263
Pennington, R., 497
Perry, R., 555
Perucchini, P., 169
Peters, A., 182
Pfeiffer, S. I., 551
Phelps-Gunn, T., 196
Phelps-Terasaki, D., 196
Phillips, D. A., 321

Piaget, J., 222, 224, 225, 226, 228, 229, 462
Piazza, C. C., 562
Pickles, A., 44
Pierce, K., 32, 33, 510, 593
Pierce, P. M., 544
Pierce, T. B., 480
Pierson, M. R., 513
Piper, M., 321, 331, 336
Piscitelli, V., 576
Piven, J., 31
Ploof, D., 72
Politsch, A., 592
Pomeroy, J., 31
Posar, A., 552
Potter, C. A., 409–411
Potter, L., 204
Potucek, J., 406
Poulson, C. L., 171, 430
Powell, S., 228, 460
Powers, M. D., 355
Press, G. A., 34
Prior, M. R., 561
Prizant, B. M., 20, 21, 103, 349, 350, 353, 373, 408, 411, 433, 441, 442, 480, 483, 491–494, 558
Provencal, S., 524
Prutting, C., 174, 191
Przybeck, T., 266

Quill, K. A., 202, 267, 273, 405, 464, 495–496, 514, 525–526
Quinn, H. P., 550, 551, 552

Rademacher, J. A., 592, 593
Raeburn, J. M., 425
Rafferty, Y., 576
Raiten, D. J., 550
Ramirez, C., 67
Ramos, O., 8
Rand, Y., 96
Rankin-Hill, L., 70
Rapin, I., 22, 35, 552
Rapp, N., 587
Rausch, J. L., 501–503
Realmuto, G., 31
Reddy, V., 230
Ree, Y., 70
Reed, N. L., 374, 388
Reichelt, K. L., 551
Reichler, R., 47
Reichler, R. J., 286
Reid, D. H., 505–506
Reid, R., 593
Reis, K., 460
Reiss, J. G., 544
Remington, N., 544
Rescorla, L. A., 287
Richard, G. J., 190, 421
Richdale, A. L., 561, 562

Ricks, D., 175
Ridgley, R., 415
Riguet, C. B., 230, 231, 234, 244
Riley, A. M., 204
Rinaldi, J., 34, 169, 257
Risi, S., 21, 45, 95, 114, 241, 284, 286, 306, 491
Risley, T., 412, 433, 442
Ritvo, E. R., 35
Rivera, C. M., 464
Robarts, J., 5
Robert, J., 306
Roberts, B., 441
Roberts, J., 483
Roberts-DeGennaro, M., 98
Robertson, K., 584
Robertson, W., 367
Robins, D. L., 12, 18, 20, 48, 305
Robinson, C., 544
Rochen-Renner, B., 47, 286
Rodier, P. M., 33, 35, 36
Roeyers, H., 257, 260, 497, 502, 503, 576
Rogers, S. J., 22, 81, 83, 230, 232, 260–261, 263, 264, 349, 351–352, 353, 355, 460
Romano, J., 519
Roper, N., 441
Rossi, P. G., 552
Roth, F. P., 170, 193, 194, 195, 206
Rothman, J., 544
Rourke, B. P., 29
Royle, J., 592
Rubel, A. J., 82
Rubin, E., 350, 353, 373, 480
Rubin, S., 307–310
Ruble, L. A., 578–579
Ruskin, E., 253, 257
Russell, A., 31
Russell, D., 331
Russell, J., 232, 264
Rutherford, M. D., 230, 232
Rutter, M., 5, 21, 44, 45, 114, 241, 284, 286, 312, 491
Rydell, P., 480
Rydell, P. J., 159, 171–172, 173, 187, 408, 433, 441, 442

Sack, S., 408, 442
Sainato, D. M., 463, 587
Saitoh, O., 32, 33, 34
Saleebey, D., 69, 73, 79, 323
Saltz, E., 225
Saltz, R., 225
Sanchez-Ayendez, M., 70
Sancilio, M. F., 226
Sandall, S. R., 94
Sandson, T., 29
Sarokoff, R., 430
Sarracino, T., 367
Sasso, G. M., 497, 502, 576, 579

Scales, B., 223, 229
Scarcella, R., 182
Scariano, M. M., 317
Schaffer, B., 200, 348, 431
Schanen, C., 8
Schein, E. H., 77
Schepis, M. M., 505–506
Schieffelin, B., 174
Schlosser, R. W., 401, 592
Schneiderman, R. P., 372
Schopler, E., 9, 47, 200, 286, 348, 431, 432, 494
Schreibman, L., 230, 419, 421, 464, 466, 468, 508, 510, 593
Schuler, A., 169, 172, 174, 175, 182, 201, 202, 279, 400, 472–473
Schultz, R. T., 33
Schumaker, J. B., 524
Schwartz, I. S., 94, 402, 406, 407, 585
Schwebach, A. J., 31
Scott, J., 306, 317
Searle, J., 174
Secord, W., 190, 197
Seltzer, M. M., 505
Semrud-Clikeman, M., 29
Serra, M., 259–260
Sevin, B. M., 419
Sevin, J. A., 419
Shafer, K., 497
Shahbazian, M. D., 8
Shapiro, T., 178
Sharpe, S., 232
Shaw, E., 355
Sheely, R. K., 461
Shellenberger, S., 96
Shelton, T. L., 67, 69, 98
Sherer, M., 425–426, 562
Sherman, T., 254, 267
Shinnar, S., 22
Shipley-Benamou, R., 422
Shonkoff, J., 321
Shore, C., 225, 460
Shores, R. E., 271, 504
Shoshan, Y., 268, 520
Shott, S., 551
Shriberg, L. D., 174, 175
Shulman, B. S., 196
Shumway, S., 20, 21
Shure, M. B., 506
Siegel, B., 253
Siegel, D. J., 185
Sigafoos, J., 402
Sigman, M., 169, 175, 178, 230, 231, 244, 253, 255, 256, 257, 258, 263, 265, 267, 269, 435, 558
Simmons, J. Q., 31, 174, 194, 269
Simon, C. S., 197
Simon, E. W., 407

Simpson, R. L., 43, 348, 349, 371, 402, 497, 498, 502, 522, 555, 556, 576, 579, 584
Singer, D. G., 226
Singer, J. L., 226
Sitter, S., 29
Skinner, D., 576
Small, A. M., 555
Smalley, S. L., 32
Smilansky, S., 224
Smith, A., 356
Smith, A. E., 416, 480, 510
Smith, C., 518, 519
Smith, I., 260
Smith, P., 231, 269, 467
Smith, T., 168, 353, 372
Snow, J., 98, 357
Snow, M. E., 178, 201
Snyder-McLean, L., 186, 407–409, 428, 442
Sobses, D., 559
Solomonson, B., 407–408, 442
Sonnenmeier, R., 373, 427, 428, 584
Sparrow, S., 21, 253, 255, 287
Speidel, K., 592
Spekman, N.J., 170, 193, 194, 195, 206
Spence, S., 294
Spivak, G., 506
Spradley, J., 110
Squires, J., 204
Stahmer, A., 230, 464, 466, 468, 510
Starrett, A., 372
Stedman, J. M., 421
Steele, M. M., 544, 555
Steiner, P., 82
Stepanek, J. S., 67, 68, 69, 98
Stevenson, G., 589
Stone, W. L., 22, 49, 112, 171, 230, 244, 260, 558
Stores, G., 562
Storey, K., 593
Storoschuk, S., 44
Strain, P., 175, 269, 271, 349, 353–354, 497, 498, 502, 504, 587, 593
Strawser, S., 480
Sulzer-Azaroff, B., 417, 469
Sundberg, M. L., 412, 416
Surrant, A., 416
Sussman, F., 439–440
Sutton-Smith, B., 223
Swaab-Barneveld, H., 506
Swaggart, B. L., 515, 517–519
Swettenham, J., 262, 264, 523
Sylvester, R., 316
Szatmari, P., 33, 194

Tager-Flusberg, H., 168–169, 177, 205, 262

Tanguay, P., 31
Tankersley, M., 593
Tannous, J., 434
Tantam, N., 9
Taubman, M., 422
Taylor, B., 419, 430
Taylor, B. A., 468
Taylor, N. D., 230
Taylor, P. A., 544
Teitelbaum, O., 19, 307
Teitelbaum, P., 19, 307
Thelan, E., 319
Thibodeau, M., 419
Thiele, E., 553
Thiemann, K. S., 520
Thompson, E. A., 70
Thompson, M. A., 70
Thompson, S. J., 230
Thorp, D. M., 468, 470
Thousand, J. S., 360, 363, 578
Tidmarsh, L., 5
Tidswell, T., 232
Timm, M. A., 504
Todd, R. D., 266
Toll, D. M., 407
Torem, C., 593
Townsend, J., 33–34, 176, 319
Trasowech, J. E., 419, 442
Travis, L., 257
Tremblay, A., 271
Trentacoste, S. V., 35
Trevarthen, C., 5, 8, 306, 307
Trillingsgaard, A., 430
Trivette, C. M., 68, 69, 98
Tryon, A. S., 466
Tsai, L. Y., 555
Tuchman, R. F., 552
Tunali, B., 429–430
Turnbull, A. P., 67, 102
Turnbull, H. R., 102
Turner, M., 367
Twachtman, D., 174, 181, 183–184
Twachtman-Cullen, D., 174, 177, 178, 181, 184, 263, 264
Tyron, A. S., 421
Tzuriel, D., 96

Ungerer, J. A., 230, 231, 244, 267, 269

Van der Gaag, R., 10, 506
Van der Wees, M., 506
Van Geert, P. L. C., 259–260
Van Hoorn, J., 223, 229, 239, 245
Van Houten, R., 419
Van Oost, P., 257
Vandercook, T., 357, 382
VanLue, M., 520
Varley, C. K., 555, 556
Venter, A., 432
Verbrugge, L. M., 324

Vernon, D. S., 524
Vig, S., 98, 101
Villa, R. A., 578
Villard, L., 8
Vincent, L. J., 98
Vitiello, B., 554, 555
Vittimberga, G. L., 405
Volden, J., 178, 181, 201, 430
Volkmar, F., 4, 5, 6, 9, 10, 12, 22, 29, 30, 31, 252, 253, 255–256, 257, 288, 550, 552, 555, 556, 559, 561
Volterra, V., 170
Vulocevic, J., 253
Vygotsky, L. S., 222, 228, 229

Wagner, S., 577
Waitling, R. L., 316, 323, 331
Waldron, C., 520
Walker, H. M., 589
Walsh, M. E., 424
Warren, S. F., 171, 412, 442
Waterhouse, L., 232, 267, 506
Watson, L. R., 22, 200, 204, 348, 349, 431, 432
Webb, B. J., 480, 524
Webb, T., 405, 407
Webster, J., 472
Wehner, E. A., 260
Weick, A., 69, 73, 79
Weidmer-Mikhail, E., 31
Weil, M., 544
Weininger, O., 223
Weintraub, S., 29
Weitzner-Lin, B., 408, 428
Werner, C. L., 70
Werner, R. R., 70
Westby, C. E., 73, 77, 96, 102, 109–111, 227, 228, 241, 261
Wetherby, A. M., 20, 21, 23, 24, 49, 103, 169, 170, 171, 179, 185–187, 203, 205, 206, 225, 227, 253, 256, 260, 306, 349, 398, 408, 411, 480, 483, 494, 558
Whaley, K., 355
White, O., 316
Whitehair, P. M., 407
Whittaker, C. A., 409–411
Wickstrom, S., 430, 470, 504
Wieder, S., 276, 279–281, 306, 329, 348, 349, 460–462, 469, 473, 480–483, 485–486, 502
Wiesner, L. A., 30, 31, 550, 552, 555, 556, 559, 561
Wiggs, L., 562
Wiig, E., 190, 197
Wilcox, M. J., 202
Wilczenski, F. L., 593
Wilde, L., 585, 586, 587

Wilens, T. E., 555
Willard, C. T., 279
Williams, B. J., 524
Williams, E., 230, 244
Williams, L., 417
Williams, T. A., 524
Williamson, G. G., 304, 306, 307, 312, 316, 317, 329
Wilson, B., 331, 336
Wilson, G. N., 546
Wilson, P. H., 307
Wilson, S., 22
Wing, L., 9, 46, 81, 175, 184, 231, 244
Winton, P. J., 102
Witt Engerstrom, I., 8
Wolery, M., 223, 352, 353

Wolf, M., 433
Wolfberg, P., 222, 223, 226, 229, 233, 234, 236, 238, 244, 460, 472–473, 588–589
Wolfe, P., 316
Wolff, S., 31
Wong, E. C., 34
Woodman, C., 544
Woods, J., 20, 21, 23, 24, 49, 440
Woodyatt, G., 402
World Health Organization (WHO), 5, 94, 95, 105, 195, 205, 207, 234, 245, 282, 291, 324, 545, 578
Wulff, S., 460
Wynn, J. W., 372
Wzorek, M., 32

Yang, A., 575
Yeargin-Allsop, M., 4
Yeates, S. R., 230
Yeung-Courchesne, R., 34
Yirmiya, N., 263
Yoder, P. J., 171, 416, 558
York, J., 357
Young, M. R., 67

Zachman, L., 196
Zalenski, S., 353
Zanoli, K., 587
Zercher, C., 472, 473
Zilbovicius, M., 33, 34
Zoghbi, H. Y., 8
Zola, I. K., 72
Zwernik, K., 357

Subject Index

AAC. *See* Augmentative and alternative communication (AAC)

AAP. *See* American Academy of Pediatrics (AAP)

ABC. *See Autism Behavior Checklist* (ABC; Krug, Arick, & Almond)

ABLC. *See* Affect-Based Language Curriculum (ABLC)

Absence seizures, 552, 567

Accommodations, 98, 574

Achenbach System of Empirically Based Assessment (ASEBA; Achenbach & Rescorla), 287–288

Action, 338

Activities, 95, 162, 235, 324–326

ADI–R. *See Autism Diagnostic Interview–Revised* (ADI–R; Lord, Rutter, & LeCouteur)

Adolescent Sensory Profile (Brown & Dunn), 336

Adolescents

    communication assessment and, 175, 191, 196

    communication intervention for, 429

    literacy learning and, 592

    medication and, 556

    seizure activity and, 552

    social relationships and, 256, 504, 505, 524

    tips for speaking skills improvement for, 444, 445

Adrenaline, 316

Affect, 213, 229, 294, 338, 438–439, 506

Affect-Based Language Curriculum (ABLC), 438–439

Age

    diagnosis and, 41

    mobility decreases and, 8

    play stages and, 227–228

    routine maintenance medical care and, 546

    social-emotional development and, 254–256

Agenda for team meetings, 99

Ages and Stages Questionnaires (ASQ; Squires, Potter, & Bricker), 204

Aggression

    communication issues and, 179

    hypothalamus and, 316

    medication and, 554–556

    peer training and, 505

    play and, 461

    self-abuse, 318

    sexual abuse and, 561

Aided communication, definition of, 399

Akinetic seizures, 552, 567

Alberta Infant Motor Scale (Piper & Darrah), 331, 336

Alcohol exposure prenatally, 35

AlphaTalker, 592

Alternative medicine. *See* Complementary and alternative medicine (CAM)

American Academy of Child and Adolescent Psychiatry, 25

American Academy of Neurology, 22, 24–25, 36, 327, 546, 552

American Academy of Pediatrics (AAP), 327, 542, 550

American Psychiatric Association, 168

Americans with Disabilities Act (P.L. 101-336), 574

Amygdala, 32, 33, 54, 314, 315, 316, 319

Analytic processing, 213, 258

Anatomical abnormalities, 32–33

Anemia, 559

Antecedent, 451

Antecedent prompting, 497, 502

Anthropometric, 567

Anxiety

    echolalia and, 173, 433

    medication and, 554–555

    play and, 461

    sensory processing and, 316

    sexual abuse and, 561

    videomodeling and, 422

Applied behavior analysis procedures, 451

Apraxia, 318, 338

Arousal, 173, 179, 338, 492

ASEBA. *See Achenbach System of Empirically Based Assessment* (ASEBA; Achenbach & Rescorla)

Asperger Syndrome Diagnostic Scale (Myles, Bock, & Simpson), 43

Asperger's Association of New England, 52

Asperger's Disorder

    Australian Scale for Asperger's Syndrome, 15–17, 27

    diagnosis of, 5, 9–10, 39–42

    DSM–IV classification of, 9

    overview of, 9–10

    peer intervention and, 505

    play and, 231

    pragmatic language and, 174

    prevalence of, 4

    social stories and, 520–521

Assertions, 435

Assessment. *See also* Communication assessment; Interdisciplinary assessment model; Social-emotional assessment; Sensory-motor characteristics assessment;

    audiological evaluations, 327

    barriers to family–professional collaboration, 98

    diagnostic assessment tools, 10–14, 21, 43–49

Assessment (*Continued*)
  disablement framework for, 94–95
  dynamic, 96–97
  ecological, 95–97, 328
  environmental factors and, 95
  examiner's role in, 96–97
  family involvement in, 69, 98–101
  IDEA and, 71
  for inclusionary education, 589–590
  of joint attention, 185–186
  lead level testing, 327
  medical, 25
  of nonlinguistic comprehension, 186–187
  of pain or illness, 560–561
  for peer tutoring, 499
  personal factors and, 95
  process, 94
  reinforcer, 403
  role of, 94
  of social-emotional development, 265–276
*Assessment of Social and Communication Skills for
    Children with Autism* (Quill), 273
Assistive devices, 326
Association for Persons with Severe Handicaps, 52
Associative play, 224, 247, 254
Atonic seizures, 552, 567
Attachment disorders, 307
Attainment Company, 85
Attention. *See also* Joint attention
  assessment of, 185–186
  brain abnormalities and, 33–34
  communication intervention and, 405, 439
  definition of, 338
  IEP and, 580
  medication and, 30, 555
  play intervention and, 465
  sensory-motor characteristics and, 314, 316–317,
    322
  shared, 176, 261, 305
  Shared Attention Mechanism, 261
  shifting, 34, 55, 176, 229, 405
  social-emotional intervention and, 481, 489
  TEACCH project curriculum and, 431
Attention-deficit/hyperactivity disorder, 30–31, 307
Audiological evaluations, 327
Augmentative and alternative communication (AAC),
    399–403, 438, 548
Australian Scale for Asperger's Syndrome (Garnett &
    Attwood), 12, 15–17, 27, 43, 305
Autism Behavior Checklist (ABC; Krug, Arick, &
    Almond), 44, 114, 287
Autism Diagnostic Interview–Revised (ADI–R; Lord,
    Rutter, & LeCouteur), 21, 44, 284–285
Autism Diagnostic Observation Schedule–Generic
    (ADOS–G; Lord, Rutter, DiLavore, & Risi),
    21, 45, 114, 241, 243, 286, 491
Autism Independent UK, 52
Autism Information Center, 78
Autism National Committee, 52
Autism Network International, 52
Autism Research Institute, 52

Autism Screening Instrument for Educational Planning
    (Krug, Arick, & Almond), 287
Autism Screening Questionnaire (ASQ; Berument
    et al.), 45
Autism Services Center, 52
Autism Society of America, 52, 305
Autism spectrum disorder (ASD)
  ADHD and, 30–31
  diagnostic criteria for, 5, 39–42
  DSM–IV classification of, 7
  early indicators of, 14, 17, 19–24
  learning disabilities and, 29
  mental retardation (MR) and, 29–30
  neurobiologic considerations, 32–36
  obsessive-compulsive disorder (OCD) and, 30
  PDD-NOS and, 10
  personality disorders and, 31
  prevalence of, 4
  schizophrenia and, 31
  Specific language impairment and, 29
  symptom expression, 4
Autism Spectrum Screening Questionnaire (ASSQ;
    Ehlers, Gillberg, & Wing), 46
Autocratic decision making, 369–370, 391

Backstepping, 451
Backward chaining, 404, 451
Barrier games, 435
Basal ganglia, 32, 33, 54
BBB Autism, 85
Behavior regulation. *See also* Self-regulation
  assessment and, 170, 186
  definition of, 170, 213
  medication and, 555
  social stories and, 518–521
Best practice guidelines for diagnosis, 22–26
Blood oxygenation level–dependent (BOLD) contrast,
    311
Body mass index, 567
Body scheme, definition of, 318
BOLD. *See* Blood oxygenation level–dependent
    (BOLD) contrast
Bombardment questions, 111
Brain
  anatomical abnormalities in, 32–34
  sensory-motor characteristics and, 310–319
Brain stem, 33, 311, 313, 317
Breathing dysfunctions, 8
Bridging emotional ideas, 278
Bright Futures Guidelines for Health Supervision
    of Infants, Children, and Adolescents
    (Green), 546
Bruxism, 8

CAM. *See* Complementary and alternative medicine
    (CAM)
Care conferences, 544–545, 567
Care coordination, 544–545, 567
Caregiver Questionnaire (Wetherby & Prizant), 103
Caregiver–Teacher Report Form (Achenbach &
    Rescorla), 287–288

CARS. *See Childhood Autism Rating Scale* (CARS; Schopler, Reichler, DeVillis, & Daly)
Case management, 567
Casein, **551**, 567
CAT. *See* Computerized axial tomography (CAT)
CCC. *See Children's Communication Checklist* (CCC; Bishop)
CDD. *See* Childhood disintegrative disorder (CDD)
Center for Outreach & Services for Autism Community, 85
Center for Study of Autism, 53
Central nervous system (CNS), 310, 314–317, 371
Cerebellar vermis, 32, 34, 54
Cerebellum, 34, 54, 314, 315, 317
Cerebral cortex, 313, 314
Cerebrum, 32, 54, 319
Checklist for Autism in Toddlers (CHAT; Baron-Cohen, Allen, & Gillberg), 12, 13–14, 19, 20, 46, 305
Checklist stories, 533
Child Behavior Checklist (Achenbach & Rescorla), 287
Child Neurology Society, 22, 24–25, 327
Childhood Autism Rating Scale (CARS; Schopler, Reichler, DeVillis, & Daly), 47, 286, 485
Childhood disintegrative disorder (CDD), 5, 8–9, 39–42
Children's Communication Checklist (CCC; Bishop), 204–205
Chiropractic care, 372
Choice learning, 415, 416–417, 435
Choosing Outcomes and Accommodations for Children (COACH), 98, 358, 391
Circle of communication, 481–483, 484, 533
CMV. *See* Cytomegalovirus (CMV)
COACH. *See Choosing Outcomes and Accommodations for Children* (COACH)
Cognitive potential, diagnosis and, 4
Collaborative Model for Promoting Competence and Success (COMPASS), 578–579
Collaborative teaming, 90
Combined placement, 582
Comic strip conversations, 511–514
Communication and language. *See also* Nonverbal learning disabilities
    attention and, 176
    barriers to family-professional collaboration and, 78–80
    complex communication, 277–278, 280
    conversational features, 177–180
    diagnosis and, 4, 5
    disengagement and, 176
    echolalia and, 29, 171–173, 181
    emotional expression and, 14
    excessive questioning, 173
    extralinguistic features of, 175, 213
    gestalt processing, 182–183
    gestures and, 169, 171, 175
    impairments in, 5
    inclusionary education and, 576, 579, 581, 583, 584
    inference making, 183–184
    intentional communication and, 169, 170, 193–194
    language barriers, 78–80

    linguistic features of social discourse, 175–176
    listening, 74–75
    literalness and, 178, 181–182
    metaphoric language, 181
    metaphorical language, 29
    nonverbal communication, 175, 183–184, 468
    orienting and, 176
    paralinguistic features of, 174–175, 213
    perseverative speech, 172–173, 183–184, 214
    play and language development, 226–229
    pragmatics, 169, 174–180, 191, 193–199, 438, 445–448
    professional jargon, 78
    pronoun reversal, 29
    reciprocity and, 177–180
    semantics, 188, 190–192, 448–450
    social relatedness and, 169, 170
    speaking effectively, 75–76
    specific language impairment and autistic disorder, 29
    theory of mind and, 168–169
    total communication, 399
    two-way communication and, 277, 279, 280
    unconventional verbal behavior, 169, 187–189
Communication and Symbolic Behavior Scales (CSBS; Wetherby & Prizant), 185, 203
Communication and Symbolic Behavior Scales Developmental Profile (CSBS DP), 20
Communication assessment
    aided communication, 399
    as characterized by DSM–IV, 168
    conversational features and, 177–180
    curriculum analysis and, 374, 378–382
    dimensions and aspects for assessment, 200
    echolalia and, 171–173
    forms of, 195, 199–205
    gestalt processing and, 182–183
    gestures and, 169, 171, 175, 186
    intentional communication and, 169, 170, 193–194
    interviews, 200–201, 208–210
    metaphoric language and, 181
    for nonverbal children, 186–187
    nonverbal communication, 175, 183–184
    observations and, 185, 198–199, 201–203
    overview of, 168
    perspective taking and, 275
    play and, 460, 464
    pragmatics and, 174–180, 191, 193–199
    preseverative speech and, 172–173, 183–184
    profiles of communication, 185–195
    record review and, 195, 199–200
    semantic assessment, 188, 190–192
    standardized tools and, 203 205
    theoretical views of language impairment and, 168–169
    theory of mind and, 168–169
    two-way communication, 277, 482
    unaided communication, 399
    unconventional verbal behavior and, 169, 187–189
Communication Assessment (Project TEACCH; Watson et al.), 204

Communication Interview (Peck & Schuler), 201
Communication skills intervention
   Affect-Based Language Curriculum (ABLC),
      438–439
   augmentative communication and, 400
   computer-based intervention programs, 434
   conversational skills expansion, 434–437
   echolalic management, 442
   family and primary caregivers and, 415, 423, 432,
      437–440
   home environment and, 437–440
   imitation and, 410
   incidental teaching and, 442
   joint action routines, 407–409, 442
   limited verbal skills support, 399–412
   milieu teaching and, 415
   minimal speech and proximal communication
      and, 410
   modeling and, 420–427, 424
   *More Than Words–The Hanen Program for Parents
      of Children with ASD*, 439–440
   overview of, 398
   Picture Exchange Communication System
      (PECS), 403–407
   prompting, 404
   reciprocal reading, 442
   reinforcement and, 403, 413–415, 417, 421
   scripting and, 428–429
   TEACCH language and communication
      curriculum, 431–433
   time delay and, 418, 442
   tips for, 445
   unconventional verbal behavior and, 433–434
   verbal skills support, 412–431
   visual supports, 400, 442, 450–451
Communicative Means–Function Questionnaire
   (Finnerty & Quill), 202
Community-based assessment model. *See also*
   Assessment; Interdisciplinary assessment
   model
   family involvement in, 114–115
   interviews, 109–112
   observations and, 112, 114–115
   overview of, 108–109
   questions for, 110–111
   record reviews and, 112, 113
Community follow-up meetings, 116
COMPASS. *See* Collaborative Model for Promoting
   Competence and Success (COMPASS)
Complementary and alternative medicine (CAM),
   371–374, 548, 550
Complex communication, 277–278, 280
Complex partial seizures, 552, 567
Compliments, 503, 524
Comprehensive programs, 349
Computer-based intervention programs, 434
Computerized axial tomography (CAT), 311
Conclusion drawing, 264
Conflict mediation, 363–364
Consensus building, 391
Consequences, 451, 521

Constant time delay, 418
Construct validity, 54
Constructive play, 224
Content validity, 54
Context, 177, 180, 185, 191
Contracture, 557, 567
Control needs, 173, 400
Control sentences, 514, 519, 533
Convergent thinking, 361, 391
Conversation Guide (Turnbull and Turnbull), 102
Conversational skills expansion, 434–437
Cooperative play, 224, 247, 254, 476
Coordinated actions, 489–490
Coregulation, 488–489
Corpus callosum, 32–33, 314, 315, 319
Correspondence training, 463
Cortex, 32, 54, 315, 317
Cortisol, 316
Creating emotional ideas, 278
Criterion validity, 54
CSBS. *See Communication and Symbolic Behavior
   Scales* (CSBS; Wetherby & Prizant)
CSBS DP. *See Communication and Symbolic Behavior
   Scales Developmental Profile* (CSBS DP)
Cultural competence, 70–74, 81–82, 111
Cure Autism Now, 53
Curriculum analysis for intervention planning
   curriculum modifications, 381
   curriculum objectives, 379–380
   IDEA and, 574
   language-based curriculum analysis (LBCA) and,
      374, 378, 380–382
   needs evaluation and, 380–381
   overview of, 374, 378–379
Cytomegalovirus (CMV), 35, 54

Decentered pretend play, 225
Decentration, 247
Decision making, 416. *See also* Intervention decision
   making
Decontextualization, 225, 247
Deficit perspective, 338
Delaware Autism Institute, 403
Delayed echolalia, 181, 183, 213, 424, 484
Delayed prompting, 404, 451
Democratic decision making, 369–370, 391
Dental care, 556–557, 565
Depression, 554, 561
Descriptive sentences, 514, 519, 533
Developmental coordination disorder, 307
Developmental Coordination Disorder Questionnaire
   (B. Wilson, Kaplan, Crawford, Campbell, &
   Dewey), 331, 336
Developmental individual difference relationship-
   based model (DIR), 481–486. *See also*
   Floor time
Diagnosis of autism
   anatomical abnormalities and, 32–33
   assessment tools, 10–14, 21, 43–49
   Australian Scale for Asperger's Syndrome (Garnett &
      Attwood), 12, 15–17, 27, 43

best practice guidelines, 22–26
Checklist for Autism in Toddlers, 12, 13–14, 19, 20, 46
childhood disintegrative disorder with shared autistic features and, 5
criteria for, 5–6, 39–42
Diagnostic Criteria Checklist for Autistic Disorder, 11–12
differential diagnosis, 28–31
Early Indicators or Red Flags of ASD Checklist, 23–24
etiology speculations, 34–36
Infant–Toddler Checklist, 20
infant–toddler diagnosis, 20–22
longitudinal studies and, 14, 19–20
Modified Checklist for Autism in Toddlers, 18–19
neurobiologic considerations, 32–36
overview of, 4
pervasive developmental disorders in DSM–IV, 7–10
physician referral and, 27
practitioner role in, 26–28, 96–97
Rett's Disorder and, 5
sensory motor diagnostic literature, 304–307
symptom expression variability and, 4
trends in, 6–7
videotaping and, 20–21, 27
Diagnostic and Statistical Manual of Mental Disorders–Fourth Edition (DSM–IV; APA)
ADHD and, 31
autism description and, 6, 27
communication impairment characterized in, 168
correlation with ICD–10, 6–7
observations and, 114
sensory-motor characteristics and, 305
social-emotional development and, 252
Diagnostic and Statistical Manual of Mental Disorders–Third Edition (DSM–III; APA), 5
Diet and nutrition, 8, 371, 550–552, 557–558, 565
Differential diagnosis, 28–31
Differential reinforcement, 415, 451
DIR. *See* Developmental individual difference relationship-based model (DIR)
Directive sentences, 514, 533
Disablement framework to guide assessment, 94–95
Discrete trials, 349, 404, 412, 451
Discrimination training, 404
Disengagement, 33–34, 54, 176. *See also* Engagement
Distal gestures, 186
Divergent thinking, 361, 391
Diversity, 67–68, 70–71
Dominant mutation, 54
Down syndrome, 175, 257, 259, 262, 307, 592
Dramatic play, 224
Drugs. *See* Medication
Due process, 71, 78
Dynamic assessment, 96–97, 162
Dynamic systems model, 319–322, 338
Dysphagia, 8

Early and Periodic Screening, Diagnostic, and Treatment Program. *See* EPSDT. *See* Medicaid/EPSDT (Early and Periodic Screening, Diagnostic, and Treatment Program) Schedule
Early Indicators or Red Flags of ASD Checklist, 23–24
EASIC. *See Evaluating Acquired Skills in Communication* (EASIC; Riley)
Echolalia
communication skills intervention and, 424, 433, 434, 442
communication success and, 187
computer-based intervention programs, 434
delayed echolalia, 181, 183, 213, 424, 484
description of, 171
as gestalt process, 182
immediate echolalia, 183, 213
inclusionary education and, 588
mitigated echolalia, 171–172, 183, 213
personal account of, 308
specific language impairment differentiation and, 29
video modeling and, 424, 434
Ecological assessment, 95–97, 162, 328
Ecomaps, 103, 106, 115, 162
Education for All Handicapped Children Act (P.L. 94-142), 574
Education of the Handicapped Act (P.L. 91-230), 574
EEG. *See* Electroencephalogram (EEG)
Effectiveness, 391
Efficacy, 391
Electroencephalogram (EEG), 8, 311, 327
Eligibility, 597
Elimination diets, 551
Embryogenesis, 54
Emory Autism Resource Center Inclusion Project, 577
Emotion recognition, 258–260
Emotional development. *See* headings beginning Social-emotional
Emotional ideas, 278, 280–281
Empathy, 268–269, 509, 510
Engagement, 229, 438, 460. *See also* Disengagement
Engrams, 318, 338
Environmental factors
assessment and, 95
communication skills intervention and, 400, 412, 413–415, 431
definition of, 95
floor time and, 483–484
inclusionary education and, 577, 581–582
milieu teaching and, 413–415
play intervention and, 461
pragmatic assessment and, 193
prevalence of autism and, 4
resistance to environmental change, 305
sensory-motor characteristics and, 321, 326, 329, 332
Epilepsy, 545, 552. *See also* Seizures
EPSDT. *See* Medicaid/EPSDT (Early and Periodic Screening, Diagnostic, and Treatment Program) Schedule

Etiology, speculated etiology for autism, 34–36
Evaluating Acquired Skills in Communication (EASIC; Riley), 204
Evaluating Communicative Competence: A Functional Pragmatic Procedure–Revised Edition (Simon), 197
Example questions, 110
Exceptional Parent Magazine, 85
Excessive questioning, 173, 187, 434
Execution, 307
Executive function, 263–264, 276, 294, 313, 490
Experience questions, 110–111
Expressive language, 438
Exteroceptive receptors, 312, 338
Extinction, 451
Extralinguistic features, 175, 213
Eye-Direction Detector, 261, 294
Eye gaze and eye contact
    assessment and, 589
    greetings and, 201, 266
    as indicator of autism, 20, 171
    nonstandard interventions and, 371
    as nonverbal aspect of conversation, 178
    social-emotional development and, 254, 255, 286, 489, 521
    social relatedness and, 6, 257, 306
    specific language impairment differentiation and, 29
    video monitoring and, 423

Face perception, 29, 33, 257–260
Facial expression
    assessment and, 589
    communication and, 277
    emotional recognition and, 506
    pain expression, 558
    play intervention and, 465
    social-emotional development and, 254, 255, 258, 259, 286
    theory of mind and, 522–524
    videotaping and, 423, 426, 517–518
Facial motor nucleus, 32, 54
Fact finding, 351
Fading, 415, 419, 428, 433, 464
False-belief tasks, 261–263, 523, 533
Family & Disability Newsletter, 85
Family and primary caregivers
    assessment process and, 69, 98–106, 108–112, 114–115, 589
    barriers to family–professional collaboration, 72–80, 98
    communication skills intervention and, 415, 423, 432, 437–440
    coping styles, 69
    cultural competence and, 70–74, 81–82
    dental care and, 556–557
    diagnosis of autistic disorders and, 19, 20, 26, 28, 42
    diet and nutrition and, 550–552
    diversity in families, 67–68
    family strengths, 68–69

health care and, 542–543, 545, 552–554, 559, 562
IDEA and, 70, 71
inclusionary education and, 577–579, 589
intervention and, 31, 350, 354, 356, 433
medical care and, 542–543
pivotal response behaviors, 268–269
play assessment and, 240–241
rapport-building with, 109–110
seizure activity and, 552–554
sensory-motor characteristics assessment and, 328, 332
sleep issues and, 562
social-emotional development and, 254, 267, 269, 277, 278, 284, 480, 490, 492, 502–503
Family-centered care
    assessment process and, 69, 98–101, 104–106, 108
    barriers to family–professional collaboration, 72–80, 98
    cultural competence and, 70–74, 81–82
    diversity in families and, 67–68
    family strengths, 68–69, 73–74
    IDEA and, 70
    implications for professionals, 82–83
    listening effectively, 74–75
    overview of, 66–67
    power imbalance and, 79–80
    professional language and, 78–80
    professional relationship development, 81–82
    speaking effectively, 75–76
    team culture and, 76–77
    tenets of, 67–70
Family Resource Associates, 86
Family Village, 86
Federation for Children with Special Needs, 53
Feed-forward information, 321
Feedback, 318–319, 321, 488, 522
Fight-or-flight response, 316
Figurative Language Interpretation Test (Palmer), 190
Fine motor skills, 306–307, 317, 329
First-order false-belief tasks, 262
First-order theory of mind tasks, 262, 294
FIRST WORDS Project, 21
Floor time. *See also* Developmental individual difference relationship-based model (DIR)
    definition of, 533
    example of implementation of, 484
    play intervention and, 460–461, 469, 473
    as relationship-based intervention, 348, 349
    value of, 483, 485, 502
FMRI. *See* Functional magnetic resonance imaging (FMRI)
Focal treatments, 349
Follow-up planning, 138–142
Food reinforcers, 421
Forced-choice questions, 435
Fragile X syndrome, 546, 567
Fragmentation in service delivery, 366–368
Frameworks for sharing, 487–488
Free, appropriate public education, 574–575, 597

Friendship, 269, 271, 273–274, 294, 498, 501, 590. *See also* Peer relationships; Social-emotional development

Frontal cortex, 34

Frontal lobe, 314

Functional brain imaging, 54

Functional Emotional Assessment Scale (FEAS; Greenspan), 279, 294, 485

Functional magnetic resonance imaging (FMRI), 33, 311

Functional play, 224, 247

Fusiform gyrus, 54

Games and sports. *See also* headings beginning Play
  barrier games, 435
  definition of, 247
  play intervention, 464, 468, 472, 473
  social-emotional intervention and, 522
  as stage of play, 224
  videotaping and, 468

Gender, 8, 34, 35, 41

General education classroom with development and supervision of inclusionary plan, 582

General education classroom with modification, 581–582

General education classroom with support of one-to-one aid, 582

Generalization
  intervention and, 351
  modeling and, 421, 424, 426, 426–427
  natural language intervention and, 412
  peer intervention and, 504
  response, 402, 419, 451
  scripting and, 430
  stimulus, 401

Genetic factors
  diagnosis and, 26, 304–305
  etiology of autism and, 35, 312, 327
  genetic testing, 545
  prevalence of autism and, 4, 35
  X chromosome, 8, 546, 567

Geneva Centre for Autism, 86

Genograms, 96, 103, 106, 115, 162

Gestalt processing, 182–183, 213

Gestalts, 401

Gestures. *See also* Manual signs; Nonverbal communication
  assessment and, 280, 286, 589
  early communication and, 169
  emotion recognition and, 506
  emotional expression and, 260–261, 277
  as extralinguistic feature, 175
  gesture dictionaries, 400, 521
  hand signals, 401, 411, 440
  handflapping, 304, 306
  joint attention and, 256
  nonverbal children and, 186
  overview of use of, 171
  as request function, 260
  two-way communication and, 280
  videotaping and, 426, 517

Gilliam Asperger's Disorder Scale (GADS; Gilliam), 47–48

Gilliam Autism Rating Scales (GARS; Gilliam), 48, 114

Gluten, 551, 567

Goal Attainment Scaling (GAS; Kiresuk, Smith, & Cardillo), 356

Graduated time delay, 417–419

Grand tour questions, 110, 162

Greetings
  ABLC and, 438
  communication assessment and, 206
  eye contact and, 266
  milieu language and, 415
  peer intervention and, 503, 504
  time delay and, 418
  video modeling and, 422, 423

Gross Motor Function Measure (Russell), 331

Gross motor skills, 306–307, 317, 329

Group play, 466, 472, 476

Growth monitoring, 552

Growth retardation, 8

Guiding, 486–487

Gum hyperplasia, 557

Hand signals, 401, 411, 440. *See also* Gestures; Sign language

Handflapping, 304, 306. *See also* Repetitive behavior

Health care
  augmentative communication systems and, 548
  care coordination, 544–545, 567
  checklist, 549
  complementary and alternative medicine (CAM) and, 548, 550
  dental care, 556–557
  diet and nutrition and, 550–552, 557–558
  growth monitoring, 552
  medical home, 542–543, 567
  medication and, 30, 554–556
  orthopedic care, 557
  overview of, 542
  pain and, 558–559
  preventive medicine, 545–562
  problem lists for, 545–546, 568
  resources, 565–567
  routine maintenance, 546, 548
  safety and, 559, 561
  seizures and, 543, 545, 552–554
  self-care and, 557–558
  sexuality and, 559, 561
  stimulant medication, 30
  strategies for, 545–562
  websites concerning, 546

Heller's Syndrome. *See* Childhood disintegrative disorder (CDD)

Hidden agenda questions, 111

Hippocampus, 314, 315, 316, 319

Holistic processing, 258

Home Assessment Interview (Watson, Lord, Schaffer, & Schopler), 200–201

Hygiene, 332

Hypersensitivity, 316, 324, 338
Hyposensitivity, 316, 324, 338
Hypothalamus, 314, 315, 316
Hypotonia, 557

ICD–10. *See International Classification of Diseases*
      (ICD–10; WHO)
ICF. *See International Classification of Functioning,*
      Disability and Health (ICF; WHO)
ICIDH. *See International Classification of*
      Impairments, Disabilities and Handicaps
      (ICIDH)
IEP. *See* Individualized Education Program (IEP)
IFSP. *See* Individualized Family Service Plan (IFSP)
Imaginative play, 476. *See also* Pretend play; Play
Imitation
      ABLC and, 438
      communication skills intervention and, 419, 439
      IEP and, 580
      imitation deficits, 260–261, 266
      milieu teaching and, 415
      proximal communication and, 410
Imitative play, 462–467
Immediate echolalia, 183, 213
Immunizations, 36
Impairments
      definition of, 338
      ecological assessment and, 162
      interdisciplinary assessment model and, 95
      language, 29
      play, 222, 232–233, 235
      sensory-motor characteristics and, 324
      social-emotional development and, 256–264
Incidental teaching, 404, 413, 414, 415, 442
Inclusion, definition of, 597
Inclusionary education
      COMPASS and, 578–579
      components of, 577
      integration facilitation, 584–593
      legislation and, 574
      leisure activities and, 592
      literacy and, 591–592
      models for, 581–584
      peer buddy programs, 583
      peer culture and, 588–591
      priming and, 585–587
      prompting and, 587
      self-management and, 592–593
      transitions and, 593–594
      unconventional verbal behavior and, 587–588
Independent play, 476. *See also* Play; Solitary play
Indiana Resource Center for Autism, 53
Individualized and appropriate education, 71
Individualized approach to inclusionary education, 583
Individualized Education Program (IEP). *See also*
            Intervention
      at-a-glance form, 107
      curriculum analysis and, 379–380
      definition of, 597
      family–professional collaboration and, 82
      inclusionary education and, 577

MAPS and, 357
      power hierarchy and, 79–80
      RDI model and, 490
      sensory-motor characteristics and, 328
      social interactions and, 591
      summer services and, 354
      team meetings and, 106
      team strategies, 579–581
      value of individual rights and, 71
Individualized Family Service Plan (IFSP), 106, 107,
            327–328
Individuals with Disabilities Education Act (IDEA)
      cultural competence and, 70–71
      IEPs and, 580
      inclusionary education and, 574, 580
      individual rights and, 71
      parent–school conflicts and, 77–78
      sensory-motor characteristics and, 305
Infant–Toddler Checklist, 20
Infants and toddlers, diagnosis of autism in, 20–22
Inference making, 183–184, 261, 264, 274, 438
Inflexibility. *See* Rigidity
Initiation, 268, 497, 509–510
Insomnia, 555. *See also* Sleep
Intake, 101–104, 122–130
Intentionality Detector, 261, 294
Interaction Analysis (Quill), 202
Interdisciplinary assessment model. *See also*
            Assessment
      activities and, 95
      barriers to family–professional collaboration, 98
      care coordination, 116, 119
      community-based assessment model, 108–115
      community follow-up meetings, 116
      disablement framework guide, 94–95
      dynamic assessment, 96–97
      ecological assessment, 95–97
      ecomaps and, 103–104, 106, 115
      environmental factors and, 95
      family and, 98–101
      genograms and, 96, 103, 106, 115
      impairments and, 95
      intake, 101–104, 122–130
      interdisciplinary consultation summary, 117–118,
            143–160
      interviews, 102–103
      limitations of, 119
      medical model, 94
      overview of, 94, 101
      participation and, 95
      personal factors and, 95
      planning for, 106, 108
      postassessment planning meetings, 115, 138–142
      preassessment planning meetings, 104–108,
            131–137
      professional's roles in, 96–97, 100, 106
      report writing and, 115–116
      sample forms and reports, 122–130, 131–137,
            138–142, 143–160
      social model, 94
      testing and, 97

Interdisciplinary Council on Developmental and Learning Disorders, 329
Internal consistency reliability, 54
International Classification of Diseases (ICD–10; WHO), correlation with DSM, 6–7
International Classification of Functioning, Disability and Health (ICF; WHO), 94–95, 162, 234, 324, 330
International Classification of Impairments, Disabilities and Handicaps (ICIDH), 94
Interoceptive receptors, 312, 338
Interpersonal problem solving, 506
Intervention. *See also* Communication skills intervention; Individualized Education Program (IEP); Limited verbal skills support; Scripting; Social-emotional intervention; Verbal skills support
    best practices considerations, 353–354
    COACH process and, 358
    combined approaches, 348
    comprehensive programs, 349
    conflict resolution and, 363–364
    coordination of, 364–371
    cost/benefits and, 351
    criteria for choice of, 350–352
    current, 348–356
    curriculum analysis for intervention, 374, 379–382, 574
    decision-making and, 359–371
    dietary treatments, 371–372
    early, 355–356
    effectiveness of, 349–352
    efficacy and, 349–352
    family and, 31, 350, 354, 356
    feasibility of, 351
    floor time and, 348, 349
    focal treatments, 349
    fragmentation and, 366–368
    generalizability of, 351
    language-based curriculum analysis (LBCA), 374, 378
    least restrictive environment and, 370
    Making Action Maps (MAPS), 356–358
    nonstandard interventions, 371–377
    "only as special as necessary" guideline, 368–369
    overview of, 348
    physiologically oriented interventions, 348
    placement and, 368
    planning programs, 356–359
    problem-solving and, 359, 360–363
    programming needs, 354–356
    relationship-based, 348
    sensory-motor deficits and, 323
    skill-based, 348
    social development and, 273
    summer services, 354
    TEACCH project and, 348, 349, 351
    training and, 351, 374
    VISTA and, 365–371
Intervention decision making
    autocratic decision making, 369–370
    conflict mediation, 363–364
    creative problem solving, 360–363
    democratic decision making, 369–370
    fragmentation and, 366–368
    "only as special as necessary" guideline for, 368–369
    Osborn-Parnes creative problem solving process, 361–363
    overview of, 359–360
    placement and, 368
    related services and, 364–371
    team polarization and, 369–370
    VISTA and, 365–371
Interviews
    communication assessment and, 200–201, 208–210
    community-based assessment model and, 109–112
    interdisciplinary assessment model and, 102–103
    play assessment and, 235–236
    sensory-motor characteristics assessment and, 328
    social-emotional assessments and, 284–285
Intimacy, 481
Intonation, 426
Iron deficiency, 559
Isolation, 230, 255, 264–265, 506

Jargon, 78
Joint action routines, 407–409, 442
Joint attention
    ASD diagnosis and, 19–21
    assessment of, 185–186
    definition of, 170, 213, 294
    as intervention goal, 408
    milieu teaching and, 413
    play intervention and, 461, 470–471
    social-emotional development and, 256–257, 263, 266, 286, 484, 493
    visual supports and, 399
Judgment stories, 533

Krug Asperger's Disorder Index (KADI; Krug & Arick), 48

Labeling, 422
Landau-Kleffner syndrome, 567
Language. *See* Communication and language
Language-based curriculum analysis (LBCA), 374, 378, 380–382
Language Development Survey (LDS; Achenbach & Rescorla), 287
Language Processing Test–Revised (Richard & Hanner), 190
LBCA. *See* Language-based curriculum analysis (LBCA)
LDS. *See Language Development Survey* (LDS; Achenbach & Rescorla)
Lead intoxication, 559
Lead-level testing, 327
Leading questions, 111
LEAP. *See* Learning Experiences … An Alternative Program (LEAP)
Learned helplessness, 268, 295

Learning disabilities, Autism spectrum disorder (ASD) and, 29
Learning Experiences … An Alternative Program (LEAP), 498
Learning styles, 439
Least restrictive environment, 71, 370, 574, 597. *See also* Inclusionary education
Leisure activities, 592
Limbic system, 54
Limited verbal skills support. *See also* Communication skills intervention
  augmentative and alternative communication (AAC) and, 399–403
  gestalts and, 401
  intervention goals, 400, 404–405, 408, 410
  joint action routines and, 407–409
  minimal speech and proximal communication approach, 409
  overview of, 399
  PECS and, 403–407
  visual supports, 399–403
Line of regard, 295
Listening, 74–75, 444, 495
Literacy, 591–592
Literalness, 178, 181–182

M–CHAT. *See Modified Checklist for Autism in Toddlers* (M–CHAT; Charman et al.)
MAAP Services for More Advanced Persons with Autism, 53
MacArthur Communicative Development Inventories (Fenson), 21, 203–204
Magnetic resonance imaging (MRI), 32
Magnetoencephalography (MEG), 311
Making Action Maps (MAPS), 98, 356–358, 391
Making requests, 418–419. *See also* Questioning
Mand-model procedures, 411, 413–415, 419, 451
Manual signs, 401
MAPS. *See* Making Action Maps (MAPS)
Medicaid/EPSDT (Early and Periodic Screening, Diagnostic, and Treatment Program) Schedule, 546
Medical assessment, 25
Medical home, 542–543, 565, 567
Medical model, 94, 162
Medication
  antianxiety, 555–556
  antiseizure drugs, 555
  overview of, 554–555
  resources on, 565
  side effects of, 555, 557
  stimulant, 30, 555
  tranquilizer drugs, 555
Medulla, 314, 315
MEG. *See* Magnetoencephalography (MEG)
Mental health, 31, 307, 554
Mental retardation (MR), 29–30, 201, 503, 554
Mentalizing, 295
Meta-representation, 225, 232, 260
Metaphoric language, 29, 181, 213
Milieu teaching, 412–417, 451

Mini tour questions, 110, 162
Mitigated echolalia, 171–172, 183, 213
Modeling. *See also* Observations; Videotaping
  definition of, 451
  milieu teaching and, 413, 415
  peer models, 421
  play intervention and, 462–464, 466, 467, 472
  scripting and, 428
  self-modeling, 423
  verbal skills support and, 420–421
  video modeling, 420
  in vivo modeling, 420
Modifications, 581–582
Modified Checklist for Autism in Toddlers (M–CHAT; Charman et al.), 12, 18–20, 27, 48, 305
More Than Words–The Hanen Program for Parents of Children with ASD, 439–440
Motivation
  communication skills intervention and, 408
  natural language intervention and, 412, 416
  play and, 229–230, 235
  PRT and, 507–508
  sensory-motor characteristics and, 319
  social-emotional issues and, 268, 487
  video modeling and, 422, 424
Motor-Free Visual Perception Test–Revised (Colarusso & Hammill), 331, 336
Motor planning, 307, 308, 313, 317–318, 329, 338
Motor skills development, 306–307. *See also* headings beginning Sensory-motor
MR. *See* Mental retardation (MR)
MRI. *See* Magnetic resonance imaging (MRI)
Mullen Scales of Early Learning (Mullen), 21
Multipointing, 451
Mumps, measles, rubella (MMR) vaccine, 36, 54
Muscle rigidity, 8
Myelin, 311, 338
Myelinization, 311

Narrative play therapy, 471–472, 473
National Alliance for Autism Research, 53
National Dissemination Center for Children with Disabilities, 53
National Parent Network on Disabilities (NPND), 86
National Research Council, 494
Native language questions, 111
Natural consequences, 521
Natural language paradigm, 412–417
Neurobiologic considerations, 32–36
Neuromaturational model. *See also* Sensory-motor characteristics
  central nervous system (CNS) and, 310, 314–317
  definition of, 338
  dynamic systems model compared with, 322
  feedback and, 318–319
  motor response, 317–318
  overview of, 310–312
  sensory input and, 312–313, 314, 316
Neurons, 312
Neurophysiologic retraining, 371
Neurotransmitters, 568

Nondiscriminatory assessment, 71
Nonlinguistic comprehension, 186–187
Nonliteral language, 178
Nonstandard interventions, 371–377
Nonverbal communication, 175, 183–184, 468. *See also* Gestures
Nonverbal learning disabilities, 29
Noun acquisition, 416

Object fascination, diagnosis and, 4
Objective finding, 361
Observation Profile (Cumine, Leach, & Stevenson), 589
Observations. *See also* Modeling; Videotaping
    communication assessment and, 185, 198–199, 201–203
    community-based assessment model and, 112, 114–115
    play assessment and, 236, 238–240
    sensory-motor characteristics assessment and, 328–329
    social-emotional development and, 279, 285–286
Obsessive-compulsive disorder (OCD), 30, 308
Occipital lobe, 314
OCD. *See* Obsessive-compulsive disorder (OCD)
Online Asperger Syndrome Information & Support, 53
Onlooker play, 224, 247
Open-ended questions, 435
Opioid properties, 551–552, 568
Oral motor skills, 306–307, 317, 329
Orbital prefrontal cortex, 34
Orienting, 34, 54, 176
Orthomolecular theory, 568
Overselectivity, 184, 213, 316, 318, 339, 508

Pacing, 486–487
Pain, 558–559
Paralinguistic features, 174–175, 213
Parallel play, 224, 247, 254
Parent Interview for Autism (PIA; Stone & Hogan), 49
Parents. *See* Family and primary caregivers
Parents Helping Parents, 86
Parietal cortex, 33–34
Parietal lobe, 33, 54, 314
Participation, 95, 162
Passivity, 463, 476
PDD-NOS. *See* Pervasive development disorder not otherwise specified (PDD-NOS)
Peabody Motor Development Scales–Second Edition (Folio & Fewell), 331, 336
PECS. *See* Picture Exchange Communication System (PECS; Frost & Bondy)
Pediatric Evaluation of Disabilities Inventory (Haley, Coster, Ludlow, Haltiwanger, & Andrellos), 331–332, 337
Peer relationships. *See also* Social-emotional development
    friendship, 269, 271, 273–274, 498, 501, 590
    inclusionary education and, 576, 583, 587, 588–591
    literacy learning and, 592
    peer acceptance, 295

peer buddy programs, 583
peer initiation, 497
peer intervention, 496–506
peer mediation, 577
peer modeling, 417, 421, 492
peer-supported play strategies, 470–474
peer tutoring, 417, 421, 498, 499, 501, 532
priming and, 587
Peptides, 568
Perceptual understanding, 274–275
Peripheral vasomotor disturbances, 8
Perseverative speech, 172–173, 187, 214
Personal factors, definition of, 95
Perspective sentences, 514, 519, 533
Perspective-taking skills, 254–255, 275, 425
Pervasive development disorder not otherwise specified (PDD-NOS)
    Asperger's Disoder and, 9
    Austistic Disorder and, 10
    criteria for, 5
    DSM–IV classification of, 10
    face perception and, 258–260
    overview of, 10
    prevalence of, 4
Pervasive developmental disorders, in DSM–IV, 7–10, 42
PET. *See* Position emission tomography (PET)
Phonology, 169
Physician referral, 27
Physiologically oriented interventions, 348
PIA. *See* Parent Interview for Autism (PIA; Stone & Hogan)
Pica, 559, 568
Picture Exchange Communication System (PECS; Frost & Bondy), 348, 400, 403–407
Pivotal response training (PRT), 268–270, 468, 470, 502, 507–510
P.L. 91-230. *See* Education of the Handicapped Act (P.L. 91-230)
P.L. 94-142. *See* Education for all Handicapped Children Act (P.L. 94-142)
P.L. 101-336. *See* Americans with Disabilities Act (P.L. 101-336)
Placement, 368
Planned pretend play, 225
Play. *See also* Games and sports
    associative, 224–225, 247, 254
    attention shifts and, 229
    challenges for children with ASD, 229–233
    classifications of, 223–225
    cooperative, 224, 247, 255, 476
    definitions, 247
    DSM–IV definition of play impairment, 222
    explanations for impairments in, 232–233
    flexibility in, 229–230
    functional, 224, 247
    group, 456, 466, 472, 476
    imaginative, 476
    independent, 476
    isolation and, 230, 255
    language development and, 226–229

Play (*Continued*)
    motivation and, 229–230, 235
    onlooker, 224, 247
    parallel, 224, 247, 254
    practice, 247
    pretend, 224–226, 230–232, 280
    repetitive behavior and, 230
    sensory-motor characteristics and, 306
    social interaction, 19, 223–224, 226–229,
        232–233, 235
    solitary, 224, 225, 247, 255
    stages of, 224, 227–228
    unoccupied, 223
    visual symbols and, 401–402
    world construction and, 223, 225
Play assessment
    activity dimensions of, 235
    challenges in play for children with ASD, 229–233
    family and, 240–241
    forms, 237–238, 242–243
    impairment assessment dimensions, 235
    interviews, 235–236
    motivation and, 229–230, 235
    observation and, 236, 238–240
    overview of, 222, 234
    participation dimensions of, 235
    play development principles and, 223–226
    play profiles, 233–234
    record reviews, 234–235
    relationship of play to language and cognition and,
        226–229
    theory of mind and, 235
    tools for, 240–243
    videotaping and, 239
Play intervention
    communication and language and, 460
    engagement and, 460
    floor time and, 460–461, 469, 473
    goals for, 462
    imitative play, 462–467
    independent play, 462–466
    joint attention and, 461, 470–471
    modeling and, 462–464, 466, 467, 472
    overview of, 460–462
    peer-supported play strategies, 470–474
    pretend play, 466–470
    prompting and, 462–463, 467, 472
    reciprocity and, 461
    reinforcement and, 463–464, 467, 471
    scripting and, 461, 466, 468–469
    video modeling and, 468, 469
Play Observation Diary (Van Hoorn), 239
Play Preference Inventory (Wolfberg), 239
*Playmates and Friends Questionnaire for
        Teachers–Revised* (Goldman & Buysse), 590
Pointing, 19, 280
Polymorphism, 35, 55
Pons, 314, 315
Positron emission tomography (PET), 33, 311
Posttraumatic stress disorder, 307

Postassessment planning meetings, 115, 138–142
Power card strategy, 522
Power hierarchy and imbalance, 79–80
Practice play, 247
Pragmatics, 169, 174–180, 191, 193–199, 214, 438,
        445–448
Praxis, 307, 317, 329
Pre-Feeding Skills (Morris & Klein), 329
Preassessment planning meetings, 104–108, 131–137
Predicting behavior, 274
Prefatory statements, 111
Preschoolers, 576
Presupposition, 111, 194
Pretend play, 224–226, 230–232, 280, 466–470
Prevalence of ASD, 4, 35, 41
Preventive medicine. *See* Health care
Primary motor strip, 339
Primary representation, 225
Priming, 585–587
Problem list, 545–546, 568
Problem-oriented medical record, 568
Problem solving
    creative blocks and, 360–361
    interpersonal problem solving, 506
    Osborn-Parnes creative problem-solving process,
        361–363
    play intervention and, 460
    problem identification and, 361–362
    as skill, 264, 277–278
Profile of Individual Play Characteristics (Wolfberg),
        239
PROGRESS curriculum, 524
Project TEACCH. *See* TEACCH project
Prompting
    antecedent prompting, 497, 502
    definition of, 451
    delayed prompting, 404, 451
    inclusionary education and, 587
    milieu teaching and, 415
    peer prompting, 497, 505
    play intervention and, 462–463, 467, 472
    prompt dependency, 405
    unconventional verbal behavior management
        and, 433
    visual communication and, 401
Pronoun reversal, 29
Pronouns, 434
Proprioceptive receptors, 308, 312, 328, 339
Proximity, 178, 497
PRT. *See* Pivotal response training (PRT)
Psychopharmacology, 568. *See also* Medication
Psychosis, 5, 8, 554
Purkinje neurons, 32, 55

Questioning
    bombardment questions, 111
    example questions, 110
    excessive questioning, 173, 434
    experience questions, 110–111
    forced-choice questions, 435

grand tour questions, 110
hidden agenda questions, 111
leading questions, 111
learning to question, 418–419, 431, 437, 440
mini tour questions, 110
native language questions, 111
open-ended questions, 435, 467
prefatory statements, 111
presupposition questions, 111
question-asking training, 417, 418–419
requests, 418–419, 431, 440, 505
Questionnaires, 103, 281–282, 330–331

Rapport-building, 109–110
RAS. *See* Reticular activating system (RAS)
RDI. *See* Relationship development intervention model (RDI)
Reasonable accommodations, 574
Receptive language, 438
Recessive mutation, 55
Reciprocal reading, 442
Reciprocity
    ABLC and, 438–439
    communication assessment, 177–180
    play intervention and, 461
    questioning and, 437
    reciprocal social behavior defined, 295
    scripting and, 427
    social-emotional issues and, 266–268, 271, 521
    video modeling and, 423
"Recommendations for Preventive Pediatric Health
    Care" (American Academy of Pediatrics), 546
Record reviews
    communication assessment and, 195, 199–200
    community-based assessment model and, 112, 113
    play assessment and, 234–235
    sensory-motor characteristics assessment and,
        327–328
    social-emotional assessment, 284
Referential looking, 295
Regression, 8, 354, 552, 553
Regular Education Initiative (REI), 574, 575, 597
REI. *See* Regular Education Initiative (REI)
Reinforcement
    antecedent prompting, 497
    communication skills intervention and, 403
    definition of, 451
    differential reinforcement, 415, 451
    food reinforcers, 421
    intrinsic reinforcement, 473
    natural language paradigm and, 416
    peer reinforcement, 497, 505
    play intervention and, 463–464, 467, 471
    praise, 413–414, 421, 463, 471
    PRT and, 509
    question-asking training and, 417
    reinforcer assessment, 403
    social-emotional intervention and, 487
    verbal skills support, 413–414
Relationship-based interventions, 348

Relationship building, 269, 271, 273–274, 280
Relationship development intervention model (RDI),
    485–491
Reliability, 97
Religious beliefs, 71
Repair strategies, 435
Repetitive behavior, 4, 6, 230, 264, 305, 481. *See also*
    Sameness desires
Report writing
    information in, 115–116
    interdisciplinary consultation summary, 117–118,
        143–160
    resource notebooks and, 115–116
    sample reports, 143–160
Request for Assistance Protocol (Peck & Schuler), 202
Requests, 418–419, 431, 440, 505. *See also*
    Questioning
Resource notebooks, 115–116
Resources
    assessment tools, 212–213
    health care resources, 565–567
    online resources, 52–54, 85, 337–338
    organizations, 52–54, 85–86
    peer tutoring articles, 532
    social skills and activities programs, 528–532
Response, 404, 452
Response generalization, 402, 419, 451
Response to name, 20, 21
Reticular activating system (RAS), 314
Rett's Disorder
    diagnosis and, 5, 7, 39–42
    gender and, 8
    intervention and, 358
    overview of, 7–8
Rigidity, 185, 229–230, 264, 461
Routine, 407–409, 427, 452

Safety, 559, 561, 566
Sally-and-Ann task, 262
Sameness desires, diagnosis and, 4, 6
Schema, 427, 452
Schizophrenia, 31, 307
School Function Assessment (Coster, Deeney,
    Haltiwanger, & Haley), 332, 337
Scoliosis, 8, 557, 568
SCORE Skills program, 524
Screening Tool for Autism in Two-Year-Olds (STAT;
    Stone, Coonrod, & Ousley), 49
Script fading, 428, 452
Scripting
    bedtime scripts, 562
    communication skills intervention and, 422,
        427–431, 435–437
    definition of, 452
    health and dental care and, 548, 557, 559
    play intervention and, 461, 466, 468–469
    social-emotional intervention and, 487
Second-order theory of mind tasks, 295
Seizures
    antiseizure drugs, 555

Seizures (*Continued*)
charting, 553
health care strategies and, 545, 552–554
medical home and, 543
resources on, 566–567
Rett's disorder and, 8
types of, 552, 567, 568
Selective serotonin reuptake inhibitors (SSRIs), 555
Self-abuse, 318
Self-care, 422, 425, 557–558
Self-injury, 555
Self-modeling, 423, 556
Self-recognition, 257–258, 295
Self-regulation
executive function and, 264
inclusionary education and, 592–593
pivotal response behaviors and, 268, 509
play and, 465
PRT and, 509
RDI model and, 490
SCERTS model and, 492–493
self- versus peer monitoring, 504, 510
social growth and, 276–280
Self-stimulation, 318, 555
Semantics, 188, 190–192, 214, 448–450
Sensorimotor History Questionnaire for Preschoolers
(DeGangi & Balzer-Martin), 330–331, 337
Sensory input, 312–313, 314, 316, 329
Sensory modulation, 316, 339
Sensory-motor characteristics
activity and, 324–326
components of, 313
diagnostic literature, 304–307
DSM–IV and, 305
dynamic systems model, 319–322
execution and, 307
feed-forward information, 321
feedback and, 318–319, 321
goal formation and, 307
handflapping and, 304, 306
IDEA and, 305
intervention and, 348
motivation and, 319
motor planning and, 307, 308
motor skills development, 306–307
neuromaturational model, 310–319, 322
observations and, 328–329
overview of, 304
personal accounts, 307–310
play and, 306
praxis deficits and, 307
proprioceptive senses, 308
relationship between sensory and motor
characteristics, 310–322
repetitive behavior and, 305, 306
vestibular senses, 308
Sensory-motor characteristics assessment
assumptions about sensory-motor functioning and,
323–324
contextual factors, 326

dimensions of disability and aspects, 324–326
impairment and, 324
interviews and, 328
overview of, 326–327
participation and, 326
record reviews, 327–328
standardized assessments, 329–332, 336–337
strengths perspective and, 323
tools for, 305, 329–332
Sensory perception, 316, 339
Sensory Profile (Dunn), 337
Sensory registration, 339
Serotonin, 555, 568
Service delivery. *See* Family-centered care
Service delivery. *See* Intervention
Sexual abuse, 559, 561
Sexuality, 559, 561, 566–567
Shaping, 404, 415, 452
Shared Attention Mechanism, 261
Sharing, 503
Shifting attention, 34, 55, 176, 229, 405
Sibling Information Network, 86
Sibling Support Project, 86
Sign language, 402, 403. *See also* Hand signals
Simple partial seizures, 552, 568
Single-photon emission computed tomography
(SPECT), 33
Skill-based interventions, 348
Skills stories, 533
Skillstreaming Curriculum (McGinnis & Goldstein),
589, 590
Sleep issues, 8, 543, 555, 561–562
SLPs. *See* Speech–language pathologists (SLPs)
Social behavior, 273
Social-emotional assessment
bridging ideas, 278, 281–282
complex communication and, 277–278, 280
dimensions of disability, 283
DSM–IV and, 252
emotional ideas and, 278, 280–282
executive function and, 276
family and primary caregivers and, 267, 269, 277,
278
friendship, 269, 271–274
gestures and, 277, 280
imitation and, 266
interviews, 284–285
joint attention and, 266
observations and, 285–286
overview of, 265–266, 273–274, 276–277, 282–283
perspective-taking skills, 275
pivotal response behavior, 268–270
reciprocity and, 266–268, 271
record reviews, 284
relationship building, 269, 271–274, 280
self-regulation and, 268, 276–277, 279–280
theory of mind and, 274–276
tools for, 273–274, 281–282, 284–285, 286–288,
294
two-way communication and, 277, 279, 280

Social-emotional development, 269, 273
  assessment and, 186
  brain abnormalities and, 33
  in children with ASD, 255–256
  in children without disabilities, 253–255
  communication and language and, 169, 170, 180, 399, 403, 409
  curriculum analysis and, 378
  definition of, 170
  diagnosis and, 4–6
  DSM–IV and, 252
  emotion recognition, 258–260
  emotional development profile, 276–282
  executive function and, 263 264, 276
  eye gaze and, 6
  face perception and, 257–260
  false-belief tasks, 261–263
  family and primary caregivers and, 254, 267, 269, 277, 278
  gestures and, 260–261, 277, 280
  imitation and, 260–261
  impact of deficits in, 264–265
  impairment areas, 256–264
  inclusionary education and, 581–583
  joint attention and, 256–257, 263
  linguistic features of social discourse, 175–176
  observations and, 279
  overview of, 252–253
  peers and, 576, 588–591
  perceptual understanding, 274–275
  perspective-taking skills, 254–255
  play and, 254, 20, 223–224, 226–229, 232–233, 235, 465
  relationship-based interventions, 348
  self-regulation and, 264
  social organization of discourse, 194–195
  theory of mind and, 261–264
  visual cues and, 402
Social-emotional intervention
  cognitive behavioral interventions, 506–507
  comic strip conversations and, 511–514
  developmental individual difference relationship-based model (DIR), 481–486
  do–watch–listen–say framework, 495–496
  floor time and, 483–485, 502
  Learning Experiences … An Alternative Program (LEAP), 498, 504
  overview of, 480–481
  peer intervention strategies, 495–506
  pivotal response training (PRT) and, 507–510
  power card strategy, 522
  PROGRESS curriculum, 524
  relationship development intervention model (RDI), 485–491
  SCORE Skills program, 524
  social communication, emotional regulation, and transactional supports model (SCERTS), 491–494
  social stories and, 514–521
  theory of mind and, 522–524
    training for, 490, 503, 505–506, 506
    videotaping and, 485, 517–518, 520
Social goals, 273
Social interaction, 214
Social Interaction Observation Guide (Peck & Schuler), 202–203
Social model, 94, 162
Social organization of discourse, 194–195
Social Reciprocity Scale (SRS), 267
Social referencing, 489
Social review, 517–518, 533
Social Skills Rating System (SSRS; Gresham & Elliot), 288
Social stories, 514–521, 548, 559
Socioeconomic status, due process and, 78
Solitary play, 224, 225, 247, 255
Spasticity, 8
Speaking effectively, 75–76
Specific language impairment and autistic disorder, 29
SPECT. See Single-photon emission computed tomography (SPECT)
Speech–language pathologists (SLPs), 69
  care coordination and, 545
  communication assessment and, 168
  curriculum analysis and, 374
  inclusionary education and, 583–584, 590–591
  intervention decisions and, 368
  medical home and, 543
  milieu teaching and, 417
  sleep issues and, 562
  social-emotional intervention and, 480
Spelling, 592
Spinal column, 313, 314, 315, 317
Sports. See Games and sports
Spotlighting, 487
SRS. See Social Reciprocity Scale (SRS)
SSRIs. See Selective serotonin reuptake inhibitors (SSRIs)
SSRS. See Social Skills Rating System (SSRS; Gresham & Elliot)
STAT. See Screening Tool for Autism in Two-Year-Olds (STAT; Stone, Coonrod, & Ousley)
Stereotypy, 555, 556, 476, 503, 463. See also Repetitive behavior; Sameness desires
Stimulant medication, 30, 555
Stimulus, 416, 419, 452
Stimulus control, 452
Stimulus generalization, 401
Stimulus overselectivity, 184, 316, 318, 339, 508
Strength perspective, 339
Summer services, 354
Superior olive, 32, 55
Symbolic play. See Pretend play
Symbolic Play Scale Checklist (Westby), 228, 241
Symbolic Play Scale (Westby), 241
Syntax, 169
System for Observation of Children's Social Interactions (Brown), 273

Systematic Observation of Red Flags for Autism Spectrum Disorders in Young Children (SORF; Wetherby & Woods), 21, 49

Taking turns, 413, 415, 425, 468, 484, 503, 508
Tardive dyskinesia, 555
TEACCH project, 201, 348, 349, 351, 431–433
Teacher Report Form, (Achenbach & Rescorla), 287
Teachers, 574, 575, 584–585, 589–590
Teams
    agenda format, 99
    collaborative teaming, 90
    curriculum analysis and, 378–381
    decision making and, 360–371
    family and, 98, 100–101
    IEPs and, 579–581
    inclusionary education and, 577–581, 584–586
    intake, 101–104
    intervention planning and, 356–359
    medical care coordination, 544–545
    medical home and, 543
    polarization of, 369
    problem solving and, 360–363
    professional's roles, 100, 106
    seizure activity and, 554
    team culture, 76–77
Temporal lobe, 314
Temporal lobes, 33
Teratogens, 55
Test of Language Competence–Expanded (Wiig & Secord), 197
Test of Perception of Emotion from Facial Expressions and Test of Perception of Emotion from Posture Cues (Spence), 294
Test of Pragmatic Language (Phelps-Terasaki & Phelps-Gunn), 196
Test of Pragmatic Skills–Revised (Shulman), 196
Test of Problem Solving–Adolescent Version (Zachman, Barrett, Huisingh, Orman, & Blagden), 196
Test of Problem Solving–Revised Elementary Version (Bowers, Barrett, Huisingh, Orman, & LoGiudice), 197
Test of Word Knowledge (Wiig & Secord), 190
Test–retest reliability, 55
Testing, dynamic assessment and, 97
Thalamus, 315, 316
Theory of mind, 168–169, 235, 261–264, 274–276, 294, 295, 522–524
Theory of Mind Mechanism, 261–262
Theory of Mind Test (Muris), 274
Time delay, 413, 414, 415, 417–420, 433, 442
Tissue donation, 26
Toileting, 557–558, 580
Tonic-clonic seizures, 552, 568
Total communication, 399, 401
Toxins, 35–36
TPBA. *See Transdisciplinary Play-Based Assessment* (TPBA)
Training, 351, 374
Tranquilizer drugs, 555

Transdisciplinary Play-Based Assessment (TPBA), 240–241
Transitions, 593–594
Treatment. *See* headings beginning Intervention; specific types of intervention
Treatment and Education of Autistic and Related Communication Handicapped Children (TEACCH). *See* TEACCH project
Tricyclic, 568
TSC. *See* Tuberous sclerosis complex (TSC)
Tuberous sclerosis complex (TSC), 55
Turn taking, 413, 415, 425, 468, 484, 503, 508
Two-person prompting, 452
Two-way communication, 277, 279, 280, 484

Unaided communication, definition of, 399
Unconventional verbal behavior, 169, 187–189, 433–434, 587–588
Unoccupied play, 223

VABS. *See Vineland Adaptive Behavior Scale* (VABS; Sparrow, Balla, & Cicchetti)
Validity, 55, 97
Valporic acid, 35, 55
Verbal skills support
    milieu teaching, 412–417
    modeling and, 420–427
    natural language paradigm, 412–417
    overview of, 412
    scripting and, 427–431
    time delay and, 413, 414, 415, 417–420
Vermont Interdependent Services Team Approach (VISTA). *See* VISTA
Vermont Rural Autism Project (VT–RAP)
    family-centered assessment process and, 69, 71, 82–83, 90
    interdisciplinary assessment model for children with ASD and, 101–119
    parent–school conflicts and, 77–78
    power hierarchy and imbalance, 79–80
    socioeconomic status of families, 78
Vestibular senses, 308, 328
Videotaping. *See also* Modeling; Observations
    ASD diagnosis and, 20–21, 27
    communication skills assessment and, 411
    dynamic assessment and, 97
    health and dental care and, 553, 557, 559
    play, 239, 468, 469
    regression and, 553
    social-emotional development and, 255, 485, 517–518
    video modeling, 421–427, 434, 468, 470
Vineland Adaptive Behavior Scale (VABS; Sparrow, Balla, & Cicchetti), 21, 749
Viruses, 35–36
VISTA, 365–371, 391
Visual cue fading, 419
Visual supports, 399–403, 442, 450–451, 514, 559, 593–594
Vitamin therapy, 551

Vocabulary knowledge, 381, 387, 592
VT RAP. *See* Vermont Rural Autism Project
    (VT–RAP)

Walker Social Skills Curriculum: The Accepts Program
    (Walker & McConnell), 589–590
Watching, 495
Websites related to autism, 52–54, 85, 329
WHO. *See* World Health Organization (WHO)
Withdrawal. *See* Isolation

Word Test 2: Adolescent (Bowers, Huisingh,
    LoGiudice, & Orman), 191
Word Test 2: Elementary (Bowers, Huisingh,
    LoGiudice, & Orman), 191
World Health Organization (WHO), 282, 305, 324,
    545

Yale Child Study Center, 53–54

Zero reject, 71

About the Author and Contributors

Patricia A. Prelock received her doctorate in speech–language pathology with a concentration in cognitive psychology from the University of Pittsburgh in 1983. Dr. Prelock is professor and chair in the Department of Communication Sciences at the University of Vermont (UVM). She holds the Certificate of Clinical Competence in Speech–Language Pathology and is a board-recognized child language specialist. Dr. Prelock was the project director for the Vermont Rural Autism Project (VT-RAP), a federally funded project designed to prepare speech–language pathologists, special educators, and related service providers to better serve children with autism spectrum disorders and their families (1997–2001). As part of the institutionalization of VT-RAP she cosponsors an annual week-long Summer Institute in Autism with the Autism Society of Vermont and teaches an assessment and intervention course in autism at UVM. Currently, she is training director for the Vermont Interdisciplinary Leadership Education for Health Professionals Program (a federal project funded through the Maternal and Child Health Bureau). She is conducting intervention research on the use of social stories and peer play with children on the autism spectrum.

Contributors

Jean E. Beatson is a registered nurse and a research assistant professor in the Department of Nursing at the University of Vermont in Burlington. She received her doctorate in educational leadership from the University of Vermont. Dr. Beatson is the clinical director and associate training director for the Vermont Interdisciplinary Leadership Education for Health Professionals (VT-ILEHP) Program.

Stephen H. Contompasis is a developmental pediatrician and an assistant professor in the Department of Pediatrics at the University of Vermont in Burlington. He graduated from Tufts Medical School and did his residency training at Dartmouth–Hitchcock Medical Center and his postresidency training at Children's Hospital in Boston. He is board-certified in pediatrics, developmental and behavioral pediatrics, and neurodevelopmental disabilities. Dr. Contompasis is the program director for the VT-ILEHP Program.

Ruth Dennis is a certified occupational therapist and a research assistant professor in the Department of Education at the University of Vermont in

Burlington. She received her doctorate in educational leadership from the University of Vermont. Dr. Dennis is also a member of the State of Vermont Interdisciplinary Team (VT-I Team) through the Center for Disability and Community Inclusion and a core faculty member for the VT-ILEHP Program.

Amy Ducker is a developmental psychologist at the Baird Center for Children and Families in Burlington, Vermont. She received her doctorate in developmental psychology from the University of Vermont. Dr. Ducker is the clinical director for the Autism Spectrum Program at the Baird Center.

Susan Edelman is a certified physical therapist and a research assistant professor in the Department of Education at the University of Vermont in Burlington. She received her doctorate in educational leadership from the University of Vermont. She is also coordinator of the VT-I Team and the Deaf/Blind Project through the Center for Disability and Community Inclusion at the University of Vermont.